THE ONTOLOGICAL FOUNDATION OF ETHICS, POLITICS, AND LAW

REVISED EDITION

Francesco Belfiore

University Press of America,® Inc.
Lanham · Boulder · New York · Toronto · Plymouth, UK

Dedication

In loving memory
of my father, *Salvatore*,
and
my mother, *Eleonora Pirrone*

Contents

Chapter 3—Public Ethics and Political Philosophy   161

Figures

Tables

Preface

In my previous book, which appeared a few years ago (*The Structure of the Mind*, UPA, 2004), I attempted to present a complete philosophical system, solidly grounded on ontological bases. This systematic exposition of my thought made it possible to cover several philosophical fields and to show the coherence of the system, but necessarily limited the presentation to a concise account of the essential points and prevented the discussion of several important details, thus justifying the subtitle: *Outlines of a Philosophical System*. For this reason, in the preface to that book, I promised the readers (and myself) that the main sections of *The Structure of the Mind* would have been developed into more extensive publications. The present book, therefore, may be considered as the fulfillment of a promise.

My philosophical system can be regarded as consisting of a basic ontological conception (which considers the Mind as an *evolving, conscious, triadic entity* composed of *intellect, sensitiveness*, and *power*), from which new concepts and views are derived concerning the products of intellect (*ideas*, which produce knowledge), of sensitiveness (*sentiments*, which are expressed as ability to aesthetic enjoyment and artistic creations), and of power (*actions*, which form human behavior). The present book is devoted to the last issue, in that it discusses in detail questions of human behavior, which is made of personal or selfish actions and of moral acts, both of which may be exerted in the private (or individual) or in the public (or social) life. Otherwise stated, this book deals with *ethics, politics*, and *law* (treated in chapters 2, 3, and 4), as indicated by the title, and excludes other areas such as epistemology, logic, language, and aesthetics. Moreover, some difficult controversial topics, like those referring to "free will" or to "the theories on consciousness", are not treated, and only the essential concepts are mentioned instead. A special mention should be made to *ontology* (treated in chapter 1), inasmuch as while this important philosophical field is not specifically treated in this book, a *concise account* of my ontological conception is given in the first chapter, as a necessary premise. This is because I firmly believe that it is illegitimate to claim to argue about a given subject matter without first attempting to know what that subject actually "*is*". Referring to the contents of this book, it would be illegitimate to pretend to discuss the behavior of human beings without first having defined what human beings actually are, as ontological entities. Indeed, I am a convinced assertor of the *ontological turn* in philosophy.

In line with the above reasoning, the main characteristic of this book is that it presents my views and concepts about ethics, politics, and law as derived from my ontological conception about the structure and functioning of the human mind (or spirit). Thus, the notions of human good, of moral norms, of society, of law, down to the separation of powers, are derived from my conception of what the human mind "*is*": an evolving, conscious, triadic entity made of intellect, sensitiveness, and power. In other words, the notions that I present are the *result of a discovery*, and not the *consequence of a choice*. Otherwise stated, ethics, politics, and law are given an *ontological foundation*; hence, the title of the book.

In keeping with the above argument, the core concepts about my ontological conception, which I treated in *The Structure of the Mind*, are summarized in the 1st chapter of this book and at the beginning of the other three main chapters, as necessary premises; this has been indicated by a specific quotation, to give the readers the suggestion for a further analysis.

The contents of this book includes both the exposition of my thought about the various topics considered as well as a brief mention of the main views of other thinkers, followed by a critical comment and a reinterpretation of their positions. This is because it is my conviction that a thinker, who presents his own philosophical thought, has the duty to explain how his thought can be related to the ideas of others and, especially, how it allows to reinterpret them. In this regard, I would like to express here my appreciation, debit, and respect toward all those thinkers whose thoughts I quote and comment, including those (indeed, especially those) with whom I disagree and whose thoughts I criticize and reinterpret.

In the text, the various works discussed are quoted as follows: (Author year: page number or range).

The text is highly structured and divided into five main Chapters (quoted as "Ch.") and many small sub-chapters (quoted as "ch."), down to the 5th level; moreover, most sub-chapters are divided into sections (*A, B, C, . . .*), each section into points (*1, 2, 3, . . .*), and each point into sub-points (*a, b, c, . . .*). This, in my opinion, helps the reader to identify the topic being discussed and to set it in the general context of the philosophical conception presented. This also results in a detailed "table of contents", from which the reader can easily get an idea about the philosophical matter treated in the book.

The various chapters are closely interrelated with one another, and the text is heavily cross-referenced throughout; the reader is therefore invited to follow the cross-references, especially those referring to the 1st chapter, which gives the basic ontological concepts.

The matter treated in this book is extensive and complex; for this reason, I made every effort to expound the arguments in as clear and simple a form as possible, in order to help the readers to easily follow the unfolding of the discourse.

Writing this book took much time and cost me much effort which, unavoidably, also involved my family, to which I am indebted for their understanding. My special thanks are due to my wife *Silvia*, who has carefully helped me in the final check of the manuscript for oversights and typing mistakes.

I am aware that any proposal of new views and theories gives rise to reflections and critical analyses. This is the way through which the endless evolution of the philosophical thought occurs. I would very much welcome the contributions of those thinkers who might be willing to offer their feedback opinions or views on my work and to give helpful suggestions and advice.

Catania (Italy), July 2006

Francesco Belfiore
E-mail: f.belfiore1@tin.it

Preface to the Revised Edition

The first edition of this book appeared in early 2007, yet the text was finished in 2006. In the six years elapsed since that time, I have written a new book, which has just appeared (*The Democratic Society and Its Founding Concepts*—2012), and have in the meantime further refined several aspects of my philosophical conception. For this reason, I felt that a new edition of *The Ontological Foundation of Ethics, Politics, and Law* should be prepared.

The main changes introduced in this second edition are of three kinds.

First, I added some new concepts and updated the terminology used, in order to get a better coherence of my thought and a uniformity of language.

Second, I quoted additional thinkers and discussed their philosophical views.

Third, I attempted to correct some oversights and to make some improvements in style.

It is noteworthy that, although many pages have been rewritten, the page-numbers of the various chapters and sub-chapters in this edition are the same as those in the previous one. Therefore, previous quotations from the first edition (made by myself and possibly by others) are also valid for this second edition.

I hope that the enrichment in concepts and in quotations as well as the improvement in style may make the present edition significantly better than the first one.

Catania (Italy), March 2012

Francesco Belfiore
E-mail: f.belfiore1@alice.it

CHAPTER 1

Premise: The Basic Ontological Conception

This chapter presents, in a concise form, the core concepts of the philosophical system that I published a few years ago (Belfiore 2004); its scope is to provide the reader with the necessary premises required to understand the contents of the chapters that follow.

1.1—A NEW ONTOLOGICAL CONCEPTION: THE MIND AND ITS COMPONENTS

1.1.1—Expanding the Meaning of Descartes' "Cogito"

1.1.1.1—Critical Analysis of the "Cogito Ergo Sum"

As it is known, the argument "I am thinking, therefore I exist" (shortly: I think, therefore I am; Latin: *cogito ergo sum*) was used by Descartes (1637: 127) to reach the first, certain knowledge: that "I am." When conceived as a *deductive argument*, Descartes' *cogito ergo sum* has been questioned (Russell 1945: 519). Yet, I think that Descartes' "cogito" should be regarded as an act of internal observation, or introspection, i.e., as an act of the mind that observes itself, through which the mind acquires the self-evident truth that the thinking agent expresses with the words: "I am." This mental process might be defined as *intuition*; however, more properly, it is an *observational process*, i.e., a process leading to the acquisition of new knowledge through the observation of an existing "object" (in this instance, the thinking mind itself).

However, an extended analysis of the "cogito" intuition gives a much richer result, as it leads to the fundamental discoveries (or self-evident truths) listed below (Belfiore 2004: 1–6).

(1) Descartes had the intuition that, if he thought then he must exist as a thinking entity, i.e., as an entity that possesses the attribute (or category) of thought (or *intellect*) through which he had acquired the new *concept or idea*.

(2) At the same time, as he refers (Descartes 1637: 124), the intuition of the "cogito" gave him great emotion and enthusiasm; that is, he felt happy. He should have then perceived in a clear and distinct manner that, in addition to the attribute of thought, he also possessed another attribute (*sensitiveness*) that consisted of his ability to feel happy (i.e., to have a *sentiment*).

(3) Soon after the "cogito" intuition, Descartes decided to carry out some *actions*, that is, he took some paper and a pen and he started to write down an account of his thought. He was able to do that because he had the *power* to do so, as he possessed arms and hands apt to write. Therefore, he should have then perceived in a clear and distinct manner that, in addition to the attributes of intellect and sensitiveness, he had an additional attribute (*power*) that consisted of his ability to carry out *actions*; this attribute should have appeared to him as something that, even if undefined and of uncertain nature, was distinct from the ability to create *ideas or concepts* (*intellect*) and from the ability to feel *sentiments* (*sensitiveness*). Notoriously, admitting the existence of arms and hands (and of all physical objects) represents a critical point. While this issue cannot be discussed in detail here, I will just underline that it suffices that we admit arms and hands are "some existing things" different from ideas or sentiments, of which we have an uncertain, initial knowledge, to be progressively developed. The same is true for the "thinking I", of which Descartes says: "But I do not yet have a sufficient understanding of what this 'I' is, that now necessarily exists" (Descartes 1641: 17).

(4) Despite the fact that ideas, sentiments and actions appeared to be different products of different mind components (the intellect, the sensitiveness, and the power), they were experienced by a single entity, as all of them entered reality as experiences of a single conscious "I", i.e., as distinct and yet inseparable products of the conscious "I". The latter appears, therefore, as a conscious entity made of the unity-distinction of intellect, sensitiveness, and power.

(5) Before the "cogito", Descartes was doubtful, after the "cogito" he became certain that he existed; before the "cogito" he was distressed by the doubt, after the "cogito" he became happy; before the "cogito" he carried out some undefined actions, after the "cogito" he carried out the action(s) of writing an account of his thought. This means that in Descartes' mind some *changes* had occurred that involved all three activities or attributes or categories of the mind (the intellect, the sensitiveness, and the power). Briefly, the *cogito* intuition shows that the mind is able to undergo *changes*. By

comparing Descartes' state of mind as it was before the changes induced by the "cogito" with the mind state after the "cogito", we note that they are not only different from each other, but that the "post-cogito" state is *richer* or more *evolved* than the "pre-cogito" state. In other words, we have the intuition, or direct experience of consciousness, that the passage from the former to the latter state entails an *evolution* of mind, whereas the reverse would be an *involution*, and that the nature of the mind is such that it *tends toward evolution*, i.e., it continuously *transcends itself*. Thus, the mind appears as a continuously changing entity that can undergo *evolution* (or *involution*).

(6) The mind components are *interrelated* to one another, inasmuch as each mind component can exist only if supported by the other two components. Thus, the *intellect*, in order to be able to think of a given "object", needs a minimum of power to perform the action of observing the "object" (i.e., the body and its relation with the surrounding physical world) and a minimum of sensitiveness to feel the desire to direct its thinking activity toward that object; the *sensitiveness*, in order to generate a sentiment (desire or aversion) toward an "object", needs to know it through the activity of the intellect, and needs also the contribution of the power (body structure and functions); the *power*, in order to generate actions, needs an idea-of-project (produced by the intellect) and a desire (created by the sensitiveness) toward the end to which the action is directed.

Thus, the mind and its components are marked by *unity-distinction* of multiple components (or *unity-multiplicity*) and *interrelation*. Moreover, the analysis of the "cogito" shows that the mind is capable of self-reflection.

It is noteworthy that reference to the cogito has been made to refer just to a well-known mind experiment. Yet, similar deductions can be drawn from the analysis of any instance of mind activity, which will show the triadic and evolving nature of the mind and the interrelation of its components.

1.1.1.2—The Mind, Its Components, and Its Products

From the above discussion, it follows that the mind can be conceived as consisting of the unity-distinction of *intellect*, *sensitiveness*, and *power*.

Each of the mind components can be conceived as acting in two opposing directions, i.e., as exerting an *outward activity* directed toward the external world, and an *inward activity* directed toward the mind itself. The outward activity of the intellect, sensitiveness, and power is a *selfish* activity of the mind, through which an agent tends to develop his own intellect, sensitiveness and power. The selfish activity as a whole represents the *selfishness* of the mind. Instead, the inward activity of the intellect, sensitiveness, and power is the *moral* activity of the mind, through which the mind understands and feels itself (and other minds) as an evolving entity, and acts accordingly. The moral activity as a whole represents the *consciousness* of the mind. Each mind component creates its own products. These concepts will be developed in the following chapters and are summarized in Fig. 1.1.

1.1.1.2.1—The Outward Mind Activity (or Selfishness). 1—The Intellect and Its Products: Ideas, Projects, and Fantasies

The intellect, through its outward activity, produces *ideas*, *projects*, and *fantasies*.

(A) Ideas.
Ideas are the product of the outward activity of the intellect directed to understand the objects and events of reality. The latter include: *(1) Physical objects* and *events*, i.e., objects and events of the physical world, concerning the human body and its relations with the physical world (which represent the *power* component of the mind) and including human *actions*, and *(2) Non-physical objects* and *events*. The latter comprise: *(a) sentiments*, generated by the *sensitiveness*; *(b) ideas* themselves, which also include fantasies (imaginary ideas) and the ideas-of-projects or, simply, projects (ideas being produced by the *intellect*, this means that the intellect thinks about itself— *self-reflection of intellect*); and *(c) moral events*, i.e., the products of the inward mind activity (moral thoughts, feelings, and acts—see ch. 1.1.1.2.4).

Objects are regarded by our intellect as static entities, whereas *events* are changing objects, i.e., objects undergoing changes. Since any existing entity is a becoming entity undergoing continuous changes (even a stone undergoes changes over, say, millions of years), this distinction is rather arbitrary or, more exactly, relative to the time-meter of humans (Belfiore 2004: 89). Actually, objects should be regarded as *slowly changing events*. However, for the sake of simplicity, the distinction between "objects" and "events" will be maintained throughout this book. To fully understand events, the difficult concept of causation should be defined. This issue, however, is outside the scope of this book (see Belfiore 2004: 91–102).

As mentioned above (ch. 1.1.1.1, *6*), due to the interrelation of the three mind components and of their products (Fig. 1, dotted arrows), ideas (and also projects and fantasies—see below) need the support, or *presuppose*, the other two kinds of mind products: sentiments and actions. Thus, the idea of an object cannot exist without the support of the action directed to observe that object (i.e., the body structures and their relation to the environment) and of the desire to direct the thinking activity toward that object. Hence, an idea actually exists as a *triplet*, and could be indicated as "$_{sentiment}$-idea$_{-action}$".

(B) Projects and Fantasies.
Besides ideas, the outward activity of intellect creates *projects* as well as *fantasies*. Projects (together with *hypotheses* formulated in scientific re-

search) and fantasies are *imaginary ideas*. Whereas ideas refer to existing objects or events (either physical or non-physical), projects envisage *new* (i.e., as yet not existing) or possible objects or events. Projects are produced by the *intellect*, are stirred up by sentiments produced by the *sensitiveness*, and are realized through the actions, generated by the *power*.

1.1.1.2.2—The Outward Mind Activity (or Selfishness). 2—The Sensitiveness and Its Products: Sentiments

Whereas the outward activity of intellect attempts to understand what the "objects" that it faces are, the outward activity of sensitiveness, when faced with an "object", creates a sentiment, which is an original product of its activity. Thus, sentiments are the result of a *founding activity* of the sensitiveness. Sentiments are directed toward the objects and events pertaining to the physical world (sphere of the *power*), including actions, as they are known through the activity of the *intellect*, or toward "non-physical objects", i.e., ideas and projects (created by the *intellect*) or sentiments themselves, created by the *sensitiveness* itself, which thus shows self-reflection.

Like ideas, sentiments are interrelated with, and need the support of the other two kinds of mind products, ideas and actions (In Fig. 1, the interrelations of sentiments are shown as dotted arrows). Thus, a sentiment (desire or aversion) toward an object necessarily needs the support of the idea of that object and of the action of observing that object. Hence, a sentiment actually exists as a *triplet*, and could be indicated as "$_{action}$sentiment$_{idea}$".

1.1.1.2.3—The Outward Mind Activity (or Selfishness). 3—The Power and Its Products: Actions

The third fundamental mind component is the *power*, whose outward activity enables the mind to carry out *actions*. We can define an action as a change or event taking place in the physical world as a result of a voluntary movement of our body, i.e., as a change in the relationship *"body"-to-"rest of the world"* (shortly: body-world) directed to realize a project (in society, actions also depend on the *socio-economic status* of the agents).

Actions, generated by the power, need some necessary premises, inasmuch as an action may occur only as the accomplishment of an idea, more properly, an idea-of-project or, simply, *project* (created by the *intellect*), and as the satisfaction of a *sentiment* (created by the *sensitiveness*); this shows the *inter-relationships* of actions with the products of the other mind components. The fact that any action implements a project entails that any action has an end; therefore, the actions of an agent are end-directed physical events, originating in his brain and extending to nerves, muscles and, ultimately, to various objects of the physical world, including other individuals.

Like ideas and sentiments, actions exist as *triplets*, since they actually consist of the realization of an *idea*-of-project, produced by the intellect, and of the satisfaction of a *sentiment* (desire to do that action), produced by the sensitiveness. Hence, an action should be indicated as "$_{idea-}$action$_{sentiment}$". (In Fig. 1, the interrelations of actions are shown as dotted arrows)

1.1.1.2.4—*The Inward Mind Activity (or Consciousness) and Its Products: Moral Thoughts, Moral Feelings, and Moral Acts*

The inward mind activity (or consciousness) can be defined as the activity of the mind that, being focused on the mind itself (or on its core or inner part), is able to have an overview of the mind as a whole. Through it, the awareness that the mind is a unitary entity arises, composed of intellect, sensitiveness, and power (Fig. 1.1), which undergoes continuous changes; the latter can be directed either toward evolution or involution. The ability of the mind to undergo *evolution* is the source of morality (ch. 2.1.4). The inward mind activity creates inward ideas (*moral thoughts*—including *moral projects*), inward sentiments (*moral feelings*) and inward actions (*moral acts*); these products of the inward mind activity may be indicated as *moral events* (chs. 2.1.1; 2.1.2). The existence of an inward and an outward mind activity shows that the mind exerts a *bidirectional* activity (*bi-directionality* of the mind). These two activities are distinct and yet linked to each other (*unity-distinction* of mind activities), for what actually occurs is a *mainly* outward or *mainly* inward activity (Fig. 2.2) (see chs. 1.2, *A1e*; 2.1.3.3.3).

The inward nature of moral events means that they have as their "object" the mind as a whole and have as their effect either the evolution or the involution of the mind. Thus, *moral thoughts* are directed to understand that the mind is a triadic conscious entity capable of undergoing *evolution* and that *mind evolution*, entailing the possibility of changes into "better" states, is the *"objective" moral good*. *Moral feelings* enable the agent to *feel* mind evolution as a *moral value*. *Moral acts* are directed to pursue the moral good (mind evolution), guided by the moral thoughts and feelings (these concepts will be developed in chs. 2.1 and 2.2). This means that the inward mind activity is reflective in nature (*self-reflection* of mind activity). Like the products of outward mind activity (ideas, sentiments, and actions), the three kinds of products of the inward mind activity (moral thoughts, feelings, and acts) are closely interrelated to one another (see Fig. 1, dotted arrows), as each of them needs the support of (i.e., *presuppose*) the other two, so that they actually exist as *triplets*, and should be indicated as moral "$_{feeling-}$thought$_{act}$", moral "$_{act-}$feeling$_{thought}$", and moral "$_{thought-}$act$_{feeling}$".

However, considering that the *inward* and the *outward* activities of the mind, though distinct, are closely interrelated, each mind product is actually a *sextet*, as it is necessarily supported by the other five mind products.

1.1.2—The New Ontological Conception in Four Propositions

Based on the above, the structure and functioning of the mind can be summarized by *four mind-defining propositions* (Belfiore 2004: 5–6):

1ˢᵗ Proposition. The mind (or spirit) is a triadic entity, consisting of intellect, sensitiveness, and power.

2ⁿᵈ Proposition. The mind components (and their products) are *interrelated* to one another, as each of them needs the support of the other two to exist.

3ʳᵈ Proposition. The mind exerts an outward activity (producing ideas, sentiments, and actions) and an inward activity (producing moral thoughts, feelings, and acts) that are *interrelated*, i.e., it exerts a *bidirectional* activity.

4ᵗʰ Proposition. The mind exists as an endlessly becoming entity that tends to *evolution*, through which it continuously *transcends itself*. Mind evolution is the objective *good*, and the source of moral principles and values which guide moral acts (whereas mind *involution* is the objective *evil*). A schematic representation of the structure of the mind is shown in Fig. 1.1.

1.1.3—The Judgment Criteria for the Products of the Mind Components

The products of the outward mind activity (ideas, sentiments, and actions) as well as the products of the inward mind activity (moral thoughts, moral feelings, and moral acts) can be evaluated by two kinds of judgment criteria: *specific criteria*, for each of the products of the mind components; and the *value criterion*, common to all mind products (Table 1.1).

1.1.3.1—Judgment by "Specific Criteria"

For the products of each of the three mind components there is a *specific judgment criterion* (Table 1.1), as indicated below.

(a) Truth criterion (true/false) for ideas. This criterion is valid for the *ideas of objects*, referring to physical or non-physical objects. [The *imaginary/fantastical ideas*, which are created by the intellect under the stimulus

of sentiments, have no judgment criterion, as they do not refer to any pre-existing object—or they may be judged as always true].

(b) Efficaciousness criterion (efficacious/inefficacious) for projects.

(c) Affective criterion (joy/sorrow) for sentiments, and *aesthetic criterion* (beautiful/ugly) for the objects of sentiments. I recall that these criteria are based on the *founding activity* of the sensitiveness.

(d) Strength criterion (strong/weak) for actions.

(e) Morality criterion (good/bad) for moral events, i.e., moral thoughts/projects, moral feelings and moral acts, which are judged as good or bad according to whether they are directed to favor or restrain mind evolution.

1.1.3.2—Judgment by the "Value Criterion", Valid for All Mind Products

The *value criterion* allows us to distinguish all mind products into *particular* or *universal* (Table 1.1).

1.1.3.2.1—Judgment of Ideas and Projects by the Value Criterion

The value criterion allows the distinction of ideas into *particular* and *universal*. I will consider separately the ideas about *physical* objects and events, and the ideas about *non-physical* objects and events.

(1) "Particular Ideas" about Physical Objects and Events versus "Universal Ideas" about Classes of Physical Objects and Classes of Physical Events (Grouping Physical Objects and Events into Classes). Our intellect groups similar objects and events into *classes of objects* and *classes of events*. Let us consider these two kinds of class separately.

[In this book, I will refer to the classes of the "macro-world" or, more exactly, of the *supra-molecular world*, which are *heterogeneous* classes that have as members the objects and events of the world as observed by humans either directly or by the aid of a microscope. Each of these classes includes several or many similar but diverse (or non-identical) "objects" (such as stones, or horses, or men—which belong to the class of stone, the class of horses, and the class of men, respectively). These classes should be distinguished from the *homogeneous* classes referring to identical objects (or particles) of the "micro-world" or, more exactly, of the "molecular-atomic-subatomic world", such as the class of oxygen molecules, or the class of hydrogen atoms, or the class of electrons, etc., whose members are identical to one another (more details in: Belfiore 2004: 56–67)].

(a) Classes of objects. Besides the ideas that refer to a particular object (or event), there are ideas that refer to the properties common to a *"class" of*

similar objects (or of similar events); an example of a class of objects is, for instance, the class of horses. An idea of a class is an idea that refers to the *common* (or shared or essential) *properties* possessed by all members of that class and that distinguish these members from the members of other classes. The common or essential properties also serve as the *inclusion criterion* for that class, inasmuch as an "object" can be included in a given class only if it possesses the essential properties that define that class. Examples of common or essential properties are: "being solid", for the class of stones; "ability to run", for the class of horses; and "being rational", for the class of men. The common or essential properties (possessed by all the similar objects belonging to a class) should be distinguished from *particular or individual properties*, specific of each member of a class, and making it a unique and unrepeatable entity (i.e., defining its *individuality*). Individual properties may consist of either: *(a)* a property (most often a minor property) possessed only by one or some members of a class (this is more easily found in the complex objects of the living world—example: "having a nevus on a cheek" for the class of men); or *(b)* the particular and unique form under which each common or essential property occurs in each member of a class (examples: the degree of *friability*, for the members of the class of stones; ability to run at a given speed for the members of the class of horses; aptitude to be more or less rational for the members of the class of men). Moreover, properties such as *structure, form, size, weight*, etc., vary among the members of a given class, thus conferring individuality to each member and making it a unique entity, although the variations of each of these properties occur within a range of values that is proper of each class.

Thus, while the common or essential properties define a class, particular or individual properties define each member of the class.

It should be underlined that, while the particular objects pre-exist to the activity of intellect (with their specific, individual properties), the class and the common or essential properties that define it are the result of the activity of intellect, i.e., they are ideas created by the intellect. Thus, a class actually is an idea of a class and results from the assembling of the ideas that refer to the various essential properties that define that class. Each idea referring to a property (which varies among the "similar objects" that form the members of a class) can be regarded as an *approximate (or imprecise) mental abstraction*. The approximation or imprecision of the idea referring to a property becomes evident if we consider, for instance, the property "weight" in relation to the class of men; it is clear that the "weight" of men can only be approximately defined, since, among the various men, body weight varies within a rather wide range of values. The same approximation applies to the idea referring to the property "color" of the members of the class of roses.

Another point is worthy of mention. The variability of the essential properties among the members of a class is such that some of such properties may be lacking in a minority of the members. An example is given by the property "being rational"; it is an essential property of the class of men, and yet it is absent in newborns and in patients affected by Alzheimer's disease (and patients with other forms of dementia), although both the newborns and the Alzheimer patients undeniably belong to the class of men. This entails that the universal affirmative propositions, such as "All men are rational", are no longer justified and should be changed into "Most men are rational", thus introducing an element of approximation or imprecision (Belfiore 2004: 143–46).

Thus, the *class* is a creation of the mind, i.e., is an *idea* consisting of a *flexible mental abstraction*, created from the observation of similar objects and which refers to one or more properties, defined *approximately*, that characterize those objects that are similar to one another with regard to those properties. The idea of a *class* is therefore an abstract and approximate scheme of what actually is a member of that class. The idea of *class*, however, is *universal*, as it is an idea that is true for all the members of that class (or most of them). Thus, the ideas that refer to particular objects at a given time are *concrete and particular ideas* whereas the ideas of classes are *abstract and universal ideas*. They are *abstract* because they refer to a mental, approximate scheme of an object or event deprived of the particularities of its properties that define it as a unique and unrepeatable member of the class, and they are *universal* because they are true for all the members of a class (or most of them), whatever the place and time of their occurrence.

(b) Classes of events. Like the idea of a class of objects, the idea of a class of events is a mental scheme representing the average behavior of a group of *similar events* (which may be events occurring in the inorganic or organic world, or events created by man, i.e., actions). The idea of a class of events is generally known as *scientific law*. Thus, the law that "insulin lowers blood glucose" indicates the average behavior of many different "events" occurring in different individuals or in the same individual at different times, each showing particular specific characteristics as concerns the degree of the blood glucose lowering and its time course. [This is true for the classes of events (or scientific laws) of the *macro-world* or, better, of the *supra-molecular world*, since in the *molecular-atomic-subatomic world* the events show regularity]. In other words, a class of objects includes similar objects possessing common properties, while a class of events (or scientific law) includes similar events, occurring according to a common *transformation pattern*. In short, a class of objects includes similar objects; a class of events (or transformation law, or scientific law) includes similar events.

Here it should be anticipated that the rules and laws created by States and other organized communities can be regarded as ideas-of-projects creating classes of similar events, i.e., classes of human actions (ch. 4.1.1).

(2) Universal Ideas of Classes of Non-Physical Objects and Events.

These classes have as members non-physical objects (mentioned above), such as *ideas* and *projects, sentiments*, and *actions* as well as *moral thoughts* and *projects, moral feelings* and *moral acts*.

For the scope of this book, the classes of *projects* are of special interest, and will be developed later. Here I will just recall that projects can be distinguished into: *(a) particular projects*, which are those projects created by, and concerning, individual minds, and *(b) universal projects*, which are those projects shared by most members of a community.

(3) Main Features of "Knowledge" of Objects and Events and of the "Previsions" of Future Facts. The following points concerning knowledge and prevision should be borne in mind, as reference to them will be made in various chapters of this book.

(a) Objects and events. The *objects* of the supra-molecular world are complex, different from one another also within a given class, and continuously changing, so that our knowledge of them is always *incomplete* (Belfiore 2004: 45–52). This is also true for *events*, which, too, are complex and differ from one another also within a given class (Belfiore 2004: 97).

(b) Classes of objects and classes of events (or scientific laws). The classes of objects as well as the classes of events (or scientific laws) of the supra-molecular world are *heterogeneous* classes, i.e., are made of "members" which differ in their properties from one another. Therefore, the *common or essential properties* possessed by the members of a class (be they objects or events) and that characterize the class can only be defined in an *approximate* or *imprecise* manner (Belfiore 2004: 56–61, 102–7).

(c) Incompleteness and approximation (or imprecision): The hallmarks of human knowledge. In the supra-molecular world, and especially in the human world, the knowledge of the *individuals* (or *members of a class*) is always *incomplete*, due to their complexity, diversity, and continuous changing, whereas the knowledge of the *classes* is always *approximate*, due to the variability of its members. In other words, the knowledge of existing objects and occurring events is marked by *incompleteness*, the knowledge and the various classes is only possible on a *statistical basis*, and the previsions of future events can only be made on a *probabilistic basis*, i.e., the knowledge of classes and the prevision of future events are marked by *approximation* or *imprecision* (Belfiore 2004: 70, 138–46, 154–58, 162).

(d) Cause-effect relationship. Contrary to the common view, that the world is made of distinct objects and events (fragmented view of the world), I maintain that there is an underlying *continuum* that unites the apparently distinct facts (Belfiore 2004: 91–100). This entails that the "cause" is not separated from its "effect", as the cause continues into its effect and cannot be distinguished from it; the same is true for human actions, which cannot be distinguished from their effects, as they continue in them (Belfiore 2004: 102). This is of great relevance in the ethical field.

1.1.3.2.2—Judgment of Sentiments by the Value Criterion

Like the other products of the mind, sentiments may be distinguished into *(a) particular* and *(b) universal* sentiments.

(a) Particular (light) sentiments. These are the sentiments felt by single individual minds in connection with particular and personal experiences. This kind of sentiment may even be showy, striking and rich in moving body expressions (like the sentiment of one who cries and gives himself up to despair for the death of a loved person) and yet it is light and superficial, linked to a particular event, and significant only to the mind that feels it.

(b) Universal (deep) sentiments. Sentiments are universal (deep) when, even if they are little showy and poor in external manifestations, they are deep, as in this instance they will overcome the particular events that have initially stirred them up, and are similar to the sentiments that would be felt by most men experiencing similar events. Thus, although deep sentiments can be felt by a single mind, they are common to most men, i.e., most men who experience similar events feel similar deep sentiments (provided they possess an adequately developed sensitiveness). Universal sentiments express themselves in literary, musical and visual art creations.

1.1.3.2.3—Judgment of Actions by the Value Criterion

Actions can also be distinguished into *(a) particular actions* and *(b) universal actions*.

(a) Particular actions are those performed by single individuals.

(b) Universal actions are those performed by all (or most of) the members of a community (or a population) by observing some shared rules.

Universal actions will be treated in greater details in chapter 3.1.1.

1.1.3.2.4—Judgment of Moral Thoughts, Moral feelings, and Moral Acts by the Value Criterion

Moral thoughts, moral feelings, and *moral acts,* i.e., the products of the inward mind activity (which can be referred to as *moral events*) may, they too, be judged by the *value criterion,* which allows us to distinguish *particular* versus *universal* moral thoughts/projects, feelings, and acts. *Particular moral thoughts/projects, feelings and acts* are those that concern the mind of one or a few individuals. *Universal moral thoughts* are those thoughts concerning a population; *universal moral projects* are those projects endorsed by and/or affecting a population (the publicly-shared moral projects are expressed in the democratic constitutional norms and laws—ch.

4.2.2.3.2, *1a*); *universal moral feelings* are deep feelings that, as such, are shared by all or most men; *universal moral acts* are those acts shared by and/or affecting a population (see ch. 1.1.3.2.5, below, and also ch. 2.2.2).

1.1.3.2.5—The Judgment by the Value Criterion (Particular versus Universal) and the Concept of Mind Evolution

The evolution of mind activities takes place through *(a)* the creation of ever new particular mind products (ideas and moral thoughts, sentiments and moral feelings, and actions and moral acts); and *(b)* the development of *particular* mind products toward *universal* mind products, through a process of progressive universalization (see also Belfiore 2004: 70, 196, 290). Thus, there is a *parallelism* between the functioning of the three mind activities.

The universalization of the mind products should be distinguished into: *(a) universalization as to objects* (e.g., the universalization of selfish ideas as well as of moral thoughts, which refers to all or most objects of a class); *(b) universalization as to agents* (which consists in the *sharing* by all or *most minds* belonging to a class—e.g., universalization of selfish sentiments, projects and actions as well as of moral feelings); and *(c) universalization as to objects and/or agents*, (e.g., the universalization of moral projects and moral acts—when these mind products are *publicly* shared, we could use for them the term *collective* instead of *shared*) (ch. 1.2, *A2a*,3). The distinction between "shared" and "collective" (or "publicly-shared") is that "shared" refers to mind products that are universal just because they are shared in an unofficial and undefined manner, whereas "collective" refers to mind products that are shared in an official, public and defined manner—as are the democratic laws, which are officially, publicly and collectively approved by most members of society (through their representatives) and, since they refer to most citizens of a class, may be defined as both *collective* (as to agents) and *universal* (as to objects) (see chs. 4.1.1.2.2 and 4.1.1.4).

The progressive universalization of mind products should not be understood as consisting of quitting "particulars" to move toward "universals", but a true *evolution* through which each *particular* mind product, which is "single-defined-concrete", contributes to the creation of the corresponding *universal* mind product, which is "grouping-undefined-abstract". In other words, *the universal is always a particularized universal*; it continuously expands as more particular instances are grouped and abstracted in it. This means that the degree of universalization reached at a given time is prospectively open to include also what presently is not yet included, because what is not yet included in the universal is what makes possible its further expansion which, in principle, is directed to reach the actually unreachable end of the full universalization.

1.2—SYNOPSIS OF THE MIND COMPONENTS, THEIR PRODUCTS, AND THEIR JUDGMENT CRITERIA

(A) Mind Components, Their Activities, and Their Products.
Here I will present *(1)* a *synopsis* of the mind components and of their activities and products (structure and functioning of the mind), and *(2)* the *terminology* of the various mind components, their activities and products.

(1) Synopsis. An overview of the mind components and their products is given in Fig. 1.1. Based on the concepts expounded in the preceding pages (ch. 1.1 and its sub-chapters), we can define the mind as follows.

(a) The mind is an *evolving, conscious, triadic entity, made of three components: intellect, sensitiveness, and power*; each of these components exerts a bidirectional (outward and inward) activity (see also Table 1.1).

(b) Through the *outward activity (selfishness)* of intellect, sensitiveness, and power, the mind produces *ideas, sentiments*, and *actions*, respectively.

(c) Through the inward activity (*consciousness*) of intellect, sensitiveness, and power, the mind produces *moral thoughts, moral feelings*, and *moral acts*, respectively, and thinks, feels, and pursues *mind evolution* as the *moral good*.

(d) The products of each mind component need the support of (i.e., presuppose) the products of the other two mind components (*interrelation, or unity-distinction, of mind components*), so that they actually exist as *triplets*; however, considering that the inward and the outward activities of each mind component, though distinct, are closely interrelated (unity-distinction of mind activities), the products of each mind activity actually exist as *sextets*, as they need the support of the products of the other five mind activities. Therefore, there are six kinds of mind products, created by six kinds of mind activity; the life of the mind consists of the interplay of such six elements.

(e) The outward and inward activities of each mind component, although distinct, are closely interrelated (*bi-directionality* and *unity-distinction* of mind activities), so that they (and their judgment criteria) necessarily co-exist (see chs. 1.1.1.2.4; 2.1.3.3.3). [Examples of this necessary co-existence could be the following ones: *(i)* The inward/moral project to give some money to a poor and sick person is a morally-good project (by the morality criterion); however, if, according to this project, in order to take the money from my bank account I should go to a bank office that is too far, instead of going to a bank office that is close to my home, the inward/moral project is at the same time an outward/selfish project that is inefficacious (by the efficaciousness criterion). Likewise, concerning the moral act and the associated action for implementing the above project, it should be noted that the inward/moral act of giving money to a poor and sick person, which is a morally-good act (by the morality criterion), is at the same time an out-

ward/selfish action that may be weak or inefficient (by the strength criterion) if I take the money from a very distant bank office. *(ii)* The outward/selfish project to lend money to a person in need by charging an excessive interest rate is an efficacious project (by the efficaciousness criterion); however, it is at the same time a morally-bad project (by the morality criterion) if the interest rate is so high as to damage the person to whom the money is lent. Likewise, concerning the selfish action and the associated moral acts for implementing the above project, it should be noted that the selfish action of loaning money at a high interest rate is at the same time a morally-bad act if it damages the recipient of the loan. *(iii)* Similarly, examples of the necessary link between the outward/selfish and the inward/moral mind products, besides for inward/moral projects and acts and for outward/selfish project and actions (see above, points "*i*" and "*ii*"), could also be easily given for the other mind products, i.e., for the outward/selfish ideas, and sentiments and for the inward/moral thoughts and feelings].

Based on the above, we can talk of the *triadic structure* and *bidirectional activity* of the mind.

(2) Terminology of Mind Components, Their Activities and Their Products. Since the various mind components can be named in various ways (e.g., "inward activity of the intellect" or "rational consciousness"), for the sake of clarity, in the following lines I will indicate the various terms used, together with their equivalents and their meaning. I will consider both *(a)* adjectives and *(b)* nouns.

(a) Adjectives.

1. "*Outward*" = "selfish" = "egoistic" = "personal": is said of the activity of the mind components (intellect, sensitiveness, and power) directed toward the "objects" external to the mind itself; it may concern the mind itself which, however, is considered as an object (not as a conscious evolving "subject" that thinks, feels, and acts, as is the case of *inward* activity—see below).

2. "*Inward*" = "moral" = "higher-order": is said of the activity of the mind components (intellect, sensitiveness, and power) that is internally directed, i.e., directed toward the mind itself considered as a conscious evolving entity that thinks, feels, and acts. Even when directed to other minds, inward mind activity looks at the inner part of them, i.e., considers them as evolving conscious triadic entities (and not as mere "objects" to be observed and possibly changed according to one's desires). Inward mind activity is "moral" because it is concerned with the mind itself, which, being capable of evolution, is the source of moral values and of moral responsibility; it is "higher-order" because it concerns the mind itself, which is the most complex and evolved among all the existing entities (chs. 2.1.1; 2.1.2).

3. "*Universal*": is a general term that applies to all mind products that refer to all or most members of a class. We should distinguish: *(i) universal*

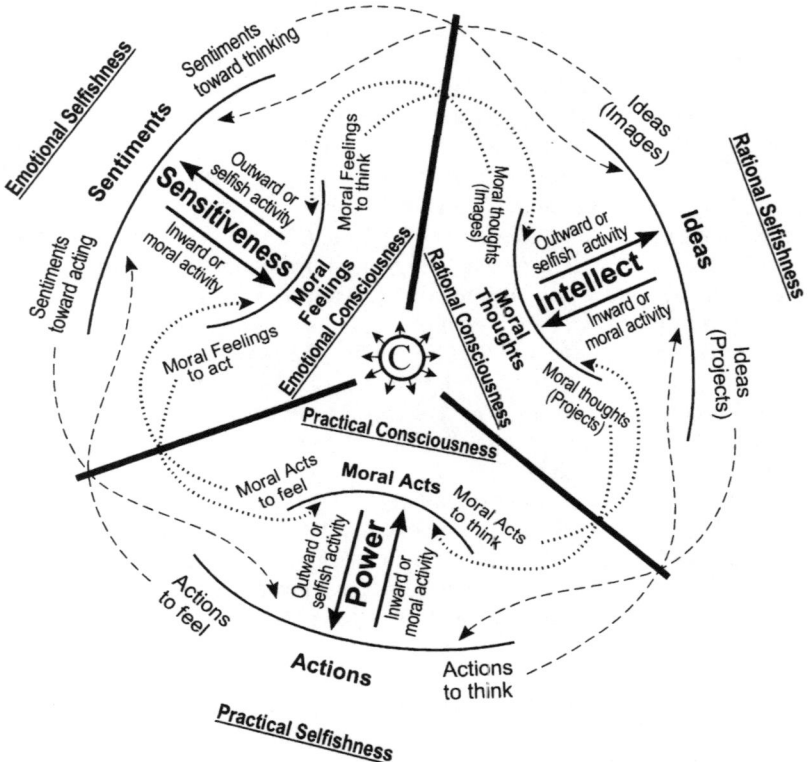

Fig. 1.1. Visual scheme of the structure and functioning of the human mind. The mind has a triadic structure and exerts a bidirectional (outward *vs* inward, or egoistic *vs* moral) activity. Its activity is evolutionary, which is the source of values and morality. (The star-like image at the center of the figure, with a "C" inside it, indicates the "Consciousness" as a whole).

as to objects (or simply *universal*), as are the universal ideas and the universal moral thoughts, whose objects are all or most members of a class; *(ii) universal as to agents* (or *shared*), as are the universal selfish sentiments, selfish projects and selfish actions, as well as the universal moral feelings, which are shared by all or most men or by all or most people of a class; and *(iii) universal as to objects and/or agents* (or *universal and/or shared or collective*), as are the universal moral projects and moral acts, which may refer to, or may be shared by, all or most men or all or most people of a class (for the difference between *shared* and *collective*, see ch. 1.1.3.2.5).
(b) Nouns.
1. "*Rational selfishness*" = "rational egoism" = "outward (or selfish) activi-

Table 1.1. The six kinds of mind products and their judgment criteria

MIND COMPONENTS and THEIR PRODUCTS (AS TRIPLETS)[1]	SPECIFIC CRITERIA		COMMON CRITERION[2]	
	Criterion	Outcomes	Criterion	Outcomes
OUTWARD ACTIVITY (SELFISHNESS)[3]				
INTELLECT: sentiment-Ideas-action (including the Ideas-of-project)[4]	Truth criterion	True/False	Value criterion	**P**= ideas of single objects/events **U**= idea of a class of objects/events[5]
SENSITIVENESS[6]: action-Sentiments-idea	Affective criterion	Joy/Sorrow	Value criterion	**P**= light sentiments felt by single persons **U**= deep sentiments shared by all/most men[7]
POWER: idea-Actions-sentiment	Strength criterion	Strong/ Weak	Value criterion	**P**= actions performed by single persons **U**= actions performed by a population[8]
INWARD ACTIVITY (CONSCIOUSNESS)[3]				
INTELLECT: feeling-Thoughts-act (including the moral projects)[9]	Morality criterion	Good/Bad	Value criterion	**P**= thoughts concerning one person **U**= thoughts concerning a population[10]
SENSITIVENESS: act-Feelings-thought	Morality criterion	Good/Bad	Value criterion	**P**= light feelings felt by single persons **U**= deep feelings shared by all (most) men
POWER: thought-Acts-feeling	Morality criterion	Good/Bad	Value criterion	**P**= acts affecting one person **U**= acts affecting a population[11]

1. Considering the *bi-directionality* and *unity-distinction* of the mind activities, the products of each mind activity actually exist as *sextets* (see chs. 1.1.1.2.4; 1.2, *A1d*).

2. "**P**" means "particular"; "**U**" means "universal". Universality of mind products includes *universality as to the objects* and *universality as to the agents* (see ch. 1.1.3.2.5). Another common criterion is the *magnitude criterion* (see ch. 2.2.1.6.1, *1*).

3. Because of the *bi-directionality* and *unity-distinction* of the mind activities, each product of the three outward mind activities, with its judgment criterion, is associated with the corresponding product of the inward mind activities and its judgment criterion.

4. The "ideas-of-project" (or *projects*) are judged as efficacious or inefficacious by the *efficaciousness* criterion, and as *particular (personal)* versus *universal (shared) projects* by the *value criterion*. [Intellect also produces "fantasies", not considered here].

5. An idea concerning a "classes of events" corresponds to what is commonly termed a "scientific law".

6. Besides producing sentiments, sensitiveness also considers the objects as "aesthetic objects" and judges them, according to the *aesthetic* criterion, as beautiful or ugly.

7. These are deep, universal sentiments expressed in literary, musical and visual arts.

8. These are *shared* actions, which are regulated by the laws of the State.

9. By the *value criterion*, we can distinguish *particular (personal) moral projects* versus *universal and/or collective moral projects* (see ch. 1.1.3.2.5).

10. They include *universal/collective moral projects* that form the democratic laws.

11. These are *universal and/or collective* moral acts (see ch. 1.1.3.2.5), which include the *universal* and *collective* acts exerted by the Executive Power of the State.

ty of the intellect": indicates the activity of the intellect producing selfish ideas and projects directed to expand and affirm the agent's self.

2. *"Emotional selfishness"* = "emotional egoism" = "outward activity of the sensitiveness": indicates the activity of the sensitiveness producing selfish sentiments, which expresses the agent's desires or aversions.

3. *"Practical selfishness"* = "practical egoism" = "outward activity of the power": indicates the activity of the power producing actions directed to satisfy the agent's desires or aversions or to realize his projects.

4. *"Selfishness"* = "egoism": indicates the selfishness as a whole, including rational, emotional, and practical selfishness.

5. *"Rational consciousness"* = "inward (or moral) activity of the intellect": indicates the activity of the intellect producing moral thoughts, directed to understand the mind itself as an *evolving*, conscious, triadic entity.

6. *"Emotional consciousness"* = "inward (or moral) activity of the sensitiveness": indicates the activity of the sensitiveness consisting of moral feelings toward thoughts/projects and actions that affect mind evolution.

7. *"Practical consciousness"* = "inward (or moral) activity of the power": indicates the activity of the power producing moral acts, directed to fulfill moral feelings and to follow moral thoughts, in this way affecting mind evolution.

8. *"Consciousness"*: indicates the consciousness as a whole, including the rational, the emotional, and the practical consciousness.

9. *"Triplet"* = refers to each of the products of the outward, or of the inward, activity of the three mind components, intellect, sensitiveness, and power; being the three mind components, though distinct, closely interrelated (*unity-distinction of mind components*), each of the three kinds of products of the outward, or of the inward, mind activity (ideas, sentiments, and actions, as well as moral thoughts, feelings and acts) cannot exist without the support of the other two.

10. *"Sextet"* = refers to each of the six products of outward and inward mind activities considered as a whole; being the outward and the inward mind activities, although distinct, closely interrelated (*unity-distinction of mind activities*), each of such six kinds of products (ideas, sentiments, and action; and moral thoughts, feelings, and acts) cannot exist without the support of the other five.

(B) Judgment Criteria.

The various criteria for the judgment of the products of the mind components are shown in Table 1.1.

To better understand the various chapters of this book, the reader should refer to the concepts and views summarized in this "Synopsis", in Fig. 1.1 as well as in Table 1.1, in order to easily frame each discussed topic into an integrated and coherent conception.

CHAPTER 2

Private Ethics: Consciousness and Moral Thoughts, Feelings, and Acts

In this chapter I will present my conception of *private* or *personal ethics*; this will be followed, in the next chapters (Chs. 3; 4), by an account of my view on *public ethics* (i.e., on *politics* and on *law*). Readers interested in other ethical or metaethical theories can refer to several available reviews and monographs (Dancy 1993; Darwall 1998; Darwall, ed., 2003; Gert 1998; MacIntyre 1998; Hooker and Little 2000; Beauchamp 2001; Sher 2001; Cahn and Markie, eds., 2002; Miller 2003; Hinman 2005; 2008; Horgan and Timmons, eds., 2006; Barcalow 2007; Shafer-Landau and Cuneo, eds., 2007; Shafer-Landau, ed., 2006–2011).

In the previous introductory chapter, I have already given a concise description of the mind as an evolving, unitary-multiple entity consisting of three components, the *intellect*, the *sensitiveness*, and the *power*, which, through their inward activity (that has as its "object" the mind as a whole, with all its content) form the *consciousness*. The latter, therefore, can be regarded as the inner part, or the core, of the mind, the apex of its activity or, in other words, as the *conscious self*. Therefore, *we can define the mind as an evolving, conscious, triadic entity that, through its inward activity, gives rise to the consciousness.*

Inward mind activity or *consciousness* creates its own specific products, i.e., *moral events*, which include *moral thoughts*, *moral feelings*, and *moral acts*; each of these mind products is judged by a specific criterion, the *morality criterion*, as well as by the *value criterion*, which applies to all mind products (Table 1.1).

2.1—CONSCIOUSNESS: INWARD MIND ACTIVITY THAT PRODUCES MORAL EVENTS

2.1.1—*Moral Events (Moral Thoughts/Projects, Moral Feelings, and Moral Acts)*

As described elsewhere (Belfiore 2004: 273–82), *moral events* are the specific products of the consciousness. We can distinguish three kinds of moral events: *(a) moral thoughts* and *moral projects* (created by the inward activity of intellect or *"rational consciousness"*), *(b) moral feelings* (created by the inward activity of sensitiveness or *"emotional consciousness"*), and *(c) moral acts* (created by the inward activity of power or *"practical consciousness"*) (Fig. 1.1). These events correspond to the selfish ideas/projects, sentiments, and actions, created by the outward activity of the intellect, sensitiveness, and power, respectively. Indeed moral events can be conceived as "higher-order" mental products, i.e., as ideas, sentiments and actions taking place at a "higher level", i.e., at a level higher than that at which the outward activities of intellect, sensitiveness, and power operate, i.e., at the level of consciousness. The adjective "higher-order" can be applied to each of the moral events, be it a moral *thought/ project*, a moral *feeling* or a moral *act*, because moral events are created through the inward mind activity or self-reflection of the mind on itself, i.e., are the result of the *reflexive activity* by which the mind thinks of, feels about, and acts on itself. This entails that moral events refer to the mind as a whole with its entire content of knowledge, sentiments, and performed actions (including the awareness of the existence of other minds and of the relationship between one's mind with them). This means that moral events have as their "object" the most complex and evolved among all the existing entities (see next chapters); hence, the definition of moral events as "higher-order" events and of *consciousness* as a "higher-level" mind component as compared to *selfishness*. This is illustrated in the Fig. 1.1, which shows that moral thoughts/projects, moral feelings and moral acts can be regarded as the products of the "inward activity" of intellect, sensitiveness, and power (see the arrows pointing at the center of the figure, as opposed to the outwardly-directed arrows); this activity is directed toward the inner part, or the core, of the mind where it gives rise to consciousness. Thus, consciousness always acts with the awareness of being the core of an individual mind (understood as an entity susceptible to changes, either evolution or involution) operating in a world populated by other minds; this entails that any moral event is performed with the awareness of the effects that it may produce on the evolution of the mind of the acting agent himself or of other minds. This awareness is the source of *moral responsibility*.

2.1.1.1—Moral Thoughts and Moral Projects/Decisions

(1) Moral Thoughts. Moral thoughts can be defined as inwardly oriented, or "high-order", ideas produced by the *rational consciousness* (Fig. 1.1). The rational consciousness, producing moral thoughts, has as its object the mind as a whole, and is aware of all the content of the mind, i.e., of the many ideas/theories, sentiments and actions as well as moral thoughts themselves, moral feelings and moral acts produced by the intellect, sensitiveness, and power; this enables it to elaborate *moral thoughts* (or a more general *moral conception*) having as their "object" the mind itself with all its content, which includes the knowledge of other minds and of the physical world (namely, the known reality as a whole). For this reason, moral thoughts are "higher-order" ideas compared to the ideas produced by the outward activity of intellect. To clarify this point, we should consider that the human mind is the most complex and evolved among all the existing entities, i.e., it is at the apex of an ideal pyramid that includes, going from top to bottom, human conscious minds, animals, plants, and physical objects. The human conscious mind is the most evolved entity and is reached only through the inward activity of intellect or rational consciousness; it is not reachable through the outward activity of intellect (rational selfishness), because the outward activity of intellect, even when directed to the mind itself (as occurs with psychological inquiry), considers the mind as an object of observation. It is only through the inward activity of intellect (rational consciousness) that the mind is considered as a "subject", i.e., is understood in its true nature, as an *evolving* conscious triadic entity, made of intellect, sensitiveness, and power, capable of *evolution* and, hence, as the source of *moral responsibility*. This dimension of the mind can only be reached through moral thoughts (higher-order ideas), and not through the (lower-order) ideas of the outward activity of intellect.

(2) Moral Projects. The rational consciousness, based on its moral thoughts, makes a synthesis and creates several or many *moral projects*, with the help of imagination. Moral projects can be regarded as inwardly oriented, or "higher-order", projects (compared to the "lower-order" projects created by the outward activity of intellect); the adjective "high-order" is applied to moral projects because the latter are based on moral thoughts, which are "higher-order" ideas (see above). Among the created projects, consciousness selects the one to be realized, i.e., consciousness takes a *moral decision*. The latter consists of a choice of one moral project among the many possible projects created by the mind. Indeed, a decision cannot take place unless there are several (actually many) projects from which to

make a choice. Actually, *any formulated project is always a "selected project"* and therefore it always entails a decision, otherwise it is still a project in formation, i.e., the activity of inward activity of intellect and imagination that ends with the selected project. Once created, moral projects stir-up special sentiments, *moral feelings* (see below, ch. 2.1.1.2), which contribute to determine whether a project is selected or not (moral decision). The selected moral project is followed by the *moral act* that realizes it (see ch. 2.1.1.3).

A moral decision expresses the adhesion of the consciousness to the selected project and reflects the inner, deeper part of the consciousness: the *self*. As such, moral decisions are characterized by *intentionality* and moral *responsibility*.

[I mentioned above that moral projects are created with the help of imagination. Indeed, imagination (or fantasy) is a very important feature of the intellect, and is required for the cognitive activity of the intellect itself (to create scientific *hypotheses*) but also for the activity of sensitiveness (to create the *fantastic objects* or aesthetic ideals and the *means* to express sentiments) as well as for the activity of power (whose actions realize one of the *ideas-of-projects* created with the help of imagination), and for the activity of consciousness (to create *moral projects*). Fantasy, however, will not be further discussed in this book—for more details, see Belfiore 2004].

2.1.1.2—Moral Feelings

Moral feelings can be regarded as inwardly oriented, or "high-order", *sentiments* created by the *inward activity of sensitiveness* (or *emotional consciousness*) (Fig. 1.1). They have as objects the other kinds of mind products (and thus, indirectly, all facts of the human world); importantly, they contribute to the selection of the projects (i.e., to the choice between moral and selfish projects), by competing with personal or selfish sentiments (desires or aversions). Since a moral project is implemented by the corresponding *moral act* (see below—ch. 2.1.1.3), a moral feeling is felt toward both the moral decision (the selected project) and the corresponding moral act.

While selfish sentiments, created by the outward activity of sensitiveness, are directed toward "objects" (physical or non-physical), moral feelings, created by the inward activity of sensitiveness, are mainly directed toward moral thoughts/projects and moral acts, which can induce evolution or involution in one or more minds. The adjective "higher-order" is applicable to moral feelings as compared to selfish sentiments because, unlike the latter, moral feelings are mainly concerned with moral thoughts/projects and acts, which are higher-order ideas/projects and actions related to the mind itself as an evolving and conscious entity, which is the source of moral responsibility and is not reachable by personal or selfish sentiments.

2.1.1.3—Moral Acts

Moral acts are the product of the *inward activity of power*, which forms *practical consciousness* (Fig. 1.1). A *moral act* consists of the realization of a moral project (i.e., of the selected moral project) and of the fulfillment of a moral feeling; as such, it too is charged with moral *responsibility*, as are the moral projects and decisions (see also below).

The adjective "higher-order" is applicable to moral acts because they (unlike personal or selfish actions), being the product of the inward activity of the power, are directed to affect (or have as their object) the mind itself as an evolving and conscious entity, by inducing either mind-evolution or mind-involution; this effect is the source of moral responsibility and is outside the reach of personal or selfish actions (produced by the outward activity of power—or practical selfishness).

2.1.2—*Defining Moral Events: Consciousness versus Selfishness*

(A) Defining Moral Events.
As stated elsewhere (Belfiore 2004: 276–81), moral events, which include moral thoughts/projects, moral feelings, and moral acts, have two unique, distinctive features: *(1)* they are always the *creation of a single individual mind*, and *(2)* they have as their "object" the *mind as a whole* (either the mind of the acting agent or the minds of others).

(1) Moral Events Are Created by Single Individual Minds. Moral thoughts/projects, moral feelings, and moral acts are always the product of a single mind. Even when a group of individuals creates a moral project or performs a moral act, this should be regarded as the result of several individual moral projects/acts occurring simultaneously. This is because a moral act, being characterized by *intentionality* and charged with *responsibility*, cannot be a "common" act.

When a moral act is carried out simultaneously by more than one individual, whether the finality of a given individual is the same as that of other individuals, or differs from it, does not modify the moral significance of his act, i.e., the moral significance of a given individual act is neither increased nor reduced by the contemporary occurrence of other similar moral acts.

When a moral project or the corresponding moral act is endorsed and/or performed simultaneously by most members of a community, this means that the moral project/act has undergone a process of *universalization as to its agents*, i.e., it has become a *universal and collective* moral project/act (see ch. 1.1.3.2.5).

(2) Moral Events Are Directed to Change the Mind. Moral events could be thought as ordered in a sequence to show that they are directed to produce some change: *moral thoughts* are the basis for *moral projects*, the latter stir-up (or are prompted by) *moral feelings*, which in turn prompt *moral acts*, which realize a change. However, in contrast to *personal or selfish actions* (created by the *outward* activity of power or *practical selfishness*), which produce changes in the physical world, *moral acts* (and the corresponding moral thoughts/projects and moral feelings), which are created by the inward activity of power (*practical consciousness*, see Fig. 1.1), are directed to produce changes in one or more minds (i.e., changes affecting one or more individuals). This means that when an individual takes a moral decision and undertakes the corresponding moral act his activity is directed to modify the state of a mind, i.e., to induce an evolution or an involution in the intellect, and/or sensitiveness and/or power of one or more individuals (including the acting agent himself). For this reason, moral events make the individual a moral subject, charged with moral responsibility.

Thus, we can say that: *(a)* moral thoughts, created by the rational consciousness (Fig. 1.1), are inwardly oriented ideas directed to understand the mind as a whole, while moral projects (and decisions) are plans for possible mind changes, to be realized by moral acts; *(b)* moral feelings, created by the emotional consciousness, consist of inwardly oriented sentiments (of attraction or repulsion) toward moral thoughts or projects and moral acts; and *(c)* moral acts, created by the practical consciousness, are inwardly oriented actions directed to change the mind of an individual (who may well be the acting individual himself) or of some individuals or of many individuals.

(B) Consciousness versus Selfishness (Fig. 1.1).
It is noteworthy that the outward mind activity (selfishness) is directed to create ideas/projects, sentiments, and actions concerned with most objects and events, with the exception of the most complex and evolved one: the mind itself regarded as an *evolving* entity. For this reason, selfishness is "inferior" to consciousness, which is concerned with the mind as a whole.

On the other hand, the inward mind activity (or consciousness) is directed to create moral thoughts/projects, feelings, and acts, which are concerned with the mind itself with all its content and its ability to undergo evolution (or involution). The mind being the most complex and evolved entity, consciousness is "superior" to selfishness (ch. 3.1.1.2, *1*).

2.1.3—*Inward/Moral versus Outward/Selfish Mind Products*

In this chapter, I will attempt to further explain the distinction between the products of the inward/moral and the outward/selfish activity of intellect, sensitiveness, and power, i.e., the products of consciousness versus those of selfishness. However, I once again underline that the inward/moral mind activity is not separated from the outward/selfish one; rather these two kinds of activity are always interrelated to each other, so that what actually occurs is a prevalently inward/moral or a prevalently outward/selfish mind activity. Thus, the mind is bidirectional (bi-directionality of mind) and yet unitary.

I will consider: (1) *Moral thoughts* and *moral projects/decisions* versus *ideas* and *personal or selfish projects/decisions*; (2) *Moral feelings* versus *personal or selfish sentiments*; and (3) *Moral acts* versus *personal or selfish actions*.

2.1.3.1—Moral Thoughts and Moral Projects-Decisions versus Selfish or Personal Ideas and Projects-Decisions

In the following two chapters, I will contrast moral thoughts versus selfish or personal ideas, and moral projects/decisions versus selfish or personal projects/decisions.

2.1.3.1.1—Moral Thoughts (and Moral Conception) versus Personal (or Selfish) Ideas (and Scientific Theories)

While the *outward activity of intellect* (*rational selfishness*) produces selfish ideas (or, simply, *ideas*) as well as the more elaborated *scientific theories*, the *inward activity of intellect* (*rational consciousness*) produces *moral thoughts* as well as the more elaborated *moral conception* (Fig. 1.1).

The characteristic feature of moral thoughts is that, although being a cognitive process, they are not concerned with the acquisition of new knowledge on some aspects of the *objective* reality (this is obtained by the outward activity of intellect through the inductive method) nor with the elaboration of the knowledge so obtained (which is made by the intellect through the deductive method); rather they aim at a supreme rational synthesis concerned with the mind as a whole, as a *subject*, with all its content and its evolving nature, leading to a conception about the *value* of the mind itself and of its evolution. This is an *evaluative* activity; it allows to recognize the preeminent place that individual minds have in reality as conscious and evolving entities, i.e., as entities whose nature tends toward evolution.

As will be discussed in chapter 2.2.1.1, moral thoughts (and moral conception) should not be judged as true or false by the *truth criterion* (this kind of evaluation applies to the outward products of intellect—ideas) but they must be judged as good or bad by the *morality criterion* (Table 1.1).

2.1.3.1.2—Moral Projects and Decisions versus Personal (or Selfish) Projects and Decisions

As stated elsewhere (ch. 1.1.1.2.1), *personal projects* are created by the *outward activity of intellect* (or *rational selfishness*), and then realized through personal actions, directed to satisfy a personal sentiment or to realize an idea-of-project or to modify the results of previous actions. Conversely, *moral projects* are created by the *inward activity of intellect* (or *rational consciousness*), and are then realized by *moral acts* directed to induce a change in one or more minds, a change that may be an evolution or an involution of the affected mind(s). Thus, moral projects and moral acts are to be judged as good or bad (by the *morality criterion*) (ch. 1.1.3.1), according to whether they are directed to induce an evolution or an involution in the affected minds (Table 1.1). [In contrast, personal projects are to be judged as efficacious or inefficacious (by the *efficaciousness criterion*), according to whether they are or not apt to reach (through the corresponding action) the end to which they are directed; and personal actions are to be judged as weak or strong (by the *strength criterion*), according to whether they are or are not efficient in producing the projected effects (ch. 1.1.3.1; Table 1.1)].

Moral decisions, which consist of the selection of the projects to be realized through moral acts, are, they too, judged by the morality criterion.

2.1.3.2—Moral Feelings versus Personal (or Selfish) Sentiments

As I have described elsewhere (Belfiore 2004: 279), we should distinguish moral feelings from personal or selfish sentiments. *Personal sentiments* are created by the *outward activity of sensitiveness* (or *emotional selfishness*—see Fig. 1.1) and express the desire or hate toward a variety of particular "objects", including physical objects and events as well as ideas, projects, actions and sentiments themselves. Selfish sentiments are judged as joyful or sorrowful by the *affective criterion*, which is a *subjective* criterion and indicates whether a given sentiment means joy or sorrow for the subject who feels it (Table 1.1). Conversely, *moral feelings* are created by the *inward activity of sensitiveness* (or *emotional consciousness*) and express the feelings that are felt by the consciousness toward moral thoughts/projects, moral feelings themselves, and the corresponding moral acts, considered as factors that affect mind evolution, i.e., that can induce either mind evolution or involution. Moral feelings are judged as good or bad by the *morality criterion* (which is an *objective* criterion) according to whether they are felt toward moral thoughts/projects, feelings and the corresponding moral acts directed to produce an evolution or an involution in one or more individual minds. Often, personal sentiments and moral feelings are in contrast, the former inducing a given person to do what he likes best, the latter inducing him to do what will produce an evolution in one or more minds (including the mind of the acting individual). The competition between personal sentiments and moral feelings will determine the moral choice, inasmuch as the final act will express the prevalence of one over the other (or vice versa).

2.1.3.3—Moral Acts versus Personal (or Selfish) Actions

In the following three chapters, I will summarize the *features of personal or selfish actions*, those of *moral acts*, and the *relationship* between these two mind products.

2.1.3.3.1—Features of Personal (or Selfish) Actions

A *personal or selfish action* is the product of the outward activity of the *power* (i.e., of the *practical selfishness*). As I stated elsewhere (Belfiore 2004: 29–31, 237–42), a personal action realizes a selected *personal or selfish project* (created by intellect by means of imagination) and satisfies a sentiment felt by the acting individual; this end is reached by inducing a *change in the physical world*. A personal project is formed by the intellect without prior or simultaneous awareness of being part of an individual mind, susceptible to evolution or involution, and without considering the existence of other individuals, who are regarded simply as physical objects. Thus, an action is a mind activity performed for *subjective or personal or selfish reasons*, which produces effects significant from the standpoint of the *selfishness* of the acting agent (but not from his moral standpoint, i.e., the standpoint of his *consciousness*). When subjected to judgment, a personal project may be judged as efficacious or inefficacious (by the efficaciousness criterion); and the corresponding personal actions may be judged as weak or strong (by the strength criterion) (Table 1.1).

An example of personal action may be my turning on a fan to alleviate the heat (Belfiore 2004: 281). If I know (i.e., if I have the *idea*) that circulating the air with an electric fan helps me to tolerate the heat, and if I wish to avoid suffering from the heat (i.e., if I feel the *sentiment* of hate toward the heat), and if I want to realize my wish, then, while I am seated on my chair, I may create in my mind the *personal project* consisting in foreseeing those actions required to turn on the fan (to rise to my feet, to go to the place where the fan is located and to turn it on), and then I can perform the corresponding *personal action*. Note that this action includes the contribution of all the three mind components, because they are closely correlated to one another, as it has already been mentioned.

2.1.3.3.2—Features of Moral Acts

A *moral act* is the product of the inward activity of the *power* (*practical consciousness*) (Fig. 1.1); it realizes a *moral project/decision* created by the inward activity of intellect (or *rational consciousness*) by selecting a project among the various possible projects created by means of imagination. As described elsewhere (Belfiore 2004: 280), a moral act is directed to induce a *change in the mind* (intellect and/or sensitiveness and/or power), which may involve one or more minds, and may consist of either a mind evolution or involution. Thus, a moral act is a product of the consciousness created for *objective reasons*, inasmuch as it induces effects significant in virtue of the evolution or involution that it causes in an existing entity, the mind, either the mind of the acting individual, or that of another individual, or that of a group of individuals, or that of an entire community. As such, a moral act is characterized by *responsibility*, as will be discussed in the following chapters. Note that whereas personal actions can affect an individual considered as a physical object, moral acts affect individuals considered as instances of the mind (i.e., persons composed of intellect, sensitiveness, power and exerting both inward and outward activity), susceptible to evolution or involution. Briefly, we can say that whereas *personal (selfish) actions are "mind-to-physical world" relations, moral acts are "mind-to-mind" relations.*

When subjected to judgment, moral acts (as the corresponding moral projects) should be judged as good or bad by the *morality criterion* (according to whether they induce mind evolution or involution) (Table 1.1). Note that moral acts, at variance with personal actions, cannot be judged by the strength criterions (as weak or strong), because being weak or strong has no relevance to the moral meaning of a moral act: indeed, a moral act that could be judged as "weak" by the strength criterion, may be morally better than a moral act that could be judged as "strong" if the former is intentionally directed to induce a greater mind evolution than the latter.

Both moral acts and personal actions can be judged by the *value criterion* as ranging from particular to universal (see: Table 1.1; chs. 2.2.2; 3.1).

Here I will give two examples of moral acts: *(1)* one affecting a mind other than the agent's mind, and *(2)* one affecting the mind of the agent himself (Belfiore 2004: 281).

(1) Example of a Moral Act Affecting a Mind Other Than the Agent's Mind. If I know that a boy is not able to go to school because his family does not have enough money, and if I wish to help him, I can decide to give him an amount of money to allow him an education, i.e., to induce an evolution of his intellect (and also of the other components of his mind). To this end, I make the appropriate *moral project*, followed by the corresponding *moral act* (going to my bank and making those actions required to transfer money to the poor boy).

(2) Example of a Moral Act Affecting the Mind of the Agent Himself. A student likes a special kind of luxurious car very much and, hence, he buys it; by doing so, he has carried out a *personal action* that satisfies one of his desires. On the other hand, it may be that the student makes a deeper consideration, namely that if he spends so much money on buying a luxurious car, he would no longer be able to pay the fees for his university course, so he renounces to buy the car and takes the *moral decision* of paying the university fees to attend the university course through which he will improve his intellectual ability (i.e., he will promote the evolution of his mind).

2.1.3.3.3—Relationship Between Moral Acts and Personal Actions

The relationship between personal actions and moral acts is worth further clarification. Both *personal (or selfish) actions* and *moral acts* are physical events or changes in the physical world carried out by *power*: the former by the *outward activity of power* (or *practical selfishness*) and the latter by the *inward activity of power* (or *practical consciousness*—Fig. 1.1). However, they differ because the former consist of the realization of *selfish projects* directed to satisfy selfish *desires or interests* of the acting agent whereas the latter consist of the realization of *moral projects* directed to fulfill *moral feelings* and to induce a change (evolution or involution) in one or more minds (Belfiore 2004: 279–80). Yet, because of *mind bi-directionality* (chs. 1.1.1.2.4; 1.2, *A1e*), most personal actions are associated to a moral act and *vice versa*, because when a personal project is realized through a personal action the consciousness of the agent is aware that some effects may be exerted on the involved minds (the agent's mind or other minds); likewise, when performing a moral act, the agent may select the way that best satisfy his selfish desires/interests. We can say that any agent-caused physical event is a personal action inasmuch as it reflects the desires of the agent and, if it induces a change in one or more minds, it is at the same time a moral act. Thus, *most personal actions* (if they involve human beings, and do not consist only of changes to physical objects) *also entail a moral act, and most moral acts also entail a personal action.* However, the weight of the two components changes along a range of situations so that at one extremity of the range there are those instances in which the agent-caused physical event is mainly or almost exclusively a personal action, because it is carried out primarily to satisfy the agent desires, whereas at the other extremity there are those situations in which the event is mainly or almost exclusively a moral act, because it is carried out primarily to induce a change in one or more minds (Belfiore 2004: 292–93) (see also Fig. 2.3).

When personal actions promote the evolution of the agent's mind, they are actually moral acts and express *morally-good egoism* (ch. 2.1.5.2.2).

Notably, a moral act actually is the *naturalistic* (physical) component of a *triplet* and co-exists with the supporting *non-naturalistic* components: moral thoughts/projects and feelings. This helps to explain *nonreductive ethical naturalism* and, mainly, *ethical nonnaturalism* (see Tables 2.2; 2.3).

2.1.4—Consciousness as the Generator of Moral Principles, Moral Values, and Moral Norms

We already know that the *rational consciousness* produces *moral thoughts* (and *moral projects*), that the *emotional consciousness* produces *moral feelings*, and that the *practical consciousness* produces *moral acts* (Fig. 1.1). Below, I will discuss moral thoughts, moral feelings and moral projects by considering them as the source of moral principles, moral values and moral norms, respectively.

2.1.4.1—Defining Moral Principles (Moral Thoughts), Moral Values (Moral Feelings), and Moral Norms (Moral Projects)

Referring to what has been discussed in the previous chapters, let us see how *moral thoughts* create *moral principles*, *moral feelings* found *moral values*, and *moral projects* give rise to *moral norms*.

(a) Defining moral principles. Moral thoughts, produced by *rational consciousness*, through *internal observation* (or introspection), make us aware that *mind evolution* is the objective moral *good*. This means that the rational consciousness produces the *moral thought* that "mind evolution is the human good", which is actually a *moral principle*. This general principle, in its turn, includes less comprehensive *moral principles*, such as the principle that "the evolution of intellect is morally-good", or the principle that "the evolution of sensitiveness is morally-good", or the principle that "the evolution of power is morally-good", and other still less extensive principles (see next chapter). The justification of the moral principle that "mind evolution is the human good", together with its *objective nature*, is discussed in chapter 2.2.1.1.1, *1*.

Thus, *moral principles* are the product of *moral thought*, generated by the inward activity of intellect (or *rational consciousness*).

It should be pointed out that good moral principles (i.e., that the evolution of the mind, or of each of its components, is the human good) are the products of *"good" moral thoughts* generated by a *"good" rational consciousness*; a *morally-bad* consciousness may produce *bad* moral thoughts and *bad* moral principles (according to which mind evolution is not the human good and is not different, or is even less good, than mind involution).

Thus, contrary to Hume's view (ch. 2.2.1.1.1), moral thought (or "reason") generated by intellect does affect human actions and behavior.

(b) Defining moral values. Through internal observation, *moral thought* makes us aware that *moral feelings* (produced by the *emotional consciousness*—Fig. 1.1) consist of the desire to realize the human good; in other words, moral feelings lead the agent to consider the human good as morally desirable or *valuable*, i.e., moral feelings "found" *moral values.* As for the moral principles (see above), so for the moral values we can distinguish general moral values (having as their object the evolution of the mind as a whole) and less comprehensive moral values, i.e., those concerning less comprehensive moral goods, such as the evolution of just one of the mind components (intellect or sensitiveness or power) or still less comprehensive moral goods (see next chapter, and Table 2.1).

Thus, *moral values* are founded by the *moral feelings*, created by the inward activity of sensitiveness (or *emotional consciousness*).

Like moral thoughts and moral principles, moral feelings and moral values may be distinguished into *good* or *bad* by the morality criterion (Table 1.1). Moral feelings (and the corresponding moral values) are *good* when they consist of the desire to realize the human good (i.e., promotion of mind evolution) whereas they are *bad* when they consist of the desire to realize human evil (i.e., restraint of mind evolution).

Moral values, felt through moral feelings, are most often in agreement with moral principles generated by moral thoughts, due to the internal coherence of the mind; yet, sometimes discordance may exist. This may happen when erroneous moral thoughts give us the false cognitive awareness that something is "good", whereas it is actually "bad". An example could be the case of Abraham, who was ready to sacrifice Isaac for doing what he (erroneously) thought was "good" (obeying God's command), even if he was certainly tormented by his moral feeling of repulsion toward "killing human beings" (besides his personal desire to preserve the life of his son). Conversely, when moral thoughts tell us that a given act is "bad", it may happen that personal desires or interests prompt us to do that act whereas moral feelings (if they are "good moral feelings" and are not too weak and overcome by personal desires) will incite us not to do the bad act; on the other hand, if moral feelings are "bad", they may prompt us to do the bad act. This entails that, like moral thoughts (which may be "good" or "bad" according to whether they recognize, or not, that mind evolution is the "good"), moral feelings may be "good" or "bad", according to whether they consist of a feeling of attraction or of repulsion for the good projects and acts. Considering that mind evolution is "the good", it follows that the "bad" moral thoughts and feelings are the expression of little evolved (or even "sick") minds (crimes committed for "motive of honor" and prompted by the agent's "moral feeling", are a typical expression of little evolved minds). It should be considered that the "bad" moral feelings are difficult to distinguish from extremely weak "good moral feelings" that are easily overcome by opposing strong personal desires and interests.

(c) Defining moral norms. Moral thoughts, through internal observation, make us aware that *moral principles* (created by moral thoughts themselves and, hence, by the rational consciousness) and *moral values* (created by moral feelings and, hence, by emotional consciousness) converge into a *selected moral project,* i.e., a project that reflects both the thought moral principle and the felt moral value; this desired project will act as a *moral norm* that guides the *moral acts* (created by the practical consciousness—Fig. 1.1) directed to realize that project and to fulfill the moral feeling that desires it. Like moral principles and moral values, moral norms can be distinguished into general moral norms, directed to realize the evolution of the mind as a whole, and less comprehensive moral norms, directed to realize the evolution of one of the mind components (ch. 4.1.2.3; Figs. 4.2 and 4.3).

Thus, *moral norms* are the *selected moral projects,* i.e., projects produced by the rational consciousness on the basis of its moral principles or thoughts, and then selected under the pressure of moral feelings (or the balance between moral feelings and personal desires); moral norms will be implemented by (or are the guide of) *moral acts.* Hence, moral norms consist of adhering to the indications of moral principles (which define the moral good) and to the demands of moral feelings (which prompt to pursue moral values).

Like moral principles and moral values, moral norms may be distinguished, according to the *morality criterion,* into *good* moral norms, when they prescribe moral acts directed to realize the human good (mind evolution), or *bad* moral norms (when they prescribe moral acts directed to realize human evil, i.e., mind involution or restraint of mind evolution).

2.1.4.2—Hierarchical Arrangement of the Various "Moral Goods"

Based on the above reasoning, we can say that the *moral good* (mind evolution) is what is defined by good moral thoughts as *moral principles,* what is felt by good moral feelings as *moral values* and what is prescribed by good moral *norms* and realized by good *moral acts.* It follows that there is a correspondence between *(a)* the various human "moral goods", and *(b)* the various moral principles, values, and norms.

The various human "moral goods" can be hierarchically arranged, inasmuch as there is a general moral good (mind evolution) that includes less comprehensive moral goods (i.e., the evolution of one or another of the three mind components); the latter, in their turn, include still less comprehensive moral goods, i.e., the evolution of one of the activities of a given mind component (e.g., the evolution of ideas in the sphere of mathematics or of biological sciences or of social sciences, etc., in the case of intellect). Thus, the relationship between the various hierarchical levels is that of a large class, its sub-classes, the sub-sub-classes, down to the class members, which are single particular ideas or sentiments or actions (Table 2.1).

The basic moral good is mind evolution. It should be underlined, however, that even more important than mind evolution is preserving the existence of the mind and avoiding its partial or total involution, i.e., avoiding physical harm or death, which represent "possibly irreversible" and "total and irreversible" mind involutions, respectively (ch. 4.1.2.3, *A*).

The three sub-classes shown in Table 2.1 (evolution of intellect, evolution of sensitiveness, and evolution of power) refer to the *outward* activity of mind, to which other classes should be added referring to the *inward* mind activity, i.e., the class referring to the evolution of *consciousness*, which comprises three sub-classes: the evolution of *moral thoughts*, the evolution of *moral feelings*, and the evolution of *moral acts*. Moreover, it should be considered that two necessary conditions are required for the evolution of the power (see below): *liberty* and *equality* of opportunity; this means that two further classes (and their sub-classes) should be adjoined, i.e., the classes whose members are those particular conditions through which *liberty* and *equality* are concretely implemented.

At this point, it is useful to define the meaning of the terms *(1)* "liberty" and *(2)* "equality of opportunity".

(1) Liberty. The complex and difficult issue of human liberty will be discussed in chapter 2.4. Here I just recall that we should distinguish *internal freedom*, which is concerned with the choice of the agent between alternative actions or moral acts (actually between alternative projects, which will then be realized through actions or moral acts), and *external freedom*, which is needed to concretely perform the decided actions or moral acts. It follows that liberty is concerned with the activity of the *power*, both with the outward activity of the power (or *practical selfishness*), which generates actions, and with the inward activity of the power (or *practical consciousness*—Fig. 1.1), which generates moral acts. This means that liberty is required for the development (or evolution) of the power. Indeed, whereas the activity of intellect and that of sensitiveness may be fully developed (from particular to universal ideas and sentiments) by the single individual, the activity of the power, being directed to the external world, may be limited or impeded by obstacles, including other minds (social relationships). Thus, liberty means absence of obstacles that interfere with the performance of the agent's decided actions and moral acts and, therefore, with the evolution of the power. However, since the three components of the mind are closely

interrelated to one another (each component needing the support of the other two for its activity—chs. 1.1.1.1, 6; 1.1.2, 2nd proposition), lack of freedom interferes also with the evolution of the intellect and sensitiveness. Thus, *liberty or freedom is a necessary condition for the evolution of the mind* in all its three components and in its outward as well as inward activity.

Which are the obstacles that may limit or impede freedom? To answer this question we should consider that (apart from natural or physical obstacles) the actions of an agent may be limited by the arrogance and violence of another agent (or other agents) who, in this way, would act against the moral norm (they would restrain mind evolution of others). Indeed, if freedom is required for mind evolution, it should be enjoyed by all individuals (or citizens, if we refer to an organized society or State). This is possible if there are norms and laws that regulate the actions of citizens to assure freedom to all of them. It follows that freedom, to exist as a condition enjoyed by all citizens, needs human actions to be regulated by shared norms and laws (which reflect shared moral principles and values). This means that, unlike personal actions, moral acts, being directed to help the evolution of mind (which needs freedom), cannot interfere with the freedom of others; otherwise they would no longer be moral acts. Needless to say, freedom cannot be conceived as "freedom from the laws", because this would mean freedom for some people (those who do not respect the laws, thus interfering with the freedom of others) and lack of freedom for those people whose actions are interfered with. Thus, *personal actions should be regulated by the laws and should be free within the laws*.

(2) Equality of Opportunity. Like liberty, equality of opportunity is needed for mind evolution because it allows the full expression of the ability of each mind component of an agent to reach the level of development allowed by its natural endowment. Since mind evolution mainly consists of the development of "particular" into "universal" ideas, sentiments and actions, we can say that equality of opportunity is required in order to have attributed, by the *value criterion*, the correct score in the scale of value going from "particular" to "universal" (Table 1.1). This is true for both the *outward* and the *inward* mind activities.

Due to the parallelism between *(a)* the various human "moral goods", and *(b)* the corresponding moral principles, values and norms, the hierarchical arrangement shown in Table 2.1 also applies to moral principles, values and norms (ch. 4.1.2.3). To show this, referring to one of the "moral goods" included in that Table, let us say, the "evolution of intellect", it suffices to recognize that the "evolution of intellect" is a "moral good" because moral thoughts have created the *moral principle* that "evolution of intellect is a moral good", and is a "moral value" because through moral feelings it is felt that "evolution of intellect is a *moral value*". This moral principle and this moral value converge into the *moral norm*: "one ought to promote the

Table 2.1. The hierarchical arrangement of the various "moral goods[1]"

CLASS	SUB-CLASSES[2]	SUB-SUB-CLASSES[3]	SINGLE CLASS MEMBERS
Evolution of *mind*	Evolution of *intellect* (universalization of ideas)	Evolution of ideas in *mathematics*	Idea-*1* Idea-2 Idea . . . *n*
		Evolution of ideas in *biological sciences*	Idea-*1* Idea-2 Idea . . . *n*
		Evolution of ideas in *social sciences*, etc.	Idea-*1* Idea-2 Idea . . . *n*
	Evolution of *sensitiveness* (universalization, or deepening, of sentiments)	Evolution of sentiments in *literary arts*	Sentiment-*1* Sentiment-2 Sentiment . . . *n*
		Evolution of sentiments in *musical arts*	Sentiment-*1* Sentiment-2 Sentiment . . . *n*
		Evolution of sentiments in *visual arts*, etc.	Sentiment-*1* Sentiment-2 Sentiment . . . *n*
	Evolution of *power* (universalization of actions)	Evolution in the *physical health*	Ability to action-*1* Ability to action-2 Ability to action . . . *n*
		Evolution in the *economic conditions*	Ability to action-*1* Ability to action-2 Ability to action . . . *n*
		Evolution in the *social status*	Ability to action-*1* Ability to action-2 Ability to action . . . *n*

1. Due to correspondence between the various "moral goods" and the various moral principles, values and norms, the hierarchical arrangement as outlined in this table also applies to the latter (see the text in this chapter; also: ch. 4.1.2.3; Figs. 4.2 and 4.3).

2. The three sub-classes in this group refer to the *outward* activity of the mind, to which other classes should be added, referring to the *inward* mind activity (*consciousness*), i.e., the three sub-classes which refer to the evolution of *moral thoughts*, the evolution of *moral feelings*, and the evolution of *moral acts*. Moral goods also comprise *truth telling* (ch 2.2.1.4.2, *D4*) and *keeping promises* (chs. 2.2.1.4.2, *D4*; 2.2.1.7.2, *C1*; 3.1.1.2, *2c*; 3.1.2.3.3), whose lack may impair the knowledge concerning past or present facts (truth telling) or future facts (keeping promises); this may affect the activity and evolution of intellect and, indirectly, of the other mind components. Moreover, it should be considered that two necessary conditions are required for mind evolution (activity and evolution of the power): *liberty* and *equality* of opportunity (see points "*1*" and "*2*" in this chapter); this means that two further classes (and their sub-classes) should be adjoined, i.e., the classes whose members are those particular conditions through which liberty and equality of opportunity are concretely implemented.

3. These sub-sub-classes of moral goods (mathematics, or biological sciences, or literary or visual arts, etc.) are pursued by the most evolved minds; in the less-evolved minds, the distinction is less evident and yet the tendency is always present.

evolution of intellect." The hierarchical arrangement of norms is analyzed in chapter 4.1.2.3 and summarized in Figs. 4.2 and 4.3.

2.1.5—The "Ground Moral Norm" and the Spheres of Decreasing Moral Responsibility

Although the ground moral norm has already been defined in the preceding chapters, the characteristics of such a norm and the responsibility for its application are worthy of further discussion.

2.1.5.1—The Ground Moral Norm: An "Open" (non-Dogmatic) Norm

We already know that the ground moral norm prescribes the promotion of mind evolution. The concept of "evolution of the mind", however, is a very complex and peculiar one. It refers to the *continuous change* of the mind; therefore, the ground moral norm does not refer to given well-defined acts, but to the extremely great variety of acts that can be performed at any of the continuously evolving stages of the mind. In other words, the ground moral norm indicates an end, which can be reached by means of different, particular moral acts, none of which, however, has *per se* a constant effect, because the effect of a moral act depends upon the conditions of the affected mind. Thus, a moral act is judged by means of the morality criterion as good or bad according to whether it induces an evolution or an involution of the mind on which it exerts its effects. This means that moral acts have not an absolute moral value but rather a relative moral value (i.e., a value relative to the condition of the affected mind). For this reason, the ground moral norm does not prescribe any definite or particular act, but any one of the many acts that, given the present evolutionary state of the involved mind(s), can promote its (or their) evolution. Thus, it is an *open* norm, not a dogmatic one.

An example may help to clarify this concept (Belfiore 2004: 310). Let us assume that the evolution of the mind is represented by moving to the West; if a person staying in London moves to New York he has performed a good moral act (he has moved West); if the same person now moves from New York to Chicago, he again performs a good moral act; finally, if he moves to Los Angeles, he again performs a good moral act. However, none of these trips is a good moral act *per se*, i.e., moving to New York, or moving to Chicago, or moving to Los Angeles are not good moral acts *per se* because if a person who lives in Chicago moves to New York, he will perform a bad moral act, because he moves East (and not West). Thus, the same moral act (in the example: moving to New York) may be good or bad according to whether, taking into account the condition of the affected mind (in the example: the place from which the hypothesized person starts his trip), it represents an evolution (moving West) or an involution (moving

East) of the mind.

The above reasoning refers to the openness of the ground moral norm toward the different situations that may occur at the different stages of the evolution of a given mind. The norm, however, is also open to the different situations that may occur in different minds in relation to their different evolutionary stages. This means that a given act may be morally good if directed to a given mind (or group of minds) that is at a stage of evolution "*x*" but may be morally bad if directed to other minds that are at a stage of evolution higher than "*x*". Thus, if the government of an underdeveloped country, whose citizens are almost all illiterate, promulgates a law that states: "All citizens of this country must go to school for a duration of 5 years," this law can be judged as a good law (because it would favor the evolution of citizens' minds), whereas if the same law is promulgated in the U.S. or in a European State it would be a bad law (because it would result in an involution of the citizens' minds). The same is true for moral acts that concern the private life, as it happens when a father considers the education of his son. If, in a poor family that may normally only afford the expenses of sending a boy to elementary school, the father decides to make a supplementary effort to send his son to high school, he has taken a *good* moral decision. If, in a rich family, that can normally afford the expenses to support the education of a boy up to university level, the father decides to stop the education of his son at the level of high school, he has taken a *bad* moral decision. Thus, the ground moral norm could be defined as an *open (non "dogmatic") norm, equal for all and yet different for each individual and situation*. This norm covers *all kinds of moral goods*, including *liberty* and *equality* (see ch 2.1.4.2; Table 2.1), as well as *truth telling* (see ch 2.2.1.4.2, *D4*) and *keeping promises* (see chs. 2.2.1.4.2, *D4*; 2.2.1.7.2, *C1*). As will be shown later (chs. 2.1.7; 3.1.2.5.3), this norm unites the certainty in basal moral choices and the uncertainty in particular (or procedural) choices.

Yet, the ground moral norm raises two important questions concerning the following points: *(1)* To which individuals should the moral norm be applied? *(2)* To which extent (or degree) should mind evolution be promoted? These questions will be treated in the next two chapters.

2.1.5.2—The Spheres of Decreasing Moral Responsibility of the Individual

2.1.5.2.1—*Moral Responsibility Toward Others*

The ground moral norm prescribes the promotion of mind evolution. This raises the question: to which extent should this norm be applied? In other words: should the "good person" promote the evolution of the minds of all individuals? Or should he promote the evolution of his own mind alone? Or, perhaps, should he promote mind evolution of his family members or of his relatives?

The first of these possibilities (promoting the minds of *all* humans) is certainly too demanding when applied to the single individual, i.e., in the field of private ethics, which is the issue treated in this chapter (although it may be appropriate in the field of public ethics, both at the national and international level—chs. 3.1.2.5.1, *3*; 3.4.1.2); it perhaps resembles the ideal of "universal brotherly love" (maintained by Christian and humanist traditions) as well as the utilitarian pursuing of *general* happiness (which seems to satisfy the demand for unselfishness and fairness). These too-demanding positions, however, have been regarded as actually impracticable, and little plausible even as ideals; in this regard, Mackie (1977: 129, 171) recalls that, according to Butler (1726: 325–61), even if we distinguish self-love and benevolence, we should note that human actions motivated by unselfishness and benevolence are directed to relatives and friends, and therefore prompted by self-referential altruism, rather than by *universal* concern. One could also recall the critics by Nietzsche (1886: 87), who underlined that, if the good is identified with the utility of the herd (the community), there cannot be morality based on neighborly love (directed to the single individuals). Mackie (1977: 142) points out the difficult problem of how to go from individualistic hedonism to universal hedonism. Indeed, there is no rational basis why one should promote *general* happiness; this could only be maintained by following the *universalization principle*, which I criticize elsewhere (ch. 2.2.1.1.3, *A1*).

Indeed, I think that *personal* (or *private*) *moral responsibility* (as distinguished from *public moral responsibility*—chs. 3.1.2.5.1, *3*; 3.4.1.2) concerns the private life, i.e., it arises within the spheres of individual relationships and acquaintances. This means that personal moral responsibility exists only toward those individuals with whom a person in some way interacts in his private life. Moreover, the degree of responsibility changes according to the degree of relationship between the moral agent and the recipient of the moral act. In other words, personal moral responsibility (toward people with comparable needs) decreases with the decrease in the degree of proximity; it follows that, considering the present organization of our Western societies, personal moral responsibility will decrease going from the agent himself to family members, relatives, friends, colleagues and association fellow-members, acquaintances, fellow-countrymen, and foreigners (Fig. 2.1).

In order to understand the reasons for this decrease in moral responsibility, it should be considered that: *(a)* the "moral good" is the effect of a moral act; *(b)* the moral act consists of the realization of a moral project; *(c)* the moral project, in turn, is based on moral thoughts (knowledge); and *(d)* the moral norm demands that one acts in the way that results in the greatest

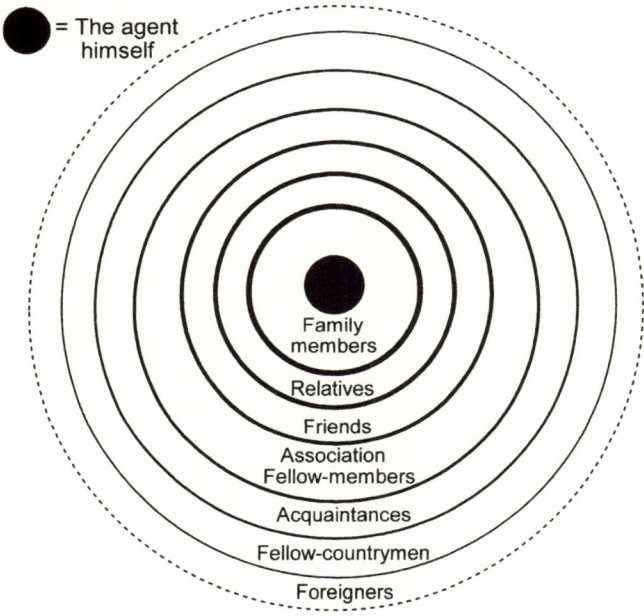

= The agent himself

Family members
Relatives
Friends
Association Fellow-members
Acquaintances
Fellow-countrymen
Foreigners

Fig. 2.1. The spheres of decreasing moral responsibility of the individual.

possible effect on mind evolution.

On these grounds, we can say that the reasons for the decrease in moral responsibility lie in the fact that with the decrease in the helper-helped closeness, there is a decrease in the *easiness* and *timeliness* in *(a)* knowing the needs, *(b)* creating the moral project and performing the corresponding moral act, and *(c)* verifying the effects of the moral act, whereas there is an increase in *(d)* the numerousness of the potential moral agents.

(a) Knowing the needs. There is no doubt that the greater the proximity and closer the relationship between the moral agent and the needy people, the easier and quicker it is to *know* the needs of the needy people and to elaborate the corresponding moral projects (a father can know the needs of his son more easily and more quickly than a distant person).

(b) Performing the moral acts. There is no doubt that the greater the proximity and closer the relationship between the moral agent and the needy people, the easier and quicker it is to perform the required *moral act*, i.e., those acts required to help the needy people (a father can satisfy the needs of his son more easily and more quickly than a distant person).

(c) Verifying the efficacy of moral acts. The greater the proximity and closer the relationship between the moral agent and the needy people, the easier and quicker it is to verify the effects of the moral act and to adjust or integrate it as needed (a father can verify the efficacy of his helping act toward his son more easily and more quickly than an agent can do concerning the help given to a distant boy).

(d) Numerousness of the potential moral agents. Less the proximity and weaker the relationship between the moral agent and the needy people, the more probable it is that there are additional moral agents who may contribute in helping the needy people; therefore, moral responsibility will be shared by many people or, so to say, it will be "diluted" (a needy boy has just one father but many acquaintances, say the inhabitants of its neighborhood, all of whom can equally help him and, therefore, share the moral responsibility toward him).

Together, these four points make the "agent-recipient" closeness an important factor for the efficiency of moral acts. Actually, for an equal amount of effort and resources, the effect on mind evolution will be greater if the rule that "moral responsibility decreases with the decrease in helper-helped closeness" is followed.

It should be noted that the modern means of communications allows most people to know about the needs of some distant individuals or populations, i.e., distant individuals or populations become like indirect acquaintances. This entails a certain degree of moral responsibility, i.e., the duty to give some help to these needy people; this is the moral basis, for instances, for the duty of the people from rich countries to give some money for helping distant needy people, especially when a natural disaster causes severe suffering to distant populations. Yet, the general rule based on the concept of the *spheres of decreasing moral responsibility* still remains valid.

The above reasoning supports the view that the greatest responsibility of a moral agent is the *responsibility toward himself* (of course, if the needs of the agent are *similar* to those of others). This is because there cannot be a relationship closer than that occurring between an agent and himself, and because without the willingness of the person who needs help to cooperate, it is difficult, and in some situations even impossible, to help him (ch. 2.2.1.6.3).

To further support the points discussed above, it may be useful to compare the relationship between a moral agent and his son with that between a moral agent and a needy boy living in the same neighborhood. The moral agent will know the needs of his son easier and timelier than the other inhabitants of the neighborhood, and can act easier and timelier; therefore, his moral acting will produce the best effects. Moreover, it is probable that when, after some time, the needs of the needy boy are known by the inhabitants of the neighborhood, not only our moral agent, but several other people might contribute in helping the needy boy. Thus, parents have a greater responsibility toward their children than toward one of their acquaintances (with a similar degree of need), because the acquainted person could and should also receive help from his parents or relatives or colleagues or other acquaintances, and also because proximity makes helping easier, timelier, and more effective. Conversely, a moral agent has relatively little moral responsibility toward a needy person living abroad, of whom he has only a tardy and incomplete knowledge, to whom he may give help with difficulty, and for whom there are many other people who could intervene to help. [The moral duty to help needy *populations* belongs to the sphere of *public morality*, and may involve the single individual as a citizen, i.e., as a supporter of a political party whose program includes (or not includes) helping the suffering populations; this issue will be discussed in chs. 3.1.2.5.1; 3.4.1.1, *2b*; 3.4.1.2].

At this point, a mention should be made to the doctrine of neighborly love (according to the biblical commandment: "Thou shalt love thy neighbor as thyself"), which has been regarded as impracticable by some thinkers (Mackie 1977: 129, 171). Actually, I think that this doctrine is acceptable if one takes into account the spheres of decreasing moral responsibility, discussed above. If we consider that our moral duty decreases as the interpersonal relationship becomes less close, then we should convene that our moral duty toward our neighbor is less than that toward, say, ourselves or our children. Thus, the biblical commandment should be interpreted as meaning that an agent should treat his neighbor in the same manner he would like to be treated by others (who look at him as a neighbor), i.e., with love but with a love weaker than that he feels toward himself and his children. In other words, the biblical commandment would say: as you expect your neighbor to help you in case of need, when your neighbor is in need, give him help, i.e., treat him as if you were in his place.

2.1.5.2.2—*Moral Responsibility Toward Oneself as the Origin of the Rights*

In the precedent chapter, I mentioned that the greatest responsibility of a moral agent is the *responsibility toward himself*. This means that, conditions being equal, a moral agent has the duty to promote first the evolution of his own mind and then the evolution of the minds of others, according to the rule of the spheres of decreasing moral responsibility, i.e., the moral agent has primarily a *duty toward himself*. Indeed, it is the duty toward oneself that gives origin to human rights because, if one has the *duty* to attempt to develop his own mind, others must at the same time recognize his *right* to enjoy those concrete conditions that make this possible (apart from natural obstacles). Likewise, our duty to help others to develop their minds entails the corresponding right of others to enjoy some help from us. This "right of others" is respected, at the individual level, through personal good deeds, and at the public level through the contribution of each citizen to the social security, health service programs, etc. (chs. 3.1.2.5.2; 4.1.2.2); in the international scenario, respecting the rights of others should be a primary *duty* of the rich States (chs. 3.4.1.1, *2b*; 3.4.1.2).

The above reasoning entails that we should reformulate the meaning of the term *egoism* inasmuch as we should distinguish two kinds of egoism (or selfishness): *(a) morally-bad egoism* (or *morally-bad selfishness*), which consists of pursuing *self-promotion* (i.e., pursuing the promotion of one's power, intellect and sensitivity) by ignoring and/or violating the rights/duties of others to develop their own minds (thus breaking the ground moral norm); and *(b) morally-good egoism* (or *morally-good selfishness*), which consists of pursuing *self-development* (or *self-evolution*) while respecting the rights/duties of others to develop their minds (in accord with the ground moral norm). Indeed, the actions prompted by the morally-good egoism are *integrated* with, and not opposed to, the moral acts stirred up by moral feelings.

Morally-bad egoism (or self-promotion) cannot be regarded as self-development (or self-evolution) because development (or evolution) means development (or evolution) of the mind as a whole (and not just of one's outward activity of power) and, therefore, necessarily includes the evolution of the consciousness, which, in turn, entails the observance of the ground moral norm.

It should be pointed out that morally-good egoism (self-evolution) should not be confused with the so-called *ethical egoism* (ch. 2.2.1.2.3, *D*), because the latter means that moral norms consist of following egoistic or selfish desires, whereas morally-good egoism means the reverse, i.e., that egoism is good if it follows the prescriptions of the moral norms.

2.1.5.3—The Limit of Moral Responsibility: The "Evolution-Allowing, Involution-Avoiding Condition"

The ground moral norm, which prescribes the promotion of mind evolution, raises the problem of defining the extent (or degree) to which mind evolution should be promoted, i.e., the problem of establishing the "limit" of moral responsibility. In other words: in order to follow the moral norm, up to which extent should an agent help others? Otherwise stated: up to which extent should he promote the evolution of the mind of others? Should he continue to help others until they reach a level equal to his own? Although this question belongs in part to the sphere of public morality (ch. 3.1.2.5.1), here I note that the moral agent needs not to help others until they reach a condition *equal* to that of the agent himself. The reason for this is that the end of the moral acts is not the *equality* among people, because individuals differ from one another in the degree and specificity of their mind evolution, linked to the difference in their natural endowment (and in environmental influences) (ch. 3.2.2.1.2). Rather, the moral agent has the duty to help others until they reach the *evolution-allowing, involution-avoiding condition.* In other words, the moral norm requires that one should help others until they become capable of developing their mind by themselves. Once the helped person reaches the *evolution-allowing condition*, most of the moral responsibility shifts from the moral agent to the helped person; now it is primarily the responsibility of the latter to further develop his own mind, i.e., he should now fulfill his *moral duty toward himself.*

The evolution-allowing condition might be compared with the enjoyment of the human rights as listed in the "Universal Declaration of Human Rights" (U. N. General Assembly, 1948) (summarized in ch. 3.1.2.5.1). However, while human rights are required for mind evolution, enjoying the evolution-allowing condition is superior to enjoying human rights for the following reasons (see also my recent book—2012: 22-23).

(1) Moral Foundation. The duty of the moral agent to help others to reach the evolution-allowing condition has a moral foundation, since it derives from the ground moral norm that prescribes the pursuit of the promotion of mind evolution. This entails a morally active behavior, inasmuch as the moral agent has the duty to actively do his best to help the mind evolution of those with whom he in some way interacts, i.e., to help them to reach the evolution-allowing condition. This is very different from the mere passive recognition that others have rights. In other words, the requirements of the evolution-allowing condition should be conceived as duties of the moral agent, rather than as rights of the recipient or, better, as rights/duties.

(2) Objectivity of the Pursued End: the Moral Good. When the moral agent favors a given person to reach the evolution-allowing condition, he knows that he is pursuing a well-defined and objective moral end: mind evolution, which is the objective moral good. The awareness that there is an end to be reached (mind evolution) induces the moral agent to give a concrete and substantial help instead of a mere formal one.

(3) Flexibility in defining the Goals. Favoring or promoting the reaching of the evolution-allowing condition means pursuing several goals, most of which coincide with the values that the declaration of human rights pro-

tects. Yet, each goal is not fixed in an abstract manner, as in the U. N. declaration, but is conceived in a flexible manner, in order to reach the goal of favoring mind evolution, taking into account the particular conditions of the helped person (degree and specificity of the evolution of his mind) and of the society in which he lives. An example may be useful. Concerning education, The U. N. declaration only says that everyone has the right to education. The moral agent who wants to help someone to reach the evolution-allowing condition knows very well that education means mind evolution. However, he also knows that promotion of education should be conceived by taking into account the characteristic and degree of evolution of the person to be helped and of the society in which he lives, so that the task is different if the person to be helped is a citizen of an underdeveloped country, where almost all citizens are illiterate (in which case promoting an education limited to elementary school might be a morally-good act), or is a citizen of a European country (in which case attending only elementary school would not be morally good). The same reasoning is true for every goal to be reached, which should be conceived with flexibility and concreteness.

It should be added that the awareness of the end to be reached (mind evolution) enables the moral agent to understand that the rights to life and to health have priority over any other right because, even more important than promoting mind evolution is preventing physical harm or death, since they mean "total and irreversible" or "partially reversible" mind *involution*.

Moreover, enjoying the evolution-allowing condition is also superior to having "enough" (Frankfurt 1987: 21) or enjoying equality of opportunities, for reasons given elsewhere (see my book—2012: 23-24).

Finally, it should be underlined that the evolution-allowing condition is difficult to implement in the diverse concrete situations. Yet, as discussed in the next chapter, uncertainty may exist about the details of the choices or the methods to follow, but not about the moral ends to be reached.

2.1.6—The Imprecision in Defining Moral Goods and the Uncertainty in Moral Choices

In the previous chapter, I mentioned that the various moral goods can be hierarchically arranged; this means that the various moral goods can be regarded as a system of *classes* and sub-classes that is composed of the most general class (mind evolution), which comprises three sub-classes (evolution of intellect, of sensitiveness, and of power), each of which, in turn, comprises several sub-sub-classes, and so on. The same is true of moral norms (which pursue moral goods), which may, likewise, be ordered into a system of classes and sub-classes (ch. 4.1.2.3). Since classes are defined by our intellect in an approximate and imprecise manner (ch. 1.1.3.2.1), so are the various classes of "moral goods" and of "moral norms"; moreover, concerning norms, it should also be considered that the acts prescribed by norms have effects that can only be foreseen on a probabilistic basis. In other words, moral goods, norms, and acts are subjected to the general rule that *human knowledge and previsions (as concerns the "macro-world") are grounded on statistical-probabilistic bases.* This has important implications, inasmuch as it introduces an element of uncertainty in moral choices, which, however, should not be emphasized. Actually, in moral choices, there are *(1)* elements of certainty and *(2)* elements of uncertainty.

(1) Elements of Certainty. Despite the imprecision in defining the classes of moral goods and their members, each class of moral goods clearly indicates an end to be pursued. Indeed, the basic class, "mind evolution", or its members (evolution of intellect, evolution of sensitiveness, and evolution of power), which are less comprehensive classes (or sub-classes) composed of less general moral goods, clearly indicate the moral ends to be pursued. These moral ends cannot be misunderstood or confused with moral *evils*, such as mind *involution*, or *involution* of intellect or of sensitiveness or of power.

(2) Elements of Uncertainty. The elements of uncertainty in moral choices are of two kinds.

(a) Uncertainty concerning the priority of possible moral acts. Each moral good being a class composed of several less comprehensive moral goods, it is uncertain, in concrete situations concerning definite person(s), which of the several moral goods that form a class should be given priority, considering that it is impossible to pursue all the moral goods that form a class at the same time and to the same extent, since moral goods are pursued through moral acts, which are competing with each other. This entails uncertain choices between competing, but not contrasting, moral acts.

(b) Uncertainty in the prevision of the effects of moral acts. Each of the moral goods (that form a class of less extensive moral goods) is pursued by creating a moral project and then converting it into a moral act directed to achieve that moral good; projects, however, are based on the acquired knowledge, which is grounded on statistical basis, and they entail previsions, which can only be made on a probabilistic basis (ch. 1.1.3.2.1, *3c*). Thus, the effects of moral acts can only be probabilistically foreseen; hence, the uncertainty about which of the possible moral acts should be preferred.

An example may be useful. A father has no doubt that he should promote the evolution of his son's mind (because his moral thoughts tell him that "mind evolution is the moral good" and his moral feelings prompt him accordingly); he clearly understands that this moral end requires that he provides for giving his son a proper education. Yet, he is uncertain about which kind of education is the most appropriate for his son, i.e., he is uncertain whether he should give his son an education primarily oriented toward the technical-scientific field or toward humanities or toward the economic area, because his knowledge about his son's aptitudes is not absolutely certain and complete (uncertainty about "priority"—see above, point "*a*"). Thus, his choice is uncertain and can only be made as a result of reflection and of discussion with the other members of the family. The same is true concerning the choice of the preferable school or university among the available ones (uncertainty about "prevision"—see above, point "*b*"). It is noteworthy that the same uncertainties are encountered by the "son" himself in deciding on the evolution of his own mind.

Here a comparison with what happens in the field of knowledge may be appropriate. I will refer to a hypothetical case concerning "medicine". Let us suppose that a patient asks his physician (who has just said to him: "you are affected by *influenza*") what the disease "influenza" actually consists of. The physician answers that influenza is a disease characterized by: fever of variable degree; coughing of variable severity; asthenia of variable intensity; a duration which most often ranges from 3 to 5 days but some time is limited to 1 or 2 days, sometimes may extend to 6 or 7 days, sometimes may be indefinable, since some symptoms (e.g., cough or asthenia) may persist for several days and then gradually disappear, etc. The patient notices that knowledge about influenza is very *imprecise*. Then he asks the physician which is the prevision about the course of his disease. The physician, again, answers that the patient's disease might last from 3 to 5 days but might also last from 1 to 7 days, that the symptoms will probably not be severe (because he is young and robust), etc. Moreover, the physician prescribes treatment "*a*" and adds that there is another treatment, "*b*", which is also effective but, considering the state of the patient, treatment "*a*" is *probably* the most appropriate one. The patient, again, notices that there is great uncertainty concerning both the prevision of the course of his disease and the preferable treatment. He, then, concludes that, being all scientific views and positions uncertain, none can be affirmed and imposed as the best one; a further step, and the patient might share with Feyerabend (1975: 295–309) the conviction that scientific knowledge is no different from (nor preferable to) other practices, such as voodoo. To show that this conclusion is unjustified, it is enough to compare the diagnosis of "influenza" with that of "advanced lung cancer" to understand that, despite the imprecision in the knowledge about the minor aspects of the two diseases and their course or response to treatment, medical science is able to clearly distinguish the former disease (which, within a short period, will disappear) from the latter (which, within a short period, will lead to death).

Thus, the uncertainty in human moral behavior (which is comparable to the uncertainty that exists in the scientific knowledge about the macroworld) concerns the "particular" choices or the methods to follow but not the general moral ends to be pursued. Therefore, never can it justify a skeptical or relativistic moral position.

I note that the search for a *precise* knowledge in ethics has been a long-lasting source of misunderstanding; examples of this search are the original Latin title of Spinoza's Ethics "*Ethica Ordine Geometrico Demonstrata*" (1677a) and the subtitle of Hume's Treatise "*An Attempt to introduce the experimental Method of Reasoning into Moral Subjects*" (1739/40).

2.1.7—An Overview on Moral Choices: "Moral" versus "Procedural" Choices

Based on the above, we should consider the following kinds of moral choices. A detailed discussion of moral choices in both the private and public spheres can be found elsewhere (Belfiore 2012: 410–19).

(1) Ground "Morally-Certain" Moral Choices. These are the *moral choices* between the *morally-good ends* (promoting mind evolution in the agent himself as well as in others—until they reach the *evolution-allowing condition*) and the *morally-bad egoistic ends* (following the agent's egoistic preferences while disregarding moral demands). These choices are *morally certain* because, regardless of their effects, they are made on the basis of a subjective decision of the conscious moral agent, of which the agent himself is certain (with the possible exception of the cases of self-deception).

(2) "Morally-Certain/Cognitively Imprecise" Moral Choices. These *moral choices* concern which of the various moral goods (which are parts of mind evolution) should be given priority, and the extent to which to pursue it. These choices are: *(a) morally certain* choices, because the choice to pursue a moral end (or not) and the extent to which to pursue it depends on a subjective decision of the moral agent, of which the agent himself is certain; and *(b) cognitively imprecise*, because they concern which of the various moral goods should be pursued first, or most, which depends on the knowledge of the *particular* condition of the *particular* individuals who are involved, a kind of knowledge that, referring to particular and concrete "objects", is always *incomplete* and *imprecise* (see also ch. 3.1.2.5.3).

(3) "Cognitively-Imprecise/Predictively-Uncertain" Procedural Choices. Once a given moral good has been chosen, uncertainty arises about which is the best *procedure* (which is defined by a *project*) to pursue it. The various possible procedures are *competing* but not *contrasting* among one another, as all of them are directed to promote a given moral good. [Projects and procedures are contrasting when they point to opposing (moral) ends]. Our knowledge of the concrete, *particular* situations being always incomplete and imprecise, and our previsions about the effect of the chosen procedure uncertain, these *procedural choices* belong to *cognitively imprecise and predictively uncertain choices* (see also ch. 3.1.2.5.3).

2.2—JUDGMENT OF MORAL EVENTS (MORAL THOUGHTS, MORAL FEELINGS, AND MORAL ACTS)

I have already stated that the mind products can be judged by a general criterion, the *value criterion*, valid for all the products of the three mind components, as well as by criteria specific to one or some of the mind products. Therefore, I will discuss the judgment of *moral events* (i.e., of *moral thoughts/projects, moral feelings,* and *moral acts*) by a criterion specific to them, the *morality criterion*, as well as by the criterion common to all mind products, the *value criterion* (Table 1.1).

2.2.1—*Judgment of Moral Events (Moral Thoughts, Feelings, and Acts) by the Morality Criterion*

As mentioned elsewhere (Belfiore 2004: 6), the *4th mind-defining proposition* (ch. 1.1.2) tells us that a fundamental characteristic of the mind is to undergo continuous changes that may consist of evolution or involution. *Evolution* means development of the ability of the intellect, sensitiveness, and power to create new ideas and theories, sentiments, and actions, respectively, and to progressively increase their degree of universalization; *involution* means a decrease in knowledge, sensitiveness, and power. From the *4th mind-defining proposition*, we also know that evolution is a fundamental trend of the mind; it is an essential aspiration of our consciousness. Moreover, since mind evolution is the basic *moral good* (chs. 1.1.1.2.4; 2.1.4.1), the evolution of mind serves as the basis for the *morality criterion*, by means of which moral events can be judged as *good* or *bad, according to whether they favor or restrain the evolution of one or more minds.*

2.2.1.1—Moral Thoughts and Moral Judgments

As we already know, moral thoughts are the cognitive contents of rational consciousness, because they are the products of the inward (or high-order) activity of intellect. Yet, they should not be judged by the truth criterion, as are the cognitive products of the outward activity of intellect (ideas and theories), because moral thoughts are concerned with knowledge, or better awareness, of the nature of the mind as an *evolving* entity, i.e., as an entity capable of undergoing *evolution* (or involution); for this reason, they should be judged by the *morality criterion* as *good* or *bad*. Thus, for instance, if a given individual, through his rational consciousness (or inward activity of intellect), comes to the moral thought or conception that his own mind as well as other minds are becoming entities that can change, and that can be changed either in the direction of evolution or of involution, of which the former is much better than the latter, we can say that his thought regarded as a scientific conception (i.e., a product of the outward activity of intellect) is *true* whereas when regarded as a moral conception it is *good*. Conversely, if an individual comes to the moral thought or conception that minds are changing entities whose direction of changing does not matter, then the thought of this individual should be judged as scientifically *false* and as morally *bad*. Of course, many intermediate positions are possible.

Moral thoughts are the basis for moral projects and related moral decisions, which are then realized through moral acts. Moral projects and moral decisions can be judged by the morality criterion as good or bad, according to whether they give rise to good or bad moral acts, i.e., moral acts that promote or restrain mind evolution (ch. 2.2.1.6; Table 1.1).

In the above reasoning, I maintain the fundamental concept that the *objective* nature of the mind as an evolving entity gives rise to the *moral good*. Indeed, it is mind evolution itself that constitutes the moral good, inasmuch as the most evolved states of the mind are "better" than the less evolved ones, in accord with the recognized meaning of the term *evolution*: "a process of continuous change from a lower, simpler, or worse to a higher, more complex, or better state" (Merriam-Webster's Collegiate Dictionary, 1993). Indeed, evolution toward *better* states appears as an *intrinsic property of the mind*. It is through moral thoughts, created by the inward activity of the *intellect* (or rational consciousness), that we learn about the evolutionary nature of the mind and become aware that mind evolution is the moral good. These concepts are worthy of further explanation, which will be given in the next chapters (chs. from 2.2.1.1.1 to 2.2.1.1.6) where I will discuss the arguments against, and those in favor of, the role of the intellect or "reason" in moral decisions.

It should be pointed out that moral thoughts are at the same time the "subject" and the "object" of moral judgments: as a thinking entity, the thought-producing consciousness is the "subject" that judges the moral thoughts of a mind as morally good or morally bad. At the same time, the consciousness-produced moral thought can be the "object" of a moral judgment by the thought-producing consciousness. It is noteworthy that the judging consciousness may be the same one that produces the moral thought that is the object of judgment (reflexivity of consciousness) or may be the rational consciousness of a mind (or person) different from the one that is being judged; moreover, due to its evolutionary nature and reflexive capacity, consciousness can judge the moral thoughts that it has previously created, and may recognize as bad a thought that it had previously judged as good (or vice versa).

2.2.1.1.1—The Supposed "Is-Ought Gap" and the "Evolution Toward Better States" as an Intrinsic Property of the Mind

1. "Reason" and the "Moral Good". It has been said that knowledge (or reason) is morally neutral (separateness of "reason" from morals). Hume (1739/40) pointed out that moral distinctions (laudable or blamable) are not derived from reason because, while reason is concerned with the discovery of truth and falsity (agreement or disagreement with the real facts or relation of ideas), actions (and passions or volitions) are not susceptible to such agreement or disagreement and therefore cannot be conformable or contrary to reason. In other words, reason is wholly inactive, and cannot be the source of so active a principle as is the conscience or the sense of morals (Hume 1739/40: 413–17, 455–69).

Hume's position seems to be untenable. Considering that moral choices entail that agents compare and relate to each other at least two objects or events, Hume's position can be accepted only for some kinds of comparisons or relations, such as those between simple objects of the inorganic word, but not for comparisons or relations involving complex objects of the living world and, especially, human beings. If, in a clothing shop, our intellect observes a white shirt and a blue one and we choose to buy the former, we can say that our knowledge about the property "color" of the shirts has not affected our choice, which may have been determined by our personal preferences. Things are different if the intellect of a man observes two "objects" such as: *(a)* a sack containing about 70 Kg of inert matter and *(b)* a human being; the observing intellect notes that they are two "objects" and also notes some differences by comparing one object with the other, e.g., it notes that they differ in color, in shape, in magnitude, etc. But this is not all that the intellect of the observing man notes; after having carefully observed and studied the two "objects", the observing intellect notes (or understands) that one of such objects, the human being, is much more (actually, almost infinitely more) complex in its structure and function than the other one. Such a difference, which is part of the knowledge that the observing intellect has acquired about the observed objects, could not be denied by any rational being; it appears as a self-evident truth, from which the notions of *moral principles, values,* and *norms* arise. Moreover, it should be noted that moral thoughts necessarily entail *motivation* because, these thoughts being *triplets* (ch. 1.1.1.2.4), are supported by the *moral feeling* to get them.

An important point is that the mind shows the capacity to undergo evolution and that mind evolution can be affected by several factors. Among the factors capable of affecting the mind, there are human actions and moral acts, through which a mind can favor or restrain its own evolution or the evolution of other minds. It follows that: *(a)* the "more evolved" *stages of the mind* are "better", or "morally better", than the less evolved ones, i.e., they represent the *objective good*; and *(b) human acts* that favor mind evolution are *morally-good*, whereas those that restrain it are *morally bad*.

The notion of mind evolution entails the following distinction: *(a) Ideas* (outward activity of intellect) are directed to understand *what exists* (included the mind itself as a *changing* entity), or can probabilistically be foreseen that *will exist*, apart from human intervention, and can be judged as (probably) *true* or *false* by the truth criterion. *(b) Moral thoughts* (inward activity of intellect) are directed to understand that the mind does not merely change but *evolves,* and that *mind evolution is a value*; they make a *comparative evaluation* between the present state and the possible states of the mind that *do not yet exist* but could exist as result of human acts, and can be judged as *good* or *bad* by the morality criterion according to whether they express the understanding that mind evolution is *the good* and that human acts should bring into existence the most-evolved among the possible states of mind. What counts is the *direction* (evolution or involution) of mind activity.

The notion of *moral good* is attained through *moral thoughts*, produced by the *inward activity of intellect* (or *rational consciousness*), and not through *ideas* (or theories) produced by the *outward activity of intellect* (Fig. 1.1); it follows that moral thoughts guide moral acts, whereas ideas (and theories) guide selfish actions. This distinction allows us to reject the position of Nelson (1991: 46–47) who, concerning the thought of Hume (1739/40) (that reason alone has no power to influence conduct and that each action involves a desire), thinks that Hume's position is an extreme one, since reason would affect our actions by providing rational strategies for the action and rational consistence and inference for rational choices. Clearly, Nelson is talking about personal or selfish actions, which, being "body-physical world" relationships, obviously are based on the knowledge of the physical world in order to be effective. In contrast, the role of "rationality" in moral decisions is that of generating *moral thoughts* (concerned with the *evaluation* of the mind as an evolving entity), which create moral principles, thus affecting *moral projects* and, consequently, *moral acts*.

To further clarify the role of reason in understanding the *good* (consisting of mind evolution), let us consider a series of three "objects of observation", consisting of three people, of whom one has been totally restrained in the development of his natural endowment (we will call him "the restrained mind"), one who has had the opportunity to develop his aptitudes to only a little degree (we will call him "the little evolved mind"), and one who has enjoyed the opportunity to reach the full evolution of his mind (we will call him "the fully evolved mind"). These three "objects" could be regarded as the stages of an evolutionary process, and could be ordered as follows:

Stage-1 = a "restrained mind" (an illiterate man, living in extreme poverty); *Stage-2* = a "little evolved mind"; *Stage-3* = a "fully evolved mind".

The difference in "value" between adjacent stages in this sequence should be an objective and self-evident truth for any rational person; i.e., any rational person should consider the possible evolution toward "better" states as the original datum noticed by observing a mind, a datum that refers to an *intrinsic property of the mind*. This is true both in the case of the observation of one's own mind or of the mind of others. Thus, *the concept of mind evolution as the objective good arises from the only reliable source of knowledge: observation (and description), not argumentation (and deduction)*. This means that an individual who does not fully understand the difference between "*Stage-1*" and "*Stage-3*" of the above series is an individual who, from the cognitive standpoint (outward activity of intellect), has a *false* idea or theory, whereas from the moral standpoint is an individual who has a *bad* moral thought or conception, which may lead him to produce moral projects not directed to respect or, better, to favor, mind evolution.

Thus, moral thought tells us that human acts that favor mind evolution (i.e., the evolution of an illiterate person into a cultivated one, or of an unfeeling person into a person with a well-developed sensitiveness, or of an extremely poor person into a well-off one) are *morally-good acts*, while those human acts that restrain the evolution of the mind are *morally-bad acts*. Morally-bad acts also include those acts that cause mind *involution*. This happens when a person is deprived of his economic goods, or physically harmed (involution of power), or is impeded in his cognitive activity by obstacles in the access to books, newspapers, and other means of information (involution of intellect), or is brutalized by a coarse environment and lack of any access to literary, musical or visual arts (involution of sensitiveness). Thus, we should consider both the morally-good "mind *evolution*" (evolution from stage-1 to stage-3 in the above series) and the morally-bad "mind *involution*" (involution from the stage-3 to stage-1).

It is noteworthy that, concerning mind involution, a further "stage" should be added to the above series: "stage-0"; so that the above series can be extended to include four "stages": "*Stage-0*", "*Stage-1*", "*Stage-2*", and "*Stage-3*". "Stage-0" would refer to ~70 Kg of inert matter; its meaning derives from the fact that the change from "stage-1" to "stage-0" would consist of the death of a person, and would represent the most extreme and irreversible "mind involution". It follows that the human acts that cause this passage, i.e., murders, are the worse among the possible bad moral acts. The reverse change, from "stage-0" to "stage-1", would represent the birth of a new human being. This step, however, while certainly representing an evolution (it consists of the change of inert matter into a new "mind"), should be evaluated by taking into account the balance between the morally-good event, consisting of the transformation of inert matter into a new human being, on the one hand, and the morally-bad situation linked to excessive world population, which entails poverty and underdevelopment. This issue belongs to *hard moral choices* (ch. 2.2.1.5) linked to the problems of abortion (ch. 2.2.1.5.2) and of environmental control (ch. 3.2.14.1).

It should be pointed out that the above reasoning, leading to the conception of the human good as something *objective*, makes it possible to evaluate *naturally-occurring state of affairs concerning human minds*, or *natural events affecting human minds*, as *good* or *bad*. Thus, the occurrence of people who live in a condition of extreme misery with high mortality due to under-nutrition or lack of water is a morally "bad" mind condition (it scores too low in the scale expressing the various possible degrees of mind evolution). Conversely, the occurrence of people who have reached a high degree of mind evolution (concerning wealth and/or knowledge and/or sensitiveness) is a morally-*good* fact (it scores high in the scale of the various possible degrees of mind evolution). In other words, a good "condition" is a stage of mind more evolved compared to a lower one. On the other hand, a good natural "event" is one that favors mind development (e.g., raining after a long period of dry weather in a poor underdeveloped country).

(2) Kant on Science and Philosophy. It is noteworthy that, according to Kant (1785: 16), in order to know what is good to do, there is no need for science or philosophy, because the practical faculty of judgment (common morality) would be advantaged over the theoretical one, which often leads to uncertainty and contradictions. I think that it is difficult to understand how an illiterate man could have the "practical faculty of judgment" to deal with the principle of universalization, which is central in Kant's moral theory, and which has been criticized (ch. 2.2.1.1.3). I think that what is unnecessary for the moral choice is the technical-scientific knowledge (outward activity of intellect), whereas the moral thoughts (inward activity of intellect) through which one understands that mind evolution is "the good", can be attained, at least in their essential parts, also by illiterate persons through the simple observation of the human person; moreover, the illiterate can also be guided in his moral behavior by his *moral feelings*, produced by the inward activity of his sensitiveness (or *emotional consciousness*) (Fig. 1.1).

(3) Comment. Referring to the main metaethical philosophical theories (Table 2.2), I note: *(a)* contrary to *moral error theories* and *moral antirealism*, moral good (mind evolution) is objective and *knowable* (through internal observation), and justifies *moral realism* and *foundationalism*; *(b)* moral thoughts concerning *mind evolution* necessarily entail *motivation*, also because these thoughts being *triplets* (ch. 1.1.1.2.4), they are supported by the *moral feeling* to get them (and by some acts); *(c)* moral thoughts are required (together with moral acts) for the creation of motivating moral feelings; *(d)* moral thoughts (together with moral feelings) are the *non-naturalistic* components that determine the *naturalistic* moral acts and that constitute the object of the *non-naturalistic realism*; *(e)* the claimed "non-moral" that would *supervene* on the "moral" actually consists of moral

thoughts and moral feelings that determine naturalistic moral acts.

2.2.1.1.2—Filling the "Is-Ought Gap" (or Connecting Reason to Morals)

(A) Gewirth's View.

Gewirth (1973-74) has attempted to show the possibility of deriving "ought-judgments" from "factual-statements" (i.e., deriving the "ought" from the "is"); this would be possible because the "ought" is defined in empirical terms and is considered as *internal* to the "is" (if the "ought" is considered as *external* to the "is", there would be a logical gap between them).

Gewirth (1973-74) points out that the argument for deriving "ought" from "is" is not affected by the content of actions, as it proceeds in the context of the generic features of actions, i.e., the features of being "voluntary" and "purposive"; this means that actions are associated to freedom and relative well-being, and that the agent regards the purpose of his action as some sort of good. This argument, in Gewirth's view, is necessary because it reflects the necessary structure of purposive actions as viewed by the agent.

Although it is true that actions require freedom and relative well-being, I note that the fact that the agent regards the purpose of his action as some sort of good has no definite meaning, because it is not stated which criterion is followed by the agent to regard the purpose of his action as "good": is this purpose "good" for him alone, or for the particular class of men to which he belongs, or for all men? Consider the purpose of the action of a thief; the purpose of his action (to steal the money of one's neighbor) may be regarded as "good" by him, or by the class of thieves, but not by an honest man nor by the members of the class of honest men. Actually, Gewirth's reasoning concerns any purposive action, but does not provide any basis to distinguish morally-good actions (promoting mind evolution) from the morally-bad ones (restraining mind evolution).

However, according to Gewirth (1973-74), the argument for deriving the "ought-statements" from the "is-statements" (describing the actions) is made of the following four steps:

(1) Actions entail some evaluative element, since the agent considers as good (based on whatever criteria) the object of his action as well as the required freedom and well-being; thus, the "fact-value" gap is already bridged in action. Again, I note that the fact that the agent regards as good the object of his action does not mean that the object is good; actually, what is bridged is the "fact-value for the agent" gap, but not the "fact-value for all men" gap.

(2) The agent regards his action's object as good and therefore regards his action as *justified*, which entails that he claims the *right* to freedom and well-being as necessary conditions of his action. Thus, action is viewed by the agent as having a normative as well as evaluative structure, in that it

involves right-claims and judgments of good. Once again, I underline that these are subjective and arbitrary right-claims and judgments that are only subjectively justified; this has nothing to do with morally justified rights.

(3) The agent who claims the rights as mentioned above must be committed to a generalization, i.e., he must admit that his claim is valid for all actions and that similar rights also belong to other rational people. Actually, I think that there is no rational basis to generalize an action, unless we first demonstrate its moral nature (the action of buying a chocolate ice-cream needs not be generalized; the action of a thief must not be generalized; whereas the action of helping needy people should be generalized). Moreover, the generalization or universalization principle can be rejected on the basis of arguments expounded in the next chapter (ch. 2.2.1.1.3, *A1*).

(4) From the above mentioned generalized right-claims, the corresponding *ought*-judgments would follow, since if one has the right to do what one wants (but I deny that one has such a right), it follows that one should avoid interfering with the freedom and well-being of other purposive agents or persons. In my opinion, the lack of any basis for such a generalization invalidates any "ought-judgment" derived from it; what could be generalized is (at most) the generic right to freedom and well-being required for any purposive action, but the moral evaluation of the various actions remains unsettled.

From the above discussion, Gewirth (1973-74) derives the *Principle of Generic Consistency* (PGC), which precepts: "Apply to your recipient the same generic features of actions that you apply to yourself." The PGC would combine the *consistency* of the universalization argument (see above, under point "*3*") with the *generic* feature of actions; it would be an egalitarian universalistic moral principle, as it requires equal distribution of the basic rights of action. My critical notes expounded above invalidate this principle.

(B) Mackie's View.

Mackie (1977: 66–73) starts his argument by referring to the thought of Searle (1964), who suggested that the gap between facts and values, or description and evaluation, or "is" and "ought", could be bridged by appealing to a peculiar class of facts, the institutional facts, which entail obligations. Mackie notes that the institutions can be described *from outside*, as brute facts like others, and handled by general logic, or they can be viewed *from inside*, by *endorsing* them and their rules; this, however, does not mean the existence of objective moral values or intrinsic prescriptions. The desires and suffering of other people can be a reason to action if one endorses an institution and its established moral traditions, which demand that one shows some concern for the well-being of others. This may have contributed to produce the concept of intrinsic requirements linked to the nature of things and, therefore, of moral obligation; this, however, would be an error since "nothing logically commits us to doing so" (Mackie 1977: 79). I think that institutions are not the source but the result of moral values endorsed by the majority of citizens; indeed, society and its institutions are the result of the universalization of the citizens' actions and moral acts, and therefore reflect desires and moral values that stir-up actions and moral acts, respectively (chs. 3.1.1.1.1; 3.1.2.1).

According to Mackie (1977: 73–77), "ought" sets up an expectation; it may have the same meaning in its different uses, so that moral "ought" does not have a meaning different from that of other "ought". Thus, in *epistemic contexts*, "ought" introduces what the reasons are for expecting a given outcome ("They ought to be across the border right now"); in the case of *hypothetical imperative*, reasons for being obliged may be the desire of the agent or the demand of the institution, seen from outside or endorsed by the agent. In *moral contexts*, there would be the supposed intrinsic reasons peculiar to the moral "ought". I underline that, in the case of the epistemic context and of the hypothetical imperative, the use of "ought" is actually improper. Indeed, in the epistemic context, "ought" indicates a probabilistic *hypothesis* or an expectation (*prevision*) about the (probable) *existence* of some object or event based on what is known; instead of "They ought to be across the border right now," one should say "I believe that they are across the border right now." In the case of the hypothetical imperative, "ought" refers to probabilistic expectation (prevision) based on the agent's desires, either spontaneous desires or desires induced by social pressures: instead of "He ought to do *x*" one should say "I believe that he will decide to do *x*". In the moral field, "ought" is properly used and refers to *envisaged but yet not existing states of the mind, which may come into existence through the agent's decision and ensuing act*; it means that "one has the duty to do *x*" because the moral act "*x*" will favor mind evolution toward a more evolved state.

2.2.1.1.3—The Universalizability Principle

The *universalizability principle* has played an important role in the attempt to link reason and morality. I will discuss this principle as conceived by *(A)* Kant (1785), *(B)* Hare (1963; 1989a), and *(C)* Nelson (1991).

(A) Kant's Universalizability Principle.
(1) Critique to Kant's Universalizability Principle. Kant (1785) attempted to create an ethics founded on reason, in which a central role is played by the *universalizability principle* (and by the principle of treating men as ends—ch. 2.2.1.1.5).

After having distinguished the "good will" from "inclinations" (ch. 2.2.1.2.2, *D*), Kant (1785: 13) affirms that acting from duty does not have its moral value in its purpose but in the *maxim* (the subjective principle of volition) by which it is determined. One should "act in accordance with a maxim that can at the same time make itself a universal law" (Kant 1785: 44). The "universal imperative of duty" can also go as follows: "act only in accordance with that maxim through which you can at the same time will that it become a universal law" or "act as if the maxim of your action were to become by your will a universal law of nature" (Kant 1785: 31).

Here I note that it is not clear how a maxim (or a law) can have moral value not based on the end that the observance of the maxim will produce. Perhaps, Kant's claim should be interpreted as if it means that the moral value of a maxim is not linked to the end as evaluated by the agent but to an end to be evaluated by an agent-neutral criterion. This, however, changes Kant's claim, because it means that moral value of a maxim is linked to its end, impersonally evaluated.

Perhaps, it is more important to underline that Kant's claim is based on the view that an action is an entity separated from its effects, i.e., a view framed into what I call a *fragmented conception* of reality. Yet, as I have attempted to show, reality is not made of separated "objects" or "events" but, according to the principle of unity-distinction, reality is a unitary and yet pleomorphic substance (unity-multiplicity of reality), in which the "cause" cannot be separated from its "effect", because cause and effect are merely two stages of the continuous change of reality (ch. 1.1.3.2.1, *3d*). Thus, if an action and its effect are not separated entities but merely two distinct aspects or stages of a unique process of continuous transformation (unity-distinction), one cannot evaluate the action separately from its effect but should evaluate the unitary event composed of the "action/effect".

Kant (1785: 2) deprives the will of all impulses that could arise from the obedience of a law (e.g., the expected results), so that nothing remains as a principle of will but the universal conformity to the law as such; thus, one should act in such a way as to will that his own *maxim* should be a universal law (see above). Kant (1785: 15) notes that without this *universalization principle* a maxim would be self-defeating: if using a false promise for one's own interest became a universal law, nobody would make promises at all (because it would be the rule that they would not be respected).

This universalization principle is the rational component of Kant's moral theory; it, however, in my opinion, is by no means rational. To discuss this point we should refer to the concept of class (ch. 1.1.3.2.1, *1*), to the class of men defined by the properties common to all men (ch. 3.2.2.1.1) and to the various smaller classes of men defined by properties that are not common to all men but that define a particular sub-class. Let us refer to the example given by Kant himself, i.e., the case of the false promise for one's own interest. It is perfectly rational that a man, who believes that he belongs to the sub-class of cunning men, thinks that he can make false promises for his own interest, and he may think that the maxim "all cunning men can make false promises" should become a "universal" law (i.e., a law referring to "all" the members of the sub-class of cunning men). Likewise, a man, who believes that he belongs to the sub-class of "strong" men, may be perfectly rational in thinking that he can obtain what he wants through violence (instead of obtaining what he is entitled to, according to the law), and he may think that the maxim "all strong men can use violence to obtain what they want" should become a "universal" law. Indeed, Kant himself actually referred to a sub-class of men, i.e., the sub-class of men who are adults and of sound mind (two properties that can only be *imprecisely* defined).

Kant (1785: 34) notes that often a man who transgresses a duty wants that the duty remains for others and that an exception should apply to him; Kant thinks that, from the standpoint of reason, this is a *contradiction* (a *universal* principle should not apply to us), but from the standpoint of a will affected by inclinations this is an *antagonism* between the inclination and the precept of reason. I think that there may be no contradiction if the man who transgresses a duty believes that he belongs to a special class defined by special properties, or even that he possesses some very special properties, which no other man has; in the latter instance, the class has only one member: the transgressor of the duty. On this basis, the transgressor can rationally affirm that he (but not others, who lack the properties he possesses) can transgress the duty.

(2) The Categorical Imperative. Kant (1785: 24–5) maintains that only rational beings have a *will*, which is the ability to act according to the conception of laws (principles); since reason is required for the derivation of actions from laws, will is nothing else than practical reason, i.e., the faculty of choosing only what the reason (independently of inclinations) recognizes as practically necessary: the good. Often, with the actual (imperfect) men, it would occur that the will is not of itself in complete accord with reason; in such cases, the determination of such a will according to objective (universal) laws is a constraint (Kant 1785: 24). The conception of objective principles (those valid for all rational beings) as constraining the will is a *command* of reason and its formula is a *categorical imperative* (Kant 1785: 24). Apart from the fact that, in my opinion, the concept of "will" is vaguely defined by Kant, my critique of the universalization principle, which I made above, invalidates the categorical imperative, which is derived from it.

(3) Duties Derived from the Universalizability Principle. Kant (1785: 31–33) mentions some *duties* derived from the universalizability principle (obedience to moral law), which I will list and comment below:

(a) Duties to ourselves (p. 31–32). The maxim of a despaired man to shorten his life cannot be a universal law because of the *contradiction* that a natural feeling directed to preserve life would be directed to destroy life. Indeed, as noted above, it is fully rational that a man belonging to the sub-class of despaired men, says: "all despaired men should shorten their life."

(b) Duties to others (p. 32). Borrowing money with the will of not repaying it, if taken as a universal law, would make meaningless any promise. Apart from the fact that Kant does not explain why keeping promises should be considered morally good (see chs. 2.2.1.4.2, *D4*; 2.2.1.7.2, *C1*; 3.1.1.2, *2c* for my view on this issue), I note that, as mentioned above, for a man belonging to the class of cunning men, it is perfectly rational to assert: "All cunning men can borrow money with the will of not repaying it."

(c) Perfection duties (p. 32–33). A talented man who neglects his gifts and searches only pleasures cannot will his maxim to be raised to a universal law, because a rational being necessarily wills that his faculties be developed to realize their natural ends. This statement of Kant is unjustified. Should the "faculties" of a young mafia man be developed to realize his "natural ends"? Which are the good natural ends? The behavior of a talented man who neglects his gifts and searches pleasure is morally bad only when his "gifts" are evaluated according to my moral principle prescribing the promotion of mind evolution, including the mind of the agent himself (see ch. 2.1.5.2.2 on the moral responsibility toward oneself).

(d) Imperfection duties (p. 33). A man who does not care for the needs of others cannot will that his maxim be raised to a universal law, because he could face contradiction when circumstances arise in which he needs the love and sympathy of others. Indeed, this appears an egoistic reason. However, this statement can be questioned by noting that a healthy, strong, and rich man may be willing to raise to a universal law the maxim "All healthy, strong, and rich men can refuse to help sick, weak, and poor men"; he may think that it is highly improbable that he himself will become sick, weak and poor, and he may decide that it is the case to risk.

(B) Hare's Conception of the Universalizability Principle.
Hare (1989a: 175–90) distinguishes three levels of moral thinking: the *intuitive* level (based on the good dispositions, principles, and attitudes that we cultivate), the *critical* level (to which we resort in hard cases or problematic occasions), and the *meta-ethical* or *logical* or *formal* level, at which a formalist view is attained. It is at the latter level that *formal questions* arise; these questions can be answered solely by appealing to the form, i.e., to their logical properties (or to our understanding of the words and concepts used), without the need for even their semantic properties (i.e., their descriptive meaning). At the formal (or meta-ethical) level, Hare (1963: 86–111; 1989a: 179–80) distinguishes two features of the term "ought": *prescriptivity* and *universalizability*; he thinks that refusing universalizability would mean to be *logically inconsistent*. Moreover, Hare (1963) notes that using "ought" in a prescriptive and universalizable sense does not link to a particular moral opinion, because ethics, which is the logic of moral arguments, is morally neutral. In other words, according to the *formalist* view, a moral judgment must be *prescriptive* (of some given action), *universalizable* (to

all similar situations), *overriding* any other judgment, and also *independent of its contents* (Hare 1952; 1981).

Concerning the last point, I underline that defining the *contents* of moral judgments (which, according to my view, is *mind evolution*) is of basic importance because, if the contents are not well defined, the universalization principle allows "limited universalization", restricted to sub-classes of men, and hence morally unacceptable conclusions (see the discussion that follows). I recall that the formalist view was contrasted also by Warnock, who maintained that morality must have *content*, even if it consists of social conventions adopted to help human coexistence; "the 'general object' of morality . . . is to contribute to betterment . . . of the human predicament, primarily and essentially by seeking to countervail 'limited sympathies' and their potentially most damaging effects" (Warnock 1971: 26).

I have already criticized the principle of universalization (see above). Concerning the "moral neutrality" of the logic moral arguments, it means to leave undefined the criterion to distinguish the logic but immoral judgments from the logic but moral ones, and that moral principles are derived, as Hare says (see above), from the dispositions and attitudes that we cultivate, i.e., from those principles used at the *intuitive* level of moral thinking; and "intuitions", interpreted according to my theory, actually correspond to what I call *deep moral feelings* (chs. 2.1.1.2; 2.1.3.2).

Hare (1989a: 181–88) notes that one is constrained to treat other people's preferences as if they were one's own; if a given preference of one's victim is stronger than one's preference, the stronger preference should override the weaker one.

This statement can be criticized because, as stated in my repeated critique to the universalization principle, the various degrees of suffering should be evaluated together with the various classes to which the agent belongs: it is rationally correct to claim that a given suffering of a man belonging to the "class of insensitive men" is different from a similar suffering of a man belonging to the "class of sensitive men".

It may be useful to comment on an example mentioned by Hare (1963: 86–111): Suppose that "A" owes money to "B", and "B" owes money to "C"; that there is a law that creditors may exact their debts by putting their debtors into prison; and that "B" is *inclined* to put into prison "A" in order to make him pay. If the question of universalizing the prescriptions is ignored, then "B" would assent to the *singular* prescription "Let me put 'A' into prison"; but, if "B" seeks to turn this prescription into a moral (*prescriptive*) one by saying "I *ought* to put 'A' in prison . . ." he must accept the *universal* principle that "Anyone who is in my position *ought* to put his debtor into prison . . ." and, consequently, that "C" *ought* to put him, i.e., "B", in prison (Hare 1963: 86–111). Hare claims that the above argument shows analogy with the Popperian theory according to which a hypothesis is falsified by a singular negative statement of facts, inasmuch as a moral principle is rejected if its consequences cannot be accepted (Hare 1963: 91).

Indeed, Hare's reasoning ignores that *universalization* can be conceived in different manners, i.e., by referring to classes of men and of facts of various amplitude, as shown by the following considerations, referring to Hare's example above.

(1) The Universalizability Principle and Agents' Differences. Let us assume that "B" is (or he thinks to be) a strong and intelligent man (i.e., a member of the class of strong and intelligent men) whereas "A" and "C" are weak and stupid men; in this situation, "B" could make the *prescriptive* and *universal* judgment: "I ought to put 'A' in prison, whereas 'C' should not put me in prison, because all strong and intelligent men have the right to refuse to pay their debts to weak and stupid men." There is no incoherence in this statement. Nor could we get him (i.e., "B") to imagine himself in the position of the weak and stupid man, because he ("B") believes that he actually is intelligent and strong, so that the condition of the weak and stupid is extraneous to him. Note that the universalization can be done by referring to ever-narrower classes, up to an extremely narrow one comprising just one member (in the above example: comprising only "B"). Reference to subclasses of the agent can be impeded if we refer not to the *maxim* that determines the action, but to the *effect* determined by the action, and if the effect is exerted on *mind evolution*, which is the *essential property* of the class of men and that, as such, is possessed by *all* men; such common or universally shared property is the property consisting of the fundamental feature of the mind, i.e., its ability to evolve toward more developed states. It should be noted that, when the difference of "B" in respect to "A" and "C" is not due to a stable property but rather to a condition that may supervene in an unforeseeable manner (say, a state of disease), the reasoning of "B" could be opposed by comparing his actual state with an imagined, possible, and future state in which he will become sick; even in this case, however, "B" may decide to risk and to continue to maintain his claim.

(2) The Universalizability Principle and Factual Differences. The above point refers to *agents' differences*, i.e., to the existence of diverse classes and sub-classes to which the agent belongs (or claims to belong). Now, let us consider *factual differences*, i.e., the possibility of distinguishing apparently similar facts or events into smaller sub-classes, each of which limits the universalization of a moral norm.

Let us assume that the debt of "A" was contracted in order to make a trip of pleasure, whereas the debt of "B" was contracted for paying medical expenses; in this situation, "B" could make the *prescriptive* and *universal* judgment: "I ought to put 'A' in prison, whereas 'C' should not put me in prison, because all debts contracted for making pleasure trips must be paid, whereas all debts contracted for coping with medical expenses should not."

It should be noted that when the actual situation of "A" is a situation that may supervene in an unforeseeable manner, say a disease, "B" cannot exclude that he himself may become sick in the future; even in this case, however, "B" may decide to risk and to continue to maintain his claim.

(C) Mackie's Interpretation of the Universalizability Principle.
Mackie (1977: 83–102) maintains that moral judgments are *universalizable* according to three stages of universalization. The *first stage universalization* (Mackie 1977: 83–90) tells us that moral judgments must be valid for all the *relevantly similar* actions (or persons or states of affairs). This means that one should rule out the mere numerical differences (those between an individual and another simply as such, and the mere generic, or irrelevant features) and consider only the *significant* qualitative difference; therefore, moral judgments should contain *variables*, and not *constants* such as proper names. Mackie (1977) observes that this kind of universalization is based on a correct logical thesis, but does not rule out egoism linked to the (actually "insignificant") agent's socio-economic status or ideals. Here I note that universalization is "logically correct" even when it is restricted to a subclass of agents (ch. 2.2.1.1.3, *A1*) defined by "insignificant" qualitative differences. The problem of establishing whether a qualitative difference (i.e., a given *property*) is significant or not is a difficult one, and can only be solved by referring to the *essential properties* that define the "class of men" and that, therefore, are common to all men (the properties of being *evolving* conscious entities made of intellect, sensitiveness, and power). This is what I do in my proposal of a new version of the universalizability principle (ch. 2.2.1.1.4).

The *second stage universalization*, according to Mackie (1977: 90–92), consists of putting oneself in another person's place; it avoids the kinds of unfairness mentioned above but, Mackie notes, it would be based on a controversial logical thesis, as it is only a practical thesis that an action should conform to moral judgments universalized in this way. I think that putting oneself in another person's place actually means considering the other person as equal to oneself, i.e., considering the "other person" as belonging to the same "class of men" to which the agent belongs (or claims to belong). I once again note that, in order to consider the other person(s) as belonging to the same class to which the agent belongs, we need to refer to the *essential properties* that define the "class of men" and that, therefore, are common to *all* men. This is the basis of my proposal of a new version of the universalizability principle (ch. 2.2.1.1.4).

The *third stage of universalization* considered by Mackie (1977: 92–97) consists of taking into equal account the different tastes and rival ideals (which is a sort of utilitarian view). Mackie (1977) notes that this kind of universalization is based on a false logical thesis, because there are no logical constrains for giving equal weight to all ideals (apart from the uncertainty about how the different ideals should be weighed); thus, what one does most often is to take into some account the various ideals. I think that Mackie is right in considering illogical this kind of universalization. I add that, actually, this is not a kind of universalization at all, and that it is unrelated to moral judgment. This is because universalization serves to find the "universal" (good) moral laws and principles, which, being universal, exclude other rival principles and ideals. Moreover, giving equal consideration to all ideals means having no moral ideal; should we, in order to attain universalization, give equal consideration to the Nazi ideal, the mafia ideal, and the democratic-liberal ideal? Indeed, it should be clarified that, while no moral "rival ideals" or "rival ends" can exist, the occurrence of "parallel moral ends" is common, inasmuch as each moral good is a class that comprises various equally good (parallel) moral goods of less extension. Thus, mind evolution comprises the evolution of intellect, the evolution of sensitiveness, and the evolution of power. These three moral goods are parallel to one another (and not "rival" to one another), and some uncertainty may only arise about which of them should be promoted more or first in the various particular situations. Moreover, uncertainty may exist concerning the choice of the best means to implement the chosen good (*procedural choices*), but not concerning the choice between a good and a bad end (chs. 2.1.6; 2.1.7).

Finally, I note that the third-stage universalization is incompatible with the first-stage universalization as conceived by Mackie (1977: 83–90). This is because one who universalizes his moral judgments by applying them to all the members of the class of men who believe in a given ideal cannot at the same time give equal weight to all ideals, i.e., to the ideal other than the one which defines the class to which he claims to belong.

Mackie (1977) underlines that, although the logical thesis for the first-stage universalization of moral judgments is correct, one should remember that substantive practical principles are independent of the corresponding logical thesis. He says that this can be understood by conceiving morality and moral language as an institution and the substantive practical principles as speaking within such an institution; "but this does not give universalizable maxims any intrinsic, objective, superiority to non-universalizable ones" and "no one is constrained to adhere to that institution"; it is a subjective decision (Mackie 1977: 98–99). Thus, universalizability does not avoid Mackie's moral skepticism or subjectivism. Here I think that Mackie is right in saying that the logic of universalization does not entail the acceptance of the moral norm that is universalized (see my critique to the universalization principle under section "*A1*" of this chapter). Yet, I dissent from his claim that endorsing a moral norm is a matter of "subjective decision." Indeed, as I showed elsewhere (chs. 2.1.4.1; 2.1.5.1; 2.2.1.1.1), the moral norm arises from the *objective* nature of the mind, i.e., from its *evolutionary capacity*.

(D) Nelson's Interpretation of the Universalizability Principle.
Nelson (1991: 47–55) criticizes Kant's moral theory. He points out that it is very difficult to ever know whether someone is acting with a morally-good will, i.e., in such a way that one's maxim may be raised to universal law (*universalization principle*); this is because we cannot exclude that someone is acting by some secret impulse of self-love or desire (Nelson 1991: 42).

Actually, in my opinion, any moral act is supported by a rational component (*moral thoughts*), that Kant identifies in the universalization principles, as well as by an affective component (*moral feelings*), which must prevail over personal desires. The possibility of simulating a morally-good act that, actually, satisfies a secret personal desire, refers to cases of deception (included self-deception), which are possible with any moral theory.

However, according to Nelson (1991: 51–52), Kant's universalization principle may be regarded as a principle of impartiality. He notes that this principle suffers from the fact that actions can be described in different ways, all of which are true. Nelson supposes that we have to decide whether to stop the treatment of a suffering dying person; this can be described as killing an innocent person (a maxim that, obviously, cannot be universalized) or as helping dying people to die peacefully (Nelson 1991: 52). The example given by Nelson actually refers to the so-called "hard moral cases", for which there is not a clear-cut decision, regardless of the moral theory followed, because they allow only a very *approximate* evaluation and, hence, diverse and even competing acceptable solutions (ch. 2.2.1.5).

Moreover, Nelson (1991: 52–54) notes that the impartiality implicit in the universalization principle seems to be based on the agent's ideals or preferences, without any concern for the views of others. Nelson supposes that one wants to preserve the environment and, therefore, he refrains from polluting even if this entails some sacrifices, while someone else thinks that no sacrifice should be done in view of uncertain beneficial effects on the environment. Which one of these two different positions should be universalized? I think that the case to which Nelson's example refers allows a right choice (preserving the environment). However, Nelson's examples refer to very complex facts and situations, for which only probable (but not certain) interpretative hypotheses can be formulated and only *approximate* evaluation and previsions can be made (ch. 1.1.3.2.1, *3*); it follows that the corresponding moral choices are difficult and uncertain (ch. 2.2.1.5). These difficult moral cases should not lead to moral skepticism, since in most occurrences in human life right moral choices can be made with only a minimum of uncertainty by following the moral norm prescribing the promotion of mind evolution (ch. 2.1.6).

2.2.1.1.4—A New Version of the Universalizability Principle

The macro-world is made of heterogeneous classes of similar but not identical "objects" (as is the class of men) and of classes of variable events (ch. 1.1.3.2.1); this entails that: *(a)* concerning the agents, several *sub-classes of men* can be conceived, which limits the universalizability of action's maxims; and *(b)* concerning facts or events, due to their great complexity and variability, it is possible to divide any class of facts (which share some similar characteristics) into *sub-classes of facts*, each sub-class sharing some unifying characteristics; moreover, the great complexity of facts or events allows several interpretative hypotheses, from which diverse and even contrasting choices can be derived. In order to evaluate human actions and acts according to the universalizability principle, we should consider separately *(A)* the *end* of the agent's action and *(B)* the *agent* of the action.

> *(A) Universalization Referred to the Class to Which the Agent's End Belongs.*

The above critique to Kant's universalization principle (ch. 2.2.1.1.3, *A1*) shows that the *universalization of the maxim that determines an action* does not work as the basis for judging good moral acts; yet, this is the only possible kind of universalization if one considers, as Kant did, that the moral value of an action is *not* linked to its purpose or end or effect. A different kind of universalization is, however, possible on the grounds of my moral conception, and is based on two concepts: *(1)* the moral value of a human act depends on its end or effect; *(2)* the universalization should refer to the effect of an act, and not to its maxim.

(1) As I noted in chapter 2.2.1.6.1, the moral value of a human act depends on its *effect on mind evolution*, the act being morally good or bad according to whether it promotes or restrains the evolution of intellect and/or sensitiveness and/or power of one or more minds. [Here I overlook that the *effect* of an act cannot be distinguished from the act itself, since the cause is linked to its effect through a *continuum*, and the same is true for the relation between human actions and their effects (Belfiore 2004: 91–100, 102)].

(2) Since the ability to undergo mind evolution is an essential property of the class of men, i.e., it is a property common to *all* men, it allows a new kind of universalization: the *universalization of the effect that is determined by an act*. In other words, considering that mind evolution is the objective human good (chs. 1.1.1.2.4; 2.1.4.1; 2.2.1.1.1, *1*), and that all men possess the ability to undergo evolution, it follows that *all men should recognize the universal moral norm that prescribes to promote mind evolution*. So conceived, the universalizability principle *does not allow any exception*. It is irrelevant whether the agent is intelligent or stupid, strong or weak, rich or poor (i.e., whether he belongs to the sub-classes of the intelligent men or of

the strong men or of the rich men, and so on); what is important is the *effect* (on mind evolution) exerted by the act performed by the agent. The statement, just made, that the universalizability principle, as I conceive it, "does not allow any exception" needs to be clarified, since it may appear to be in contrast to my assertion that, due to the variability of the essential properties that define the members of a class, the universal affirmative propositions, such as "All 'x' are . . .", are unjustified; the explanation of this apparent contrast is given below (under section "*B*").

A central point is that any moral conception should be based on a definition of what a man actually is. Kant defined man as a rational being and based his moral norm on the *universalizability of the maxims* that determine actions. I define man as an evolving conscious entity consisting of intellect, sensitiveness, and power, and ground my moral norm on the *universalizability of the effects* that are determined by human acts.

It is noteworthy that the acts that promote mind evolution form a class, which can be divided into *sub-classes of acts* that promote the evolution of a single mind-component, such as the sub-class of acts that promote the evolution of the intellect, the sub-class of acts that promote the evolution of the sensitiveness, and so on. Moreover, smaller sub-sub-classes can also be created, which include those acts that promote the evolution of an aspect of the intellect or of the sensitiveness, etc. (ch. 2.1.4.2). Despite some differences between these acts, difficult to evaluate (given the complexity of the mind), all of them contribute to the evolution of the mind as a whole.

The force of the universalization principle, as I conceive it, derives from the objectivity and self-evidence of the "good" on which it is based (mind evolution), and from its inescapability. On this basis, a "bad man" who would like to kill a rich man for taking his money (thus inducing an extreme and irreversible mind *involution*, as killing means transforming a man into inert matter) should deny that there is an extreme difference between the value of a man and that of ~70 Kg of inert matter, i.e., he should deny what appears to the rational consciousness a self-evident truth.

On the grounds of the above reasoning, I would substitute Kant's moral rule (1785: 31) "act only in accordance with that maxim [the subjective principle of action] through which you can at the same time will that it become a universal law" with the moral rule: *act to promote mind evolution (in yourself and in others), which is the "good" for all men.*

   (B) Universalization Referred to the Class to Which the Agent Belongs.

I recall that universalization means referring to all the members of a class; the class of a moral agent can be variously defined: we may refer to the class of mammals, that of men, that of intelligent men, that of sensitive men, that of strong men, that of rich men, that of men who believe in a given ideal, etc. Moreover, within a given class, say, the class of "intelligent men", several sub-classes can be defined, depending on the degree of intelligence, the field in which intelligence expresses itself, etc. Since we are in search of a norm for human action, we can ignore the class of mammals, which comprises, besides men, also living beings other than men; yet, we cannot ignore the sub-classes into which the class of men can be divided. Indeed, a man belonging to any of the possible sub-classes can universalize his moral judgments by considering them valid for *all* the members of his own class. Indeed, Kant himself actually referred to a sub-class of men, i.e., the sub-class of men who are adult and of sound mind (two properties that can only be *imprecisely* defined). Referring to a sub-class is logically correct and may also be morally-good, provided that one considers as valid for *all men* those moral judgments that concern the properties *common to all men* (i.e., the *essential properties* that define the class of men), and as valid for all the members of a given sub-class (e.g., the sub-class of intelligent men) those moral judgments that concern the property specific of that sub-class (intelligence, in the above example). Thus, it is logically correct and morally good to say: "All intelligent men should have the right to be selected to become professors at university" (of course, within the class of "intelligent men" one should consider the various degrees of intelligence, etc.). To make a universal statement concerning *all men* (that is, concerning all the members of the class of men), i.e., to state "all men should have the right (or duty) to . . .", one must first identify the essential properties that define the class of men and that therefore are possessed by all its members. As I showed elsewhere (chs. 1.1.1; 1.1.2; 1.2), this property of the human mind consists of being an *evolving* conscious entity made of intellect, sensitiveness, and power. This fundamental property of all men gives rise to the universal moral norm (and to universal human rights and duties). Indeed, mind evolution is the moral good for any man, regardless of his intelligence, sensitiveness, and power (perhaps, in the case of a less intelligent, sensitive, and potent man, the promotion of mind evolution is even more valuable). Recognizing mind evolution as the moral good for all men is the basis for *equality* in treating human beings. On the other hand, a moral statement referring to all the members of a *sub-class of men* can only be made when referring to the *diversity* that exists among men, which gives rise to different merits and which concerns differences in the *degree and specificity of mind evolution* (this difficult issue is treated in chs. 3.2.2.1.1; 3.2.2.1.2).

As mentioned above (section "A"), the universalizability principle, as I conceive it, "does not allow any exception"; this statement needs to be clarified, since it may appear to be in contrast to my assertion that, due to the variability of the essential properties that define the members of any class of the macro-world (such as the class of men and that of man's ends), the universal affirmative propositions, such as "All 'x' are . . .", are unjustified and should be changed into "Most 'x' are . . .", thus introducing an element of approximation or imprecision (ch. 1.1.3.2.1). To clarify this point, we should recall that variability concerns all the properties of all the members of all the classes of the macro-world (or supra-molecular world, to which the human world belongs), with two notable exceptions, concerning two properties: *existence* and *becoming*. Existence and becoming are properties possessed by all existing entities and define the class of existing things (ch. 1.1.3.2.1). It follows that these two properties are possessed by all men; in man, however, the becoming is not a mere change, as may occur in physical objects, but consists of an *evolution*, as it entails a progressive increase in the complexity of the functions of the evolving conscious entity (the human mind, made of intellect, sensitiveness, and power). Becoming, or evolution, is a property possessed by *all* human beings, from newborns to old people (included to subjects affected by Alzheimer disease or other forms of dementia), even if to a various extent. When the mind does not undergo any change, then it does not exist anymore; this is what happens in the so-called "brain death", which, accordingly, is the only clinical condition recognized by law as the "death" of an individual. Accordingly, that referred to mind evolution is a true universalizability, and is a kind of universalizability that truly does not allow exceptions. Thus, the apparent contrast is eliminated and the coherence of my conception is reestablished.

2.2.1.1.5—Treating Men as Ends

According to Kant (1785: 37), whereas "things" have a worth linked to someone's inclination, rational beings are ends in themselves; they are *persons*. From this, Kant derives the practical imperative that men should be treated as ends and never as means. The actions of all rational beings obeying universal maxims given by themselves to themselves makes the *realm of ends* possible, i.e., the systematic union of rational beings through a common law (abstracting from personal differences and private ends).

Here I object that Kant's above-mentioned statements seem unjustified, since he does not explain in which sense we should treat people as ends. In contrast, my moral theory indicates that the human person, being an evolving mind, has the fundamental end of a progressive and *continuous evolution* of his intellect, sensitiveness, and power (in their outward and inward activities); a society governed by laws assuring to all citizens the rights derived from the fundamental moral norm (prescribing the promotion of mind evolution) is the *true realm of ends*. I would substitute Kant's moral rule or "practical imperative" "So act that you use humanity, whether in your own person or in the person of any other, always at the same time as an end, never merely as a means" (Kant 1785: 38) with the moral rule: *Act so that you promote mind evolution, either in your own person or in that of others.*

Kant (1785: 42) maintains that what is related to human inclinations, needs or desires has a *market price*; what is related to the taste or purposeless pleasure has an *affective price*; what is related to the condition under which something can be an end in itself has no price (relative worth) but a *dignity* (intrinsic worth). I find it strange to compare man with the objects of his desires or purposeless pleasure; I think, again, that this is the result of a lack of reference to the ontological conception about human beings and the structure of the mind. Indeed, man, consisting of a *conscious, evolving entity* made of *intellect, sensitiveness, and power*, is the most evolved and, hence, valuable of the existing entities, an entity that has absolute value and that is the source of any other value; this prompts the *inward activity of sensitiveness* (or emotional consciousness—Fig. 1.1) to generate the *moral feeling* named "respect" or the wish to consider that entity as having "dignity". Man so defined is the *source* of any other value, such as the value assigned to the things that are the object of human needs (belonging to the sphere of the *power*) or the value assigned to the things that are the object of desires and pleasure (belonging to the sphere of the *sensitiveness*). Moreover, as noted by Murphy (1988), Kantian theory, based on the ability of rational choices, raises the important question whether human beings lacking this ability, such as infants and mentally retarded individuals, have dignity, or if they merit respect. This problem does not arise when my theory is followed, since the ground moral norm of *promoting mind evolution* (to the maximum possible extent) is valid for all humans; indeed, the less developed the minds with whom we interact, the bigger our effort should be to promote their evolution.

2.2.1.1.6—*Other Views About the Reason-Morals Relationship*

Moore (1903) has attempted to define what is "good". He underlines that objects or notions that are complex can be defined by enumerating the simple properties, qualities, and parts that compose it. Conversely, "good" is a simple notion, just as "yellow" is, and simple notions cannot be explained; they are the starting point to explain complex objects and notions. Moreover, Moore (1903) notes that "good" is an adjective and, therefore, what is good must be a substantive. While what is regarded as good (*the* good) can be definable, "good", regarded as the quality that belongs to a thing, cannot be defined; it is a simple and indefinable quality (as is the perception of yellow).

At least two comments on Moore's view are in order. *First*, let us consider three "things", of which thing *A* is yellow, thing *B* is red, and thing *C* is good; what is important for the moral philosopher is to understand the difference between *A*, *B*, and *C*. Indeed, C differs from A (and from B) for a reason different from the reason by which A differs from B, because C has a moral *value* that A and B does not have. Moore's theory says nothing about this difference. I underline that a "thing" that has higher moral value than another one actually is a *stage of mind evolution* higher than a previously and lower one. *Second*, Moore talks of objects and notions, and considers the "good" as a quality that belongs to a "thing"; yet, besides "things" (see above), there are other entities that may be good or bad; they are events, more exactly those particular events that are human actions or, to use my terminology, human *moral acts*, which are good or bad according to whether they promote or favor mind evolution or involution.

Some thinkers maintain that ethics is linked to each society and is not trans-cultural or universal; they think that at least some of the virtues proposed by Aristotle are linked to the particular features of the Greek society (greatness of soul appears a more Greek than universal virtue, and contrasts with Christian humility). Conversely, Nussbaum (1988) notes that Aristotle's conception of virtues was thought in an objective manner, justifiable with reference to reason and to *grounding experiences* common to all men. Here I add that the *true* grounding experience, shared by *all* men and *specific* to man, is that of being minds composed of intellect, sensitiveness, and power, capable of *evolution*. This truth is obtained by intellect (or reason) through internal observation (Ch. 1).

Other works concern: the form and content of moral judgments (Brink 1989: 25–29); the limits of what should be done (and often is not done) and of what is considered as imperative (without regard of the effects) (Kagan 1989); the way of practical reasoning toward justice and virtues (O'Neil 1996); and the relationship of morality and universality (Potter and Timmons 1985). Lack of space prevents me from commenting on these works.

2.2.1.2—Moral Feelings and Moral Judgments

According to my conception, moral feelings can be judged (through moral thoughts) by the morality criterion as good or bad according to whether they are directed to favor good or bad moral acts (ch. 2.2.1.6.1; Table 1.1). On the other hand, moral feelings are the source of moral values, i.e., they "found" moral values (ch. 2.1.4.1, *b*). Yet, the role of moral feelings in moral judgments has been variously considered. I will discuss some views against the role of moral feelings in moral judgments, followed by a discussion of the role of moral feelings as conceived in selected classical and modern philosophical works. It is noteworthy that the role of moral feelings (as such and also as part of the moral *triplets*) in moral judgments allows us to reinterpret some ethical philosophical positions, such as *ethical expressivism or non-cognitivism, sensibility theories, motivational internalism or externalism*, and even *motivational reasons* (see Tables 2.2 and 2.3).

2.2.1.2.1—Arguments Against the Role of Moral Feelings in Moral Judgments

These are the arguments in favor of the thesis that moral judgments and decisions are grounded on reason; these arguments have been treated in chapter 2.2.1.1.

Here some comments on Nozick's "pleasure-machine" may be added. Nozick (1974: 42–45) notes that, if pleasure was the good that matters to us, and if neuro-psychologists had created a machine capable of any kind of pleasant experience, or producing in the world the results we want, one should desire to be hooked up to that machine for life; likewise, we should desire to continuously take psychoactive drugs that give pleasant sensations. Instead, Nozick notes, we desire to live in contact with reality. Although I fully agree with Nozick's view, I think that a fuller explanation for the refusal of machines or drugs giving pleasure can be obtained by referring to my theory. Four points should be considered. *(1)* The pleasure produced by a machine or by a drug is always a light and particular pleasure, which cannot develop or evolve into a deep and universal sentiment, like those expressed in literary, musical, and visual arts. *(2)* Pleasure-driven actions are unrelated to moral ends, as they are directed to satisfy personal desires or sentiments. *(3)* What is related to morality are not personal *sentiments* produced by the *outward activity of sensitiveness*, but *moral feelings* produced by the inward activity of sensitiveness (or *emotional consciousness*—Fig. 1.1). *(4)* Continuous enjoyment of the low pleasure produced by *sensitiveness* under the stimulus of a machine or of a drug would prevent us from developing the components of the mind (which is the fundamental moral end), i.e., from developing *sensitiveness* (creation of sentiments deeper than those given by the pleasure-machine), *intellect* (production of knowledge), and *power* (practical activity), all of which can be restrained by continuously experiencing false sensations and perceiving a false state of affairs.

2.2.1.2.2—The Notion of "Moral Feeling" in Classical Philosophical Works

(A) Epicurus.
Epicurus (~341–271 B.C.) was one of the first thinkers to maintain that the good is what is pleasant (*good = pleasant*). Yet, he pointed out that a pleasant and happy life is not the one devoted to superficial or sensual pleasure (which would be eventually disappointing), as life should also pursue honorability, justice, and prudence.

I comment on Epicurus's thought by noting that the distinction between "superficial" or "sensual" pleasure and other higher pleasures, such as honorability, justice and prudence, can be given a solid ontological basis if we regard *(a)* pleasure and happiness as *personal sentiments* produced by the *outward activity of sensitiveness* and directed to satisfy personal desires, and *(b)* honorability, justice, and prudence as behavioral features stirred-up by *moral feelings* produced by the *inward activity of sensitiveness* (or *emotional consciousness*) and directed to promote mind evolution (chs. 1.1.1.2; 2.1.3.2; Fig. 1.1).

(B) Hume.

Hume (1739/40: 470–76) held that morality is felt rather than judged; according to him, feelings arising from virtues are agreeable whereas feelings arising from vices are uneasy. He thought that good and evil are nothing but "particular" pains and pleasures; actions, sentiments or characters are virtuous or vicious when they cause pleasure or uneasiness of a particular kind. [A similar view had been held by Spinoza in his *Ethics* (1677a: Part IV, Def. I and II, and Prop. VIII)]. Hume's view includes two points, which can be explained by my theory as follows: *(1)* The claim that morality is *felt* (and not judged of, or thought) should be interpreted as referring to *moral feelings* produced by *emotional consciousness* (Ch. 1; ch. 2.1.1.2) [I recall that moral feelings, due to the internal coherence of the mind, are most often in agreement with the indications derived from reason or intellect—ch. 2.1.4.1, *b*]. *(2)* The rather vague statement that morality is based on feelings (pains or pleasure) of "a particular kind" should be explained by recalling the difference between *personal sentiments*, produced by the *outward activity of sensitiveness* and directed to satisfy personal desires and interests, and *moral feelings*, produced by *inward activity of sensitiveness* (or *emotional consciousness*) and directed to promote mind evolution.

I note that the position of Hume (1739/40) includes a contradiction: on the one hand, he argues that enforcement of moral laws is necessary to ensure law observance by the essentially *selfish* man; on the other hand, he thinks that we link the idea of virtue to that of justice because of *sympathy*, i.e., the natural disposition to share the feelings of others. This contradiction can be explained if we refer to my theory, since "selfishness" expresses *personal desires*, produced by the *outward activity of sensitiveness*, whereas "sympathy" expresses *moral feelings*, produced by the *inward activity of sensitiveness* (or *emotional consciousness*) (ch. 2.1.3.2; Fig. 1.1) and directed to promote mind evolution, in the agent himself and/or in others.

(C) Bentham.

Bentham (1789: 38–41) maintained that *pleasure* and *absence of pain* are the only human ends that have values, a pleasure of longer duration or greater intensity being of greater value than one of shorter duration or less intensity. He said: "Nature has placed mankind under the governance of two sovereign masters, pain and pleasure" (Bentham 1789: 11).

Bentham's view can be questioned for at least three reasons.

(1) Pleasure can be correctly evaluated only if it is framed into a conception about the structure and functioning of the human mind; Bentham seems to lack such a conception. By referring to my theory, we can say that pleasure is the pleasant form of *sentiment* and, therefore, it is the product of the *outward activity of sensitiveness*; as such, it should not be evaluated only according to its intensity and duration but also according to the *value criterion* (ch. 1.1.3.2.2), which allows us to distinguish pleasures with varying degree of universalization, from light and particular pleasures to deep, fully universal pleasures, which may be expressed in literary, musical, and visual arts and which enable the human soul to "understand" the arts (Table 1.1).

(2) Besides pleasure (produced by sensitiveness), there are other "human ends", such as *knowledge* (produced by *intellect*) and the economic and socio-political achievements (produced by *power*); these mind products, too, can have a varying degree of universalization, from particular to universal (chs. 1.1.3.2.1; 1.1.3.2.3; Table 1.1).

(3) The *moral end* does not consist of enjoying an intense and long pleasure nor of possessing a given knowledge or enjoying a given economic and political status; although possessing a certain degree of knowledge and welfare is an objectively good status compared to lower intellectual or welfare states, the moral ends of human moral acts consist of *promoting the endless evolution of intellect, sensitiveness, and power* in order to achieve ever more universal knowledge, sentiments, and ability of practical actions. Thus, moral acts are prompted by moral feelings, and differ from personal actions, prompted by personal sentiments, because the former are concerned with mind evolution, the latter are not.

(D) Kant.

Kant (1785: 2) conceives the *good will* as something good in itself, independently of what it accomplishes or of its adequacy to accomplish some proposed ends; it sparkles like a jewel in its own light. Kant (1785: 2) claims (rather arbitrarily, I think) that, assuming as a principle that in the natural constitution of beings there is no organ that is not the fittest and most suited for its purpose, it follows that, if happiness was the true end of human beings, who have reason and will, nature would have made a poor arrangement in appointing reason as the executor of such an end, which would be better attained by instinct and inclination than by reason. Thus, reason's proper function must be to produce a will that is good in itself (not a will that is good merely as a means); *good will* would be established by reason and would attain a purpose determined by reason, even though this injures the ends of inclinations (Kant 1785: 10).

Although I agree that happiness is not the true end of human beings (ch. 2.2.1.6.2), I underline the weakness of the above reasoning about the axiom on the fitness of each organ for its purpose, and the conclusions derived from it. Indeed, I think that Kant's distinction between "good will" and "inclinations" becomes clear and justified if we identify "good will" with what I call *moral feelings* (produced by *emotional consciousness*—Fig. 1.1) and "inclinations" with *personal sentiments or desires* (produced by *emotional selfishness*); this entails that "good will" is not created by reason, as Kant claims. Indeed, the Kantian attempt to derive "good will" from reason is not convincing, as I will try to show in the following lines.

According to Kant (1785: 13), to act morally one must act *from duty*, and not just according to duty when duty coincides with one's inclination; he says that "an action from duty has its moral worth not in the purpose to be attained by it but in the maxim in accordance with which it is decided." Love as inclination cannot be commanded; beneficence from duty, when no inclination impels it, resides in the will (and not in propensities of feeling) and can be commanded. According to my conception, acting "from duty" means acting by following *moral feelings* (produced by *emotional consciousness*), whereas acting according to one's inclinations means acting by following one's *personal desires* (produced by *emotional selfishness*) (chs. 2.1.1.2; 2.1.3.2). The claim that inclinations cannot be commanded whereas acting from duty can be commanded raises the big problem of freedom of will; while this problem is discussed elsewhere (ch. 2.4), here I just mention that human decisions depend on the prevalence of *moral feelings* over *personal desires*, or vice versa.

Kant (1785: 13) maintains that *duty* is the necessity of an action executed from *respect* for moral law. Kant attempts to clarify what he means as "respect" by saying that this term would not refer to some "obscure feeling" because, though respect is a feeling, it would not be one received through any outer influence, but is one self-worked by a rational concept and, therefore, it differs from the feelings that can be named inclination or fear.

This rather obscure explanation can be substituted with one based on my moral theory by stating that "respect" for moral law, actually, is *moral feeling* produced by *emotional consciousness*, and that "inclination or fear" corresponds to *personal sentiments* (desires or aversion) produced by *emotional selfishness*.

(E) Croce.
Croce's moral conception (1909: 309–63, 440–51), too, seems grounded on what I name *moral feelings* (even if directed to *universal ends*).

2.2.1.2.3—The Notion of "Moral Feeling" in Modern Philosophy

(A) Ross's Prima Facie Duties.
Ross (1930: 16–47) underlines the inadequacy of utilitarianism, in all its variants. According to him, a man "fulfills a promise" because he thinks that he ought to do so, without thinking of its total consequences; he thinks,

in fact, much more of the past than of the future. Moreover, one helps a victim not because this produces more good than not doing so, but because one thinks this is his duty (Ross 1930: 16–18). In these two examples, Ross does not explain *why* one thinks that he ought to fulfill promises or should think that it is his duty to help a victim.

Ross (1930: 19) points out that utilitarianism ignores such relations as promisee-to-promiser, creditor-to-debtor, wife-to-husband, child-to-parent, friend-to-friend, fellow countryman-to-fellow countryman, etc., which are foundations of *prima facie* duties (I discuss them in ch. 2.2.1.7.2, *C*).

Ross's attempt to explain the origin of what he calls *prima facie duties* is rather obscure, and can be interpreted, based on my theory, as suggesting that duties actually originate from *moral feelings* produced by human *emotional consciousness* (chs. 2.1.1.2; 2.1.3.2). This is suggested by Ross's statement that duties are not based on logical principles; moreover, his statements that duties are based on "what we really think about moral question" and on "reflection on our moral convictions" should be interpreted, according to my theory, as saying that duties are based on "what we really *feel* about moral question" and on "reflection on our moral *feelings*." Ross adds that duties are apprehended as self-evident by reflection; they contain something that we do not merely think but know (they are like mathematical axioms), and this forms the standard by reference to which the truth of any moral theory has to be tested (Ross 1930). I think that the supposed "axioms" are actually *deep moral feelings*.

Ross (1930: 19–21) proposes the following list of *prima facie* duties (which I will further comment on in ch. 2.2.1.7.2, *C*): *(1) Duties resting on previous acts of the agent*, which include *duties of fidelity* (resting on a promise) and *duties of reparation* (resting on previous wrongful acts). *(2) Duties of gratitude*, which rest on previous acts of other men (these, I think, are not duties at all). *(3) Duties of justice*, which arise from a distribution of pleasure or happiness not in accordance with the merits. *(4) Duties of beneficence*, which rest on the possibility to improve the condition (virtue, intelligence, pleasure) of others. *(5) Duties of self-improvement*, which rest on the possibility to improve our own condition. *(6) Duties of nonmaleficence*, consisting of not injuring others. Ross does not provide any rational explanation for these six kinds of duties; therefore, based on my moral theory, I think that these duties arise from *deep moral feelings* (which, as we already know, are most often consistent with our *moral thoughts*).

Ross (1930: 30–32) notes that in the actual world, the various duties are compounded together in highly complex ways, so that judgments about *particular* duties are not self-evident as the *prima facie* duties are. Therefore, he thinks that we should study the situation, reflect about the characteristics and implications of the various acts, and form a considered opinion about which duty is the most incumbent. According to Ross, we should be content with what appears as the greater likelihood. I think that Ross is right in underlining the complexity of real situations. As I pointed out elsewhere (ch. 1.1.3.2.1), in the supra-molecular world (and especially in the human world), "objects" and "events" are complex, variable or irregular across the various instances, and continuously changing; therefore, they can only be known with *approximation*; moreover, our forecasts are always probabilistic. It follows that, when we attempt to evaluate the implications of the various possible acts, our evaluation can only be made with *approximation* or *imprecision*; this is especially true in the so-called hard moral cases, as I discuss in chapter 2.2.1.5.

Ross (1930: 137–40) attempts to define the relationships between the intrinsically good things, which include virtue, pleasure, allocation of pleasure to the virtuous (and of pain to the vicious), and knowledge; he points out that pleasure is not always good in itself, because what is good or bad is more properly defined by all the relevant facts, some of which may be good whereas others may not be (example: a sentient being may be in a state of pleasure that is undeserved, or that is the realization of a vicious disposition). Thus, pleasure creates only a presupposition of goodness that may be outweighed by other elements in the total fact. I note that pleasure, like happiness, is the result of the agent's personal actions (directed to satisfy personal desires) and of luck, and is unrelated to the "good". What Ross calls pleasure linked to good relevant facts is actually what I have defined as *moral feeling* (produced by *emotional consciousness*), which prompt moral acts directed to promote the human good, i.e., mind evolution (chs. 2.1.1.2; 2.1.3.2; 2.1.4.1). Accomplishing moral acts prompted by moral feelings (directed to promote mind evolution) produces a feeling of "clean conscience", which is different from the "pleasure" arising from the satisfaction of personal desires through personal actions.

Ross (1930: 141) also notes that there are complex states of mind that we think "good in themselves" and that are compounded of the above mentioned moral goods (virtue, knowledge, and pleasure); thus, "aesthetic enjoyment" would be a blend of pleasure with insight into the nature of the object that inspires it, and "mutual love" would be a blend of virtuous disposition of two minds toward each other with the pleasure that arises from such disposition and the reciprocal knowledge. I object that "aesthetic enjoyment" is only indirectly linked to the "good", and the same is true for "mutual love". This is because both these conditions (being able to aesthetic enjoyment and harboring deep love) indicate a well-evolved state of mind (more exactly: indicate a mind with a well-developed *sensitiveness*, producing deep *sentiments*); this evolved state of sensitiveness should be judged as "morally good" ("good in itself," to use Ross's expression) if compared to less evolved states of the sensitiveness, but "morally bad" if compared with even more evolved states of sensitiveness. The occurrence of such morally-good states of the mind should be distinguished from good moral acts, of which they represent the ends. Indeed, moral acts are directed to promote the (endless) evolution of mind, including sensitiveness, i.e., are directed to promote the *evolution of sensitiveness* (to make it capable of generating ever deeper sentiments, including aesthetic enjoyment and mutual love), together with the evolution of intellect and power (chs. 2.2.1.6.2; 3.2.5.1). [Ross's claims that aesthetic enjoyment is associated with an insight into the nature of the object that inspires it, and that mutual love is a pleasure that arises also from the reciprocal knowledge may ingenerate the false conviction that "knowledge" plays an important role in the field of aesthetics and of love. Indeed, "knowledge" belongs to the sphere of intellect and is distinct from the aesthetic activity generated by sensitiveness; it plays only a minor supporting role in the sphere of aesthetic creativity and enjoyment—Belfiore 2004: 203–7].

(B) Ayer's Emotive Moral Judgments.

Ayer maintains that the validity of ethical judgments must be regarded as *absolute* or *intrinsic* and not empirically verifiable (Ayer 1936: 105), as these judgments have no objective validity and only express certain feelings of the speaker about certain objects (Ayer 1936: 108) (often based on the fear of God or of enmity of society—Ayer 1936: 112–13), so that their relevance is purely "emotive" (Ayer 1936: 108). Ethical statements would be comparable, *mutatis mutandis*, to the aesthetic statements (Ayer 1936: 103). This means that *normative* ethical concepts (unlike the *descriptive* ethical concepts, which belong to psychological or sociological sciences) cannot be controlled by observation, but only by mysterious "intellectual intuitions," which may conflict amongst one another (Ayer 1936: 106). It follows that arguments on moral questions are possible only if a system of values is presupposed; if an opponent disagrees with us, we can only feel that our system of values is superior but without being able to demonstrate this, i.e., we resort on mere abuse (Ayer 1936: 111).

I think that Ayer's position, according to which ethical judgments are purely "emotive" and are controlled only by "intuitions", should be interpreted as vaguely referring to what I call *moral feelings*, which, together with *moral thoughts and projects* and *moral acts*, represent one of the three kinds of products of the consciousness. Moral feelings, however, contrary to the ethical judgments as conceived by Ayer, are not derived from fear of God or social expectations, but are the expression of the intrinsic properties of the human consciousness which, as such, are common to all men (apparently discordant moral feelings among different individuals most often express a different degree of evolution of emotional consciousness, so that discordant positions tend to converge as mind evolves). However, when an opponent disagrees with us, we should first distinguish whether the disagreement concerns issue not related to morality (e.g., sexual behavior); concerning issues of moral relevance, when a disagreement arises, we should resort to moral thoughts (produced by rational consciousness), which, through internal observation make us aware that mind evolution is the objective moral good. Due to the internal coherence of the mind (ch. 2.1.4.1, *b*), moral feelings are most often in keeping with moral thoughts. However, when a contrast occurs between a speaker and his opponent on a moral issue, moral thoughts allow us to show that one of the two is right (the one whose moral project is directed to promote mind evolution) and the other is wrong (with the exceptions of the "hard moral situations"—ch. 2.2.1.5); yet, contrasting opinions may remain concerning minor aspects or details about the *procedural choices* for reaching moral ends (ch. 2.1.7).

(C) *Act-Utilitarianism, Rule-Utilitarianism, Consequentialism, and "Rational" Desires.*

(1) Act-Utilitarianism. Mill (1861) is an authoritative proponent of *utilitarianism*, a doctrine that has been much developed by many thinkers (see in: Brandt 1992; Scarre 1996); he holds that the foundation of morals is the *utility* (or *happiness* or *pleasure*) and maintains the *greatest happiness principle* (Mill 1861: 7).

(a) The core concepts of utilitarianism. Mill (1861: 6–26) held that actions are right in proportion as they tend to promote happiness, the latter including not only mere pleasant sensations but also the "higher pleasures" of intellect, imagination, and moral sentiments, as judged by "those who are qualified" or by their majority (pp. 7–11) (yet he did not say who the "qualified" evaluators are!). Thus, besides the "quantity", the "quality" of the various kinds of pleasure should also be considered, and the "higher" pleasure is preferable to the "lower" one. Also, what counts is not the agent's happiness but the happiness of all those who are concerned (*overall happiness*).

Mill's views raise problems. Concerning the "quantity" of pleasure, it is well known the difficulty in measuring it (see below, under "*c*"). As to the different quality of pleasures, Mill, besides to the "higher pleasure," also refers to "the conscientious feelings of mankind" (p. 29), without explaining the difference between pleasure (even the "higher pleasure") and the sense of clean conscience. I think that Mill failed to make the essential distinction, grounded on the structure of the mind, between: *(i) personal sentiments*, created by the *outward activity of sensitiveness* (or *emotional selfishness*) and expressing personal desires, and *(ii) moral feelings*, created by the *inward activity of sensitiveness* (or *emotional consciousness*) and having *mind evolution* as their object (chs. 2.1.1.2; 2.1.3.2; Fig. 1.1). The satisfaction of the former gives selfish pleasure whereas following the demand of the latter gives the non-selfish feeling of having a clean conscience. It is the latter kind of "pleasure", not the former, that is morally relevant. Moreover, concerning pleasure linked to *personal sentiments*, the degree of their deepness (universality) should also be considered (ch. 1.1.3.2.2; Table 1.1), because the high pleasure linked to deeper sentiments (as are those expressed in literary, musical, and visual arts) is morally better than the sensorial, light pleasure linked to particular personal experiences, as the former indicates a more evolved sensitiveness. However, we should distinguish between: *(i)* having a *sensitiveness* capable of generating deep and universal *sentiment*, which is a morally better status compared to having a sensitiveness generating only light and particular sentiments, and *(ii)* performing *good moral acts*, which are those acts that promote the *evolution of sensitiveness* toward the production of ever-deeper sentiments (of course, good moral acts are also those that promote the evolution of the other mind-components, i.e., the *intellect* and *power*). I also note that, considering pleasure and happiness as the moral ends would entail that, being the love of the loved person one of the major causes of happiness, we should be engaged in helping our relatives and friends to obtain the love of the persons whom they love; obviously, this would not be an appealing moral norm (ch. 2.2.1.6.2).

Mill (1861: 4) thought that happiness or pleasure is the good to be pursued and that whatever can be proved to be good, must be a means to something admitted to be good without proof; according to Mill (1843; 1861), what is good would be what is a proper object of pursuit. As correctly noted by Mackie (1977), this is an invalid affirmation that cannot be derived from the fact that each person desires his own happiness. Mackie (1977: 146) underlines that the content of a moral system is "more malleable, more a matter of choice, than utilitarianism, in any form, makes it appear . . . We are, then, free to mould or re-mould our moral system so as better to promote whatever it is that we do value." My comment here is that, whereas we are free to promote whatever we value, the problem is to establish whether what we appreciate has moral (obligatory, or binding) value or is just the object of our personal desire. Indeed, without the recognition of the *objective* human good (mind evolution), there is no way to distinguish the morally-good from the morally-bad (or morally neutral) values, principles, and acts. As I pointed out elsewhere (ch. 2.2.1.6.2), happiness, or the desire to be happy, is not directly linked to morality; it is certainly one of the major factors that affects human behavior but it is not the factor related to the *morally-good* behavior. What is morally relevant is the promotion of the ability to feel happy (or unhappy), i.e., the promotion of the evolution of the sensitiveness (together with the evolution of the other mind-components). Indeed, happiness is something unrelated to morality and depending on many factors, including good or bad luck. Thus, as underlined also by Mackie (1977: 140), *utility* or general *happiness* is not a peculiarly authoritative or self-justifying starting point for moral reasoning.

(b) Virtue. Mill (1861: 37) notes that *virtue* was originally and naturally not a part of the end (happiness) but a means to the end; yet, because of its

conduciveness to pleasure (because the consciousness of virtue is a pleasure), it became with time an end and is now desired as part of happiness. Something similar happened with money or with power, whose worth actually depends solely on the things they allow to obtain, but which have become a part of the end (a part of happiness) and are desired for themselves (Mill 1861: 37). Thus, human nature would desire only what is part of happiness or what is a means of happiness.

Here Mill fails to distinguish what is the *objective good* (happiness in his view, mind evolution in my conception) from the *good acts* or behavior (*virtue* in his terminology, good *moral behavior* or *acts* in mine) that promote or pursue it. Virtue (good moral acts) is not desired and does not give "pleasure"; it conforms to what is required by good *moral feeling* and may give the non-selfish feeling of having a clean conscience.

(c) Impracticability of utilitarianism. Act utilitarianism, as Mackie (1977: 129–31) notes, by taking *general* happiness as the standard of a right action, seems to satisfy the demand for unselfishness and fairness; yet, like the doctrine of neighborly love (see the biblical commandment "Thou shalt love thy neighbor as thyself"), it is impracticable because of its indeterminacy and uncertainty concerning the following aspects.

First. It is uncertain whether one should take into account the happiness of a part of or all human beings (including future generations), which would be too high an expectation. This point is related to the concept of *general* happiness. Mackie (1977: 132) observes that, as pointed out also by Butler (1726: 325–61), even if we distinguish self-love and benevolence, we should note that human actions motivated by unselfishness and benevolence are directed to relatives and friends, and therefore prompted by self-referential altruism rather than by *universal* concern. Mackie (1977: 142) underlines the difficult problem of how to go from individualistic hedonism to universal hedonism. Indeed, there is no reason why one should promote *general* happiness, because this could only be made by following the *universalization principle*, which I have criticized elsewhere (ch. 2.2.1.1.3, *A1*). The same critique applies to the claim of Sidgwick (1874: 418–22), who defends the objectivity and intrinsic value of happiness by noting that when the egoist offers the proposition that his happiness or pleasure is objectively desirable or good, he gives the ground needed for proving this; for his happiness cannot be more objectively desirable or better than the similar happiness of others; thus, he should admit that there is something intrinsically good. Here I recall my critique to the universalization principle (chs. 2.2.1.1.3, *A1*; 2.2.1.1.4), based on the consideration that the "rich man" (or the "cunning man") might assert that "all the rich (or cunning) men have the right to be happy", thus escaping the rule of promoting "general" happiness. Also, pursuing *general* happiness should be the moral task of public institutions and not of the single individual, who is entitled to focus his moral acts primarily on his neighbors and the people with whom he interacts during his life (see the rule of the spheres of decreasing moral responsibility—ch. 2.1.5.2).

Second. How to measure the happiness of different people and of a single person in different times is a difficult problem. However, I note that difficulty in measuring and in the exact evaluation is a general problem when one is facing human facts, so that it cannot be regarded as a drawback of utilitarianism. It would be unrealistic to pretend to find a precise method allowing to measure happiness with exactness; since, in the *supra-molecular world*, all calculations and previsions can only be made with *approximation*, including the calculations and previsions in scientific fields such as biology, medicine, sociology, and political science (ch. 1.1.3.2.1), one should be content with *approximate* evaluation.

Third. The distribution of happiness (in addition to its quantity) is difficult to evaluate, also in consideration of the fact that material goods have a diminishing marginal utility. This, however, is a problem concerning the *public* aspect of utilitarianism and will be discussed in chapter 3, devoted to political philosophy (ch. 3.2.2.2.2, *A3a*).

Fourth. Finally, there is the problem of how to take into account the merit, which is an incentive to increase the aggregate of happiness. This point, like the preceding one, concerns the public aspect of utilitarianism and will be discussed in chapter 3.

(d) Public aspects of utilitarianism. Mill (1861: 19) believed that those who are in a position to act as *public* benefactors should pursue *general* happiness or utility, whereas the single individual should pursue *private* utility (the happiness of those few persons with whom he interacts).

While the public aspects of utilitarianism will be discussed in chapter 3, some comments are here anticipated. Mackie (1977: 147) underlines that his skeptical position does not mean that an individual is free to invent a moral system at will, since a moral system of rules must be accepted and followed by the society of which the individual is part. Here two points should be commented. *First*, the moral system accepted by the society is a public (community-shared) moral system based on shared principles (which may differ, at least in part, from the principle endorsed at the individual or private level—ch. 4.1.1.3.2, *B*). *Second*, the central problem is how to establish whether the shared principles are actually morally good or bad; I think that this problem can only be solved by referring to an *objective* human good, as the one proposed in my moral theory: *mind evolution* (chs. 1.1.1.2.4; 2.1.4.1; 2.2.1.1.1, *1*).

Moreover, pursuing "overall happiness" (i.e., the utility for the whole society) by those who may act as "public benefactors (as suggested by Mill—1861: 19), "does not take seriously the distinctions between persons" (as noted by Rawls—1971: 24) when it allows that in a society some people are charged by burdens for the greater benefit or utility of *other* persons (Rawls 1971: 29). Williams (1973: 116–17) notes that utilitarianism does not recognize the great value of the *agent life projects* to which he is committed; this would alienate agent's persons and could be regarded as an attack to their integrity.

I add that pursuing "overall happiness" by "public benefactors" is a problem belonging to political philosophy, and that the drawback of this view is avoided if one follows the *public moral norm* that I propose: "*To assure that all citizens enjoy an evolution-allowing, involution-avoiding condition*" (ch. 3.1.2.5.1, *3*).

(2) Rule-Utilitarianism (Harsanyi 1985; Hardin 1988; Scarre 1996). According to Brandt (1963: 109) and others, utilitarianism should be distinguished into *act-utilitarianism* (classical utilitarianism), which holds that the rightness of an action is fixed by the utility of its consequences, and *rule-utilitarianism*. The latter holds that the rightness of an action is fixed by its conformity with a general, learnable (by people with ordinary intelligence) set of moral rules or principles whose general acceptance results in utility for the whole society or have the *best* consequences. In other words, rule-utilitarianism takes into account not the direct effects of an action on general happiness but the effect of the adherence to the rule prescribing that action (or to a set of accepted rules). This form of utilitarianism would allow avoiding some unacceptable conclusions of act utilitarianism (that it is right to harm a few innocent people if this increases the happiness of many others). Yet, as noted by Mackie (1977: 137–39), rule-utilitarianism can be regarded as "extensionally equivalent to act-utilitarianism," and can "collapse into act-utilitarianism," unless one considers only those rules that are accepted and endorsed by public opinion (even if the problem of indeterminacy in happiness measurement remains). Besides the fact that rule-utilitarianism may be made to collapse into act-utilitarianism, I note that rule-utilitarianism does not solve the problem common to any kind of utilitarianism, i.e., why one should consider happiness or utility as morally good. Moreover, the proposal to follow those rules accepted and endorsed by public opinion, does not tell us why these rules should have moral value; in addition, it should be noted that rules endorsed by public opinion actually refer to *public* morality (which will be discussed in chapter 3, devoted to political philosophy), and not to the *private* or *personal* morality (with which I am here concerned).

(3) Consequentialism. As it is known, consequentialism extends the utilitarian concept of "good" to include, besides happiness and pleasure, also other issues such as knowledge, inter-personal relations, etc. (and even equality and respect of rights) (Scheffler, 1988; Pettit 1993; Darwall 2003). However, as summarized by Mackie (1977: 159), in evaluating an action we should consider the means, the end, the side effects, and the further conse-

quences, the latter two being often indicated as second effect; hence, we have the *principle of the double effect* (the end and the second effect) (Mackie 1977: 160–68). Bentham (1789: 86) maintained that the agent directly intends the means and the goal, but he only obliquely intends a known second effect. The principle of double effect has been endorsed by Catholic moralists, such as Aquinas (*Summa Theologica*, II–II, Q. 64, Art. 7), because it allows the defending of absolute moral rules, i.e., rules that absolutely prescribe or prohibit directly intended actions (means and ends) without including the obliquely intended side effects or further consequences (being the latter less certain than the chosen means and ends and sometime depending on the behavior of others). However, Mackie (1977: 166) pointed out that the distinction between means and side effect is often difficult, so that relying on it may be morally corrupting. He recalls the view of Anscombe (1958; 1961) that rejection of the principle of double effect has been the corruption of the non-Catholic moral thought, while its abuse has been the corruption of the Catholic moral thought. I underline that the distinction between the means, the end, the side effect, and the second effect (or further consequences) results from the *fragmented* view of reality, i.e., from the view that reality is made of *fragments*, separated both spatially (*objects*) and temporally (*events*), a view that should be rejected in favor of my conception of reality as made of a unitary and yet pleomorphic substance, i.e., a unitary substance that assumes multiple forms and undergoes continuous changes, so that the cause is linked to the effect through a *continuum* (ch. 1.1.3.2.1, *3d*); the same is true for the relation between a human action and its effect. Indeed, the cause (the human act) cannot be separated from its effect (end) and second effect (that occur along time), nor from the associated causes and side effects (that occur across space), as the cause continues, through a temporal and spatial *continuum*, in its effect and then in its second effects and is associated to contributing causes and side effects. The apparently primary cause together with its (always present) contributing causes are often indicated as "background conditions", so that we can say that actually it is a state of the world (the so-called cause) that, through a *continuum*, transforms itself into another state of the world (the so-called effect). It is because of our *fragmented view* that we distinguish a cause from the other contributing causes as well as a given cause (human action) from its means, effects, secondary effects, and side effects. Thus, due to the complexity, variety, and continuous changes of the "objects" and "events" of the human world, the distinction between what we call cause, means, effect, and secondary effect can only be made with *approximation*; therefore, no clear-cut rules of action can be formulated on these grounds.

(4) "Rational Desires". Brandt (1979:110) analyzes the genesis of pleasures and desires to show what a fully rational (or informed) person would want, what is desired by all rational people, or what is desired by some ra-

tional persons in some circumstances. He recalls that, according to Hume (1739/40: 413–17), a desire is irrational only if it is directed to an object that does not exist or if one chooses means insufficient for the desired end. Brandt (1979: 113), however, defines as irrational the desires that would not be present if confronted with relevant available information, i.e., if they do not survive "cognitive psychotherapy." Brandt (1979: 115–26) lists four types of causes that may lead to "mistaken desires" (or aversions): *(a) false beliefs* [a student may desire to begin working for a Ph.D. based on the (false) belief that doing so he will please his parents]; *(b) culture-transmission* (conditioning by parents, teachers, peers, films, television); *(c) untypical examples* (irrational generalization of untypical examples or experiences that, as such, should not be generalized); and *(d) early deprivation* (lack of satisfaction of desires early in a child's life can lead to insatiable and irrational desires in adult life).

Brandt's analysis, like Hume's recalled statement, refers to the relationship between desires or, in general, *sentiments* (produced by the *sensitiveness*), and *knowledge* (produced by the *intellect*). This relationship can be better clarified by referring to my conception about the structure of the mind, i.e., by taking into account that, due to the close relationship between the mind components (chs. 1.1.1.1, 6; 1.1.2, 2nd proposition), *sensitiveness* needs the support of *knowledge*, since nothing can be desired or hated if it previously is not known (therefore, a false knowledge may lead to "irrational" desires).

Brandt (1979: 126) asks himself whether the notion of "rational desire" approximates the concept of intrinsic good, and suggests that perhaps this is not the case. Brandt here is right, because a desire (even if "rational"), or the object of a desire, is unrelated with human "good", which coincides with mind evolution. On the other hand, Brandt (1979: 128) defends the utility of the concept of rational desire and notes that the term "good" or "intrinsically good" entails generalization, inasmuch as if something is good it must be good for everybody. Here Brandt refers to the *universalization principle*, which I have questioned elsewhere (ch. 2.2.1.1.3, *A1*) because it also allows limited generalization.

(D) Selfish and Unselfish Desires and Ethical Egoism.
Foot (1972: 157–67) questions the Kantian claim that moral judgments are categorical imperatives. This author notes that some rules (as those based on habits or traditions) do not give the reason to act according to them, and she thinks that moral rules are of this kind; it follows that the amoral man may deny that there is any reason to follow moral rules. According to Foot, it would not be our rationality but rather our "feeling" (perhaps affected by moral teaching) that gives the moral "should" a special sense.

Indeed, my moral theory provides both *(a)* a rational (and objective) basis for morality based on the understanding, through *moral thoughts*, of the ability of the mind to undergo *evolution*, and *(b)* an explanation of the role of the "feeling" by defining it as *moral feeling* produced by *emotional consciousness* and directed to promote *mind evolution* (chs. 2.1.1.1; 2.1.1.2; 2.1.4.1).

Egoism (i.e., *selfish desires*) has been proposed as the driving motive of human actions (Feinberg 1978: 547–58). *Egoistic hedonism* would consist of the desire for pleasure or pleasant experience (Bentham 1789: 38–41; Broad 1952: 218). The apparently disinterested *unselfish desires* (e.g., helping others) would be explained by the pleasure enjoyed in receiving gratitude or in feeling self-esteem or a good conscience (Feinberg 1978). These theories do not consider the difference between different kinds of desires nor do they explain why helping others should entail the pleasure of good conscience. Actually, the rather unclear distinction between selfish and unselfish desires is due to the lack of reference to the structure and functioning of the mind. Indeed, if we refer to my conception of the structure of the mind it becomes clear that "selfish desires" are *personal desires*, which are produced by the *outward activity of sensitiveness* (or *emotional selfishness*) and stir-up personal actions (directed to satisfy the desires by inducing changes in the physical world), whereas "unselfish desires" are *moral feelings*, which are produced by the *inward activity of sensitiveness* (or *emotional consciousness*) and which stir-up moral acts, directed to promote *mind evolution*.

The so-called *ethical egoism* is a normative theory according to which humans ought to pursue their own well-being (Feinberg 1978: 547–58). This theory is arbitrary (why should humans pursue their well-being?) and incomplete (why should humans pursue *only* their well-being?). As I have already pointed out, humans should pursue mind evolution because it is the absolute and objective human good (chs. 1.1.1.2.4; 2.1.4.1; 2.2.1.1.1, *1*), which includes all the kinds of moral goods. This means that humans should pursue the evolution of all the three mind components, i.e., the evolution of the *intellect* (developing knowledge), the evolution of the *sensitiveness* (to produce ever deeper sentiments), and the evolution of the *power* (which includes the promotion of well-being). Moreover, evolution should be pursued not only with reference to the agent's mind (see the concept of *morally-good egoism* in ch. 2.1.5.2.2) but also to the minds of others. This means that in pursuing the evolution of his mind the agent should not interfere with mind evolution of others; moreover, he should help those who do not enjoy the evolution-allowing condition.

(E) Men Shared Desires.

Nelson (1991: 53) underlines that some interests or desires, such as not being maimed or injured, may be common to all men, whereas in several fields the agent should consider also the interests, values or viewpoints of others to get impartiality. As I have repeatedly stated, values common to all men (and, therefore, universalizable) are those linked to the *essential, shared property* of the class of men, i.e., the property of being *evolving conscious minds* composed of intellect, sensitiveness, and power. These common properties give rise to the ground moral norm, which prescribes the promotion of mind evolution and forbids maiming or injuring (which entail a severe restraining of mind evolution—or induce severe mind *involution*).

Nelson (1991: 54) also maintains that men act morally when they obey laws which all of them are willing to accept as universally binding; in this way, they would act both as sovereign and as subjects. In evaluating this statement, I note that obeying publicly-shared laws refers to the public morality, linked to the acts one performs as a citizen of a democratic State (ch. 4.1.1.3), which should be kept distinct from private morality. Moreover, Nelson does not explain why the interests or desires common to all men (or those shared by a community) should be judged as *morally good*, i.e., he does not provide a philosophical justification for one's moral obligation to obey the laws accepted by all other men. In my view, laws accepted by all as binding are those laws that express shared moral principles and values; the latter, in turn, may be good or bad according to whether they are directed to promote or to restrain *mind evolution*; it is the task of the morally more evolved, "dissenting" citizen to attempt to correct shared moral principles and values that are morally bad, thus promoting the evolution of the common consciousness (ch. 4.1.1.3.2, *B*).

(F) Explaining Moral Emotions: Guilt and Resentment.

Gibbard (1985; 1990: 45–46) proposes a non-cognitivist theory of morality based on the claim that to call something (an action, belief or emotion) *rational* is to endorse it, i.e., "to accept norms that permit it." This would be a "psychological state that we are far from entirely understanding" (Gibbard 1985; 1990: 55). Moral questions would concern the rationality of certain moral emotions, such as guilt and resentment. An act is morally wrong if it is rational for the agent to feel guilty for doing it, and for others to resent him for doing it (Gibbard 1985; 1990: 47). Thus, what we have to explain is not what a norm for guilt or resentment is, but what accepting that norm is or means (Gibbard 1985; 1990: 46). From the moral point of view, an action should be regarded as wrong in the *subjective* sense, i.e., in light of what the agent has good reason to believe (Gibbard 1985; 1990: 42). Since some wrong actions may be made under extenuating psychological circumstances that exempt the agent from blame, *blameworthy* would be a more appropriate term than morally wrong; another distinction is that wrong is prospective, as it refers to the acts open to the agent, whereas blameworthy is retrospective, as it refers to the agent's acts made with insufficient moral motivation (Gibbard 1985; 1990: 44).

Gibbard's above theory clearly consists in the attempt to explain the reason for such emotions as guilt and resentment. When interpreted according to my conception, this means that morality, as thought by Gibbard, is based on what I call *moral feeling* (produced by *emotional consciousness*— Fig. 1.1). So conceived, morality cannot be "understood", since it can only be understood through *moral thoughts*, produced by *rational consciousness*; and, indeed, Gibbard (1985; 1990: 55) points out that accepting a norm is a significant kind of *psychological* state that we do not fully understand. Gibbard (1985; 1990: 56) claims that there are two different and often conflicting psychological motivations, i.e., the *normative motivation* (the norms a person accepts), involving the psychological *normative control system*, and the *animal motivation* (appetite), involving the *animal control system*. This rather uncertain distinction can be explained according to my theory by interpreting the normative motivation as due to *moral feeling* produced by the *inward activity of sensitiveness* (*emotional consciousness*), and the animal motivation as due to *personal sentiments* (desires, preferences, interests) produced by the *outward activity of sensitiveness* (*emotional selfishness*).

The distinction made by Gibbard (1985; 1990: 59–60, 68–75) between a norm that is *accepted* by an agent (because regarded as rational) and a norm that is *internalized* under social pressure, can be explained by referring to the distinction that I make between *personal morality* and *public or shared morality* as expressed by the social habits or by the laws of a democratic State (primarily by constitutional norms) (ch. 4.1.1.3.2, *B*).

(G) Assumptions on Moral Sensibility and Principles.
Harman asks himself whether moral principles can be tested and confirmed in the same way as scientific principles are. He notes that we need assumptions about physical facts to explain observations that support a scientific theory whereas to explain moral observations we need "assumptions" about the psychology or moral sensibility or moral principles (Harman 1977: 6). Thus, Harman thinks that morality is based on moral sensibility or moral principles; yet, he does not define what "moral sensibility" is. In my view, "moral sensibility" should be identified with what I call *moral feelings* that (as I discuss in chs. 2.1.1.2; 2.1.3.2) are those feelings directed to promote *mind evolution*. Harman's claim that moral (and scientific) principles consist of "assumptions" is in contrast with my view about the role of the *inward activity of intellect* that takes place at the level of the *rational consciousness* and that produces *moral thoughts* (through which we learn what the objective human good is: *mind evolution*). Indeed, I think that moral thoughts (and projects) play an important role, inasmuch as they provide the rational basis of morals and, due to the *internal coherence of the mind*, they are most often in accord with moral feelings (ch. 2.1.4.1, *b*).

(H) Generalized, Agent-Neutral Desires.
Nagel (1980) argues that the objectivity of values must be conceived in a manner different from that concerning physical or mental phenomena; he

thinks that to discover whether there are objective values we must try to arrive at normative judgments from an impersonal standpoint, i.e., we should *detach from our individual perspective.* To this end, *generality* must be considered inasmuch as if there is a reason for an individual to do something, then there is a general form of such a reason that applies to anyone in similar circumstances (Nagel 1980). For instance, we could ask ourselves whether pleasure and pain have any value when considered from an objective standpoint; Nagel (1980) believes that they have an agent-neutral value, i.e., that anyone has a reason to want to stop pain and to pursue pleasure, and this is a self-evident claim.

Nagel's position seems to be based on the claim that values are objective if they are agent-neutral and, consequently, have *generality*; it should be noted, however, that generality is also possessed by desires that hardly can be regarded as values, such as egoistic desires. Moreover, generality is another way to name the *universalizability principle.* Like this principle, generality does not necessarily entail reference to all men, as it may be conceived as referring to some sub-class of men (ch. 2.2.1.1.3, *A1*). Moreover, he does not provide any explanation as to why some *general* desires are values and others are not, nor does he explain why some values are *moral* values. Indeed, I think that desires should be evaluated from the moral point of view according to whether they are directed to promote or to restrain mind evolution. On this basis, we can say that the desire to avoid pain can be regarded as a moral value because pain is linked to some harm to our physical integrity, which is a basic requirement for mind evolution.

Nagel (1980) also notes that the desire to stop pain is simply *evoked* in the person who feels it, and is not the result of a *decision.* He adds that humans "are not limited to the particular point of view that goes with their personal position inside the world. They are also . . . objective selves; they cannot help forming an objective conception of the world with themselves in it." This seems to mean that some desires, as the desire to stop pain, are objective in the sense that they arise from the characteristics that human beings actually possess. When considered from my standpoint, this is true in the sense that human *moral feelings* are linked to the way in which human beings are made. Finally, Nagel (1980) points out that, despite the diversity of values among different cultures, agreement can be achieved and social prejudices transcended in the face of strong pressure, which suggests that something real must exist. Here Nagel omits to make an important distinction, i.e., that agreement should be pursued, and can be achieved, with regard to those values linked to the *essential properties* of the class of men (conceived as *evolving* conscious entities made of intellect, sensitiveness, and power) and therefore common to *all* men (ch. 3.2.2.1.1), whereas agreement should not be pursued with regard to *particular properties* specific to individuals or groups, because they express the diversity among human beings (i.e., their identity or personality), which enriches the human world (ch. 3.2.2.1.2).

2.2.1.3—Further Theories on Moral Judgment, Moral Thoughts, and Moral Feelings

2.2.1.3.1—Neither Utilitarianism nor Kantianism: Categorical Desires

Williams (1976) questions both utilitarianism and Kantianism and insists that each person has his own character consisting of his desires, concerns, and projects; he notes that some desires do not depend on the assumption of the person's existence ("categorical desires"). I think that what Williams names desires and concerns should be interpreted as what I name *personal desires* (produced by the *outward activity of sensitiveness*), whereas what Williams names categorical desires should be interpreted as what I name *moral feelings* (produced by the *inward activity of sensitiveness* or *emotional consciousness*) (ch. 2.1.3.2). The distinction made by Williams is, however, not clear and is not supported by a basic philosophical conception.

Williams (1976) criticizes *utilitarianism* because it abstracts from the separateness of persons (inasmuch as it pursues total utility or the agglomeration of satisfactions) and also from the identity of the agent who produces a given state of affairs. Williams's view is right, but I think that it should be given a different interpretation. One should distinguish *private* or *personal morality* from *public* or *institutional morality*; while the latter should pursue maximal, total "utility" (always avoiding that the pursuit of the utility of the majority is made at expenses of others), the former should take into account the concrete situation of the agent and his relationship with those who are affected by his acts. Indeed, family members, relatives, friends, colleagues, and acquaintances can be regarded as members of mini-communities which have non-written rules (ch. 3.1.2.3.3) and which establish different degrees of moral responsibility, as I discuss in chapter 2.1.5.2.1. Moreover, the nature of the true utility is not defined by Williams' theory; once again, I point out that the true "utility" is *mind evolution* and that the true "morally-good acts" are those directed toward the *promotion* of mind evolution.

Williams (1976) also notes that utilitarianism makes the unreasonable demand on the agent that he gives up what is required by his own ground project if the latter conflicts with the impersonal utility-maximizing principle. Here I note that, when "utility" is conceived as mind evolution, personal projects conflicting with mind evolution are to be judged as morally bad.

Williams (1976) also questions *Kantianism*, because it is based on the rational application of the impartiality principle, based on an inadequate account of the individual, as it ignores the particular characteristic of the agent and his circumstances and relations to others; this would be also true for the moral decisions taken under the condition of "ignorance", as conceived by Rawls (1971: 118–23). Williams (1976) notes that, for the Kantian thinkers, personal relations should presuppose moral relations; but this is not always true, as conflict may arise between personal relations and moral demand. If a potential rescuer in saving some people gives preference to his wife, this is morally right, because in some circumstances one's sentiments and attachment to other people express themselves in the world in ways that are incompatible with the impartial view. I underline that here, once again, one should distinguish private or *personal morality* from public or *institutional morality* (see above, and also ch. 4.1.1.3.2, *B*); a "private" rescuer has greater responsibility and duties toward his wife than toward the wife of another man, due to the non-written rules of the mini-community represented by the family (ch. 3.1.2.3.3), as well as for reasons linked to the concept of the spheres of decreasing moral responsibility (ch. 2.1.5.2.1). Conversely, an "institutional" rescuer should treat equally all the people in danger, and different treatments should be based on objective reasons, i.e., on the probability of a successful rescuing.

Finally, I recall that the impartiality principle (or *universalizability principle*) should refer to the moral acts that have a true moral end, i.e., that are directed to promote *mind evolution* (ch. 2.2.1.1.4).

2.2.1.3.2—Self-Interest Theories

Parfit (1984: 493–502) analyzes what makes someone's life go best, i.e., the *theories about self-interest*. He considers several theories, which I report below, together with my critical comment.

(1) Hedonistic Theory. This identifies the good with pleasure or happiness. I have already criticized this theory in chs. 2.2.1.2.2 and 2.2.1.2.3, and will discuss it again in ch. 2.2.1.6.2.

(2) Preference Hedonism (Parfit 1984: 493). Preference hedonism regards pleasant experience (and not merely "pleasure") as the most preferred experiences, so that, for instance, a suffering man may prefer thinking in torment than being confusedly euphoric (although euphoria is more pleasant). My comment is that the distinction between the desire of "thinking in torment" and the desire of being "confusedly euphoric" actually refers to the distinction between the light and particular sentiments and the deep and universal sentiments, respectively (ch. 1.1.3.2.2). From the moral point of view, the desire to think (even if in torment) is an *objectively better moral status* than the desire to be confusedly euphoric, because the former desire is deeper than the former, i.e., it possesses a higher "degree of universality"

(i.e., it expresses a *more evolved sensitiveness*). The choice in favor of the deeper sentiment (the desire of thinking, even if in torment) is prompted by a *moral feeing* (created by *emotional consciousness*—Fig. 1.1) (chs. 2.1.1.2; 2.1.4.1, *b*). Moreover, due to the close inter-relationship between the mind-components, the *moral feeling* that prompt the individual to prefer thinking (even if in torment) is supported by the *moral thought*, created by *rational* consciousness, through which consciousness becomes aware that thinking (even if in torment) is an objectively better moral status than being confusedly euphoric, because it expresses a much *more evolved intellect* (see chs. 2.1.1.1; 2.1.4.1, *a*).

(3) Desire-Fulfillment Theories. Parfit considers three versions of this theory.

(a) The unrestricted theory (Parfit 1984: 494). This theory maintains the implausible view that what is best for someone is what would best fulfill *all* of his desires throughout his life. The implausibility of this theory exempts us from criticizing it.

(b) The success theory (Parfit 1984: 494–96). This theory appeals to *all* of someone's desires about his own life, and not to the present preferences, introspectively discernible. Thus, according to the success theory, undesired facts are bad for a person even if he does not know them (example: the unknown failure of one's children) or even if the undesired facts occur after his death. I think that the unknown and undesired facts cannot be evaluated by the agent, and therefore they cannot be for the agent a matter of moral evaluation and choice; these facts could only be evaluated by other persons who know the agent's desires. In any case, moral relevance will depend on the kind of "objects" of the agent's desires, since the satisfaction of desires about one's life cannot have, *per se*, moral value (ch. 2.2.1.6.2). Thus, the agent's desires about his own life will be "good" if they prompt acts that contribute to *mind evolution*.

(c) The summative theory (Parfit 1984: 496–99). Both preference-hedonism and success theory are *summative*: if one could indicate with a positive number each desire that is fulfilled and with a negative number each desire that is not fulfilled, one could get the total net sum of desire fulfillment (Parfit 1984). Yet, it is well known that desire fulfillment (like pleasure) cannot be exactly measured and, therefore, summed. A better version of the summative theories is the *global theory* (Parfit 1984: 497), which appeals to global, rather than local and particular, desires and preferences, i.e., desires and preferences that are about one's global life or about a part of one's life considered as a whole. Parfit refers to the example of a drug addict who (contrary to what could be expected on the basis of summative theory) prefers to fulfill his desire of not being an addict (a desire referring to his life as a whole) to the sum of the many particular desire-fulfillments that he could get each morning, being an addict. Here a com-

ment similar to what I made above, under point "2", is in order: the pleasure given by drug assumption is particular and light whereas the pleasure of not being an addict is a deeper sentiment. Again, having deep sentiments is an *objectively better moral status* than having light sentiments, because the former expresses a *more evolved sensitiveness* (ch. 2.2.1.6.2). The choice in favor of the deeper sentiment (the desire of not being an addict) is prompted by *moral feeing* (created by *emotional consciousness*—Fig. 1.1). This *moral feeling* (leading to the preference not to be an addict) is supported by the *moral thought*, created by *rational consciousness*, through which the consciousness becomes aware that not being an addict is an *objectively better status* than being confusedly euphoric (chs. 2.1.1.1; 2.1.4.1).

(*d*) *Objective-list theory* (Parfit 1984: 499–500). This theory maintains that there are things that are good or bad whether or not one desires them; these are those things that are in harmony with reason or that we have good reason to desire. On this theory (which appeals to facts and their value), one wants not to be deceived because this is bad for him, whereas on success theory (which appeals to what a person prefers) the reverse is true, i.e., it is bad for someone to be deceived because he does not desire this. This theory affirms the existence of "objective" good without, however, defining it; according to my theory (ch. 2.2.1.1.1, *1*), a given event or fact is morally better than another if the former corresponds to, or causes, a more evolved status of the involved minds.

After having examined several conflicting theories, Parfit (1984: 501–2) concludes that, perhaps, it is possible to combine what is most plausible in them. Thus, instead of claiming that the good is what is wanted or that one wants what is good, it is preferable to claim that to have "knowledge", to be engaged in "rational activity", to experience "mutual love", and to be "aware of beauty" is both what is good for someone and what is wanted by him. Parfit's conclusion is rather vague and is focused on "knowledge" and "rational activity", as well as on "mutual love" and awareness of "beauty". It should be noted that Parfit does not provide a philosophical justification of his statements. Based on my theory, we can say that Parfit's focus is on the products of the *intellect* and *sensitiveness*, and that, curiously, Parfit seems to ignore the practical achievements in the private or public life, obtained through *actions* produced by the *power* (e.g., the achievements in the economic or political fields). However, if one is in search of what makes life a *morally-good* life, one should note the following: (*a*) each stage of intellect, sensitiveness, and power development is *objectively* more good than the lower development stages; (*b*) the morally-good agent's acts are those directed to *promote* the endless development or evolution of the intellect, the sensitiveness, and the power of the mind of the agent himself as well as of the minds of others.

2.2.1.3.3—Rawls' Constructivism: The Higher-Order Interests of Free and Equal Persons

(1) Rawls' Reflective Equilibrium. Rawls (1971: 18–19, 42–43) has searched for a compromise between *prima facie* general moral principles (as accepted by our moral consciousness) and the *prima facie* (or intuitive) acceptable particular moral judgments to find a "reflective equilibrium." Here my comment is focused on two points: *(a)* relying on vague defined "*intuitions*" means to renounce to what is the specific task of philosophy, i.e., attempting to find moral principles grounded on rational (and possibly objective, or even ontological) bases, unless we identify "intuitions" with *moral feelings*, as defined in my theory; *(b)* instead of searching for a compromise between contrasting general moral principles and particular judgments, the philosopher should search for a coherent set of principles allowing justified moral judgments. This is what I attempted to do by defining the objective *moral good*, consisting of *mind evolution*, and the consequent *moral norms*, directed to *promote mind evolution* (chs. 1.1.1.2.4; 2.1.4.1; 2.1.5.1; 2.2.1.1.1, *1*;) and by ordering the various "moral goods", the various "moral acts", and the various "moral norms" in three systems of classes and subclasses, each system including all the kinds of "moral goods" (ch. 2.1.4.2; Table 2.1), all the kinds of "moral acts" (ch. 2.2.1.7.2, *E*), and all the kinds of "moral norms" (ch. 4.1.2.3; Figs. 4.2 and 4.3), respectively.

(2) Constructing versus Discovering Principles. Rawls (1980) contrasts his Kantian *constructivism* with *rational intuitionism*. The latter assumes that first moral principles are self-evident, that the basic moral concepts are not analyzable in terms of non-moral concepts, and that agreement in judgment is founded on the recognition of self-evident truths about good reasons. These reasons would be fixed by a *moral order* that is known by rational intuition. Conversely, *constructivism* is centered on first principles of justice derived from the conception of the person as free and equal and moved by their *highest-order interests*, as are those of the parties in the "original position" (as illustrated by the procedure of construction in justice as fairness). In constructivism, first principles are defined as reasonable or unreasonable rather than as true or false (as they would be defined by rational intuitionist) (Rawls 1980). In justice as fairness, the principles of justice adopted by the parties in the original position are designed by them to achieve a public and workable agreement on matter of social justice; they are *constructed*, and not *discovered* (Rawls 1980).

I think that the problem with Rawls's view is that he does not explain what the *highest-order interests*, from which the first principles of justice are derived (or constructed), actually are. Rawls (1980) points out that the parties in the original position do not recognize any antecedently given principle of justice; they just select the principles most rational for them in their circumstances. He notes that this should not be regarded as an approximation to moral facts, because there are not moral facts to which the principles adopted could approximate, and the principles are always the result of construction (Rawls 1980). Therefore, if there are no given principles of justice or moral facts, the *highest-order interests* of the parties in the original position are the determinants of the parties' choices. But, what actually are the higher-order interests? Rawls adds that the first principles of justice depend upon the *general beliefs about human nature* and society that are allowed to the parties in the original position, and that may change. Yet, if this is true, it means that the chosen principles are, indeed, "discovered" (and not "constructed"), since they depend on what human nature actually is. Indeed, I think that no ethical theory is possible if it is not based on what humans are as ontological entities. Referring to my theory, this means that ethical principles should be based on the conception of humans as evolving conscious entities made of intellect, sensitiveness, and power. On these grounds, I think that the *highest-order interests* of the parties in the "original position" actually are those "interests" that express *moral feelings*, produced by *emotional consciousness* (chs. 2.1.1.2; 2.1.3.2; 2.1.4.1, *b*) and directed to promote those principles that will favor *mind evolution*. Likewise, the *general beliefs about human nature* reflect what I name *moral thoughts*, created by *rational consciousness*. Moral thoughts are well defined in my moral theory: they are those thoughts (focused on the mind itself) that tell us that we are becoming minds, capable of endless *evolution*, and that *mind evolution* is the objective *moral good* (chs. 1.1.1.2.4; 2.1.1.1; 2.1.4.1, *a*; 2.2.1.1.1, *1*).

(3) The Objectivity of Rawls' Principles. In Rawls's view, objectivity is to be understood by reference to a suitably constructed social point of view, and not as recognition of a prior and independent moral order (Rawls 1980). To the objection that the notions of reasonableness and objectivity cannot be the result of an agreement or choice, Rawls replies that we should distinguish the parties in the original position from the citizens. The parties' agreement singles out the facts to count as reason, subjected to all the conditions of the original position, which represent the "reasonable" and the "rational". These facts "count as reason not for the parties, since they are moved by their *highest-order interests*," but for the citizens, who are bound by first principles and by what their duties are, and must act in the light of reasons of justice (Rawls 1980). I note that this is a rather vague definition of what the "reasonable" and the "rational" is; indeed, Rawls does not provide what is the central point of any moral theory: a clear definition of what the "good" is. Actually, the "parties in the original condition," which can be

regarded as the equivalent of a constituent assembly, are called to define the general moral principles that should guide the entire community; these principles express the moral thoughts and feelings shared by the majority of a community and are routed in the nature of men conceived as evolving conscious entities made of intellect, sensitiveness, and power.

(4) Rawls's General Principles as Categorical Imperatives. Rawls (1971: 221–27) believes that his conception of *justice as fairness* may be given a Kantian interpretation, mainly by relating it to Kant's notion of *autonomy*. He notes that acting autonomously means to choose the most adequate expression of the agents' nature as "free" and "equal rational" beings; this is what happens when the choice is made from behind the "veil of ignorance" (Rawls 1971: 118–23). Acting heteronymously means to act on principles linked to a "particular" (personal or social) condition. The original position may be thought of as the point of view from which noumenal selves see the world (Rawls 1971: 225). The principles of justice apply to us whatever in particular our aims are; which means that these principles are "categorical imperatives" (Rawls 1971: 222–23). Moreover, "justice as fairness" includes the premises concerning the elementary facts about persons and their place in nature, i.e., takes into account that the parties know that they are subject to the conditions of human life (Rawls 1971). Thus, the choice made by the parties in the original position is like a *procedural interpretation* of Kant's conception of autonomy and categorical imperative (Rawls 1971: 226).

The above reasoning is based on the undemonstrated assumption that men are "free", "equal", and "rational". But, why should we accept this assumption? Rawls does not demonstrate it. If being rational entities means acting according to the universalization principle, then I question it (see below, point "5"). However, I underline that, according to my conception, human beings are minds (or spirits) made of an evolving intellect, sensitiveness, and power (and exerting both outward and inward activities); they possess *common properties*, derived from their ability to undergo *evolution*, and *have common rights*, linked to their common nature (those rights whose enjoyment allows mind evolution) as well as *individual rights*, linked to the *degree* and *specificity* of mind evolution, as it occurs in each individual (chs. 3.2.2.1.1; 3.2.2.1.2). Thus, both the rights independent of "particular positions", which I indicate as common or *universal rights*, and those dependent on "particular positions" (or particular properties of individuals), which I indicate as *individual rights*, should be recognized.

(5) The "Veil of Ignorance" and the Universalization Principle. Rawls maintains that the parties in the "original position" make choices from behind a "veil of ignorance" (Rawls 1971: 118–23), i.e., independently of their particular position but in accordance with the general principles in which they believe, i.e., principles referring to men conceived as "free and equal

rational beings" (Rawls 1971: 222). These choices are comparable to those made by rational beings that follow the *universalization principle* and, therefore, are subjected to the critique that I made elsewhere about this principle: it allows limited universalization, referred to sub-classes of men possessing particular properties (chs. 2.2.1.1.3, *A1*; 2.2.1.1.4). Fully universalization (extended to all the members of the class of men) is possible if reference is made to the *common properties* that define the class of men and that, therefore, are common to *all* men. To make this, it is required to refer to a conception about what a man actually is. According to my theory, these *common properties* derive from the fact that men are *evolving* conscious entities made of intellect, sensitiveness, and power.

However, I underline that the choices made from behind the veil of ignorance would lead to the definition of general or universal principles of justice (or moral values) and the corresponding universal rights that should be recognized to *all* men because of their *common properties*. Yet, there are also the particular, individual rights that should be recognized; they arise from the *individual properties* that define the identity of each individual, linked to the degree and specificity of mind evolution as it occurs in the various individuals. Indeed, as I note elsewhere (ch. 3.2.2.2.2, *A2a*), the equality in the enjoyment of universal rights (arising from the common properties) serves to reveal the diversities of individual properties, from which individual rights arise; in short, *equality serves to reveal diversities*.

Finally, Rawls (1971: 226) claims that the choice made from behind the "veil of ignorance" (in the original position) would be like a *procedural interpretation* of a Kantian choice as equal rational beings (i.e., a choice independent of particular, individual situations). Yet, to reach this end, it is not necessary to resort to the hypothetical "veil of ignorance," as a simpler procedure is available and consists of applying the following rule: *To make a "universal" choice, use a proposition whose subject is the term "All men"; to make a "particular" choice, use a proposition whose subject is the term "All 'x' men"* (where '*x*' indicates the particular condition or property to which the choice refers). This is because any attribute or right or duty that can be recognized to *all* men must necessarily refer to the properties common to all men (the property of being able to undergo *evolution*, according to my theory) and therefore expresses the agent's conception of human nature (again I underline that a conception of human nature is always required to make any reasoning about humans). Thus, we could say: "*All men* have the right to receive a good education" (because we know that humans are evolving entities and that education induces an evolution of their intellect and sensitiveness). Conversely, we could say: "All intelligent men have the right to be preferred as university professors." Of course, both the universal or "all-men" propositions and the particular or "all-*x*-men" propositions may express good or bad moral statements, depending on the moral conception and moral feeling of the agent.

(6) Rawls's Principles as Applying to the Basic Structure of Society. Rawls (1971: 222) points out that his veil-of-ignorance doctrine adds to the Kantian conception the feature that the principles chosen are to apply to the basic structure of society; moreover, he holds that the person's choice as a noumenal self is assumed to be a collective one, and that the unanimous agreement is expressive of the nature of even a single self and does not override a person's interests (Rawls 1971: 226). I think that Rawls' claim that the person's choice as a noumenal self can be assumed to be a "collective one," and that it is taken by "unanimous agreement" indicates that the choices made in the original position applies to *public morality* (i.e., the morality based on publicly-shared moral principles) (chs. 4.1.1.3.2, *B*; 4.1.2.1); these choices can be compared to the choices made by a constituent assembly, and rarely, perhaps never, are taken by an unanimous agreement, so that the "shared" moral principles are actually shared by a majority of the choosing people. This entails that some citizens may not agree about the shared moral principles, and a *conflict between private (or personal) and public moral principles* may arise. An example is the refusal of justifying the death penalty by many citizens in democratic countries where it is publicly justified; or the conscientious objector who refuses to participate in military operations, even when they are justified by the public or shared laws. In these instances, the dissenting citizen has certainly the right (indeed, the duty) to promote, by democratic means, his view, with the aim to obtain that the laws are improved (if the dissenting citizen is morally better than the other citizens); in this way, he favors the evolution of the community consciousness, as reflected in the shared norms (ch. 4.1.1.3.2, *B*).

[For other aspects of Rawls's thought, see ch. 3.2.6.1].

2.2.1.3.4—Other Theories

(A) Plurality of Values and Qualitative Contrasts.
Taylor (1982) underlines that there is a diversity of moral goods and a plurality of values; therefore, he criticizes both utilitarianism and formalism, which are based on the false belief that there is a single domain of what is moral and a single set of evaluation procedures for determining what we ought to do.

Taylor (1982: 129) notes that *utilitarianism* exerts an epistemological appeal, because it allows us to make rational choices, i.e., those choices that get the most favorable results in terms of human *happiness*, the latter conceived according to the universalization principle that the happiness of each agent counts for one and the happiness of no agent should count for more than one. Here I would like to note that happiness, although certainly a value pursued by men, is not a *moral* value.

On the other hand, Taylor (1982: 130) argues that *formalism* offers the advantage that we can ignore the problematic distinctions between different qualities of action or modes of life, and can rely primarily upon the universal applicability of maxims or the universal attribution of moral personality. However, Taylor notes that, historically, the principle of universalization has sometimes been understood as valid within a community, thus allowing discrimination and domination; anyway, he thinks that there are some moral ideals and goals that cannot be coordinated with universalism, such as less than universal solidarity or personal excellence, and that formalism ignores other languages of moral praise, condemnation, aspiration or aversion. I agree with Taylor about the inadequacy of the universalization principle (chs. 2.2.1.1.3, *A1*; 2.2.1.1.4). As to the ideals and goals that, according to Taylor, cannot be coordinated with universalism, I think that we should distinguish which ones of such ideals and goals belong to the sphere of morality and which ones belong to other spheres of mind activity; I will comment on this matter just below (after the list of Taylor's "qualitative contrasts").

Taylor (1982: 133, 135) argues that, central to our moral thinking, are the "qualitative contrasts" between morally higher or lower, noble or base, admirable or contemptible actions or feelings or modes of life; these contrasts may be summarized as follows:

(a) Personal integrity (expression of what one truly feels as important and worthwhile) against the temptation of *conforming* to established standards.

(b) Adherence to charity (according to the Christian model) against the temptation of *refusing charity*.

(c) Pursuing liberty against *renouncing liberty* because of the obstacle of ignorance or lack of courage.

(d) Following rationality against *irrational illusions*.

Recognizing the value of integrity, charity, liberty, and rationality entails the *obligation* to pursue them. This would be somewhat similar to Kant's categorical imperative.

My comment here is that integrity, charity, liberty, and rationality form a group of heterogeneous values, some of which are *moral* values while others are not. Thus, charity and liberty are certainly moral values, since the former consists of helping others (i.e., consists of promoting the evolution of the minds of needy people) and the latter is required to allow that everybody can do what he thinks useful to promote mind evolution. Concerning integrity, conceived as related to what one truly feels as important and worthwhile, all depends on what one feels as worthwhile: some people may think or feel as worthwhile something that actually is morally bad because it restrains mind evolution. With regard to rationality, which refers to the activity of the *intellect*, one should distinguish what is the *objective good* (being intelligent and rational is objectively better than being very little intelligent and rational) from the *morally-good acts* (those directed to promote the evolution of the intellect and the knowledge of one or more minds). It follows that a little-intelligent individual who behaves in a little rational way is not necessarily a morally-bad man, unless he has voluntarily neglected to cultivate his intellect, in which case he is morally responsible for the loss of the intellectual improvement that can be obtained by cultivating intellectual activity, but not for being born with little intelligence.

Taylor also considers other qualitative contrasts, besides the moral ones, such as: *(a)* appreciation for Mozart's music and insensitivity to it (the latter implying a non-moral condemnation) (Taylor 1982: 136–37); *(b)* admiration* (people who are beautiful or have charisma or are winners) and *contempt* (for people with opposite qualities) (Taylor 1982: 137–38); *(c)* contrast referring to *awe* (i.e., respect or veneration for those who pursue high goals) (Taylor 1982: 138). Moreover, there would be still other qualitative distinctions, such as, for instance, that of being "cool", being "macho", etc. These points should be commented separately. Concerning the respect for those who pursue high goals, it will all depend on what these "high" goals are. The ability to appreciate music is linked to *sensitiveness*, and can be evaluated like rational ability, as discussed above. With regard to *admiration*, we should distinguish admiration for beautiful people (which depends on the degree of development of the aesthetic taste, produced by *sensitiveness*) from the admiration for those who have charisma or are winners, whose meaning will depend on how people use their charisma or in what field and with which means they become winners.

Based on the above, Taylor (1982: 142) remarks that ethics is not a homogeneous domain, and the kinds of moral good that we recognize as moral are diverse; besides utility and happiness (utilitarianism) and the universal attribution of moral personality (formalism), there are many and diverse goals, which may even contrast among one another, so that we have to assess their relative validity or establish an order of priority. Taylor's position reflects a failure in distinguishing *moral goals* (those prescribed by the fundamental moral norm, i.e., the promotion of the evolution of the mind components: *intellect, sensitiveness,* and *power*) from the other human *personal goals* (linked to the satisfaction of human desires, produced by *sensitiveness*). All the various moral goals are linked to the existence of the three mind components and can be viewed as a single goal: promotion of the evolution of one or more of the mind components; moreover, the various "moral goals" or "moral goods" can be ordered into a system of classes and subclasses, all included in the most general class consisting of *mind evolution* (ch. 2.1.4.2; table 2.1).

According to Taylor (1982: 143–44), one of the reasons why some qualitative contrasts are neglected is that they are not easily accounted for on a naturalistic basis, i.e. cannot be explained by scientific analysis, as they are rather regarded as subject-related properties that express the way we feel, not the way things are. This, he thinks, is because motivated human actions are unsuitable to be analyzed as physical things are, and should be explicated by marking qualitative contrasts, as they are not morally neutral. Taylor's statement that qualitative contrasts concern "the way we feel, not the way things are" is questionable, since moral values (qualitative contrasts) are the product not only of our moral feelings but also of our moral thoughts and moral conception (ch. 2.1.4.1). Moreover, instead of speaking of qualitative contrasts one should speak of a continuous scale of values that goes from "non-care for others" to "extreme charity", from "renouncing liberty" to "extreme love for liberty", and from "full irrationality" to "extreme rationality"; this continuous scale of values reflects the various stages in the endless evolution of the mind.

(B) Conversation, Narratives, and Tradition.
MacIntyre (1981) criticizes: *(a)* the modern social tendency to the partition of human life into a variety of segments by dividing work from leisure, private from public life, the corporate from the personal, etc.; *(b)* the atomistic view of analytical philosophers, who consider complex actions and transactions in terms of simple components; and *(c)* the existentialist view, which separates the individual from his context and considers the life as a series of unconnected episodes, which leads to a liquidation of the self.

MacIntyre (1981: 205) maintains that the identity of the self resides in life conceived as a whole, in the unity of a narrative which links birth to life to death. To understand human actions and intentions, we should order them both causally and temporally with reference to the setting to which the agent belongs. The *narrative history* is the basic and essential genre for the characterization of human actions (p. 208). *Conversations* are the context in which speech-acts and purposes are made intelligible and, like any human transaction, are enacted narratives (MacIntyre 1981: 210–12). We all inherit from our family, city, and nation a variety of debts, inheritances, rightful expectations and obligations that constitute the given of one's life, his moral starting point (MacIntyre 1981: 220) (see also chs. 3.1.2.5.3, *3*; 3.2.11.1, *2*).

I agree with MacIntyre's view that personal identity is closely linked to that of others both in a spatial sense, as it is linked to the identity of the community, and in a temporal sense, as it is linked to the inheritance of the past and the expectations of the future. The point is that we should find, within this view, a *morality criterion* for distinguishing the good from the bad human acts.

MacIntyre (1981: 219) says that what is good for man depends on the success or failure of a narrated or to-be-narrated quest; the good life is the life spent in searching for the good life, and the virtues necessary for this searching are those which will enable to understand what the good life for man is. For MacIntyre (pp. 220–23), *traditions* should be conceived as live traditions, which continue a not-yet-completed narrative; virtues would enable one to pursue his own good and the good of the shared tradition of which he is the bearer. MacIntyre (1981: 223–25) adds that moral dilemmas often offer alternatives both of which may lead to the good; moreover, who faces a dilemma often cannot do everything that he ought to do because, according to him, "ought" (contrarily to the Kantian ought) does not always imply "can", so that the agent has to do what is better for him as an individual, parent of a child, citizen, etc. This, however, MacIntyre notes, would not mean that what is chosen (like the choice of a particular medical treatment for a particular patient) is not susceptible of objective truth or falsity. MacIntyre (1981: 190–91) proposes to pursue "internal goods" whose "achievement is a good for the whole community who participate in the practice." He seems to think that the good for man is that embedded in the tradition of one's community (family, friends, and society). However, he does not provide a criterion for distinguishing what is good, what is bad, and what is morally neutral in the tradition. He is right when he criticizes the atomistic view that considers human behavior in terms of single components, but he makes the opposite mistake to consider all aspects of human life as an undistinguished whole: the product of the tradition of a community and of the conversation among its members. I think that we should distinguish the products of the three mind components, identify the outward mind activity as distinct from the inward activity, and consider the fundamental characteristic of the mind: its ability to undergo *evolution*, which is the source of moral principles, values, and norms. In this way, we will be able to recognize that there is a unique set of moral values valid for all traditions (those linked to the promotion of mind evolution), and that the other beliefs, preferences, and practices may freely vary among different cultures and traditions, as they are linked to the *degree* and *specificity* of mind evolution which characterize any individual as well as any community (chs. 3.2.2.1.1; 3.2.2.1.2).

(C) Helping the Suffering Populations.

Singer (1971/72) draws our attention to the fact that in some parts of the world there are people in danger of dying from lack of food, shelter, and medical care, and that neither individuals nor governments of rich nations make the necessary effort to significantly help the suffering people, despite the development of communication, which makes both individuals and governments aware of the presence of suffering people in even distant parts of the world. To morally evaluate these facts, Singer refers to the following assumptions (that he thinks should be uncontroversial), which I list below together with a short comment:

(1) Suffering and death from lack of food, shelter, and medical care are bad.

I think this statement is really uncontroversial, since life and health are the basic conditions for the existence and development of the mind, i.e., for the objective human good as defined elsewhere (chs. 1.1.1.2.4; 2.1.4.1; 2.2.1.1.1, *1*).

(2) If we can prevent something bad without thereby sacrificing anything morally significant, we ought, morally, to do it.

(3) There should be no difference whether someone is the only person who can provide help or whether there are many who can help.

(4) Due to principles of impartiality, universalizability, and equality, we cannot take into account the proximity or distance of the people to be helped (this may entail a psychological difference but not a difference in moral obligation).

To shortly comment on the last three points, I underline that the claim (point "2") that one should help suffering people only if he can do this without sacrificing anything morally significant, should be evaluated by considering that, from the objective moral standpoint, there is no difference between the "good" of the agent and that of others, i.e., between the evolution of the agent's mind and that of the minds of others; this would entail that one should give until his condition equals that of the recipient. This heavy moral demand is in accord with what Singer (1971/72) calls the *strong version* of the *principle of preventing and relieving bad occurrences.* This heavy demand, however, is not actually required (see below).

Things will appear different if we consider Singer's assumptions expounded above, in points "*3*" and "*4*". Whether or not there are other men who can help does matter, because: *(a)* if they are willing to help, one should coordinate with such men the helping actions; *(b)* if they are not willing to help, one should attempt to convince them to participate in helping. Perhaps more important is to comment on the assumption that the distance of the suffering people does not matter, due to the universalizability principle (point "*4*"). Indeed, this principle leads to the moral demand that even distant people must be helped, but it does not say anything about the way in which the help should be realized. Here one should take into account the real situation in which the men who should help actually are: they are citizens of an organized State. Therefore, they act both as individuals and as citizens of a State, and this is also true for their moral behavior. In other words, one should distinguish: *(1) private or personal morality* from *(2) public or institutional morality.* I will discuss these two points separately.

(1) Private (or Personal) Morality. Personal morality refers to the moral responsibility that arises within the spheres of individual relationships and, according to the principle of the *spheres of decreasing moral responsibility* (ch. 2.1.5.2), actually decreases starting from family members to relatives, friends, colleagues and association fellow-members, acquaintances,

fellow-citizens, fellow-countrymen, and foreigners, i.e., moral responsibility decreases with the decrease in the degree of proximity of the moral agent and the needy people. Moreover, it is not morally required that one should give to the needy people until their condition equals the condition of the helper; the moral rule is that one should help others until they become capable of developing their mind by themselves, i.e., until they reach the enjoyment of the *evolution allowing condition* (ch. 2.1.5.3).

It should also be considered that help should not be limited only to economic help, directed to improve the *power* of the recipients, because, given that the moral goal consists of the evolution of the mind components, one should also help the needy people to develop their *intellect* and *sensitiveness*; although economic help favors the development of intellect and sensitiveness (due to the interrelation of the three mind components), specific help is also needed to assure that the needy people will receive adequate education in the scientific and human fields and be treated with understanding and sympathy. These considerations suggest that a more realistic moral demand is close to that entailed by what Singer (1971/72) calls the *moderate version* of the *principle of preventing and relieving bad occurrences*; yet, even in its moderate version, the principle would require that we give to a high extent. In this regard, I note that one should not expect to realize within a short time a world in which morality is developed to its maximum (the evolution of the human world is endless); indeed, the life of the mind is characterized by an endless evolution of its components, intellect, sensitiveness, and power, each of which, at any state of its evolution, is always incompletely developed. Thus, both the individual citizens and the governments should do their utmost to help the suffering populations and to progressively increase their helping effort, without being discouraged by the impossibility to reach, within a short period, a morally ideal condition.

(2) Public (or Institutional) Morality. Public morality is the other aspect to be considered. Singer (1971/72) argues against the claim that aiding suffering populations is the responsibility of governments and not of the private citizen. He thinks that if no one or very few give voluntarily help, the government may assume that its citizens do not care about helping the needy people and would not be willing to adopt those acts required to help needy populations. I would like to underline that each individual who is a member of a society ordered as a State, has the obligation of acting both as an individual and as a citizen. As individual, due to the development of the means of communication and information, he cannot ignore distant suffering people, as they become somewhat like his acquaintances; therefore, he is, to some extent, involved in helping these people (see above, under point "*1*"). The degree of involvement can only be *approximately* defined, since approximation marks all the spheres of human activity, including the moral sphere (ch. 1.1.3.2.1). At the same time, as a citizen, each individual has the

duty of promoting those political parties and programs that take into account the problem of helping the needy populations; the results that can be obtained in this way (through the intervention of governments) is much greater than the results of personal help.

On the other hand, governments have the moral duty of helping needy people belonging to the populations that they govern, by giving equal weight to comparable need of all involved people, according to the principle of impartiality, which here should be fully applied. Moreover, governments are in a favorable position for knowing the needs of distant populations (present in the international arena) and for providing the required help. They have, therefore, the duty to provide, through a concerted international intervention, for the basic needs of distant populations. Both in the domestic and in the international areas, the moral duty of governments should be that of ensuring that all people can enjoy the evolution-allowing condition, in order to implement the ground moral norm, which prescribes the promotion of mind evolution.

Singer (1971/72) points out that, due to the severity of famine and other disasters in some parts of the world, citizens of rich countries should be working full-time to relieve the suffering of the unfortunate populations. This may be regarded as too demanding a claim, since a moral code, to be followed, should not be too far beyond the capacity of the ordinary man, a view maintained also by Sidgwick (1874: 220–21) and by Urmson (1958: 214). Yet, Singer (1971/72) thinks that helping suffering and starving people is a duty and not a charity (or a supererogation), i.e., it is not something that would be good to do but neither wrong not to do (as it is the case for making other people happy). This, indeed, is in keeping with the statement by Aquinas (*Summa Theologica*, II–II, Q. 66, Art. 7) that whatever a man has in superabundance is owed, of natural right, to the poor for their sustenance. My comment on this point is that the burden of helping needy populations may be reduced to a tolerable degree if: *(a)* we distinguish between private (or personal) and public (or institutional) morality (see above); *(b)* we consider that, within the sphere of personal morality, the moral responsibility slightly decreases with the decrease in the proximity of the needy people to the moral agent, also because proximity makes helping easier, timelier and more effective (ch. 2.1.5.2.1); *(c)* all rich countries contribute in the helping program; and *(d)* the helpers should make the maximum effort to help needy populations to progressively approach the evolution allowing condition, and (as already stated above, under point "*1*") should persist in this action without being discouraged by the impossibility to reach, within a short period, a morally ideal state.

Singer (1971/72) also maintains that refusing to help needy populations is not justified by the fact that, without effective population-growth control, any help would only have transient effects, since this consideration should prompt us to work to relieve famine and to control population growth. I agree on this point and add that the control of population growth is a goal that lies within the sphere of *public or institutional morality*, as it may be reached only by acts adopted by the involved governments (such as pressure by the governments of the giving countries and concrete acts by the government of the recipient country, including educational and intervention programs).

(D) Moral Luck.

Nagel (1979) underlines that, although it is intuitively thought that one is responsible only for what is under his control, actually we often make moral judgments without excluding external factors, beyond our control, that influence to a large extent our actions. He mentions the moral difference between rescuing someone from a burning building and dropping him from the twelfth-story window while trying to rescue him. In such cases, we can speak of *moral luck*. Nagel (1979: 35) notes that when moral luck is considered, it seems that the area of genuine agency, and therefore of legitimate moral judgment, shrinks to an extension-less point. He distinguishes the following four types of moral luck.

(1) Luck in the Way Things Turn Out (Nagel 1979: 28). Examples: a truck driver who blames himself for having accidentally run over a child; or the claimed difference between an attempted murder and a successful murder. Nagel (1979: 29) makes a special mention of the *decisions under uncertainty*; when someone launches a violent revolution against an authoritarian regime, the outcome is uncertain and yet it is the outcome that may change our moral judgment from positive to negative (even if this, although it may have a legal use, seems irrational to me).

(2) Luck in One's Circumstances (Nagel 1979: 33). One may behave in a good or bad way according to the circumstances he encounters: think of a citizen of Nazi Germany compared to that of a democratic State.

(3) Luck in Antecedent Circumstances (Nagel 1979: 35). Even the stripped-down acts of the will itself are the product of antecedent circumstances outside the control of the will.

(4) Constitutive Luck (Nagel 1979: 32). According to Kant, the qualities of temperament and personality (inclinations, desires, etc.) are not morally relevant, as they can be controlled by an effort of the will. Yet, at least to some extent, these qualities are largely a matter of constitutive bad fortune.

Let us discuss separately first the points "*1*", "*2*" and "*3*" and then point "*4*". As to points "*1*", "*2*", and "*3*", Nagel's position can be questioned by referring to two important considerations. *First*, any action is an event that results from the interaction "human body"-to-"rest-of-the-world"; therefore, a role of the "external" factors concerning the rest of the world is unavoidable. These factors, however, reduce but do not abolish the area of "genuine agency"; moreover, it is always possible to evaluate in an *approximate* manner (as it is always unavoidable when dealing with the complexity of human events) the role played by these factors. *Second,* what is more important is that the "area of genuine agency," i.e., the area governed by our *free will,* actually does not exist since what we call *free will* actually is a *non-free will,* resulting from the physical and chemical phenomena occurring in the brain; yet, moral responsibility is compatible with a non-free will, as the moral responsibility for a fact consists of having the awareness of being the causal agent (most often a contributing causal agent) of that fact (ch. 2.4.2).

Concerning the fourth point ("constitutive luck"), constitutional inclinations and desires do play a role in determining moral acts, inasmuch as, according to my theory (chs. 2.1.3.2; 2.1.3.3), the *moral decision* (determinations of the will) and the consequent moral act are determined by the prevalence of *moral feelings* over *personal desires* or inclinations, or vice versa. It follows that a man who constitutionally possesses strong and bad inclinations must possess even stronger good moral feelings to operate in a morally-good way.

Nagel (1979: 37) concludes by underlining that the problem is that the idea of a free agent is incompatible with actions being events and people being things; perhaps it is that we cannot simply take an external evaluative view of ourselves, of what we most essentially are and what we do; our acts remain ours, and we remain ourselves despite the reason that point to external influences. I think that, perhaps, the problem raised by Nagel coincides with that of understanding what the so-called "free will" actually is, i.e., of establishing whether free will is actually free (ch. 2.4).

(E) Trans-Cultural Judgment: The Values Necessary for a Society to Exist.

Rachels (1986: 18) notes that different societies have different moral codes (cultural relativism); accordingly, there is no objective standard to judge such codes, so that no *trans-cultural judgment* is justified (Rachels 1986: 22). However, Rachels maintains that the disagreement between cultures is less dramatic than is often thought, as it is due not to a difference about values, but to a difference about beliefs. It is the *belief* that after death the souls of humans inhabit the bodies of cows (so that a cow might be inhabited by our grandma!) that leads some populations to regard the eating of cows as wrong, in contrast to our habit; yet the difference does not concern values, as we agree that we should not eat one's grandma (Rachels 1986: 23–24). That beliefs can affect moral behavior is better explained by my moral theory, inasmuch as Rachels' beliefs should be interpreted as corresponding to what I call *moral thoughts* (the rational component of morality), which affect *moral feelings,* which in turn affect *moral acts* (ch. 2.1.4.1).

Moreover, according to Rachels (1986: 25–26), some values, such as the protection of infants, prohibition of murder, and truth telling, would be common to all cultures, because they are necessary for a society to exist, whereas other values and practices are merely cultural products that are neither right nor wrong. Thus, Rachels distinguishes values common to all cultures and values that are the product of specific cultures; he, however, justifies this distinction by defining common values as those necessary for a society to exist. This is a vague definition that may lead to justify any kind of value (repression by police may be regarded by some people as necessary for the survival of society). I think that a better basis for such a distinction is the one that I propose in chs. 3.2.2.1.1 and 3.2.2.1.2, based on the distinction between the universal or essential properties of the class of men (their ability to undergo *evolution*—or involution—of the intellect, sensitiveness, and power), which give rise to *universal values and rights,* and the particular properties that vary among individuals or groups and are linked to the individual (or group) *degree* and *specificity* of the evolution of the intellect, sensitiveness, and power, which give rise to *individual values and rights.*

   (F) Moral Saints.

Wolf (1982) argues that the perfectly moral person, the moral saint, being heavily committed in pursuing moral ideals and values, may neglect other genuine values of human life such as "intellectual inquiry" and "artistic creation"; thus, moral values are not the highest ones as a guide to human actions. If we refer to my moral conception, we note that Wolf's statement is not tenable, because the moral end pursued by the moral person consists of promoting *mind evolution,* which means promoting the evolution of *intellect* (which is linked to the "intellectual inquiry"), and/or *sensitivity* (which may lead to aesthetic enjoyment and to "artistic creation") and/or *power* (which leads to welfare and political achievements). Thus, the moral person (moral saint) cannot neglect "other genuine values of human life," as thought by Wolf; it is, however, possible that the moral person devotes his life in promoting the evolution of the minds of others, while neglecting to some extent his own mind (example: a man who spends all his money on allowing his friend, but not himself, to attend university education), in which instance one could say that the moral person has neglected "other genuine values" as far as his life is concerned, but that he has pursued these values with regard to the lives of others; and, from the moral point of view, there is no difference between the agent's life and the lives of others, with some limitations, as discussed in chapter 2.1.5.2.

   (G) Other.

Some thinkers have only studied and described the moral views and beliefs of human societies through time (Westermarck 1906-8; 1932). I object that studying and describing some moral views or beliefs does not justify, nor does it condemn, them. Nielsen (1990) has defended the independence of ethics from religion, which is a fully justified position.

   Warnock (1971: 76–86) argues that the function of morality is to counteract the bad effects of various limitations, such as limitation of resources, of rationality, and, especially, of sympathy for others (which is overwhelmed by egoism). Similar theses were maintained by Plato (~380 B.C.) in the dialogue *Protagoras* (in a mythical form) as well as by Hobbes (1651) who proposed the social contract as a solution. Similarly, Hume (1739/40: 484–500) conceived justice not as the result of a natural disposition of humans but as a useful device to make possible cooperation among essentially selfish people who face a limitation of resources. I think that limitation of resources is not the central point. Even if men had an unlimited amount of natural resources, competition would equally arise with regard to the goods created by human activity (inventions); competition about who is the inventor, who will benefit more of an invention, competition about who is the most intelligent or sensible or potent man, etc. Actually, the origin of society and of the competition and cooperation occurring in it is the result of the structure and functioning of the mind (ch. 3.1.1.1.1).

Warnock (1971: 76–86) maintains that morality does not consist of following some rules but of a set of moral virtues; it would be based on knowledge, organization, coercion, and good dispositions, the latter including both non-moral virtues (industriousness, courage, and self-control) directed to counteract various kinds of human weakness as well as moral virtues (non-maleficence, fairness, beneficence, and non-deception). I think that the picture drawn by Warnock is rather confused and could be clarified by referring to my theory. Indeed, "organization" and "coercion" belong to the sphere of public institutions and can be directed either to favor or to restrain the pursuing of moral ends (development of citizen's minds). On the other hand, "knowledge" and "good disposition" belong to the sphere of private or personal morality; moreover, whereas "courage" is an individual property unrelated to morality (the courageous man, like the cowardly one, may be morally good or bad), "industriousness" and "self-control" (which, together with courage, would counteract human weakness) refer to the moral duties that the agent has toward himself (i.e., they refer to the development of his own mind) (ch. 2.1.5.2.2). Finally, "non-maleficence", "fairness", "beneficence", and "non-deception" refer to the duty that the agent has toward other minds.

2.2.1.4—Refusing Morality

2.2.1.4.1—Nietzsche's Thought

As I will try to demonstrate, the position held by Nietzsche can be interpreted as a refusal to admit moral principles and values. Below, I will briefly comment on some of Nietzsche's main thoughts, by referring to my moral theory.

(1) Freedom and Responsibility. Nietzsche (1878: 34–35) claims that we make man responsible first for the effects of his action, then for his actions, then for his motives, then for his nature; then we discover that his nature cannot be responsible either, inasmuch as it is itself an inevitable consequence of past and present things. Thus, the history of moral feelings can be regarded as the history of an error called *responsibility*, which in turn rests on an error called *freedom of the will*. Here Nietzsche says something right when he criticizes the concept of free will (ch. 2.4.1); he is, however, wrong when he denies the existence of responsibility and calls it an "error", since moral responsibility is compatible with the lack of internal freedom (ch. 2.4.2).

(2) The Good and the Bad. Nietzsche (1878: 36) notes that to prefer a low good (e.g., sensual pleasure) to one esteemed higher (e.g., health) is regarded as immoral, likewise to prefer comfort to freedom; yet, the hierarchy of the good is not fixed and changes with time and cultures (preferring revenge to justice was moral according to earlier cultures). Moreover, according to him (Nietzsche 1878: 36–37), good and evil have a double prehistory. First, men who had the power to requite goodness with goodness and evil with evil and who practiced requital were called *good* and were regarded as noble individuals or masters; men who were powerless and could not requite were taken for *bad* and were regarded as the base or slaves (in Homer, both the Trojans and the Greeks are *good*). Then, he continues, in the soul of oppressed, powerless men every other man was regarded as hostile, exploitative, cruel; he became the evil. When this concept of good and evil predominates, the downfall of individuals, their clans and races, is near at hand. Present morality would have grown up on the ground of the ruling clans and castes.

Nietzsche's statements about the *good* and the *bad* cannot be accepted and are derived from an arbitrary interpretation of history. Actually, one should note that through history, going from one culture to the subsequent one, i.e., from the time of Greeks to that of Romans, to Middle-Ages, to Modern era, to the Contemporary age, morality (which is produced by the consciousness) has evolved, like other mind products such as knowledge (produced by the intellect); and it may be true that requital of evil with evil has been regarded, for a long time, as not bad. Human consciousness (or *inward* mind activity) has evolved through time, producing new and more evolved moral thoughts and moral feelings, thus overwhelming the conception of the ancient populations, dominated by the *outward* mind activity (selfishness). Those who live today have duties linked to the moral conception of our time; they cannot refer to old times to endorse a conception of the good and the evil that actually would represent a regress of the human consciousness to the early stages of its development. Moreover, it is not true that at the time of the Greeks or of the Romans the potent man who practiced requital was "good" and the powerless man who could not requite was "bad"; nor is it true that, with time, the powerless men regarded every other man as evil, because history shows that powerless men have found "good" and "bad" men both among the potent as well as among powerless people. Indeed, Nietzsche's attempt to find an explanation for the "good" and the "bad" reveals Nietzsche's inability to conceive moral principles and values.

(3) Slaves and Masters, Men and Over-men. According to Nietzsche (1878: 49–50), between *slaves* and *masters*, or between a weak and a powerful part, rights exist to the extent that the possession of the slave is useful to the master (or the preservation of the weak part is useful to the powerful one). Thus, even the weaker part has some rights, although they are modest (hence, the statement by Spinoza—1670: 200—"the rights of an individual extend to the utmost limits of his power"). More than that of the masters, it is the concept of the *over-men*, as opposed to the *common man*, that is central in the conception of Nietzsche (1883-85: 12–13). In this regard, he says that man is something that should be overcome. Like the ape for man, so man shall be for the over-man just a laughingstock or a painful embarrassment. The over-man shall be the meaning of the earth! So, one should not believe those who speak of otherworldly hopes! They are poison mixers. Nietzsche asks himself: what is the greatest experience you can have? He replies: it is the hour when even your happiness, your reason, your virtue, justice, and pity arouse your disgust.

Here Nietzsche is totally, arbitrarily and unjustifiably wrong. His over-man, so insufficiently defined (he would be the meaning of the heart!), actually is a despicable man who: *(a)* is against reason, thinking, inferring, reckoning, coordinating cause and effect (Nietzsche 1887: 84); against benevolence, pity, consideration, moderation, modesty, indulgence, industriousness, public spirit, and general welfare (Nietzsche 1886: 86) as well as against justice, (Nietzsche 1878: 49); and *(b)* is in favor of wilderness, adventure, prowling, hostility, war, cruelty, and joy in persecuting, in attacking, and in destroying (Nietzsche 1887: 84, 85) as well as in favor of the prevalence of the powerful over the powerless (Nietzsche 1878: 36–37).

This confirms that Nietzsche is insensible to any kind of moral principle and value, except the principle of free exercise of unjustified power, that is, of *violence*. While I discuss in chapter 3.1.2.4 the negative value of violence, here I underline that Nietzsche does not explain what is the value of the over-man, what is his role and what are his ends; he lacks a basic philosophical conception. Perhaps more important is the fact that he does not provide a rule for identifying the over-man. Actually, in a community, there are individuals with different degrees of mind development (ch. 3.2.2.1.2); however, it is only if *all* individuals have equally enjoyed an evolution-allowing, involution-avoiding condition, i.e., if all citizens have concretely enjoyed the same fundamental human rights and observed the same fundamental duties toward others, that it is possible to identify those individuals who have reached a higher development of one or more of their mind components (intellect, sensitiveness, or power) because of a genuinely higher natural endowment (chs. 3.2.2.1.2; 3.2.2.2.2, A2a). Yet, Nietzsche's over-man looks like he who, while believing that he is an over-man, refuses to submit himself to the only verification process that can ascertain his "higher status": conducting his life by enjoying the same fundamental rights and observing the same duties toward others as *all* other citizens. Indeed, we could say that equality in rights protects not only the "slaves" from the "masters" but also the "masters" from the "slaves", inasmuch as it allows that *all* individuals can develop their potential natural endowment, thus revealing their true value (in the case of masters, revealing a "higher value"), while avoiding the accusation that their status is the result of unjustified privileges.

Other Nietzsche's thoughts, concerned with the issues of *political philosophy*, such as justice (1878), society (1887), and democracy and general welfare (1886), will be discussed in chapter 3.2.4.3.

2.2.1.4.2—Moral Skepticism

(A) Values: Are They Subjective?

Mackie's moral view (1977: 15) can be defined as *moral skepticism*, according to which moral values (like the aesthetic values) are not objective, as they are not part of the fabric of the world. Mackie (1977: 17) notes that his view should be distinguished from moral subjectivism (which is a positive doctrine that regards moral judgment as expressing feelings or attitudes of the speaker), since moral skepticism is a negative, ontological doctrine that says that those entities called objective values do not exist.

I note that Mackie's claim that moral values "are not part of the fabric of the world" is arbitrary because, before making this statement, one should first analyze the structure of the world (read: the structure of the mind) and then conclude that no things were found that could be named moral values. Yet, Mackie does not make this analysis in his book, in which he expounds his moral skepticism. Indeed, referring to my ontological conception of the mind (Fig. 1.1), we can note the following. *(a)* The *inward activity of intellect* (or *rational consciousness*), through internal observation or introspection, gives us the information (*moral thoughts*) that the mind, and therefore each individual mind, is a *becoming entity* capable of undergoing *evolution* toward ever more complex stages, each of which appears to be (as a self-evident observational datum) more evolved, of more *value*, or more "*good*", than the preceding one (chs. 2.1.4.1; 2.2.1.1.1, *1*). *(b)* The *inward activity of sensitiveness* (or *emotional consciousness*) generates *moral feelings*, which prompt *moral acts* (produced by the *practical consciousness*) capable of favoring or restraining mind evolution; therefore, we can distinguish good or bad moral thoughts, feelings, and acts according to whether they are directed to favor or restrain mind evolution. Thus, in the "fabric of the world" there are two kinds of objective entities: *(a)* the *evolved stages of the mind* (say: the state of a cultivated, intelligent, sensitive, well-off man), which are more "*good*" then the less evolved stages (say: the state of an illiterate, coarse, extremely poor man); *(b)* *moral events* (thoughts, feelings, and acts), which, if they are directed to favor mind evolution, are *good*, i.e., they possess moral *value*. These are ontologically objective entities (stages of the mind and moral events), which allow us to contrast Mackie's thesis that in the moral reasoning there is something that cannot be objectively validated, as well as his *error theory*, according to which the claim that moral reasoning points to something objectively prescriptive is false (Mackie 1977: 35).

Mackie (1977: 83–102) also questions the universalizability principle by pointing out that it may be merely the result of the general agreement about a value (inter-subjective value) and yet it may not be objective. I agree that the universalizability principle is questionable; my critique to this principle is expounded in chapter 2.2.1.1.3, *A1*.

Mackie (1977: 27–29) criticizes the categorical imperatives, which, he thinks, can be conceived as hypothetical imperatives in which the conditional clause (which refers to desires, wills, purpose or ends by the speaker or by the society, either a real or an ideal society—see Kant's kingdom of ends) has been omitted. The conditional clause may also be the will of God; indeed, Anscombe (1958) underlined that moral values are survivals outside the thought that makes them intelligible, namely the belief in a divine law. My critical comment on the categorical imperative is given in chapter 2.2.1.1.3, *A2*. Here I add that the "conditional clause" is actually the way in which the human mind is made, i.e., the fact that the human mind is capable of undergoing *evolution*, which is an *objective* fact.

Mackie (1977: 36–38) underlines that the radical differences between the moral judgments of different societies make it difficult to consider these different judgments as based on objective truths; even if these differences may disappear if we restrict our consideration to the general basic values, he thinks that the latter are mainly based on *intuition* or *moral sense* and not on reason. Mackie is right in admitting that the differences between the various societies disappear when only the basic values are considered; he, however, does not define what these basic values are and regards them as a product of *intuition* or *moral sense* without even defining what the latter two terms actually indicate. Indeed, the basic moral values are those linked to the fundamental property of all men, i.e., *mind evolution*, and they are the source of all the *universal human rights* and *duties* (ch. 3.2.2.1.1). Concerning the possible meaning of the terms "intuition" and "moral sense", used by

Mackie (see above), I would suggest that the first could be regarded as referring to *moral thoughts* and *moral conception*, and the latter to *moral feelings*, which, because of the internal coherence of the mind, are most often in accord with moral thoughts (ch. 2.1.4.1, *b*).

Mackie (1977: 38) argues that if objective moral values exist they should be entities different from anything else existing in the universe, and should possess "non-natural" qualities, according to the term used by Moore (1903: 62–69); also, to be aware of them, we should possess some special faculty, different from that which we use to know everything else, i.e., what has been named the "faculty of moral intuition". Here it seems that Mackie, actually, says that moral values are not "physical objects" with "natural qualities", which can be known through physical observation; since moral values are not physical objects, he notes that, if they exist, they should have "non-natural qualities". In this regard, I recall that, besides physical objects, there are "non-physical objects", such as thoughts, projects, sentiment, etc., that, although possessing properties different from physical objects, are "part of the fabric of the world," i.e., are part of reality. Actually, moral values arise from the fundamental property of the mind consisting of its *evolutional capacity*; this is a special quality that refers to the mind as a whole, and can be understood by *moral thoughts* produced by *rational consciousness*. This allows us to reject Hume's claim (1739/40: 413–17), recalled by Mackie, that reason cannot be an influencing motive of the will, since *moral thoughts* (produced by the inward activity of intellect) are the basis for *moral projects* which, in turn, guide *moral acts* (ch. 2.1.4.1) (also because moral thoughts, being *triplets*, entail moral feelings). Based on my theory, we can also explain what Mackie regarded as a difficult problem, i.e., what is the link between a natural fact (a cruel action) and the moral fact (that a cruel action is wrong); or, in other words, what signifies, *in the world*, that an action is wrong *because* it is a piece of deliberate cruelty. Mackie thinks that to understand this we should postulate a faculty that enables us to see the features of cruelty and wrongness, and the mysterious link between them. We could reply to Mackie that the violent death of a healthy person is a *morally-bad* event, because it consists of an extreme and irreversible *involution* of a mind (i.e., the conversion of an individual into inert matter), and that the moral act of the murderer is wrong because it causes this extreme mind involution; thus, there is no "mysterious link" between the bad event and its wrongness nor do we need some special "faculty" to understand this.

Mackie (1977: 43) points out that the claimed objectivity of the good derives from the mistake of considering the desires (often internalization of social pressures) as depending upon goodness, instead of understanding that goodness depends on desires. The latter statement would indicate that Mackie considers happiness as the human good, which would make him a utilitarian. In any instance, desires are objectively existing entities, which exist in individual minds, and are, therefore, part of the fabric of the world. Yet, desires and happiness are not directly linked to morality, as I discuss in chapter 2.2.1.6.2. When Mackie says that goodness depends on desire, he fails to distinguish "desires", which are produced by the outward activity of sensitiveness (emotional selfishness), from *moral feelings*, produced by the inward activity of sensitiveness (emotional consciousness), which, due to the internal coherence of the mind, are in keeping with *moral thoughts*, produced by the inward activity of intellect (rational consciousness).

(B) About the Meaning of "Good".
Moore (1903: 62–69) maintained that the term "good" in ethical theory denotes something simple and indefinable, a non-natural quality, whose meaning is subjected to the "open question" argument (whichever the meaning we attribute to "good", we can always ask ourselves whether it is really "good").

Geach (1956), in discussing the general meaning of "good" (i.e., the meaning in both moral and non-moral contexts), points out that this term is an *attributive adjective*, to be distinguished from *predicative adjectives*. Mackie (1977: 52) notes that attributive adjectives are operators on predicates. According to him, in the sentence "x is a big flea," "big" is an *attributive* adjective because this sentence is not equivalent to "x is big and x is a flea"; on the other hand, in the sentence "x is a red book," "red" is a predicative adjective because this sentence is equivalent to "x is red and x is a book."

I think that *attributive adjectives* are those adjectives that entail a comparison (or a relation) between similar but not identical individual objects that are members of one of the *heterogeneous classes of the macro-world (or supra-molecular world)* (ch. 1.1.3.2.1, *1*). Example: "x is a big flea" means that x is a member of the class of fleas and that, compared with the other members of such a class, x is big (or that x is bigger than many other xs). On the other hand, the *predicative adjectives* are those adjectives that refer to a property of the objects (or particles) that are identical to one another and that are members of one of the *homogeneous classes of the molecular-atomic-subatomic world* (ch. 1.1.3.2.1, *1*). In the latter instance, since the homogeneous classes are made of identical particles, the property indicated by the adjective is identical for all the members of a class and therefore no comparison is possible. Example: "x is a red substance" means that x is a substance made of particles (molecules) which have (or which generate) red color. The sentence "x is a red book" may be misleading, because in this instance "red" is predicative although the book is an individual object that is a member of the heterogeneous class of books. This is because the sentence should be more correctly written as follows: "x is a book whose cover is made of a red material"; so written, the sentence shows that "red" actually refers to identical particles of the homogeneous classes of the molecular-atomic-subatomic world, whose members are the molecules of the substance that gives the red color to the book cover.

In the attempt to explain the meaning of attributive adjectives, Hare (1952: 100; 1967) notes that they may refer to "functional words," i.e., to words that refer to objects that are known to be used to do something. A carving knife is known to serve to cut meat into slices, and therefore a good knife is one that cuts well; in this sense, "good" would mean "efficient". Thus, good means having the properties that are commendable in the kind of object in question (commendable would derive from commend, which means "to mention as worthy of . . . being pronounced to be good"—Hare 1967: 77). May I note that "efficient" indicates that an object serves well for the scope of the agent, so that a murderer could define "good" a big knife suitable for killing people; this way of defining the term "good" is, therefore, unrelated to the moral good. As observed by Mackie (1977: 53), Hare's definition entails circularity and could be defined as an egocentric commendation; moreover, "good" may be used leaving indefinite whose interest the requirements of the good thing satisfy (perhaps those of typical people).

According to Mackie (1977: 57), "good" may not always be attributive (attached to a noun), as it may be used with reference to unspecified things or events ("that is a good thing, or a good event"). He notes that, for those who believe in objective moral values, "good" is such as to satisfy the intrinsic requirements of a thing (Mackie 1977: 59). This perhaps is close to the concept of "good from the point of view of the universe" (Sidgwick 1874: 382, 420), or to the concept of "dignity" as conceived in Kant's ethics (Kant 1785: 42), according to which the requirements are intrinsic to what has dignity (the good will). As I stated elsewhere (ch. 2.2.1.1.1), a good natural "event" is one that favors mind development (raining after a long period of dry weather), and a good "thing" is a stage of mind evolution that is higher compared to a lower one; on the other hand, the man-caused events (*moral acts*) are good or bad depending on whether they favor or restrain mind evolution.

(C) Defining the Object of Morality.

Mackie (1977: 120) notes that the moral thought of Protagoras, Hume (1739/40), Warnock (1971), and perhaps that of Hobbes (1651) actually consists of the explanation of already existing and conventionally accepted moral ideas. Here Mackie is right; yet, I object that conventionally accepted moral ideas are not "truly moral" unless they have some objective support that justify their moral and, therefore, obligatory character. Those who maintain that moral laws are required because they assure some utility to society, does not explain why utility should be pursued and why the rules that assure utility should have an obligatory force. The truth is that, without a fundamental moral norm (in my view, the norm that prescribes the pursuing of mind evolution) rooted in an ontological conception, no ethical theory is possible.

The position of Mackie (1977: 106) is that no objective moral truths can be postulated: "Morality is not to be discovered but to be made: we have to decide what moral views to adopt, what moral stands to take." He thinks that, considering that a man's conscience may tell him to do the vilest things (as noted by Anscombe—1958), the *content* of morality consists of the conscience of men that is formed by taking into individual minds those principles "which have been useful" (reinforced by evolution, education, and politics) (Mackie 1977: 120–24). I object that, if there are principles "which have been useful," we should ask ourselves *why* and *for whom* these principles are useful; if they are useful because they satisfy some personal desires, they have not the obligatory character of a moral norm and could be refused by any individual; if they are useful because they bring about something "good" (mind evolution, in my theory), then they must possess some qualities that make them "moral" principles; yet, nothing is said by Mackie about these qualities. Mackie (1977: 113) hypothesizes that a preferential survival of individuals or groups with stronger sentiment of sympathy for others may cause an evolutionary development of such sentiment. This, however, does not explain why sympathy for others should entail preferential survival; indeed, the opposite is much more probable. In any case, sentiments and desires cannot be the base of obligatory moral norms.

Mackie (1977: 121–23) also points out that, in recent decades, deep changes in human condition have occurred (in part linked to the technological development, widespread information, and worldwide mutual dependence), which have caused changes in moral thought; thus, some obligations, such as patriotism, may no longer be tenable. Thus, morality is to be made and also to be changed to cope with the changed human conditions. I object that the changes in moral obligations through time or across space are only apparent. It should be considered that moral acts are directed to promote mind evolution and, therefore, they must take into account the status (degree of evolution) of the minds to which they are directed. The socio-political organization is the way through which the previously particular human actions get some degree of universalization (and the universalized actions, in turn, favor the promotion of the intellect and sensitiveness of the community); the State-nation was one important step in the progressive universalization of human actions, and it was a morally-good act to defend it from outside invaders or oppressors (patriotism). With the evolution of the process of universalization of human actions, many adjacent nations became first allied to one another, and then they attempted to join with one another to form a unique State (this is the process presently in progress in the European Union). Consequently, the patriotism linked to the single State-nation today not only would be untenable but it would be morally bad, because it would restrain the evolution toward ever-larger union of nations (with the final scope to realize the fully universalization of human actions, i.e., the Universal Republic). Indeed, today the patriotism survives in some still underdeveloped countries, where the evolution toward the universalization of human actions is still at a low stage, the stage of the construction or consolidation of the State-nation. Thus, although moral obligations may change their immediate scope in relation to the degree of evolution of the minds of the agents and of their community, they are always directed to favor the progressive evolution of minds, according to the *ground moral norm*, which, as shown by these considerations, has the merit of being *flexible*, i.e., an *open, non-dogmatic norm* (ch. 2.1.5.1), because it takes into account the degree of evolution of the involved minds.

(D) The "Practical Morality" of a Moral Skeptic.
Mackie (1977: 169–200), from his morally skeptic position, attempts to sketch a practical system of morality. He considers as a good life the life that satisfies our interests and the interests of those who participate in the good life; it should be a way of life that we welcome and approve. Although different people have different views of a good life, Mackie (1977: 170–71) thinks that "For any individual a good life will be made up largely of the affective pursuit of activities that he finds worthwhile," either for himself or for other people about whom he cares. This view, based on egoism and self-referential altruism, entails the existence of cooperation but also of competition and conflict (in contrast with the ideal of universal brotherly love, maintained by Christian and humanist traditions but regarded by Mackie as actually impracticable). Mackie (1977: 200) defines his approach as a *rule-right-duty-disposition utilitarianism* (or egoism), based on some conception of the flourishing of human life.

We could summarize Mackie's position by saying that a good life is made up of the *affective* pursuit of activities that one finds *worthwhile*, and that the worthwhile things are those that satisfy our *interests* or the interests of those about whom we care. It is surprising that a moral skeptic proposes a system of "practical morality"; I think that the moral skeptic should simply state that there are not moral values, and nothing else. Considering Mackie's theory, we are entitled to ask: why should one consider himself bound to respect the affective pursuing by others or what they find worthwhile? It remains to be defined to which kind of value the term "worthwhile" refers, i.e., whether it refers to *moral* values or to personal preference and desires, which have no relation with morality. Once again, I have to stress that no moral norm can be binding unless it prescribes the pursuing of what is *objectively* good for men, i.e., the promotion of the evolution of their mind or spirit (chs. 1.1.1.2.4; 2.1.4.1; 2.2.1.1.1, *1*). However, Mackie considers several points related to morality, which I summarize and comment on below.

(1) Rights. Mackie's rejection of objective values carries with it the de-

nial that there are self-subsistent rights; thus, rights arise from the need of each individual of a secured area in which he is free to make choices that contribute to the pursuit of his own happiness (which is a large and central part of the good life). Moreover, rights would not be determined *a priori*, but as a result of a conflict and compromise between rival ideals (Mackie 1977: 174). It seems to me that these are unjustified statements, since they do not *justify* the claim that one has the *right* to pursue his happiness nor do they explain why happiness is a moral "good"; moreover, a compromise between rival ideals (which have not previously been shown to be *moral* ideals) may lead to an agreement that cannot have any *morally* binding character.

(2) *Ownership*. Systems allowing private property have been regarded as necessary to exert some virtues, such as generosity. This point is primarily concerned with public morality and, therefore, will be treated in chapter 3.2.3.4, 2. Here I would like to mention that, under any political system, each citizen owns a certain amount, even if a small amount, of resources (say: his salary), which enables him to manifest and exert those virtues, such as generosity, which, as pointed out since the time of Aristotle (~330 B.C.) (see: Aristotle, *Politics*), are somewhat linked to property. Only the magnitude of the generous acts may be linked to property or, better, to the wealth of the moral agent, not generosity *per se*. Indeed, it should be noted that the generosity of the poor man has a higher moral value than that of the rich man.

(3) *Liberty*. Liberty could be defended not on the basis of a supposedly self-evident principle of non-interference (by the public power or by others) but on the basis of principles of legitimate interference, which are those that harmonize with the general conditions for a good life; moreover, adjudication between the various rivals and possibly conflicting claims of freedom would be required (Mackie 1977: 181–82). My definition of liberty is given in chapter 2.1.4.2, *1*. Here I add that, since Mackie does not give a solid definition of what a morally-good life is, it remains indeterminate what the principles of liberty, that harmonize with it, are; this is also true for the adjudication between rival claims of freedom and the criterion for such an adjudication.

(4) *Truth Telling*. According to Mackie (1977: 182–183), people live as members of various social circles, large and small, with different kinds and degrees of cooperation, competition, and conflict; thus, truth telling is appropriate in the cases of cooperation but not in the cases of competition or conflict. On the other hand, lies are parasitic upon truth telling, since one is believed only if it is known that he generally tells the truth. I think that in a society governed by rules, laws, and norms, interpersonal relationships should consist only of cooperation and competition but not of conflict, because conflict means a fight outside the ordinary rules. In a society so con-

ceived, there is no place for lies (except lies told for pity or courtesy), since lies mark the change of honest competition into fraudulent competition. Thus, Mackie's statement (1977: 183) that "a prudent man will not squander his limited stock of convincing lies, but uses it sparingly to the best effect" should be changed into "a prudent cheat will not squander his limited stock of convincing lies." Indeed, a lie causes a false belief in the interlocutor, thus lowering his degree of knowledge and affecting the evolution of his intellect (the same is true for keeping promises) (see chs. 2.2.1.4.2, *D4*; 2.2.1.7.2, *C1*; 3.1.1.2, *2c*).

Mackie (1977: 183) is right when he states that agreements are essential for allowing cooperation and regards keeping agreements as necessary. Yet, I point out that the duty of keeping agreements is not linked to the fact that they are voluntary and in general deliberate, as held by Mackie. Rather, it results from the nature of the agreement, which, like a promise, is a rule issued (and shared) by the mini-community made of the participants in the agreement or in the promise (ch. 3.1.2.3.3), and should be observed for the same reasons that other rules or laws should be, i.e., because failing to keep promises produces the objectively bad effect of destroying the mini-community, thus inducing an involution of the degree of universalization of the agents' actions (which change from "social" actions into "individual" actions). Moreover, failing to keep a promise causes some damage (mind involution) to the involved individuals, who expected that the promise was kept (see chs. 2.2.1.4.2, *D4*; 2.2.1.7.2, *C1*; 3.1.1.2, *2c*).

(5) Virtues. Although Mackie (1977: 186–87) underlines that virtues are difficult to define, he suggests three sources to define them: *(a)* the way of behaving that is conventionally admired at a particular place and time; *(b)* one's own conception of good; and *(c)* acting in accord with reason. In my opinion, neither the admiration by others nor one's own conception of good can be morally relevant (except for the agent who has that conception of good); behavior in accord with reason relies on the *universalization principle*, which I have criticized elsewhere (chs. 2.2.1.1.3, *A1*; 2.2.1.1.4). Actually, "virtues" indicate several qualities or properties of the mind, some of which, such as courage, are not related to morality (neither a courageous man nor a cowardly one is necessarily morally good or bad), while others, such as fairness, clearly are.

(6) Evading Moral Rules. Mackie (1977: 190–92) poses the question: why should one not at the same time both profit from the moral system and evade it, especially when one can do so with impunity and even without detection? Mackie does not think that there is an easy answer; he maintains that "nearly all of us do have moral feelings and do tend to think in characteristically moral ways" and that "these help to determine our real interests and well-being." From this, it would ensue that, if someone has little or no moral tendencies, it may be prudent for him to act immorally (Mackie 1977:

192). However, the disposition that is advantageous to have would be the one that can be seen as virtue, i.e., the one that harmonizes with knowledge, in the light of some conception of good, and with some respect for the way of life of society (Mackie 1977: 192). Although this is a rather vague statement, Mackie seems to maintain that we follow moral rules because we have moral feelings; the latter, however, are conceived as subjective and arbitrary, whereas I think that they are deep moral feelings of all men, are in keeping with moral thoughts, and prompt us to do those acts that promote mind evolution (see also below, under point "7"). It follows that the man with little or no good moral feeling, who acts immorally, is objectively morally bad, even if he may think that he is "prudent".

(7) The Right to Life. According to Mackie (1977: 195), the right to life (and the correlated duty not to kill) is fundamental but not absolute, as shown by the cases of wars or revolutions; deliberate killing (including the death penalty) cannot be accepted, because it is "a special outrage against the humane feelings which are a central part of morality." Both these statements are untenable.

First, the right to life and the corresponding duty not to kill is fundamental and absolute for the *private* morality, and is based on the objective fact that killing means an induction of extreme and irreversible mind *involution* (see also the next paragraph). On the other hand, wars, revolutions, and "coups d'État" belong to the sphere of *public* ethics, which is treated in chapter 3 (they are not related to murdering and can never be used to deny that the right to life is an absolute one). They are always morally bad; most often they entail the existence of a responsible and guilty part, the one corresponding to the offending State, or to the tyrant, or to the promoters of a "coup d'État" against a democratic government. In complex cases, where it may be difficult to distinguish the offending part from the offended one, it is the conviction of each part that establishes its moral position. Concerning euthanasia and abortion, I agree with Mackie (1977: 196–99) that these are controversial moral questions; I would add that these are hard cases in which the complexity common to all human events reaches its top, and that, therefore, can only be evaluated with approximation (ch. 2.2.1.5).

Second, saying that killing cannot be accepted because it is "against the humane feelings" is too weak a justification. Indeed, based on my theory, killing represents the extreme *involution* of the mind (an individual is converted into inert matter), which is the extreme, *objective evil*; moreover, the fact that killing is against humane feeling acquires moral relevance if we refer to *moral feelings* as I conceive them, i.e., as the product of the *emotional consciousness* (Fig. 1.1), directed to stir-up *moral acts* that promote mind evolution (which is the *objective human good*), in accord with moral thoughts (chs. 1.1.1.2.4; 2.1.4.1; 2.2.1.1.1, *1*). *Moral feelings* so conceived are distinct from *personal sentiments* or desires (created by the *emotional selfishness*), which prompt actions directed to satisfy them (ch. 2.1.3.2).

Concerning the risk for life connected to activities useful for the flourishing of human life (bridge building, road travel), Mackie (1977: 196) says that it can be tolerated. Indeed, it is not fully tolerated, as shown by the fact that those responsible for accidents are punished. Instead, I recall that any human activity, indeed life itself, is linked to a certain risk for life; as human society develops, global risk progressively diminishes (the duration of life increases), although the risk may greatly decrease in some fields (infectious diseases) and may increase in others (road travel). Regressing toward less-developed stages of human life, besides being hardly possible, would be associated with an *increased* global risk for life. However, in most instances, with very few exceptions, any single death or injury is the result of the carelessness of someone who is responsible for it.

(8) Morality Toward Non-Participants. Mackie (1977: 193) underlines that morality (as he conceives it) is concerned with "the well-being of active, intelligent, participants in a partly competitive life, and . . . [has been introduced] as necessary limits on competition for the benefit of all the competitors"; this would entail the exclusion of duties toward non participants (children, the unborn, the aged, the sick, the insane, etc.). It would only be a gratuitous extension of morality that covers them. These morality extensions would be due to the natural dispositions in morality which manifest themselves as disgust toward cruelty and sympathy with pain and suffering (including the pain and suffering of animals). Here Mackie's position is unacceptable with regard to his conception of both morality and society: society is not made by the "active, intelligent participants . . . for the benefit of all the competitors" (Mackie 1977: 193), but rather it is made by *all* participants, since it is the form under which human actions and moral acts become *universal* (i.e., extended to *all* citizens) or, at least, reach the best approach to universality (ch. 3.1.1.1.1). Moreover, the scope of universalized human actions and moral acts is primarily to promote mind evolution of all citizens (moral acts) and only secondarily to satisfy the legitimate desires and preferences of parties, groups, associations, etc. (actions). It follows that the "non-participants", who are the weaker part of society (children, the sick, the poor, etc.), are not only an integral part of society, but are also those who should receive more attention and help (e.g., education to children, medical care to the sick, enough money to the poor), in order to assure those conditions that allow the evolution of their mind. Thus, helping the "non-participants" (i.e., the weak people) is a duty, and not "gratuitous extensions of morality" due to the human "disgust at cruelty and sympathy with pain and suffering" (Mackie 1977: 194); moreover, were the help to needy people based on sentiments such as disgust and sympathy, it would have no *moral* character and, therefore, would not bear any obligation, and could be disregarded by those who do not feel such sentiments.

2.2.1.5—Hard Moral Choices and Moral Dilemmas

2.2.1.5.1—General Considerations

Moral dilemmas are a much-debated subject [see in: Gowans (ed.) 1987; Greenspan 1995; Mason (ed.) 1996]. A true moral dilemma arises when there are two conflicting norms (or two conflicting obligations deriving from a norm—the so-called symmetrical cases), of which neither overrides the other (Sinnott-Armstrong 1988). Some thinkers believe that moral dilemmas entail inconsistency in the moral system in which they arise because, according to them, a set of rules would be inconsistent if there are circumstances (or possible worlds) in which not all the rules are satisfiable (Marcus 1980); this would also compromise the role of norms in guiding practical actions. The inconsistency, it is held, may be logic and/or deontological (Lemmon, 1962; Williams 1965; Van Fraassen 1973; McConnell 1978; Marcus 1980; Donagan 1984).

The claim that so-called moral dilemmas indicate inconsistency of the moral system is based on the false assumption that events of the human world can be known and evaluated with exactness. Indeed, as I point out elsewhere (ch. 1.1.3.2.1, *1*), in contrast to what happens in the realm of chemistry and physics (i.e., in the molecular-atomic-subatomic world), which is made of *homogeneous* classes whose members are *identical* particles (molecules, atoms, electrons, etc.) and of *regular* events, the human world is much more complex, as it is made of *heterogeneous* classes each of which includes: *(a)* complex "objects" that are *similar but not identical* to one another, and *(b) variable* events. It follows that, while in the field of chemistry and physics we can reach *certain* knowledge and previsions, in the sphere of the human world both knowledge and previsions are characterized by *incompleteness*, *approximation*, and allow only a *statistical-probabilistic approach*; moreover, there are difficult situations in which not even an approximate knowledge is possible (indeed, difficult situations also occur in the field of physics, even if rarely—see the so-called "deterministic chaos"). The same is true of moral judgments: they refer to "objects" and "events" that are complex and variable, even within a class, and therefore can only be judged from the moral standpoint with *approximation*; in some very difficult situations, not even an approximate moral judgment can be made: these are the situations in which the so-called moral dilemmas arise. This, however, does not make the moral system inconsistent, because full consistency is not possible, considering the way in which the human world is made and the ability of the human mind.

Some thinkers believe that in moral dilemma situations, whatever the choice, the agent will experience remorse and guilt and, therefore, he subjectively faces a real moral dilemma (Williams 1965; Marcus 1980). Some deny that subjective emotions (moral residue) can serve to prove the existence of moral dilemmas (McConnell 1978; 1996). Still others maintain that remorse and guilt are justified only if the agent feels to have made a wrong choice, or that the agent may experience guilt when he is causally, even if not morally, involved in a morally-bad situation (Zimmerman 1996). I agree with the last statement, because moral responsibility consists of the awareness of being the causal (or con-causal) agent of an event; this position is linked to the conception of human will as being not internally free (chs. 2.4.1; 2.4.2).

Several kinds of moral dilemmas have been considered: *epistemic dilemmas* (when the agent does not know which of the opposing duties has a priority), *ontological dilemmas* (when the opposing requirements actually have no priority), *self-imposed dilemmas* (the conflicting situation is caused by the agent himself), *dilemmas imposed by the world* (the conflicting situation is not caused by the agent himself), *obligation dilemmas* (when there is an obligation to two opposing actions), *prohibition dilemmas* (when there is a prohibition of two opposing actions), *single-agent dilemmas* (when a single agent faces a moral dilemma), *multi-personal dilemmas*, or impersonal moral conflicts (when, for two or more agents, it is impossible that all of them do what each of them ought to do) (McConnell 1978; 1988; 1996; Marcus 1980; Donagan 1984; Smith 1986; Vallentyne 1989).

2.2.1.5.2—Abortion: A Typical Hard Moral Case

Thomson (1971/72) examines the difficult question of whether abortion is morally permissible. She does not contest the claim that the fetus is a person and that, as such, he has the right to live; she argues, however, that having the right to life does not guarantee the right to use another person's body. Her example is the following: suppose that one awakes and finds that a sick violinist has been attached to his kidneys and that if the violinist is detached before the completion of a nine-year period he will die. Thomson thinks that if one unplugs himself from the violinist one is not unjust to him, because no one has given the violinist the right to use the kidneys of others; one has not the right not to be killed but rather the right not to be killed unjustly.

I think that in discussing this difficult problem, we should clearly define the terms "right" and "duty" with reference to their moral and legal meaning. Moreover, we should distinguish: *(1)* the complexity of human facts, and *(2)* the varying degree of morality among individuals.

(1) The Complexity of Human Facts. Due to the great complexity of

human facts and the underlying *continuum* that unites the apparently distinct facts [see my critique to the *fragmented view* of the world (ch. 1.1.3.2.1, *3d*)], which also applies to the distinction between actions and their effects, moral judgments can only be made with *approximation or imprecision*. For practical reasons, i.e., in order to make possible shared evaluations and judgments, the legal system attempts to transform approximation into an *artificial exactness* by arbitrarily fixing clear-cut distinctions between facts and between the apparently diverse stages of their continuous evolution. This happens, for instance, when the law establishes a fixed age at which a citizen is regarded as an adult, although the transition toward adulthood is a *continuous* process that occurs at different ages and takes a different time in different persons. Although the law makes provisions for reducing the approximation (or increasing the precision) in the evaluation of human facts (referring to the above example, the law may recognize particular cases of delayed achievement of adulthood), approximation still remains.

Returning to the problem of abortion, the central point is at which time (in the *continuous* evolution which goes from the zygote to the embryo, the fetus, and the newborn) the new organism should be regarded as a *person*. The truth is that there is no such an evolutionary stage, occurring at a fixed time, at which the embryo (first 2 months of pregnancy) or the fetus (2 to 9 months of pregnancy) changes from a biological matter into a person. Rather, the formation of a new individual is a continuous process in which we can arbitrarily fix some steps: *(a)* the spermatozoon and the oocyte (each of which contains half of the encoded instructions for the formation of the new individual), *(b)* their fusion to form the zygote (which contains encoded the complete set of instructions for the development of the new individual), *(c)* the embryonic phase of development (first 2 months) that ends with the differentiation of most tissues and organs, and *(d)* the subsequent development of the fetus that ends with the birth. There are no sudden changes, occurring at a given instant; some events that apparently take place at a sharply defined time-point, such as the union of the two gametes to form the zygotes (fertilization), actually occur as continuous processes that only if time is arbitrarily measured by the "human meter" can be regarded as occurring in a short time interval. Thus, all the attempts to establish an exact time-point (or even an approximate time) at which the embryo or the fetus becomes a person are vane; such are the proposals of those who think that the embryo is a person from the time of fertilization or from the time when the first brain cells differentiate or from the time when most organs and tissues are differentiated (end of the 2nd month), etc. On these grounds, in order to make it possible to take *publicly-shared decisions* (i.e., legal decisions), some legal systems, e.g., the Italian one, "arbitrarily" fix at the 90th day of pregnancy the limit within which abortion is allowed for reasons other than severe threats to the life of the mother or severe diseases of the fetus.

(2) The Varying Degree of Morality Among Individuals. From the ground moral norm, we know that everyone has the moral duty to promote the evolution of his mind, which includes as basic the moral duty to preserve his life. If one has the moral duty to preserve his life, he has also the moral right to enjoy those conditions that allow preserving his life; correspondingly, the others have the moral duty to concretely recognize his right. If we consider the embryo or the fetus as a person (as the Catholic doctrine holds), these considerations would also apply to the right of the embryo (<2 months of pregnancy) or of the fetus (>2 months of pregnancy) to his life. On this basis, abortion should be forbidden as morally bad. According to this view, referring to the above example, we should say that one has the moral duty to remain connected with the violinist who needs our kidneys for his life (see above), and that the violinist has the moral right to remain connected. In evaluating this hypothetical case, one should also consider that remaining attached to the violinist, while has the morally-good effect of allowing the violinist to live, also entails a morally-bad consequence consisting of some restraint in the mind evolution of the person who remains attached to the violinist. Yet we should note that allowing the violinist to remain connected to one's kidney certainly would imply a very high degree of morality, which would be possessed by very few people in the world. Therefore, a moral norm that would prescribe a full respect for life (which entails avoiding abortion—and to remain attached to the violinist, in the above example) would be endorsed by a minority of individuals. While each individual is fully entitled to follow this restrictive moral norm in his *private moral life*, the laws enacted by most legal systems on this matter (but the same is true for the laws concerning other issues) take into account the various degrees of morality occurring among individuals, and prescribe a less stringent norm allowing abortion, at least in the first stage of pregnancy or when certain conditions are met; this in order to reach a *publicly-shared decision* (law) endorsed by the majority of citizens. Thus, one may follow his moral thought (*moral principle*) and moral feeling (*moral value*) according to which he has the *moral duty* to avoid abortion (or to remain attached to the violinist, in the above example) without having the corresponding *legal obligation*.

The above reasoning is based on the fact that very few people reach a very high level of morality. This is similar to what happens in other spheres of mind activity, since very few people reach a very high level of knowledge or of sensitivity or of power (very few people reach the level of Galileo or Einstein in the field of knowledge—which is a product of *intellect*—or of Dante or Beethoven in the field of art—which is a product of *sensitiveness*). On these grounds, one could say that the difference between the two couples of facts "life of violinist/nine year sacrifice" and "death of violinist/no sacrifice" is not recognized as relevant by most legal systems and, therefore, no legal obligation is established in favor of one or the other situation. The difference becomes significant in the case, hypothesized by Thomson (1971/72), that the violinist needs to use your kidneys for only one hour; even in this situation, Thomson maintains that the violinist would have no *right* to remain attached to your kidneys; rather, you ought to allow him to use your kidneys for one hour, otherwise you are self-centered, callous, indecent in fact, but not unjust. Again, I would say that "self-centered, callous, indecent" should be interpreted as "morally bad", and that "not unjust" should be interpreted as "not legally unjust" or as "not having broken any law." [I recall that the difference between "moral" and "legal" responsibility refers to the *moral gap* between private or personal morality and publicly-shared morality; this *moral gap* has an important role in the promotion of the evolution of consciousness of a community brought about by the individuals with a more evolved consciousness (ch. 4.1.1.3.2, *B*).]

(3) The Rights of the Fetus as a Person. If one assumes that the fetus is a person, the question arises whether killing the fetus violates its right to life. This question was posed by Thomson (1971/72); she thinks that abortion should be justified in cases of pregnancy due to rape (because the mother has not given the unborn a right to use her body) but should not be justified when a woman voluntarily indulges in intercourses and is aware of the possibility of a pregnancy (in this case, the unborn would have the right to use the mother's body). I object that in the case of rape, it is true that the mother has not given the unborn a right to use her body, yet it is also true that it was not the unborn who has abused of the mother's body but the author of the rape. Actually, the unborn finds himself in a body that he did not choose; why should the unborn pay for a guilt of the author of the rape? Indeed, this is one of the hard moral cases for which no clear-cut evaluation can be made. Perhaps a possible solution may be found by considering, with a rather arbitrary criterion, the embryo (less than 2 months of pregnancy) as an entity whose evolution has not yet reached the stage of fetus (more than 2 months of pregnancy), at which it can be regarded as a person.

Intermediate between the pregnancy due to rape and the desired pregnancy is the case of parents who have a child despite having taken all reasonable preventive measures. Thomson (1971/72) thinks that these parents have the right to decide to stop pregnancy if avoiding abortion will cause them large sacrifices; they may decide to avoid abortion and to behave as Good Samaritans, but this is not their duty. I think that Thomson's statement is rather arbitrary, as it is not justified on a philosophical basis.

Thomson (1971/72) distinguishes three kinds of conduct: *(a)* the *Good Samaritan* conduct (making large sacrifices to help others, like allowing the violinist to remain connected for a long time), *(b)* the *Minimally Decent Samaritan* conduct (making mild sacrifices to help others, like allowing the violinist to remain connected for one hour), and *(c) less than Minimally Decent Samaritan* conduct (refusing to help others). I note that this is a moral (and not legal) evaluation of conduct; Thomson recalls that in the U.S. there is no law that compels one to be even a Minimally Decent Samaritan, although in Europe such a law exists.

To further clarify her point, Thomson (1971/72) refers to the story of Kitty Genovese who was murdered while 38 people watched or listened but did nothing to help her; a Good Samaritan is a person who perhaps would have taken the risk of directly intervening to help her; a Minimally Decent Samaritan would have perhaps called the police. She says that those who are against abortion even in the cases of rape pretend that women act as Good Samaritans but do not extend this claim to other fields. May I note that the example might not be fully appropriate; the 38 people who watched or listened while Kitty Genovese was killed, even if they did not intervene, certainly judged the killers as guilty (murderers), which entails that we should judge those who kill a fetus (the women who decide to terminate a pregnancy) as guilty. Moreover, murder consists of someone who destroys the life of a person, whereas sexual rape consists of someone who offends a person while giving rise to a new life; the new life is not responsible for the offense, as it is not the cause of the offense but rather the result.

Thomson (1971/72) underlines that the above discussion about abortion is based on the assumption that the embryo/fetus is a human being from the moment of conception; if this assumption is not true, then the above arguments do not apply to early abortion. I think that it is perhaps impossible to establish the exact time when the life of a *person* begins, since (as already stated) the formation of a human being is a continuous evolutional process; for this reason, decisions about abortion are typical examples of hard moral decisions for which no clear-cut evaluation is possible.

Feinberg (1986) is another thinker who has discussed the problem of abortion. He examines the conflict between the claim to life of the fetus and that of the woman to abortion; according to him, the claim of the woman may be regarded as a right to choose, like the right to liberty and, as such, the right to an abortion may be limited by the right of others (the fetus).

Feinberg (1986) thinks that the claim of women can be based on the following rights:

(a) Right to bodily autonomy, which is limited by the fact that the fetus is an independent moral subject.

(b) Right to property, limited by the fact that the fetus cannot be regarded as being a property of the mother (or of the father).

(c) Right to self-defense, which can be invoked only in the case of a woman subjected to rape.

I think that these rights are too light when compared to a human life; they cannot overcome the *duty* to promote mind evolution and, even more, to *avoid mind involution* (abortion, entailing the death of the fetus, is an extreme and irreversible mind *involution*), because mind evolution is the moral good. Again, only if one, rather arbitrarily, considers the embryo (< 2 months of pregnancy) as an entity whose evolution has not yet reached the stage at which it can be regarded as a person, can abortion be justified.

As noted by English (1975: 242), the prevailing morals, laws, and customs, allow that one may cause an injury roughly proportional to the injury to be avoided. Feinberg points out that this is justified by the fact that an aggressor is the part that is guilty, whereas, in the case of abortion, the fetus is not guilty and, indeed, it is not even an aggressor. According to Feinberg, one may be justified in killing even an innocent aggressor only if this is needed to save one's own life or to avoid a serious injury; he refers to the example by Thomson (1976) of a baby used as an innocent shield by an aggressor, a situation that would justify the assailed to kill the baby to save his own life. Yet, Feinberg (1986) thinks that the example is not appropriate, since the fetus is not an innocent shield of an aggressor; the fetus may at most be conceived as a non-aggressive, non-culpable threat.

Warren (1973) thinks that the right to life of a person does not impose a corresponding duty to others to do whatever is necessary to keep him alive. I contest this statement, since to each right of a person there must be a corresponding duty of others to concretely recognize that right; otherwise, what would a right mean? This entails that one should at least do what is possible (even if not whatever is necessary) in order to recognize that right; and avoiding abortion is certainly something possible and tolerable. The point is that Warren's statement fails to distinguish *legal rights* (to which it seems to refer) from *moral rights*.

Moreover, Feinberg (1986) notes that in the case of voluntary intercourse, the mother has some responsibility in becoming pregnant, which makes the condition of the fetus different from that of the violinist, in the above example by Thomson. Feinberg describes seven conditions entailing increasing responsibility of a woman for her pregnancy: *(1)* total non-voluntariness (rape), *(2)* contraceptive failure (fault of the manufacturers), *(3)* no one's fault (normal risk in contraceptive use), *(4)* negligence in the use of contraceptives, *(5)* recklessness, *(6)* indifference toward possible pregnancy, and *(7)* completely voluntary pregnancy. He thinks that a woman would be non-responsible for her pregnancy (and therefore she has the right to an abortion) in cases *1, 2,* and *3* whereas she would be responsible for her pregnancy (and therefore would have no right to abortion) in cases *4, 5, 6,* and *7.*

My position on this matter is that evaluating the mother's right to abortion against the right of the fetus to life is a very difficult task, because there are contrasting claims to be taken into account; it is one of the hard moral cases in which only *approximate* evaluations can be made. On the grounds of the above reasoning, I think that the conclusions reached by Feinberg are acceptable if we refer to abortion before the first 2 months of pregnancy, but cannot be accepted in later stages of gestation, when the fetus should be considered as a person.

2.2.1.5.3—Other Examples of Hard Moral Cases

(A) Hard Moral Cases in Private Life.
Williams (1973: 97–99) criticizes utilitarianism by referring to two examples: that of *George* who has the possibility to get a bad job (working in a laboratory for chemical and biological warfare), of which he is in need of to help his wife and his children; and that of *Jim* who, being in a south American town, meets captain Pedro who is going to kill some Indian protestors and who promises that if Jim accepts to kill one Indian the other Indians will be let off. Williams notes that, according to the utilitarian view, George should accept the job and Jim should kill the Indian.

If we evaluate these two examples according to my theory, we should conclude that *George* should not accept the job, because by accepting it, he contributes (even if to a small extent, because the effective use of the weapons will depend on the decisions and actions of many others, which can only be *approximately* known or foreseen) to the potential deaths that can be caused by the use of the chemical and biological weapons; and death is the extreme and irreversible form of mind *involution* (transformation of one or more men into inert matter). However, George could accept the bad work only if he is in extreme need of it, as, for instance, in the case of needing money to buy food for his family or medicines for his sick son. Indeed, the case of George (as that of Jim) belongs to the *hard moral situations*, which may only be *approximately* evaluated and that allow more than one justified solution (ch. 2.2.1.5.1). Concerning the case of *Jim*, I think that all will depend on whether captain Pedro is firm in his decision or not. If captain Pedro is firm in his decision, then Jim should kill the Indian; if captain Pedro's decision is not firmly taken, Jim should not kill the Indian because captain Pedro may change his decision, and this change may be favored by a firm refusal by Jim to kill the Indian. However, because the will of captain Pedro can only be known with approximation, the situation can only be approximately evaluated, so that both the actions open to Jim may be performed with morally-good intentions (see also ch. 3.3 on Difficult Moral Choices in Public Life).

However, Williams (1973: 100–101) underlines that there are other effects of George's and Jim's decision that should be considered and that are difficult to evaluate, including the *effect on others* who might know their decision, or the *effects on future opportunities* in their life, or the *psycho-*

logical effects on the agents themselves (i.e., the agents' feeling bad for their decision). The latter point, from the utilitarian point of view, should be clarified. Indeed, Williams notes that the agent feels bad after his choice because he thinks he has done the wrong thing; yet, Williams adds, this point raises some problems from the utilitarian standpoint, because this bad feeling should not arise considering that the choice was a good one for the utilitarian and because the bad feelings should not count, since nothing is advanced by having them. The same would be true for the bad feeling of someone who has to decide to "remove" a minority from a community to satisfy the desires or interest of the majority. I think, however, that the agent's bad feeling should count from the utilitarian standpoint, because it should be regarded as affecting the "utility", conceived as pleasure or happiness. Another effect that, according to Williams (1973: 106–7), should be considered is the *precedent effect*, i.e., the psychologically effective principle that one morally can do what has been done by someone else, especially if the latter is a public agent. Moreover, Williams (1973: 95–99, 108) recalls that utilitarianism (consequentialism) admits the *negative responsibility*, charging the agent not only for what he has done but also for what he has not prevented. Yet, referring to the example of Jim, I think that killing the Indians is not a direct result of Jim's refusal to kill one of them, but is indeed the result of Pedro's decision to kill all the members of the Indian group (the utilitarian is unable to distinguish between one's projects and actions and someone else's projects and actions).

I think that Williams's reasoning shows the great difficulty in evaluating human actions and moral acts and their effects; this is true both when one attempts to evaluate the effects on "utility" or the effects on mind evolution. This is because, in contrast to what happens in the molecular-atomic-subatomic world, the events occurring in the supra-molecular world, including human moral acts, are very complex, different from case to case, and concern continuously changing situations. Therefore, they can only be known *approximately*. Indeed, referring to the above examples, who can exactly evaluate George's need for money, and who can exactly know the scope for which the weapons are made, for defense or for offense? Who exactly knows the true will of captain Pedro? Likewise, the effects can only be *approximately* foreseen: who knows with certainty the future use of the weapons? Who exactly knows what Pedro will actually do? For these reasons, *hard moral situations* allow more than one justified solution.

(B) Hard Moral Cases in Public Life.

Hard moral cases in public life most often occur in relation to the political competition and the administration of the executive power or to the war; they will be treated in chapter 3.3.2.

2.2.1.6—Judgment of Moral Acts

2.2.1.6.1—Good versus Bad Moral Acts

Considering that *moral acts* are directed to produce mind changes (changes in the mind of the agent himself or in other minds), they can be judged, by the *morality criterion*, as *good or bad according to whether they are directed to promote or to restrain mind evolution,* i.e., the evolution or development of one or more mind-components (intellect, sensitiveness, or power) of one or more minds (Table 1.1).

When judging the moral acts by the morality criterion, two aspects should be taken into account.

(1) The Magnitude of the Effects. In addition to the kind of effect of a moral act (mind evolution or involution), the *magnitude* of the effect should also be considered (giving 1 dollar to a poor man is not the same as giving him 10,000 dollars). This means that moral acts should also be judged as *small* or as *big*, according to whether they produce a small or a big effect on mind evolution (or involution). The *small* versus *big* distinction (*magnitude criterion*) actually applies to the judgment of all mind products. Thus, when judging an idea or a moral thought, produced by the *intellect*, or a sentiment or a moral feeling, produced by the *sensitiveness*, or an action or a moral act, produced by the *power*, besides the specific criteria (ch. 1.1.3.1; Table 1.1) and the general *value criterion* (ch. 1.1.3.2; Table 1.1), we should also consider whether each of the mind products represents or causes a *small* or a *big* advancement in the evolution of the outward or inward activity of *intellect* (ideas and moral thoughts), or of *sensitiveness* (sentiments and moral feelings), or of *power* (actions and moral acts) (ch. 1.1.3.1; Table 1.1).

It should be noted that the small-*vs*-big distinction can only be made on an empirical basis and with *approximation*, as is true for any evaluation and prevision concerning human facts and, more generally, the facts of the macro-world or *supra-molecular world* (ch. 1.1.3.2.1).

(2) The Cost to the Agent. Besides the *magnitude* of the effect of a moral act, its *cost* to the agent should also be considered; thus, a poor man who gives one dollar may be comparable to a rich man who gives 10,000 dollars. Again, the cost can only be evaluated with *approximation* (see above). Actually, the *magnitude* of the effect and the *cost* to the agent should be regarded as two closely related aspects of any moral act. Indeed, they should be considered together to give rise to the *magnitude-related-to-cost* parameter of evaluation.

2.2.1.6.2—*Promoting the Evolution of Sensitiveness versus Promoting Happiness*

As already stated, good acts are directed to promote the evolution of one or more mind components (belonging to one or more minds). With reference to the promotion of the evolution of *sensitiveness*, it should be stressed that this should be distinguished from the promotion of happiness. Promoting the evolution of sensitiveness by a good *moral act* means to enable an individual (the acting individual or other individuals) to feel an ever greater number of sentiments of ever greater deepness; in other words, promoting the evolution of sensitiveness means enhancing the ability to feel sentiments toward others, and to be capable of aesthetic enjoyment and artistic creation. This should be distinguished from the pursuing of the satisfaction of personal sentiments or desires through *personal actions*, so that an individual will feel happier. In other words, the development of sensitiveness, and not the achievement of happiness, is the scope of a moral act. Indeed, it may well happen that a moral act, directed to develop sensitiveness, may contrast, rather than favor, happiness; this may happen when an individual chooses to perform a moral act that contrasts with his own desires or interest. Thus, the achievement of happiness by actions and the pursuing of mind evolution by moral acts are quite distinct and separate mental events, the former belonging to the sphere of the *outward activity of the power* or *practical selfishness*, the latter to the sphere of the *inward activity of the power* or *practical consciousness* (see also below: ch. 2.2.1.6.3).

As noted elsewhere (Belfiore 2004: 291), it should be underlined, however, that the desires or wishes that contrast with the development of the mind are never deep and universal sentiments, but rather particular and light sentiments; this is because there is an *internal coherence of the mind* that makes it impossible that great, deep sentiments are in contrast with the development of mind capacities and therefore with the finality of moral acts; this is more so also because being able to feel great, deep, universal sentiments is just one of the scopes (together with the development of intellect and power) of moral acts. To clarify this point, let us compare a light and particular sentiment, such as the desire to spend most of one's time and money frequenting women of easy virtue, with a deep and universal sentiment, like the one expressed by Dante toward Beatrice ["Her eyes were shining brighter than the Star . . . / . . . 'O Lady of virtue, thou alone through whom / the human race exceedeth all contained / within the heaven that has the lesser circles" (the last two lines mean: the humane race raises itself above all earthly things) (Dante, *The Divine Comedy*, Inferno, canto II, lines 55 and 76–78)]. While the former sentiment is clearly in contrast with the moral prescription of pursuing mind evolution (from the moral standpoint, the majority of time and money should be employed to attend school, to read books, to frequent theaters and concert halls, etc.), the latter sentiment is a deep and universal one that, as such, represents a high stage in the evolution of sensitiveness, i.e., it represents one of the scopes of moral acts and is the result of Dante's effort to cultivate and develop his own sensitiveness (apart from his natural endowment).

2.2.1.6.3—Pursuing Mind Evolution as the Source of Human Rights

As repeatedly stated, the scope of moral acts is to induce or favor the evolution of one or more minds; this entails that the finality of moral acts includes the development of the mind of the acting individual himself. Indeed, the scope of moral acts is an *objective* one, so that favoring the development of a mind is always a morally-good act, regardless of whether the mind toward which the moral act is directed is the mind of the acting individual or the mind of another individual. This means that a human being is morally responsible not only toward other human beings but also toward himself. This raises the question whether the *moral responsibility toward oneself* is greater or lower than that toward others. This question should be answered by referring to the rule of the *spheres of decreasing moral responsibility* (ch. 2.1.5.2.1), according to which, for the same kind of mind change (i.e., all things being equal), the responsibility toward oneself comes prior to the responsibility toward other individuals; the latter kind of responsibility will decrease starting from relatives to friends, to association fellow-members, to acquaintances, to fellow-citizen, to fellow-country-men, and to foreigners.

The moral duty that each man has toward himself, i.e., the duty to promote the evolution of his own mind, entails that he is entitled to enjoy those rights that make it possible for him to attempt to develop his own mind. In other words, the moral duty of a human being to develop his own mind is correlated with the duty of other human beings to favor or, at least, not to restrain, his mind development; hence, the source of human rights. Thus, the moral responsibility toward one's own mind is the source of the fundamental human rights, i.e., of those inalienable and indefeasible rights that belong to any individual.

It may be useful to stress once again that the right of an individual does not include the achievement of his happiness. The relationship between "rights" and "happiness" should be understood as follows. All men have the right to be free (within the limits of laws, i.e., while respecting the freedom of others) and, if they are free, they will certainly pursue their happiness (again, while respecting the pursuing of happiness by others). Therefore, *pursuing happiness is a right that descends from the right to be free.* Happiness as such, however, is not a moral end. Nobody can claim the right to be happy; no man (or woman) can have the right to obtain the love of his beloved woman (or man), while he (or she) has the right to do what he or she wants (within the limits of the laws and social rules) in the attempt to obtain the love of the loved person (chs. 2.2.1.2.3, *C1a*; 2.2.1.6.2). However, all other things being equal, happiness is a "sentiment" morally preferable to sadness; this preference is based on an entirely subjective criterion, based on the *founding activity of sensitiveness*, i.e., the same subjective criterion that allows the distinction of joy from sorrow, and of beautiful from ugly (Table 1.1).

My moral conception provides us with an objective criterion to judge moral acts as good or bad. Of course, the application of this criterion in concrete and particular instances encountered in everyday life may not always be simple, as both the human mind and society are very complex entities; this entails that all evaluations and decisions are marked by *approximation* and *imprecision* and, therefore, may give rise to *discussion* and justify *different positions* about details or particular moral choices (*procedural decisions and choices*) but not about the general moral ends to be pursued (*moral decisions and choices*) (chs. 2.1.6; 2.1.7).

The above concept may perhaps be illustrated by the following considerations (Belfiore 2004: 292): the ground moral norm that I propose is for human beings *what a compass is for a sailor*; although the use of a compass is not enough for a sailor to do his task, as he also needs to know how to trim the sails, how to face the winds, the waves, etc. (for which he has to take *procedural decisions and choices*), nevertheless a compass remains a fundamental and necessary guide that indicates which is the right direction to follow (i.e., the compass acts like the ground moral norm, which prompts the agent to take the *moral decisions/choices* that direct his activity toward mind evolution). Indeed, in any circumstance, the ground moral norm indicates to the moral agent what his duty is: to do his best to help the development of the involved minds.

2.2.1.7—Classes of Good Moral Acts

Good moral acts can be ordered into a system of classes and sub-classes, as shown in the following chapters.

2.2.1.7.1—The General Class of Good Moral Acts

This is the class whose members are *all* the human moral acts directed to favor or promote the basic moral good: mind evolution. This large class includes several sub-classes, discussed below.

2.2.1.7.2—The Sub-Classes of Good Moral Acts

The classes and sub-classes of *good moral acts* include those moral acts directed to pursue the class and sub-classes of *moral goods*, discussed in ch. 2.1.4.2 and shown in Table 2.1. I will briefly discuss the moral goods as conceived by some thinkers (sections "*A*" to "*D*") and then I will mention the sub-classes of good moral acts according to my theory (section "*E*").

(A) Aristotelian Virtues.
The virtues recognized by Aristotle and the corresponding spheres of human experience (shown in brackets), as summarized by Nussbaum (1988), are listed below, together with a short comment based on my moral theory. I divide these virtues into two groups depending on whether, according to my opinion, they are correlated, or not, to morality.

(1) Virtues Correlated to Morality.

(a) Justice (distribution of limited resources). Justice is clearly related to morality, since a fair distribution of resources is necessary to avoid leaving some people without the minimum of resources they need to attempt to promote the development of their mind. I note, however, that justice is not limited to the sphere of distribution of resources (distributive justice), as it clearly extends to other spheres of human experience.

(b) Generosity (management of one's personal property in respect to others). This virtue is linked to morality, since it means a propensity toward helping those in need in their effort to develop their mind.

(c) Expansive hospitality (management of one's personal property in respect to hospitality). Hospitality may be assimilated to the propensity toward helping those who are temporarily in need.

(d) Truthfulness (truthfulness in speech). The moral relevance of truthfulness, and the related issue of keeping promises, is discussed below in this chapter (section "*C1*") and also in chs. 2.2.1.4.2, *D4*; 3.1.1.2, *2c*; 3.1.2.3.3.

(e) Intellectual virtues, such as perceptiveness, knowledge, etc. (intellectual life). These virtues are of moral relevance if they are regarded as an effort to promote the evolution of intellect (knowledge). If, on the other hand, they refer to the constitutional intellectual ability of an individual (natural endowment), they should be regarded as an *objective morally-good condition* (a condition that can be little improved by moral acts); at the same time, they represent particular properties that characterize an individual mind (see below, under point "*2*").

(f) Practical wisdom (the planning of one's life and conduct). This virtue is certainly of moral relevance, since it means the project of one's life, which may be directed to promote the evolution of the mind or to reach low-level pleasures.

(g) Proper judgment, contrasted with enviousness, spitefulness, etc. (attitude toward the good and ill fortune of others). Enviousness and spitefulness are morally-bad sentiments that prompt bad moral acts toward those to whom they are directed.

(2) Virtues not Correlated to Morality.

These virtues are part of the particular properties that characterize an individual mind, i.e., they express the particular degree and specificity of the evolution of the intellect, sensitiveness, and power that occurs in each individual and that is linked to his natural endowment (ch. 3.2.2.1.2). These virtues include:

(a) Courage (fear of important damages, especially death). Courage is not related to morality: a courageous man is not necessarily a morally-good man, nor a cowardly man is necessarily a morally-bad man.

(b) Moderation (bodily appetites and pleasures). Bodily appetites and pleasures, even if enjoyed in full, are not necessarily bad, provided that they are not pursued to the detriment of those virtues and attitudes directed to promote mind evolution.

(c) Greatness of soul (attitudes and actions with respect to one's own worth). This virtue is unrelated to morality, as it is merely a personal characteristic: a magnanimous man is not necessarily a morally-good man, nor a petty man is necessarily a morally-bad man.

(d) Mildness of temper (attitude to coping with slights and damages). Again, mildness in coping with slights and damages is an individual property not related to morality.

(e) Easy grace (social association of a playful kind), contrasted with coarseness, rudeness, insensitivity. This virtue and the opposite aptitudes (coarseness, rudeness, etc.) are morally irrelevant individual characteristics, unless they are conceived as unwillingness toward the promotion of mind sensitiveness.

(f) Friendliness, as contrasted with irritability and grumpiness (social association more generally). Neither friendliness nor grumpiness is morally relevant, unless they are associated to the unwillingness to help others to promote their mind evolution.

Nussbaum (1988) supposes that a first objector to Aristotle's conception could maintain that even if the grounding experiences are largely shared, the corresponding virtues may be differently defined by the various societies and cultures. The possible reply to this objection, according to Nussbaum, is that the virtuous person should be able to reach a balance between general rules and the *particular* features of his concrete context. Thus, the virtue-based morality would acquire some of the relativistic features without losing its objective nature.

Nussbaum considers that a second objector could claim that the spheres of grounding experience (even the basic ones, such as the fear of death or the bodily appetites and desires) are actually a creation of the various societies and cultures. To this objection, Nussbaum (1988) replies that, despite differences, common basic human experiences can be recognized across different cultures.

My comment here is that common human experiences are grounded on the *essential properties* of men, linked to their nature as *evolving, conscious* entities made of *intellect, sensitiveness,* and *power* (chs. 1.1.1; 1.1.2; 3.2.2.1.1); this gives rise to the *ground moral norm* (chs. 2.1.4.1; 2.1.5.1) and to the *universal rights/duties* (ch. 3.2.2.1.1) of men. On the other hand, the particularities which characterize the various societies and cultures are linked to individual properties of human beings (or of groups, or communities, or populations), i.e., to the degree and specificity of their mind evolution, which give rise to the individual (or group) rights (ch. 3.2.2.1.2).

Finally, Nussbaum (1988) notes that a third objector might maintain that the alleged grounding experiences are not necessary to human life or may even be a sign of bad life; thus, generosity presupposes private property, which is deemed as bad by the Marxist conception. I observe that, with reference to the private moral life, generosity does not presuppose private property, as it refers to those acts that a man performs to help a neighbor who, for any reason, is in a situation of need. These acts are also possible to a man who owns only his salary (ch. 3.2.3.4, *2*); the wealth of the helper can only affect the *magnitude* of his moral acts (ch. 2.2.1.6.1).

(B) Kantian Duties.

Kant (1785: 31) mentions some *duties* derived from the universalizability principle (obedience to the moral law): *(1) Duties to ourselves, (2) Duties to others, (3) Perfection duties,* and *(4) Imperfection duties.* My comment on these duties is given in chapter 2.2.1.1.3, *A3.*

(C) Ross' Duties.

Ross (1930: 21–22) proposed the following list of *prima facie* duties (already mentioned in ch. 2.2.1.2.3, *A*).

(1) Duties Resting on Previous Acts of the Agent. They include *duties of fidelity* (resting on a promise) and *duties of reparation* (resting on previous wrongful acts). These duties include, among others, those arising from the relations promisee-to-promiser, creditor-to-debtor, and wife-to-husband (in the latter instance, I think that actions prompted by love should be added—see also point "*4*", below). These duties can be explained according to my moral theory by considering that failing to fulfill a promise will cause an involution in the promisee's mind (chs. 2.2.1.4.2, *D4*; 3.1.1.2, *2c*; 3.1.2.3.3). This may refer to an involution of *power* (as in the case of the debtor promise) or to an involution of power and/or *intellect* and/or *sensitiveness,* according to the nature of the promise. Repairing previous wrong acts compensates a previously caused mind involution produced by the wrong act. Moreover, it should be considered that a promise is like a law or rule issued

in a mini-community made of two or more members [the promisee(s) and the promiser(s)]; thus, failing to fulfill a promise is like breaching a law and has the same negative moral meaning: restraining the universalization of actions, which occurs through the organization of individuals into a society.

(2) Duties of Gratitude. These duties rest on previous acts of other men. I note that gratitude is not a "duty"; if someone saves my life, I have no "duty" to do anything for him. However, saving my life is a morally-good act (it avoids the extreme *involution* of my mind linked to the transformation of myself into about 70 Kg of inert matter); therefore, if I am a morally-good person, I should appreciate through my moral thoughts and should love through my moral feelings the morally-good acts and the agent who has made them (in the example: my rescuer); hence, gratitude is the *awareness* of having been the object of a morally-good act and the *moral feeling* toward the agent of such a good act (these feelings may prompt me to do some acts expressing gratitude).

(3) Duties of Justice. They arise from the distribution of pleasure or happiness not in accordance with the merits. Compensating those who are disadvantaged, in order to make some evolution of their minds possible, is fully explained by my moral theory. More exactly, one should not pursue an "equal" distribution of happiness but a distribution of resources (money and opportunities) such as to make it possible for *all* men to enjoy an evolution-allowing, involution-avoiding condition, as discussed in chapter 2.1.5.3.

(4) Duties of Beneficence. These virtues rest on the possibility to improve the condition (virtue, intelligence, pleasure) of others. Concerning "intelligence" (and some of the virtues), this position is in accord with my moral theory, which indicates as a moral end the promotion of mind evolution. "Pleasure", however, is not a "moral good" or a moral end; in place of enhancing "pleasure", we have the duty to enhance the ability to feel pleasure, i.e., to develop *sensitiveness* (ch. 2.2.1.6.2).

A special case is that of the relation parent-to-child (above mentioned); here the parent's duty of promoting children's mind evolution is strengthened by the very close relation between parents and children, according to the theory of the spheres of decreasing moral responsibility (ch. 2.1.5.2.1). Moreover, children are not merely persons with whom the parents enter into relation but they are persons *generated* by the parents; this entails that abandoning children is a moral bad act, because other people may not be ready to substitute a parent in helping the abandoned children, or they may have other burdens that make it difficult to also help the abandoned children. Moreover, family is a mini-community with rules established by tradition, rooted in deep human sentiments, and recognized by the State legal system; therefore, abandoning children, besides an act of private immorality, should be regarded as an act that breaks the existing legal systems, both the mini-system represented by the family and the larger one represented by the State legal system; and breaking the existing legal system is an immoral act because it entails the *involution* from universal actions exerted in an organized society to particular actions exerted by isolated individuals.

Moreover, in these instances, actions dictated by love should also be considered. Love-prompted actions are not duty-dictated moral acts, as they are stirred up by the love for a person (one's own child), which is a personal sentiment (produced by the sensitiveness) that might even be dangerous (as it happens when a parent *oppresses* his child with an excessive love).

(5) Duties of Self-Improvement. These duties rest on the possibility to improve one's own condition. Promoting the evolution of the mind of the agent himself (duty toward oneself) is in accord with my moral theory (ch. 2.1.5.2.2).

(6) *Duties of Non-Maleficence.* They consist of not injuring others. Injuring entails a restrain of mind evolution; avoiding the restraining of mind evolution is a basic duty in my moral theory.

Ross does not provide any rational explanation for the six kinds of "prima facie duties" listed above; therefore, based on my moral theory, I think that these duties should be regarded as arising from *moral feelings*. However, due to the internal coherence of the mind (ch. 2.1.4.1, *b*), these duties are also in accord with moral thoughts, i.e., they (at least most of them) are directed to favor mind evolution, which is the moral good indicated by the moral thoughts.

(D) Nussbaum's Human Features Related to Morality.
Nussbaum (1988) identifies eight features of our common humanity related to morality and to good moral acts, each of which is listed below, accompanied by a short interpretation.

(1) Mortality. All humans know it, and this would shape their lives. In my opinion, mortality is a property possessed by all existing things, which, even if with different speed, continuously change and, with time, will disappear. This certainly shapes human life as a whole; its link to morality consists of the fact that human acts causing the death of an individual are morally bad, because they actually cause the most extreme and irreversible involution of the mind.

(2) Body Features and Experiences. These include body possibilities and vulnerability as well as experiences such as hunger, thirst, desires, and the five sense perceptions; they would be pre-cultural and show large overlap across societies. I think that the human body is the basic structure that belongs to the sphere of the *power*; preserving body integrity, by taking into account its possibilities, vulnerability, needs (hunger and thirst), and functions (sense perceptions), is a basic moral requirement, as it allows the development of the *power* itself and of the other mind components, to which power gives the necessary support.

(3) Pleasure and Pain. These would be pre-cultural, universal human

experiences. I note that pleasure and pain are linked to human happiness, not to morality (ch. 2.2.1.6.2). However, they may acquire moral relevance if we consider that pain may be a signal of body injury or suffering (see point "2", above), or if we consider the ability to feel pleasure or pain, which indicates the degree of evolution of sensitiveness, whose development is one of the ends of moral acts.

(4) Cognitive Capacity. This would be a basic human feature, although it is later shaped by acculturation. My comment here is that cognitive capacity is a characteristic of each individual and, as such, is not linked to morality; it may acquire moral relevance if one conceives the cognitive capacity as an expression of the function of the intellect that is susceptible to evolution and whose development should be one of the ends of moral acts.

(5) Practical Reason. All humans would ask themselves how they should live and act. This point is fully relevant to morality, since the human practical activity is divided between personal actions, which satisfy personal desires, and moral acts, which are guided by moral thoughts and stirred up by moral feelings and which are directed to promote mind evolution (ch. 2.1.3.3). Choosing between personal desires and moral feelings is central to the moral behavior of any individual.

(6) Early Infant Development. Infant experiences of desire, pleasure, loss, one's own finitude, envy, grief, gratitude, all would be to a large extent common to all humans. Here I note that infant development and experiences, which are certainly basic in human life, may affect all aspects of human soul, not limited to the moral sphere.

(7) Affiliation. By nature, humans would be social animals and, therefore, share the need and desire for friendship and love. In my opinion, interpersonal relationships express the tendency or desire of human beings to organize themselves into a society, in order to realize the universalization of actions, which is one of the human moral ends (ch. 3.1.1.1.1). On the other hand, friendship and love are linked to the activity of sensitiveness and are unrelated to morality (unless understood as desire to help others).

(8) Humor. Humor and play would be basic needs of humans, who are called "laughing animals." This is one of the human individual characteristics; yet, it is not related to morality, since a man with little humor is not necessarily a morally-bad man, and vice versa.

(E) Sub-Classes of Good Moral Acts According to My Theory.
In my view, the class and sub-classes of good moral acts include those moral acts directed to pursue the class and sub-classes of moral goods, as discussed in chapter 2.1.4.2 and shown in Table 2.1.

As noted for moral goods, the ordering of moral acts into classes and sub-classes entails their hierarchical arrangement.

2.2.1.8—The Selfishness/Consciousness Balance (or Outward versus Inward Mind activity)

From the structure and functioning of the mind as illustrated in the preceding chapters, we can conceive the activity of each mind component, and of the mind as a whole, as divided into: *(1)* the *outwardly oriented* activity, indicated as *selfishness*, which comprises the rational, the emotional, and the practical selfishness; and *(2)* the *inwardly oriented* activity, indicated as *consciousness*, which comprises the rational, the emotional, and the practical consciousness (Fig. 1.1). This is the *bi-directionality* of the mind.

On these grounds, although minds are different from one another and despite the fact that each mind property varies across the innumerable individual minds, going from one extreme to the opposing one through a continuum, we could attempt to conceive two typical and opposing types of mind, one characterized by the prevalence, or greater evolution, of the inward activity (or consciousness), and the other characterized by the prevalence, or greater evolution, of the outward activity (or selfishness). The former could be defined as the mind of a *morally-good person*; the latter could be defined as the mind of a *selfish person*. Fig. 2.2 shows all the intermediate positions from the full prevalence of consciousness to the full prevalence of selfishness, through a continuum. The above reasoning indicates the importance of the *selfishness/consciousness balance* (or of the outward versus inward mind activity) in defining the moral profile of human beings (chs. 2.1.3.1; 2.1.3.2; 2.1.3.3). It should be underlined that the selfishness/consciousness balance is not fixed for a given individual, since the ability to undergo evolution entails that this balance may vary through time; moreover, this balance may vary in the same individual according to the diverse situations and the different facts faced by that individual and the corresponding choices that he has to make (ch. 2.4.1.3).

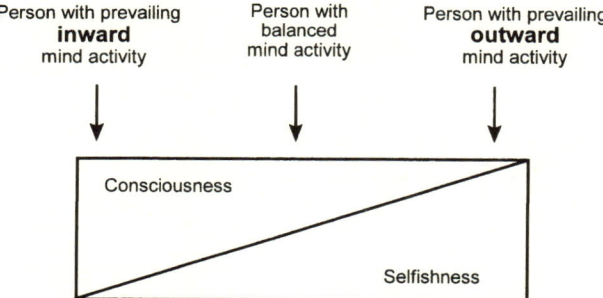

Fig. 2.2. Balance between consciousness and selfishness (or inward and outward mind activities), as it may occur among people. [The various instances of activity of an individual, too, may be mainly of inward or outward nature, but are always mixed].

2.2.1.9—An Overview of the Main Metaethical Theories

In the last decades, several metaethical theories have been posed or further developed. An overview of these doctrines is given in the table that follows.

Table 2.2. Moral Facts (MFs) and Moral Properties (MPs) according to the main metaethical philosophical theories. An overview[1].

Moral antirealism: MFs and MPs are not objective	
Moral error theories: MPs do not exist (Mackie 1977; Joyce 2001), as also shown by their lack of explanatory role (Harman 1977; Wright 1992). Moral knowledge is impossible.	*Moral expressivism or non-cognitivism*: MPs are expression of emotional attitudes (Ayer 1936; Gibbard 2003), or of *prescriptivism* (Hare 1952; 1963; 1981), or of *nondescriptivist cognitivism* (Timmons 1999; Horgan and Timmons 2000b), and may be based on an "expressivistic logic" or "logic of attitudes" (Blackburn 1984; 1993; 1988; 1998; Gibbard 1990: 83–102; 2003; Dreier 1996; Sinnott-Armstrong 2000; Unwin 1999; 2001), as moral sentences would have no logical truth-value (Geach 1960; 1965).
Intermediate positions	
Constructivism: MFs are defined by interpersonal conventions (Harman 1975), or by an idealized observer (Firth 1952; Milo 1995; Smith 1994), or by reflection (Korsgaard 1996)	*Sensibility theories*: Moral concepts are response-dependent (RD, like redness), rather than response-independent (RI, like squareness); MPs have been conceived either as being RD or RI. Moral response might be either "elicited" or "merited" by MPs (McDowell 1985; Wiggins 1987).
Moral realism: MFs and MPs are objective. Moral judgments express propositions that just represent moral facts (*moral cognitivism*); they necessarily entail motivation (*motivational internalism*) (Foot 1972; Williams 1979; McNaughton 1988; Smith 1994; McDowell 1979; Little 1997) (which may lead to a Kantian position—Korsgaard 1986; 1996), even if we have no explanation for this (Shafer-Landau—2003: 165–228), or they do not entail motivation (*motivational externalism*). Moral judgments and motivational desires are separate entities (*Humean theory of motivation*) (Zangwill 2003), which has been challenged (Little 1995). Other aspects concern *normative reasons*[2] and *moral knowledge*[3].	

Ethical naturalism: MFs are like the objects of natural sciences (Boyd 1988; Railton 1986)		*Ethical nonnaturalism*: MFs and moral principles are objective but unlike those of the natural world, and may be known in an *a priory* way (Hampton 1998; Shafer-Landau 2003; 2006). An MP is multiply realizable (it is not necessarily related to the corresponding nonmoral property) (Blackburn 1971;1985), and it would be disjunctive (Jackson 1998), so that a nonmoral situation may be right or wrong[4].
Reductive ethical naturalism: MFs may be identical, or may be reduced, to the facts of natural world (Railton 1986; Jackson 1988)	*Nonreductive ethical naturalism*: MFs are not identical or reducible to the facts of natural world; they are knowable a posteriori and may have, or not, causal/explanatory role (Boyd 1988; Harman 1977; Railton 1986; Sturgeon 1985; Cuneo 2006). An MP is multiply realizable (it is not necessarily related to the corresponding nonmoral property) (Blackburn 1971; 1985), and it would be disjunctive (Jackson 1988), so that a nonmoral situation may be right or wrong[4].	

Table 2.3. My views on Moral Facts (MFs) and Moral Properties (MPs)

Moral antirealism:	
It should be rejected. MFs and MPs are real and related to mind evolution/involution	
Moral error theories: They are wrong. The *good* and the *evil* are objective (mind evolution/ involution) and play explanatory role (good/bad thoughts and/or feelings cause good/bad acts) and can be known.	*Moral expressivism or non-cognitivism*: It might refer to what I name moral feelings (engraved in human soul). *Prescriptivism* and *nonde-scriptivist cognitivism* might refer to rather unjusti-fied rational attitudes (which do not allow logical truth-values). In contrast, my *moral thoughts* allow the (approximate) knowledge of the objective good.
Intermediate positions	
Constructivism: This position too is based on be-liefs prompted by moral feeling, engraved in the human soul.	*Sensibility theories*: These theories lack full objectivity, in contrast to my own, which indicates the objective "good" (mind evolution).

Moral realism:
I agree with this position. MFs and MPs are objective and "real", as they are moral acts, prompted by moral feelings and moral thoughts, which can be known (*moral cogni-tivism*). Mind products being triplets, judgment (thoughts) necessarily entail motivation (feelings) (*motivational internalism*). Yet, as judgments (thoughts) coexist with motiva-tions (feelings) in determining acts, there is also a motivation external to judgments (*mo-tivational externalism*). Thus, contrary to Hume's position, both thoughts and feelings contribute to motivation. Moral knowledge is based on mind observation (which makes *foundationalism* possible), in contrast to *intuitionism* or to *coherentism* (based on the coherence of a system of judgments), and resists *moral disagreement*. This explains why *normative reasons*, unlike *motivational reasons*, are explanatory of actions and acts.

Ethical naturalism: It is wrong. MFs are not just *natural*, but include actions or acts (which belong to the *natural*) and moral thoughts and feelings (which are *real* but not *natural*)		*Ethical nonnaturalism*: This position considers MFs as objective and yet unlike natural ones, knowable *a priory*, and *supervenient* on non-MFs. It perhaps refers to the moral thoughts and feelings that de-termine MFs.
Reductive ethical naturalism: It is wrong. MFs cannot be re-duced to natural facts, as they include actions or acts (which belong to the *natural*) and moral thoughts and feelings (which are *real* but not *natural*).	*Nonreductive ethical natural-ism*: This position considers MFs as not identical or reducible to natural facts; yet it defines in a vague manner what MFs actually are.	

NOTES TO TABLE 2.2:

1. For a general review, see Shafer-Landau and Cuneo (eds., 2007).

2. *Normative reasons*, unlike *motivational reasons*, should be explanatory of actions (Williams 1979; 1989; Joyce 2001: 106–134), yet reasons might be both motivational and normative (Dancy 1995; 2000: 98–137). Moral facts (e.g., Hitler's wrongness) do have a causal role (Sturgeon 1985), which is denied by others (Harman 1986) or under-stood as a teleological explanation (Hampton 1998); or some moral facts, but not others, may have causal explanatory power (Cuneo 2006). The moral disagreement does not undermine moral realism (Stevenson 1963; Brink 1989: 104, 197–209).

3. *Moral knowledge* is possible by postulating basic, non-inferential, or self-evident beliefs (*foundationalism*), known by intuition (*intuitionism*: Audi 1997; 2004), or by Rawls's reflective equilibrium to reach a coherent system of beliefs (*coherentism*: Dan-iels 1979), a view that has been criticized as not truly justificatory (Singer 1974; Brandt 1979: 1–23). Based on Putnam's "Twin Earth thought experiment" (1973; 1975), Horgan and Timmons (1991; 1992a; 1992b; 2000a) have discussed the meaning of moral terms.

4. These concepts are relevant to the complex notion of *supervenience*, that is, with the supervenience of the moral on the non-moral or descriptive (Blackburn 1985; Savel-los and Yalcin, eds., 1995; Kim 2002).

2.2.2—Judgment of Moral Events (Moral Thoughts, Feelings, and Acts) by the Value Criterion

According to the *value criterion* (ch. 1.1.3.2.5; Table 1.1), moral events can be judged as *particular* or *universal*, as described below.

Moral thoughts are "particular" if they concern (or are about) a single mind or person (or few people) and "universal" (universal as to their *objects*—see ch. 1.1.3.2.5) if they concern most members of a population (or most members of a class). Moral thoughts also include *moral projects*, which concern non-existing (or yet not existing) "objects"; they are "particular" if refer to, and/or are created by, a single person, and "universal" or, better, *universal and/or collective* if they refer to, and/or are created (or thought) by, most/all members of a population or of a class (universal as to *objects* and/or *agents*—see ch. 1.1.3.2.5). The laws of democratic States are examples of universal/collective moral projects (see ch. 4.1.1).

Moral feelings are "particular" if they are *light* feelings, as such felt by single persons, whereas they are "universal" (or *shared*) if they are *deep* feelings that can be felt by a single mind and yet are shared by most men (provided they possess an adequately developed emotional consciousness).

Moral acts can be distinguished into "particular" or "universal" not only according to the number of the acting individuals (universality as to the *agents*—see ch. 1.1.3.2.5) but also according to the number of the affected individuals toward whom the moral act(s) is/are directed (universality as to the *objects*—see ch. 1.1.3.2.5). Indeed, *moral acts* are always the creation of a single individual mind (see ch. 2.1.2, *A1*). (For the *magnitude criterion*, see ch. 2.2.1.6.1). Some examples may be useful (Belfiore 2004: 300). If I give some money to an extremely poor individual, I make a particular moral act. If I give money to a charity institution that helps, say, 100 people, my moral act has some degree of universalization. If a manager of a firm takes a moral decision, followed by the corresponding moral act, directed to help in some way all the employees (say 1000 people), he has made a moral act of a greater degree of universalization; if the firm is a large one, with (say) 50,000 employees, the degree of universalization is clearly still greater, and may further increase in the case of very large firms with a very high number of employees. As to the number of the acting agents, it is not morally relevant because the moral significance of a given individual act is neither increased nor reduced by the contemporary occurrence of other similar acts (ch. 2.1.2, *A1*). Yet, when moral acts are made collectively because they are endorsed by all or most members of a class (e.g., the members of the Executive power of the State—see ch. 4.1.1) they are *universal/collective* moral acts (see ch. 1.1.3.2.5). Thus, the universality of the *moral projects/decisions* and the corresponding *moral acts* may refer to the agents and/or the affected people. (This topic belongs to *public ethics*—see ch. 4.1.1).

2.3—SUPER-NORMAL AND ABNORMAL MORAL BEHAVIOR

2.3.1—Supererogation

As I described elsewhere (Belfiore 2004: 308–11), considering that good moral acts promote or favor the development of one or more minds, and that mind development is an endless process, there is the possibility of moral acts of progressively increasing beneficial effect, up to moral acts that can be regarded as unusual or exceptional for both their effects and the "cost" paid by the acting agent. The behavioral tendency to go beyond the call of duty by doing these unusual or exceptional moral acts forms what is indicated with the term *supererogation*. Thus, *supererogation* is the tendency to go beyond the call of duty and consists of such actions that can be defined as beneficence, charity, volunteering, forgiveness, toleration, heroism and saintliness (Schumaker 1977; Heyd 1982; Mellema 1991). Without entering into details, I will just mention that, on the basis of my conception, supererogation should be regarded as the performance of "high cost" moral acts of great "magnitude", which produce very remarkable effects with reference to both the degree of induced mind evolution and/or the number of involved minds. It has been claimed that supererogatory acts include beneficence, charity, volunteering, forgiveness, toleration, etc.; however, considering that there is no distributive justice in most, perhaps in all, countries, I believe that the above-mentioned acts can be regarded as supererogatory only if they are of some magnitude and of high cost whereas minor acts, such as giving 5 cents to a poor man, may not indeed qualify as supererogatory. Thus, without placing any sharp limit, we can say that moral acts progressively approach the supererogatory dimension as their effects and the burden of the acting agent increase to an unusual or even exceptional extent; in the most extreme instances, these supererogatory moral acts tend toward heroism and saintliness.

2.3.2—Moral Formalism

The ground moral norm, as defined in my moral theory, provides us with a rule that indicates the *finality* of a moral act: the evolution of one or more minds or, in greater detail, the evolution of one or more mind components, which means the development of the intellect and/or sensitiveness and/or power. As I described elsewhere (ch. 2.1.5.1), this finality can be reached by means of different, particular moral acts, none of which, however, has *per se* a constant effect, because the effect of a moral act depends upon the conditions of the affected mind. Thus, a moral act has not an absolute value *per se* but is judged as good or bad according to whether it induces an evolution or an involution of the mind(s) on which it exerts its effects. Judging a particular moral act *per se*, instead of judging it on the basis of its concrete effect produced in one or more minds (i.e., confounding the moral act with its effect), is the basis of *moral formalism* as opposed to true morality.

Morality consists of performing true moral acts, which promote mind evolution; moral formalism is the strict adherence to some particular rules of behavior, consisting of the performance of acts that are considered by the agents as having moral significance *per se* (without any regard to their actual effects) but that are actually only formal acts deprived of any moral content. The examples given in chapter 2.1.5.1 help to clarify this concept.

Since religion provides individuals with what may be regarded as the faith-based counterpart of moral principles, a *religious formalism* exists that, like moral formalism, consists of the strict adherence to some particular behavior made up of acts that are considered by the agents as having religious significance *per se*, without any regard to their actual religious or moral content (Belfiore 2004: 310).

2.3.3—Fanaticism

In previous chapters, I stated that *moral feelings* could be regarded as *inward sentiments* produced by the inward activity of sensitiveness (or *emotional consciousness*) (ch. 2.1.1.2).

As noted elsewhere (Belfiore 2004: 310–11), moral feelings, like any other sentiment, may be showy and yet particular and superficial, or they may be little showy and yet deep and universal. When moral formalism is adhered to with showy and yet particular and superficial moral feeling, *fanaticism* arises. Thus, fanatic individuals often unjustifiably assign a great moral value to particular, formal rules and to the corresponding acts that actually have little or no meaning by themselves, and tend to impose on others with violence the observance of these rules and the performance of the corresponding acts.

It should also be noted that a deep, universal moral feeling cannot give rise to fanaticism, since if it is truly deep and universal, it is always directed toward truly *moral* acts with a truly *moral* end (induction of evolution in one or more minds) (ch. 2.1.4.1, *b*). Rather, deep, universal moral feeling can lead to great moral acts or to moral supererogation. However, it should be pointed out that some individuals, whose unusual moral behavior may at first appear to be driven by moral feeling and who may engage themselves in moral acts approaching heroism and sanctity (acts that sometimes are beyond their reach), might actually be psychologically disturbed individuals.

Examples of fanaticism, moral, religious, or mixed, are (Belfiore 2004: 311): *(a)* the drastic condemnation of those individuals whose habits differ under certain particular aspects from ours (supposed witches, foreigners, divorcees, homosexuals, etc.), without any rational analysis that shows an actual dangerous effect (for one or more minds) of the condemned behaviors; *(b)* violent imposition on others of particular acts or habits that, although meaningless, are uncritically considered as morally significant (adhering to a political party or a religious doctrine, wearing the "burka", etc.).

2.4—HUMAN FREEDOM

We have already learned from previous chapters (1.1.1.2.3; 1.1.1.2.4; 2.1.1.3) that the mind can induce changes in the physical world by means of *actions*, produced by the *outward activity of power* (or *practical selfishness*), as well as changes in one or more minds (including the mind of the acting individual himself) by means of *moral acts*, produced by the *inward activity of power* (or *practical consciousness*—Fig. 1.1). Each action and each moral act expresses the *intention* or *will* of performing that action or moral act; this means that any action or moral act has *intentionality*.

The will to perform a given action entails selecting, from the various possible ideas-of-projects, created by the outward activity of intellect (or rational selfishness), the one to be realized, i.e., making a *practical choice* or *decision*. Likewise, the will to perform a given moral act entails selecting, from the various possible moral projects, created by the inward activity of intellect (or rational consciousness), the one to be realized, i.e., taking a *moral choice* or *decision*. Thus, the big problem arises whether the choice from the various possible ideas-of-projects or the various possible moral projects is *free* or *determined* or, in other words, whether human beings possess or not *free will*, i.e., whether they are internally free or not.

2.4.1—The Claimed Freedom of Human Conduct

I will discuss separately *(1)* the factors determining *personal decisions and actions* and *(2)* the factors determining *moral decisions and acts*.

2.4.1.1—Personal Decisions and Actions, as Determined by the Prevailing Sentiment

As mentioned elsewhere (Belfiore 2004: 279–80, 312–13), a *personal action* realizes an idea-of-project referring to one or another of the desires or wishes (sentiments) that one has; the project to be realized by the action is chosen among several others by a *choice* or *decision*. The action (and the corresponding decision) is directed to realize the *prevailing desire*, the one that (after having evaluated all the involved factors) is felt with greater intensity, because there is no reason why one should do otherwise (i.e., why one should choose to satisfy a sentiment other than the one felt with more strength).

At this point, I think it is useful to recall that ideas-of-projects (and the related actions) can be primarily directed to satisfy a sentiment or to realize an idea-of-project or to modify a preceding action, although in any case they include all the three kinds of products of the mind components (intellect, sensitiveness, and power). However, in some instances, it will be the intellectual component, i.e., ideas or theories, that prevails (e.g., a scientific project is primarily an elaboration by the intellect, toward which, however, the subject feels some attraction and which requires some actions to be realized). In other instances, it will be sentiments that prevail; thus, the project to undertake a trip to meet one's loved one is primarily directed to satisfy a sentiment, although it includes some intellectual and power contributions, such as the knowledge of the loved person as well as the elementary knowledge required to be able to undertake a trip and the little power required to make the trip. Still in other instances, it will be the power component that prevails, as when one undertakes a favorable financial operation to increase his own power, as represented by money, although this requires some contribution by the intellect and sensitiveness, such as the elementary knowledge necessary to perform the operation and some positive feeling toward it. In all instances, however, the sentiments or desires toward a given idea-of-project play a relevant role in the practical choice.

Personal actions are free if there is no physical impediment to their occurrence, namely if there is no impediment or interference in the chain of events (better, along the transformation pathway) from the brain events corresponding to the prevailing sentiment felt by the agent to the final event corresponding to the satisfaction of the desire through the accomplishment of an action. There is no "internal" uncertainty about which of the many desires felt by the sensitiveness of an individual should be given the preference, because the one which prevails, as such, is the most strongly felt one. Thus, when one chooses to buy a chocolate ice cream instead of a vanilla one, this is because he desires the former more than the latter. Unless there is some impediment, such as the unavailability of vanilla ice cream or some block in brain physical-chemical processes, the choice is free. The choice, of course, may be a more complex and thought-involving one, such as the choice by a student of a given university faculty over another one; this choice is externally free, unless it is limited by some impediment, such as the lack of money that may prevent the student from choosing the course whose fees are higher than those of other courses.

2.4.1.2—Moral Decisions and Moral Acts as Determined by the Prevailing Moral Feelings

It should be considered that any moral act is the realization of a moral choice or decision; the latter consists of selecting, from the various possible *moral projects* elaborated by *rational consciousness* (on the basis of *moral thoughts*), the one to be realized. Although the selection of a moral project is a very complex mental operation, its mechanism is comparable to that concerning the selection of personal projects. As the latter selection is determined by the prevailing sentiment, so the selection of a moral project is determined by the *prevailing moral feeling*, generated by *emotional consciousness*. Thus, if the prevailing moral feeling is "good", it will prompt the choice of the moral project that, when realized through a moral act, will best promote mind evolution; if the prevailing moral feeling is "bad", it will prompt the choice of the moral project that, when realized through a moral act, will restrain mind evolution.

Yet, the process just described is only the first step leading to the moral act, because moral projects may contrast with personal projects, so that a competition between them arises. Thus, after having selected the moral project, another selection is required: that between the moral project, prompted by moral feeling, and the competing personal project, prompted by personal desires or sentiments. This is the fundamental moral choice, which opposes *personal projects* (prompted by *personal sentiments*, produced by the *outward activity of sensitiveness* or *emotional selfishness*) to *moral projects* (prompted by *moral feelings*, produced by the *inward activity of sensitiveness* or *emotional consciousness*—Fig. 1.1). This fundamental choice, which actually is determined by the prevalence of the moral feeling over the personal sentiment, or vice versa, would be, according to some thinkers, a "free choice"; this issue will be discussed in the next chapter (2.4.1.3).

Once the choice has been made, if the moral feeling has prevailed over personal sentiments, the resulting moral act will be (externally) free if there is no physical impediment to its occurrence, namely if there is no impediment or interference in the chain of events going from the brain events, corresponding to the prevailing moral feeling felt by the agent, to the final event, corresponding to the fulfillment of the moral feeling through the corresponding moral act. The same is true for personal actions resulting from the prevalence of personal desires over moral feelings.

2.4.1.3—The Fundamental Moral Choice: Moral Projects versus Personal Projects (The Claimed "Free Will")

In the attempt to define the essence of a moral choice or decision we could say that it consists of the sequence of two steps: *(a)* the selection of the "best" moral project, made by referring to its effects (exerted when it will be realized) on one or more minds, and *(b)* the choice between the selected moral-project and the competing personal project (made by referring to subjective reasons, primarily to subjective desires). The selection of the best moral project (i.e., the project that induces the most favorable effect on the evolution of one or more mind components in one or more minds) depends primarily on the ability of the acting person to understand and evaluate the actual effects of the selected moral project (this will depend upon the moral thought created by the *rational consciousness*, or *inward activity of intel-lect*—Fig. 1.1) as well as on the moral feelings of the moral agent. There is no significant reason by which an individual should select a moral project other than the one that he thinks is the best one (of course, his choice may actually be wrong if his moral thought is bad or little developed) and toward which he feels the strongest moral feeling. The difficulty for the acting indi-vidual arises when, as it often happens, the selected moral project, directed to induce an effect in one or more minds, contrasts with the personal project created to satisfy a personal desire. It is this fundamental choice that is charged with moral responsibility and that makes the choosing individual a moral subject.

We could further clarify the fundamental moral choice as follows. *Mor-al feelings*, produced by the emotional consciousness, are directed toward a moral project, i.e., a project whose realization by means of the correspond-ing act affects one or more minds. *Personal sentiments* or desires, produced by the emotional selfishness, are directed to personal projects and prompt the corresponding personal actions. Therefore, choosing between moral pro-jects and personal projects, i.e., taking a moral decision, is choosing be-tween the moral feeling, felt toward a given moral project, and the personal sentiment, felt toward a competing personal project. Is this moral choice (or moral decision) *free*?

Before answering this question, I recall that we should distinguish an *external freedom* and an *internal freedom*.

External freedom consists of the lack of any impediment in the chain of events going from the brain changes corresponding to the prevailing senti-ment (in the case of a personal action) or to the prevailing moral feeling (in the case of a moral act) felt by the choosing subject to the final effect to which the action or the moral act is directed.

Internal freedom, on the other hand, is related to the choice between the action prompted by *personal sentiments* and the moral act prompted by *moral feelings*. To answer the question whether the choice between the de-mand of *personal sentiments* and that of *moral feelings* is a free choice, we should consider that such moral choice is determined by which of the two competing "forces" (the sentiment or the moral feeling) is the stronger one. As mentioned elsewhere (Belfiore 2004: 314–18), this entails that the choosing individual is not free in the sense commonly given to this term, because the choosing individual cannot change the strength of the senti-ments or of the moral feelings that he experiences. No one has the power to modify one's sentiment (of attraction, repulsion or indifference) toward a personal project directed to visit a given city, nor can one modify one's moral feeling (of attraction, repulsion or indifference) toward a moral project directed to help a poor boy. Yet, these two "forces" may compete with each other; this happens when making a trip to visit a given city entails spending an amount of money that one could give to help a poor boy. Nevertheless, many thinkers maintain that men are free in doing what they do and that this freedom is the basis of their moral responsibility. Maintaining that the choice between a moral project and a personal project is free implies that the choosing agent (or "mind"), faced with a moral project for which he experiences a weak moral feeling of attraction and a contrasting personal project for which he experiences a strong sentiment of attraction, has the ability to make a choice independent of both these contrasting emotional forces, although a choice so conceived appears as based on an undefined and perhaps mysterious criterion.

In the attempt to understand whether an *internal freedom* is possible, let us consider the following example: John's consciousness is faced with two possibilities, either to spend some money on a trip to visit Paris, or to give the money to a very poor sick boy. John feels the moral desire to help the poor boy and, at the same time, feels the contrasting desire to visit Paris. I think that the final decision will depend on which of these two "emotional forces" is stronger. Other thinkers, however, believe that John's consciousness is able to choose between these two contrasting forces (personal sentiment and moral feeling) without relying on them, so that, although John's desire to visit Paris is his strongest feeling, he ultimately can decide to help the poor sick boy. Now the problem arises in defining what is the entity that takes this decision and what determines it. I think that the decision is taken at the level of consciousness (which is the "core" of the mind), where the awareness of the two competing "forces" arises. If this decision were not the result of the prevailing emotional force (personal sentiment or moral feeling), then what would be the factor(s) that determine(s) the decision? An answer could be: reason tells John that helping the boy is a morally-good act (because it induces an evolution of the boy's power, thus enabling him to cure his disease and to provide for his needs), so that John will decide to do it (or John's consciousness adheres to this moral project). I think, however, that this explanation cannot be accepted because the role of reason (which certainly exists) is performed before the time of the choice, during the elaboration of both the personal project (outward activity of intellect) and the moral project (inward activity of intellect). Indeed, any project is elaborated by reason (intellect) so that, at the time when the consciousness is faced with the choice between the personal and the moral project, the task of reason has already been accomplished. Referring to the example cited above, when John is faced with his choice, reason has already made him aware that going to Paris will give him joy whereas giving money to the poor sick boy helps the development of the boy's mind. What determines John's choice must be an intrinsic property of his consciousness, i.e., a property that leads him to adhere to the moral project (to help the poor boy) instead of the attractive personal project (to visit Paris). This property, however, if present, must be a constitutive characteristic of John's consciousness; therefore, it is the prevalence of this property that determines John's choice, which again means that John was not free to choose otherwise. Conversely, if we hypothesize that John's will or consciousness is not determined by the prevalence of moral feeling over personal sentiments (or vice versa) nor by the prevalence of the (rather mysterious) hypothesized property, then we should postulate the presence of still another, second property in John's mind, a property that operates before the former one and that has determined it; for this second property, a similar reasoning could be made, so that a third property should be postulated, and so on. The fact is that if an entity is able to make a choice, it must have some structural, inherent property that determines the choice (so that the choice is not free). An entity that is capable of making a "free choice" understood as a choice not determined by one (or more) intrinsic property of the choosing entity itself, should be an entity with no properties, i.e., it should be an entity deprived of any property, which is as if one says that it should be a *non-existing entity*! In other words, a choosing entity must have some *intrinsic* and at least relatively *constant* property that determines the choices: this must be an *intrinsic* property to ensure that the choice (and the linked responsibility) is made by the choosing entity; it must also have some *constancy*, as some continuity in time is one of the characteristics of a conscious and responsible mind.

May I recall the deterministic conception, excluding free will, held by Spinoza (see also my recent book 2012: 41-43); he said that "an individual . . . acts as it was conditioned by nature, and cannot act otherwise" (1670: 201) (see also Spinoza's later works, 1677a; 1677b). Spinoza, however, seems to conceive the human mind as exerting only the selfish activity, ignoring the moral activity and the competition between these two activities.

It should be pointed out that, in a given individual, the prevalence of moral feelings (or inward sentiments) over personal sentiments, or vice versa, is not the same for all situations in which a choice is to be made. As noted elsewhere, in the consciousness of an individual, prevalence of moral feelings or personal sentiments may change at each of the many and different situations encountered with time. Indeed, although moral feelings and personal sentiments depend on the structural characteristics of a given individual mind (i.e., on the characteristics of the outward and inward activity of his sensitiveness), which must show some constancy, it is also true that, with the continuous becoming of the mind (which is contributed by education and environmental stimuli), the balance between moral feelings and personal sentiments may change with time in favor of the former (*evolution of consciousness*) or of the latter (*involution of consciousness*).

2.4.2—*Moral Responsibility in the Absence of Internal Freedom*

(A) Moral Responsibility and the Second Effects and Side Effects of Human Actions and Moral Acts.

Before discussing the difficult problem of moral responsibility, we should recall that Mackie (1977: 203–8) distinguishes human actions and moral acts into: *(a) directly intentional* (i.e., directly intended under a given description representing a feature sought by the agent); *(b) obliquely intentional* (i.e., intended under description representing a feature not sought but accepted by the agent); *(c) voluntary* (i.e., arising from, and immediately expressing, a desire, without involving any intention or belief); and *(d) nonvoluntary* (i.e., made by compulsion, or ignorance, or lack of skill). It is commonly held that an agent is responsible only for his *intentional* actions or moral acts; yet, it is uncertain whether an agent is responsible for the second effects or the obliquely intended effects of his actions or moral acts, and whether he can be held responsible for his negligence itself or also for the unforeseen results (Mackie 1977: 208–15). Actually, as I pointed out elsewhere (ch. 1.1.3.2.1), due to the complexity of the human world and of human actions and moral acts, any evaluation can only be made with *approximation*; this is also true for the evaluation of responsibility: we can only attempt to limit the degree of approximation or imprecision, without pretending to reach any clear-cut conclusion.

(B) Moral Responsibility and the Freedom of Human Actions and Moral Acts.

The commonly accepted principle that moral responsibility must be associated with human freedom has prompted many thinkers to attempt to show that the fundamental moral choice is "free". Yet, the incontrovertible facts that human behavior is closely associated with changes occurring in the brain, and that the changes occurring in the brain are of physical and chemical nature and, therefore, governed by determinism, make any attempt to show moral freedom a hopeless task. I just recall that both "compatibilist" and "incompatibilist" theories have been put forward, the former of which maintain that freedom is compatible with causal determinism, while the latter hold that freedom is incompatible with causal determinism. The *principle of indetermination* has also been invoked to defend the view that human moral choices are free and not governed by necessity. However, it should be underlined that the principle of indetermination cannot apply to the problem of human actions for at least two reasons. This principle, in fact, concerns sub-atomic particles whereas brain events are changes that occur at the molecular (often macro-molecular) level. Moreover, according to the principle of indetermination, the sub-atomic particles seem to be governed by still unclear mechanisms, or by randomness or casualness, whereas human choices are claimed *not* to be random events but conscious, responsible, and "free" choices. Thus, even if subatomic particles have been claimed to exert possible macro-effects, these cannot explain free will. Here I will briefly expound the following two concepts (Belfiore 2004: 323–30).

(1) The Apparent Freedom of Moral Choice Results from the Extreme Complexity of the Brain. Due to the *extreme* complexity of the physical-chemical changes that, in the brain cells, are associated with the activity of the mind-components (intellect, sensitiveness, and power, each exerting a bidirectional—outward and inward—activity), human rational activity is unable to follow and to understand the work of the brain. For instance, the intellect is unable to follow all the steps that link an afferent stimulus (bringing a signal from the sensory organs to the brain) to the elaboration of that signal in the brain, and the following efferent stimulus (response of the brain) bringing a signal from the brain to the muscles (that induces some change in the physical world). Therefore, in order to fill the gap represented by the many steps that we are unable to understand, we are attracted by the hypothesis that the response of the brain is due to a "free" choice or decision. The unwillingness to accept the above view (that freedom is only apparent) is due to the general unawareness of the extraordinary complexity of the brain structure and functioning (and of life mechanisms in general).

(2) "Being Morally Responsible for" as Synonym of "Being the Causal Agent of". To understand this statement, it is useful to analyze the activity of all the mind-components, as follows.

(a) When, in a given individual, the *outward* activity of his *intellect* reaches an excellent degree of development, we recognize that this individual is a great scientist; we respect him for this reason, and he feels some justified pleasure for being aware of his intellectual excellence. Examples of intellectual excellence may be Galileo, Newton, and Einstein.

(b) When, in a given individual, the *outward* activity of his *sensitiveness* reaches an excellent degree of development, we recognize that this individual is a great literate or musician or visual artist; we respect him for this reason, and he feels some justified pleasure for being aware of the excellence of his sensitiveness. Examples of excellence of sensitiveness may be Dante, Shakespeare, Beethoven, and Michelangelo.

(c) When, in a given individual, the *outward* activity of his *power* reaches an excellent degree of development, we recognize that this individual is a great statesman or politician; we respect him for this reason, and he feels some justified pleasure for being aware of the excellence of his *power*. Examples of excellence in the field of power may be Pericles, Caesar Augustus, and Napoleon.

(d) When, in a given individual, the *inward* activity of his intellect and/or sensitiveness and/or power (activity of *consciousness*) reaches an excellent degree of development (and prevails over the *outward* mind ac-

tivity), we recognize that this individual is a very good man; we respect him for this reason, and he feels some justified pleasure (feeling of a clean conscience) for being aware of the excellence of his consciousness performance (i.e., moral behavior). Examples of excellence in the field of consciousness activity may be Saint Francis of Assisi and mother Teresa of Calcutta.

Thus, we assign a different kind of merit to those who excel in the field of the *outward* activity of intellect, or of sensitiveness, or of power (selfishness), or of the *inward* activity of intellect, or of sensitiveness or of power (consciousness), and we feel a different kind of respect for them. Let us reflect on the following example. Consider a physician who cures a patient whose conditions progressively worsen, so that a second physician is consulted who understands that the diagnosis made by the first physician is wrong, makes the correct diagnosis but informs the patient's parents that by then it is too late to save the life of the patient, who soon after dies. Nobody could deny that the first doctor will feel some remorse for having been unable to make the right diagnosis, thus saving the patient's life; yet, it is not his fault if he is less clever (read: if he has a less-developed intellect), assuming that he has not been less active than the second doctor in studying during the medical courses or during the training period, or in following the programs of continuous medical education. Therefore, we must recognize that the first doctor feels guilty for something (his degree of intellectual capacity) that does not depend on his free will.

On the grounds of the above reasoning, we can say that the feeling of a clean conscience or of guilt is the awareness of being the causal agent of a good or bad moral act, regardless of whether the causal agent is in turn "caused" (i.e., governed by determinism) or "uncaused" (i.e., "free"). So understood, the concept of moral responsibility is compatible with the determinism that governs the brain and therefore all mind activities. In this regard, I recall that, as noted by Mackie (1977: 222–23), many theologians, from St. Augustine onwards, have been compatibilists, i.e., have thought that human choices retain their moral meaning even if they are fixed in advance, being foreseen by God. This is in keeping with my view about the *existence of moral responsibility without freedom.*

2.5—THE PRIMACY OF ETHICS

Before closing the part of this book devoted to private ethics, some general comments are in order. I will briefly make a comparison between *(1)* ethics and the other products of the mind components, and *(2)* ethics and religion.

2.5.1—Ethics and the Other Products of the Mind Components

We already know that consciousness is the innermost or the inward part of the mind, or its "core". It is at the level of consciousness that the awareness concerning the extremely complex structure and functioning of the mind as an *evolving, conscious entity* arises; this awareness, in turn, gives rise to *ethics*, based on the *ground moral norm*, which prescribes the promotion of mind evolution. It follows that *ethics*, and the *consciousness* that creates it, can be regarded as having a *primacy* among the products and the components of the mind, respectively. The consciousness-created ethics makes man aware of what he is and of the place that he holds in reality: the central or highest place, being the most evolved among the known entities. Ethics suggests to man what he is (the most evolved of the evolving entities), where he is (at the apex of the known entities), where to go (toward an endless evolution), and what to do (to promote mind evolution).

The *ground moral norm* (that prescribes the promotion of mind evolution) provides men with a *guide* without imposing any dogma or rigid rule; it is like a map for a traveler or a compass for a sailor (more exactly: it is like the information that a traveler obtains from a map, and a sailor from a compass). The compass tells a sailor where is north and where is south; the ground moral norm tells man what is the "good" (mind evolution) and what is the "evil" (mind involution), what is morally good (promoting mind evolution) and what is morally bad (restraining mind evolution).

The primacy of the inward mind activity (*consciousness*), and of *ethics* among mind products, becomes apparent if we compare a moral philosopher who has "discovered" the "objective" human good (mind evolution) with a scientist or a technical expert working in a particular scientific field. Both the moral philosopher and the science-expert have made valuable advancements in the sphere of knowledge (activity of intellect); yet, the moral philosopher is like the sailor with a compass, who is aware that he is going north, whereas the science-expert has certainly explored some part of the sea, he may even have discovered some new island, and yet he does not know where he is going; he is a somewhat bewildered man. This is the condition of most modern scholars in the technical-scientific area: they gain new knowledge through the *outward* activity of intellect, which looks at particular, specific fields located, so to say, at the periphery of the mind, far from the core of the mind; in contrast, the moral philosopher acts in the domain of the *inward* activity of intellect or *rational consciousness*. Indeed, many individuals in modern society, despite their remarkable achievements in specific fields such as physics, chemistry, biology, medicine, economics, and socio-political sciences, appear as dwarfs when measured with the meter of moral values. A more widespread diffusion of moral philosophy would develop the rational consciousness (moral thoughts), thus promoting the moral growth of humans.

2.5.2—Ethics and Religion

Philosophy can be defined as the product of the greatest effort made by human intellect to understand reality, or as the most general or supreme theory about reality for which some support by observational data or rational deductions is possible. Yet, due to the limitedness of human minds, what is known is much less than what is unknown, and the endless evolution of the mind enables the human intellect to make only small advancements, so that knowledge of reality as a whole remains an unreachable end; it will always remain unknown to us. Since knowledge of the whole is required to fully understand the meaning of its parts, we can say that the reality as a whole is for us the true "noumenon". The incompleteness of human knowledge leaves some fundamental questions without an answer, such as those about the ontological conception of the universe, the meaning of human life, the true end of human beings, etc. The philosopher is content with what can be obtained by human reason, and is *neutral* about the possible hypotheses concerning what remains unknown. *Ethics*, as conceived in this book, provides men with a guide based on *moral principles* and *values* derived from the *evolving* nature of the mind as known through internal observation. Most people, however, prompted by the insuppressible *desire* (produced by *sensitiveness*, primarily by its inward activity or emotional consciousness) to give some answer to the fundamental questions about human fate or the interpretation of the whole universe, believe by *faith* in some *indemonstrable hypotheses*, commonly called *religions*, which are collective creations made by human *intellect* through its imaginative ability. In particular, they believe in an intelligent entity, *God*, whose decisions or *will* are primarily regarded as *(1)* the causes of all those phenomena that are unexplainable to men, and *(2)* as the sources of moral values. This has been an old tendency of man.

(1) God's Will as the Cause of Unexplainable Phenomena. As mentioned elsewhere (Belfiore 2004: 328), an example concerning a biological phenomenon (interpreted by ignorant men as due to a free choice of a divine entity) may be taken from the "Iliad". During the Trojan War, a severe epidemic developed among the Greeks who besieged the city of Troy. Now we know that this was the effect of the diffusion of some pathogen bacterium, but at that time this was not known and, due to the inability to follow the cause-effect chain of events in which the epidemic was inserted, Homer postulated that it was the decision and subsequent act of an offended and angry "God" (Apollo). Likewise, the cessation of the epidemic (which may have been due to the death of the more susceptible individuals and the survival of the resistant ones) was again attributed to the decision of a pitiful goddess, "Juno" (Homer: Iliad, Book 1).

(2) God's Will as the Sources of Moral Values. This concept has been mentioned in various previous chapters. However, I note that, in the course of history, God has also been invoked to support pseudo-moral values that actually served the interest of the dominant class, as occurred at the time of the absolute monarchies. In contrast to the "divine" moral laws, my moral theory shows that men, by looking within their *consciousness* (i.e., through the *inward activity* of their mind), have the possibility to understand their true nature as *evolving conscious entities* (made of intellect, sensitiveness and power) and to discover what is the objective *moral good* (mind evolution), from which *moral principles*, *values*, and *norms* are derived.

CHAPTER 3

Public Ethics and Political Philosophy

3.1—HUMAN ACTIONS AND MORAL ACTS: THEIR JUDGMENT BY THE VALUE CRITERION

I have already mentioned that human *actions* and *moral acts* are the product of the outward and inward activity of the *power*, respectively (ch. 1.1.1.2; Fig. 1.1), and that they can be judged by *specific criteria* (i.e., criteria specific to actions and to moral acts) as well as by the *value criterion*, applicable to the products of all the three mind components (ch. 1.1.3; Table 1.1).

The judgment of actions and moral acts by the value criterion will be discussed in the pages that follow.

3.1.1—Distinction of Actions into Particular and · Universal by the Value Criterion

Like ideas and sentiments, *actions* can be judged by the *value criterion* by assigning them a place in a continuum, ranging from "particular" to "universal" actions. Yet, contrary to ideas and sentiments, which can reach universalization in the mind of a single individual (such as a scientist or a poet), actions performed by a single individual are always *particular* actions. To become *universal*, the actions need cooperation between individuals, i.e., an action is universal if it is performed by *all* (or *most*) the individuals belonging to a class, who follow some rules or laws. Here class of individuals means all the individuals belonging to a community. It follows that the *degree of universalization* of human actions will increase with the increase in the size of the community whose members perform their actions by following the same rules or laws, i.e., going from the City to the Region, to the

State, and, prospectively, to the Universal Republic.

3.1.1.1—Society as the Result of the Universalization of Human Actions

3.1.1.1.1—The Origin of Human Society

Most thinkers have attempted to explain the origin of human society by resorting to the theory of *social contract*, conceived either as a historical event or, more convincingly, as a metaphor. It has been pointed out that the agreement on which the contract is based may be directed to maximize self-interest (Hobbes 1651; Buchanan and Tullock 1962; Gauthier 1986), a doctrine that has been named *contractarianism*; or it may be directed to affirm some shared rational or moral assumptions (Kant 1797; Rawls 1971; 1993), a doctrine that has been named *contractualism*. Moreover, both self-interest and rational or moral assumptions can be regarded as those conceived by the stakeholders as they actually are (Buchanan and Tullock 1962; Gauthier 1986) or by idealized (more intelligent, sensible, informed, educated, etc.) stakeholders (Rawls 1971). I will discuss in the next chapters the views of the main proponents of the doctrine of the social contract; here, as mentioned elsewhere (Belfiore 2004: 245), I note that two concepts are basic to this doctrine: *(a)* the *contract* would be a *contingent* agreement freely stipulated by men living in the original "state of nature" (which, in the most extreme conception, is viewed as a war of all against all); *(b)* the contractors agree to give up part of their rights to a sovereign government in order to reach a *scope*, i.e., to gain some benefits, be they a better defense of their *self-interest* or the adherence to some *rational or moral rules*. The limitation of rights in favor of the government may be extended or relatively small according to the authoritarian conception of the social contract (Hobbes 1651; Rousseau 1762), or the conception based on a more limited role of government (Locke 1690; Kant 1797; Rawls 1971), respectively. In contrast to this theory, I think that the organization of human beings into a society is not *contingent* but *necessary*, and its scope is not to gain some *benefits* but to reach the *universalization of actions*.

To clarify this point, we should recall the conception of the mind as an evolving entity made of intellect, sensitiveness, and power, whose evolution mainly consists of the progressive universalization of ideas (from particular ideas to fully universal ideas, as are scientific laws), sentiments (from particular sentiments to fully universal sentiments, as are those expressed in literary, musical, and visual arts), and actions (from particular or individual actions to the fully universal actions, as are those exerted by all the members of a large community such as the State or the supra-national organizations). Universalization of actions can only occur if individuals organize themselves into a community or society in which all members will perform similar and coordinated actions, by following some *collectively shared* laws, rules and commands, in this way developing their power. In contrast, a man who lives in isolation has only very little power and his actions are just individual or particular.

The above reasoning shows that society is not the result of a free and contingent agreement (contract) but is rather the necessary result of the structure and functioning of the mind. In fact, the mind components tend to develop or to evolve toward universality: in this way, the intellect evolves to produce science, the sensitiveness evolves to produce arts, and the power evolves to produce society with its institutions and laws.

Universalization of actions takes place through the organization of individuals into a *society* and through the creation of public *institutions*; this is closely associated with the creation of *laws* and to the process of *adjudication* (laws and adjudication will be treated in Ch. 4).

The *universalization of actions* may be of *various degrees*. Indeed, although the concept of "degree" of universalization may appear odd at first, it should be considered that the term "universalization" refers to something that can be extended to *all the members of a class*, which, as concerns actions, means *all the members of an organized community*. Since communities can be ordered into a sequence according to their increasing extension (mini-communities, cities, provinces, regions or lands, States, and supranational organizations), it follows that, between the individual and the State (or the supra-national organizations), there are intermediate steps with an increasing degree of universalization. Likewise, in the spheres of *intellect* and *sensitiveness*, between the particular idea and the fully universal scientific law, or between the particular sentiment and the fully universal sentiment (as expressed in literary, musical, and visual arts) there are intermediate states of universalization of ideas and of sentiments.

The *full* universalization of human actions will be reached when all men will organize themselves into a Universal State. As noted elsewhere (Belfiore 2004: 247), human nature is such that not only do humans organize themselves into States, but they also tend to a Universal State which includes all men; this tendency is shown by the proneness to establish international relations between the existing States; these relations, whichever their initial character (even a non-friendly one), always represent the first step toward a progressively more developed relationship, prelude to a true Universal State. In our time, the "United Nations" (or U. N.) is the institution that better represents the tendency of human actions toward full universality. [A further detailed discussion of human society can be found in my recent book: *The Democratic Society and Its Founding Concepts* (2012: 16–306)].

*3.1.1.1.2—Relationships Between Communities of Different Degrees of
　　　　Universality*

Here I will consider the relationship between communities of increasing
extension, which, if we consider both political and non-political communities, include: *(a)* the single individual, regarded as a single-member community; *(b)* family, relatives, friends; *(c)* associations of various nature (cultural, economic, professional, sports, charitable, etc.); *(d)* enterprises, trade associations, etc.; *(e)* universities, banks, etc.; *(f)* cities and their institutions; *(g)*
provinces, regions, lands, etc., and their institutions; *(h)* the State and its
institutions, and the international organizations and institutions (Table 3.1).
Each of these communities has its rules or laws that define the universal
actions that can be performed within it. In other words, the rules and laws of
a community define and limit the *allowed freedom of action*; the latter can
be conceived as an absence or removal of any limitation of one's right by
others (Berlin 1969; Narveson 1988), or as the right to act in an autonomous
and conscious manner, according to one's principles (Young 1986; Benn
1988; Dworkin G. 1988), although these are actually two complementary
aspects of freedom.

　　The allowed freedom of action must be defined referring to each of the
communities into which society is organized. As noted elsewhere (Belfiore
2004: 249), a hypothetical individual who lives alone in the world would be
free to do what he wants and what he can, which means that no other man
(who does not exist in this hypothetical condition) interferes with his actions, which, therefore, are limited only by the resistance of the physical
world. His actions, however, are particular actions. When a man meets another man, both are attracted by the possibility of enhancing their power by
exerting parallel or converging actions, which is possible if they follow
some rules upon which they agree. At this point, a mini-society is born and
some common rules exist; this entails that actions can now be distinguished
into *individual or personal actions* (performed by a single individual according to his own wishes and will) and *common actions* (those regulated
by the common rules). Now, the single man is free to perform personal actions that do not interfere with those of the mini-society, whereas the mini-
society (the two men together) is free (or has the right) to exert common
actions, without interfering with individual ones. Thus, any of the communities mentioned above (associations, cities, States, etc.) is free (or has the
right) to perform those common actions allowed by the rules on which the
community is based, without interfering with the actions exerted by other
communities of a higher or a lower degree of universalization or by single
individuals.

Table 3.1. The structure of human society as made of communities and institutions of increasing "degree of universality" (which represent the increasing universalization of *actions* and *moral acts*, produced by the *power*)

COMMUNITIES	DEGREE OF UNIVERSALITY (MEANING)	NATURE OF THE BINDING RULES	CHAPTERS[1]
The individual	Minimal (*Support of power* to mixed activities)	Private: Rules created by the individual for himself	3.1.1.1.2; 3.1.2.3.3
Family, relatives, friends	Very small (*Support of power* to mixed activities)	Private: Rules (unwritten) stirred-up by natural or affective links	3.1.1.1.2; 3.1.2.3.3; 3.1.1.2, *2bc*
Associations (professional, sports, charitable, etc.)[2]	Middle-low (*Support of power* to mixed activities)	Private: Rules (written or unwritten) that regulate relationships of various nature	3.1.1.1.2; 3.1.2
Universities: -Economics, Political Sciences, Law Departments; -Scientific Depts; -Art Depts. Scientific and cultural associations	Middle-high (*Support of power* to the activity of *intellect* and of *sensitiveness*)	Intermediate: Rules that regulate relationships concerning the activity of intellect and of sensitiveness	3.1.1.1.2; 3.1.2
Banks Enterprises; Trade associations; Consumer associations, etc.	Middle-high (Ways of the *ECONOMIC organization of the activity of power*)	Private: Rules that regulate relationships of economic nature	3.1.1.1.2; 3.1.2; 3.2.3.2, *1b*
Cities (and their institutions)	High (Ways of the *POLITICAL organization of the activity of power*)	Public: "Laws" that regulate public life in a city	3.1.1.1.2; 3.4.1.1, *1*
Provinces, regions, lands, etc. (and their institutions)	Very high (Ways of the *POLITICAL organization of the activity of power*)	Public: "Laws" that regulate public life in provinces, regions, lands, etc.	3.1.1.1.2; 3.4.1.1, *1*
State (and its institutions); International Institutions (e.g., U. N.)	Maximum (Ways of the *POLITICAL organization of the activity of power*)	Public: 1. "Laws" that regulate public life in a State; 2. "International agreements"	3.1.1.1.2; 3.1.2; 3.4.1.1, *1*

1. In this column, references are given concerning the chapters in which the various kinds of "communities" are discussed.

2. Among "associations", we could include minority groups (ch. 3.1.1.2, *2a*) that exist in many modern Western societies.

Indeed, the various communities, and the rules on which they are based, may be ordered in a scale of *increasing degree of universalization*, going from the single individual to cities, province, regions, States, and international organizations. Thus, it can be stated that *each community* (including the single individual, considered as a one-member community) *is allowed (or has the right) to exert those actions defined by the rules on which the community itself is based, which should not interfere with the rules of other communities of a smaller or a greater degree of universalization.*

It is noteworthy that the various communities with increasing extension should be conceived as *ontologically distinct entities* reflecting the functioning of the mind, whose evolution takes place through progressive stages of universalization. It follows that each community is autonomous and free within its sphere of action but should not interfere with communities of higher or lower degree of universalization. This is because, since legitimate rules are those shared by the largest possible percentage of the members of a community (see next chapters), any attempt to enforce in a community rules that define actions which have not been agreed upon by that community, but by a different one, would be illegitimate. This is especially true for the possible interferences with the smallest possible community, the single individual. For this reason, as pointed out by Locke (1689; 1690), freedom (allowed by rules or laws of the community) is a fundamental right of the individual, and any limitation of freedom must be justified (Mill 1859; Gaus 1996). The only justification for limiting individuals' freedom should be based on the laws agreed upon by the members of the various communities with different degrees of universalization, which ranges from the single individual to the city, province, region, State, and international organizations.

3.1.1.2—Public Selfish Actions versus Public Moral Acts as the Binomial Motor of Human Society

In this chapter I will discuss two issues: *(1)* dualism between public selfish actions and public moral acts, and *(2)* finalities of public moral acts.

(1) Dualism Between Public Selfish Actions and Public Moral Acts. I have already stated (ch. 3.1.1.1.1) that society is the result of the tendency of human actions toward universality; it follows that political activity in society should follow the universality principle which, in real life, should be conceived as the *principle of the best approach to universality* (ch. 3.1.2.1). This means that public actions, and the laws that regulate them, should express the projects shared by the largest possible percentage of citizens. On the other hand, public actions are directed to affect mind evolution of the citizens; therefore, they are indeed public *moral acts*, directed to implement public moral projects (as are or should be laws), under the pressure of moral

feelings. This "moral activity", however, may be associated to actions directed to ends different from the common good, i.e., to satisfy (legitimate) desires or interests of single individuals or groups or political parties; these public actions are "selfish actions", opposed to "moral acts". Thus, we can say that society is driven by a binomial motor or by a duality of forces: "moral" projects and acts (morality) versus "selfish" projects and actions (selfishness). This expresses the *bi-directionality of the mind activity* (chs. 1.1.1.2.4; 1.1.2; 1.2, *A1a*) as well as the *unity-distinction* that links its two kinds of activities: its outward-selfish and inward-moral activities.

It is of note that both morality (or consciousness) and selfishness may be morally "good" or "bad". Selfishness is "good" if the individuals and groups that act in society fulfill the duties toward themselves (chs. 2.1.5.2.2; 2.2.1.6.3), consisting in promoting the development of their own minds while avoiding restraining other minds' evolution (*morally-good selfishness or egoism*); if selfishness leads to an abuse of the rights of others, thus restraining the evolution of their minds, it would be *abusive* or *morally-bad selfishness* or *egoism*. Likewise, morality is morally good if it is directed to promote mind evolution in the agents themselves and/or in others (*morally-good morality*), whereas it is morally bad if it is directed to impose to others a given arbitrary moral standard not shared by the majority of citizens, as it may occur in non-democratic societies (*oppressive* or *morally-bad morality*). In society, what is needed is the integration of the morally-good morality and the morally-good selfishness; this means that the *public-moral* activity should also be directed to favor the (good) *private-selfish* one.

The selfish activity of individuals, groups, parties, etc. includes the economic activity, which is studied by the complex discipline named *economics* (Hausman 1994; Davis et al. 1998; Arrow et al. 2002; Hausman and McPherson 2006). The economic activity concerns the outward (selfish) actions exerted by individuals or groups or parties that, however extended they may be, are always only a part of the community; therefore, their actions cannot reach a full degree of universality, i.e., they will always concern only a class (however large) of citizens. Moreover, the economic selfish actions are directed to the "objects of the external world"; even when they are directed at other individuals, they consider them as "objects" that may favor or impede the reaching of desired ends, without considering their interiority and their nature of *conscious evolving minds*, i.e., of persons. Conversely, moral activity includes both the moral acts directed to promote mind evolution as well as the morally-good selfish actions; it follows that moral activity reaches a higher degree of universality than selfish activity. Indeed, *universal actions* (or the actions that are the best approach to universality) as exerted in the political activity are at the same time *public moral acts*, as they are directed to affect the mind evolution of citizens; they are directed to the mind as a whole, which represents the most evolved among the existing entities. It follows that the public moral acts of politics should reach, or at least approach, *full universality* because they are directed to *all* (or most) citizens and because they, being directed to affect the minds of citizens, include all kinds (or classes) of possible actions and acts.

From the above, it follows that the *moral activity* of the mind (consciousness) is *superior* to the *selfish activity* (or selfishness), because the latter is unable to reach and to include the mind as a whole (ch. 2.1.2, *B*). Indeed, we could say that moral activity regulates and limits selfish activity. Hence, politics is superior to the economic activity; the latter is regulated and limited by politics, because politics (but not the economic activity) is concerned with the mind as a whole.

It should, however, be stressed that the primacy of politics over economic activity can be achieved and defended in the sphere of a given State. In the present time, economic activity has expanded to a supranational dimension (it has reached a significant degree of globalization), whereas political activity is still primarily based on States, and international institutions are still not fully established. In this unbalanced situation, economic activity may attempt to overcome politics or to exert undue pressure on it.

It should also be considered that, when we evaluate events occurring in society, we should distinguish *private* (personal or of group) moral responsibility, referring to actions exerted by individuals or by groups in their private life, from *public* moral responsibility, referring to moral acts exerted by public institutions and public officials or by citizens in the public life.

(2) The Finalities of Public Moral Acts. As mentioned elsewhere (ch. 3.1.2.5.1, *3*), public moral acts should be directed to pursue the mind evolution of all citizens and to ensure that all citizens concretely enjoy the evolution-allowing, involution-avoiding condition. Besides this, it should be noted that the organization of single individuals into a society and the pursuing of the best approach to universality in the public activity is something morally good in itself. This is because it represents the *evolution* from particular, individual actions to universal, public actions (universalization of human actions), inasmuch as the particular actions of individuals become universal actions of the community. In other words, the organization of individuals into a society represents the *evolution of the power*, which, together with the evolution of the intellect (from particular ideas to universal scientific laws) and of the sensitiveness (from particular and light sentiments to universal and deep sentiments, as are those expressed in literary, musical, and visual arts), forms the *moral good*. For this reason, respecting the laws and avoiding breaking the legal system in a democratic, constitutional State is morally good, i.e., is in accord with the *ground moral norm*. Conversely, breaking a law, besides other effects linked to the specific moral value that any law protects, has the general morally-bad consequence of contributing to undermine the good functioning of the legal sys-

tem which, being the means through which human actions approach universality, has an intrinsic moral value.

The above reasoning applies not only to the whole society or to the State, but also to the smaller or informal communities, including *(a)* minorities, *(b)* family, and *(c)* other mini-communities (see also: ch. 3.1.2.3.3; Table 3.1).

(a) Minorities. In a democratic, constitutional State, minorities are those groups that, for various reasons (political, ethnic, religious, cultural, etc.), may not share some habits and traditions of the majority of society. In these groups, there may be particular customs, usages, and ways of life that act as unwritten rules, which may give rise to expectations; as such, these unwritten rules should not be unexpectedly ignored (without having first discussed the matter with the people with whom an agent interacts), because this may cause damage in those people who expected that those rules were respected. Even the habits and tradition of the society as a whole may give rise to expectations and, therefore, to some moral responsibility.

(b) Family. A family is a mini-community with rules established by tradition, rooted in deep human sentiments, and recognized by the State legal system. Therefore, abandoning children, besides an act of private immorality, should be regarded as an act that breaks the existing legal systems, both the mini-system represented by the family and the larger one represented by the State, which is morally bad (see above).

(c) Other mini-communities. A promise is like a law or rule issued in a mini-community made of two or some members [the promisee(s) and the promiser(s)]. Indeed, a promise creates a mini-society formed by the promisee and the promiser. Failing to keep a promise has two morally negative effects (see also chs. 2.2.1.4.2, *D4*; 2.2.1.7.2, *C1*; 3.1.2.3.3): *first,* it may cause a damage (mind involution—involution of power in the case of a promise concerning an economic matter) to the person who expected the promise to be kept and who organizes his activity on the basis of this expectation; *second,* it breaches the mini-society that arises from the promise (a mini-society made of the contractors and regulated by the "rule" of which a promise essentially consists). Since society is the way through which human actions evolve toward universality, any breach of rules that govern a society, including the rule of a promise, is morally bad (it has a moral meaning somewhat similar to that of breaking a law of the State—see above). Therefore, promises are a source of moral (as well as legal) obligation.

3.1.2—Social Institutions

We already know that individuals organize themselves into a society in order to make it possible to achieve the *universalization of actions*, generated by the *power*. This organization of individuals into a society gives rise to *social institutions*, which represent the forms under which the power organizes its functioning. Here the term "social" means "consisting of, or referring to, a community made of two or more individuals" (this term could be extended to include the single individuals if we consider the individual as forming a mini-community in which he has relations with himself). When considered in a broad sense, the institutions can be distinguished into various types (Table 3.1). The following distinction is worth some comment.

(1) Institutions Belonging to the Power. Some institutions are part of the power itself and represent the social structures under which the *power* organizes its activities. They include: *(a) political* (and administrative) institutions of the State, Regions, Cities, etc., which are concerned with all the members of the respective communities; and *(b) economic* institutions (banks, concerns, industries, trade associations, etc.), which represent the forms under which various groups of individuals organize their power.

(2) Institutions Belonging to the Relationship of Power with the Intellect and the Sensitiveness. These are the institutions that represent the support of the power to the functioning of the intellect and sensitiveness (required because of the interrelation between the various mind components—chs. 1.1.1.1, 6; 112, 2nd proposition). They include: *(a)* the institutions which represent the support of the power to the intellectual activity directed to understand or to know the functioning of the power itself (such as university faculties or study centers of Economics or Political Sciences); *(b)* the institutions that represent the support of the power to the activity of intellect in various scientific fields and that comprise a wide range of entities such as universities (scientific faculties), research centers, scientific associations, etc.; and *(c)* the institutions that represent the support of the power to the activity of sensitiveness (artistic activity), such as universities (art faculties), art academies, etc.

3.1.2.1—The "Principle of the Best Approach to Universality" and the Public Justification of Social Institutions

Considering *(a)* that individuals organize themselves into a society in order to achieve the *universalization* of their actions, and *(b)* that the degree of universality of the products of the mind components is evaluated by the *value criterion* (Table 1.1), it follows *(c)* that *the degree of universality of a social institution should be evaluated by the value criterion*. This criterion allows judging whether a rule (or law) and the action that it regulates is a *particular* one (i.e., referring to and exerted by a single individual or a few people) or is a fully *universal* action (i.e., referring to and exerted by *all* the members of a community). Moreover, from the conception that society and the institutions into which it is structured have the scope of achieving the universality of actions (and of the corresponding *projects*), it follows that only the institutions that express truly universal actions (and projects) are justified. Thus, in the case of a State government, the *full* public justification would entail that the laws (and the corresponding actions) on which that government is based and according to which it functions are agreed upon by *all* the members of that State.

However, as noted elsewhere (Belfiore 2004: 251–52), the achievement of full universality is a fortunate but highly improbable condition; therefore, we can say that a social or political institution, say a government, is publicly justified if the laws on which that government is based and according to which it functions are agreed upon by the largest possible *majority of the members* of the community or society (organized into a State), which represents the largest possible degree of universalization, or *the best approach to universality*. This is realized in today's Western democracies through political voting (by universal suffrage) by which parties that enter political competition are divided into the majority party (or parties), which becomes the party in power, and the minority party (or parties), which becomes the opposition party.

The above reasoning allows us to make the statement that *the public justification of a government lies in the universality of the actions regulated by its laws*; however, considering that full universality is never reached in the real world, we may state that *a government is publicly justified only if the actions defined by its laws express the highest possible degree of universality*. In other words, we can put forward the *principle of the best approach to universality of public actions*.

Since in a large community "direct democracy" (i.e., decisions taken by all the members of a community) is not possible, public actions are regulated by the laws enacted by the "government", which represents the community. This entails that a government, to be publicly justified, must actually reflect the largest possible majority of community members. Moreover, considering that *power*, as all three mind components, is a continuous *changing and evolving entity* (see the 4th proposition defining the mind, in ch. 1.1.2), a mechanism is required in order to verify that the government in charge actually reflects the changes that, through time, occur in the projects and aspirations of the largest possible percentage of community members. From the above considerations, the following two points ensue (Belfiore 2004: 251–52).

(1) In order for *continuous change* to be possible, a verification process, represented by political voting, must be repeated at specified time intervals to cope with the changes occurring in the mind of the community members, including both the members belonging to the majority party and those be-

longing to the opposition party. The time interval for the election of the assemblies that issue ordinary laws (such as the parliament) must be rather short (3, 4, or 5 years) to allow that changes in the mind of the members of the community are timely reflected in the kind of majority that is in power. On the other hand, for the constitutional norms, which concern general principles and values of long-lasting validity, no fixed time interval should be established for the verification of their validity, and changes should be introduced when requested by a large majority of citizens or their representatives, through special procedures provided for by the constitution itself.

(2) The majority party, which is in power, must guarantee freedom (within the existing laws) and must respect and consider the activity and the opinions of the minority party, which is in opposition. This is because, if the opposition party is oppressed, it cannot grow and possibly gain the power in the future, i.e., a possible *change* in the political government is prevented, which is against the evolving nature of the mind. Moreover, the participation of the minority party in the political life of the government enhances the general relevance of government acts, which become closer to a full universality, i.e., *it enhances the degree of universality* of government acts. My proposal of a *gradational democracy* (ch. 3.1.2.1.2) is directed to enhance the participation of the minority party in political activity.

3.1.2.1.1—Advantages of the "Principle of the Best Approach to Universality of Public Actions"

My conception of society, based on the *principle of the best approach to universality of public actions*, has the merit of avoiding some problems that arise with the social contract theory, which have prompted the formulation of various proposals (Rawls 1971; Gaus 1996; Hampton 1997; D'Agostino and Gaus 1998). Indeed, my conception makes any exclusion of individual or groups irrational and unjustified, because any exclusion prevents the achievement of the full universality of actions, which is the fundamental scope of society and of its institutions. This is true both of the risk of selecting those entitled to be part of the contract (Vallentyne 1991), which might favor the predominance of a race (Mills 1997) or of a gender (Pateman 1989), and of the risk of excluding those who cannot reciprocate the benefits gained by contracts, such as poor or disabled individuals (Kittay 1999). Exceptions may only be extreme cases, such as those of severely mentally disable individuals, unable to make any decision and to adhere to a rule or law (the problem of the severely mentally disabled people should be solved on a moral basis). Another issue has been raised (Hampton 1997), concerning the possibility that poor, despairing initial conditions of those involved in the stipulation of the contract may lead to acceptance and even to justification of bad regimes such as the totalitarian ones. Again, I note that, by following the above-stated *principle of the best approach to universality of public actions*, this is possible only if the majority of contractors, for exceptional reasons, actually want to *transitorily* support a totalitarian government; however, if such a government refuses to subsequently submit itself to the judgment of citizens by the voting process, in order to verify if it still represents the largest possible majority of the community members, it becomes unjustified, because the laws and the actions of such a totalitarian government could no longer be regarded as the best approach to universality. However, the danger that poor and despairing conditions of citizens, as hypothesized by Hampton (1997), may prompt them to make bad political decisions is real.

3.1.2.1.2—The "Best Approach to Universality" and the Proposal of a "Gradational Democracy"

In a democratic system, the degree of the approach to universality (both for the approval of a draft bill or for the election of a candidate) is measured by the percentage of favorable votes. It follows that any percentage of votes greater than 50% may be regarded as the best approach to universality, because even a percentage of 50.01% represents a better approach to universality compared to the alternative possibility, which, in this instance, has necessarily obtained less than 50% of favorable votes. Now, focusing our discussion on the approval of a draft bill, the problem arises as to whether it is justified that a law approved with, say, 51% of favorable votes (and against 49% of unfavorable votes) should be obeyed by *all* citizens (as any law should be). Before further discussing this issue, it should be remembered that, outside the field of mathematics, physics, and chemistry, "full universality" is an unreachable end in all spheres of human activity. Referring to the sphere of knowledge, we can say that in biology or medicine, scientific laws have only a statistical valence, and scientific previsions are based on probability rather than on certainty (ch. 1.1.3.2.1) (e.g., diagnoses and prognoses of a physician are made on statistical and probabilistic bases); things are even worse in the field of social or psychological sciences. In other words, a large part of human activity is marked by *approximation*. Likewise, referring to the sphere of politics, full universality (say, 100% of favorable voted obtained by a party or by a draft bill) is an unreachable end or a rare event. Yet, we should strive to attain the *best approach* to universality, which, as stated above, may go from 50.01% to the unreachable 100% of favorable votes. This means that there is a very large range of "degrees of universality". This entails that, in cases of low degrees of universality, a significant percentage of citizens (up to 49.99%) may consider a law as imposed by a small majority; to some extent, this means that there is the danger of a sort of "dictatorship of the majority". This danger should be reduced by the moral responsibility of the majority to recognize and respect the rights, opinions, and activity of the minority party, in order to pursue the greatest possible degree of universalization of its political actions (ch. 3.1.2.1). This, however, will depend on the choices of the majority and, therefore, cannot represent a guarantee for the citizens belonging to the minority party. In order to limit the consequence of this unavoidable lack of full universality, I propose the following scheme of a democratic system that could be named *gradational democracy*.

It should be recalled that the various "laws" can be hierarchically ordered according to the extension of the moral principles and values that they express and the numerousness of the citizens whom they concern (ch. 4.1.2.3; Figs. 4.2 and 4.3). This is confirmed by the distinction, recognized in many democratic States, into constitutional norms (considered as supreme) and ordinary laws. Usually, the constitutional norms are approved or modified by a qualified majority (often, by a two-thirds majority) and, sometimes, through a special procedure (e.g., double voting with a fixed time interval). I think that this distinction of "laws" into two categories (constitutional and ordinary laws) does not suffice, and I propose that a third or a fourth category be added, according to the schemes expounded below, under points "*1*" and "*2*", for the reasons given under point "*3*".

(1) 1st Scheme of Gradational Democracy: Three Ranks of Laws. "Laws", understood in a broad sense, should be divided into three categories or ranks: *(a) norms* (or 1st rank laws), which should include those "laws" that express moral principles and values and that, therefore, pursue the various "moral goods"; *(b) major laws* (or 2nd rank laws or, simply, *laws*), which should include those "laws" that implement moral principles and values expressed by norms; and *(c) minor laws* (or 3rd rank laws—or *rules*, according to the terminology I use in ch. 4.1.2.3 and in Fig. 4.3), which should include those laws that concern the implementation of the major laws and all those minor laws required for a routine legislative activity. These three categories of "laws" should be approved by majorities of votes of different extents: norms, major laws, and minor laws should obtain more than 80%, 65%, and 50% of favorable votes, respectively (Fig. 3.1, top panel). A system based on these different percent values of favorable votes would assure that the major laws are enacted with the involvement of a large percentage of representatives and, hence, with the contribution of at least a part of the opposing party. Of course, these are only proposed percentages, which are rather arbitrarily fixed. They are based on the consideration that the difficulty in obtaining the number of favorable votes required for passing a law increases with the increase in the percentage of favorable votes that should be exceeded; in practice, it is difficult to obtain a

percentage of favorable votes higher than 80%. Moreover, while fixing a high percentage of required favorable votes assures that the minority part is involved in the major decisions, when the percentage of required votes is too high (say, 95%), even small groups may prevent the approval of a good law; thus, the balance between opposing demands should be taken into account.

An important point is that a law of lower rank cannot be in contrast with a law of higher rank, because the former is part of the latter and serves to implement it (ch. 4.1.2.3; Fig. 4.3).

The above reasoning refers to the enactment of "laws" by a legislative assembly (parliament), i.e., to legislative power. Yet, the same concepts should also be applied to executive power; to this end, administrative acts should also be divided into three categories of decreasing importance, and each Ministry (or Department) should be directed by a Minister, who should be the president of a council made of six members (including the Minister), which should be elected by the citizens in such a way as to roughly represent the parties (or groups of parties) present in the political arena. This would allow that decisions are taken with one of three possible degrees of universalization, represented by a minimum of 3, or 4, or 5 favorable votes (in the first instance, the three votes should include the vote of the Minister, which should have a special "weight").

(2) 2nd Scheme of Gradational Democracy: Four Ranks of Laws. This scheme would differ from the 1st one because "laws", according to their "weight", would be divided into four categories or ranks: *(a) norms* (or 1st rank laws), *(b) major laws* (or 2nd rank laws), *(c) middle laws* (or 3rd rank laws), and *(d) minor laws* (or 4th rank laws—or *rules*). In this instance, the minimum percentages of the favorable votes that should be exceeded for enacting the four categories of "laws" should be: 50%, 60%, 70%, and 80%, respectively (Fig. 3.1, bottom panel).

Concerning executive power, administrative acts should also be divided into four categories of decreasing importance, and each Minister should be the president of a council made of eight elected members (including the Minister). This would allow that decisions are taken with one of four possible degrees of universalization, represented by a minimum of 4, or 5, or 6, or 7 favorable votes (in the first instance, the four votes should include the vote of the Minister, which should have a special "weight").

A similar subdivision of "laws" into three or four categories and a distinction of three or four minimum percentages of favorable votes required for taking decisions should be adopted for *bylaws* enacted by *local* and *regional governments*.

I am aware of the fact that the distinction of "laws" into three or four categories is a very difficult matter. Yet, I think that the task of a philosopher is to create a scheme and indicate the finalities of a democratic-constitutional system, whereas its practical implementation should be accomplished with the contributions of experts in the fields of legal, political, economic, and social sciences; these multiple contributions are required to fix the many concrete details of this complex process, whose characteristics may also change according to the country involved and the stage of its evolution.

A central point is that the distinction of laws into ranks should be established by a "1st rank law", i.e., by a constitutional norm, which, as such, is approved by the highest of the required percentages of favorable votes.

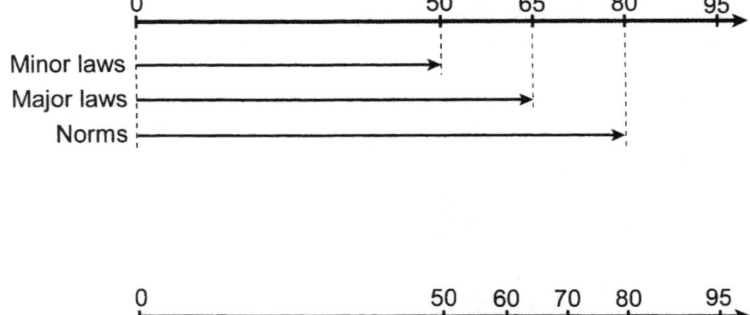

Fig. 3.1. Proposed minimum percentages of favorable votes that should be exceeded in order to pass the various categories of "laws", i.e., "laws" of different rank (see the text for explanation).

(3) Reasons for Adopting the Proposed "Gradational Democracy". I will shortly discuss the following points.

(a) Experience accumulated through decades indicates that often, governments in Western democracies are elected by a very small majority of votes. When the difference between favorable votes and unfavorable ones is very small, it may merely express a difference occurred by chance, which means that a true majority does not exist. Yet, a government so elected is entitled (actually has the duty) to handle all kinds of affairs and to take any kind of decision, including such potentially disastrous decisions as that con-

cerning the initiation of a war or the participation in it. This might be felt by the minority as an undue imposition. Indeed, a government that, actually, has been elected by chance, can drag the governed country into risky ventures. The system that I propose will reduce to a minimum the percent of citizens who suffer from undesired and much-demanding laws, because it provides a mechanism through which "laws" have a *degree of universality* roughly proportional to their importance for the life of society. This would enhance the social stability and cohesion.

Referring to the case in which a government is elected by a very small majority of votes, someone could object that my proposal, by limiting the function of such a government to just the enactment of "minor laws" and the accomplishment of minor administrative acts, would greatly limit the political activity of a country, as it would produce a sort of semi-paralysis. My answer would be that this is by no means a negative effect of the proposed system, but is actually a positive consequence, as it entails that the extent of activity of a government is roughly proportional to the degree of the majority that supports it, i.e., the extent of the activity of a government reflects the "political reality" of the country; if the population of a country is politically indecisive, so should be the activity of its government. The awareness of this consequence may stimulate the voters to take clearer decisions.

(b) There is, still, another positive consequence of the system that I propose, inasmuch as it allows us to solve some difficult problems that can arise in public life. Suppose that a candidate to a central public office (e.g., the office of Premier) is elected by a majority of, say, 55% of votes and that he is indicted and then sentenced by a court for a wrongdoing he has committed (here I ignore the important issues of whether the indictment or the sentence occurs before or after the election, and whether the sanction includes the disqualification from holding public offices). Here a difficult situation has arisen: should the "sentence of the court" prevail (in which instance the elected candidate should leave the office)? Or should the "will of citizens" prevail (in which instance the candidate should retain his office)? The system that I propose provides us with a rule for settling this problem. If this problem arises in a country where there is the system with three categories of "laws", described above (point "*1*"), then one should consider whether the "law" in accordance with which the candidate was condemned belongs to the category of the *norms* (approved by a majority of votes higher than 80%), or to that of *major laws* (approved with a majority of votes comprised between 65 and 80%), or to that of *minor laws* (approved with a majority of votes comprised between 50 and 65%). If the law in accordance with which the sentence has been passed is a norm or a major law, then it possesses a higher degree of universality than the "decision" expressed by citizens through the voting (55%); if the law in accordance with which the sentence has been passed is a minor law, then its degree of

universality is similar to that of the decision expressed by citizens. In this instance, however, the law should prevail over the decision of voters based on the principle that, *with regard to specific, particular decisions, the will of representatives should prevail over that of represented citizens* whereas with regard to general and simple choices, the will of citizens should prevail (as is the case when simple decisions are taken by a referendum). However, intermediate cases may occur, for which it may be uncertain which solution should be adopted. The principle just mentioned is based on the fact that, compared to citizens, representatives have the duty to devote more time and more care in studying the specific matter about which they have to decide and, therefore (conditions being equal), their decisions are superior to that of voting citizens. Another reason is that representatives make general decisions that must be officially defended, which means that representatives must take a public responsibility for their decisions, contrary to the voting citizens, who are "protected" by the secrecy of the vote. Moreover, it should be considered that the voters' decisions are *short-term decisions* (lasting 4 or 5 years) whereas the decisions expressed by the laws are *long-term decisions*. Only in the case that the percent of votes obtained by the candidate (say, 70%) is higher than the percent value of favorable votes required for the approval of the law in accordance with which he has been condemned (say, >50% or >60%) should the decision of the voters prevail. Another possibility would be to compare directly the percent of favorable votes obtained by the candidate and the percent of favorable votes by which the law (in accordance with which he has been condemned) was approved. This, however, would mean to make too particular evaluations, which might entail to give significance to very little difference in the percent of favorable votes that may be the result of chance. Moreover, there is a more serious point to be considered, i.e., that what actually counts is not the percentage of favorable votes obtained by a law, but the awareness of the voters (parliament members) about the rank of the proposed law that should be approved or rejected. Thus, a "minor law", even if approved with, say, 90% of favorable votes, is always "inferior" in rank to a "norm", which is approved with, say, 82% of favorable votes. This is because the distinction of laws into ranks should be a constitutional "norm" (1st rank law), which, as such, has been approved with a high percentage of favorable votes and, hence, should prevail over a "minor law", whichever the percentage of favorable votes obtained, by chance, by the latter.

However, what I think is significant is that the above reasoning suggests a possible criterion for *comparing the degree of universality* of public choices, which enables us to evaluate competing "decisions" (in the example given above: the decision of parliament and that of the voters).

[The above reasoning applies only to those politicians who occupy a central political office, for which all citizens of the country are asked to express their vote, because those who occupy non-central political offices, for which only the citizens living in a given part of the country (a city, a region, etc.) can give their vote, even if they are elected with a high majority of the "local" votes, are actually elected by a small percentage of the citizens of the entire country; hence, for them, the law in accordance with which they might have been condemned should always prevail].

3.1.2.2—The "Voting Act" and Its Meaning

3.1.2.2.1—Making the "Voting Act" Free and Responsible

The public justification of a government is based on the voting process, i.e., on the choice made by each adult member of a community about the political program to be realized and about the persons who should realize it. The simple action of voting, as simple as it is, requires that each citizen possesses: *(1)* a minimum of ability to perform *actions* (created by the *power*); and (due to the relationship of power with intellect and sensitiveness) also *(2)* a minimum of *knowledge* (created by the *intellect*) as well as *(3)* a minimum of *desire* and interest toward public life (created by the *sensitiveness*) (Belfiore 2004: 259–60). I will briefly discuss these three points, and then I will add, under point *(4)*, a short comment.

(1) The Role of Power. The need for a minimum of *power* to make the vote meaningful is undeniable. Indeed, some economic power, which can be symbolized by private property or, more generally, by money, is needed because if an individual is extremely poor so that he has not even enough money to support the alimentary need of himself and his family, he will not be able to spend money (i.e., he has not the power) to access the necessary information about community life (say, by buying newspapers, books, and a television set). Some thinkers have underlined that an individual may significantly participate in a voting if he is free and that freedom is closely related (or in fact coincides) with private property as linked to a free-market economy (Hayek 1978; Gaus 1994a). This system, however, may lead to an equilibrium entailing a high rate of unemployment (Keynes 1936), so that economic systems in which a significant control role is played by (a democratic!) government has been envisaged (Rawls 1971). I think that the role of the government should consist in assuring that all citizens enjoy the evolution-allowing condition (ch. 3.1.2.5.1, *3*).

(2) The Role of Intellect. The participation of *intellect* is required in order to ensure that each member of the community acquires as much information as possible. To this end, community members should have the power and freedom to access free and pluralistic education system and they should also be able to benefit from free and pluralistic information, including free-

dom of speech, of press, and of the information broadcasted by radio and television. The right to free and pluralistic information is very important. The reason for this lies in the fact that information spread by the press and television can be regarded as the continuation of education in the historical, social, economic, and political fields. However, education given in Schools and Universities primarily concerns events of the past for which, through time, experts have gained enough knowledge and have reached or approached some degree of agreement in interpretation and evaluation. In contrast, recent social, political, and economic events are still in progress or have too short a history, so that a minimum of agreement about their interpretation and evaluation is not available. For this reason, the only possible way to make citizens aware of the current events in public life is to provide them with pluralistic information, i.e., with information, interpretation, and evaluation coming from diverse sources and therefore expressing different points of view, so that citizens can draw the conclusions that they find more appropriate. Freedom of press is important to the point that some thinkers have maintained that journalists should enjoy special rights, such as the rights to protect the confidentiality of their sources of information (Dworkin 1978), to be protected against liability for defamation (Stewart 1975), to obtain and publish information about trials (even if the judges believe that this is not compatible with a fair trial), and to seek and publish information that may appear to violate the privacy of persons (Murphy and Coleman 1990: 89). It has been pointed out, however, that the right of citizens to know what a reporter has discovered should be exerted with caution because it has many implications (Dworkin 1978).

(3) The Role of Sensitiveness. The participation of *sensitiveness* is required to enable each member of the community to feel the desire and interest for the life of the community. Both knowledge and interest concerning public life depend on the natural endowment of the individuals and by the stimulatory effect exerted by the education system.

(4) Comment. From the above it is apparent that the public justification of a government, i.e., its democratic nature, is linked to the vote given by citizens. In an ideal world, it would be possible to have a fully justified (i.e., a fully democratic) government supported by the totality (100%) of votes, given by absolutely independent, completely informed, fully motivated voters, i.e., by voters expressing a *fully-reasoned, deeply-felt, and enduring decision.* Yet, in the real world, under the pressure of momentary and superficial beliefs, desires and interests, voters may express a *little-reasoned, impulsive, and mutable decision.* Thus, the ideal conditions rarely occur; often, each of them is only partially realized. Thus, it is highly improbable that the following conditions are all satisfied to a full extent: *(a)* concerning the sphere of the *power*, that each voter is not affected, at least to some extent, by the pressure of more or less "potent" individuals or groups with which he

is linked by relationships of various nature; *(b)* concerning the sphere of *intellect*, that each voter is informed in an absolutely complete and objective manner; *(c)* concerning the sphere of *sensitiveness*, that each voter is so keen on political life to devote all his knowledge and utilize his power (independence) in order to give a free and responsible vote. What actually happens is that the above conditions are fulfilled to a certain extent; it follows that there is no government that can be judged as *fully* democratic, but each government can only be assigned a given place in the scale that goes from "totally non-democratic" to "fully democratic". Thus, instead of asking: is government "*x*" democratic? One should ask: which is the degree of democracy of government "*x*"? Due to the parallelism between the mind components, the impossibility for a government to be fully democratic is similar to the impossibility for scientists to know everything and for artists to create any possible form of art. This is because the evolution of the mind toward more evolved states is an endless process. In practice, each legal system has its legal procedures that ensure that a political voting can be judged as democratic or not. This is somewhat similar to the legal definition of when one comes of age; although laws can fix the limit at, say, 18 years, actually this depends on many factors, such as natural endowment, degree and nature of education, emotional experiences, good or bad examples of relatives and friends, and other environmental factors. Thus, laws provide a practical means to decide in a yes-or-no manner in matters where, from the philosophical standpoint, only approximate evaluation referring to a continuum scale of values can be made. It is to be hoped that with the evolution of the mind of the various communities, there will be a progressive evolution toward ever-higher degrees of democracy in the various "democratic" States, even if a "perfect" democracy will never be reached.

It should also be recalled that, since mind evolution also includes the evolution of consciousness, it is to be hoped that evolution toward an ever-higher degree of democracy is associated with an evolution toward an ever-higher moral content of the activity of democratic governments.

3.1.2.2.2—The Meaning of the "Voting Act"

The democratic system based on universal suffrage, in which each individual gives one vote, has been criticized as a system that ignores the difference between individuals by assigning equal weight to the vote of a valued personality (say, a great writer or a keen scientist) and to that of an illiterate and stupid person. This, however, is by no means true. As noted elsewhere (Belfiore 2004: 251), in democratic, vote-based systems, each person gives one vote but may also, at the same time, affect the vote of other people, such as relatives, friends, colleagues, acquaintances, and still other community members, with whom he interacts, with whom he discusses political issues, and on whom he exerts his cultural influence. This influence will certainly be greater in the case of an educated and intelligent person than in the case of an illiterate or stupid one, and is roughly proportional to the "cultural weight" of each individual. The value of personality is, thus, preserved (unless the valued individual decides by himself not to exert any influence). Thus, the vote should be regarded as the minimal, basal "unit" to measure political weight, and represents a right that should be recognized to each adult citizen of a democratic State.

Rather, the reverse may be true, i.e., that the very rich or potent individuals may exert an excessive weight in political life; the same may be true, according to Posner (1990: 354–55), for "organized groups" (ch. 4.2.5, *C1a*). In this regard, I recall that Hart (1961: 195) maintained that an approximate equality in strength is required to make possible or even necessary "a system of mutual forbearance and compromise which is the base of both legal and moral obligation." He also believed that "no individual is so much more powerful than others, that he is able, without co-operation, to dominate or subdue them" (Hart 1961: 195). In my opinion, such approximate equality may exist with regard to physical strength but not with regard to the *power* of the various individuals, and the possibility should be considered that some individuals or groups acquire an excessive power, which may interfere with the normal functioning of a democratic State. Indeed, I think that very potent individuals or groups might exert undue pressure over the government and other social or political institutions, and might even be able to overcome the control by the legal system, thus undermining the fundaments of democracy. For these reasons, a limit to the economic power of individuals or groups should be established by specific laws, which should have the rank of constitutional norms (see ch. 3.2.3.2, *1a*). I underline that, to this end, laws against monopolies do not suffice, because even respecting these laws, individuals or groups may reach an excessive power. It is the task of experts in economics, sociology, political science, and law, to establish the *upper limit of allowed economic power*; the scope should be to avoid that the powerful individuals or groups reach so high a power to be able to threaten the authority of the State. Moreover, the most powerful citizens should be prohibited to access political competition to become members of the legislative or executive organs, by fixing an *upper limit of economic power for accessing political competitions*. Of course, these limits should be high enough to avoid that they restrain free enterprise and the selfish activity linked to the *morally-good egoism* and the duty toward oneself (ch. 2.1.5.2.2). In this regard, it should be considered that, beyond a certain limit, the further growth of economic power is no longer supported by the active *selfish forces* that stimulate the economic activity. However, a solution should be envisaged for those individuals or groups that reach the allowed upper limit to avoid that they could feel economically damaged.

3.1.2.3—The "Rating" of Actions (and of the Laws that Regulate Them) and the Public Justification of Power

3.1.2.3.1—The Rating of Actions and of Laws

I have already discussed that, by applying the value criterion, actions (and the laws that define them) can be evaluated, or rated, as far as their degree of universality is concerned, i.e., they can be assigned a value in the continuous scale that goes from particular actions (performed by one or a few individuals) to a fully universal action (performed by all the individuals of a given class, which may be represented by the citizens of a city, a province, a region, or a State) (ch. 1.1.3.2.3; Table 1.1). Two kinds of "universality" (and two kinds of "degree of universality") should be considered for an action and for the law that regulates it: *(a)* the degree of universality as expressed by the extension of the class of individuals who (in a various percentage) support that action and the corresponding law (e.g., the classes formed by the citizens of a city or a region or the entire State), and *(b)* the universality expressed by the percentage of the citizens (within a given class) who support that action and the corresponding law. Thus, a public action corresponding to a law enacted by a city government may be supported by 80% of the citizens of that city, thus possessing a relatively high degree of universality; yet this action/law has a lower degree of universality compared to an action corresponding to a law enacted by the State government of which a city is part, because the state is made by a larger number of citizens than a city (actually, a city can be considered as a sub-class of the class of individuals represented by the State).

Thus, as concerns the degree of universality of law within the class of citizens that has enacted it (cities, regions, or the State) (see above—point "*b*"), the correct rating is given by the percentage of votes supporting it. Yet, since modern democracies are representative democracies, each law results from two interrelated orders of votes: the votes given by all citizens to a general political program promoted by a political party, and the votes given by the members of parliament for passing the various bills.

3.1.2.3.2—Publicly Justified Power

From the above discussion, it follows that a government (and therefore the laws that it enacts) is publicly justified if it is supported by the highest possible percentage of votes, which means that it possesses the highest possible degree of universality or that it represents the best possible approach to universality.

On the other hand, a modern society is structured into several levels of government (cities, provinces, regions, and the State) and, therefore, can be regarded as having a *pyramidal structure*, inasmuch as in it there are communities composed of an *increasing* number of members allowing an increasing degree of universality, each with a certain number of rules (and corresponding actions) governing the community that has created them. Based on the number of members, at the apex of the pyramid we could place the *single-individual*, whose rules concern the various actions that a single individual can perform in his private life; then, there are the cities and provinces, with their own rules and actions; at a more general or universal level, there are the regions (or lands), and then the State, each with its own rules, laws, and norms regulating public actions (Table 3.2).

As noted elsewhere (Belfiore 2004: 255), the laws of each of these communities, while concerning all its members, cannot interfere with the rules/actions internal to the communities of higher or lower degree of universality. This is because such interference would be a case of *wrong-rating* of rules and actions, and therefore it would be *violence* (see below). This means that the State cannot interfere with the rules/actions created by the provinces or cities in which it is structured and concerning the internal lives of these communities. Of course, the State can interfere with the government of a minor community (say, a city government) that claims to impose its rules and actions outside its sphere of activity or its territory, say in the entire State, because this would be a case of wrong-rating of the rules and corresponding actions by the city government.

The problem of the relationship between the *individual rights* and the rules or laws of the community, which has been debated by several thinkers (Gaus 1983; Benn 1988; Kymlicka 1989b), should be discussed in this context. It should be stressed that each law is justified in the community that created it, i.e., that supports it by the majority of its member. Therefore, the actions promoted by an individual (with the possible exception of non-adult or mentally non-healthy people), if they are actions that do not interfere with those of others, cannot be limited by the community laws, be they laws of State or city government or other institutions, as any such limitation would be arbitrary *violence*.

Table 3.2. The pyramidal organization of political communities with increasing "degree of universality" (i.e., number of members), in a hypothetical State composed of 20 individuals

COMMUNITIES WITH INCREASING DEGREE OF UNIVERSALITY	SPHERES OF INFLUENCE[1]																			
Individuals (twenty)	1	2	3	4	5	6	7	8	9	10	11	12	13	14	15	16	17	18	19	20
Cities (four) (Low degree of universality)	The rules of this city concern 5 citizens					The rules of this city concern 6 citizens						The rules of this city concern 4 citizens				The rules of this city concern 5 citizens				
Regions (two) (Intermediate degree of universality)	The laws of this region concern 11 of the 20 citizens											The laws of this region concern 9 of the 20 citizens								
State (one) (High degree of universality)	The laws of the state concern all the citizens (20 individuals)																			

1. Note that the legitimate sphere of influence of the laws and rules is that exerted within the boundaries that limit each box. Any attempt to extend the influence outside this box, in any direction, i.e., crossing the boundaries that delimit the spheres of legitimate influence, would be violence. In other words, violence arises when the law-regulated actions of a community extend their effect to other communities of higher or lower degree of universality, whose members have not agreed upon the (offending) law-action.

3.1.2.3.3—Informal Mini-Communities

In this chapter, I will briefly comment on *(1)* informal mini-communities that exist in a society, and *(2)* the effects of breaking the rules on which these mini-communities are based.

(1) The Various Types of Informal Mini-Communities. These are the small communities that arise from unwritten agreements, or from habits and traditions, or from natural affective links; they may be transitory or relatively stable. Apart from the "single individual", which could in principle be regarded as a single-member community whose member is only related with himself, informal mini-communities include the following entities (Table 3.1).

(a) Mini-communities arising from an oral agreement made between two or a few individuals, consisting of a (reciprocal) promise or on giving one's word; these mini-communities create the relation promisee-to-promiser. An agreement made between two individuals gives rise to the smallest possible mini-community.

(b) Mini-communities arising from an event linking two or more individuals, such as lending money, which create the relation creditor-to-debtor.

(c) Mini-communities arising from habits or traditions, such as the trust relation between host and guest, or the parish (or vicar) and a parishioner, or the teacher and his students, or between colleagues, etc. [The role of these trust relationships is recognized by most legal systems, which consider breaching these relations as an aggravating circumstance in case of wrong-doing].

(d) Mini-communities arising from natural affective links, such as the family (based on motherly, fatherly, and filial love), or relatives, friends, colleagues, etc.

These informal mini-communities are founded on unwritten or tacitly accepted rules that, like the written rules of formal, official communities, should be respected because they create obligations and corresponding expectations. They may also include the cases of *promissory estoppels* (Kessler and Gilmore 1986), i.e., cases where legitimate expectations are induced without explicit promises.

(2) Effects of Breaking the Unwritten Rules of Mini-Communities. The agreements made between two or more individuals, or the tacitly accepted rules arising from traditions or natural affective links, are actually the rules on which a mini-community is founded. Breaking such rules has the following morally negative effects.

(a) Failing to respect a rule of an informal mini-community (such as failing to keep a promise, or to respect the duties as a father, etc.) will cause mind involution in those involved individuals who expected that the rule be obeyed and who organized their activity or their life on the basis of this expectation. This mind involution may refer to involution of power (i.e., economic damage, as in the case of the debtor promise) or to involution of power and/or intellect and/or sensitiveness, according to the nature of the broken rule.

(b) Rules on which informal mini-communities are founded are rules tacitly issued (and shared) by the members of the mini-community, and should be observed for the same reasons that other rules, laws or norms should be (chs. 3.1.1.2, 2; 4.2.1.2.2), i.e., because failing to keep a promise produces the objectively bad effect of breaking or destroying the mini-community. Since any kind of "society", including mini-communities, is the way through which human actions evolve toward universality, any breach of rules that govern a society is morally bad, because it induces an *involution*

of the degree of universalization of the agents' actions (which change from "social" actions into "individual" actions), i.e., it induces an *involution of the power*, which is against the precepts of the ground moral norm.

(c) The unwritten or tacitly accepted rules on which mini-communities are founded should be respected because any action of one individual that breaks the tacitly agreed-upon rules is an example of wrong-rating of actions, inasmuch as an action by one individual, which as such is an *individual action*, is rated as if it is a rule of the mini-community (i.e., it is imposed to all the members of the mini-community); therefore, such an action is actually a *violence*.

(d) Finally, it should be pointed out that most mini-communities entail a close relationship between its members (e.g., the relationship between the members of a family), which has moral relevance for reasons linked to the concept of the spheres of decreasing moral responsibility (ch. 2.1.5.2.1)

3.1.2.4—"Arrogance", "Violence", and Publicly Unjustified Power

As the correct rating of laws (and of the corresponding actions) is the ground of justified political *power*, so the *wrong-rating of laws (and of corresponding actions)* is the ground of unjustified political power, which actually consists of *arrogance* and/or of *violence*.

Arrogance consists of publicly unjustified collective moral *projects/decisions*, i.e., of unjustified laws (laws are publicly-shared projects—ch. 4.1.1.1), as are the laws enacted by authorities who do not represent the majority of citizens or the laws that are not correctly rated (ch. 3.1.2.3).

Violence consists of public *actions* exerted as implementation of publicly unjustified laws, i.e., of publicly unjustified collective projects.

Both arrogance and violence also occur in the field of private morality, when individuals make projects/decisions unjustified by the existing laws and when they turn these projects/decisions into practice through actions.

Thus, *arrogance and violence consist of a wrong-rating of laws and of corresponding actions by the value criterion* (Table 1.1), and are opposed to the publicly justified *power*, based on laws approved by the majority of community members, and on the corresponding actions. Thus, the opposition of correct versus wrong rating of actions actually means opposition of *power* versus *violence*.

As noted elsewhere (Belfiore 2004: 255–56), wrong-rating of laws and actions may occur both *(1)* within a community and *(2)* between communities of different degrees of universality; in both instances, wrong-rating of laws and corresponding actions may consist of *(a)* over-rating or *(b)* under-rating.

(1) Wrong-Rating of Laws and Corresponding Actions Within a Community.

(a) Over-rating. This happens when a party that is not the majority party (or a mini-community or a powerful group of individuals or even a single individual) attempts to impose its "laws" and the corresponding actions to the entire community.

(b) Under-rating. This occurs when the government of a community (be it a city, a region, or a State) attempts to impose its laws (and corresponding actions) to the *social institutions* or to the *informal social groups* existing *within* that community and therefore possessing a lower degree of universality (entities that include diverse institutions, associations, etc., and that may be of various nature: economic, cultural, religious, etc.), down to the single individual, thus limiting their liberty and disturbing their activity and, therefore, interfering with their autonomy (within the general laws). In this regard, it should be underlined that the "central power" cannot know the needs and desires nor can it substitute the creativity and richness of initiatives of the several political entities, the many economic and cultural organizations, and the innumerable individuals that belong to a large community. It follows that wrong-rating of laws and political actions is a *violence that is often associated with incompetence.* A historical example of an extremely centralized power (associated with a non-justified government) that interfered with the activity of citizens and of various social structures through a centrally elaborated plan can be found in the communist Russia and East European countries (before the events of 1989); with time, the centralized plans have proven to be ineffective (ch. 3.2.8.1.1).

(2) Wrong-Rating of Laws and Corresponding Actions Between Communities of Different Degrees of Universality.

(a) Over-rating. This happens when a community attempts to impose its laws or rules (and the corresponding actions) to a community of a higher degree of universality. This kind of wrong-rating occurs when the government of, say, a city attempts to impose its laws over and against the laws of a (legitimate) government of the region or of the State.

(b) Under-rating. This happens when a community attempts to impose its laws or rules (and the corresponding actions) to a community of a lower degree of universality. This is the case when, for example, a State government attempts to impose its laws to the internal affairs of a region or of a city (or when a regional government attempts to impose its laws to the internal affairs of a city), thus interfering with its autonomy (within the general laws of the state). In these instances, the term "under-rating" is justified because a law of, say, the State, which has a high degree of universality, is regarded as if it is a law of a community with a lower degree of universality, such as a region or a city, and therefore valid within the sphere of activity of that community (region or city).

Under-rating of laws, referring to the tendency of central governments to regulate the life of smaller communities, is often associated with the tendency to implement centrally-governed, radical, fast, and complex changes. Against this tendency, some thinkers (Popper 1945; Hayek 1976) underline that any government should consider the fallibility of any assumption due to unavoidable ignorance of most particular facts and should refrain from sharp and fundamental changes in favor of small progressive adjustments. While this is a fully justified view, I would note that it is, in part, covered by the concept of under-rating of laws (which entails *violence* and is unavoidably associated to *incompetence*—see also above), and is in some way linked to the concept of the *approximation* and *imprecision* of human knowledge and forecasting (ch. 1.1.3.2.1).

(3) Comments on the Wrong-Rating of Laws and Corresponding Actions. It should be underlined that the distinction into the several communities with different degrees of universality should be regarded as an *ontological distinction*, because it represents the forms under which the power, as a mind component, organizes itself in a given historical period.

Wrong-rating of laws and corresponding actions regularly occurs in the States governed by tyrannical regimes. Yet, it is noteworthy that wrong-rating may "informally" occur also in apparently democratic regimes when powerful economic or political groups, associations, or parties make undue pressure in a soft manner to impose laws and actions that favor their interests, outside the sphere of their legitimate competence.

Wrong-rating of actions (which are created by *power*) may be compared to wrong-rating of ideas (created by *intellect*) or of sentiments (created by *sensitiveness*). Over-rating occurs when particular ideas are proposed or presented as universal ideas or scientific laws, or when the expression of particular sentiments is proposed or presented as the expression of universal sentiments (literary, musical, and visual arts); under-rating occurs when universal scientific laws or great artworks are regarded as particular ideas or as an expression of particular sentiments, respectively.

Wrong-rating of actions (as well as of ideas or sentiments) is morally blameworthy, because it, by interfering with the liberty and autonomy of individuals or groups or institutions or other social entities, restrains mind evolution. It may be performed as a consequence of a distorted conception of political power, i.e., as a result of a *bad moral thought*, and/or as a consequence of a *bad moral feeling*, or both (ch. 2.1.4.1).

3.1.2.5—Ethics and Politics, Duties and Rights

3.1.2.5.1—The Ethical Aspects of Politics: The "Evolution-Allowing Condition" as the Public Moral End

(1) Ethics and Politics. As underlined by Mackie (1977: 235), ethics and politics are concerned with choices, actions and interpersonal relations, so that the choice of a political goal is essentially a moral choice. Indeed, any kind of law-regulated actions of citizens should be considered at the same time *(a) universal and collective moral acts* directed to induce a change (which, in a democratic State, should consist of evolution) in many minds, i.e., in all or most members of the community, and *(b) universal* (or *shared*) good *selfish actions* directed to satisfy the desires or interests of the acting agents. They are a *collection* of universal moral acts because they are the sum of several single moral acts stirred-up by shared moral feelings and thought (as expressed by the laws), made by all or most citizens (moral acts are always the product of single individuals—ch. 2.1.2, *A1*). They are *universal/hared* selfish actions in the sense that they are actions that, though directed to satisfy the desires or interests of some agents, or groups, or parties, are integrated with universal moral acts (the term "universal" is, then, here used in the sense of "integrated with universal moral acts"). This is because *selfish* actions (directed to satisfy the desires or interests of the acting agents, groups or parties) and collective *moral acts* (which, together with the selfish actions, determine political activity) do not necessarily oppose each other. Indeed, selfish actions, if exerted by respecting the norms and laws of a democratic State, are in accordance with the law-regulated collective moral acts, as they express the *morally-good egoism* (or *morally-good selfishness*) and the duty toward oneself (ch. 2.1.5.2.2). Thus, universalized selfish actions and collective moral acts should be *integrated together* (ch. 3.1.1.2, *1*). Indeed, *public-moral* acts have the scope of favoring the (good) *private-selfish* actions. Only the selfish actions that interfere with the actions of others, thus restraining their mind evolution, are against the moral norms as well as against the norms and laws of a democratic State.

From the fact, discussed above, that law-regulated actions or social events are at the same time "*universal (shared) selfish actions*" and "*universal and collective moral acts*", it ensues that *politics and morality cannot be distinguished from each other.*

(2) Ethics and Political Parties. From the above, it follows that in the political activity, the selfish and the moral component should be harmoniously integrated together, as the morally-good selfishness is part of the moral good and, therefore, is included in the demands of the ground moral norm. In the real world, this ideal harmonious integration is rarely fully achieved. This entails that, although political parties justify their identity

based on several aspects of their political programs, there are only two fundamental and enduring political positions (see also Belfiore 2004: 262; 2012: 307-408), as outlined below.

(a) Prevalence of *moral thoughts* and *feelings* (and hence of *moral principles* and *values*, which define the *duties* to others, especially the duty of *equality* of opportunity), over *selfish (personal or group) ideas, desires and interests*, directed to promote the evolution of the acting agents by ensuring the enjoyment of *rights* and of *freedom* of initiative; shortly, this means prevalence of *morality/duties/equality* over *selfishness/rights/freedom* (this is the position usually known as political Left).

(b) Prevalence of *selfish (personal or group) ideas, desires and interests* over *moral thoughts* and *feelings*, leading to a reverse situation, which is characterized by the prevalence of *selfishness/rights/freedom* over *morality/duties/equality* (this is the position usually known as political Right). The point is that both situations can be good or bad according to whether what prevails is the "good morality" (adherence to the shared moral standards while respecting freedom) and not the "oppressive morality" (imposition of an arbitrary moral standard to all while restraining freedom); or the "good selfishness" (defense of rights and freedom while respecting the duties and the equality of opportunity) and not the "bad selfishness" (defense of rights and freedom while ignoring duties and equality). This distinction of the two driving forces of political life is based on the bidirectional functioning of the mind (selfish ideas and sentiments created by the *outward mind activity* versus moral thoughts and moral feelings created by the *inward mind activity*—Fig. 1.1).

The above reasoning indicates that political parties should be evaluated according to a political as well as a moral criterion. The *political criterion* is linked to the prevalence of morality/duties/equality over selfishness/rights/freedom or vice versa. The *moral criterion* is linked to the prevalence of the *good* versus the *bad* morality, or of the *good* versus the *bad* selfishness, as defined above.

The distinction that I propose is based on *ideals* (e.g., pursuing the common good, in accord with the prescriptions of the ground moral norm, which entails pursuing freedom, social justice, and solidarity), which are immutable *ends*. In contrast, the old political distinctions were based on *ideologies*, which are *methods* or *procedures* to reach an end and which, as all procedures, have effects that change with the changing situations in which they are applied; in the political field, the effects of procedures change according to the conditions of society and the degree of its evolution. Moreover, procedures refer to actions, moral acts, and practical activities that should assure the reach of some ends but that, actually, are marked by uncertainty, as the effect of all human actions and acts can only be probabilistically foreseen. Thus, in the evaluation of a political party, one should consider two factors: *(a)* the ideals or ends pursued (common good versus selfish interests), and *(b)* the method(s) proposed to reach the pursued ideals or ends. While the judgment based on the pursued ideals should be categorical, denying legitimacy to those parties that pursue bad selfish interests or oppressive morality (which are both against the common good), between parties pursuing good ideals or ends but differing for the proposed methods there should be a fair confrontation and competition directed to convince citizens that the proposed program is preferable to the competing one(s).

(3) The "Evolution-Allowing Condition" as the Public Moral End. From the above discussion, it follows that the prevalence of good over bad *moral thoughts and feelings* and/or of good over bad *selfish (personal or group) ideas and desires/interests* leads to the creation of laws directed to promote the common good (*mind evolution* of most citizens). This goal can only be reached by following the norm that prescribes to ensure that every individual concretely enjoys the *evolution-allowing, involution-avoiding condition* (described in ch. 2.1.5.3); this means that ensuring that all citizens concretely enjoy this condition should be the public moral end of a democratic State. It might seem, at first, that the enjoyment of the evolution-allowing condition is equivalent to the enjoyment of the human rights, as defined in the "Universal Declaration of Human Rights" (U. N. General Assembly, 1948). But this is not true (see also Belfiore 2012: 22-23, 303).

[By summarizing the U. N. declaration, we can say that it states that everyone has the following main rights: to life, liberty and the security of person; not to be subjected to torture or to cruel treatment; to be equal before the law; to a remedy by a tribunal for acts violating his rights; to a fair and public hearing by an independent and impartial tribunal; to the respect of his privacy, family, home, correspondence, honor and reputation; to freedom of movement and residence; to seek and to enjoy in other countries asylum from persecution; to own property; to freedom of thought, conscience and religion; to freedom of opinion and expression; to freedom of peaceful assembly and association; to take part in the government of his country; to equal access to public service in his country; to social security and economic, social and cultural rights indispensable for the free development of his personality; to work (under just conditions), to free choice of employment, to protection against unemployment, to just and favorable remuneration; to a standard of living adequate for the health and well-being of himself and of his family, including special care and assistance for motherhood and childhood; to free education].

Certainly, all the rights recognized by the U.N. are required for mind evolution. However, while nobody could question the goodness of each of the rights included in the U. N. declaration, it is also true that no philosophical justification or foundation is given for them; this entails that one could ask: Why should these rights be respected? Which are their ends? How can they be concretely implemented? These questions could not be asked concerning the pursuing of the evolution-allowing condition for all citizens. Indeed, as mentioned in ch. 2.1.5.3, ensuring the enjoyment of the evolution-allowing, involution-avoiding condition means much more than ensuring the enjoyment of the universal *human rights*, because of the following motives: *(a)* it is the prescription of a moral norm solidly grounded on ontological bases, which gives the *reason* why this condition should be enjoyed and requires a *morally active behavior* (and not merely a passive recognition of the rights of others); *(b)* it consists in pursuing a well-defined *end* (mind evolution), which is the objective moral good; and *(c)* it makes possible that the *various goals* and the means to reach them be conceived in a flexible way, by taking into account both the extremely diverse natural endowments of individuals and the concrete conditions (degree and specificity of development) of each citizen and of the society as a whole.

Being prescribed by the ground moral norm, the requirements of the evolution-allowing condition should be conceived as duties of the moral agents, rather than as rights of the recipients or, better, as rights/duties. Thus, we could say that the requirements of the evolution-allowing condition consist of the *universal human rights/duties justified by moral reasons, aimed at the objective moral good, and flexible in their practical implementation.*

It should be underlined, however, that even more important than the enjoyment of the condition allowing mind evolution is the enjoyment of a condition that avoids mind involution. In this regard, of basic importance is preserving the existence of the mind and avoiding its partial or total involution, i.e., avoiding physical harm or death, which represent "possibly irreversible" and "extreme and irreversible" mind involutions, respectively. Thus, the rights to life and to health should be given priority over any other right.

Defining the various goals to be pursued in order to realize the evolution-allowing condition is difficult in practice, and entails some degree of uncertainty (as always occurs with matters concerning the human world—ch. 3.1.2.5.3). Indeed, defining the evolution-allowing condition by taking into account the diverse situations occurring in a given society may require the contribution of experts in various fields. Yet, these difficulties may entail uncertainty about the details of the choices or the methods to follow, but not about the ends to be reached.

It is of interest to contrast the prevalence of morally-bad selfish desires/interests with the prevalence of morally-good thoughts and feelings. The prevalence of morally-bad selfish desires (although limited by constitutional norms) may interfere with fundamental rights of minorities while favoring the interest of the individuals belonging to the majority party, and in particular some of them (extreme individualism). Conversely, the prevalence of morally-good thoughts and feelings (i.e., of moral principles and values) cannot have this effect (at least in a democratic society with an evolved common consciousness), since moral thoughts and feelings, as stated above, lead to the creation of laws directed to promote mind evolution of *all* citizens, by ensuring that all citizens concretely enjoy the evolution-allowing condition. Nor can the prevalence of moral thoughts and feelings lead to a limitation of individual freedom or of the spirit of enterprise, because the latter are required for the evolution of individuals (see the above-mentioned morally-good selfishness and the duties toward oneself—ch. 2.1.5.2.2) and are favored by the enjoyment of the evolution-allowing condition, which is the scope of those laws stirred-up by moral feelings.

3.1.2.5.2—Duties as the Source of Rights

We know that the ground moral norm prescribes the promotion of the evolution of the mind, including the agent's mind as well as the minds of others (even if to a different extent, according to the rule of the spheres of decreasing moral responsibility—ch. 2.1.5.2.1). If a citizen has the *duty* to attempt to develop his own mind he must have at the same time the corresponding *right* to enjoy those concrete conditions that make this possible. Likewise, the duty of all citizens to help the needy people to develop their minds (by enjoying the evolution-allowing condition) entails the corresponding right of the needy people to receive some help from the other citizens and from the State (chs. 2.1.5.2.2; 3.4.1.1, *2b*; 4.1.2.2). Hence, the duty of citizens to respect the "right of others" by contributing (e.g., through taxation) to such morally-good ends as social security, health service, etc.

3.1.2.5.3—The Imprecision in Defining Public Moral Ends and Norms as Source of Discussion and Diverse Opinions

In a previous chapter (2.1.4.2), I mentioned that the various moral goods (all of which are included in the "basic good" represented by mind evolution) can be hierarchically arranged into a system of classes and sub-classes (Table 2.1). I have already defined the basic public moral end (consisting in the enjoyment, by all citizens, of the evolution-allowing condition—ch. 3.1.2.5.1, *3*). The public basic moral end, and the various less comprehensive moral ends comprised in it, are pursued by following the various public moral norms (and laws, rules and commands) which, again, can be hierarchically ordered into a system of classes and sub-classes (ch. 4.1.2.3; Figs. 4.2 and 4.3). Thus, there is a parallelism between the various kinds of public moral ends (or moral goods) and the norms and laws that prescribe to pursue them. Since classes are defined by our intellect in an approximate and imprecise manner (ch. 1.1.3.2.1), so are the various classes of "moral goods" and of "moral norms". This introduces an "element of uncertainty" in the choices concerning public (as well as private) life. Uncertainty also arises from the imprecision with which the effects of human actions and moral acts can be foreseen. I have already discussed this issue concerning private ethics (chs. 2.1.6; 2.1.7). Here I will briefly consider the public aspects by discussing *(1)* the various public moral choices, and *(2)* the mechanisms of choices; then I will mention *(3)* some theoretical positions about uncertainty in public moral choices.

(1) The Public Moral Choices. These choices are similar to those made in the private moral life, which have been described in chs. 2.1.6 and 2.1.7, with the difference that they are made by public agents or by the citizens when they give their vote. Here, I briefly recall that these choices include the following ones (for more details, see Belfiore 2012: 410-19).

(a) The Ground "Morally-Certain" Moral Choices. These are the choices between pursuing morally-good ends (i.e., promoting mind evolution of all or most citizens) and the extent to which pursuing them, versus pursuing morally-bad egoistic ends, while restraining the mind evolution of other citizens. In the public sphere, these choices are made by the collective governmental organs and by their single members when taking public decisions. Similar choices are also made by the citizens when they make public choices by expressing their vote. Individual choices (by the members of collective organs or by citizens) are made through reflection (and discussion); collective choices (by collective organs) are made through harsh discussion (about morally-opposed ends) and the use of majority rule. These choices being between opposed ends, are *contrasting choices*. They are *morally certain* because the choosing agents know with certainty whether they want to act in the direction of the good ends (even if subjectively conceived) or not.

(b) The "Morally-Certain/Cognitively-Imprecise" Moral Choices. These choices concern which moral good to pursue first or most among those that compose the ground moral good (i.e., evolution of intellect, or of sensitiveness, or of power, or still less comprehensive moral goods); this requires the adoption of a priority criterion that is unavoidably uncertain. These choices may also concern the extent to which a given moral good should be pursued. These choices may be competing but not contrasting, since all of them point to a moral good. The choosing agents are again the collective organs, their members, and the voting citizens. Individual choices (by the members of collective organs, or by the voting citizens) are made through reflection (and discussion); collective choices are made through discussion (on the most needed moral good) and the use of majority rule. These choices are *morally-certain* (the choosing agents know whether they want the good) but *cognitively-imprecise* (due to the unavoidable uncertainty about

the knowledge of the actual needs of society).

(c) The "Cognitively-Imprecise/Predictively-Uncertain" Procedural Choices. These choices concern the selection of the most appropriate procedure(s) for implementing (to the decided extent) the chosen moral end(s). The various possible choices are *competing* but not *contrasting* among one another, because all of them are directed to select the best procedure to promote a given moral good (they could be contrasting if some of the proposed procedure were against the implementation of a good end, which entails a previous bad moral choice, of the type discussed above, under point "*a*"). The choosing agents, once again, are the collective organs, their members, and the voting citizens. Individual choices (by the members of collective organs, or by the voting citizens) are made through reflection (and discussion); collective choices are made through discussion (on the most appropriate procedure) and the use of majority rule. These are procedural, and not moral, choices (the moral end to be pursued has already been selected); moreover, they are *cognitively-imprecise* (due to the unavoidable uncertainty about the knowledge of the particular concrete conditions, and the ensuing needs, of the involved society) and *predictively-uncertain* (because the effects of any procedure, as those of any human action, can only be foreseen on an uncertain, probabilistic basis—see ch. 1.1.3.2.1, *3d*).

An example may be useful. Suppose that in a given State, there is a region whose population, for various reasons, suffers from unemployment and extreme poverty. The "government" may have no doubt that the poor and unemployed people should be helped, because this means promoting the evolution of their mind. Yet, the government is faced with the competing projects (possible laws that define *procedures*) directed to use the available resources to give unemployment benefits, or to favor the birth of a concern so that the unemployed can have a job, or to establish a vocational school to enable the unemployed to acquire some competence and thus to find a job elsewhere, etc. These possible projects and related procedures, although competing with one another, are not contrasting because all of them are directed to promote the evolution of the mind (mainly the power component of the mind) of the involved citizens. Contrast between projects would exist if one of the above projects were opposed by a project directed to extend taxation to the unemployed, which would further restrain the mind evolution of the involved citizens. Thus, concrete moral choices are characterized by *uncertainty* and can only be made as a result of reflections, discussions and debates involving the citizens and their representatives, and leading to *opinions* and not to certainties, which requires the adoption of majority rule.

(2) The Mechanism of the Choices. The ground moral choices are the result of the balance between the prevailing selfish desires and the prevailing moral feelings. The "objects" of both selfish desires and moral feelings are the objects, events, and facts of the world, and the beliefs about them

produced by the activity of intellect. Thus, both the emotional and the rational activities of the mind participate in the choices. Yet, while ideas and beliefs are marked by uncertainty and imprecision (see above), selfish desires and moral feelings, though they may contrast with each other, cannot be uncertain or imprecise (the agent is aware of his desires and feelings).

(3) Theoretical Positions About Uncertainty in Public Moral Choices. It is well known that the philosophical current known as *postmodernism* questions any truth-claim and the presumption of reaching an even approximately objective and shared knowledge concerning human facts (see: Natoli and Hutcheon, eds., 1993; Kramer 1997; Bertens and Natoli, eds., 2002; Drolet, ed., 2003; Malpas 2005). Starting from my conception of knowledge as a *subject-object relationship* (2004: 107–114), I have concisely treated postmodern philosophy elsewhere (2004:335–342). Here I note that, from what is said above (point *"1"*), it is apparent that imprecision and uncertainty concern the procedural choices and the choices regarding the priority to assign to the various moral goods (choices that can be made based on discussion and majority rule), but not the *fundamental moral choice* (to pursue the moral good or not), which is the choice that confers meaning to human life. In other words, we have certainty as concerns *general* moral ends, but have uncertainty as concerns the *particular* moral choices regarding the priority of the various moral good and the procedures for their implementation in a given concrete situation. This applies also to the claims of several thinkers (Gadamer 1976; Habermas 1979; Carr 1986: 60–65) who have emphasized the element of uncertainty in human life and maintain that, being a true foresight of human acts actually impossible, human experience has a narrative character, based on guessing, assumptions, discussions, and interpretations. This has led some of them to make assertions like "Morality which is no particular society's morality is to be found nowhere" (MacIntyre 1981: 265–66) (see also ch. 2.2.1.3.4, *B*).

Hermeneutics is another philosophical current that leads to uncertainty in the knowledge of human facts, as it maintains that facts should be interpreted (see: Mueller-Vollmer, ed. 1988; Ormiston and Schrift, eds. 1990; Grondin 1991). I have treated this issue elsewhere (2012: 429-32). Here I just note that, since every mind product is a *triplet* (see ch. 1.2), it can only be understood if we *interpret* it, i.e., if we attempt to discover the two mind products that support the one under scrutiny. Since, considering together the outward and the inward mind activity, each of the mind products can be regarded as a *sextet* (see ch. 1.2), for each mind product under scrutiny we should attempt to discover the five supporting ones. Politics being essentially a moral activity, what should mainly be interpreted are the public moral thought, feelings and acts of politicians and of political institutions. Thus, in order to understand human facts (in the public as in the private sphere), in addition to *observation* (direct or indirect) we need *interpretation*.

3.2—POLITICAL CONCEPTS AND THEORIES: CRITIQUE AND REINTERPRETATION

In this chapter, I will discuss some basic political concepts, as well as the main political theories [for a general reflection on political thought about ancient, modern, and post-modern theories see: Thiele 1997]. Besides an introductory discussion of the concept of human beings as members of the *class of men*, the issues considered include the concept of *equality* (and its relationship with *meritocracy* and *fraternity*) and that of *property*, while *liberty* (whose meaning at the individual level has been treated in ch. 2.1.4.2, *1*) will be discussed in its public aspects in the subsequent chapters, together with the various political theories. For each issue considered, I will expound my conception, together with the reinterpretation, from my point of view, of the thought and positions of some other authors; this is because it is my conviction that a thinker, who presents his own philosophical thought, has the duty to explain how his thought can be related to the ideas of others and, especially, how it allows to explain and reinterpret them.

3.2.1—General Concepts: 1. The Centrality of the Idea of Class to Understand Men and Society

The *concept of class* is central for the understanding of men and society; therefore, the reader is invited to bear in mind the points expounded in chapter 1.1.3.2.1, concerning the essential or shared properties that define a class and the particular properties that characterize its members.

In the chapters that follow, I will apply the concepts of "essential properties" (which are shared by all, or most, the members of a class and that define that class) and of "particular or individual properties" (specific of each member of a class) to the *class of men*. We already know which are the *essential properties* of the class of men, because we know that men are *evolving minds*, each of which consists of *intellect*, *sensitiveness*, and *power*. Each individual mind, however, evolves through particular and unique ways and up to a certain level, linked to his natural endowment (and to environmental factors), so that each individual differs from any other by his *degree and specificity of mind evolution*. Thus, the degree and specificity of mind evolution give rise to the *particular or individual properties* that define the personality or the identity of each human being. These concepts will be developed below, in chs. 3.2.2.1.1 and 3.2.2.1.2.

Besides defining the single personality, the particular or individual properties help us to also understand what a "community" is: a community consists of a group of individuals among whom the variations of some individual properties are less pronounced than among individuals belonging to different communities.

3.2.2—*General Concepts: 2. Equality*

3.2.2.1—Equality and Diversity

Society is regulated by laws, which means that laws regulate the activity of all citizens and, thus, affect the development of their mind components. Therefore, a basic problem related to the creation of laws is whether all citizens should be considered as *equal* to one another or not, i.e., the problem concerning the equality of citizens arises.

Based on my conception of the mind, equality should be referred to the mind components, i.e., to the intellect, sensitiveness, and power, and to their continuous becoming. Moreover, based on the concept of class (see above), human beings (and, therefore, the individuals who are citizens of a State) can be considered as the members of a class, the class of men, so that they must have *common properties*, shared by all men, and particular or *individual properties* specific to the single individual; this means that between individuals (or citizens) there are both *equalities* and *inequalities* or *diversities*, as will be discussed in the next two chapters.

3.2.2.1.1—*Equality of Human Beings: Their Common Properties and Universal Rights*

As we already know, all men share the common properties that define the class of men, i.e., they are conscious entities consisting of the same mind components (intellect, sensitiveness, and power) undergoing continuous changes, which, according to the ground moral norm, should be directed toward the evolution of mind. It follows that all men have the fundamental and indefeasible right to benefit from those concrete conditions required to allow the development of their mind (i.e., to enjoy the *evolution-allowing, involution-avoiding condition*).

The counterpart of this statement is that each man has the duty to promote or favor the development of both his own mind and the minds of the men with whom he interacts. Otherwise stated, all men have the duty of favoring mind development of all men (even if with the limitation linked to the rule of the "spheres of decreasing moral responsibility"). Hence, the following motto could be launched: *people of all the world, promote mind evolution of all people of the world!*

This means that all individuals have, to the same extent, the right to enjoy, among others, freedom, good education, free information, health services, and equal opportunity to access an adequately remunerated work. *These are the universal human rights*, which, in this way, are given a moral foundation (ch. 3.1.2.5.1, *3*). These rights are linked to the essential properties of the class of men, and their enjoyment means the enjoyment of the *evolution-allowing, involution-avoiding condition*. In fact, enjoying the rights just mentioned is the necessary requirement to make it possible for everyone to attempt to develop his mind components according to the moral norms, without any unjustified and arbitrary limitation.

The above definition of the fundamental rights that must be equally enjoyed by all men provides a solid basis to reinterpret several theories directed to explain equality between individuals, as will be discussed in the chapters that follow. As mentioned elsewhere (Belfiore 2004: 305), I just note that many difficult problems of the present time (such as migration, rebellions, and even some form of guerrilla warfare) are, at least in part, due to the fact that *too many people living in the so-called third world are deprived of the fundamental rights common to all men*, as they have no or very little possibility to develop, even to a minimum extent, their intellect (through education in the scientific field), their power (by means of adequately remunerated work) and their sensitiveness (through education in literary, musical, and visual arts, and by treating them with understanding and sympathy).

3.2.2.1.2—Diversity of Human Beings: Their Individual Properties and Rights

Although each man, as a member of the class of men, has properties common to all members of the class, each individual possesses individual characteristics, linked to the *degree* and *specificity* of the evolution of his intellect, sensitiveness, and power; thus, individuals (or groups) may differ from one another according to the following possibilities (see also, Belfiore 2004: 305–8):

(a) Prevalence of one mind component over the others. This means that an individual may possess the aptitude to primarily develop his intellect, and therefore he will mainly act in the broad field of knowledge; another one may possess the aptitude to primarily develop his sensitiveness, and therefore he will mainly act in the field of arts; still another may possess the aptitude to primarily develop his power, and therefore he will mainly act in the field of business or politics.

(b) Difference in the various activities of a given mind component. This means that, within the group of individuals who primarily develop intellect,

some may be more prone, say, to mathematics while others will prefer, for instance, biology or medicine or social sciences; among those who primarily develop sensitiveness, some will be prone to literary arts, others to musical arts, others to visual arts; among those who primarily develop power, some will be prone to business, others to politics or social relations, and so on.

(c) Degree of development of mind components. By enjoying the fundamental rights discussed above (ch. 3.2.2.1.1), i.e., by enjoying the evolution-allowing condition, each individual will reach a certain level in the scale of mind development. From this it follows that each individual has the right to affirm and express his own value (or degree of mind development). However, it should be stressed that assigning a place in the scale of mind values to a given individual is a very difficult task and is only possible if the fundamental rights discussed above (and, therefore, the evolution-allowing condition) are actually enjoyed to their full. In other words, one should distinguish the level of mind development actually reached by a given individual (or community) and the potential level, i.e., the level that would have been reached if the fundamental human rights had been fully enjoyed; otherwise, pretending to assign a place in the scale of mind values may become one of the greatest injustices that can be committed against a given individual (or community).

(d) Combination of multiple factors. Finally, differences among individuals (or communities) may be due to a combination of two or more of the above factors.

In real life, diversity is much more complex than it appears from the scheme just described, as it results from the almost infinite, different ways of thinking, the great variety of preferences and artistic creations, and the innumerable forms of habits, behaviors, and social assets. However, each individual (or group of individuals) has rights linked to his own individual properties, that is, linked to the degree and specificity of the evolution of his mind; these properties make him a unique member of the class of men. This means that each individual has the right to implement his own particular personality and therefore the right to unequal (individualized) treatment.

From the above discussion, it follows that there are universal human rights, linked to the common properties of the class of men, and individual (or group) human rights, linked to the peculiar properties of each member or group or community. For each right of individuals or communities there is a corresponding duty of the other individuals or communities to recognize and respect that right. Therefore, instead of talking about human rights we should talk of human rights/duties. Indeed, I think that we should give more weight to duties than to rights; this is because the recognition of the rights of others may be compatible with inactivity (or very little activity) of the moral agent, whereas recognition of our duties entails the obligation to be active moral agents. For this reason, instead of (or besides) the universal declaration of human rights, what is needed is a *universal declaration of human duties* (the duties linked to the moral obligation to promote mind evolution).

From the above discussion, it descends that *all individuals have the fundamental rights linked to the essential properties of the class of men* (properties that, as such, are common to all men); in addition, *each individual has the rights linked to his individual properties* that make him a unique member of the class of men, i.e., that make his personality. Therefore, there are *universal human rights*, linked to the common properties of the *class* of men, and *individual human rights*, linked to the peculiar properties of each *member* of that class.

3.2.2.1.3—Equality versus Diversity of Human Beings

From the above discussion, it follows that all human beings, as such, are bearers, to an equal extent, of rights linked to their common properties, i.e., as beings made of an evolving intellect, sensitiveness and power (and exerting both an outward and an inward activity); in addition, through life, each individual expresses personal merits and thus acquires individual rights, linked to his individual properties (degree and specificity of his mind evolution, as they result from *natural endowment* and *environmental factors*).

The balance between *(a)* the *common basal/universal* human value and rights and *(b)* the *individual/acquired* value (or merit) and rights is variously evaluated. In an ideal condition, in which each citizen concretely enjoys the evolution-allowing condition, and judgments are made in a wise and honest way, an equal weight should be conferred to the basal/universal and the individual/acquired value and rights (Fig. 3.2, top panel). In the real world, things are different. The super-individualist most often confers greater weight to the individual/acquired merits and rights and will minimize the basal/universal value and rights (Fig. 3.2, middle panel). In contrast, considering that in the real world the evolution-allowing condition is seldom concretely enjoyed, I think that greater weight should be conferred to the basal/universal human value and rights, even if the individual/acquired merits and rights should also be considered to some extent (Fig. 3.2, bottom panel). This latter option is supported by the conception of human beings as evolving conscious triads, made of intellect, sensitiveness, and power, whose evolution is the objective *good*. Indeed, if the evolution of the human being is the absolute good, the human being itself should be regarded as the basic, fundamental part of what is the good, because it is not possible that the degree of evolution of the individual is better than the individual himself. Otherwise stated, conferring a greater weight to the basal/universal value and rights than to the individual/acquired ones derives from the profound ap-

preciation of the human person as a conscious entity bearer of ideas, sentiments, memories, projects, and hopes and, hence, as the most valuable of
the existing entities.

An important issue is that the possibility of compensation decreases
with the age of individuals (ch. 3.2.2.2.2, *B2*). This confers great importance
to the prescription that the evolution-allowing condition be enjoyed from
the first years of life.

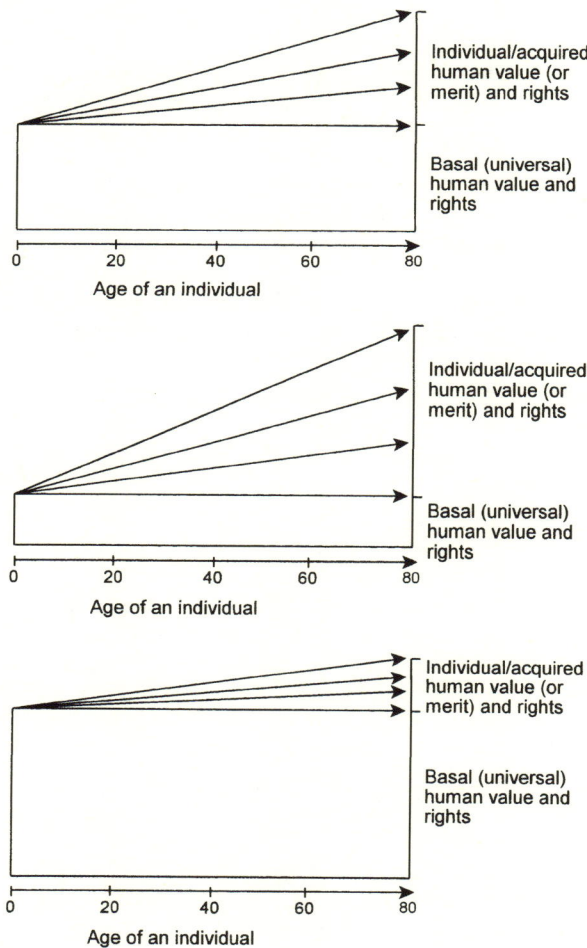

Fig. 3.2. Changes of the basal (universal) and individual/acquired values and rights
through life.

3.2.2.2—Theories of Equality: A Critical Analysis

3.2.2.2.1—Overview

Equality has proven to be a difficult concept to deal with. As mentioned elsewhere (Belfiore 2004: 305, 307–8), equality has been conceived as *formal equality* based on *rational principle* (it is rational to treat equal cases equally) (Aristotle ~330 B.C., "Nicomachean Ethics" and "Politics"); or as *moral equality*, grounded on various moral principles entailing that equal respect, dignity, worth, and consideration should be due to all men (Hobbes 1651; Locke 1690; Rousseau 1755; Kant 1785; Dahrendorf 1962) even if, under various respects, differences among them should be recognized (Vlastos 1962; Dworkin 1977; Nagel 1991; Kymlicka 2002); or as *presumptive equality*, based on the criterion of universal reciprocal justification (i.e., a criterion accepted by all and refused by no one) (Scanlon 1998) and on the assumption that all men should receive equal share of goods in public distribution, irrespective of apparent differences (unless evident and recognized reasons—such as disability, desert, etc.—justify an unequal distribution) (Benn and Richard 1959; Williams 1973). Moreover, equality has been regarded as based on moral assumptions (Williams 1973) or as linked to distributive justice (Brown 1988).

On the other hand, the need to take into account the diversity among individuals has increased the difficulty encountered in defining equality (Rae 1981), and has led to theories such as the theory of proportional equality, i.e., equality proportional to individual merits (Rae 1981; Nagel 1991; Sen 1992), and the theories that emphasize the many variables (or equality indexes) involved and the consequent various possible conceptions of equality (Rawls 1971; Westen 1990; Temkin 1993).

Moreover, it has been underlined that simple equality may entail negative aspects, such as: the possibility of unequal satisfaction or the decrease in the incentives of efficiency (Okun 1975); limitation of the possibility of changing the existing system with a better one (Sen 1970); and possible repression of pluralism and democracy (Cohen 1989). Accordingly, considering the difference between individuals, a complex conception of equality, based on a pluralistic view of life, should be adhered to (Walzer 1983), which raises the problem of how to realize equality in the presence of differences among individuals (Taylor 1992) as well as the problem of the time within which equality should be achieved (McKerlie 1989). On these grounds, it has been pointed out that equality (and justice) should be comparative, avoiding confusion between equality and universality (Raz 1986), and that patterned principles of justices should be avoided in favor of an "entitlement theory" of justice (Nozick 1974: 150–82).

3.2.2.2.2—The Analysis of the Concept of Equality

(A) Defining Equality.

(1) The Idea of Equality. According to Williams (1962), the statement of fact that men *are* equal is too *strong* and actually *false*, whereas the statement or principle that men *should* be equal (in virtue of their common humanity) is a *weak* interpretation of the principle of equality, which, however, tells us that some general reason must be given when men are treated differently. In my opinion, this position is rather unclear; human equality is better understood if we refer to the fundamental property that, according to my conception, is the essence of all men and is shared by all of them: the property of being conscious entities made of intellect, sensitiveness, and power, and capable of undergoing *evolution.* The property of being capable of evolution, while explaining men's *equality*, at the same time does not contrast with men's *diversity*, because each man evolves according to his own natural endowment (and the environmental factors), i.e., along an individual way through which he will acquire some specific properties and will reach different levels. The ability to undergo evolution defines what men have in common much better than the characteristics indicated by Williams (1962), such as the use of language, utilization of tools, living in society, the capacity to feel pain and to feel affection for others, the desire for self-respect and the *moral ability*, because these characteristics actually *vary* among different individuals. Moreover, Williams (1962) maintains that human beings should be considered from the human point of view, i.e., the life, actions or character of a man should be considered by taking into account what they mean for him when regarded from his point of view. This appeal to the subjective point of view is not justified. In contrast, reference to the ability to undergo *evolution* provides us with an objective criterion for evaluating men with reference to both their *equality* and their *diversity*.

(2) Equality as a Descriptive Concept. Oppenheim (1970), after having mentioned that equality may refer to persons, or to the treatment of persons, or to the rules themselves, and that a rule of distribution may be conceived in several ways, suggests that a rule of distribution is egalitarian if it equalizes holdings, or at least reduces the difference between them. He notes that, to reach this goal, we should not take fixed amounts from the more advantaged (in some instances this may increase the difference) but should reduce the percentage difference between the holdings (thus, a sale tax is inegalitarian).

Oppenheim's view suffers from the lack of reference to a basic philosophical conception. If we refer to the structure of the mind, it becomes clear that a rule of distribution of resources is a rule that regulates the distribution of the means through which the *power* manifests itself (or, to be more exact, one of the means through which the power manifests itself, the other means belonging to the sphere of the socio-political status). Bearing in mind that in a society citizens differ from one another as far as their aptitude to primarily develop one or another of the three mind components is concerned, it follows that we should consider separately the distribution of resources *(a)* among those citizens primarily engaged in developing their power (i.e., active in the fields of business or socio-political activity), and *(b)* among all citizens, irrespective of their preferential aptitude to develop the *power*, or the *intellect* (lovers of natural or human sciences) or the *sensitiveness* (craftsmen, and those who are engaged in literary, musical, or visual arts).

(a) Among the citizens primarily engaged in developing their power, the distribution of resources cannot be equal, since (apart from the consideration that equal distribution of resources is utopian) individuals differ in their natural endowment, and this difference is manifested (besides others) in the diverse ability to develop one's economic power. In this regard, it should be recalled that the accumulation of capital is required for the economic development of a society. Thus, instead of an egalitarian rule of distribution of resources, we should adopt the rule that each individual should concretely enjoy an *evolution-allowing, involution-avoiding condition* (chs. 2.1.5.3; 3.1.2.5.1, *3*), i.e., should enjoy a sufficient amount of resources (and also of scientific and humanistic education) to allow him to develop his mind according to his natural aptitude and endowment. The rule of assuring an evolution-allowing condition should substitute the rule of assuring the "basic needs", or of equalizing benefits as concerns those whose basic needs are unsatisfied (Vlastos 1962), or of pursuing a "minimum entitlement egalitarianism" (McKerlie 1989). Once the *evolution-allowing, involution-avoiding condition* is reached, the amount of resources should be allowed to freely vary among individuals, according to their ability (correctly exerted) or merit. Thus, the *egalitarian* rule that "all should enjoy an evolution-allowing condition" serves to enable each individual to express his own diversity, which leads to a diversified (or *correctly non-egalitarian*) society. Therefore, we could say that *equality serves to reveal diversities*.

(b) Referring to all citizens considered as "whole persons" (irrespective of their preferential aptitude to develop their power, intellect or sensitivity), equal distribution of resources is even more absurd. Indeed, it is absurd to pretend that a university professor or an "artist" should possess the same amount of resources as a successful businessman or a manufacturer of cars or other industrial products. Instead, what is required is that a sufficient degree of scientific and humanistic education is assured to all citizens (in addition to a sufficient provision of resources), in order that each of them can enjoy an *evolution-allowing, involution-avoiding condition*, which entails not only the enjoyment of a sufficient amount of resources (sphere of power) but also a sufficient education in the field of science (sphere of intellect) and of arts (sphere of sensitiveness). These considerations underline that the

scientist or the artist does not aspire to possess the same amount of resources as others (and, especially, as a businessman), but he perhaps aspires to be able to produce significant scientific works or artistic creations. This may help to explain the observation of Hospers (1961: 424) that equal distribution of money does not lead to equal happiness, and happiness itself is something that cannot be distributed. The latter point refers to the fact that happiness is not a moral or political end, as it depends mainly on luck (chs. 2.2.1.2.3, *C1a*; 2.2.1.6.2; 3.2.5.1, *1a*).

(3) Equality as a Moral Ideal or Principle. Two positions will be briefly considered.

(a) Equality as a moral ideal. Frankfurt (1987: 21) maintains the *doctrine of sufficiency*, i.e., that what counts from the moral standpoint "is not that everyone should have the same but that each should have *enough.*" To have *enough* means that a certain requirement or *standard* has been met (Frankfurt 1987: 37). [In this regard, Parfit (1997) underlines that priority should be given to the improvement of the status of the poorer and weaker members of society]. Moreover, in an affluent society it may be that the worst off has no unsatisfied needs or claims (Frankfurt 1987: 35–6). Frankfurt's doctrine of sufficiency is flawed by vagueness. We agree that everyone should have enough; but how can we quantitatively define the term "enough"? Which is the "standard" to be met? Does "enough" refer only to economic resources? We can answer these questions by referring to my moral and political theories: "enough" should be understood as referring to all those conditions (economic and non-economic) that allow each citizen to promote the evolution of his own mind according to his natural endowment, i.e., each citizen should enjoy the *evolution-allowing, involution-avoiding condition,* so that the different levels reached by the various citizens will depend on their different personal abilities.

Frankfurt (1987: 23) thinks that pursuing equality may have negative effects, as it may entail a limitation of liberty, may divert a person's attention from what he really cares about, and may even lead to alienation. I note that these undesirable effects may be produced by pursuing absolute equality (primarily understood as economic equality) but not by pursuing equality of the right to enjoy the conditions for mind evolution; when this fundamental right is enjoyed (which entails the enjoyment of all the universal human rights—ch. 3.2.2.1.1), everybody can reach the position suitable to his personality and should be satisfied with it.

Frankfurt (1987: 24–5) observes that equality has been defended on the grounds of the principle of diminishing *marginal utility*, which is based on the false assumptions that for each individual the utility of money diminishes at margin and that the utility functions of all individuals are the same. He adds that marginal utility may not diminish for money, because of its unlimited protean versatility (p. 26); for some goods it may even increase with time (an individual may acquire a special taste or the capacity for obtaining gratification) (p. 26). Moreover, marginal utility may also increase when there is a *utility threshold* that has to be reached (Frankfurt 1987: 27–30). Thus, the last dollar added to a saving program allows to reach the amount required to buy a certain good; a good acquired last can be combined with a good acquired before to make a more useful complex object; and equal distribution of a limited but essential good leaves everyone below the survival threshold. Therefore, egalitarian distribution may fail to maximize utility (Frankfurt 1987: 30). I note that all the above reasoning refers to absolute economic equality, and is not valid when we refer to equality in the right to enjoy the conditions allowing mind evolution.

(b) The principle of equality. Singer (1993: 21) defends the ethical principle of equal consideration of interests; he observes that a difference in ability between people does not justify any difference in consideration, as equality is a basic ethical principle, not an assertion of fact. Although the latter assertion is true, I would note that a basic ethical principle cannot be merely stated but must be given a philosophical justification; in this regard, see my discussion of equality as concerning the rights that must be respected to assure all citizens an *evolution-allowing, involution-avoiding condition*, i.e., a condition that enables people to attempt to successfully develop their mind (ch. 3.2.2.1.1).

Singer (1993: 23–25) defends a *minimal* principle of equality, rather than a thoroughgoing egalitarian principle, which would be difficult to implement (it is difficult to give equal consideration to the interest of one's family and to those of strangers). I object the following. *(a)* The term "minimal principle" is too vague to be meaningful, and the principle of equality does not entail that one should give equal consideration to all. I think that the principle of equality should be conceived not as a "minimal principle" but as a "thoroughgoing principle" when applied to the basic rights that assure an *evolution-allowing, involution-avoiding condition*; conversely, it should not be applied at all when referring to the differences (in degree and specificity of mind evolution) that individuals who have equally enjoyed an evolution-allowing condition have manifested. *(b)* It is not true that one should give equal consideration to the interest of one's family and to those of strangers, because one should follow the rule of the *spheres of decreasing moral responsibility* (ch. 2.1.5.2.1).

(4) Differences Between Races and Genders. Singer (1993: 26–38) recalls that there is evidence supporting difference in intelligence (as measured by IQ) between races that may have at least a partial genetic basis (besides being contributed by environmental factors); likewise, there is some evidence of sexual difference, as men would have a greater mathematical and "visual-spatial" ability and aggressivity whereas women would have a better verbal ability and creativity. Singer (1993: 30–31) argues, however,

that this does not support any racist view, for several reasons: *(a)* difference refers to the average values and is associated with substantial overlapping, and thus it says nothing about individuals; *(b)* we should make a higher effort to help those who score low; and *(c)* basic human interests (basic needs, freedom, avoiding pain, developing one's ability, etc.) are not related to the degree of intelligence, as stated by the words of T. Jefferson (1809: 492) that "whatever be their degree of talent, it is no measure of their rights." I think that what is lacking in the above reasoning is the distinction between: *(a) universal human rights*, linked not only to the "basic" needs but to all those needs that must be satisfied in order to concretely enjoy an evolution-allowing condition; and *(b) individual rights*, linked to the individual properties, i.e., the properties that each individual (having enjoyed an evolution-allowing condition in a similar, or at least comparable, degree as others) has expressed.

(5) Equal Consideration versus Equal Opportunity (see also below, in section "*B*"). Singer (1993: 39) argues that the moral principle of equal consideration of interests is superior to that of equal opportunity, because to achieve genuine equal opportunity one should secure that everyone has the same kind of school education, the same kind of home (a quiet room to study, availability of books), and the same help and support by parents, things that are difficult to control. I point out that Singer's equal consideration of interests and needs is a vague expression, which corresponds to what I call the *evolution-allowing, involution-avoiding condition* (chs. 2.1.5.3; 3.1.2.5.1, *3*); the latter, although very difficult to turn into practice, indicates very well what is the ideal goal that a modern and democratic State should attempt to realize. Considering that a full *evolution-allowing, involution-avoiding condition* is presently not yet enjoyed by all citizens, governments should attempt to compensate for the disadvantaged conditions (for instance, by providing special assistance in schools to students belonging to the poorer classes). Singer (1993: 40–42) thinks that, to realize equality, income should be related to the interests and needs, not to the ability (according to the Marxist slogan "From each according to his ability, to each according to his needs"). Yet, Singer notes, unless done in all countries, this would result in a "brain drain" through emigration; according to him, what could be done is to reduce the income difference to a moderate degree, without reaching the point at which most talented people would emigrate. I object that imposing limits to the income is always difficult, and may also be unjustified, because equality cannot be reached by assuring to all a similar income, since factors other than the economic ones should be considered. As mentioned elsewhere (ch. 3.2.2.1.2), it should be born in mind that people, by following their natural aptitudes, will primarily develop their intellect (i.e., their knowledge) or their sensitiveness (i.e., their ability in the field of "arts") or their power (i.e., their economic and socio-political

status). This leads to a diversity among people and shows that equality concerns the enjoyment of basic rights (enjoyment of the evolution-allowing condition) and actually serves to allow that natural diversities can be freely and fully expressed. In my opinion, what is important is that all citizens concretely enjoy an *evolution-allowing, involution-avoiding condition*, so that any individual can reach the degree and specificity of evolution according to his natural endowment.

Singer (1993: 42) suggests that it would also be worth trying to reward the effort made to work near one's upper limit of ability, rather than the degree of one's ability. This, however, would be difficult to realize and even unjust; if the work of two people has the same "value" (say, a value of "10"), why should one be paid more than the other in consideration of his greater effort? Moreover, how should the "effort" be measured? I think that it is the duty of all to make a reasonable, constant effort to work as efficiently as possible; providing that all individuals equally enjoy an evolution-allowing condition, they should be allowed to reach different levels of evolution along different ways, according to their natural endowment.

(6) Equality and Time. Egalitarianism may require equality in the distribution of *resources* (possessions and services like wealth, property, and medical care) or in the distribution of *welfare* (i.e., in the happiness or desire-satisfaction) (Dworkin 1981). McKerlie (1989) distinguishes various forms of egalitarianism, among which there are: *(a) complete-lives egalitarianism*, which refers to equality between the total amount of resources and welfare that people receive during the complete life (thus giving importance also to what has happened in the past); *(b) corresponding-segments egalitarianism*, which compares corresponding segments of different lives, say youth with youth, maturity with maturity, and old age with old age; and *(c) simultaneous-segments egalitarianism*, which aims at achieving equality between parts of lives during the same time period. According to McKerlie (1989), this last view, although it does not compensate for past inequalities and raises the question of how to conceive personal identity, would be the most acceptable, even if it may be advisable to balance equality between complete lives and the equality between parts of lives.

The above views show how difficult the attempt is to realize the *absurd project* directed to satisfy the claim that living conditions of all citizens should be *equal*. As I have stated elsewhere (ch. 3.2.2.1.1), egalitarianism should be directed to assure that all citizens *equally* enjoy, in a concrete manner, an *evolution-allowing, involution-avoiding condition*; this is a basic or starting condition that enables a citizen to develop his mind to the maximum extent allowed by his natural endowment, thus reaching a final condition *specific* for that citizen (and therefore *different* from a citizen to another), as it will depend on the prevalence of one of the mind components over the other two as well as on the degree and specificity of the development of each of the mind components. A citizen should be compensated if he has not enjoyed an evolution-allowing condition (ch. 3.2.6.1.2, *3*; see also below, under "*B2*" and "*C2*") (although the possibility of this compensation decreases with the increase in citizen's age) but, if he has enjoyed this condition, he should not be compensated for the different positions that he reaches; on the other hand, such a compensation would be very difficult as it should be made by comparison with an abstract scheme of the citizen.

(7) Complex Equality. Referring to equality, Walzer (1983: 3–30) underlines its complexity, since one should consider a *multiplicity of goods*, which is matched by the *multiplicity of distributive criteria*, procedures, and agents.

Among *goods*, Walzer (1983: 3) includes such a variety of things as membership, power, honor, ritual eminence, divine grace, kinship and love, knowledge, wealth, physical security, work, leisure, rewards, as well as other materially conceived goods such as food, shelter, clothing, transportation, medical care, commodities of every sort, and odd things (paintings, rare books, etc.). I think that Walzer is right in underlining the multiplicity of goods; however, the lack of reference to a basic philosophical conception prevented him from understanding that what he considers as "goods" can actually be divided into three groups, each group including the products of one of the three mind components. Thus, of the various "goods" mentioned above, some belong to the sphere of the *power* (physical security, medical care, food, shelter, clothing, work, transportation, and other commodities); others belong to the sphere of the *intellect* (knowledge, in all its forms); others belong to the sphere of the *sensitiveness* (kinship, love, leisure,—to which art in all its forms should be added); the remaining (honor, ritual eminence, divine grace, rewards, painting, perhaps rare books) are of uncertain allocation. Among the latter, "honor" may be linked to power, or to knowledge, or to artistic endowment; "painting" may refer to the economic value of paintings or to the ability to enjoy their artistic beauty; "rare books" may refer to their economic value, or to the ability to appreciate them for their cultural content, or to enjoy them as beautiful objects, etc. I note that some essential goods, such as education, information, freedom or equal opportunity, are not mentioned by Walzer. However, once the distinction of the alleged "goods" into three groups (according to their belonging to one or another of the three mind components) is made, it becomes apparent that the problem of distribution concerns only the goods belonging to the sphere of power, since knowledge, love, or artistic enjoyment cannot be distributed, whereas the means (power) for attempting to develop knowledge or artistic taste can be distributed. In other words, power can be distributed, whereas knowledge and sensitivity cannot.

Walzer (1983: 4–6) underlines that the multiplicity of *distributive criteria* and of *agents* requires principles that justify a choice, and that it is not known whether the ideal rational man would choose impartially. He thinks that principles of justice are pluralistic, as different social goods should be distributed for different reasons, with different procedures, by different agents. Here I observe that, while the distributing agents should be identified, directly or indirectly, with the public power and institutions, the distributive criteria, which may vary according to the kind of good involved, should be directed to assure that all citizens enjoy the concrete and various conditions that allow the development of their minds.

According to Walzer (1983: 10–13), in different historical periods, a given social good has been dominant and has been monopolized by a given group. In a capitalist society, capital is dominant and readily converted into prestige and power; in a technocracy, technical knowledge plays the same role. Indeed, I note that in an organized state, the power is exerted under various forms, so that we have political power, economic power, or military power; moreover, being the mind components interrelated to one another (chs. 1.1.1.1, 6; 1.1.2, 2nd proposition), we should add academic power (due to the support of knowledge to power), religious power (due to the support of sentiments, in this instance religious sentiments, to power), etc. In Western democracies, capital is the main measure of economic power, and the "new goods" that through time gain dominance are the products of the various advances in technical knowledge.

Walzer (1983: 10–13) underlines that social claims may have the following ends: *(a)* against *monopoly*, *(b)* against *dominance* of a given good, and *(c)* against both monopoly and dominance of a good (this is the model of every revolutionary ideology: with the French Revolution the dominance of noble birth and of feudal landholding was substituted by the dominance of bourgeois wealth). Let us comment the first two points.

(a) Claims against monopoly. According to Walzer (1983: 13–16), the dominant good should be redistributed (because *monopoly* is unjust). This would lead to a regime of simple equality in which everything is up for sale, and citizens have an equal amount of money. Yet, with time, the educated-talented group will claim that the good that it controls should be the dominant one. This, however, would require a continue State intervention to constrain incipient monopolies and new forms of dominance, which may lead to dominance of political power, hence the need for constitutional checks and balances. Here my comment is that a society in which citizens have an equal amount of money is utopist and undesirable because, once it is assured that all citizens enjoy a condition allowing the development of their minds (i.e., the *evolution-allowing, involution-avoiding condition*), each citizen's mind will evolve in a specific way and will reach a different level according to its individual properties. The truly "talented minds" will emerge and play their role in society, without substituting the "capitalist minds", since all the many and diverse kinds of mind activities contribute,

each in its own field, to the government of society. A society made of citizens enjoying the evolution-allowing condition and governed only by one dominant class is unrealistic.

(b) Claims against dominance of a given good. Walzer (1983: 16–17) maintains that, since the *dominance of a good* is unjust, the way should be opened to autonomous distribution of all goods. This would lead to a *regime of complex equality* (Walzer 1983: 17–20) or to a complex egalitarian society, in which there may be many small inequalities but "inequality will not be multiplied through the conversion process; the autonomy of distribution will tend to produce a variety of local monopolies, held by different groups." Moreover, according to Walzer (1983: 18–19), conversion of one good into another, with which there is no intrinsic connection, would mean invading the sphere where another company of men and women properly rules, so that the use of political power to gain access to other goods is a tyrannical use; principles of justice should be internal to each distributive sphere. I note that the basis for defining undue conversion is to understand the different nature of the various goods, i.e., to define their belonging to the sphere of power or of intellect or of sensitiveness, and to recognize the rich diversity existing within each sphere (various fields of knowledge; various forms of sentiments and of literary, musical, and visual arts; and various forms of economic and political power).

Walzer defends his concept of "complex equality," which requires that different goods are accessible to different companies of men and women for different reasons and in accordance with different procedures. There would be no single distributive criterion that can match the diversity of social goods; however, the three main criteria would be: *free exchange*, which creates a market in which money acts as a dominant good; *desert*, which is not applicable to love, or to personal influence, or to political offices (whose distribution to deserving men by some central agency would violate our understanding of democracy) nor to pictures (as it would be unacceptable that, through some agency or the state, pictures be assigned only to artistically cultivated people); and *need*, which is a criterion appropriate mainly for distributing social wealth in a poor society (Walzer 1983: 21–26). My comment is that the only and necessary "distributive criterion" is that everyone should enjoy an *evolution-allowing, involution-avoiding condition*, which makes it possible to avoid the needy condition and to express one's own desert through equality of opportunity.

(B) Equality of Opportunity.
(1) The Concept of Equal Opportunity. Equal Opportunity is a complex concept (Tawney 1964; Lucas 1966; Schaar 1967; MacLeod 1975; Galston 1980; Fishkin 1983 and 1987). Westen (1985) points out that equal opportunity is actually a verbal formula consisting of four simple elements, three covert elements referring to "opportunity" (i.e., the agent, the goal, and their

relationship) and one derivative element related to "equality". He adds that opportunity means absence of insurmountable obstacles (race, sex, etc.) or surmountable obstacles (religious belief, social class, etc.) to reach the goal. Moreover, obstacles in the way of reaching a goal may include: *(a)* the social disadvantage of poorer training (Goldman 1977), *(b)* the disadvantage linked to poorer natural endowment (Goldman 1977), and *(c)* the totality of features that distinguish one person from another (Dorn 1979: 112). While in the latter case goals would be reached by pure lottery (Dorn 1979: 112), I think that the disadvantage linked to poorer training should be avoided by allowing equal access to adequate education and training to all willing people (this is realized by assuring that all people can enjoy those conditions that allow *mind evolution*). If this is done, differences in training will only depend on unwillingness, a cause that should be included among those considered under point *(b)*, i.e., poorer natural endowment. The latter should not be compensated, because the scope of the equality in opportunity is that the goal be reached by those who possess specified qualities. Compensation of these differences would mean annulment of the differences in personal properties and therefore of personality. On these grounds, I do not endorse the statement of Westen (1985) that two agents have an equal opportunity to reach a goal if they are both free from the same specified obstacles, even if each of them may face different obstacles of his own, such as different training or ability. Indeed while Westen's statement is correct with regard to differences in natural ability, it is not correct with regard to differences in training (not due to unwillingness), since access to an adequate training is part of the concept of equal opportunity.

(2) Equality of Opportunity from a Liberal Standpoint. Galston (1986: 89) underlines that the principles of social justice require that the goods and services referring to the "basic needs" are distributed on the basis of need, whereas the opportunities "outside the basic needs" are allocated according to the principle of *equality of opportunity*. I think that the distinction between "basic needs" and "opportunities outside the basic needs" should be clarified. Firstly, the meaning of the term "basic needs" should be redefined, i.e., basic needs should be regarded as those needs that must be satisfied in order to allow mind evolution. Indeed, satisfaction of the basic needs means enjoyment of the *evolution-allowing, involution-avoiding condition*. So defined, basic needs include equality of opportunity, because the latter is a necessary condition for allowing that an individual evolves according to his natural endowment (and not according to arbitrary admissions and exclusions). In other words, basic needs coincide with the fundamental human rights (derived from the fundamental moral norm prescribing the promotion of mind evolution). The *equality* in the enjoyment of fundamental rights serves to allow mind evolution, through which individuals express their *diversity* (ch. 3.2.2.1).

Galston (1980; 1986) gives his conception of justice. According to him, justice is based on the conception of the *good life* for individuals (Galston 1986: 91), be it identified with happiness or moral freedom or rational life or, better, the fullest possible development of the individual potential capacities (Galston 1986: 92). Yet, Galston's "capacities" of individuals may include both good as well as bad dispositions. To define what is a good life, we should first define what is life; better, to define what is good for humans, we should first understand the structure and functioning of the human mind and its ability to undergo evolution. This allows us to distinguish good "potential capacities" (those directed to promote mind evolution) from the bad ones (those directed to restrain mind evolution).

Galston (1986: 94–96) underlines that, although the principles of justice and equal opportunity require that individual chances are linked to desert, which in turn should be linked to the *natural* differences (but not the *social* ones), actually factors such as wealth or one's family social status are outside the individual control; therefore, he thinks that the distinction between natural and social differences should perhaps be reinterpreted as the distinction between relevant and irrelevant factors for the treatment of people. This statement is worthy of further discussion. I think we should distinguish: *(a) individual properties* (or natural endowment), which define the personality of an individual and whose development should be promoted to the fullest possible extent, after the fundamental moral norm (which prescribes the promotion of mind evolution); *(b) restraints to mind evolution*, which include both the *unchangeable restraints to mind evolution* (e.g., physical handicaps such as paralysis, amputations, deafness, etc.) and the *changeable restraints to mind evolution* (the so-called social factors). The common view is that restraints to mind evolution should be *compensated*; I think that what should be compensated (to the fullest possible extent allowed by scientific and technical achievements) are the unchangeable restraints whereas the changeable restraints should not be compensated, but avoided through prevention (ch. 3.2.6.1.2, *3*; see also this ch., under "*A6*" and "*C2*"). Of course, a society in which all restraints to mind evolution are avoided or prevented is an ideal one, very difficult to achieve in the real world. Yet, the fundamental moral norm and the principle of justice tell us that this is the end to which a society should tend. As, in the field of intellect, our knowledge continuously evolves and yet will never reach the knowledge of the entire reality (which remains for us a "noumenon"), so in the field of public moral activity the social justice continuously evolves toward a full equality of treatment, which, however, will never be fully achieved. The point is that a society in which there are "restraints to mind evolution" to be "compensated" is an unjust society, and the extent of the existing restraints is a measure of the existing injustice. It is noteworthy that, although society has the duty to attempt to correct injustice by attempting to compensate for the still existing restraints to mind evolution, the compensation cannot be complete. A 60-year-old man, who did not enjoy the opportunity of receiving higher education, cannot be fully compensated for his lack of education; compensation is always incomplete, since only partial compensation is possible. For this reason, restraints to mind evolution should be prevented, since with the advancement of the age of the involved people, compensation becomes progressively more difficult, or even impossible.

It has been observed that if, in the future, technical progress will allow the changing of genetic properties of individuals, then, as underlined also by Williams (1962), "equality of opportunity will merge with broader issues of absolute equality and the morality of genetic intervention" (Galston 1986: 95). Although the issue of genetic intervention is a very complex one, I would note that genetic intervention should be directed to cure some definite pathological conditions (which will restrain mind evolution of the individual and are due to some accidental causes), and not to change individual properties that define *personal identity* or personality. This is because the fundamental moral norm prescribes the promotion of the evolution of individuals according to their natural endowment, and not the modification of individuals' endowments to be developed. Moreover, who should decide how to change genetic properties? According to which principles? Toward which standard? In other words, genetic interventions could be compared to the interventions of plastic surgery: both should be limited to correct pathological defects, not to implement an arbitrarily chosen standard of personality or of beauty, respectively. Thus, personal identity is determined by the mixture of genes as it results from randomness, which is actually a pre-established order unknown to human beings (or that human beings are unable to know).

(3) Views Against Equality of Opportunity. Equality of opportunity has been criticized along various lines (Galston 1986: 105–6).

(a) Nozick (1974: 235–38) put forward the view, which was defined by Galston (1986: 91) as *hyper-individualism,* according to which there are only individuals who agree to give to, and to receive from, one another. Galston (1986: 105) objects that being excluded from an equal chance to develop one's potential talent by education and training makes it unlikely and difficult to enter the system of exchange. I note that Nozick's conception means the prevalence of the stronger individuals (those with entitlements) over the weaker ones, i.e., the prevalence of the individual with more *power.* Yet, many competitions are unrelated to power; examples might be an opening of a position of university professor (which is related to the sphere of intellect) or an opening for the directorship of an orchestra (which is related to the sphere of sensitiveness). If the hyper-individualism is intended as meaning that some individuals actually deserve to prevail over others (because they possess some properties that others do not possess

or possess to a lesser degree), then respecting the principle of equal opportunity is the only means to show that they actually possess the properties that they claim to possess.

(b) Some *communitarians* maintain that competitions set human beings apart from one another, in a rather destructive struggle (Schaar 1967); this view is opposed by Galston (1986: 105), according to whom competitions may also promote mutual respect and may stimulate progress. I think that what may set human beings apart from one another is the arbitrary and unjust allocation of positions, which does not respect the principle of equal opportunity.

(c) Finally, there is a *democratic* objection: equal opportunity cannot apply to the sphere of politics, because the proper exercise of power consists of the direction of the city in accordance with the civic consciousness of the citizens (Walzer 1983: 287). Galston (1986: 107) observes that "the purpose of elections is not just to register opinions but also to identify excellence . . . [Thus,] the distribution of power in democracies is not wholly distinct from, but rather partly governed by, the merit-based principle of equal opportunity." I observe that political activity belongs to the sphere of the *power*; therefore, "excellence" in politics means "aptitude to achieve much power" as expressed by the number of votes obtained. In other words, in politics "excellence" means "power", and "power" means "number of votes" (because the number of votes is a measure of the *degree of universality* of the future political decisions and actions of a candidate or of a party). Thus, the need to assure equal opportunity should be focused on the stages prior to the voting, which consist of the access to the candidature and of the availability of resources for propaganda. At these stages, the opposition of a few powerful and influential people may restrain the candidature of a potential successful candidate (i.e., a candidate who might obtain a high number of favorable votes); yet, as far as availability of resources is concerned, it should be pointed out that, while it is certainly true that the support of a few economically potent people may greatly help a candidate (and a party), it is also true that a similar help can be obtained by a large number of small economic supports. However, at the pre-voting stages, equality of opportunity is necessary to avoid that an apparently successful candidate (and party) does not actually represent the majority of the citizens (i.e., does not represent *the best approach to universality*), which would mean *violence* (ch. 3.1.2.4). It follows that appropriate laws and rules are required to assure equal opportunity to the candidates as well as to the parties. Concerning parties, the problem arises whether the resources (e.g., money, access to mass media, etc.) should be available to the competing parties in an equal measure or in proportion to their political weight, i.e., the known number of supporters. This, however, is a false problem, because each voting serves just to verify which is the "political weight" of each party at the time when

the voting is carried out; therefore, before the voting, all parties should be considered on an equal basis. The "weight" resulting from the previous round of voting should not be taken into account because the voting process is directed to verify if the previous situation has changed; the "weight" resulting from opinion polls should not be taken into account because they are partial, non-official, and are often carried out by interested groups. The only official, publicly justified "opinion poll" is the voting process. Yet, a real problem remains; it consists of establishing the minimal requirement for considering a group of citizens as a political party. This is an issue that should be regulated by appropriate laws and rules, which should take into account the socio-political situations of a given country. Presently, the conditions under which the voting process occurs are unsatisfactory in all countries and are far from being based on the principle of equal opportunity. Thus, political competition lies in a sphere where social justice is still little developed.

(C) Inequality, Equality, and Partiality.

(1) Inequality. According to Temkin (1986; 1993), the size of someone's complaint can be evaluated as *relative to the average*, or as *relative to the best-off*, or as *relative to all those better-off*; moreover, this evaluation can be made by means of various principles of equality, as follows: *(a)* The *maximin principle of justice* (institutions should maximize the average level of the worst-off group); *(b)* the *maximin principle of equality* (how bad the worst-off group fares with respect to inequality and how large this group is); *(c)* the *additive principle of equality* (inequality is measured by summing up each individual complaint and taking into account the magnitude of each complaint); *(d)* the *weighted additive principle* of equality (inequality is measured by adding together people's complaints, after first attaching extra weight to them); *(e)* the *relative to the best-off person view* of complaints; *(f)* the *relative to all those better-off view* of complaints. Temkin (1986; 1993) also recalls that economists evaluate inequality by using statistical measures, which include the following: *(a)* the *range* (which expresses the *relative to the best-off person view* of complaints and the *maximin principle* of equality); *(b)* the *relative mean deviation* (which expresses the *relative to the average view* of complaints and the *additive principle* of equality); *(c)* the *Gini's coefficient* (which expresses the *relative to all those better-off view* of complaints and the *additive principle* of equality); and *(d)* the *variance*, the *coefficient of variation*, and the *standard deviation of the logarithm*, each expressing, in its own way, the relative to the average view of complaints and the weighed additive principle.

My comment is that the above methods to evaluate inequality among all citizens may be useful for *descriptive* purposes, i.e., for analyzing the distribution of resources within the society, but they are not relevant for *prescriptive* purposes, i.e., for moral or political purposes, since the moral end is to assure that all citizens enjoy the *evolution-allowing, involution-avoiding condition*; therefore, a political of social justice should be directed to improve the status of those citizens who still do not enjoy this status.

(2) Equality and Partiality. Nagel (1991: 3–20) has pointed out that ethics and the ethical basis of political theories arise from the requirement for integration of the *impersonal standpoint* (which demands universal impartiality and equality) with the *personal standpoint* (which produces individualistic motives); public institutions and their theoretical justifications would be the way in which the demands of the impersonal standpoint are externalized. I note that, although Nagel's distinction of the impersonal from the personal standpoint is acceptable, he does not give a satisfactory definition of what these two standpoints are nor does he frame them into a general philosophical conception. I think that a necessary premise in this field is the reference to an ethical theory, in turn framed into a general philosophical conception. By referring to my moral theory, we can say that the *universal standpoint* does not demand "universal impartiality and equality," but rather demands that public actions actually change into *moral acts*, i.e., that public actions are directed to *equally* assure to all citizens the enjoyment of those conditions allowing each of them to promote the evolution of his mind according to his natural endowment; the evolution of mind, then, generates (or reveals) justified *diversities* among individuals.

Nagel (1991: 63–74) maintains that equality should consider the condition of *non-responsibility*, since it is bad that people should be unequal in advantages or disadvantages for which they are not responsible. The latter include the conditions in which they are born and in which they must lead their life, conditions that, therefore, fall under the egalitarian principle. Here I refer to my view about the *unchangeable and changeable restraints to mind evolution* (see above, under "*B2*"), the former should be compensated to the fullest possible extent (chs. 3.2.6.1.2, *3*; 3.2.6.3; see also above, under "*A6*") whereas the latter should be prevented because their compensation is difficult or even impossible with the advancement of age of the involved people (see above, under "*B2*").

At variance with the absolute priority to the worse off according to the *difference principle* of Rawls (1971: 65–73) (generalized into the *lexical difference principle* as suggested by Rawls—1971: 72—and modified by others), Nagel (1991: 73) prefers a "somewhat weaker preference for the worse off, which can be outweighed by sufficiently large benefit to sufficiently large numbers of those better-off." My view in this matter is sharply different: society has the overriding duty to assure all citizens the *equal* enjoyment of those conditions that enable them to develop their mind according to their natural endowment, which makes the expression of natural *diversities* possible.

3.2.2.2.3—Equality as Related to Meritocracy, Fraternity, and Friendship

(1) Meritocracy. In a society in which all citizens enjoy the *evolution-allowing, involution-avoiding condition*, each citizen reaches a different degree of mind evolution, according to his natural endowment. Meritocracy refers to a socio-political system in which, in all the spheres of activity, the "weight" of each citizen is proportional to its "merits". In an ideal world, this would be right. Yet, it should be pointed out that, in the real world, the evolution-allowing condition is difficult to implement in practice to the full extent and that in most societies a certain percentage of citizens does not enjoy that condition; this entails that these citizens should be compensated for their undeserved disadvantages (chs. 3.2.2.2.2, A6, B2, C2; 3.2.6.1.2, 3; 3.2.6.3). This should always be kept in mind when evaluating apparently different merits. Moreover, it should be considered that the lack of evolution-allowing condition is progressively more difficult to be fully compensated as the age of the involved people advances (ch. 3.2.2.2.2, B2). Indeed, Young (1958), who first used the term "meritocracy", underlined that meritocracy may have a negative sense when it refers to what might happen if we place gaining formal education over all other considerations; this would lead to the exclusion of those who are unable to get higher education and to the rise of a new discriminatory social class. I observe, however, that this may only happen in a society in which the evolution-allowing condition is not enjoyed by all citizens.

Oppenheim (1970) notes that meritocracy is not extended to all kinds of benefits, as, for instance, equal suffrage means political participation regardless of merit. This view cannot be accepted; as I discussed elsewhere (ch. 3.1.2.2.2), the vote is the minimum amount (the atom) of political power that must be recognized to all citizens. The different "weight" of the various citizens is exerted through the influence that they exert on the formation of the political choice of others.

(2) Fraternity and Friendship. Lucas (1965) maintains that *equality* is incompatible with *fraternity* (brotherliness). *Fraternity*, Lucas argues, entails respect for the common humanity, but this would contrast with the fact that we do not like to lose our individuality (individual differences), and also with the fact that we cannot have (in a large society) fraternity with many people, as personal relationships are emotionally absorbing and time demanding. Both the points of this strange view can be rejected on the following bases.

(a) Fraternity does not entail ignoring individual differences but rather demands that each individual should not defend his own interests ignoring or damaging other people but should recognize to his "brothers" the right to enjoy an evolution-allowing condition and should help the development of

their mind, so that they can express their differences or diversities.

(b) Nobody pretends that a person has fraternity with many (or with all) people but merely with the people with whom he interacts. I developed this point in chapter 2.1.5.2, where the concept of the *spheres of decreasing moral responsibility* is discussed. It is the duty of public authorities, which exert universal actions (or actions that should represent the best approach to universality), to give equal consideration to *all* citizens.

3.2.2.2.4—The Confutation of the Concept of Equality

(1) A Critique of Contemporary Egalitarianism. Equality of human rights and human worth has been a subject of much debate (Finnis 1980; Gewirth 1982; Nielsen 1985; Baker 1987; Nickel 1987; Winston 1989; Pojman 1997), not to mention the classical works of Rawls (1971), Nozick (1974), Dworkin (1977), and Walzer (1983). Pojman (1997) critiques the attempts to find a solid foundation to egalitarianism; he recalls Hobbes's statement (1651: 51) that "The value or worth of a man is, as of all other things, his price—that is to say, so much as would be given for the use of his power— and therefore is not absolute but a thing dependent on the need and judgment of another." Pojman (1997) maintains that the doctrine of equal human worth is actually based on metaphysical systems or is simply a leftover from a religious world (i.e., equal human worth comes in at creation or is due to grace) and that, as such, cannot be accepted by secular egalitarians. He analyzes and rejects the arguments in favor of equal human worth put forward by various theorists such as Bentham (1789), Carritt (1947), Peters and Benn (1959), Vlastos (1962), Rawls (1971), Feinberg (1973), Nozick (1974), Gewirth (1978; 1982; 1996), Plantinga and Wolterstorff (1984), Nielsen (1985; 1988), Gauthier (1986), Machan (1989), Nagel (1986; 1991), and others [see in: Blackstone (ed.) 1969]. He concludes that none of them has put forward solid arguments supporting equal human worth.

I think we should distinguish: *(a)* equality in human *rights*, *(b)* equality in human *worth*, and *(c)* inequality in individual *merit* or *desert*.

(a) Equality in human rights derives from the *fundamental moral norm* prescribing the promotion of mind evolution, inasmuch as universal human rights are those rights whose enjoyment is required to enable each man to promote the evolution of his mind. Otherwise stated, all men have the same right (and duty) to attempt to develop their mind to the fullest possible extent.

(b) Equality in human worth descends from the *essential property* common to all men, i.e., the property of being conscious entities, composed of intellect, sensitivity and power, capable of evolution. As such, humans (all humans) are the most valuable among the existing entities. Yet, by

equally enjoying the evolution-allowing condition, each individual develops his own mind along specific ways and up to a certain level, which differs among the various individuals. Hence, some difference in worth actually exists among individuals; yet, this difference is small compared to the great worth that should be basically recognized to any human being (ch. 3.2.2.1.3). This introduces the following point on inequality.

(c) Inequality in individual merit arises from the particular, *individual properties* that characterize and define the personality of each man and which enable each man to develop his mind along his own way, different from the ways of others, so that people reach diverse levels. What is equal among human beings is their right to develop their mind by enjoying the evolution-allowing condition, not the level reached through their evolution. However, a central point is that individual merits, making the differences among the members of a community, can be meaningful or valid only if all involved individuals have equally enjoyed the fundamental rights (i.e., the evolution-allowing condition); otherwise, claiming individual merits may only be an expression of *arrogance*, and recognizing and implementing individual merits may only be an act of *violence*. Since the evolution-allowing condition is difficult to fully realize in practice, inequality among citizens should always be treated with prudence and modesty.

Pojman (1997) underlines that even Rawls's position may not lead to egalitarianism. Concerning Rawls's threshold principle that "once a certain minimum is met, a person is entitled to equal liberty on a par with everyone else" (Rawls 1971: 443), Pojman (1997: 293) notes: why consider just one threshold of rationality and not, say, five or six? He argues that it would be possible to weigh the votes behind the "veil of ignorance" according to criteria of assignment. Moreover, Pojman (1997: 293) notes that Rawls's *difference principle* (inequalities must serve the greatest advantage of the least advantaged) (Rawls 1971: 65–73) may be replaced by Harsanyi's average utility principle (1976) or Frankfurt's *sufficiency principle* (1987), and may permit a hierarchical, elitist society. Here my comment is that what Pojman regards as an elitist society is actually a society in which, through the recognition of *equal* respect and *equal* fundamental rights to all citizens (allowing mind evolution), each citizen has reached the position (degree and specificity of mind evolution) that met his specific individual properties and endowment.

(2) Justice Does Not Imply Equality. Nozick (1974: 236) admits that perhaps it would be better and fairer if a person with less opportunity enjoyed equality of opportunity. However, he notes that to reach this end, we should use resources, which can be obtained by convincing people to choose to devote some of their holdings to this end; and the entitlements of some people cannot be overridden in order to acquire the necessary resources. Nozick's position seems to me a weak one. Why should we con-

sider as prevailing the rights ("entitlements") of the advantaged people over the rights of others, i.e., over the rights of the disadvantaged to enjoy equality of opportunity? Only an extreme libertarian conception ignoring any moral principle could accept this view.

Nozick (1974: 235–38) argues that life is not a race with some person judging the swiftness, because there is no centralized process that judges people's use of the opportunities they have; rather, there are different persons separately giving other persons different things. Here Nozick is decisively wrong, since in any organized society or State (perhaps even the most primitive communities) there is "a centralized process that judges people" according to some rules and principles (not to mention the judgment of our consciousness). A society composed of "different persons separately giving other persons different things" would not be a "society" at all.

To "show" that the entitlement conception cannot be easily overridden, Nozick (1974: 237–38) quotes two inconsistent examples. *(a)* If the woman who later became my wife rejected another suitor for me, would the rejected less intelligent and less handsome suitor have any legitimate complaint about fairness? *(b)* Is it unfair that a child be raised in a home with a swimming pool, even if he is no more deserving than another child whose home is without one? Indeed, the first example is based on the confusion of fairness with luck, since fairness and equality of opportunity are something that society and the State should assure to all citizens, whereas obtaining (or not obtaining) the love of a person is a matter of good luck in which the State cannot (and should not) play any role. The second example refers to a foolish matter (possessing or not a swimming pool), whereas the equality among citizens refers to those more serious conditions (not only economic in nature) that allow mind evolution. What is overriding is the norm prescribing the promotion of mind evolution, because this norm is derived from the structure and functioning of the mind or, better, from the intrinsic property of the mind as an evolving entity. In contrast, there is no justification supporting Nozick's claim that, since general rights (to life, to equal opportunity, etc.) would require a substructure of things and materials and actions over which other people may have rights and entitlements, such general rights would not exist, because no rights could exist in conflict with this substructure of particular rights (Nozick 1974: 238).

Nozick (1974: 233) holds that the entitlement conception of justice in holdings makes no presumption in favor of equality, because if the distributional facts did arise by a legitimate process, they are legitimate; moreover, according to him, arguments supporting that equality should be built into any theory of justice are not convincing. Here the objection is that the entitlement conception of justice is questionable, and that the legitimacy of the "legitimate process" leading to distributional facts is by no means proved.

Nozick (1974: 233) criticizes Williams' view (1962) according to which when a description of an activity contains an "internal goal", the only proper grounds for the performance and distribution are linked to the effective achievement of that goal; thus, referring to the case of medical care, Williams maintains that the proper criterion for the distribution of medical care is medical need. Nozick (1974: 234) asks: why should the internal goal of an activity take precedence over other goals, e.g., the person's particular purpose? Why should society pay to distribute medical care according to the need? Should society do the same for the barbering? Certainly, Nozick admits, medical care is more important than barbering, but other activities are important, e.g., provision of food, and yet farming does not have an internal goal that refers to other people in the way doctoring does. Here my objection is that the reason for distribution of medical care or the provision of food is not to be found in the "internal goal" and that it cannot be denied referring to "person's particular purpose." Both views, although opposite to each other, are flawed by the lack of reference to any ontological conception. Indeed, the reason for the distribution of medical care and for the provision of food to needy people is that both these measures are directed to assure and promote mind *evolution* (preventing death, which is the extreme *involution* of the mind, and assuring a minimum of body efficiency required for any mind activity).

(3) Against Equality. Lucas (1965; 1977) thinks that the demand for equality is incoherent and incompatible with other more valuable ideals. He distinguishes two principles of equality.

(a) The principle of formal equality (or principle of *universalizability*). Lucas (1965) considers this principle as incoherent because of the infinite variety of human personality, which always creates differences between two people. Here Lucas is right (see my criticism to the universalization principle in ch. 2.2.1.1.3, *AI*). Lucas (1965) also underlines that the *principle of universalizability* has political implications, since laws are always issued in universal terms and justice does not consider all factors involved in a given case. This is not entirely true, because any evolved legal system generates laws that refer to classes of actions as narrow as possible and provide measures to modulate (as carefully as possible) the judgment according to the particular features of the circumstances and of the involved people.

Lucas (1965) also holds that laws cannot be equal, as they should consider some *relevant* discriminations (a doctor who is going to cure some people may be allowed to exceed the speed limit imposed by the law). This rather strange statement originates from the failure to distinguish the *essential properties* common to all men (the property of being entities capable of *evolution*), on which equality of treatment is based, from the *individual properties* possessed by single individual or by groups of individuals, which gives rise to diversity and to unequal (individualized) treatment (ch. 3.2.2.1). An individual who, by respecting the rights/duties linked to men's essential property, on the one hand, and by following his natural endowment, on the other, has developed his mind in the way required to become a doctor, has acquired some particular rights (and some particular duties!) linked to his particular status. The same is true for all individuals with regard to their particular status. The point is that a given particular right (or duty) is recognized to (or imposed on) *all* individuals who undergo the same kind of evolution and are in the same position.

(b) The principle of equality of respect (or *universal humanity*). Concerning the principle that, since people are similar (i.e., share a common humanity), they should be similarly treated, Lucas (1965) observes that human beings are similar in some respects (because they are featherless bipeds, sentient and rational agents, perhaps children of God) but different in other respects (i.e., in respect of height, age, sex, intellectual ability, and strength of character). He notes that the common humanity entails that they should be treated humanely (i.e., they should not be killed, tortured, imprisoned, exploited, frustrated, or humiliated) or, in other words, that they should be treated alike in some respects but not in all (Lucas 1965). Again, I note that Lucas' distinction between similarities and differences between people is weak; actually, men's common properties (linked to their property of being conscious minds capable of evolution), on which the equality of treatment is based, entails much more than the right not to be killed, or tortured, or exploited, etc.; moreover, the differences between people, on which unequal (individualized) treatment is based, are only valid if the rights/duties linked to the common properties have been respected, i.e., if the evolution-allowing condition has been concretely enjoyed by all people (ch. 3.2.2.1.2).

Concerning the socio-economic aspects (*wealth*) of the principle of *equality of respect* (or *universal humanity*), Lucas (1965) recognizes some (but not all) egalitarian conclusions, such as that it is unjust that some people have "too little." Once again, this is a weak definition of what people are entitled to enjoy. According to my theory (chs. 2.1.5.3; 3.1.2.5.1, *3*), each citizen should enjoy those concrete conditions (not limited to the economic field) that allow the evolution of his mind according to his natural endowment.

The differences in *prestige*, on the other hand, derive from the individual achievement due to natural endowment (provided equal enjoyment of basic rights has been assured to all). Prestige actually consists of the association of: *(a)* cognitive recognition (created by the intellect) of a high achievement reached by a given individual in any of the spheres of human activity, be it intellectual, artistic, or practical activity; *(b)* a feeling (generated by the sensitiveness) that such an achievement is of value; and *(c)* a respectful behavior (generated by the power, and prompted by the cognitive recognition and the felt value) toward the individual who has reached the high achievement. Thus, prestige arises from the possession of those individual properties that express a high degree of mind evolution and that are the basis for the right to unequal (individualized) treatment (ch. 3.2.2.1.2).

Lucas (1965) also argues that any organized society needs a system of coercion, i.e., a strong State apparatus that entails differences in *power*. I object that differences in power, linked to the system of coercion, belong to the sphere of public activity, i.e., they are differences linked to the function that an individual exerts as a public official (not as a private citizen). These differences are linked to the organization of the State, and not to the principle of equality between citizens. The same is true for differences linked to the position of being a judge or a legislator. These, therefore, are not examples against the principle of equality of citizens, which refers to the fundamental rights required for mind evolution. Lucas (1965) says that these examples show the internal inconsistency of the ideal of "absolute" equality, an ideal that, indeed, nobody actually pursues.

Finally, Lucas (1965) argues that *liberty* would be inherently unfair, as any person wants to be free to make his own choices. Here I object that the right to liberty derives from the duty to develop one's own mind and from the fact that liberty is required for mind development; yet, since *all* human beings have the duty to develop their mind, *all* of them have the right to liberty (ch. 2.1.4.2, *1*). It follows that the right to liberty of each individual should be limited by the respect for the liberty of others; otherwise, the exercise of liberty of one individual may cause a restraint of mind evolution of others. In other words, the right to liberty should not be exerted through irresponsible choices but through choices that take into account the limitation requested by moral norms, necessary to favor mind evolution of all citizens to the maximum possible extent.

3.2.3—General Concepts: 3. Property

It is known that *property* refers to the possession of various kinds of "goods" (lands, natural resources, means of production, manufactured products, and intellectual or artistic creations), and comprises *private property* (available resources assigned to individuals) and *communal property* (resources assigned to the community). The latter might be distinguished into the *common property* (resources usable by all members of the community) and the *collective property* (resources administered by the community). The *corporate property* might be regarded as an intermediate form of property, because resources are assigned to some individuals, and not to the community (thus resembling private property), and yet resources are assigned to *many* individuals (thus resembling communal property).

It should be stressed that the existence of *private* property in a society is regulated (i.e., guaranteed and defended, but also limited) by the *public* laws and, therefore, can only exist within an organized community.

3.2.3.1—Private Property: Main Theories on Its Origin

I will mention both *(1)* classical theories, and *(2)* modern theories.

(1) Classical Theories. Locke (1690: 287–88) based property (of lands) on the principle of the first occupancy plus one's labor (thus denying property right to nomadic populations); the first occupancy theory is strengthened by the consideration that the first occupants did not exclude anyone, due to initial abundance of land (and of resources in general) (Pufendorf 1673: 84). In Locke's view (1690: 294–96), labor would incorporate the object of the labor into one's self. Locke (1690: 288–89) also justifies the initial appropriation by underlining that, if the use of lands by industrious men had to be defined by some common decision, men would have probably starved despite the availability of resources; indeed, Locke (1690: 291) defends the industrious and rational man against the covetousness of the quarrelsome contentious. After appropriation has been established, a period of growth, accumulation, and exchange of the surplus goods would follow, which Locke (1690: 299–302) justifies because they favor the market and the general prosperity. Finally, a period would ensue, in which inequalities arise so that institutions are needed that protect property (Locke 1690: 350–52). I note that Locke's theory is descriptive rather than justificatory, and that nothing justifies Locke's affirmation that, if the use of lands by industrious men had to be defined by some common decision, probably men would have starved despite the availability of resources. According to my theory, the first occupancy is justified by the fundamental moral norm, which prescribes the promotion of the evolution of mind components (intellect, sensitiveness, and power, be they the mind components of the agent himself or those of others) because, in order to promote the *power*, it is necessary to cultivate the land. In this view, the first occupants are the initiators of this process of power development. The point is that, as discussed below (see ch. 3.2.3.2), the owner of a land should understand that he is not the exclusive owner (but rather a sort of *administrator* of "his" land) because all members of society have rights (even if to a different extent and of a different nature) on the land and because he himself and his land are integrated into a society whose laws should regulate the property in a way that guarantees the (different) rights of all citizens toward the land, i.e., the rights of all the "cooperators" in the activity of the land; these cooperators include: the *proprietor(s)-cooperator(s)*, the *administrator(s)-cooperator(s)*, the *workers-cooperators* and the *consumers-cooperators*.

Other thinkers have pointed out that property is not a product of natural law, but that it is created by a sovereign State (Hobbes 1642: 26–27) or by a convention entered by all the society members, and is actually the result of an "artifice" (Hume 1739/40: 491). The last thinker maintains that, at some time, it may be accepted as more useful for the community to recognize the existing properties instead of continuously fighting for the acquisition of resources; in this context, the role of public institutions serves to stabilize the existing situation (Hume 1739/40: 484–513; Buchanan J.M. 1975). Hume's theory has the advantage of avoiding conflicts directed to modify the status of the existing possessions, yet it would allow the recognition of some unacceptable existing situations (e.g., slavery). Like Locke's theory, Hume's position does not provide any justification of private property. Moreover, Waldron (1994) notes that the sense of justice, which arises from the social convention recognizing the existing possessions, may turn against the equilibrium that engendered it. Here my comment is the same as that expounded above in regard to Locke's views.

According to Rousseau (1762) and Kant (1797), there may be an initial period of uncertainty and provisional appropriation, as discussed also by Ryan (1984: 80); yet at some time property should be regulated by the consensus of the community, i.e., of the people affected by the way in which resources are used. Kant (1797) added that the property right should be fairly integrated with the interest of the other members of society. I note, however, that nothing is said about *why* property should be regulated by the consensus of the community or about *how* it should be integrated with the interest of the other members of the society. Recognizing the failure to justify the origin of property, Mill (1848: 7) noted that we should leave out of consideration the actual origin of property. However, Mill (1848: 14–15) argued that, compared to communism, the regime of individual property might be better if we consider this regime not as it is (with its sufferings and injustices) but as it could be made by conforming to the principles on which the justification of property rests. These justificatory principles, however, remain unclearly defined.

(2) Modern Theories. Nozick (1974: 150–82) is a defender of the historical entitlement theory. He derives the rights to property from the fundamental principle of *self-ownership*. He argues that each individual owns his talents and therefore the goods produced by his talents. However, the initial acquisition of property could not be based only on self-owned talents because, referring to a land, one can improve it with his work and talent but cannot create it. Therefore, to justify the initial acquisition of property over part of the external world Nozick adopts Locke's view that one is entitled to appropriate parts of the external world if one leaves enough and as good for others or if the appropriation leaves people overall well or better. An appropriation would be legitimate if it does not worsen the overall condition of anyone (*test of legitimate appropriation*). However, the condition that

should not be worsened is regarded only as a material condition, without taking into account other possible immaterial aspects, e.g., those linked to autonomy, dignity and liberty. Nozick thinks that, if the land was initially acquired by the use of force, the acquisition is illegitimate, in which case the possible initial illegitimate appropriation should be compensated by returning the goods to the legitimate owners when they are known, or through a one-time redistribution (based on the difference principle of Rawls), after which the principle of free exchange should be followed. When the previous property is legitimate, then any distribution resulting from free exchange is just, as justice is based on history, not on the ends (historical conception of justice). However, it has been observed that to rectify illegitimate appropriations would entail returning most of the New England territory to the American-Indians (Lyons 1981) and an adequate compensation to African-Americans (Valls 1999). I note that, besides the problem of the initial appropriation, one should consider that the principle of free exchange might lead to unacceptable results, because the exchange may occur between parts that are not equally free, as it happens when one of the parts is in need.

I agree with those who observe that we cannot know who will prove to be most able to productively utilize the previous common good. It could be possible that those who are excluded from the property of, say, a land, would be more able than those who appropriated it and, therefore, the appropriation could be illegitimate. Moreover, instead of starting from Nozick's premise that the world is initially un-owned, one could assume that the world was initially jointly owned, so that each person has equal right over the use of the land (Exdell 1977; Cohen 1986). Actually, it seems that *there is no system that passes the test of legitimate appropriation.* Thus, those who appropriate an originally common or un-owned good should compensate those who are left without property (Van Parijs 1992: 9–11); moreover, it has been added that with private property and market systems, many people would live perhaps worse than under a socialist system; and it is morally unacceptable that some should be worse off in order to allow *others* to live better-off.

The fact that free market, or unrestricted capitalism, may cause some untalented people to become very poor is accepted by Nozick because, in his view, untalented people would be very poor also if the goods were left un-owned or for common use (but not, I object, if the goods were collectively administered). Under this view, some consider the desert and maintain that poverty in a market system is due to idleness and lack of initiative (Nozick 1974; Hayek 1976) or that, at least, private property and the market system would reward the virtues of enterprise, prudence, and industriousness (Munzer 1990: 285–88).

Actually, the positive effects of the market system arise only if there are rules that govern private property, such as avoiding monopolies. Thus, I agree that the distribution of property remains a central issue (Waldron 1988: 323–42), otherwise a capitalist society may deny any right to the poor (indeed, it may deny "rights of property altogether"—Green 1895: 170).

Mackie (1977: 174–80) argues that the right to the ownership of property cannot simply derive from the natural law to property, as conceived by Locke (1690) and more recently by Nozick (1974), since the proviso that there should be enough goods left for others cannot be satisfied in all places and in all times; moreover, one's labor cannot be the basis for property because almost all goods embody directly or indirectly the labor of indefinitely many people. Moreover, inheritance would not be a legitimate way of acquiring property. Thus, Mackie thinks that the ownership of property is a cluster of rights that are not simple and absolute (they cannot be derived from self-evident first principles), as they should be created and modified through time by the interplay of various considerations and various pressures; the same would also be true for the occupation of territory by national groups. I note that Mackie does not tell us *how* the principles that justify property should be created and modified through time, thus leaving, like other thinkers, the concept of property rather undefined.

It has been argued that different ownership of means of productions may be the legitimate result of different preferences and choices (Elster 1983). I note that this is true only if all citizens enjoy the evolution-allowing condition. Others have maintained that differences in ownership may be the illegitimate result of previous injustice, such as being educated in a poor family (Roemer 1988: 62–63, 149–56); they note that these differences, which may persist under the transitory stage of socialism, will disappear under communism, which, however, does not maintain that differences in natural endowment should be compensated (Roemer 1982a; 1988: 160, 168). I object that the illegitimate results of a previous injustice can be avoided if all citizens enjoy the evolution-allowing condition.

3.2.3.2—A Justificatory Theory of Private Property

Here I briefly present my theory on the justification of property. I will discuss separately *(1)* the property of land, *(2)* the property of man-made means of productions, and *(3)* the acquisition of property by inheritance.

(1) The Property of Land. I begin by noting that the *initial* appropriation of land took place in a time when there were few people and a large availability of land. It is also reasonable to suppose that the initial appropriation occurred before the establishment of an organized society. In these conditions, appropriation was certainly justified because Locke's provisos were met and because land appropriation is the first, necessary step to initiate the cultivation of land, thus enhancing the *power* of the community (including

the land-owner and the others), as prescribed by the ground moral norm. With the growing of population, however, at some time, two new problems arose.

(a) The duty of socially optimal utilization of the owned land. The owner of a given land has the *duty* to cultivate the land in the best way in order to increase the production of goods and, therefore, the *power* of those who will utilize the land products (the initial owner and also others—see below). This duty descends from the ground moral norm, which prescribes the promotion of the evolution of mind intellect, sensitiveness, and power. Thus, the proprietor of a large land cannot leave it uncultivated (latifundium), because this would restrain the development of the power of many citizens. Thus, if the proprietor of a latifundium does not provide for an appropriate cultivation of his large land, the government should intervene and, if no other ways prove to be effective, the proprietor may be expropriated (agrarian reform). The same is true for any large estate. Suppose that a rich man buys about 50% of the apartment buildings in a town, and then decides to evict all the tenants and to keep all the apartments vacant; if there are not enough apartments available in that town, this may have bad consequences for many citizens. For this reason, in these conditions, the State should intervene and may even impose an obligatory, controlled renting. This is what happened for several years in Italy, after the 2nd world war, due to severe housing shortage. The ground for the intervention of the State lies in the fact that *ownership or property is founded and guaranteed by the organized society (State) and must meet its demands and needs.* It should also be pointed out that the possessor of a large amount of money (a large capital) has the same social duties, and is subjected to the same limitation, as the possessor of a large estate. He too has the duty to consider the social effect of the ways in which he utilizes his money, since the latter may be utilized in an active manner, i.e., it may be employed in a socially useful way, by creating enterprises and concerns that provide employment for several or many citizens, or it may be utilized in a passive manner only, i.e., by passively enjoying the yield or gain that it may produce. Thus, there is just one principle that should apply to the possessors of large amounts of resources (be they land or estate or capital): *The possessors of large amounts of resources have the duty of utilizing them in a socially optimal way* (see also ch. 3.2.8.2.1, 4). Of course, this does not apply to the owners of small lands or estate or capital, but to the owners of land, estate, or capital large enough to entail that their non-optimal utilization produces effects that have social relevance, i.e., which interfere with the mind evolution of citizens. Moreover, the above example shows that the very rich and potent individuals or groups may exert an excessive weight in the political life and might even be able to overcome the control by the legal system, thus undermining the fundaments of democracy; for this reason, an *upper limit in*

the economic growth and power of individuals or groups should be established by specific laws, which should have the rank of constitutional norms (ch. 3.1.2.2.2). Of course, this limit should be high enough to avoid that it restrains free enterprise and the selfish activity linked to the *morally-good egoism* and the *duty toward oneself* (ch. 2.1.5.2.2). In addition, a solution should be envisaged for those individuals or groups that reach the allowed upper limit to avoid that they could feel economically damaged.

(b) *The concept of cooperator-owned property.* The duty to cultivate the owned land in the best way, in its turn, entails (unless the owned land is very small) that the owner needs the cooperation of others; more exactly, he needs the work of others, who could be defined as *workers-cooperators*, as distinguished from the "owner". The nature of this cooperation is a very important point. There is no reason to consider the "workers-cooperators" merely as property-less workers, whose rights are limited to receive a (often small or arbitrarily fixed) salary; actually, "workers-cooperators" are entitled to a partial ownership of the products of the land that they contribute to cultivate (this is the justification and the meaning of their salary). Indeed, the owner of the land and those who cooperate with him to cultivate it are the members of a *community or social group* (or of more than one community, i.e., the administrators, the workers, etc.) which, while may vary in magnitude, may be regarded as a social group of a magnitude intermediate between that of the informal mini-communities (ch. 3.1.2.3.3) and that of the fully universal community, i.e., the society as a whole, represented by the State and its organs (Table 3.1). All those who cooperate with the owner to cultivate a land are entitled to share (even if to a different extent) the products. Of course, there may be differences in the degree of responsibility and in the value of the work made by the various cooperators. It is the task of specialized experts (economists, sociologists, experts in political science, and jurists) to define the details concerning the rights of each class of cooperators and the ways in which these rights may be enjoyed; the task of political philosophy is to establish that both the "owner" of the land and the workers-cooperators are members of an *informal community or social group* and, as such, they share some rights about the enjoyment of land products, so that they can be defined as a sort of *co-owners*. The distribution of the products should be made taking into account the principle that each man has the right to an *"evolution-allowing, involution-avoiding"* amount of resources, considering the stage of the development of the society (the *"evolution-allowing, involution-avoiding"* amount of resources in a medieval society is certainly different from that of a modern, technological society) (chs. 2.1.5.3; 3.1.2.5.1, *3*).

There is still another category of "cooperators" to be considered: the *consumers* of the products obtained from a land; they could be defined as *consumers-cooperators*. Again, while it is the task of specialized experts to define the details concerning the rights of the consumers and the way in which these rights can be enjoyed, I underline that consumers are true cooperators in the activities linked to the utilization of the land; without consumers, the land would not produce more than the direct utilization of the products by the "owner" and the workers-cooperators, which means that the power of all the involved minds (individuals) would be restrained, thus violating the fundamental moral norm. The consumers-cooperators have the right to buy the land products at an appropriate price (which may entail, for instance, that monopoly be contrasted), and to be correctly informed about the properties of the acquired products, etc. Thus, the consumers-cooperators too are members of the *informal community or social group* (with its implicit or unstated rules—ch. 3.1.2.3.3; Table 3.1) arising from the activities linked to the utilization of a given land, and should be regarded as *co-operators*. The recent trend of the "consumers" to organize into associations is the way through which they claim their rights as "cooperators", and hence *co-owners* (in a broad sense), of the land (but the same is true with regard to firms, enterprises, and concerns) whose products they consume.

Thus, a land is owned by the members of an informal community (or social group) that includes: the proprietor(s), who could be defined as *proprietor(s)-cooperator(s)*; the administrator(s), who could be defined as *administrator(s)-cooperato*r(s); the "workers", who could be defined as *workers-cooperators*; and the consumers, who could be regarded as *consumers-cooperators*. All these cooperators should be regarded (in a broad sense) as *co-owners*. The property so conceived may be defined a *cooperator-owned property*; thus, a given land is owned, even if with different rights and duties, by all those who cooperate in its activity, i.e., by all its cooperators.

It should be underlined that *all* the members of the informal community (or social group) mentioned above have rights on the land products; this view contrasts with that of libertarians who often think that the land-owner is entitled to establish the salary he wants to give to workers. The landowner cannot take undue advantage of the need of the workers for a salary; this would be something like a gunman who imposes what he wants to a disarmed man. Actually, a salary is just if, considering the amount of resources available, the stage of development of the society (or State) to which all the cooperators belong, and the difference in the role exerted by each cooperator, it reaches (or is the best possible approach to) the "mind evolution-allowing" amount.

By following the above-described theory, no member of the society will actually be excluded from the enjoyment of the products of the land, because all are potentially involved, at least as possible consumers.

(2) The Property of Man-Made Means of Production. These means of production include factories, firms, products of intellect or sensitiveness, etc. Here the same principles and reasoning mentioned above for the activi-

ties linked to the utilization of lands should be followed; thus, there is the *duty of optimal utilization of the owned goods* and the property should be conceived as a *cooperator-owned property*. The difference is that here the means of production are not appropriated by the owner but created by him; this entails that his (partial) ownership is not under dispute. However, even in these situations, the rights of *all* the co-owners should be taken into account, including the rights of the "administrator(s)-cooperator(s)", the "workers-cooperators", and the "consumers-cooperators".

Thus, the right to ownership should be understood as the right to a "non-exclusive ownership"; this is because the right to property is founded by the laws of the society (which guarantee and limit it), so that the ownership is always a "co-ownership" shared (to a various extent) by all the cooperators and, potentially, by all the members of the society.

(3) Acquisition of Property by Inheritance. This issue will be treated in chapter 3.2.8.2.1, 2.

3.2.3.3—The Communal Property

Marx (1861-1863) was a convict defender of collectivistic property (communism), which, however, has been strongly criticized. Communism will be treated in chapter 3.2.8. Here I will just mention that, according to some thinkers, the centralized, common administration of resources (as proposed by socialist theories) cannot be efficient, considering the innumerable production factors that should be controlled; the socialist regime would also be economically inefficient because:

> [E]xperience shows that nothing is operated with less economy and with more waste of labour and material of every kind than public services and undertakings. Private enterprise on the other hand naturally induces the owner to work with the greatest economy in his own interest. (von Mises 1951: 183)

Moreover, Hardin (1968) drew attention to what he called the "tragedy of the commons," which consists, among others, of the fact that each commoner will tend to take as much as possible from the common resources while being unwilling to undergo self-restraining to reach long-term common benefits. Moreover, it has been claimed that privatization of common resources may benefit some people without making other people worse off (Pareto-improvement). Locke (1690: 296–97) made a comparison between England of his time (where there was prevalence of private property) and the pre-colonial America (where land was in common use by natives), and affirmed that a King in America lived worse than a laborer in England. In this regard, I think that one should consider that the difference between England and America of that time was due to the large difference in mind evolution between the populations of those two countries, so that Locke's comparison is not meaningful.

Mackie (1977: 178) observes that, since the good for men consists of the pursuit of diverse ideals or private goals, a common property handled by a single authority is not practicable, and separate ownership of property would be appropriate. He notes that, if there is not a natural law of property, there is at least the natural law that there should be some law of property.

While most aspects of the communal property will be discussed in chapter 3.2.8, here I will note that the concept of communal property should be discussed by referring to the ontological conception of the human mind as an evolving conscious triadic entity made of intellect, sensitiveness, and power. Property, like money, is one of the ways in which the *power* expresses itself; it follows that all the activities linked to the utilization of, say, a land (which include the activity of the administrators, workers, and consumers—ch. 3.2.3.2) concern the sphere of the power. (Of course, the same reasoning applies to the property of factories, firms, etc.). Considering the triadic nature of the human mind and the diversity among individuals (ch. 3.2.2.1.2), we may reasonably suppose that the citizens (because of their diverse natural endowment and aptitude) will not be equally interested in the activities linked to the utilization of the land. In fact, we should consider that about one-third of citizens may have the aptitude to act in the sphere of power (the others being perhaps interested in acting in the sphere of intellect or in that of sensitiveness); moreover, among the citizens prone to act in the sphere of power, some will prefer politics while others will prefer economic activity (to which the utilization of a land belongs); among the latter citizens, some will prefer economic activities different from the direct engagement in the activity linked to the utilization of the land (say, commerce, banking, etc.), so that the citizens actually interested in the land-linked activity will represent only a limited percentage of the totality. This entails that the citizens "excluded" from the possession of land (or of factories or firms) are actually a minority. It should be noted, however, that while the number of citizens directly involved as administrators or as workers of a land (or of a factory or of a firm) is limited, the number of citizens involved as consumers is larger and may even extend to cover most citizens. On the grounds of the above considerations, the essential difference between a system based on private property and one based on communal property is that the "administration" of the means of productions (land, factories, firms, etc.) is exerted by private individuals or groups in the former case, and by "public administrators" in the latter; in both instances, however, the "administrators" represent a small percentage of the citizens, and in both instances the nature of the property is essentially "public", in the sense that the administrators (who actually are "administrators-cooperators") should recognize and respect the rights of the workers (or "workers-cooperators") as well as those of the consumers (or "consumers-cooperators"), as regulated by laws based on the concepts expounded above. Recognizing the "public" nature of the so-called private property, when regulated by appropriate laws, protects citizens from the possible "abuse of power" while preserving the greater efficiency of the systems based on the "private property" understood as exclusive ownership. The important difference concerning the way in which "profit" is distributed will be treated in chapter 3.2.8.2.1, *3*.

3.2.3.4—Property, Liberty, and Virtues

I will consider *property* in relation to *(1)* liberty, *(2)* the virtue of generosity, and (3) the affirmation of the self.

   (1) Property and Liberty. The system of private property (with a minimal governmental economic role) has been defended by claiming that it allows more *liberty*; yet, others argue that it might actually limit freedom of the poor (Cohen 1979/1991). The same is true for the independence of individuals: private property may favor the *independence* of those who own some amount of resources, and yet it may also limit the independence of the poor, who own nothing.

   The above considerations indicate, as noted by Cohen (1979/1991), that the relationship between property and liberty is rather complex. I think that we should understand that property is one of the ways in which the *power* expresses itself and, as such, it can *directly* affect only liberty in the sphere of the power but not in the sphere of intellect or sensitiveness (ch. 2.1.4.2, *1*). Indeed, even a poor man can have and express his thoughts, desires, and preferences (unless factors other than the wealth of individuals intervene). Property could affect liberty in the sphere of intellect and sensitiveness *indirectly*, by influencing (limiting and manipulating) education and information of citizens. This is because, due to the close relationship between the mind components, both the intellect and sensitiveness need some support by the power to develop their activities. For this reason, as noted by Friedman (1962), the private, multiple controls of intellectual products and information broadcasting greatly enhance the freedom of a society. Yet, I think that the problem of liberty in all its aspects and in all spheres of mind activity is linked to just one and fundamental provision: the enjoyment of the *evolution-allowing, involution-avoiding condition* by citizens; the enjoyment of this condition entails that a citizen has enough *power* (under any form), together with free, adequate, and objective instruction and information in order to develop his *intellect* and *sensitiveness*. Thus, whichever is the form of property (private or communal), if citizens enjoy the evolution allowing condition they will be free, otherwise they will not be free. Rather, the superiority of private property (when regulated by laws that guarantee an evolution allowing condition to all citizens), as compared to communal property, is that it has proven to be more efficient, thus producing a greater evolution of the power (i.e., greater wealth) of citizens and of society.

(2) Property and the Virtue of Generosity. Like Aristotle (~330 B.C.), who thought that property favors some virtues (such as responsibility and prudence), Aquinas (1272: 216) underlined the link between property and the virtue of generosity, and maintained that property laws couldn't ignore the necessities of poor people. Yet, as I mentioned in chapter 2.2.1.4.2, *D2*, it is only the magnitude of generosity that is linked to property, not generosity *per se*, because one can be generous toward those who are less advantaged even if one possesses very little, say only a modest salary (or even less); in this regard, I quote the motto of G. B. Dusmet, archbishop (1867–1887) and then cardinal (1888–1894) in Catania (Italy): "Even if I possess just a small loaf, I will divide it with the poor." Indeed, the acts of generosity exerted by non-rich people indicate a *greater* virtue than those exerted by rich people.

(3) Property and the Affirmation of the Self. Bentham (1802: 111) underlined that property is required for the affirmation of the self, as it allows one to make his general plan of conduct based on relatively certain expectations, so that the claim of redistribution should be questioned. I object that what is needed to make one's own general plan of conduct, based on relatively certain expectations, is a certain amount of power, which may or may not be linked to property (let us consider a physician, or a university professor, or a handicraftsman, etc.). In any case, if property is required, then redistribution is necessary in order to allow that all (or most) citizens can make their own general plan of conduct. Indeed, what is needed is, again, the enjoyment of the *evolution-allowing, involution-avoiding condition.* The same comment applies to the claims of other thinkers who have regarded property as necessary for the expression of one's personality. Hegel (1821: 235–36) said that "The rationale of property is to be found not in the satisfaction of needs but in the supersession of the pure subjectivity of personality. In his property a person exists for the first time as reason"; and Green (1895: 171) maintained that property is required in order to favor the development of responsibility, even if Green also underlined the need for respect for the property possessed by others.

3.2.4—Political Thought of Hobbes, Hume, and Nietzsche

Before discussing the political thought of these authors, it should be borne in mind that they lived in the *pre-democratic era*, i.e., in a time anterior to the practical implementation of *universal-suffrage-based, constitutional democracy*, which guarantees the freedom of speech, press, and association, equal opportunity in competitions for public offices, and the rule of law. It should be recalled that full universal suffrage (extended also to women), which is the necessary condition for the full *universalization of actions* (chs. 3.1.2.1; 3.1.2.2.2), was adopted only after the 1st world war in Britain and in France, after the 2nd world war in Italy, and only in 1971 in Switzerland. The full universal suffrage was preceded by stages of progressive universalization of human actions, during which the suffrage was "partial" because it was limited by factors such as property or income qualification (predominance of the rich classes), or degree of education (predominance of the educated people), or race/ethnicity (generally, predominance of white people), or gender (manhood predominance). Lack of "universal-suffrage-based, constitutional democracy" means lack of *publicly-shared moral principles and values* and, consequently, lack of *shared moral norms* (constitutional norms), derived from the *ground moral norm* (prescribing the promotion of mind evolution), in turn framed into the ontological conception of the human mind as an *evolving conscious triadic entity* made of intellect, sensitiveness, and power. This lack of principles, values, and norms was associated with the predominance of the most powerful individuals or groups or classes; this predominance was based on power and actually meant *violence*. The thinkers considered in this chapter did not critically evaluate this state of violence but rather attempted to justify it; this is shown by the conception of the social *contract* (Hobbes 1651: 78), stipulated in order to overcome the fear of death (which concerns all people) and to satisfy the desire of a "commodious living" (which primarily concerns the rich classes), or by the conception of a *convention* (Hume 1739/40: 487), made in order to assure the "enjoyment of such possessions as we have acquired by our industry and good fortune" (which, again, mainly concerns the rich classes). In the case of Nietzsche, as we will see, there is also a total insensitivity toward any human principle or value other than the exercise of unjustified personal power (i.e., violence) guided by wild, selfish instincts.

3.2.4.1—Hobbes

It is well known that Hobbes (1651: 74–76) held that men are rather similar to one another as far as the strength of body and the faculties of mind are concerned, so that, in the natural condition, no one could gain domination over the others; rather, being humans dominated by competition, they would be in a condition of war of every man against every man. In this state of continuous war, force and fraud are virtues and, because there is no common power, there is no law, and where there is no law there is no justice or injustice nor the notions of right and wrong (Hobbes 1651: 78). I object that actually men are not similar to one another as far as the strength of the body and, especially, the faculties of mind are concerned; even the power component of the mind, which is not represented only by the physical force of the body, varies in strength from individual to individual. Therefore, in the state of nature, prevalence of stronger men over weak ones would occur. Prevalence of strength, however, would occur in most but not in all instances. This is because, besides the power, the human mind also comprises the intellect and the sensitiveness, whose inward activity (which gives rise to *consciousness*) creates *moral thoughts* and *moral feeling*, respectively, through which men become aware that "the others" should be helped and not hindered, and that they may be regarded as friends and allies rather than as strangers and enemies. Moreover, the human mind soon becomes aware that individual power itself may be increased through cooperation with others, because human actions acquire a higher degree of universality. Thus, as the human mind develops or evolves, it naturally (and necessarily) leads human beings to organize themselves into a society (ch. 3.1.1.1.1). Hobbes' conception arises from a poor understanding of the complexity and richness of the human soul. According to Hobbes (1651: 77), what a man thinks of fellow subjects and citizens is shown by the fact that he rides armed and locks his doors, what he thinks of his children and servants is shown by the fact that he locks his chests; similarly, Kings and persons of sovereign authority have their weapons pointed against their neighbor kingdoms. These affirmations are superficial and misleading. Indeed, a man rides armed and locks his doors because he thinks that there may be just *some* individuals (a small minority) who might be thieves or, anyway, "bad persons". Similarly, a man locks his chests because children are not yet able to understand what they do, or because *some* servants may not be trustworthy (not to mention the cases when servants are treated as slaves!). Even the reference to weapons pointed against neighbor kingdoms is not always true, even if this issue concerns international relationships, a field in which human organization has developed and develops slower than in the domestic area (ch. 3.4.1).

Hobbes (1651: 78) believes that, if justice and injustice were inherent human faculties, they would have been possessed by a man living alone (as are human passions) but instead they are only acquired when men live in a society. This appears to me as a strange statement. Justice (like, for instance, generosity) refers to the relations among individuals and, consequently, it is obvious that it cannot exist if a man lives alone (an unrealistic hypothesis!). This, however, does not show that justice is not an inherent human faculty, but rather indicates that the evolution of the human mind leads at the same time to the organization of individuals into a society and to the pursuing of justice, both of which are irreducible tendencies of the human mind.

Notoriously, Hobbes (1651: 81–82, 108–9) maintains that men (in order to avoid the war of everybody against everybody) lay aside their rights by voluntary transferring them, through a *contract*, to a sovereign authority (*sovereign power*), consisting of a man or an assembly, with sufficient right and strength to enforce contracts and covenants and to ensure peace and the security of one's person; the *contract* so stipulated should be respected (*keeping of promise*) to avoid a *violation of faith*; the multitude united by the contract in one person (or assembly) is called a *commonwealth*. This is the contract theory about the origin of human society, to which I oppose my conception of society as arising from the tendency of human actions and moral acts toward universalization (ch. 3.1.1.1.1).

According to Hobbes (1651: 79–81, 89–98), the *right of nature* (or *jus naturale*) would be the liberty of doing what one believes to be useful for himself; a *law of nature* would be a general rule dictated by reason (and stirred up by the fear of death and the desire of a commodious living— Hobbes 1651: 78) directed to forbid what is destructive to life. Hobbes recognized *nineteen laws of nature*, including the following eight (pp. 79–81, 89–98): pursuing peace, limiting of one's liberty to meet the liberty of others, performing the covenants made (breaking them would be injustice), having gratitude for free gifts, striving to be sociable by considering others, pardoning past offenses, and directing the punishment just to correct the offender (otherwise it would be cruelty), to which a last one should be added, i.e., submitting controversies to an arbitrator. These "laws of nature" (which actually are rules of practical morality) have a very poor motivation (fear of death and the desire of a commodious living). I think that the laws that regulate the life of a society or of a State should all be directed to promote the endless *evolution of the mind* of all citizens, an end that can be realized by assuring that all citizens concretely enjoy an *evolution-allowing, involution-avoiding condition* (chs. 2.1.5.3; 3.1.2.5.1, *3*).

3.2.4.2—Hume

According to Hume (1739/40: 484–500), unlike the internal satisfaction of the mind and the external advantages of the body, the enjoyment of possessions (acquired by industry and good fortune) are exposed to the violence of others and are therefore marked by *instability*, enhanced by the *scarcity* of goods and by man's *selfishness*. To ensure stability of external goods and their peaceable enjoyment, men have used an *artifice*, i.e., they made a *convention* or *agreement* whereby all members of the society agree to regulate their conduct by certain rules. This view actually is a version of the utilitarian explanation of the origin of society as the result of a contingent *contract* (or convention), stipulated in order to reach a scope: the satisfaction of the desire of a peaceful enjoyment of external goods. Here again, I contrast this view with my conception about the origin of human society as arising from the necessary evolution of human actions and moral acts toward universality, linked to the structure and functioning of the human mind (ch. 3.1.1.1.1).

Hume (1739/40: 490–91) wrote:

> After this convention, concerning abstinence from the possessions of others, is entered into, and everyone has acquired a stability in his possessions, there immediately arise the ideas of justice and injustice; as also those of property, right, and obligation. The latter are altogether unintelligible without first understanding the former.

Thus, the "convention" would explain the origin of justice and that of property, which would be a moral (not a natural) relation of an object with its possessor. I think that the sequence proposed by Hume (that the stability of possessions generates the idea of justice and the idea of property) is unacceptable because, in my opinion, the idea of possession, that of justice, and that of property are closely related to one another and represent the product of the outward activity of power (personal actions), directed to expand the personal possessions, together with the inward activity of power (moral acts), directed to assure all citizens enough power to enable them to develop their own mind. Indeed, the idea of justice is antecedent to that of possession, because the "convention" that stabilizes the existing possessions can be agreed upon only if the existing possessions are regarded as "just", i.e., acceptance of the "convention" means that the criterion upon which the existing possessions are based is just (because it favors, to the greatest possible extent, the mind evolution of citizens); moreover, it is equally possible that the convention considers as just a different criterion and thus will stabilize some possessions while rejecting or modifying others.

Hume (1739/40: 574–91) maintained that the natural obligation to justice is the interest, and that we partake of injustice even when it affects others by *sympathy* toward them; everything in human actions that gives uneasiness is called *vice*, and everything that gives satisfaction is called *virtue*. In contrast, I think that justice means the application of the rules and laws that descend from the fundamental moral norm (prescribing the promotion of mind evolution) and that, therefore, are directed to assure all citizens a condition that is the best approach to the *evolution-allowing, involution-avoiding condition*. Moreover, vices and virtues comprise both some individual properties unrelated to justice and morality (e.g., being courageous or cowardly) and some related to it (being generous in helping others or mercilessly selfish) (ch. 2.2.1.7.2, *A*).

3.2.4.3—Nietzsche

I will briefly discuss Nietzsche's views about *(1)* justice, *(2)* society and the "bad conscience", and *(3)* constitution, democracy, and general welfare.

(1) Justice. Nietzsche (1878: 93) claims that the initial character of justice is barter, requital and exchange. He thinks that when there is no supreme power, reaching an understanding and negotiating becomes the claim of both the parties with approximately equal strength (to avoid mutual injury); this would explain why revenge, being an exchange, initially belonged (like gratitude) to the realm of justice. Then, he continues, men have forgotten the original purpose of the so-called just actions, and it has gradually come to appear that a just action is a selfless one. Nietzsche's explanation of justice is absurd. Lacking any ontological conception about the structure of the mind, Nietzsche seems to be able to recognize only the outward activity of the mind components in their particular expression, primarily the particular (personal) actions (generated by the power) as guided by particular, selfish, and wild instincts (generated by the sensitiveness). This is the condition marked by very little mind evolution, in which public life consists not of truly universal actions but only of violent actions exerted by powerful individuals or groups, and in which there are not moral thoughts, moral feelings, and moral acts. In times when there was not yet a universal (publicly justified) power, revenge might have been regarded only as "probably" justifiable, but not fully "just" (who would have judged if a revenge was "just" or exaggerated?). Justice is not a practice of revenge by people who have forgotten the barter nature of the apparently just actions; justice is a necessary product of human consciousness which, through the moral thoughts and feelings, produces moral principles, values, and norms (ch. 2.1.4.1), and consists of the observance of such principles, values, and norms through acts directed to morally just ends (chs. 2.1.5.3; 3.1.2.5.1, *3*).

(2) Society and the "Bad Conscience". Nietzsche (1887: 84–85) regards the "bad conscience" as the serious illness that man contracted when he underwent the stress of finding himself enclosed within the walls of society and peace. According to him, in this new condition, men lost their former guide, i.e., the unconscious and infallible instinct of the wild, free man (toward wilderness, adventure, prowling, hostility, war, cruelty, and joy in persecuting, in attacking, and in destruction), and were reduced to thinking, inferring, reckoning, and coordinating cause and effect, i.e., they were reduced to their "consciousness", which is their weakest and most fallible organ! All the above-named instincts, Nietzsche continues, which could no longer discharge themselves outwardly, turned inward (*internalization* of man) leading to the development of what was later called "soul". Those fearful bulwarks (including punishments), with which the political organization protects itself against the old instincts of freedom, brought about that all

those instincts turned backward against man himself; that is the origin of the "bad conscience" (Nietzsche 1887: 85). Here two comments are in order. *First*, Nietzsche seems to conceive human conduct as consisting only of *personal actions* (produced by the *power*) stirred up by *personal sentiments*, primarily the primitive and wild ones, mentioned above (produced by the *sensitiveness*); he seems to ignore the existence of human *moral acts*, stirred up by *moral feeling* and supported by *moral thoughts* and *moral conception* (chs. 2.1.1; 2.1.4.1; 2.1.5.3; 3.1.2.5.1, *3*). Moreover, the view of Nietzsche that the human soul is the result of the "internalization" of the old, wild instincts is arbitrary, and the same is true for his hypothesis about the origin of the "bad conscience". I think that the wild instincts celebrated by Nietzsche should be interpreted as the deviant conception of a strong desire to affirm one's personality, a sort of creative vitality; this strong desire, however, would be a *morally-good* one if directed to promote the evolution of one's mind and if associated with the promotion of the minds of others [see the concept of morally-good egoism (ch. 2.1.5.2.2), and the integration between selfish actions and collective moral acts (ch. 3.1.1.2, *1*)]; conversely, it would be morally bad if directed to those bad ends indicated by Nietzsche (war, cruelty, joy in persecuting, in attacking, in destruction, etc.), which might satisfy wretched and cruel personal desires and interests. *Second*, Nietzsche's conception of society (as stressing the citizens by repressing within its walls the old, wild instincts) indicates the inability of Nietzsche to understand society as the human organization that allows the universalization of the actions of citizens (ch. 3.1.1.1.1); he viewed society as an agglomerate of individuals, each attempting to exert his personal power against all others and repressed by the political organization.

(3) Constitution, Democracy, and General Welfare. Nietzsche (1886: 85) argues that, since the number of those who command is less than that of those who obey, *obedience* has been largely cultivated and it is now an almost innate instinct of the average man, who is thus ready to accept commands by parents and teachers, laws, class prejudices, or public opinion; this would occur at the expense of the art of command, thus limiting human development. Nietzsche's statement appears incoherent. It seems that obedience has been cultivated among those who obey (the average men); thus, how could this occur at the expense of the art of command, which is possessed and exerted by those who command? Although it is possible that the diffusion of obedience may somewhat extend to, or in some way affect those who command, this seems a weak and unjustified assumption.

Nietzsche (1886: 85) also thinks that those who command suffer from bad conscience and deceive themselves as if they command in order to obey to ancient or higher commands; there would be moral hypocrisy in Europe, where men glorify such attributes as public spirit, benevolence, consideration, industriousness, moderation, modesty, indulgence, and pity. However, since leaders are indispensable, people today make attempts to add together clever herd men by way of replacing commanders: this is the origin of *parliamentary constitutions* (Nietzsche 1886: 86). Once again, I think that Nietzsche makes arbitrary statements and deductions. If Nietzsche's view is correct, why should those who command suffer from "bad conscience"? "Bad conscience" can only derive from the awareness of having ignored the moral principles and values written in the human soul (consciousness), expressed by *moral thoughts* and *moral feelings* and giving rise to moral acts. Indeed, it is the attempt to define the shared moral principles and values (common to at least the majority of citizens) that has led to parliamentary constitutions. Perhaps, Nietzsche recognized primarily the value of *power* and, therefore, he admired those who command because of their *power* which, however, if not approved by the majority of citizens, actually is *violence* (ch. 3.1.2.4); this is shown by Nietzsche's admiration for Napoleon.

Nietzsche (1886: 87–88) also maintains that, if the good is identified with the utility of the herd (the community) and the "bad" with what can harm it, there cannot be morality based on neighborly love (directed to single individuals). According to him, it is after society has become secure against external dangers, that the fear of the neighbor develops and creates new perspectives of moral judgment; what raises an individual above the herd and intimidates the neighbor is regarded as evil, and the modest, submissive, conforming mentality, the mediocrity of desires, the lamb even more than the sheep, is given moral value and honors. Here one should object that fear for the neighbor is easier to occur in an unorganized agglomerate of individuals, and not in a society which, as such, is organized and has laws that control violence, while respecting the true power (recognized by the majority of citizens); those who raise themselves "above the herd," if they exert true and justified power and not violence, may indeed not be regarded as "evil" but may rather inspire confidence in everybody and may exert beneficial effects on mind development of other citizens. It is the conception of society that seems to be lacking or distorted in Nietzsche.

According to Nietzsche (1886: 118–20), *general welfare* is not ideal, not a remotely intelligible concept, but only an "emetic"; what is fair for one *cannot* be also fair for others, and the demand of one morality for all is detrimental to the higher men. Here one should ask why what is detrimental to the "higher men" but useful to the community should be regarded as "emetic", while the reverse (what is useful for the "higher men" but detrimental to the community) should be regarded as good. To maintain this view, Nietzsche should have defined at length who are the "higher men", and what is their role and its justification; conversely, the concept of "higher men" is left unclear. However, Nietzsche (1886: 89) adds that in Europe, with the help of religion, we have reached the point where we find even in political and social institutions the expression of such a morality: the *de-*

mocratic movement, which is the heir of the Christian movement. Nietzsche's restricted view, focused on power or, better, on *violence*, prevents him from appreciating publicly justified power (recognized by the majority of citizens) and the moral value of pursuing the general welfare or, more exactly, the general evolution of the mind in all its three components.

3.2.5—Utilitarianism

3.2.5.1—Happiness, Utility, and Welfare as Moral Ends

(1) The Core Concepts. It is well known that *utilitarianism* is a moral and political conception aimed at promoting the policy that maximizes human happiness and social welfare (see also ch. 2.2.1.2.3, *CI*); i.e., it maintains that moral acts and policy are good if they are directed to produce the highest possible degree of happiness and welfare for the individuals (Bentham 1789; Mill 1861; Smart and Williams 1973; Sartorius 1975). Moreover, under this theory, individual *rights* can be defended because they make individuals (and society) happier; thus, they are a means to reach a utility.

It has been pointed out, however, that the claim to realize the greatest happiness for the greatest number of individuals is unsound, because these two goals may be actually incompatible in several instances (Rescher 1966: 25–28; Griffin 1986: 151–54). Moreover, utilitarianism would fail to give a solid justification of why happiness and welfare are indeed real "good", worthy to be pursued (Smart and Williams 1973; Sen and Williams 1982). The same comment applies to *consequentialism*, which takes into account the consequences of our actions on others, without saying why some consequences should be regarded as *good*.

In commenting whether the goals that utilitarianism indicates are worthy of being pursued, I will focus on the issues discussed in the points that follow.

(a) Happiness is not a moral good *per se*; it consists of the satisfaction of personal desires created by the sensitiveness and, therefore, can be regarded as morally neutral end belonging to the personal or private activity. Indeed, as I pointed out elsewhere (chs. 2.2.1.2.3, *C1a*; 2.2.1.6.2; 2.2.1.6.3), if happiness was the end to be pursued, the moral norms should prescribe that one should be engaged in helping others to obtain the love of the loved one! Happiness, however, has an indirect link to morality in the public sphere, inasmuch as moral ends include the development of sensitiveness (ability to feel an ever-deeper happiness—or an ever-deeper sadness, depending on the circumstances) and the enjoyment of liberty and other conditions required for pursuing personal ends, including happiness.

(b) Welfare, on the other hand, is linked to morality because promoting

the welfare of citizens actually means promoting the evolution of one of their mind components, the *power*, which is one of the moral ends.

(c) Pursuing the utilitarian end, i.e., maximizing the total utility, may entail a disadvantage for single or few individuals, a consequence that could never occur with my ethical and political theory, which prescribes the promotion of the evolution of all minds (with special attention to the less-developed ones) by making any effort to ensure that all (or the largest possible percentage of) citizens can enjoy the *evolution-allowing, involution-avoiding condition* (or the best approach to it).

(d) Utilitarianism confers equal value to legitimate as well as to illegitimate (or unjust, or bad) preferences, such as those inspired by egoism, or by prejudices (including racial prejudice) or by hate. In contrast, according to my moral system, we can clearly define as immoral all those desires and preferences which are directed to restrain the evolution of the involved minds. It has been suggested (Rescher 1966: 59; Raphael 1981: 47–56) that, in giving equal consideration to the preferences of everyone, we should exclude the egoistic or illegitimate ones, thus integrating equality of treatment with deontological principles. Yet, to exclude illegitimate preferences, we should first define them; as mentioned above, my moral theory allows us to clearly identify the illegitimate or bad preferences: those that entail restraining of mind evolution.

(e) According to the utilitarian view, a bad action would be less bad (or even good) if it is liked by many people, which is an unacceptable position (Scarre 1996: 155); this, again, is avoided by my moral theory, according to which the goodness or badness of an action does not depend on the fact that it is enjoyed by one or many people; it follows that oppression of minorities is morally unacceptable, also because the disadvantaged people (who may lack the resources necessary for attempting to develop their mind) should be the primary object of public moral acts (in order to bring them to the level of the evolution-allowing condition). This is in keeping with the view that a given amount of resources produces a greater utility in those who have less (Hare 1978: 124–26; Goodin 1995: 23); consequently, resources initially assigned to a given individual should be redistributed to others if this produces a greater utility (Hare 1978), and the State, in order to give equal consideration to all citizens, should attempt to improve the condition of the most disadvantaged (Mackie 1984).

Whether we consider happiness as pure pleasant sensations, or as satisfaction of preferences, it is difficult to define and to measure, especially when we have to evaluate the preferences of other people (who in political philosophy are the citizens). This difficulty has been regarded as a flaw of the utilitarian theory; actually, it is not. This is because any measurement referring to events in the human world is always empirical and approximate, due to the extreme complexity of the facts to be measured; even in the field of natural science most evaluations are approximate (ch. 1.1.3.2.1). For this reason, even mind evolution, which is the true moral end according to my theory, can only be evaluated in an empirical and approximate manner (ch. 2.1.6). This, however, means only that, in making moral and political choices, there may be uncertainty and different opinions about particular aspects (or details) concerning which is the most appropriate means or method or procedure to be adopted (*procedural choices*), but not about which is the end to be reached (chs. 2.1.6; 2.1.7). The uncertainty about details is also due to the fact that any choice is based on previsions, which, in turn, are based on *probability* and, therefore, are uncertain (ch. 1.1.3.2.1).

(2) Equal and Unequal Concern for All People. Hare (1984; 1989b: 79–95) underlines that, although utilitarianism requires equal concern for all people and gives equal weight to their interests, certain rights may initially demand unequal concern for people. He notes that if a girl, "Ann", wants to resist the profound desire of "Tom" now for a mere whim, with the plan to accommodate him later, she should have the law-protected right to do so, even if this means to show more concern for her than for him (Hare 1989b: 80). This would be explained by the *two-level utilitarian theory* (the critical and the intuitive level): "equal concern at the *critical level* can yield principles which, in particular cases at the *intuitive level*, may require partiality or unequal concern" (Hare 1989b: 83).

I think that the cases of unequal concern, like the one exemplified above, should be explained in a different way. We should distinguish *(a)* the nature of concern, on the one hand, and *(b)* the equality of concern, on the other.

(a) The nature of concern. In the above example, the concern of "Ann" is directed toward the satisfaction of personal desires (the desire of "Tom" to obtain the love of Ann, and the desire of Ann herself to enjoy the condition of being desired) and, as such, is unrelated to ethics. Indeed, Ann is exerting her right to be free to accept the love of Tom if and when she wants; in particular, Ann is satisfying her desire to resist for some time the wish of Tom, instead of satisfying immediately Tom's wish at the expense of not resisting for some time, as she actually desires. The satisfaction of personal desires or *sentiments*, generated by the *sensitiveness*, is not the source of moral rights or duties, unless personal desires interfere with the *mind evolution* of the involved persons. Referring to the case of "Ann", whether the desire of Ann, but not that of Tom, is satisfied, or vice versa, may be related to their happiness (or unhappiness) but is morally irrelevant, because morality, as far as the affective sphere is concerned, is related to the *evolution of sensitiveness* and the consequent ability to feel ever *deeper and more universal sentiments*, and not with the satisfaction of sentiments and desires, which largely depends on luck and is related to happiness (ch. 2.2.1.6.2).

(b) The equality of concern. Referring again to the above example, Ann seems to show more concern for herself than for Tom. This is not morally bad because, other things being equal, moral concern for others *roughly* decreases starting from the agent himself to his family, relatives, friends, colleagues, partners (in economic, cultural, or charitable associations and institutions), acquaintance, neighbors, fellow-countrymen, and other distant human beings (these are the *social groups*, diverse for numerousness, composition, and links, into which human beings spontaneously organize themselves). The reason for such decreasing moral concern and responsibility is given elsewhere (ch. 2.1.5.2.1). Here I note that Ann is justified in showing more concern for herself than for Tom.

It is noteworthy that, according to Hare (1984; 1989b: 79–95), the interest of ordinary humans, including egoists, are likely to be furthered *in general* if they follow moral habits of thought, i.e., if they adopt moral language and moral thinking. This view is somewhat close to the socio-biological theory of Singer (1981), according to which the power of reason evolves because it helps us to secure, by its more selfish applications, the survival of the genes that produce it. The truth of these two statements derives from the fact that, in any situation, moral habits are those that promote the *evolution* of the involved minds (i.e., the development of their intellect and/or sensitiveness and/or power), and that even the *good* selfish application of reason most often causes an increase or evolution of the agent's power (ch. 2.1.5.2.2); these objective effects lead to more evolved minds, and the more evolved minds are actually favored with regard to their survival, thus giving rise to a virtuous circle.

(3) Acceptance-Utility and the Egalitarian Principle. Hare (1978; 1989b: 106–20, 182–202) argues that, perhaps, the best principle of justice is the one with the highest acceptance-utility, i.e., the one that "makes just reward vary (but not immoderately) with desert, and assesses desert according to service to the interests of one's fellow men" (Hare 1989b: 199). He also notes that this principle will be just if it has been selected by a formal just procedure, and if it takes into account the circumstances of particular societies; thus, in a supposedly happy slave-society, both slaves and slave-owners may be conservative and know their place; trying to inoculate the egalitarian principle may result in "the vast majority merely becoming unsettled and therefore unhappier. Then, we ought not to try to inculcate such an egalitarian principle" (Hare 1989b: 200). This would mean that it is important to take into account the thoughts and dispositions of the citizens, and that the rhetoric appeal to "right" may lead to class war, whereas principles based on critical thinking and the facts and circumstances of a given society may solve the problems preserving peace (Hare 1989b: 201–2).

Hare's above reasoning is flawed by the failure to understand that the *true* and *objective* human good is *mind evolution*, and by the false belief that human good coincides with happiness. When human good is conceived as mind evolution, it becomes clear that a slave-society is always morally bad, even in the (improbable) case in which slaves are satisfied with their condition, because the status of being slave restrains the evolution of the minds of slaves; similarly, renouncing higher education for the whim of spending all the time searching for pleasure is morally bad, because it prevents mind evolution. Thus, a slave society should be changed, even if this may produce some (transitory) unhappiness.

3.2.5.2—"Rule Utilitarianism" and "Government House Utilitarianism"

The so-called *rule-utilitarianism* (Harsanyi 1985; Hardin 1988; Scarre 1996) attempts to overcome the difficulties of act-utilitarianism (e.g., lack of consideration for the minorities) by stating that one should follow the *rules* that maximize utility, instead of doing single acts that maximize utility (ch. 2.2.1.2.3, *C2*). Apart from the fact that the advantage of considering the rules (instead of the single actions) will disappear if rules are particularized to the point that they refer to a single act or to a few acts (Hare 1963: 130–36; Lyons 1965), I note that rule-utilitarianism does not avoid the difficulty arising from the fact that it, unduly, regards as the moral end the happiness or the satisfaction of desires or preferences, which are not moral ends.

Government House utilitarianism is another theory according to which only the governmental elite follows the morally right utilitarian decisions, while the general population is encouraged to adhere to the conventional social rules (Williams 1973: 138–40; Sen and Williams 1982: 1–21). Apart from the fact that this is against public justification which is due in a democratic government (Goodin 1995: 60–77; Bailey 1997: 152–53), once again this theory does not solve the central problem of defining what is the true moral end (which I identify with the evolution of minds). Moreover, according to my view, the difference between the government and the single citizens is that the former should pursue the moral good (mind evolution) of all citizens, whereas the latter should pursue the mind evolution according to the rule of the spheres of decreasing moral responsibility (ch. 2.1.5.2.1).

3.2.6—Liberal Equality and the Compensation for Inequalities

3.2.6.1—Rawls' Theory

The thought of Rawls (1971) can be called *intuitionism*, as it is based on some *intuitive principles*, i.e., on the beliefs about some moral and political general principles (such as liberty and equality), which should be arranged according to a criterion of priority. The principles and rules maintained by Rawls (1971) will be discussed in the chapters that follow.

3.2.6.1.1—Rawls' First Principle (Equal Right to Liberty)

According to this principle (Rawls 1971: 53–54, 220, 266; 1993: 5; 2001: 42), each person has an equal right to the basic liberties compatible with the liberties of others.

In discussing this principle I underline what the basic flaw of Rawls thought is: he starts from some "intuitive" principles that actually are "arbitrary" principles, lacking any philosophical foundation. In my view, the right to the basic liberties derives from the fact that liberty is necessary to make it possible for each individual to attempt to develop his own mind (and to favor the evolution of other minds) (ch. 2.1.4.2, *1*), as prescribed by the *ground moral norm*; therefore, each person has the right to enjoy these liberties and the duty to employ them to pursue mind evolution (ch. 3.1.2.5.2).

3.2.6.1.2—Rawls' Second Principle (or Difference Principle)

This principle (Rawls 1971: 57–65, 72, 266; 1993: 6; 2001:42–43) says that social and economic inequalities are allowed only if they are *(a)* to the greatest benefit of the least advantaged, and *(b)* attached to offices and positions equally open to all under conditions of fair equality of opportunity. Thus, the less advantaged should be able to exert a sort of veto over those inequalities that aggravate their position (Rawls 1977). This principle would be directed to ensure a condition of full equality of opportunity; to this end, we should attempt to eliminate any cause of inequality that is not the result of one's free choice and consequent action and behavior. Rawls (1971: 87) affirms that no one should gain or lose from his arbitrary place in the distribution of natural assets or his initial position in society without giving or receiving compensation. Thus, we should attempt to compensate for both the inequalities due to natural causes (natural lottery) and those linked to the social position. Rawls (1971: 65–73) thinks that this can be achieved by the *difference principle.*

In criticizing Rawls' difference principle, I underline that, like other Rawls' positions, it suffers from the lack of reference to a basic philosophical conception. Let us first consider the point that positions should be equally open to all under conditions of fair equality of opportunity. The basis for this point, in my view, is that without the openness of positions and the equality of opportunity, many talented people would be unjustifiably prevented from developing their mind, while the access to positions would be offered to those who are unable to cover them efficiently (which may have various mind-restraining effects on citizens, according to the nature of the position). However, more important is the affirmation that social and economic inequalities are allowed only if they are to the greatest benefit of the least advantaged. Here several critical observations are in order.

(1) A *first* observation is that Rawls limits his consideration only to the socio-economic differences, which in my theory correspond to differences in the sphere of the *power*, while he neglects to consider also the differences concerning the *intellect* and the *sensitiveness.* I observe that economic differences *must* normally exist between individuals (or citizens) because, being the mind composed of intellect, sensitiveness, and power, it is unavoidable that those who, due to the specific properties that define their individuality, are prone to primarily develop their intellect (say: philosophers, or scientists) or their sensitiveness (say: artists such as poets or musicians) have a lower economic status than those who are prone to primarily develop their power (say, businessmen). It would be strange to pretend that a businessman should enter a new enterprise only if this is to the greatest benefit of, say, university professors (who, compared to businessmen, are certainly much less advantaged from an economic point of view). However, a university professor who has what is necessary for the needs of himself and of his family is not interested in becoming as rich as an important businessman, but is rather interested in performing and publishing interesting and new studies and researches, which will allow him to enhance his reputation as a scientist. Therefore, the State should be aware of the diversity of interests linked to the three components of the human mind and, consequently, should attempt to offer all citizens *equal* opportunity to develop their *different* aptitudes, i.e., the State should make equally possible for people to primarily develop their power, or their intellect, or their sensitiveness, according to their aptitude (ch. 3.2.2.1.2). This means that citizens, by enjoying an *equal* basic condition, will reach *different* positions in the socio-economic status; the latter, therefore, should not be equal but should correctly reflect the differences between the properties of citizens, i.e., the differences in their personality. These differences should *not* be compen-

sated for. Thus, it is the disadvantage of those citizens whose condition is "below" the *evolution-allowing, involution-avoiding condition* that should be compensated for. Indeed, it should be underlined that *equality in the evolution-allowing condition should be assured to all citizens in order to make possible the expression of inequalities among them.*

This means that, while a basic income is necessary for all (since a minimum of power is required as a support to the intellect and the sensitiveness, due to the interrelation of mind components—chs. 1.1.1.1, 6; 1.1.2, 2nd proposition), the State should attempt to facilitate and promote enterprise in business for businessmen, higher education and scientific research for philosophers and scientists, and higher art education and creativity for artists.

(2) A *second* observation derives from the first one and concerns the definition of those who are "the least advantaged"; they are not those who possess much less power than other people but those individuals (or citizens) who possess not enough to be able to successfully attempt to promote the evolution of their mind (taking into account the degree of development of the society to which they belong). These citizens should be helped to reach the *evolution-allowing, involution-avoiding condition*, as prescribed by the ground moral norm.

(3) A *third* observation concerns the compensation for inequality (see also chs. 3.2.2.2.2, *B2*, *C2*; 3.2.6.3); Rawls thinks that such compensation should take into account the disadvantages not due to personal choices, i.e., both those due to initial socio-economic position as well as those linked to natural inequalities in assets and endowment. While compensation for the initial social position (through taxation or other means) is justified and indeed necessary, compensation for inequalities in natural assets should be discussed by referring to different conditions. Let us consider, in addition to the "willing-talented" man, four main possibilities: *(a)* the "willing-untalented" man (the willing individual with poor natural endowment in the sphere of intellect, or sensitiveness, or power, or in all three spheres); *(b)* the "indolent-talented" man (the indolent individual who may have normal or even high natural endowment); *(c)* the "disable" man (who has a normal or high endowment but who is physically handicapped); and *(d)* the "unlucky" man (victim of natural disasters or other unlucky events). Concerning the case of the "disable" and "unlucky" individuals, there is no doubt that the State, the society, and each involved person have the duty to compensate these individuals for their disadvantage, to the maximum possible extent, to allow or help the development of their minds.

Concerning the other two situations mentioned above (points "*a*" and "*b*"), some thinkers believe that the "indolent-talented" individuals should not be compensated because their indolent behavior (and the consequent disadvantaged condition) is the result of their free choice. Since I deny the existence of a truly free will (ch. 2.4.1), I think that the sluggard behavior of these people is the result of their natural endowment (as is the case for intelligent or stupid men) and, therefore, we should discuss together the "indolent-talented" and the "willing-untalented" man under the definition of the "untalented man". I think that attempting to *fully* compensate the untalented man for his poor natural endowment would be arbitrary and unjustified. Indeed, the fundamental moral norm (chs. 2.1.5.1; 2.1.5.3; 3.1.2.5.1, *3*) prescribes the promotion of mind evolution; this means that the State should take all the measures that facilitate the development of the minds of citizens so that each of them may reach the maximum level allowed by the natural endowment that defines and characterizes his personality. Thus, the untalented man should be helped to enable him to develop his mind to the greatest possible extent. Once this has been done, attempting to compensate for the differences in natural endowment would be absurd. To which level should we attempt to bring the untalented man? Should we torment him by exerting on him an intolerable pressure to force him to reach a level that he is actually unable to reach? And, in which sphere of mind activity should we compensate the untalented man? In the sphere of *intellect* activity, perhaps by forcing him to study advanced mathematics, or nuclear physics, or to make biomedical research, even if this makes him desperate? Or in the field of *sensitiveness*, by forcing him to study poetry or music even if this is for him a torment? Or in the field of *power*, by forcing him to enter business or politics, against his nature that leads him to hate these activities? This would mean to attempt to change the natural personality of citizens and to force them to approach an abstract and arbitrary concept of personality. Thus, untalented men should be "compensated" or, more exactly, helped to develop their mind up to the level of the evolution-allowing, involution-avoiding condition; the latter condition allows mind development in the case of the talented man, and the enjoyment of a decent and humane state in the case of the untalented man, who should have guaranteed a minimum development of his intellect (education in knowledge), of his sensitiveness (education in arts), and of his power (money and social status) to allow him to participate in (and not to be excluded from) the life of the community to which he belongs. This condition should, therefore, be defined (even if approximately, as is always the case in the human world) by taking into account the degree of evolution of the community; for instance, in an underdeveloped country, an education limited to elementary school would suffice, whereas in a European country it would not. Starting from this condition, which should be assured to all, each individual will be able to further develop his mind through the specific ways and up to the level allowed by his natural endowment (and by environmental factors).

3.2.6.1.3—Rawls' Rule of the Priority of Liberty (First Priority Rule)

This rule (Rawls 1971: 214–20, 266) says that liberty can be restricted only for the sake of liberty, and not for the sake of other primary "goods" (thus, a less than equal liberty must be acceptable to those with the lesser liberty). Rawls does not give any justification of this rule. My theory provides us with a full justification of the priority of liberty, because liberty is the basic requirement for enabling the citizen to attempt to develop his own mind (and the minds of those citizens with whom he interacts), according to the *ground moral norm* (ch. 2.1.4.2, *1*).

3.2.6.1.4—Rawls' Rule of the Priority of Justice (Second Priority Rule)

The rule of the priority of justice over efficiency and welfare says that justice is prior to efficiency and to maximizing the sum of advantages, and that fair opportunity is prior to the difference principle (Rawls 1971: 263–66, 266–67). In brief, according to Rawls' conception of justice, liberties are prior to equal opportunities, the latter are prior to equal resources, and inequalities are allowed only if they favor the less advantaged. Once again, my theory furnishes a justification for the priority of justice over efficiency and welfare. If we bear in mind the prescription of the ground moral norm (promoting mind evolution), it becomes clear that social justice means correction or attenuation of those disadvantaged conditions that may impede or restrain mind evolution of some citizens, whereas pursuing efficiency or maximizing the sum of advantages may merely further increase the welfare of those who are well-off (see also the marginal utility principle—ch. 3.2.2.2.2, *A3a*).

Rawls maintains (1971: 11) that his conception of justice is the result of the hypothetical *social contract*; the latter would be stipulated under a condition in which the contractors are *behind a veil of ignorance*, i.e., no one knows his status with regard to his place in society or his natural assets and abilities (his intelligence, his strength, etc.), so that no one knows which is his allowed access to both the *social primary goods* (income, wealth, power, rights, liberties) and *natural primary goods* (health, intelligence, and talents) (Rawls 1971: 118–23). In this condition (the *original position*), any decision would be taken according to a principle of justice (by considering human beings equal as moral persons), as no one can favor himself because no one knows which is his position. In Rawls' view, a choice taken in this condition would be a rational choice (1971: 11), directed to maximize what one could obtain if he is in the minimum or worst condition. However, correcting his previous view, Rawls explains that the concept of rational choice should be understood in the sense that "the account of the parties, and of their reasoning, uses the theory of rational choice (decision), but that this theory is itself part of a political conception of justice, one that tries to give an account of reasonable principles of justice" (2001: 82, note). Moreover, Rawls maintains that in the original position one would choose what he calls the *difference principle* (1971: 65–73). Justice would result from a *reflective equilibrium* between the choices made from an impartial perspective (such as those made in the original position, from behind a veil of ignorance) and our intuitive principles (Rawls 1971: 18–19, 42–43).

Rawls' theory of justice seems questionable to me. Rawls himself recognized that: *(1)* the choice in the original position can be conceived and described in different ways, and *(2)* the contract stipulated in the original position should be regarded as a *useful device* to extract the consequences of our moral intuitions from an impartial perspective. Let us discuss these two points separately.

(1) The Choice in the Original Position. Rawls (1971: 15–19) claims that this choice would be made according to a principle of justice, by considering human beings equal as moral persons. But, why should it be so? Let us consider two possibilities. *(a)* The choosing people believe in the principle of human equality and, therefore, they will make an egalitarian choice. *(b)* The choosing people sincerely believe in the principle that it is morally good that the more endowed men dominate the less endowed ones; in this case, if the choosing people are *morally-good* persons, they will make a non-egalitarian choice. Moreover, as noted by Mackie (1977: 95), when one chooses from behind a veil of ignorance, he could egoistically choose a principle that makes the large majority of citizens happy at the expense of a small minority, since the probability would be in his favor. Here, again, the main problem arises: without reference to moral principles solidly grounded on philosophical bases, no theory of morality and justice can be built. Principles based on *intuition* are rather arbitrary and, therefore, not morally binding.

(2) Rawls' Contract as a Useful Device (Rawls 1971: 19). Why should we think that such a device "helps us" to extract the consequences of our moral intuitions from an impartial perspective? One who believes in the principle of human equality does not need the contract device to make an egalitarian choice. A Rawlsian thinker might observe that choosing from behind the veil of ignorance (and therefore by ignoring one's own status) will force the contractors to make an egalitarian choice for an egoistic reason. However, since the "original position" is, obviously, a hypothetical (and not real) condition, actually the choosing individuals in the real world do know their status; therefore, it is simpler to say that those who believe in the egalitarian principles should choose accordingly, otherwise they are contradictory and morally bad. Thus, the meaning of the choice from behind the veil of ignorance is, at best, uncertain.

3.2.6.2—Dworkin's Theory

Dworkin (1981: 311) maintains that the distribution of social goods should be endowment-insensitive and ambition-sensitive. To this end, he hypothesizes a scheme in which everyone participates in an ambition-sensitive auction by having assigned an equal purchasing power (say: 100 units of purchasing power); the results of such an auction should satisfy everyone, because they meet the envy-test, as they depend on the participant choice under equal conditions (Dworkin 1981: 285). This means that natural disadvantages should be compensated for before the auction takes place. Since this is difficult to do, Dworkin (1981) proposes to use insurance against both disability as well as unequal natural talent. In his scheme, taxes would be a way to collect the insurance premium, while the welfare services, including unemployment help, would be the way to compensate for the disadvantages covered by the insurance. This would not be a full compensation (first-best), which would be very difficult, but a satisfactory one (second-best). In brief: Dworkin hypothesizes an initial equal distribution of resources (100 units of purchasing power), a condition that is then modified in a choice-sensitive manner by the hypothetical auction, and that is compensated for natural disadvantages by the insurance policies. Dworkin's conception would represent a *third way*, superior to both traditional socialism and free-market libertarianism (Dworkin 1993; 2002: 1–10, 320–50; Giddens 1998).

It has been noted that Dworkin's theory attempts to compensate for inequalities after they arise and does not provide for initial equality among people (the counterpart, in the real world, of the hypothetical 100 units of purchasing power hypothesized in the above example). This is because the achievement of a true initial equality, with compensation for both natural and social inequalities, would entail radical changes in the economic organization of Western societies; thus, after all, Dworkin's theory appears as politically conservative (MacLeod 1998: 151).

Dworkin's position has also been criticized by noting that it is very difficult, or even impossible, to measure natural or social advantages or disadvantages, and that a given quality may be of different value in different situations and at different times. This, however, is not a serious critique, since in the sphere of human sciences (as in that of natural sciences) all knowledge is always characterized by *approximation* (ch. 1.1.3.2.1) and, therefore, the measurement of natural or social advantages or disadvantages can only be made in an approximate manner. However, as it occurs in science, approximation of knowledge does not prevent us from utilizing it for acting the most appropriately possible; indeed, it would be absurd that, because we cannot exactly define advantages and disadvantages, we should not employ approximate evaluations. The main point is that the concept of "compensation" for inequalities depends on the conception of equality; Dworkin's theory seems to be directed to reach a sort of absolute socio-economic equality, i.e., (referring to the typology of individuals mentioned in ch. 3.2.6.1.2, *3*) to reach an equal socio-economic level for the "willing-talented", the "willing-talented-disable", and the "willing-untalented" individuals, allowing disadvantaged conditions only for the "indolent-talented" individuals (whose condition would depend on free choices). Apart from the consideration that, in my view, due to the lack of true freedom (ch. 2.4.1), indolence should be regarded as a lack of talent (ch. 3.2.6.1.2, *3*), the major problem is that equality should not be intended as concerning the distribution of resources but as referring to the right of all citizens to enjoy those concrete conditions that make the promotion of mind evolution possible. Therefore, equality concerns the *initial conditions* of citizens, not the final result in the distribution of resources; this is because *equality* of the *basic rights* (linked to the *common properties*, shared by all men) is contrasted by the *diversity* of the acquired, *individual rights* (linked to the *individual properties*, i.e., to the *degree* and *specificity* of mind evolution that characterize each individual and define his personality). The *degree* of mind evolution refers to the various degree of natural endowment with regard to the intellect and/or the sensitiveness and/or the power that characterizes each individual; the *specificity* of mind evolution refers to the prevalence of the aptitude to primarily develop the intellect (natural or humanistic sciences), or the sensitiveness (arts), or the power (business and politics). Indeed, the value of *equality* in basic rights depends on the fact that they allow that the *diversity* among individuals can be expressed. Thus, we should defend *equality in basic rights* and *diversity in individual rights*; to defend equality in individual rights too would actually mean to restrain mind evolution, because mind evolution can only occur in ways specific to each individual, so that attempting to achieve equality among individuals would actually mean restraining their free mind evolution.

3.2.6.3—Other Views on the Compensation for Inequalities

(1) Further Theories to Reach Equality. In order to realize social equality, other theories have been put forward. *(a)* The *stakeholder society theory* proposes that a stake (of, say, $80,000) should be given to everyone when they graduate from high school, and this program should be supported by a 2% wealth tax (Ackerman and Alstott 1999). The use of the stake should be restricted to positive ends, such as education or investment (Haveman 1988). *(b)* According to the *basic income theory* (Van Parijs 1992; 1995), an unconditional basic income (say $5,000/year) should be assured to everybody. *(c)* The *egalitarian planner theory* (Roemer 1993; 1996) proposes

that, while measuring the degree of disadvantage is very difficult at the individual level, it would be possible for groups; thus, based on a list of factors that affect circumstances not due to individual choices (age, gender,
socio-economic status, disability, etc.), society should be divided into *types*,
approximately homogeneous for such factors, and then the attempt should
be made to equalize inequalities between types (leaving uncompensated the
diversities within each type, which would be due primarily to individual
choices). *(d)* The *coupon capitalism theory* (Roemer 1994; 1999) maintains
that each young adult should receive a share of the nation's profit as a port-
folio of stocks in the nation's firms, which with one's death should revert to
the Treasury to be used for the next generation. *(e)* According to the *com-
pensatory education theory* (Roemer 1999), adequate resources should be
utilized to compensate for the education of children from poorer families in
order to actually equalize their opportunities of learning and education.

I think that for each of these proposals there are *pro* and *contra*; moreover, it is also possible that their validity changes with the characteristics of
the various societies. I will not comment on them, leaving this difficult task
to economists, sociologists, experts in political science, and jurists. Rather, I
underline the importance of defining the end that, with any such proposal,
should be reached. This end is not the achievement of an equal socio-
economic status for all individuals, but the enjoyment of equal basic rights,
to enable each citizen to promote the development of his own mind to the
greater possible extent, through the way specific to his natural endowment.

(2) The Property-Owning Democracy. The liberal egalitarianism (or
welfare-state capitalism) of Rawls and Dworkin represents a conception of
the welfare state different from that of classical liberals (which results from
a compromise between the libertarian free-market and the Marxist-egalitar-
ian state planning), as it attempts to realize a full practical implementation
of the equality principle. But the welfare state cannot perhaps fully realize
the principles of liberal egalitarianism; Rawls himself (1971: 242, preface to
1999 ed., p. xv; 2001: 135–138) suggests that the *property-owning democracy* (which attempts to achieve an *ex ante* equality in distribution, thus
lessening the need for ex post correction—Krouse and McPherson 1988)
would be better than the welfare-state capitalism (which accepts initial inequalities and attempts to correct unequal income distribution *ex-post*). Yet,
it is unclear how to practically implement the property-owning democracy.
It is also noteworthy that, to reach the ends of liberal egalitarianism, an adequate *state capacity* would be required (Rothstein 1992; 1998). Moreover, I
note, once again, that the supporters of the property-owning democracy
seem primarily concerned with the inequality in the economic field, which
belongs to the sphere of the *power*, paying less attention to the other spheres
of human activity (*intellect* and *sensitiveness*).

(3) The Liberal Position. Liberals support the *neutrality of the State* po-

sition, i.e., they think that the State should not define a scale of values but should only assure freedom, justice as fairness, equal treatment, equal opportunity, and respect of individual rights and individual choices (primary goods), leaving each individual free of making his personal choices under his responsibility; these principles have been defended, from different points of view, by several thinkers (Ackerman 1980: 11, 61; Dworkin 1985: 222; Rawls 1988; 1993: 192–94; Kymlicka 1989a; Nagel 1991: 116). I argue that the State should actively intervene to ensure that all citizens concretely enjoy the *evolution-allowing, involution-avoiding condition* (or the best possible approach to it), whereas it should be neutral toward the further evolution of citizens, from that condition onward. The enjoyment of the evolution-allowing condition by all citizens is difficult to implement in practice. In this regard, it has been pointed out that liberals sometimes underestimate the need for material resources in order that some primary goods are effectively enjoyed (Nagel 1973; Schwartz 1973; Kymlicka 1989a); yet, despite it being difficult to define and to implement, the evolution-allowing condition should be the ultimate end of the State.

3.2.7—Libertarianism

Capitalist freedom (free market) has been defended because it would promote maximal *utility* and hence the best use of resources (Buchanan and Congleton 1998) as well as civil and political *liberties* (Hayek 1960: 121; Gray 1986: 62–68), even if Gray has recently changed his thought to include post-liberal views (Gray 1995). Thus, market freedom is conceived as a means to reach an end. [Libertarians, who defend personal freedom, should be distinguished from the neo-conservatives (Carey 1984); the latter defend traditional values such as patriotic feeling, family, respect for authority and military power, and may restrict personal liberty of living according to a permissive style. In most instances, conservatives tend to preserve social inequalities and are against any change or innovation, including the help to those citizens who, for various reasons, are in a disadvantaged condition (Brittan 1988: 213, 240–42)].

I will briefly discuss the following points.

(1) Nozick's Entitlement Theory. Preeminent in this field is the *entitlement theory* (Nozick 1974: 150–82), which affirms that: *(a)* provided that people's holdings are the result of *just acquisition*, they can be the object of *free transfer* ("from each as they choose, to each as they are chosen"—Nozick 1974: 160), and *(b)* unjust acquisition or transfer should be corrected through a *rectification of injustice*. Only a minimal State would be justified (limited to the protection against force, theft, and fraud, and to the enforcement of contracts), as a more extensive role of the state would violate a

person's rights and would be unjustified (Nozick 1974: ix).

The principle of *free transfer* is based on the claim that free exercise of property right entails the entitlement to dispose of one's holdings as one best prefers (of course avoiding force or fraud). Possible "unjust" consequences of the free transfer (i.e., of free market), even if due to undeserved inequalities, should not be compensated because the particular rights over things fill the space of rights, leaving no room for general rights (Nozick 1974: 238); thus, any liberal redistribution of resources to help the disadvantaged would violate property rights and would be unjustified.

I agree with those who think that Nozick does not give us a satisfactory explanation of his assumptions; he proposes a *libertarianism without foundations* (Nagel 1981). Indeed, while there is no doubt that, if people's holdings are the result of *just acquisition*, they can be the object of *free transfer*, I think that the acquisition of holdings should be critically evaluated with reference to its origin (ch. 3.2.3.2) and that the free transfer should be controlled to avoid possible unacceptable results (i.e., that some people live at a level below that of the evolution-allowing condition).

(2) Libertarianism as the Result of an Agreement. Some thinkers maintain that libertarianism is based on the adoption of some conventions or agreements that mutually advantage the contractors (such as the agreement about avoiding to harm one another) and that are regarded as a sort of moral code (moral artifice); they, however, would be generated as a rational constraint from the non-moral, utilitarian premises, as there would be no natural moral duties toward others (Gauthier 1986: 4, 55–58; Narveson 1988: 110–21; Buchanan and Congleton 1998). To ensure that those who agree to such conventions or agreements actually respect them, coercion is required to enforce the agreements (Vallentyne 1991: 264–65).

This view is reminiscent of the "social contract" theory; like the latter, it is based on the false belief that *society* as a whole and the various *informal communities or social groups* that arise within it (with their implicit or unstated rules) result from a non-necessary, *contingent* agreement stipulated in order to reach *a scope* (some sort of mutual advantage). Actually, as I point out elsewhere (ch. 3.1.1.1.1), *society* as a whole and the *informal communities (or social groups)* within it arise as the necessary result of the trend of human actions toward universalization. The universalization of human actions being a component of *mind evolution*, the organization of human beings into a society (and its informal communities or social groups) is actually governed by the ground moral norm prescribing the promotion of mind evolution. This means that it is a moral duty of humans to organize themselves into a society (and its informal communities or social groups) and to recognize the rights of all cooperators in the activities linked to the utilization of resources, in order to increase to the maximum possible extent the power of the members of the society (citizens) and to allow that they have enough power to also develop their intellect and sensitiveness according to the specific mind properties that characterize their personality.

(3) Libertarianism and Liberty. Libertarianism can be conceived as a theory that defends *liberty* as the primary value, which should not be limited for assuring equality or justice (Raphael 1970: 140–41; Gordon 1980: 134), and opposes any social or legal limitation of individual freedom (Rothbard 1982: v–vi). Methods have been proposed to measure freedom, either as the number of free choices that are allowed (neutral conception of liberty), which has proven to be difficult to implement (Steiner 1994; Carter 1999), or as the value or importance of the matter about which a particular liberty is concerned, evaluated on subjective criteria (degree of desire) or on objective criteria (Raz 1986: 13–16; Connolly 1993: 171–72). Libertarians maintain that a free market assures more freedom than the welfare state; however, it has been noted that this freedom is of those who have property, to which a reduced freedom of those left property-less corresponds. Indeed, it has been underlined that the sentence that free enterprise constitutes economic liberty is demonstrably false (Cohen 1979/1991; Goodin 1988: 312–13).

Concerning the libertarian conception of liberty, I think that two points should be discussed: *(a)* the concept of the primacy of liberty and *(b)* the extension of liberty.

(a) The concept of the primacy of liberty. The primacy of liberty is a concept that should be clarified. Liberty (considered as external freedom—ch. 2.4.1.3) is actually concerned with the *power*, since being "free" means being able to freely use one's own power to perform some actions or moral acts (ch. 2.1.4.2, *1*). However, each individual has the *right* to have the power and the freedom required not to do what he desires (including futile or extravagant or harmful actions) but to attempt to promote the evolution of his mind, according to the prescription of the ground moral norm. All this is included in the concept that each human being has the right to enjoy the evolution-allowing condition.

(b) The extension of liberty. To follow the ground moral norm, liberty and *enough* power should be assured to *all* citizens. The libertarian system, which limits the freedom of property-less poor workers, who do not have enough resources to develop their minds, is against the ground moral norm.

(4) The "New Right". From 1980 onward, the *New Right* (Mead 1986; Barry 1990) has claimed that liberal egalitarians and their welfare state fail to appreciate individual responsibility and creativity while favoring the irresponsible or indolent, thus reducing efficiency. A post-liberalism has been invoked that should defend freedom and equality of citizens not only from the government but also from the oppressive social practices (Gray 1995; Hampton 1997). I object that responsibility and creativity are neglected if one attempts to reach an equal distribution of resources but not if,

by following my theory, one attempts to assure that all citizens enjoy those *basic rights* that allow them to freely develop their own mind to reach the level allowed by their "specific properties", i.e., their natural endowment and individual ability. In this way, differences in responsibility and creativity will become fully manifest and efficiency is preserved. In other words, equality should concern the basic rights, which entails that each individual enjoys an *evolution-allowing, involution-avoiding condition.*

In the years following 1980, in many countries, there has been the prevalence of the *New Right*; this was not due to the wide acceptance of the libertarian principles and the rejection of the liberal-egalitarianism (this position would have few supporters indeed—Lomasky 1998), but rather to the assumptions described below.

(a) The welfare state entails growing and unaffordable expenses as well as excessive demands (up to the imposition of giving an organ, such as a kidney, to patients who need it). I object that expenses are affordable if they are limited to the amount allowed by the general economic condition; the principle should be to reach (or to approach to the maximum possible extent) the "evolution-allowing" amount of resources for everyone, compatibly with the available resources and avoiding the crash of the economic system. Pretending that a kidney should be given to a patient who needs it would be to pretend to realize the absolute perfection in the moral field, which is really too much (perfection is not reached in any human activity, e.g., in the field of knowledge). Thus, while giving a kidney to a patient who needs it is certainly an exceptionally good moral act, it cannot be imposed on, or expected from, everybody. Moreover, referring to the above example (giving a kidney), one should distinguish private from public behavior. At the private level, the moral agent should act by adhering to his moral principles and values (within the limit established by the laws of the legal system) and by following the rule of the spheres of decreasing moral responsibility (ch. 2.1.5.2.1) (which takes into account the closeness of the helping person and the helped one—in the example: the relationship between the kidney donor and the recipient). At the public level, the government should attempt to increase the impartial availability of organs to all citizens, for instance through a campaign directed to encourage organ donation.

(b) States do not have the capacity to effectively implement liberal principles (Glazer 1988), a view expressed also by left-wing thinkers (Rothstein 1998). This might be true if liberal principles should be implemented in a rigid and abstract manner, but not if they are implemented in a wise manner (see the following point "*c*").

(c) It has been claimed that liberal principles in practice often result in a heavy charge to the responsible and hard-working people and a premium to the indolent ones, and that the welfare state ultimately promotes passivity,

exclusion, and dependence from the State. This critique is not justified. Indeed, wisely implemented liberal principles are not a charge to the responsible individuals and a premium to the indolent ones, because the indolent individuals should receive only an *"evolution-allowing, involution-avoiding"* amount of resources (or the best approach to this amount), taking into account the available resources of the society. This ensures equality in the basic or starting condition, not in the level reached by each citizen. To give an example: it should be assured that all talented young people are able to attend university studies but it should not be assured that all students reach the university department by a luxurious car. So conceived, liberal principles do not result in too heavy a charge to the responsible (or willing-talented) individuals. Most importantly, however, is the consideration that assuring everybody an *"evolution-allowing, involution-avoiding" amount of resources* is not enough; we should also assure the enjoyment of all the basic human rights, so that all citizens are in an *"evolution-allowing, and involution-avoiding"* condition. This is the necessary condition for demonstrating (at least approximately) that successful individuals are such because they are really willing-talented, and not because they have enjoyed privileges that others have not. Thus, assuring the enjoyment of basic rights to all is in the interest of society (because it allows the selection of the true willing-talented individuals) and also in the interest of the willing-talented individuals who, in this way, are entitled to reject any contestation of their status.

(5) Roads to Serfdom. Hayek (1944) was one of the most influential defenders of free-market economy and regarded centralized or socialist economy as entailing the risk of non-democratic output (it would be "the road to serfdom"). Indeed, I think that both free market and socialist economy might be regarded as roads to serfdom, so that a 3rd option should be chosen. I will discuss these issues in the points that follow.

(a) 1st road to serfdom: The centrally planning of economic activity. In his critics to the centrally-planned economic systems, Hayek (1944) underlined the risk that they lead to non-democratic governments and to economic disasters. He was right because the centrally-planned economic system consists of some sort of control on the economic activities of citizens, and thus limits their freedom and interferes with the evolution of their mind along the ways and up to the level determined by their individual identity, while imposing abstract and arbitrary standards and goals to be reached. Hence, it is against the prescription of the ground moral norm. In brief, the centrally-planned economy controls the *development* of the economic activity of citizens, who are oppressed by the central planning power. Hence, a centrally-planned economy would represent a road to serfdom.

(b) 2nd road to serfdom: The free market economy. To avoid the interference of the government with the economic activity of citizens (which

limits their development according to their natural endowment), the free-market economy has been invoked, in which the central control is reduced to the minimum. Free market, however, leads to severe inequalities in the economic status of citizens so that a part of them will not enjoy the *basic rights and conditions*; therefore, free market limits the economic activity of many citizens who cannot attempt to develop their activity according to their natural endowment. For these citizens, the free market too (like the centrally-planned economy) represents a road to serfdom.

By criticizing the free-market economy, I do not deny that it contains positive aspects. To clarify this point, I will comment on the claims of Smith (1776), as expressed in this passage:

> [E]very individual . . . intends only his own gain, and he is in this, as in many other cases, led by an invisible hand to promote an end which was no part of his intention. Nor is it always the worse for the society that it was no part of it. By *pursuing his own interest* he frequently promotes that of society more effectually than when *he really intends to promote it.* (Smith 1776: 291–92; emphasis added)

Let us consider Smith's two statements expressed by the emphasized words.

Smith's *first* statement that every individual, by pursuing his own interest, frequently promotes that of society should not surprise us. Indeed, I think that individuals, by pursuing their own interest, *always* (rather than frequently) promote that of society. This is because, being society made of many individuals, its interest results from the sum of the interests of its members. Moreover, selfish activity (pursuing one's own interest) consists of the development of one's power, which, together with the development of intellect and sensitivity, is part of mind evolution, whose promotion is prescribed by the ground moral norm; in other words, selfish activity, provided that it is a *morally-good* selfish activity, is the way through which the agent accomplishes the *duty toward himself* (ch. 2.1.5.2.2), and should be integrated with, and not opposed to, the collective moral acts (ch. 3.1.1.2, *1*). It may be added that, when individuals work for their own interest, they are more efficient compared to the people working for public or governmental undertakings (von Mises 1951: 183), because they are prompted by selfish forces. Yet, all depends on how individuals pursue their interest and on whether all citizens enjoy the evolution-allowing condition, which enables them to develop their economic activity. If each citizen pursues his own interest without interfering with the interest of others (as regulated by the shared norms and laws) and if all citizens enjoy an equal condition, pursuing one's activity means pursuing the interest of society. If, on the other hand, these conditions are not met, pursuing the interest of some citizens may entail contrasting that of others (which means restraining mind development of others). Thus, in order to make that the pursuing of one's interest coincides with the interest of society, interest should be pursued by observing the shared norms and laws, which are directed to promote the common good (mind evolution of all, or most, citizens). Thus, the interests of society are met if the selfish interest is pursued by respecting the system of shared rules (which reflect the shared moral principles and values).

Smith's *second* statement, that every individual, by pursuing his own interest, frequently promotes that of society "more effectually than when he really intends to promote it," needs to be interpreted. I think that when a citizen "really intends to promote" the interests of society he actually intends to promote the common good and, therefore, he is exercising a *moral* activity (i.e., he is implementing moral principles and values as expressed by the shared moral norms), and not an *economic* activity (i.e., he is not attempting to increase his power). It follows that in this moral activity the citizen is *not* engaged in promoting the "interests" of society but in helping all citizens to develop their minds, i.e., he is engaged in ensuring that all citizens concretely enjoy the evolution-allowing condition. This is the reason why the government of a democratic State, which should pursue the common good, should not manage the economy but should act to create the conditions of equality of opportunity that allow all citizens to develop their economic activity, according to their natural endowment. The government should limit itself to manage those economic activities that serve to create the condition of equal opportunity, i.e., public or social services such as medical service, education, information, means of communications and transportation, citizens' security, access to energy, etc. (ch. 3.2.8.1.1, *1*). These economic activities of general interest might be exerted by the government either directly or indirectly, but they should always be exerted under the control and the responsibility of the government.

[May I recall at this point that, for different reasons, weapon industry should also be controlled by the government, and not by private individuals or groups; this is because if weapon factories are owned by individuals or groups, the latter may exert economic and political pressure directed to promote the use of the weapons, which ultimately favors violence in the domestic field and war in the international scenario. This, obviously, would be against the prescription of the ground moral norm].

Smith held that pursuing self-interest or the desire to bettering our condition is something natural. He says "the desire to bettering our condition . . . comes with us from the womb, and never leaves us until we go into the grave" (Smith 1776: 203); the consequences of this selfish desire would be naturally limited by the mechanism of competition. Compared to this natural desire that drives human actions, government intervention in the economic field could appear as something of arbitrary or unnatural. I note that, even in the presence of correct competition (i.e., avoiding monopoly), the risk that a part of citizens is excluded from the benefit of the free market persists, and can only be avoided by central or governmental intervention, which should be aimed not at directly performing economic activity but to assure equal conditions to all. Thus, government intervention is moral in nature, as it is directed to implement moral principles and values (assuring equal opportunity to all) through the legal norms and laws. These moral principles and values are at least as strong and natural as selfish desires; they too "come with us from the womb, and never leave us until we go into the grave," as they express the voice of our conscience. Indeed, the desire for bettering our condition represents the *outward* or selfish mind activity, which is counterbalanced by moral principles, values and acts, which represent the *inward* or moral mind activity; both are essential components of the human soul, which always exerts a *bidirectional activity* (Fig. 1.1).

(c) Away from serfdom: The centrally-planned basic conditions. Serfdom is avoided, and free economic activity preserved, if the government acts to ensure that all citizens equally enjoy the basic right and conditions, i.e., enjoy the evolution-allowing, involution avoiding condition. Once this condition is assured to all, then the activity of citizens should be allowed to be freely exerted, as wished by the defenders of the free-market economy. Thus, what should be controlled by the government is the *starting condition* of citizens, not their free activity through which they express the degree and specificity of their mind evolution.

3.2.8—Communism and Marxist Theories

3.2.8.1—Classic Communism and Historical Materialism: The Core of the Theory

Marxism (see also: Belfiore 2012: 357–84) stresses the principle that laborers have a right to the products of their labor, and defends the *common ownership of the means of production* (Marx and Engels 1848; Marx 1875), which is the basis of the so-called *economic democracy*. Marxism aims at abolishing private property; not the "property of the pretty artisan" but, as Marx and Engels said (1848: 484–87), the bourgeois private property:

> [The bourgeois private property is] . . . the final and most complete expression of the system of producing and appropriating products, that is based on class antagonisms, on the exploitation of the many by the few. In this sense, the theory of Communists may be summed up in the single sentence: Abolition of private property. (Marx and Engels 1848: 484)

Moreover, Marx and Engel added:

> You are horrified at our intending to do away with private property. But in your existing society, private property is already done away with for nine-

tenths of the population; its existence for the few is solely due to its non-existence in the hands of those nine-tenths. (Marx and Engels 1848: 486)

Marxists affirm that private property should be abolished because there is no moral right to it and to the private control of the means of production (Cohen 1988); the latter should be under the control of society as a whole. This would lead to *abundance of resources* so that the problems of distributive justice no longer arise (Buchanan 1982: 56–57, 122–26).

> Within the co-operative society based on *common ownership of the means of production* [emphasis added], the producers do not exchange their products; just as little does the labour employed on the products appear here *as the value* of these products, as a material quality possessed by them, since now, in contrast to capitalist society, individual labour no longer exists in an indirect fashion but directly as a component part of the total labour. The phrase 'proceeds of labour', objectionable also today on account of its ambiguity, thus loses all meaning. (Marx 1875: 529)

In this view, when the condition marked by "harmony of ends" and of abundance of resources is realized, there will not be the need for justice, rights, laws, political parties or representative democracy, because Marxists believe that the need for justice and for defense of rights arises when these conditions are not met, and individuals are seen as right-bearers, a condition that leads to conflicts (Buchanan 1982: 76; Sandel 1982: 30–33).

> In the higher phase of communist society, after . . . the productive forces also increased with the all-round development of the individual, and all the springs of cooperative wealth flow more abundantly—only then can . . . society inscribe on its banner: From each according to his ability, to each according to his needs! (Marx 1875: 531)

Concerning freedom, Marx and Engels (1848: 486) said:

> [F]reedom is meant, under the present bourgeois conditions of production, free trade, free selling and buying . . . This . . . [has] no meaning when opposed to the Communistic abolition of buying and selling, of the bourgeois conditions of production, and of the bourgeoisie itself.

Marxists underline that the implementation of Rawls' difference principle is difficult because, among others, it could be opposed by political or economic power centers; thus, the *socialization of the means of production* may be a more realistic way (DiQuattro 1983). Marxists also observe that the redistribution of resources cannot eliminate the difference between the capitalist and the worker, because the former can affect the life of the latter but not vice versa. Some thinkers believe that a better self-determination of workers can be realized under a mixed system of private and public property and worker democracy (Goodin 1982: 91–92; Weale 1982: 61–62).

In order to facilitate the criticism toward the above Marxist views, these can be summarized in the following statements: *(1)* the means of production should be equally owned and should be controlled by the society as a whole (*socialization of the means of production*); *(2)* this would lead to abundance of resources, which would allow to follow the rule "from each according to his ability, to each according to his needs"; and *(3)* in these new conditions, there would not be the need for justice and defense of rights. These statements will be discussed in the chapters that follow.

3.2.8.1.1—Socialization of the Means of Production

The ownership of the means of production by society as a whole (and, consequently, its management by the government) lacks a solid justification. I discussed elsewhere (ch. 3.2.3) the origin and justification of property, and I have shown that, apart from small estates, factories or enterprises (which can be managed by single individuals), each ownership is actually a community or social group (with its stated and unstated rules), whose members are all the individuals who cooperate in its activities, so that all are co-operators and co-owners, even if, obviously, with different roles and, consequently, with different duties and rights. My view refers to a society in which there are *multiple ownerships*, which arises spontaneously, under the pressure of the interest of the various individuals or groups involved (in the respect of the existing laws). The Marxist claim (that all the means of production should be owned by the government) seems to me as arbitrary and without foundation (see below). *The ownership, management, and control* of the means of production by the government, as defended by Marxists, could be justified if it assured a greater efficiency and, hence, a greater production, without limiting the liberty and the other values that should be recognized to the citizens. The history of communist governments in the countries of East Europe has proved that this is not the case. However, besides this historical consideration, there are philosophical reasons against a central or governmental management of economy. Indeed, the *government economic activity* is ontologically distinct from the *economic activity of private individuals or groups*, and pursues different ends, as it appears from the following considerations.

(1) The Government Economic Activity of General Interest. It should be borne in mind that a government as a whole is composed of a parliament, which makes laws (which are general or *universal* projects), and of an executive apparatus, which administers the organs of the state (by following the laws that regulate their function) in order to create some *general or universal conditions* that assure the enjoyment of the basic rights to *all* citizens. The basic rights are those rights that make the promotion of the *evolu-*

tion of the mind possible for citizens, in accordance with the *shared moral norms* (as stated by the constitutional norms), produced by the *public or common consciousness*. In other words, the activity of government enterprises is directed to serve a *moral end*: the provision of those public services that make the development of the mind equally possible to all citizens. This means that the government is entitled, indeed has the duty, to control and manage, either directly or indirectly, the "public or social services" (health service, education, information, liberties, means of communications, means of transportation, equal opportunity, citizens' security, access to energy, etc.) (see also ch. 3.2.7, *5b*). In short, the activity of government enterprises primarily consists of public *moral acts* (inward activity of power), whose ends are at the same time *universal ends* (they concern *all* citizens) and *moral ends* (favoring the *evolution* of the minds of citizens), and are primarily guided by the shared *moral principles* and stirred-up by the shared *moral feelings* (inward activity of intellect and sensitiveness, respectively), as expressed by the constitutional norms. Thus, the activity of government enterprises, consisting primarily of moral acts guided by moral principles and stirred-up by moral feelings, is the product of public or common *consciousness* (in other words, is the product of the inward activity of power, intellect, and sensitiveness). In defining the activity of government enterprises as "primarily" consisting of public moral acts, I want to recall that, as mentioned in chapter 2.1.3.3.3, moral acts are not separated from the selfish or personal (or group) actions, since any event initiated by the human mind can be "primarily" a moral act or "primarily" a selfish-personal action and yet it is always a combination of the two. In the case of government enterprises, this means that, while pursuing a primarily public moral end, they should also pursue a "selfish" policy consisting in producing the public moral end by spending as few resources as possible (e.g., a government hospital, while it should primarily pursue its public moral end, consisting of the cure of patients, should also attempt to rationally utilize the available resources in order to reduce "expenses" to the minimum, which is a "selfish" end).

(2) The Economic Activity of Individuals or Groups. The economic activities that spontaneously develop in a society consist of innumerable "centers of economic activity", which perform *actions* (generated by the outward activity of the *power*) that are: *(a) particular*, because they are promoted by individuals or by groups of individuals, and *(b) selfish or personal*, because they are prompted by *personal (or group) sentiments* (desires, preferences, or interests), produced by the outward activity of *sensitiveness* of the involved people, and because they realize *projects* created by the outward activity of their *intellect*. Thus, while the activity of government enterprises mainly consists of *universal and moral acts*, the activity of personal or group enterprises mainly consists of *particular and selfish actions*. Again,

this particular and selfish activity is not free from moral restraints; on the contrary, it should always be somewhat limited and shaped by the moral demands.

Personal sentiments function as powerful, vital, willing forces (*selfish forces*) that promote personal or group actions, i.e., the economic enterprises of individuals or groups. In contrast, state or government enterprises should be stirred-up primarily by the shared moral principles and feelings, while the *selfish forces* play only a secondary role (see above). This entails that government enterprises have a minor vitality and, hence, a minor efficiency.

(3) The Government Economic Activity of Non-General Interest. In a given State, the individual or groups will create *diverse* "centers of economic activity" across the territory and in the various sections of the life of society, according to their aptitudes and abilities; in addition, individuals and groups, being distributed approximately evenly across the territory of the State, they know all the economic characteristics of each part of the territory and can take them into account in their economic enterprises. In contrast, when the central government attempts to exercise economic activity, its activity is regulated only by general, *abstract plans*, and is, therefore, unable to utilize the various economic chances present in the diverse areas of the State, or to match the many and different needs of the several social groups, and does not reflect the actual heterogeneous economic capacity of the population. Moreover, the *selfish forces* (mentioned above) will play a minor role, because the individuals engaged in the activity of the government enterprise are not working for themselves, but for an abstract entity: the society or State. Thus, while the individuals and groups are willing, informed, and concrete managers, the State or government (outside the provision of public or social services) can only be an unwilling, misinformed, and abstract manager; hence the inefficiency of the centrally controlled economic systems. Moreover, it should be noted that the function of the State is, among others, to *regulate*, through laws, all the innumerable private enterprises (or "centers of economic activity") existing in the society, and to equally provide all of them (through governmental enterprises) with the public services required for their development. Thus, when the State substitutes the managers of the various private enterprises it actually exerts *violence*, since it crosses the boundary of its legitimate power (ch. 3.1.2.4). The "social ends" that, according to the Marxists, would be reached by the socialization of the means of production, can be achieved by conceiving the "private" enterprise as actually co-owned by all those who co-operate to its activity, i.e., all cooperators, including the *proprietor(s)-cooperator(s)*, the *administrator(s)-cooperator(s)*, the *workers-cooperators*, and the *consumers-cooperators* (ch. 3.2.3.2).

(4) The Ontological Distinction of Private versus Public Economic En-

terprises. From the above reasoning, it follows that economic enterprises can be distinguished into *private enterprises* (created and managed by private individuals or groups) and *public enterprises* (created and managed, directly or indirectly, by the government). This distinction is grounded on ontological bases, in the sense that private enterprises *are* personal, selfish economic activities generated by the *personal* (or *group-linked*) *outward activity of the power*, i.e., by the *practical selfishness*, and, as such, must be run by individuals or groups, whereas public enterprises *are* universal, morally-oriented economic activities, generated by the *shared* (or *public*) *inward activity of the power*, i.e., by the *common practical consciousness*, and, as such, must be run by the government. Thus, my position (which defends the autonomy, within the laws, of the spontaneously arising, innumerable "centers of economic activity") is ontologically founded on the structure and functioning of the mind; it tells us that considering as distinct the *private* (personal or group-promoted) economic activity from the *public* (or shared) economic activity is *the result of a discovery, not of a choice,* i.e., it is not the result of a choice made in order to achieve a scope (which in this case would be a better organization of the economic activity). In contrast, the Marxists' claim that the State should manage the entire area of economic activities is based on an analysis restricted to the meaning of the "surplus value", and is the result of a prevision and, as such, is marked by uncertainty. Indeed, it is a claim maintained with the scope of reaching an end: a better social justice; the historical experience of the communist countries has shown that this prevision has proven to be false in several countries and that the management by the State of economic activities (which ontologically belongs to individuals or groups) leads to economic inefficiency, and therefore it appears as no longer justified. We could say that the failure of the socialist economic system can be understood as the consequence of the error of having ignored the ontological distinction between the private or selfish economic activity, produced by the *outward activity of the power* (or *practical selfishness*), from the public moral economic activity, produced by the *inward activity of the power* (or *practical consciousness*—Fig. 1.1); therefore, the Marxists' claim that the State should manage the entire area of economic activities is based on an *ontological error,* i.e., on the failure to distinguish the *practical selfishness* from the *practical consciousness.*

Thus, we can say that classic Marxism pursued a morally-good end, *social justice,* which is *in accord to the ground moral norm.* Yet, because of an ontological error, Marxism also maintained that this "good end" should be reached by a *wrong means or method,* consisting of the centralization of the means of production and the political power; this leads to *suppression of liberty* (both economic and political) and to economic inefficiency (restraint to the evolution of the power), which is *against the ground moral norm.* Indeed, social justice can only be reached if it is associated to economic and political liberty as well as to *equality* in basic rights, which allows the expression of the *diversity* among individuals.

3.2.8.1.2—The Alleged Abundance of Resources and the Need for Justice

The Marxist views that the "Marxist system" would lead to abundance of goods (which would avoid the need for distributive justice) is unrealistic, since several resources, such as land and other natural resources, are, in fact, limited. But I think that still more important is the fact that, even in the presence of abundance of resources, there would always be among human beings the struggle for taking the largest possible amount of resources, regarded as an expression of their personal ability. The same struggle would occur for reaching an ever-higher degree in public administration, or in the academic world, or in the military career, etc.; briefly, in *any* sphere of human activity. This is because the struggle for attaining a "higher position" is the expression of the attempt to develop personal *power* (which is part of the *selfish mind activity*); this attempt, when made by respecting the moral (and legal) norms assuring equal rights to all, is permitted, indeed it is morally good, because it is a way to promote the evolution of one's mind (power is one of the mind components, together with intellect and sensitiveness). In short, the attempt to develop one's power is part of the duty toward oneself (ch. 2.1.5.2.2). Again, I note that the Marxist position lacks any ontological foundation.

The above critique to the Marxist claim about the possibility to achieve abundance of resources, and my arguments in favor of the unavoidability of the (correct) struggle for power among human beings, show that the Marxist prevision that in their system there would not be the need for justice is untenable. Indeed, the struggle for power results from personal, selfish *actions*, prompted by personal *sentiments* (produced by the *sensitiveness*). Therefore, the struggle for power is linked to the ontological structure and to the functioning of the mind, so that a theory of justice and a defense of rights is and will always be required in human society; this has become to be recognized by the modern, analytical Marxists (ch. 3.2.8.4).

3.2.8.2—"Exploitation" versus "Just Distribution"

Marxists affirm that private property gives rise to the wage-labor relationship, which is inherently unjust, because it entails *exploitation* and *alienation*.

Exploitation would arise because the laborer is the only person who creates the value or, better, creates the product that has value; since the capitalist takes for himself part of this value, he exploits the laborer, i.e., he takes for himself a *surplus value* inasmuch as he returns to the laborer as wages less than the laborer produces (Marx, 1861-63; Cohen 1988: 214–28). Of course, this is true if the worker is forced (e.g., by need) to work for the capitalist, as it most often occurs (Reiman 1987). This would mean to use the labor of workers as a means in favor of others (the capitalist), which is against the Kantian principle of never using man as a means. [Some thinkers also consider the citizenship-exploitation, i.e., the exploitation that derives from inequalities between rich and poor countries, as well as the exploitation linked to the inequality between the employed and unemployed (Van Parijs 1993: 123–47)].

Two distinct points should be discussed: *(1)* the existence and nature of the "surplus value" and *(2)* the transfer of the "surplus value".

3.2.8.2.1—*On the Existence and Nature of the "Surplus Value"*

Marxism holds two main concepts: that laborers in private enterprises, factories or farms are the only persons who create the value (the work products); and that the capitalists return to the laborers (as wages) less than the laborers produce and take for themselves the difference, which would be a *surplus value*. These and other issues are discussed in the following points.

(1) Are the Laborers the Only Persons Who Create the Value of the Products? Considering the laborers as the only persons who create the economic value (of the produced goods) is unjustified. Before discussing this topic, I note that a distinction should be made between the low-level workmen and the people who occupy a higher-level position in the organization of a private enterprise, factory or farm (such as the managing and executive personnel); the latter will certainly receive a higher remuneration than the low-level workman who, according to Marx, would receive a wage just sufficient to cover the basic needs for sustaining himself and his family. However, for the sake of simplicity, I will consider together all the people who work in an enterprise, factory or farm, and I will indicate them as "workers". Now, I note that, if the workers were the only people who contribute to create the products and their value, why should they need to cooperate with the capitalist? If, on the other hand, the capitalist actually plays a role, then he has the right to take a part of the produced "value"; in this instance, the problem would be to avoid that the capitalist takes too much, i.e., to avoid an unjust distribution of the produced value. A just distribution can be reached or approached through the organization of workers into trade unions, capable of defending the workers' rights. Yet, if the capitalist (and, therefore, the capital) has a role, what does this role consist of?

To answer this question, we should examine the process of capital accumulation. Let us suppose the case of a worker who has a parsimonious style of life, which allows him to save part of his salary; he started to work when he was 20 years old so that, when he reaches the age of 50, he has worked for 30 years and has accumulated a certain amount of money; in other words, he possess a "capital". Let us suppose that this novel "capitalist" buys the machines required to produce the good "x" and engages 5 workers, thus creating a small factory. I think that nobody could deny that the novel capitalist has the right to take a part of the produced value. If the novel capitalist contributes in some way to the activity of the small factory (say: by taking care of the book-keeping, or by taking care of the sale of the products, or even by having elaborated the project for creating the small factory), then he would actually act as a worker and should take a part of the value produced, and the only problem would concern how much he should take, i.e., the distribution of the created value. Even when the capitalist seems to only play the role of making his money or capital available to buy the required machines, and of supporting the factory, he also exerts the *control of efficiency* (see point "*3*", below); thus, the income he earns (called *profit*) can be regarded as the counterpart of the wages earned by workers.

(2) Capital Formation Through Saving, Legacy, and Gifts. Formation of capital may primarily occur through *saving* as well as through *legacy* and *gifts*; it may be augmented through profit. Profit will be treated below under point "*3*". Here the cases of *saving* and of *legacy* and *gift* will be discussed.

(a) Saving. Accumulation of capital by saving is justified, provided that the income source is justified.

(b) Legacy and gifts. Capital arising from a legacy or gift raises two problems, one concerning the person who gives, the other concerning the person who receives. The person who gives has most probably accumulated his capital through profit, a case that will be discussed below, under point "*3*". The person who receives a capital as a legacy or gift enjoys an advantaged position compared to others. Is this justified? I think that it is, provided that the capital received is taxed to the due extent, in order to contribute to assure the "*evolution-allowing, involution-avoiding condition*" to *all* citizens (chs. 2.1.5.3; 3.1.2.5.1, *3*). To understand the nature of legacies and gifts, it may be useful to consider them as advantages resulting from good luck (occurring in the sphere of the *power* of the recipient) and to compare them with other advantages that may occur in the spheres of activity of the other mind components (*intellect* or *sensitiveness*). Indeed, a young man, who has received a capital as a legacy from his father or as a gift from a rich man of whom he had the good luck of becoming a friend, is advantaged in undertaking economic enterprises (i.e., in the attempt to promote his *power*) compared to a man who did not have this good luck. Similarly, a young scientist, who has the good luck of having a father or of meeting a master of

great intelligence and scientific value, will receive from him a wealth of information and a scientific guide that will allow him to realize greater intellectual achievements (i.e., to realize a greater development of his *intellect*) compared to others who did not have this good luck. This is not bad, provided that the possibility of intellectual development is made available to *all* willing-talented people (i.e., provided that the "evolution-allowing condition" is assured to all citizens). The same is true in the field of *sensitiveness* and artistic activity. Thus, in the effort to promote one's mind evolution, either in the field of intellect, sensitiveness, or power, one may be helped by good luck, thus reaching a level of development higher than the level that one would otherwise have reached. This is not morally bad, provided that: *first*, all citizens have the concrete opportunity to promote the evolution of their mind; *second*, the help received through the good luck is publicly recognized, thus respecting the truth (about one's capability and position) and doing justice to the less fortunate people; *third*, what has been obtained by legacy or gift, be it a capital or a large estate or a factory or a firm, is utilized in the most possible productive way and is managed as a *cooperator-owned property*, i.e., by taking into account the rights of all those who co-operate in the activities linked to its utilization (ch. 3.2.3.2).

(3) The Surplus Value and Profit. Profit is the main source of capital accumulation; this is because saving can only give rise to small capitals, and legacy and gifts can only transfer a capital that was previously accumulated through profit. Profit is derived from the so-called "surplus value". Certainly, there is more than one source of surplus value, which has not been considered by Marx (Schumpeter 1942: 269). Here I briefly discuss the surplus value as conceived by Marx, i.e., as the difference between the value created by the labor and the value of the wages paid by the capitalist. In the case that the capitalist does not play any role in the activity concerned with his factory, the problem arises about the justification of the profit, i.e., whether or not he has the right to earn the profit. To clarify this problem, we should consider that the capitalist, even when he does not directly play any role in the activity of his factory, plays the important role consisting of *(a)* investing his capital to create a factory and to support it (e.g., by affording the expenses for buying new machineries), and *(b)* exerting the best possible *control of the efficiency* of the factory. Thus, the capitalist owner of a factory exerts a role, indeed a fundamental one, as he makes the supreme choices about the *birth*, the subsequent *support* and the *efficiency* of the factory. Thus, we may schematically distinguish three groups among all the cooperators of a factory: the workmen, the managers, and the proprietor(s)-capitalist(s) ("consumers" are not considered here—ch. 3.2.3.2). These groups of people make choices and take responsibilities of increasing importance for the existence and success of the factory and, hence, the part of the produced value taken by these groups should increase from workmen to man-

agers to owner-capitalists. The latter should take a remarkably larger part because of their role in the foundation and in the sustaining of the factory [provided that the prescriptions of the ground moral norm have been accomplished, i.e., after that *(a)* the universal rights to enjoy an evolution-allowing condition have been assured to all by paying adequate salaries and the due taxes, and *(b)* the individual rights, linked to personal qualities, have been respected]. Of course, the proportion of the income that should be taken by the workmen, by the administrators, and by the proprietor(s) may vary, in relation to the economic conditions of the factory and of the society as a whole; yet, the rule should be respected that even the lowest income should be compatible with an evolution-allowing condition.

The above reasoning has been made by referring to a factory; however, it is also valid for farms, where the possession of a land is the counterpart of the possession of a building and of machineries in the case of a factory.

(4) The Meaning of Capital. Said in a concise manner, capital can be regarded as one of the measures of the *power* of the individual who owns it. The ability to accumulate a large capital consists of the aptitude to develop one's power. However, as discussed in chs. 1.1.3.2.3 and 3.1.1.1.1, the development of the *power*, and of the *actions* that it generates, means the evolution from particular power and actions concerning individuals to ever-more general or universal power and actions involving ever-larger groups of individuals. Thus, if an initially poor man succeeds in becoming the proprietor of a factory, he has developed his power; yet, his evolved power now involves several people, i.e., all those who cooperate (the *cooperators*) in the activity of the factory. Indeed, there are important limitations to the ownership of a factory by a capitalist, because any factory actually is owned by the *capitalists*, the *managers*, and the *workmen* (and also the *consumers*), all of whom are somehow co-owners and cooperators of the factory, even if to a different extent, and all together will form a "community" or "social group" (ch. 3.2.3.2). Thus, the capitalists as well as the managers and the workmen have social responsibilities and duties, and are not allowed to neglect the efficiency and productivity of the factory, because this would have "social" consequences, as also noted by Arneson (1993). Moreover, a big capital should not be left non-invested; this would correspond to a large landed property left uncultivated. Both the unutilized capital and the uncultivated land represent a form of potential power, which, by following the ground moral norm, should be converted into actual power that extends to many citizens: the *cooperators*; in other words, those who possess a big capital or a large estate or factory should fulfill the *duty of utilizing the resources in a socially optimal way* (ch. 3.2.3.2). The law of a democratic State should contrast these situations by establishing some form of control. Indeed, as a capital or a factory increases in magnitude, its role becomes ever more of public relevance and the ownership ever more subjected to,

and limited by, public or social demands. These limitations should be imposed and regulated by the government laws. In this regard, it should be stressed that even the largest factory represents a form of universalization of power and actions inferior to that represented by the State, which, referring to its territory, represents the fully universalized power.

3.2.8.2.2—*Transfer of the "Surplus Value"*

It has been affirmed that any transfer of surplus value is unjust; this, however, would mean to defend the libertarian principle of self-ownership (Cohen 1990a: 366–69), because it would entail that, if workers are forced to pay tax to support the infirm or the disabled or the unemployed, they would be exploited. To avoid this unacceptable conclusion, it has been pointed out that forced aid to the disabled could be regarded as an insurance policy that everyone buys to his own benefit (Reiman 1989), and that the "surplus" paid is under the control of those who produce it (the workers as a class) (Holmstrom 1977). Although each of these arguments affirms something of reasonable, I think that the main reason why paying taxes to support those in need is not exploitation is that the payment of taxes in a democratic State is decided by the laws enacted by parliament, which represents all the citizens, including the workers. Moreover, these taxes are directed to help those in need and, therefore, pursue a moral end, i.e., these taxes help the needy people to reach the evolution-allowing condition, in accordance with the prescription of the ground moral norm. This is a situation very different from that of the capitalist who takes for himself a certain amount (the so-called surplus value), because the capitalist does not need this amount to reach the evolution-allowing condition (he stays above this condition).

It has also been suggested that the worker exploitation could be condemned by referring to the principle of *distribution according to the needs* (rather than the principle of self-ownership), i.e., the capitalists would exploit the workers because they take part of what the workers produce not because of their needs (Arneson 1981; Cohen 1990a). As noted by Roemer (1982a; 1982b; 1982c), the true injustice consists of the unequal access to the means of production. This position is rather close to that of the liberal-egalitarians.

It should also be noted that the principle of giving goods *to each according to his needs* would not contrast with the condemnation of exploitation (forced transfer of surplus value) because Marxists believe that under communism there will be an abundance of resources that cover all needs (Geras 1989; Cohen 1990b). Due to the illusoriness of the state of abundance, the principle "*to each according to his needs*" may perhaps be interpreted as a principle of justice, i.e., a principle of equal satisfaction of needs or equal welfare (Elster 1983). Thus, the need principle would presuppose a rule for distribution of the resources, which is somewhat reminiscent of the liberal egalitarian position (Elster 1983; 1985: 231–32).

I object that the distribution according to the needs can work if there are people in need; after basal needs are satisfied (after the evolution-allowing condition is enjoyed by all citizens), which criterion should be followed for distributing the available "surplus"? The thesis of exploitation would be correct if the capitalist did not exert any function in a factory or farm. Yet, as I discussed above, the capitalist does exert an important function, which justifies his taking a part of the produced value. Indeed, we can say that the workers contribute to the production process by their manual labor, managers by their administrative and decisional work, and the capitalist (or capitalists, in those factories or firms owned by more than one person) contributes by buying the means of production, by supporting their functioning and by controlling the efficiency. The manual labor, the administrative and decisional work, and the buying/supporting/controlling the production apparatus are *actions* of different complexity entailing different responsibility, and express different levels of *power*. Briefly, the central point is that the workers (who are the less advantaged of the cooperators of a given factory or firm) should receive an amount of resources consistent with the evolution-allowing condition; once this condition is met, the distribution of resources should express the ability and willingness in developing one's own power.

3.2.8.3—Alienation

Alienation, besides exploitation, would be a consequence of private property and, according to Marxist thinkers, is due to the fact that private property and capitalism would prevent the development of human life toward its potentialities and excellence (Lukes 1985: 87), because workers are forced to give up not only the surplus value but also the control over their work and the products they produce (Doppelt 1981). Marxism, on the contrary, would favor human potentialities and excellence, which has been indicated as the *perfectionist* conception of alienation, i.e., wage-labor would prevent perfecting human personality (Lukes 1985: 87). Potentiality and excellence are, however, regarded as activities directed to production, as labor under socialism would be an end-in-itself and the life's prime want (Campbell 1983: 138; Elster 1985: 522). However, it has been pointed out that there are other values in human life with which the enjoyment of unalienated work may compete (Arneson 1987; 1993).

In my opinion, alienation arises when individuals are forced to spend most of their time and effort in exerting just one of the three mind components. Therefore, the work as conceived by the Marxist theory (i.e., uniquely directed to production) actually is alienating, because it consists of spending most of the time (at the time of Marx, laborers worked too many hours per day) uniquely in performing *actions*, generated by (and directed to promote) the *power* component of the mind; it is alienating because it prevents the evolution of the other two mind components, i.e., the *intellect* (by expanding one's knowledge) and the *sensitiveness* (by expanding one's artistic culture and experiences), thus changing the worker's mind almost into a single-component mind.

It should be noted that prevalence of one mind component over the other two components occurs in most individuals and characterizes their personality (ch. 3.2.2.1.2). When the prevalence is pronounced and yet not forced, but is the result of natural aptitude, it indicates an *unbalanced mind*. When the prevalence is forced and excessive, it leads to an *alienated mind*. An unbalance of mind occurs when a man spontaneously (by following his natural aptitude) devotes all his time and effort to perform *actions*, generated by the *power*, while neglecting the sphere of *intellect* and *sensitiveness*; or when he spontaneously devotes all his time and effort to pursue *knowledge*, generated by the *intellect*, while neglecting his affective life (family, friends, beauty, art enjoyment), generated by the *sensitiveness*, and the practical activity consisting of actions, generated by the *power*; or when he spontaneously devotes all his time and effort to follow his *sentiments* (family, friends, beauty, art enjoyment and/or creation), generated by the *sensitiveness*, while neglecting the sphere of *knowledge*, generated by the *intellect*, and the practical activity consisting of *actions*, generated by the *power*. Thus, we can say that the *natural* excessive prevalence of one mind component over the other two leads to an *unbalanced mind*; the *forced* restriction to act mainly in the sphere of one mind component leads to *alienation*. Unbalanced minds and, especially, alienated minds could be defined as almost "single-component minds"; these can be of three types: single-component minds restricted to *power* (this is the type described by Marxists), single-component minds restricted to *intellect*, and single-component minds restricted to *sensitiveness*; each type, in turn, may be the result of natural aptitude or forced restriction. Thus, the Marxist's alienated mind can be defined as a nearly single-component-mind compulsorily restricted to power; Marxist's alienation is aggravated by the fact that, besides being restricted to only the sphere of power, workmen have little possibility to develop their power over time. Thus, the alienated workmen are *nearly single-component-minds, compulsorily restricted to power and restrained in their evolution*. It should be noted that, in a democratic State, there is the moral duty to ensure that all citizens enjoy the evolution-allowing condition (or the best approach to it), so that alienation is avoided or, at least, limited to an ever-smaller percentage of the less advantaged people.

3.2.8.4—Analytical Marxism and Non-Marxist Theories of
      Socialism

Whereas the classic communist theory, known as *historical materialism*, has
become in the last decades ever less accepted and followed, a new version
of it, known as *analytical Marxism* has gained new vitality (Roemer 1986;
Roberts 1996; Cohen 2000). Moreover, there are non-Marxist theories of
socialism. These include the conception named *social democracy*, which is
very close to, or coincides with, *liberal egalitarianism*, the former being
mostly concerned with *social equality* (equality in public life), the latter
with *distributive justice* (equality in the share of resources), although these
two conceptions may indeed be complementary and not opposing. Social
equality means that social classes and market inequalities (which, within
certain limits, might not be regarded as unfair) should not determine difference in political influence, public recognition, and access to public services,
nor should they affect the relationship with others (Walzer 1983; Miller
1994; 1999). It has been underlined that the State, which is often unable to
correct unequal incomes generated by the market (unfair distribution),
should prevent that these private inequalities affect social equality (Kaus
1992). I have already expounded my view about social equality and distributive justice (ch. 3.2.6), centered on the enjoyment of the *evolution-
allowing condition* by all citizens.

It has been noted that, in the modern society, needy people should be
considered in addition to exploited workers, so that one has to choose between the principle of self-ownership, embedded in the theory of exploitation, and the opposing principle of equality of benefits to support the very
needy or disadvantaged people (the disabled, the elderly, homosexuals, minority groups, etc.) (Cohen 1990a; Arneson 1993). As I have pointed out
elsewhere (ch. 3.2.6.1.2, *3*), the problem of disadvantaged people should be
solved by assuring everybody an equal enjoyment of the *evolution-allowing
condition* (or the best approach to it), which entails compensation for inequalities.

3.2.9—Communitarianism

Instead of elaborating abstract principles of justice that should be valid for
all societies, communitarians defend a sort of cultural and moral relativism
by maintaining that one should adhere to the particular conception of the
common good shared by the particular, local community to which he belongs (Walzer 1983; Bell 1993). It has been noted that this position is
somewhat reminiscent of Hegel's appeal to reconcile people with the existing communities in the world (Hardimon 1992). This, however, does not

mean supporting moral relativism because, as noted by Walzer (1983; 1987: 24), although the conceptions of justice and goodness are, to some extent, specific of each community, this relativism is limited by a non-relativistic, universally-valid *minimal code*, which prohibits slavery, genocide, and gross cruelty. Thus, it has been noted that a few universal principles of justice do exist (*thin* universal moral code, e.g., avoiding slavery and genocide), which should be recognized by all communities, but that other practices and ways of life, such as the caste systems or the authoritative theocracies, though illiberal, should be allowed if they express shared habits and beliefs, the latter defining a *thick* relative moral code (Walzer 1994; Bell 2000).

In my opinion, the claim that only the shared moral principles and values of the community to which one belongs should be pursued has no philosophical justification. Indeed, this claim arises from the lack of any objective foundation of ethics. If we refer to my conception of the human good as *mind evolution*, which is an objective event (recognized by the intellect and felt as good by the sensitiveness), and of human rights/duties as linked to the moral norm that prescribes to pursue mind evolution, it becomes clear that moral principles and values (so conceived) have universal validity. Walzer's thin moral code actually refers to acts that interfere heavily with mind evolution and can be understood as such by all men. It follows that the caste systems or the authoritative theocracies are morally unacceptable in *all* communities or societies, because they restrain the evolution of the minds of many or most citizens and, therefore, are morally bad. In this regard, however, two points should be considered. *First*, the morally-bad systems should not be changed by using coercion or violence, because this would produce more evil than the bad systems themselves; rather, the right choice is to help these systems to undergo an *internal* evolution, which should be pursued by means of cultural, political, or even economic pressure, hopefully exerted by the international community; the scope should not be to impose a given conduct from outside but *to favor the internal evolution of the minds*. This is in keeping with the view that life should be led from the inside, by adhering to some principles of justice and conception of the good, not by external constriction (Lomasky 1987: 253–54; Dworkin 1989: 484–87). *Second*, it should be recognized that mind evolution can only occur through ways *specific to the various individuals or communities* and linked to their specific "properties" that define their diverse identities; this diversity makes the richness of the human world (ch. 3.2.2.1.2).

Central to the communitarian position is the *individual-community relationship*. In contrast to liberals, who would like to promote a *politics of neutrality* (the justice-compatible individual preferences are regarded as equal), communitarians prefer a *perfectionist* politics, i.e., a *politics of common good*, which pursues the community-defined and adopted good, against which the individual preferences are evaluated (Unger 1976; Sandel 1982: 182; 1984a; Taylor 1985b: 190–221). Moreover, in contrast to liberals, who defend the right of the individual to critically evaluate any circumstance, i.e., the right to rational revisability of the individual (Buchanan A. 1975), communitarians maintain that the individual regarded as detached from the community in which he lives would be *empty*, because the self is actually situated or embedded in the community and realizes itself by adhering to social practices and exercising its particular social role (Taylor 1979: 14–23; MacIntyre 1981: 204–5; Sandel 1982: 58, 150, 152).

I think that the individual-community relationship is rather complex; it includes two aspects: *(1)* the influence of community on the individual, and *(2)* the role of the individual in the society.

(1) Influence of Community on the Individual. Here we should recall that a community or society is the means by which individual actions get universalization by following the shared laws (ch. 3.1.1.1.1). It follows that a community or society, through its shared laws, exerts an influence on the individual actions and behavior similar to that exerted by scientific laws (universal ideas) on individual ideas: in both instances, the influence is morally good if the scientific laws and the community laws are truly universal or, to be realistic, are the best approach to universality; this means that scientific laws should be true for all (or most of) the events to which they refer, and that community laws should be shared by the majority of community members (as it occurs in a democratic State). In these conditions, community laws are primarily directed to pursue the shared *common good*. The latter reflects the degree of evolution of the consciousness of the community; if the consciousness of the community is evolved enough, it will recognize that the true common good consists of the *evolution of the minds* of the community members (this is the *objective* human good—chs. 1.1.1.2.4; 2.1.4.1; 2.2.1.1.1, *1*). If the consciousness of the community is less evolved, the shared common good will consist of a more or less incomplete conception of mind evolution. Thus, at the time of the Romans the shared common good did not exclude slavery; the more evolved modern consciousness of Western democracies does exclude it. So conceived, the common good reflects the degree of evolution of the community's consciousness, as reached through the evolution which occurred in the preceding historical periods. The influence so exerted by the community on the individual will be more or less good, depending on the degree of the evolution of the common consciousness. If the latter is evolved, the influence of the community on a given individual will be good, and it is exerted not only by the community members living in the same period of that individual, but also by all the preceding generations. The same is true for the influence exerted by the accumulated scientific knowledge on the intellect of an individual.

Of course, the community influences the individual also through laws and rules that regulate desires, preferences, interests, habits, and traditions specific to the community; these laws and rules are justified, provided that they are shared by the majority of citizens and that they do not contrast or interfere with the pursuing of the common good (mind evolution).

(2) The Role of the Individual in the Community or Society. Each individual contributes to the formation and evolution of the community or society to which he belongs. He contributes both to the community's consciousness (primarily reflected by the constitutional norms) and to the community's habits, preferences, and ways of life. In particular, consciousness, like the mind as a whole, evolves with time; therefore, an individual living at a given time period may dissent from the laws pursuing the common good as conceived at that time (constitutional norms). This dissenting citizen, while having the duty of observing the shared laws, even if he does not endorse some of them (because the laws shared by the majority of the community members represent the best approach to universality), has also the right to propagandize his ideas (see ch. 4.1.1.3.2, *B*). Thus, the individual does not realize his self by adhering to the community, which influences him; rather, he establishes a double-way relationship with his community, which he actively influences and by which he is actively influenced.

3.2.10—Political Liberalism and Liberal Nationalism

3.2.10.1—Political Liberalism

While *classical liberalism* defends tolerance and the autonomy of the individual (Mendus 1989: 56), *political liberalism* consists of a restricted form of *liberalism*, according to which the principles of liberty and the difference principle are still valid but are accepted by different groups (thus gaining an *overlapping consensus*) for different reasons (Rawls 1987) and could also be accepted by those groups who refuse the autonomy of the individual (Rawls 1985; 1993; Galston 1991; Moon 1993). Since there may be a plurality of different groups or communities in society, freedom of conscience is needed to adhere to one or another group. Thus, freedom of conscience should be limited to the political conception concerning public identity (public rights and responsibility), without including private beliefs, habits, and attachments that define private identity (Rawls 1985). As summarized by Kymlicka (2002: 236), Rawls maintains that people can be communitarians in private life and liberals in public life. It has been noted, however, that there is no clear-cut distinction between public and private conceptions, so that the freedom about political matters in some ways affects private matters (Janzen 1990; McDonald 1991; Kukathas 1992; Mason 1993; Callan 1997; Spinner-Halev 2000; Tomasi 2001). The fact is that Rawls (1987) is concerned with the view that liberal principles may not be shared in a democratic society and, therefore, if liberalism insists on these principles it could be regarded as another sectarian doctrine.

All the above reasoning is concerned with the problems whether liberal principles can be imposed to reluctant groups without ceasing to be liberal, and whether it is possible to distinguish liberty in public life from liberty in private life. Both problems can be solved if we refer to my moral theory, based on my ontological conception. There are universal moral principles and values and corresponding rights/duties that apply to all men, because they descend from the common properties that characterize the class of men: the properties of being *evolving* conscious entities consisting of intellect, sensitiveness, and power. Thus, the ground moral norm (prescribing the promotion of mind evolution) and the corresponding norms and laws directed to realize the evolution-allowing conditions, should apply to all men and all groups or communities. Indeed, as noted by Sandel (1996: 6–17), some liberal principles are shared by several Western democracies (whose identity, therefore, cannot be based on these principles). The communities that refuse to accept these principles and laws should be helped to undergo an internal evolution of their minds. With regard to minorities within a State, this can be made by means of educational, cultural, and moral pressure and through laws; concerning independent States in the international arena, this should be made by means of cultural, moral, and even economic pressure directed to favor the mind evolution of their citizens, always avoiding the use of force or violence, because this would produce more evil than the condition that should be changed.

On the other hand, habits or practices referring to properties specific of individuals, groups, or communities, provided that they do not restrain mind evolution and are not in contrast to universal rights/duties, should not be limited because they *enrich the human world*; indeed, they should promote the unity among different groups, because diversity should generate attraction and not repulsion.

Thus, reference to my views (i.e., assuring the *evolution-allowing, involution-avoiding condition* to all) helps to solve the contrasts between different groups, especially the contrasts between majority and minority groups (discussed by Hirsch—1986) and between genders (MacKinnon 1987), and avoids that the communitarian or perfectionist State favors the majority against minorities or disadvantaged groups, as feared by others (Kymlicka 1989a; Phillips 1993).

Reference to my moral theory also helps to reinterpret the claim that principles are not enough for the stability of a State (Paris 1991), and that there must be a common form of life and an accepted common good in order for citizens to accept the demand of the State as legitimate, which cannot be achieved with the liberal principles based on individual rights (Taylor

1986; Miller 1995). Indeed, I note that the legitimate individual rights (and duties) are those based on the common good, and the true common good is that based on the essential properties common to *all* men (mind ability to undergo evolution), and consists of mind evolution.

Communitarians maintain that liberals have an atomistic view of individuals as self-sufficient, minimizing the role of the social environment, i.e., the social condition for individual freedom (Taylor 1985b; Wolgast 1987). It has been pointed out that a liberal, neutral state would be unable to create the social conditions (good functioning of such institutions as family and educational institutions, social-cultural pluralism, etc.) required for supporting a valuable way of life; these social conditions, on the other hand, would be realized by a perfectionist state (Raz 1986: 162), because individual judgments and even personal identity are formed in a community of shared language, thoughts, and practices through criticism, discussion, and confrontation (Sullivan 1982: 158–73; Beiner 1983: 152; Crowley 1987: 282). Habermas (1979: 198–99) argues that discursive criticism is required to enable a revision of the externally determined or traditionally fixed people' needs; he does not accept that the definition of the good should be left to politics and the State (Habermas 1985; 1996). Accordingly, it has been noted that public discussion may well occur in groups within the social environment, and that it is not necessarily a matter belonging to politics and State (Kymlicka 1989a).

The above appeal to family, educational institutions, cultural pluralism, criticism, and discussion, whether regarded as pertaining to social or political spheres, can be interpreted by recalling the reciprocal influence between the individual and society, mentioned above; family, educational and other institutions are the means through which the community affects the individual, whereas criticism and discussion are the means through which the individual(s) affect(s) society. I underline that through criticism and discussion the members of a community will find *within themselves* (mainly through their rational and emotional *consciousness*—Fig. 1.1) the *objective* human good, linked to the property of the mind as an *evolving* entity, and the ensuing ground moral norm prescribing the *promotion of mind evolution*.

3.2.10.2—Liberal Nationalism

For the *liberal nationalism* (Spinner 1993; Tamir 1993; Miller 1995; 2000), the basis for the solidarity in the society and the stability of the State is not based on shared liberal principles but rather on the *nationhood*, i.e., on shared culture, language, and educational public institutions. Indeed, adjustment of boundaries to approach the existing national identities has been a widespread process, which has been successful in some regions of the world and less in others (Anderson 1983; Gellner 1983; Kymlicka 2004). However, it has been pointed out that sometimes a State, in order to promote the prevailing language, culture, and other values that define a national identity, may indeed use non-liberal means and even violence; this may be in contrast with the liberal conception of the State (Brighouse 1998).

The problem with liberal nationalism is that the nationhood is based on some characteristics or properties (culture, language, ways of life) that are specific of a nation and that, therefore, are *particular* human properties that define a particular human group. In contrast to the *universal* human properties (linked to the ontology of human beings, as conscious entities capable of undergoing *evolution*), which are common to all individuals (as members of the class of men) and, as such, give rise to *universal* moral principles and values (and ensuing rights/duties), the properties that define nationhood are *particular* properties, whose value cannot be imposed upon other nations or upon those individuals who do not recognize it. Of course, the properties that define the identity of a nation can legitimately be loved, and the confrontation with other nations can be conceived as a sort of fair competition; but, when the particular properties of a community are given so large a weight as to being regarded as the basis for the national identity, most often they are associated to an aggressive behavior toward other nations. To avoid this risk, it has been proposed that nationhood could only be based on the shared territory, history, and future, allowing the co-existence of various ethnicities, religious beliefs and cultural conceptions (Kymlicka 1995b); to this end, criteria for distinguishing liberal from illiberal forms of nation building have been developed (Kymlicka and Opalski 2001). Yet, I think that the risk that a nation will attempt to value its own properties as better than those of other nations, or even that it will attempt to impose them, will remain. Indeed, being based on *particular* properties, *the concept of nationhood tends to divide and not to unite.* To avoid this, it is necessary to distinguish: *(a)* the *universal rights/duties*, linked to the ground moral norm which, in turn, descends from the conception of the human good as mind evolution, which should be valid for *all* men and *all* States; and *(b)* the *particular ways of life*, linked to the particular properties (aptitudes, preferences, culture, and way of life) that define the various populations or nations and that, provided they are not in contrast to the moral norms, should be allowed to freely flourish because they contribute to the richness of the human world. Perhaps, the love for one's own nation should be associated with the appreciation of other nationalities, within a conception of diversity as something that attracts and unites and not as something that divides.

It has also been maintained that a shared self-understanding is difficult to be achieved on a vast national scale; hence the opportunity of *decentralized power* and local governments (MacIntyre 1981: 221; Sandel 1984b); this would be especially true considering the modern trend toward multicul-

turalism, supra-national institutions, and the end of the nation-state (Guéhenno 1995). However, it has been noted that, even at a local level, there
may be various and conflicting conceptions of good and of the ways of life
that make necessary toleration of minorities (Taylor 1992). Again, I underline that the conception of *good* should be the same for all men and for all
governments (be they local, regional or State governments, or supra-
national organizations), whereas the particular properties (aptitudes, preferences, culture, and ways of life) specific to minorities should be not merely
tolerated but indeed appreciated, because the diversities between individuals
and communities enrich the human world (provided they are not in contrast
with the ground moral norm).

3.2.11—Citizenship Theory

3.2.11.1—Citizenship Theory and Civic Virtues

Citizenship theory attempts to combine the liberal principles with the communitarian emphasis on the role of the community (Heater 1990; 1999;
Beiner 1995; Shafir 1998; Van Gunsteren 1998), and stresses the role of
civic virtues, i.e., the kinds of behavior and cooperation that are needed for
the good functioning and the stability of the democratic States (Macedo
1990: 138–39; Galston 1991: 215–17, 244). The main civic virtues are those
based on liberal principles of justice and true care and respect for the others
(Spinner 1993; Calhoun 2000), together with a shared sense of common
nationhood and language (Miller 1995; Wright 2000; Kymlicka 2002).

    Civic virtues, which should supplement citizen rights (civil, social and
political) (Marshall 1965), would include *general* virtues, *social* virtues,
economic virtues, and *political* virtues (Galston 1991: 221–24); of primary
importance would be the aptitude and willingness of citizens to engage in
social and political *conversation*, in order to be able to understand, control,
and criticize the government that they have elected (Galston 1991: 121–27;
Bohman 1996: 58–59, 116–18; Barber 1999) and, through public reasonableness, to reach a common decision about the topics discussed (Rawls
1993; Gutmann and Thompson 1996; D'Agostino 1996; Macedo 1990;
1999) or, at least, a compromise (Gutmann and Thompson 1996; Mouffe
2000). Thus, democracy, rather than being based on the mere vote, is now
conceived as based on deliberative discussion, i.e., is now a communicative,
or *deliberative*, or *discursive democracy* (Habermas 1979; Dryzek 1990;
2000; Christiano 1996: 133–50; Miller 2000: 8–23; Young 2000). Discursive democracy would favor mutual understanding (Habermas 1979) and
the participation of minorities to the formation of opinions (Chambers and
Kymlicka 2001: 90–110) (chs. 2.2.1.3.4, *B*; 3.1.2.5.3, *3*).

What is the meaning of *citizenship theory* and what is the role of *civic virtues*? Let us start from the concept that the vote is of basic value to democracy (ch. 3.1.2.2). The vote expresses an *evaluation* of what the party in power has done and, especially, a *prevision* about what each of the competing parties will be able to do if it wins the competition. This evaluation and prevision process requires *knowledge* of what has been done by the party in power as well as by the opposition party and the *prevision* of what the winning party will do. Thus, a useful political discussion should be contributed by two components: *(1)* the *willingness of citizens* to engage in it, and *(2)* the *knowledge* and *prevision* concerning political events.

(1) The Willingness of Citizens. As noted in chapter 3.1.1.1.1, society and its organization as a State are the forms under which *selfish actions* and *moral acts* (created by the outward and the inward activity of *power*, respectively) reach or approach universality, similarly to what happens in the sphere of scientific knowledge or in that of the arts, which are the forms under which universality is reached or approached by *selfish ideas* and *moral thoughts* (created by the outward and the inward activity of *intellect*, respectively) and by *selfish sentiments* and *moral feelings* (created by the outward and the inward activity of *sensitiveness*, respectively—Fig. 1.1). Thus, the willingness of citizens to engage in political discussion expresses the degree of evolution of their mind as far as their outward and inward activities of *power* are concerned. More exactly, we should note that the knowledge reached through political discussion (made of *ideas* and *moral thoughts*, created by the outward and the inward activities of *intellect*) serves to create *selfish or group projects* and *moral projects* (again created by the outward and the inward activity of *intellect*) that will then be realized by political pressure on the government and especially by means of the vote.

It has been observed that often people are little interested in public discussion and political deliberation (Heater 1990: 215; Glendon 1991: 129). However, to correctly evaluate citizens' participation in political matter, one should refer to the ontological conception of the mind as an evolving, *triadic* entity (ch. 1.2). On these grounds, it seems reasonable to expect that, in a "balanced" society, about one third, or 33.33%, of citizens will be primarily and actively engaged in the function and development of one of the three mind components, and that those citizens primarily engaged in the activity and development of one mind component (about 33.33% of total) will rely on (and trust) the other two thirds, or 66.66%, of citizens as far as the activity and development of the other two mind components are concerned. Thus, contrary to the common view, active participation in political life (including the participation in voting), which belongs to the sphere of *power*, should represent the main engagement for about 33.33% of the citizens. Similar reasoning applies for the participation of citizens in the activity and development of *intellect* as well as of *sensitiveness*, each of which should be the primary engagement for about 33.33% of citizens. Of course, it is good that more than one-third of citizens, though primarily engaged in the activity and development of one of the three mind components, will participate, to some extent, also in the activity of the other two mind components; this may especially occur in coincidence with particular events that attract the general attention, like voting in the field of politics (or the occurrence of a great discovery in the scientific field). However, it is only when the percentage of citizens actively participating in political life and in voting falls below 33.33% that an abnormal disinterest for political life can be diagnosed. This disinterest may be due to an *unbalance* between the three mind components among citizens (with prevalence of the intellect and/or sensitiveness over power), or to a (hopefully transitory) slowing in the evolution, or even to an involution, of the *power* component of citizens' minds.

(2) Knowledge and Prevision of Political Events. It has been proposed that civic virtues should be promoted through educational programs by the government (Sandel 1996: 305; Kymlicka and Norman 2000). I note, however, that promoting civic virtues is a very complex task: it should include a stimulation of citizens' willingness and desire toward political discussion (which concerns the sphere of *sensitiveness*), as well as the provision of adequate knowledge and information about political events (which concerns the sphere of *intellect*). In order to allow an adequate knowledge of political events, the government and all public institutions should be open toward the citizens, and should allow that citizens have access to all the relevant information about their activity; in addition, a system of free, pluralistic, and correct information is required, which should include information spread by the press, the radio, and the television (concerning the special meaning of the information media, see ch. 3.1.2.2.1, *2*).

In addition to knowledge of political facts, prevision of future events would also be required; yet, we already know that both knowledge and prevision can only be based on a statistical-probabilistic approach, thus entailing *approximation* and *imprecision* (ch. 1.1.3.2.1); however, approximation and imprecision, which justify discussion and different opinions, concern *particular* facts, and do not prevent us from making the right choices as concerns the pursuing of general or *universal moral ends*, i.e., mind evolution (in all its aspects) for the largest possible percentage of citizens (ch. 3.1.2.5.3).

The above discussion shows how difficult it is to realize the condition for a fully informed and meaningful voting. Actually, the condition for an ideal or perfect voting is an unreachable end. Indeed, we can say that an ideal or perfect condition is an unreachable end in all spheres of mind activity. Thus, an ideal and perfect set of *moral thoughts* (inward activity of intellect), of *moral feelings* (inward activity of sensitiveness) and of *moral acts* (inward activity of power) as well as a complete and perfect *knowledge* (outward activity of the *intellect*), a complete literary, musical, and visual art production, expressing all possible human *sentiments* (outward activity of the *sensitiveness*), and a total or perfect ability to *action* (outward activity of the *power*), are all unreachable ends that can only be slowly and progressively approached through an endless process of evolution.

3.2.11.2—Civic Republicanism

The above discussion also helps to interpret *civic republicanism* (this term derives from reference to the active participation in public life in the ancient republics, such as Athens and Rome). This political conception considers the active participation in political debate and decision as a primary value, ensuring the highest form of human living-together (Oldfield 1990: 6). In my view, this position is an extreme one, since political activity refers to just one of the three mind components, the *power*, both its inward and outward activities (i.e., the *practical mind activity*—Fig. 1.1), and should be given the same "weight" as the activities referring to the other two mind components, *intellect* and *sensitiveness* (i.e., to the *rational* and *emotional mind activities*). This consideration provides support to the view that probably many people actually prefer other private or intimate values, such as love, family, friends, work, the arts, etc., values that civic republicans seem to minimize or deny (Galston 1991: 58–63; Kymlicka 2002: 298), and that the interest for political debate and deliberation may grow only in time of voting or during deep or dramatic political changes (Ackerman 1991).

3.2.11.3—Teaching and Learning Civic Virtues

It has been noted that, to be enjoyed by citizens, political participation should not be conducted on too-large a scale, so that it may be closer to citizens, and should not be affected by the power of money, media and experts (Herzog 1986: 483–90; Kymlicka 2002: 297). Moreover, undue prevalence of self-interest, prejudices and non-care for disadvantaged groups should be avoided (Fierlbeck 1991; Mulgan 1991). Free *market* has been suggested to promote the citizen initiative, responsibility and civic virtues while restraining the tendency to passivity and dependence from public power that a welfare State would favor (Mead 1986). Others, however, underline that the market does not promote the sense of justice nor public discussion about social or political problems, and might indeed favor the exclusion of undesired minorities (Fierlbeck 1991; Mulgan 1991).

It has been suggested that formative projects for developing civic virtues should be realized by appropriate private or public institutions (Glendon 1991; Glendon and Blankenhorn 1995). These should include the following: *(a) social associations*, such as family, church, neighborhood, charity or other associations (Elshtain 1981; Ruddick 1984; Glendon 1991; Walzer 1992a), even if all these associations may also teach egoism, prejudice or despotism, or non-care for others (Mouffe 1992; Walzer 1992a; Rosenblum 1998); *(b) school* and the educational system (Gutmann 1987: 51; Weinstock 2002), provided that they are detached from, and even critical to, any familial, ethnic, religious, habitual, or traditional point of view (Callan 1997: 133; Levinson 1999).

All the above views, considered together, show how difficult a problem the teaching of civic virtues is. In my opinion, what is important is that any educational or formative program spreads the conception that political activity should be directed to assure the supremacy of the moral ends (favoring mind evolution of all citizens by assuring an *evolution-allowing, involution-avoiding condition* to all of them) over the selfish interests, even if the latter, when respecting the moral ends, play the important role of promoting individual and group welfare and are linked to the "duty toward oneself" (ch. 2.1.5.2.2). These educational programs should contrast the tendency of some religious or ethnic groups (e.g., the Amish community) to preserve their identity by subtracting their children from a liberal education (Macedo 1990: 53–54; Spinner-Halev 2000). Some maintain that these groups or communities, if they are peaceful and do not attempt to affect the rest of society, should be allowed to lead their way of life (Spinner 1993: 98). This view cannot be accepted, because it allows the cultural development of young people to be restrained (Gutmann 1980). I would like to add that restraining the education of young people means to restrain their mind evolution, which is against the prescription of the ground moral norm. In this regard, I recall that the rights of individuals or groups are linked to their duty to promote the evolution of the minds (including the mind of the agents themselves and the minds of others) (ch. 3.1.2.5.2); this duty, in turn, is linked to the essential properties of the class of men (linked to their ability to undergo *evolution*), which are *universal* properties, common to all men. On the other hand, *particular* properties, which characterize individuals or groups, give rise to the right to freely express them; however, some particular properties (like the wish of subtracting children from school—see above) are against the fundamental moral norm, as they restrain mind evolution, so that the attempt to impose them gives rise to "bad claims" that, as such, should be contrasted (ch. 3.2.12, *3*).

3.2.12—Multiculturalism

Multiculturalism attempts to cope with the heterogeneity of modern society, composed of diverse ethnic-cultural groups, by recognizing these groups and their rights and traditions, instead of ignoring or excluding them (Gutmann, ed., 1992; Goldberg 1995; Kymlicka 1995a; Willet 1998). In Western democracies, several types of ethnic-cultural groups have been distinguished (including small immigrant ethnic-religious groups that voluntarily isolate themselves from the larger society, such as Hutterites, Amish, or Hasidic Jews) (Walzer 1983; Carens 1989; Bauböck 1994; Rubio-Marin 2000; Kymlicka 2001; 2002).

It has been observed that the emphasis of multiculturalism on those rights linked to the community gives it some similarity with communitarianism (Van Dyke 1977; McDonald 1991; Addis 1992). Indeed, at least some ethnic-cultural groups share with the majority group the belief in the same basic liberal principles; in addition, they want recognition and respect of their identity (language, culture, religion and habits) that allows the true enjoyment of those principles (Kymlicka 1989b; 1995b; Spinner 1993; Tamir 1993; Miller 1995; Raz 1998). The attempts to promote the inclusion of all citizenships within a common culture by extending to all the basic social rights (Marshall 1965) has proved to be unsuccessful in eliminating differences, which would suggest that a differentiated citizenship is required (Young 1990; 2000). Differentiated citizenship has been opposed by arguing that the concept of citizenship is inherent to the community as a whole (Porter 1987: 128). Some thinkers have argued that adhering to the language and culture of a community can be regarded as a free choice, which should entail acceptance of the consequences, whereas others question that this can be regarded as a free choice and underline that changing language and culture is a very difficult task (Kymlicka 1995a,b). It has been suggested that the differences in the economic status (economic hierarchy) should be corrected by a politics of redistribution, whereas differences in the social status (status hierarchy) should be corrected by a politics of recognition (Fraser 1998), although often the two should be combined, as the politics of recognition should supplement that of redistribution (Fraser 1998; Banting 2000; Young 2000). (On *multiculturalism* see also my recent book, 2012:162–81).

In commenting on the above issues, I start by noting that the ethnic-cultural-religious differences may be a problem for the minority groups, since the majority group, in a democratic State, is the group in power; thus, the true problem concerns the ethnic-cultural-religious minorities or, to be more exact, the claims of these minorities. These claims can be distinguished into three groups, as described below.

(1) Claims Concerning Rights of Minorities. The rights of minorities are directed to assure them the enjoyment of the *evolution-allowing, involution-*

avoiding condition, and consist of the universal human rights (as defined elsewhere—chs. 3.2.2.1.1; 3.2.2.1.2). The rights of minorities entail the existence of corresponding *duties* of the citizens belonging to the majority group (and of the government) directed to assure the concrete enjoyment of those rights. These rights/duties are linked to the *essential properties* common to all individuals, as members of the class of men, properties that consist of the fact that men are conscious entities composed of intellect, sensitiveness, and power and capable of undergoing *evolution*. These rights and duties are of *moral* nature, and descend from the *ground moral norm*, which prescribes the promotion of mind evolution (ch. 2.1.5.1); they may also be *legal* rights/duties if they are included in the constitutional norms of a democratic State, as should be the case when the consciousness of the majority of the members of a community (which is reflected in the constitutional norms) is sufficiently evolved or developed. The *evolution of consciousness*, of course, occurs through time, so that there may be periods in history and places in the world in which the consciousness of the majority of the members of a community is not evolved enough to recognize the fundamental rights of the minorities. Examples of this are the acceptance of slaves during the Roman Empire or, for several decades (until the late 19th century), in some American States. In these instances, what can be done is that the citizens with a more evolved consciousness (who dissent from some of the shared moral principles and values, and from the corresponding norms) actively propagandize among the community members, by democratic means, their moral thoughts and feelings (thus acting as promoters of the evolution of the consciousness of the community) until these are accepted by the majority of citizens and included into the constitutional norms (or their equivalents) (ch. 4.1.1.3.2, *B*).

(2) Justified Claims. These are the claims that derive from the wish to express the particular properties (preferences, habits, culture, traditions, and programs) that characterize a group and define its identity. This means that these claims consist of the *right to freedom* in expressing the particular properties of a community. It should be noted that each individual or group can only develop and evolve in a way specific to its constitutional identity and natural endowment, so that attempting to repress the expression of the particular properties of an individual or group actually means to restrain his mind evolution, which is against the ground moral norm.

On the other hand, it should be considered that it is in the interest of all the communities living within a State to be able to communicate and to cooperate with one another, at least to some extent, because this will lead to a better functioning and development of the entire society. This entails, among others, that each group should actively engage itself in learning and understanding the *languages* of other co-existing groups (because language is an extremely important means for communication and cooperation) and should also accept to reciprocally change, to the necessary extent, their habits and traditions to avoid that excessive differences may interfere with the general organization of the public activities (examples: the habit of having a rest after lunch may interfere with the organization of the work). Thus, a reciprocal effort of each of the coexisting groups to meet one another is very useful for the good functioning of a State and for its evolution, and is, therefore, morally good. Of course, there are many ways to reach this goal in each concrete instance of co-existence of different groups; while it is the task of sociology, economics, political science, and law to define the particular ways by which this goal can be reached in any concrete situation, the task of political philosophy is to define the reason by which co-existing groups should attempt to reach, or at least approach, this goal.

It has been claimed that: *(a)* the politics of recognition, by underlining cultural differences, may make the politics of redistribution difficult (difficulty in obtaining jobs, etc.), so that the latter politics should be favored (Barry 2001); and *(b)* recognition of minorities' rights might lead to, or favor, social conflicts (Schlesinger 1992; Schmidt 1997). These claims are unjustified if a reciprocal effort of each of the coexisting groups to meet one another is made (as stated above) and if the diversities among the different groups (unless they are against mind evolution) are regarded as something that enriches the human world, as something that should generate attraction (and not repulsion) between groups, and that should unite rather than divide. Indeed, diversity among groups, communities or populations means the creation of diverse and various forms of literary, musical and visual arts, beliefs, religious faith, clothing, preferences, habits, traditions, perspectives, and ways of life. How poor and boring the world would be if all communities and populations (and individuals) were almost equal to one another! Indeed, *diversity is the necessary condition for the life of humans.* If men did not differ from one another, that is, if they were identical to one another, like the clones of a unique prototype, they could not exist as human beings and could not give rise to the human world as we know it. On these grounds, *interculturalism* arose; it is the philosophical conception that appreciates diversity and that attempts to harmonize and accord diverse groups or communities, which may differ from one another with regard to several properties, linked to ethnicity, religious beliefs, culture, language, etc.

Concerning the relation between the majority group and the minorities within a democratic State, it should be recalled that a democratic government has not the right to simply enact laws and implement rules shared only by the majority group or political party (this would be a dictatorship of the majority), but it has the moral and political duty to attempt to reach as large a consensus as possible, i.e., to realize the *better approach to universality,* which is only possible if the desires and needs of the minority groups are recognized and respected to the largest possible extent (ch. 3.1.2.1.1).

Moreover, it would be very useful that laws of major importance (especially those dealing with fundamental rights) are passed by qualified majorities, according to the concept of "gradational democracy" (ch. 3.1.2.1.2).

The above reasoning helps to reinterpret and explain the following views. *(a)* Liberal-democratic States should behave as *civic nations* by benignly neglecting the ethnic-cultural diversity, and not as *ethnic nations* that aim at promoting their own ethno-national culture (Pfaff 1993: 162; Ignatieff 1993). *(b)* A complete separation of State and ethnic-culture should be realized (Walzer 1992b). *(c)* What happens in most Western democracies, which actually attempt to promote their own *societal culture* (i.e., their language, culture, and institutions), should be avoided (Kymlicka 2001; 2002), even if this may favor equality and solidarity (Tamir 1993; Miller 1995; Canovan 1996). *(d)* The politics of recognition actually strengthens solidarity (by avoiding exclusions) and promotes political stability (Kymlicka 1998; 2001), whereas denying the recognition of minorities and the respect of their identity leads to instability and conflicts (Gurr 1993; Lapidoth 1996).

(3) Unjustified or "Bad" Claims. It may happen that some individuals or, more importantly, some groups or communities claim to have rights linked to their specific properties that actually are unjustified. In some instances, these claims are directed to preserve some illiberal and oppressive habits, such as denying education to children or to women, or confining women to home and opposing women emancipation (Okin 1999; Deveaux 2001; Shachar 2001). These "bad minority claims" are clearly unjustified, because they are directed to restrain mind evolution; Kymlicka (2002: 340) has termed them "bad rights". These bad claims can be made both by majority or minority groups. Concerning minority groups, one should distinguish *unjustified claims*, which entail *internal restrictions* of individual rights, from *justified claims* (which actually are *rights*), allowing *external protection* of minority groups against the pressure of the majority (Kymlicka 2001: 22).

The unjustified claims can be defined as those claims that are directed to *restrain mind evolution* of individuals belonging either to the claiming group itself or to other groups; they may be of two kinds:

(a) Unjustified or bad claims that actually restrain mind evolution. The attempt to impose this kind of "bad claim" may lead to two sorts of consequences: *internal restrictions*, when these claims of a community are directed to its own members; or *external impositions*, when these claims of a community are directed toward another community or State. Examples of *internal restriction* are: the well-known case of the Amish people, who would like to withdraw their children from school before the age of 16, in order to prevent that they abandon their religious tradition or even the community; or the case of some States, where the access to education and

other rights are denied to women. Examples of *external imposition* are the cases when habits or rules of conduct that restrain mind evolution are imposed by a community to another one; in other words, when a community attempts to impose its "bad claims" on other communities. Clearly, these claims cannot be accepted, because they are against the universal human rights, as they would cause a severe restraining of mind evolution.

(b) Unjustified or bad claims that arbitrarily contrast individual or group rights. These are those claims that contrast the implementation of the properties that are specific to individuals or communities and that define their identity. This, again, may lead to both internal restrictions and external impositions. Examples are the attempts to contrast the culture, habits, preferences, traditions, religious beliefs or, shortly, the "way of life" of other individuals or communities. Since mind evolution can only occur through ways specific to each individual or group (according to the natural endowment), restraining the implementation of the properties specific to individuals or communities actually means restraining their mind evolution.

(4) Intercultural Policy. The above discussion should help to cope with the coexistence of communities with different identities, because it shows that diversity is a necessary condition for the life of humans and because it suggests a criterion for coping with the diversity among individuals and communities. Indeed, the above reasoning suggests that diversity linked to the individual or group properties should be respected, through a politics of recognition, and also encouraged, appreciated, and loved, as it may only produce an enrichment of the human world. Indeed, as I have already noted, restraining the implementation of the properties specific to an individual (or group) actually means restraining the evolution of his mind.

Some thinkers underline that, in addition to a politics of recognition, a politics of redistribution is also required toward those communities that, for several reasons, may suffer from a low economic status (Fraser 1998; Barry 2001). However, it should be noted that the politics of redistribution should be directed to correct differences in the economic status of individuals or groups, irrespective of their belonging to one or another of the cultural communities or ethnic groups.

Thus, the "bad claims" (both those which directly restrain mind evolution as well as those which arbitrarily contrast the implementation of individual properties) should not be recognized but should rather be efficiently contrasted.

From the above discussion, it follows that problems arise *(a)* when individuals or communities attempt to impose "bad claims" to other individuals or communities, or *(b)* when individuals or communities deny other individuals or communities the right to implement their particular rights (that is, to express their own particular properties). This should not be permitted. However, preventing or correcting these "bad claims" is always a difficult task.

At the individual level, each "good" individual should do his best to persuade and educate the people who claim "bad rights" and with whom he interacts during his life.

At the public level, in the case of communities existing within a State, prevention or correction can be made through appropriate laws (example: a law imposing that all children should go to school) associated to educational programs.

The difficulty is greater in the case of communities belonging to different States. In these instances, preventing or correcting the imposition of bad claims should not be done by using coercion or violence, because violence may produce more evil than the imposition of bad rights itself, as it may mean war. From my standpoint, war, being always associated with many deaths, should be regarded as causing the greatest possible involution of many individual minds, namely the transformation of human beings into inert matter. Therefore, restraining the imposition of bad rights should be pursued by means of cultural, political, or even economic pressure by the international community; the scope should not be to impose a given conduct from outside but to favor the internal evolution of the minds.

A special case is that concerning the groups (or individuals) defined by their ideals or points of view. Mackie suggests that a good form of society should be able to accommodate cooperation, competition, and conflict between followers of different ideals. He underlines that there are different and opposing points of view which lead to opposing evaluation: "terrorist gunmen" versus "fearless freedom fighters"; "defenders of law and order" versus "fascist thugs"; "incorruptible idealists" versus "ruthless fanatics"; "guardians of freedom" versus "imperialist exploiters" (Mackie 1977: 238). I note that we should distinguish the ideals from the ways (or *procedures*—ch. 3.1.2.5.3, *1c*) through which they are pursued. Ideals should be moral ends and, therefore, according to my ethical conception, they should consist of the many aspects of the main moral end: mind evolution. Thus, referring to the couples mentioned by Mackie, the couple "terrorist gunmen"-"fearless freedom fighters" refers to the ideal of *freedom*, which is the basic condition for promoting mind evolution; the couple "defenders of law and order"-"fascist thugs" refer to the observance of laws (principle of *lawfulness*), which is required for the functioning of the State (which means evolution of human actions toward universality and pursuing of the moral ends as defined by the constitutional norms); the couple "guardians of freedom"-"imperialist exploiters" refers to the defense of *international freedom* from the threat of non-democratic or tyrannical States. These are ideals shared by most people because they are clearly morally good; indeed, an "immoral" ideal would not be an ideal at all. Problems arise with regard to the ways (or *procedures*) through which ideals are pursued. In short, violent means are not justified, because they cause more evil than that caused by the condition that the violent actions attempt to change; in most cases terrorist actions cause the death of several or many people, which means the complete and irreversible *involution* of many minds. Likewise, defense of freedom in the international scenery should not be pursued by means of an "imperialist" policy, often associated to violence or even to war, but through cultural, political and even economic pressure (the latter only of moderate degree) directed not to make impositions from outside but to induce an internal evolution of minds. Violence might be justified in very special circumstances, such as when citizens fight for liberty under a non-democratic or tyrannical government (ch. 3.2.14.2); an example may be the fight of Resistance Movements in Europe during the occupation by the Nazis. Otherwise, political changes can be obtained by non-violent means, even under difficult conditions, as shown by the struggle guided by Gandhi in India.

Mackie points out that, when divergent moral principles exist (as may often occur in the field of peripheral or non-core principles of morality such as those concerning sexual behavior), the morality of one part of society should not be imposed by law to society as a whole; rather, the law should limit its role to enable the followers of rival ideals to live together by limiting their conflicting claims, considering that moral ideals are such for those who adhere to them, and are not objective values to impose on others (Mackie 1977: 234–35). Actually, "sexual behavior" is not a "peripheral part" of morality, but is unrelated to morality, and is one of the expressions of the specific properties that define the identity of individuals and groups. [Indeed, sexual behavior may have some relation to morality in the sense that sexual pleasure is a light and particular sentiment compared to the sexual pleasure that is associated to, and part of, a profound love; the latter (as compared to the former) is a deeper sentiment possessing "a higher degree of universality" and, therefore, is an expression of a more evolved mind and, hence, is morally better]. The law should impose on all citizens those norms (which actually are moral norms) that favor mind development, whereas it should favor compromise between all other claims linked to preferences, desires, or interests; these claims are not moral claims because they are unrelated to mind evolution.

3.2.13—Feminism

Feminism concerns most fields of political theory considered from the feminist point of view (Butler and Scott 1992; Jaggar and Young 1998; Phillips 1998; Tong 1998; Card 1999). The main focus has been about: *(1)* the elimination of sexual difference from social and political life, i.e., the defense of *gender equality* (Kittay 1995; Rhode 1997), and the related *public man/private woman* debate (Elshtain 1981; Boyd 1997; Landes 1998); and *(2)* the *ethics of care* (Gilligan 1982; Kittay and Meyers 1987; Larabee 1993; Held V. 1995; Clement 1996).

(1) Defense of Gender Equality. The problem of gender equality is a special case of the problem of equality between different and co-existing communities, with the special notation that the female gender comprises about half of all human beings. While I refer to chapter 3.2.12 for a discussion concerning co-existing communities, here I recall that, according to the ground moral norm, all human beings, independently of their gender or their particular properties, should *equally* enjoy those concrete conditions that allow mind development, i.e., should enjoy an evolution-allowing condition.

(2) Ethics of Care. It has been noted that, historically, morality has been conceived differently by the two genders, since men's ethics would be centered on *justice* (i.e., would be based on universal moral principles, rights, and fairness) whereas women's ethics would be centered on *care* and responsiveness to particular cases and to relationships (Baier 1987; Friedman 1987; Tronto 1987; 1993; Blum 1988). Men would have a moral voice of *justice* based on a duality of principles and practice whereas women look at human needs and their moral voice is one of *care* (Gilligan 1982) and would not depend on general moral principles (Noddings 1984; Ruddick 1984; Grimshaw 1986; Hekman 1995). An *ethics of care* is also defended by Noddings (1989), who claims that we should attempt to understand rather than to judge. Yet, general theories or principles seem necessary in order to know for whom and for what we feel responsible, and when a demand is legitimate or has priority over other ones (Grimshaw 1986; Sher 1987; Tronto 1993; Bubeck 1995; Bowden 1996). Moreover, the ethics of care would make it difficult to define the reason why we should care for strangers (Gilligan 1982; Deveaux 1995).

I think that the feminist position can be interpreted by referring to my moral theory if we recall that *moral acts* (moral behavior) are guided by moral norms, which are directed to implement *moral principles* (created by *moral thoughts*) and *moral values* (created by *moral feelings*). In men, moral principles (and, therefore, moral thoughts) may prevail over moral values (and, therefore, over moral feelings), whereas in women the reverse may be true, i.e., moral feelings and values prevail over moral thoughts and principles.

Concerning the principles created by *moral thoughts* (i.e., created by the inward activity of intellect), I recall that a central point in the functioning of intellect is represented by the creation of the ideas of class, which refer to all similar objects or events that share some common properties. Thus, we should assume that men are more prone to endorse general laws or principles that refer to a class, like the one expressed by the proposition "we should help all needy men" (this proposition refers to the class of needy men), whereas women are more prone toward the particular and similar objects that are members of a class; referring to the above example, women would be more prone to care for the particular members of the class of needy men, so that they would say: "we should help this needy man '*a*' and that needy man '*b*'." The latter statement, in the case of women, is not primarily supported by the general principle "we should help all needy men", but by emotional factors, as are the moral feelings, created by emotional consciousness (Fig. 1.1). In this regard, it should be remembered that moral feelings (like sentiments) are directed to "particular" objects (Belfiore 2004: 26–27), i.e., particular human minds or persons, whereas moral thoughts (like ideas) tend to go from particular to universal. Therefore, the *ethics of care* can be defined as an ethics in which moral feelings (which are mainly directed to particular individuals) prevail over moral thoughts (which are mainly directed to define general principles) and prompt the agent to directly care for needy persons (minds) with whom he interacts.

"Care" means feeling "responsibility for" and the desire to help those who are in need by doing the acts required for promoting the evolution of their minds, under all aspects. On these grounds, Noddings's remark (quoted above) that women attempt to understand (rather than to judge) should be reinterpreted by giving the term "understand" the meaning "understand the particular conditions of those who are in need." The importance of caring for others (directed to promote their mind evolution) derives from the fact that whichever is the judgment about a person, i.e., be he a "good man" or a "bad man", our moral behavior toward him should always be the same: promoting his mind evolution to the maximum possible extent or, shortly, caring for him. In this view, even the sanction against a "bad man" should be directed to educate him, i.e., to promote his mind evolution.

Noddings (1989) is against individualism and competitive life; she maintains that, instead of the ideology of individualism leading to a competitive life, we should attempt to stand by both the competing or opposing parties, the apparently good and the apparently evil, and try to reconcile them. This statement is acceptable only in part: it is good that we attempt to understand and reconcile competing or opposing parties, but we should not reconcile the "good" and the "bad" man; rather, what is desirable is, first, that we have moral norms that, without being dogmatic, should allow us to distinguish the "good" from the "bad" men and, then, that we approach the "bad man" with understanding and care, and do our utmost to help him to undergo mind evolution (i.e., to change from "bad" to "as good as possible").

The above discussed *ethics of care* also helps to understand the role given by women to any *subjectively-felt hurt* (Harding 1982), which would impose the excessive duty of responding to all claims and expectations (Dancy 1992). Indeed, the role given by women to the subjectively-felt hurts can be another consequence of the prevalence of moral feelings over moral thoughts (see above). On the same basis, we could explain the view (Ruddick 1984; 1987) that women's maternal attitude is mainly directed toward holding or keeping existing relationships rather than toward acquiring new relations and pursuing new goals; in fact, existing concrete relationships are primarily the objects of moral feelings, while new projected relations and goals are primarily the objects of moral thoughts.

3.2.14—Other Issues

3.2.14.1—Environmental Policy

As noted by Parfit (1984: 356), any intervention on the environment will affect posterity, which can be regarded as a set of people whose identities are not yet fixed. Hare (1989b: 236–53) thinks that we have a duty to posterity, including the duty to ensure that there is posterity; he maintains that we should use the Golden Rule of moral reasoning (we should consider what we would wish to be done to us, were we in the position of the victim of a certain action) to delimit the classes of beings that can have morally relevant interests and rights. Thus, we should avoid polluting the environment by burying hazardous waste in it if we consider like ourselves the people who will live after our death; and this reasoning might be extended to include sentient animals (Hare 1989b: 236–53). Once again, I observe that the reason for respecting the environment is not merely to respect the *wishes* (or desires or preferences) of the future generations to the same extent as we respect our own wishes, but to preserve or, better, improve the environment in order to favor the *mind evolution* of the future generations of human beings, in accordance with the prescription of the ground moral norm. Indeed, the concept of evolution can be extended to cover all living species, since any living organism is susceptible to undergoing some degree of evolution. So conceived, however, the evolution of the lower species should be subordinated to that of the higher species and, especially, to the evolution of the highest species, the species of humans. This would entail the establishment of a hierarchy of species, which is a difficult task that can only be accomplished with *approximation*, as it occurs in most spheres of human intellectual activity, except for the supremacy of human beings, which seems undeniable.

According to Hare (1989b: 246–49), when conflicting interests of different individuals or groups are affected, environmental moral choices should be made by comparing the *strength* of the various interests as well as their quality. Although this method is somewhat defective, because one cannot accurately envisage what the various options would be like in practice and because posterity is ignored, Hare notes that it is less defective than a pure democratic method, which does not take into account the strengths of the preferences. Non-utilitarians may use other methods, such as the "difference principle" of Rawls (1971: 65–73) or the duties of beneficence and non-maleficence of Ross (1930: 19–21) (chs. 2.2.1.2.3, *A*; 2.2.1.7.2, *C*). According to my view, environmental moral choices should be directed not to respect the wishes and interests (or the strength of these wishes and interests) of the involved individuals or groups, but to favor or promote the evolution of the involved minds (including the posterity's minds).

3.2.14.2—Rebellion

Hare (1989b: 21–33) considers the conditions under which illegal political activity, i.e., rebellion, can be justified. He distinguishes: *(a)* the *criminal*, who breaks the law for his own advantage; *(b)* the *rebel*, or "politically motivated law-breaker," who breaks the law to change it, for universal or group-related political reasons; and *(c)* the *revolutionary*, who attempts by illegal means to change the entire government system. Illegal political activity would be justified only for grave reasons and when there are no legal means to reach the goal, and should be undertaken by evaluating its short- and long-term effects.

I think that *rebellions* and *revolutions* can be justified only (and with caution) in tyrannical non-democratic States, provided they are directed to change the system into a democratic one; this is because non-democratic States prevent any political change, oppress citizens, and restrain their *mind evolution*.

In a democratic State, *revolutions* are always unjustified, whereas *rebellions* (by non-violent means) should be evaluated on the basis of the end that they pursue; the end, in turn, should be evaluated against the existing constitutional norms, which express the shared (by the majority of citizens) moral principles and values, and reflect the degree of evolution reached by the consciousness of the community. Two situations are possible: *(a)* the end pursued by the rebel represents an evolution compared to the end to which the existing constitutional norms are directed to (*morally-good rebel*); or *(b)* the rebel's end represents actually an involution compared to the existing status (*morally-bad rebel*). Examples of morally-good rebels are represented by those who fought slavery in those American States where it was legal or tolerated, or those who fought in order to obtain the right of voting for women in those States where this right was not recognized. Example of morally-bad rebels is represented by those who fought for limiting constitutionally protected rights and liberties, as did the fascist groups called "squadristi" in Italy, in the period preceding the establishment of the fascist government. It should be underlined that the morally-good rebel should never use violence (which most often produces more evil than the condition that it tends to change); in this regard, Gandhi (who indeed acted in a non-democratic situation) represents a classic example of radical political changes obtained without the use of violence. Therefore, most often the morally-good rebel coincides with the *civil disobedient*.

An important issue concerns who should judge whether the end of a rebel is a good or a bad one. There is no doubt that the end of a rebel should be "publicly" evaluated, i.e., should be evaluated against the moral principles and values shared by the majority of the community; the only hope of the morally-good rebel or civil disobedient is that his protest may serve to promote the evolution of the consciousness of the community, so that the majority of citizens will endorse his end, and this may lead to change the existing constitutional norms (of course, some minor problems may just require some change in ordinary laws). In this way, the morally-good rebel serves as a promoter of the evolution of the consciousness of the community (ch. 4.1.1.3.2, *B*).

3.3—Difficult Moral Choices in Public Life

3.3.1—General Considerations

Two kinds of difficult moral choices should be distinguished: *dirty-hands cases* and *moral dilemmas*. "Dirty-hands cases" are the kind of difficult moral choices in which the choice is due to the agent's decision, taken on the basis of his *previsions*; moral dilemmas are a kind of difficult moral choices in which the agent's choice is affected by coercion exerted by *circumstances* (either the will of other agents or factual situations) (Table 3.3). Difficult moral choices may occur in political life as well as in private life (Stocker 1990: 9–36), and also include cases occurring in the private realm of economic activities (Held 1984).

Table 3.3. Difficult moral choices: Classification and examples

	DECISION (BASED ON PREVISIONS)	COERCION (DUE TO CIRCUMSTANCES)
Private	Dirty-hands cases (e.g., a man kills a criminal who is going to kill his friend)	Moral dilemmas (e.g., a mother of two children chooses the one to save, given that she cannot save both of them—Stocker 1990[1])
Public	Dirty-hands cases (e.g., a politician performs some immoral acts, based on his prevision that this will prevent greater evil)	Moral dilemmas (e.g., a military commander, during a battle, abandons some of his men to avoid a sure[2] greater damage—Stocker 1990)

1. This example refers to the case of Sophie's choice, taken from Styron (1979).
2. If the "greater damage" is not sure, but is only a probable prevision of the commander, the case would be one of the public "dirty-hands cases".

While private cases are discussed in chapter 2.2.1.5, here public cases will be considered.

There is no doubt that dirty-hands cases may be faced in political actions. In one of Sartre's work (Sartre 1948: 218), a character representing a political leader admits: "Well, I have dirty hands. Right up to the elbows.

I've plunged them in filth and blood. But what do you hope? Do you think you can govern innocently?", thus pointing to the dilemma of dirty hands as a central feature of political life. A typical example may be that of an official who tortures someone to force him to say where his fellow soldiers have hidden a time bomb among an innocent population (Walzer 1973).

Sorell (1999: 91–117) discusses whether the norms of personal morality are equally valid in political life. He recalls that the events of political life are often unpredictable and difficult to handle; public institutions must be ready to face emergencies (such as terrorism or military invasion) by using normally immoral acts of pre-emptive violence, such as assassinations or sabotage (if there is no other means to avoid the evil, and provided that the information about the danger is accurate). Of course, Sorell says that only emergencies can excuse taking actions that in normal conditions would be wrong.

In my opinion, it is not true that the *unpredictability* of events and the arising of *emergencies* are characteristic of public or political life, as they also apply to private or individual life. The difference is that in private life (i.e., in events affecting only the agent) unpredictability and emergencies are handled through a relationship of the individual with himself, whereas in political life they are handled through a relationship between the rulers and the other citizens (this is true not only with regard to the State but also, with some difference, with regard to smaller communities, such as associations, or even the family). Below, I will discuss: *(1)* the unpredictability of events, *(2)* emergencies, and *(3)* guilt and difficult moral choices.

(1) Unpredictability of Events. Human projects, and the ensuing actions and acts, are based on *evaluation* of the present condition and on *prevision* about possible changes, both of which are not certain but only approximate and probable, respectively. This is true both for the efficaciousness of the projects and for the consequences of the actions or acts. It should be recalled that in the biological and social world, not only the previsions but also the so-called "scientific knowledge" is marked by incompleteness and approximation (ch. 1.1.3.2.1). Indeed, a project is very seldom *fully* efficacious, and a given action or act very seldom produces *all* the expected consequences in their full extent; most often, the actual results of projects and actions correspond to the expected ones only to some extent or degree. Thus, we can say that the *index actual/expected results* is always lower than 1. In private life, this index could be named *results/desired-end index*; in public life, it could be named *realization/promised-end index*.

In private life, the projects about one's future life and the actions directed to realize them may lead to delusory results, i.e., may produce a too low *results/desired-end index*, for which the agent can only complain to himself and to fate (or to others, when it is the case).

In political life, the project of a politician or of a political party (i.e., the *promises* contained in a political program) and the subsequent actions directed to realize it may lead to results that correspond to the expected ones to a more or less extent. Here the evaluation of results is made by people (citizens) different from those (politicians) who prepared the project and attempted to realize it. In evaluating the results obtained by a politician or a political party, citizens should consider that the *realization/promised-end index* is usually less than 1. In the case that citizens think that the realization/promised-end index is too low, they should distinguish whether this is mainly due to inefficaciousness of the project, to weakness of the actions, or to deliberate deception in the elaboration of the projects and/or in the accomplishment of the political actions. Only in the latter instance (entailing deception) politicians can be judged as morally bad. In the other two instances, they should be judged as of little value (i.e., incapable of dealing with the universal actions that are performed in a State); in both instances, dirty-hands cases (i.e., bad moral choices and acts, made in prevision of a greater good end) cannot occur.

(2) Emergencies. Emergencies may occur both in private and in public life. Both a wise individual and a wise government have projects for those emergencies that can be approximately foreseen (in the case of a government: war, natural disasters, etc.). Yet, actually occurring emergencies may present unexpectedly or may have unexpected characteristics, and may require rapid decisions not supported by preexisting detailed or specific projects (or plans), or for which no satisfactory solutions actually exist. Thus, circumstances may occur which give rise to dirty-hands cases.

In private life, this may happen, for instance, when a man who sees that three children are going to drown in a river, saves two of them by taking each of them with one of his hands, so abandoning the third child to certain death (private moral dilemma); or when a man, who evaluates as very probable that his friend is being killed by a bad man, prevents the criminal's action and kills the bad man (private dirty-hands case).

In public life, we can imagine the case of a military commander who, during a battle, abandons some of his men to avoid a sure greater damage (public moral dilemma); or the case of a politician who does immoral acts, based on his prevision that this will prevent greater evil (public dirty-hands case) (Table 3.3).

(3) Guilt and Difficult Moral Choices. As pointed out by Sorell (1999: 91–117), utilitarian moral theories deny that actions can be morally intrinsically wrong regardless of their consequences; therefore, there is no basis for guilt in dirty-hands cases. On the other hand, non-utilitarian moral theories help to explain the feeling of guilt as an expression of a good character facing a moral conflict in cases of dirty hands but do not help in deciding what is permissible in times of emergencies (Sorell 1999: 91–117).

I think that when dealing with guilt in difficult moral choices, we should distinguish: *(a) moral dilemmas* from *(b) dirty-hands cases* (as defined above and in Table 3.3).

(a) Concerning *moral dilemmas,* there is no reason why an agent involved in them should feel guilty. Indeed what an agent involved in a moral dilemma feels is deep sorrow for the morally-bad event associated with the difficult moral choice imposed by circumstances. Thus, the man who can save only two of three children (referring to the above example) feels a deep sorrow for the death of the third child, which is an objectively bad moral event (death is an extreme and irreversible mind *involution*). This is shown by the fact that a deep sorrow may also be felt by the people who may have observed the death of the third child. The sorrow of the man who failed to save the third child may be greater because he was personally involved in the bad moral event (the sorrow could be even greater if the man was the father of the dead child, because of the love that links the father to his children). The same reasoning applies to the case of the commander who abandons a group of his men (see the above example).

(b) In contrast to moral dilemmas, *dirty-hands cases* entail a decision of the agent, taken on the basis of *his* evaluation and prevision. However, both evaluations and previsions can only be made with approximation (ch. 1.1.3.2.1); moreover, once an agent has performed the action that he decided to perform, the doubt will remain that the situation could have been better if the agent had taken a different decision. This entails that the agent feels responsible for the consequences of his action; hence, his sense of guilt.

It has been said that the distinction between private and public (political) morality, i.e., the claim that what is immoral in private life may be legitimate for reaching political ends, has arisen in the modern era (Allett 1995). I think that a more significant distinction should be made between those public dirty-hands cases occurring in modern democratic-constitutional States, in which there are publicly-shared moral principles and values, and those occurring in non-democratic non-constitutional (old and modern) States, in which no such principles exist, as will be discussed in the next chapters.

3.3.2—Views About Dirty Hands Cases

3.3.2.1—Dirty-Hands Cases in Non-Democratic Non-Constitutional (Old and Modern) States

In non-democratic non-constitutional States, there are no publicly-shared moral principles and values, which in the democratic constitutional States are acknowledged in the constitutional norms. Therefore, suspected dirty-hands cases occurring in public life can only be evaluated by private moral principles, i.e., by moral principles held by individual citizens; these principles, although they might actually be largely shared by citizens, lack public justification through voting. I will briefly comment the position of Machiavelli and that of Hobbes.

(1) Machiavelli. Machiavelli (1513; 1531) maintained that the political office itself requires power (including dirty and ruthless deeds) and popular support and submission. As underlined by Tinder (1986: 110), the merit of Machiavelli is that he focused on the tension arising from the awareness that there is a moral law but that rulers on some occasions must break it; hence the advice to the prince to learn how not to be good and to use this knowledge according to the necessity of the case (Machiavelli 1513: 48); similar advice was given to republican rulers (Machiavelli 1531: 194–95). In my view, we should recall that Machiavelli lived in the pre-democratic pre-constitutional era, when no publicly-shared moral principles governing political actions existed, i.e., when public life occurred in an "amoral" environment, actually ruled by strength and violence. Thus, the "moral" rules for political actions were imposed by the rulers themselves, and the single political actions could only be judged by citizens on the basis of individual (non-publicly-shared) moral principles. Considering that, as discussed elsewhere (ch. 4.1.1.3.2, *B*), *public* moral principles (for judging public actions) may be different from *private* moral principles (for judging private actions), the situation was very complex, since *public* actions could only be judged by *private* principles. For this reason, it is difficult to evaluate Machiavelli's moral sensitivity. Indeed, according to Walzer (1973), Machiavelli's moral sensitivity is uncertain, because he does not define the emotional state of the man with dirty hands (who should experience some guilt), although the original reluctance of such a man to dirty his hands seems to imply some pangs of conscience. Walzer (1973) considers the position of Machiavelli (1531) as representing the neoclassical tradition of conceiving dirty hands, as distinguished from the Protestant and the Catholic traditions. [The *Protestant* tradition would be represented by Weber (1918) according to whom the good politician may do bad in order to do good, and surrenders his soul; he is a good man with dirty hands and is perhaps a hero, but a tragic hero; the *Catholic* tradition would be exemplified by the "just assassin", who kills for some claimed moral reason and acknowledges his responsibility and accepts the corresponding punishment]. Machiavelli's claim (1531: 108) (that when the deeds accuse, the consequences or results excuse) would mean that if the politician succeeds the citizens come to agree that the result was worth it; eternal praise is the supreme reward for not being good (Walzer 1973).

My comment here is that performing some acts that are immoral on the basis of private morality is a vague statement, since "private morality" may vary from one individual to another; thus, we can only say that performing some acts that are immoral on the basis of "apparently prevalent" private morality does (or does not) entail reluctance and sense of guilt in a public official according to whether he, from his personal point of view, judges that act as immoral or not (this is because there are not publicly-shared moral norms or laws).

(2) Hobbes. Hobbes (1651: 81–82, 108–9) assumed that citizens have transferred their rights of nature to the sovereign, which consequently represents citizens, personifies their union, and is authorized by citizens to do whatever it wants to assure peace and security. In this view, dirty hands would in part be justified by the responsibility of those holding offices toward those they represent. Yet, as noted by Sorell (1999: 104), Hobbes's conception is like a device for diverting responsibility for the sovereign's action to the parties of the contract, so that they cannot complain of iniquity. Again, I note that in a non-democratic State, the sovereign itself is arbitrary and amoral, and creates an amoral social environment (ruled by strength and violence and lacking publicly-shared moral norms) in which the possible cases of dirty hands can only be judged by private moral principles.

3.3.2.2—Dirty-Hands Cases in Modern Democratic Constitutional States

3.3.2.2.1—Dirty Hands and Democracy

(1) General Considerations. Considerations about dirty cases in democracy will be focused on the following points.

(a) Dirty hands and the democratic environment. According to Thompson (1987: 11–39), democracy provides a cleaner environment for political activity, because it entails *shared responsibility*, allows *control over political actions*, and makes *acting against wrong behavior* possible.

It has also been claimed that democracy might have some negative aspects, inasmuch as it might introduce a sort of *sectarianism*, since a politician may defend the interest of groups or of the party or constituency that he represents, instead of pursuing the general interest and justice (Mansbridge 1990: 147–70). I note that, in a democracy, sectarianism is limited by the constitutional norms, which are directed to promote the common good and ensure the control of citizens over government activity (by guaranteeing free and pluralistic information and public access to the government activity), even if some degree of discretion of the party in charge always remains, because of the indeterminacy of the constitutional norms.

Moreover, obstacles to prevent dirty hands in a democracy are *secret decisions* (Sorell 1999: 112), which may be required in some areas (e.g., controlling crime, or preventing and facing war or terrorism). I think, however, that secrecy should be kept to the minimum required by State security, and should be kept within the limit set up by the constitutional norms. Indeed, I think that the extensive role that, unfortunately, secret decisions and actions still play in the democratic societies is due to the existence of true or potential external "enemies", which requires covert operations of security services; with time, when the evolution of consciousness of humans will lead toward the Universal Republic (and a universal constitution), there will not be external enemies any longer, and the need for secrecy will be limited to only a minor role, as required by the internal security linked to the activity of police and judicial investigations.

(b) Utilitarianism versus Kantianism. It has been maintained that utilitarianism is a *public philosophy* (suitable for public life and political power) whereas Kantian (or absolutist or virtue) theories would better serve private or personal morality; this is because the consequentialism, suitable for public decisions (and to some extent allowing bad means to reach good ends), conflicts with the attachment to rules, projects and emotional demands that dominate private life (Smart and Williams 1973; Hampshire 1989; Goodin 1995). I do not see such a distinction; instead, I note that we should distinguish *public morality*, based on publicly-shared moral principles and values, and *private morality*, based on individual moral principles and values; divergence or conflict between public and private morality may occur, as discussed in chapter 4.1.1.3.2, *B*.

As noted by Hollis (1982), moral dilemmas may arise from the refutation that in some public roles it may be legitimate to break *prima facie* moral rules. Sutherland (2000) challenges the view that moral standards can sometimes be violated in politics. He recalls that, as underlined by Benn (1983), the dirty-hands problem assumes the consequentialist pretence that a leader can anticipate the cost/benefit of his decisions, i.e., can predict future scenarios; actually, a leader can only make "probable" judgments and previsions. This is in keeping with the view that, being a true foresight actually impossible, human experience has a narrative character, based on guessing, assumptions and interpretations (Gadamer 1976; Carr 1986: 60–65). On these grounds, "the legitimacy and rationality of secret unilateral decision-making—outside a compelling emergency situation—begins to seem dubious" (Sutherland 2000: 210). I note that the uncertainty of the previsions may have two rather opposite consequences: it justifies, to some extent, the difference between the result achieved and the prevision-based promises of politicians, i.e. it justifies the fact that the *realization/promised-end index* is usually less than 1 (ch. 3.3.1, *1*); on the other hand, it charges politicians with great responsibility, which may be of two types, i.e., it may be *political responsibility*, in the case of an *incapacity in deciding*, leading to inappropriate decisions, or a *moral responsibility*, when a decision is deliberately taken for reasons other than the pursuing of the common good.

(c) Leaders-followers relationship. McDonald (2000) notes that, in *small groups* (face-to-face groups), the disposition of the others can be discerned, and there may be a reciprocal advantage in rational agents tying their hands ("I will tie my hands if you will tie yours"). On the other hand, in *large-scale groups*, leaders and followers are distant, and there is a great power imbalance, since leaders have control and knowledge that their followers lack, so that the relation with leaders is based on trust (McDonald 2000). To verify the trust relationship between leaders and followers, Baier (1986) proposed a test consisting of whether the trust relationship survives the unmasking (through adequate information) of the motives and methods of a trusted person (this would produce the transparency existing in the small, face-to-face groups—see above). Moreover, a distinction should be made between cases when the damage is made to the followers from the case when damage is made to others (McDonald 2000). In the latter case, if the "damage to others" is useful to the followers, it is possible that it is in agreement with the trust link; of course, even in this instance, causing damage to others is always wrong.

(2) Occurrence of Dirty Hands Cases. Dirty hands cases may occur with regard to *(a)* political activity as well as *(b)* the discretion of public officials.

(a) Dirty hands and political activity. Shugarman (2000) quotes some *examples* that would suggest that dirty hands are a common practice in politics and that they are acceptable in a democratic system. He recalls that an official involved in the Iran-Contra scandal said that by their very nature covert operations are a lie; moreover, a head of a branch of Canada's security services said that breaking the law (opening of hundreds of pieces of regular mail without court authorization) in his section was so commonplace that it was no longer thought of as illegal. Several other examples of dirty hands in politics in recent years have been illustrated and discussed (Thompson 1987; Collins 1997; Greene and Shugarman 1997; Judt 1998), and some thinkers consider dealing with corrupted bosses as events common in the political activity (Howard 1977).

I underline that the fact that dirty-hands cases do occur in the political life does not entail that they are justified or justifiable; many decisively bad actions occur in the world (e.g., murders), and the fact that they occur does not cancel the fact that they are morally bad. Indeed, all the above-mentioned positions that attempt to justify dirty-hand cases fail to distinguish the cases of dirty hands occurring in non-constitutional States from those occurring in the modern constitutional States. In the *non-constitutional States*, dirty hands cases occur in the absence of publicly-shared moral principles, values, and norms, since the public life is driven by force and violence (as defined in ch. 3.1.2.4); in the modern *constitutional States*, dirty hands cases occur despite the presence of publicly-shared moral principles, values and norms, because the latter are not fully recognized and implemented. This is due to two reasons. *First*, the constitutional States cover only the area of Western democracies but not other areas of the world in which non-democratic States are still present, which entails that in international politics force and violence still play a major role. *Second*, even in the domestic area of constitutional democratic States, the shared moral principles, values, and norms are recognized and implemented only to a certain extent, proportional to the degree of development of the consciousness of the community. With the progressive evolution of the community's consciousness, the use of force and violence (a major expression of which consists of the security and secret services) will progressively decrease to a minimum (say, will be limited to the necessarily covered operations that accompany the capture of a criminal), even if perhaps it cannot completely disappear because the evolution of consciousness (and of the mind as a whole) is an endless process, which will never reach its full end.

(b) Discretion of public officials. Applbaum (1992; 1999) discusses the complex problem of the discretion of public officials, i.e., the problem concerning when and to which extent officials can exercise discretion to pursue their substantive views when these views dissent from those of superiors or legislators or most citizens. Public officials deal with mandates to act that are often ambiguous, conflict-ridden, and are indeed shaped in part by the very actions of the official (Warwick 1981; Applbaum 1992; 1999). It has been noted that there are also other "second-order" reasons, such as the judgment of the authority or the outcome of a procedure (Raz 1979); there may also be third-order reasons arising from the seeking agreement about legitimacy in the face of different conceptions of justice. Thus, three orders of reason would be at work: the good, the just, and the legitimate (Applbaum 1992; 1999). I think that public officials should always distinguish their private behavior, which should be directed to reach their personal ends and should be controlled by their private moral principles and values, and their behavior as public officials, which should be directed to pursue the shared ends and should be controlled by the publicly-shared moral principles and values, as defined by the constitutional norms and other laws. Due to the indeterminacy of norms, laws, rules, and mandates to act (chs. 4.1.1.1; 4.2.3; 4.3.1.1, *1a*), there will always be room for discretion, which, however, should be kept to the lowest possible minimum, by pursuing the scope of adhering to the spirit of norms, laws, rules and commands as closely as one's ability allows.

3.3.2.2.2—The Alleged Justification of Dirty Hands

(1) Weber's Position. Weber explicitly maintained that the ethical demands in politics should reflect the fact that "[P]olitics operates with very special means, namely, power backed up by violence" (Weber 1919: 119), and that "The decisive means for politics is violence" (Weber 1919: 121). He thinks that "The proponent of an ethic of absolute ends cannot stand up under the ethical irrationality of the world. He is a cosmic-ethical rationalist" (Weber 1919: 122); moreover, according to him, concerning political actions "[I]t is not true that good can follow only from good and evil from evil, but that often the opposite is true. Anyone who fails to see this is, indeed, a political infant" (Weber 1919: 123).

Weber's position is the consequence of a distorted (pre-constitutional) conception of politics and of the State; he perhaps (consciously or unconsciously) did not endorse the principles of the constitutional State. Indeed, if, as Weber thinks, the means of politics are "power backed up by violence" or merely "violence" (see above), then dirty hands cases in politics are unavoidable. The objection is that politics operates by power backed up by violence only in absolutist States but not in constitutional democratic ones.

(2) Arendt's Thought. In the following pages, I will present *(a)* a discussion of Arendt's views and, then, *(b)* a general comment on them.

(a) Arendt views on dirty hands. Arendt (1954) asserted that the end of politics is the preservation and continuation of the world, so that, if principles of truth, goodness or virtue conflict with this end, they can be ignored and deception and fraud (i.e., dirty hands) allowed. I think that both the claims contained in this statement are generic and arbitrary. The end of politics is not merely the preservation and continuation of the world (which kind of world should be preserved and continued, according to Arendt?) but to progressively improve the world by promoting its *evolution*, i.e., by attempting to ensure an evolution-allowing condition for all human beings (in accordance with the ground moral norm).

Arendt (1958: 77) adds that goodness in public life is no longer good but becomes corrupt and produces corruption. I think, however, that this may occur if one fails to distinguish public from private moral behavior. Thus, if a public official, prompted by his goodness, uses his public power to benefit one of his friends (instead of using his own resources to help his friend), he will certainly accomplish a corrupted act. This would be due to the fact that private goodness should be expressed by helping friends and acquaintance with one's own resources whereas public goodness should be expressed by politicians by promoting those political decisions and administrative acts directed to help all those who are in need. Thus, contrary to the claim of Arendt, *goodness is always good.* Indeed, Arendt (1955) does consider the private versus public distinction, since she says that there are distinct private and public moral goods, on the one hand, and private and public selves, on the other, in contrast with the unitary view of Kantianism (Kant 1795); the problem is that she has an arbitrary and unacceptable conception of the public "good", which would coincide with, or at least would include, immoral behavior (see below).

To support the view that public good differs from the private one, it has been pointed out that, for instance, publicly denouncing a friend who did something wrong would be indefensible (Elshtain 1993). This, however, is a superficial and vague statement. One should distinguish three different cases: *first*, the case of an essentially good friend who accidentally performed a (not too-much) wrong action, which has not produced great harm (e.g., he has stolen a little amount of money from a very rich man) and which he will not repeat (we can foresee this because we know him), so that by avoiding to denounce him we only prevent the sanction but we do not cause further harm; *second*, the case of a friend who has committed a murder for which an innocent is going to be condemned; and *third*, the case of a friend who reveals himself as a serial killer and who has already killed two people and is going to kill another one. In the first case, avoiding denouncing a friend may be in part justified by the sentiment of friendship (which would make denouncing a friend too distressing) and in part by the difference between private and public moral judgment. The former is based on one's own *privately acquired knowledge*, i.e., the knowledge about one's friend, which allows one to foresee that the friend will not repeat the bad action; the latter, conversely, is based on the *publicly demonstrable facts*, i.e., on the demonstrated fact that the friend has stolen some money, and it cannot take into account the statement of a friend of the thief because any friend, as such, may not be objective. On the other hand, in the latter two cases, one must denounce his friend (after having officially terminated the friendship), otherwise he becomes co-responsible of the condemnation of an innocent or of the further crimes committed by the criminal friend. Of course, between the first hypothesized case and the other two ones there may be innumerable intermediate situations, some of which may entail morally difficult choices, which can only be settled with approximation, as it happens in many fields of human activity (ch. 1.1.3.2.1).

Arendt (1958: 77) affirms that rigid moral imperatives are unsuitable to govern practical judgments of political life, and that "trespassing is an everyday occurrence which is in the nature of action's constant establishment of new relationships within a web of relations . . ." (Arendt 1958: 240). Pursuing truth in the political realm would actually interfere with freedom and would be associated with "frequently tyrannical tendencies" (Arendt 1954: 239–40). Moreover, she says that in public life "the ability to lie . . . belongs among the few obvious, demonstrable data that confirm human freedom"

(Arendt 1954: 250); in other words, the ability to lie would mean the ability to create meanings irrespective of truth and indicates the capacity for freedom, imagination, and creativity (Arendt 1951; 1954). Once again, I note that these are arbitrary statements. Why should the "establishment of new relationships within a web of relations" require trespassing moral norms? Why (and how) should "the ability to lie" confirm human freedom? Why should lying indicate capacity for freedom, imagination, and creativity? To avoid a severe negative moral judgment about Arendt, I hypothesize that, in making these statements, she had in mind the fact that politicians make promises (projects) based on evaluations and previsions that are uncertain, and that therefore may be realized only in part, i.e., that the *realization/promised-end index* is most often below 1 (ch. 3.3.1, *1*). The same hypothesis helps to understand the otherwise incredible claims put forward by Arendt (1954), that lying and deceit are intrinsic to politics, which is a world of opinions and plurality (contrasting with reason and truth, which deal with the solitude of the mind). This would mean that deliberate falsehood is a legitimate means to achieve political ends; she says:

> [L]ies are often much more plausible, more appealing to reason, than reality, since the liar has the great advantage of knowing beforehand what the audience wishes or expects to hear . . . whereas reality has the disconcerting habit of confronting us with the unexpected, for which we were not prepared . . . the audience to which the lies are addressed is forced to disregard altogether the distinguishing line between truth and falsehood in order to be able to survive. (Arendt 1972: 7)

The fact that Arendt says that politics is a world of opinions and plurality strengthens my hypothesis (indeed my hope!) that she actually means that politicians most often make evaluations and previsions, which can only be probable but not certain.

Arendt (1971) also contrasts reason and truth with politics and practical judgment, as she thinks that reason cannot be expected to lead to any moral proposition or code of conduct or a final decision of what is good or evil; according to her, in a man, it would not be the consistency of principles but the weightiness of his person that counts (Arendt 1955). Here Arendt seems to adhere to the view of Hume (1739/40) according to which the reason is neutral with regard to moral choices. I reject this claim and maintain that moral acts (and corresponding projects) are necessarily supported by moral *thoughts* (which create *moral principles*) and by *moral feelings* (which create *moral values*) (chs. 2.1.4.1; 2.2.1.1.1, *1*). Moreover, what Arendt calls weightiness of a person actually is the aptitude to primarily develop one's power, i.e., it is the proneness to operate in the spheres of politics or economic activity, shortly, the bent for action, and therefore can be either good or bad according to whether it is directed to promote or to restrain mind evolution.

(b) General comment on Arendt's thought. Bradshaw (2000) underlines that the position of Arendt (1954) on lying in politics may have some historical precedents in the thought of Machiavelli (1513; 1531) and Plato (~360 B.C.); especially pertinent would be the similarity with the "noble lie", or the myth of metals, in Plato's *Republic*. Stocker (1990: 9–36) recalls that even Aristotle (~330 B.C.) in his *Nicomachean Ethics* recognizes the distinction between contemplative life, driven by reason, and active life, driven by opinion and marked by contrasts and by possible dirty-hands cases that make the contrasting virtues of moderation and justice possible. I note that Plato, Aristotle, and Machiavelli lived in the "pre-constitutional" era, when no publicly-shared moral principles existed and the public life was driven by force and violence (as defined in ch. 3.1.2.4); since their time, the common human consciousness has undergone remarkable evolution. Yet, they never overtly justified dirty-hands cases. Therefore, their thought cannot be used to support the morally questionable conception of Arendt, who lived in a time when human consciousness was much more evolved (compared to that of the time of Aristotle or Machiavelli) and constitutional moral norms had been introduced in most Western States.

Bradshaw (2000) also suggests that the position of Arendt (1954; 1955; 1958) is somewhat similar to that of *postmodernism*, which considers human beings as the result of historical development and social processes while denying that there is something certain and definitive and therefore denying that dirty-hands cases of transgression can be identified and judged. I reject this moral relativism and its supporting post-modern views, primarily because they lack any reference to a basic ontological conception (Belfiore 2004: 335–42); I oppose my objective conception of the *good* (as *mind evolution*) and of *moral norms* (as those norms prescribing the *promotion of mind evolution* both in private and public life). Uncertainty may exist concerning the details or the choices about minor or particular facts but not concerning the general, universal moral ends to be pursued (ch. 3.1.2.5.3, 3). In any case, the uncertainty should be faced with good faith, not with deceiving intentions.

(3) Walzer's View. Walzer (1973) wrote that in politics it is easy for a leader to get his hands dirty, and often it is right to do so and sometimes we want him to do so. He refers to the example of a political leader who has to decide whether to buy votes by a corrupted ward boss; Walzer says that, if the stakes are high enough, the leader will ignore his scruples and will make the deal, and we want him to make it, precisely because he has scruples about it (he would not be bad because he has scruples). If we are the supporter of the good political leader, we view the campaign in a certain light, and we hope that he will overcome his scruples and make the deal; we want him to make it, precisely because he has scruples (Walzer 1973). If such a politician is induced by particular situations to do what is morally wrong, he

will acknowledge this and bear his guilt. Here is the moral politician: it is by his dirty hands that we know him (Walzer 1973). Walzer (1973), however, maintains that we should deny power to the greatest liars, except those few leaders whose extraordinary achievements make us forget the lies they told. I reject this view, for reasons given in ch. 3.3.2.2.4.

(4) Other Views. Several other thinkers have claimed that politicians can somewhat violate the moral standards valid outside politics (Coady 1991), or that they are licensed by us to pursue the good in an arena where they can succeed only if they operate partly beyond the range of our understanding and our control (Hollis 1982). Other thinkers consider dealing with corrupted bosses as events common in the political activity (Howard 1977). Yet, Shugarman (2000) points out that the defenders of dirty hands (Machiavelli 1513; 1531; Trotskii 1936; Merleau-Ponty 1969; Hollis 1982; Benn 1983: 167) have a war-like view of politics, or that they conceive politics as a warrior's realm. In this regard, I recall that Machiavelli (1513; 1531), in the elaboration of his theory, referred to Italy of his time, where there was widespread corruption and lawlessness, and there was no constitutional constraint. Trotskii (1936: 28) claimed that distinguishing peaceful struggle from war is a pathetic evasion. Clearly, this way of thinking ignores the difference between the pre-constitutional authoritarian regimes and the constitutional democratic systems, and reflects the lack of publicly-shared moral principles, as codified in the constitutional norms. Hollis (1982) underlines that there are evil men about, and that to check them the apparatus of the State should be used dishonestly; actually, the violence of the "evil man" can be won by the legitimate force of a democratic-constitutional State.

3.3.2.2.3—Against Dirty Hands

As underlined by Shugarman (2000), dirty hands or bad deals cannot be accepted by those who believe in democratic principles and procedures. The claim that it is democratic for a democracy to disenfranchise itself is logically and practically incoherent (Greene and Shugarman 1997: 173). Indeed, the term democratic should not be used when the majority violates the basic democratic rules and values (Dahl 1991: 163–75). Others underline the risk of a contagion effect of accepting leaders who rig elections, which may favor diffusion of wrong practices (Coady 1995).

(1) Absolutist Views. The positions based on *moral absolutism*, like those of Anscombe (1981) and Donagan (1997), are opposed by several thinkers (Nagel 1971/72; Nielsen 1981; 1990: 128–62; 1992).

Nagel (1971/72) points out that there are circumstances in which the cost to follow absolutist moral rules may be too high (e.g., failure to prevent a looming disaster), so that one may face a *moral dilemma*, and it may be impossible to choose a course free of guilt and responsibility for evil. In contrast to this view, Brandt (1971/72) maintains that there are moral rules and evaluations that allow to make the right choice. Hare (1971/72), on the other hand, argues that what may appear as a moral dilemma is actually a conflict between ordinary moral principles (in part shaped by education) and higher-level moral principles, and that the conflict can be resolved at that level. I believe that, due to the complexity of the human world and the uncertainty about our previsions, moral judgments (like the judgments about the truth of our knowledge) and the ensuing choices can only be made with some *approximation* so that in the harder cases it may be impossible to distinguish which is the better choice; in these cases, if the moral or political agent makes the choice that he thinks is probably the best one, no moral guilt should be attributed to him.

(2) Utilitarian Views. Most thinkers follow *non-absolutist views*. Nielsen (1992; 1996a) questions the claim of some thinkers (Walzer 1973; Williams 1973; Nagel 1979: 53–90, 128–41) that, in cases of dirty hands, politicians must do wrong in order to do right, which would be a paradox. He underlines that the political agent has to choose what, considered the circumstances, appears as the lesser of two evils (the *lesser-evil argument*), and that, in so doing, the agent will do what he ought to do, and in doing what he ought to do he cannot do wrong; perhaps he may feel guilty, but to feel guilty is not necessarily to be guilty (Nielsen 1992; 1996a). I think that the position of Nielsen is right. However, in order to be able to follow the "lesser-evil argument" we need a criterion for evaluating the degree of evilness of each possible choice. While in some extreme instances the degree of evilness is clear (e.g., choosing between the sure death of one or of 10 people), in other cases it may be a difficult task both because the consequences of our choices are probable but not certain and because it is difficult to evaluate which consequence is the worst one. Although the badness or the goodness of a choice can only be evaluated with *approximation*, my moral theory, by identifying the goodness of a choice with its effect on the evolution of the involved minds, provides us with a useful tool for determining which of two choices is most probably the better one.

By following Barry (1991: 40–77), Nielsen's conception (1981; 1992; 1996a), based on doing the lesser evil, can be defined *weak consequentialism* or, considering that it is based on the evaluation of objective situations, *contextualism* (Haber 1994; Nielsen 1996a; 1996b: 25–56). The need to consider the objective circumstances for any moral evaluation is clearly stated by my moral theory; in fact, if goodness coincides with the evolution of the mind, any stage of mind evolution is "good" if compared with the less evolved stages of mind and is "bad" if compared with the more evolved stages.

Cragg (2000) underlines that dirty-hands cases may also arise in the business community (where, indeed, they are endemic the world over) because private businesses may have public consequences; he underlines that dirty-hands cases should be regarded as deviations from normal and symptoms of a moral pathology in business environment whereas moral values such as efficiency, honesty, and fairness should be recognized as lying at the foundations of market economy. Moreover, according to De George (1993), bribery undermines the proper functioning of both the democratic process and the marketplace.

It has been claimed that bribery is a way of life in some developing countries and, therefore, it would be a necessity in some international business transactions (Lane and Simpson 1984). While this issue (which, actually, belongs to the sphere of international politics) may be linked to the lack of an international government (and international constitutional norms), it has been noted that the necessity of offering bribes in international business might have been exaggerated, since it has been shown by an American study (De George 1993) that prohibiting bribery would result in a loss of business of less than 1% of 250 companies surveyed. I think that this shows that often some dirty-hands cases are "justified" by an act of self-deception, i.e., by convicting oneself that there is not a clean choice and that, therefore, the "dirty-hands choice" is justified. The same interpretation applies to the claim that, in public life and in private business, "heroic" leaders are needed who should be prepared to use morally reprehensible means. As pointed out by Shugarman (1990), this claim is linked to the pessimistic view that political life (and business transactions) is carried out in an atmosphere of warfare, rivalry, duplicity, and violence; again, this pessimistic view may be the result of a pre-constitutional conception of political life and of an exaggeration of the difficulties in international transactions, and may indicate self-deception or morally-bad tendencies.

(3) The Constitutionalist View. I will briefly consider *(a)* the constitution norms as related to political activity, and *(b)* the participatory versus elitist democracy.

(a) Constitutional norms and political activity. Anderson (1993) underlines that constitutionalism demands that political activity can be publicly controlled, evaluated and sometimes condemned. Moreover, constitutionalism entails *deliberative democracy*, and the latter demands that both ends and means of political actions are *legitimate* only if addressed in legitimate deliberative procedures, subjected to retrospective evaluation, so that any attempt to evade the deliberative phase of decision and the retrospective judgment is an offense to the political system (Thompson 1993). Moreover, political actions are *moral* if they meet other standards, i.e., if they apply to all citizens equally, are based on relevant reasons, and are publicly justified (Thompson 1987: 96–122). Thus, democracy is viewed as both a policy

delivery system and as a public conversational evaluative system (Braybrooke and Lindblom 1970; Braybrooke 1974; Braybrooke et al. 1996).

The retrospective-deliberative process "is the only hope that society has to be educated by the past in order to face the challenges of the future" (Sutherland 2000: 223).

Shugarman (2000) affirms that, in democratic politics, dirty-hands cases should be considered as very extreme exceptions. Bok (1978) underlines that, before departing from the accepted norms, one has to verify that the action reduces harm, assures fairness, and respects trustworthiness. Shugarman (2000) recalls that even Camus (1954), in depicting his "rebel", justifies violence (and does not think that the rebel should feel guilty, as claimed by Walzer—1973) only in exceptional circumstances, to fight injustice and oppression; after the goal has been reached the "just assassin" is willing to be executed to avoid further violence or to prevent that he might be rewarded. Camus's rebel is not a man in power, but he fights against power. Thus, violence and deception should be limited to the minimum necessary.

Once again, I underline that in constitutional democratic States, it is possible to promote big changes through legal and peaceful ways; peaceful ways might also be effective in non-democratic environments. This is shown by the examples given by Gandhi's challenge to British Imperial rule and M. L. King's civil rights struggle (May and Collins-Sharratt 1994: 243). I would add that what characterizes the thought of the dirty-hands defenders is that they (consciously or unconsciously) refer to a non-democratic non-constitutional State, in which no publicly-shared moral principles, expressed in the constitutional norms, exist. Since democracy and constitutionalism have appeared in recent times (although in different times in various States), we can say that dirty-hands defenders refer to the *pre-constitutional era*. Considering that constitutional norms are freely shared by the majority of citizens (i.e., they are norms endorsed by the majority of citizens by conviction, and not by constriction), and therefore are the best approach to universality, they should be accepted by all citizens. Indeed, those citizens who may not agree with a given constitutional norm, are not justified if they use violence or illegal means to change it, because they enjoy the possibility (deriving from the freedom guaranteed by the constitution) to propagandize their ideas and to contribute to initiate the legal process, as provided in the constitution itself, to change a given constitutional norm. This is the mechanism through which the evolution of the human consciousness is transferred into constitutional norms. However, even in the pre-constitutional era, i.e., in the absence of publicly-shared moral principles, actions occurring in public life can be subjected to moral judgment (no human event can escape moral judgment!), which in these conditions can only be based on private (individual) moral principles. Thus, corruption, bribery, cruelty, murder, etc., will always be condemned by many (hopefully by most) citizens, i.e., by those citizens with a more developed consciousness.

(b) Participatory versus elitist democracy. Shugarman (2000: 233) stresses the importance of distinguishing two kinds of democracy: *(a) the participatory democracy*, characterized by the continuous, ongoing, participation of citizens to political discussion and decisions (Shugarman 2000: 233), as first defended by Dewey (1916) and then by others (Williams 1962; Macpherson 1972; Dworkin 1977; Dahl 1991; Rawls 1993; Gewirth 1996); and *(b) the elitist democracy*, in which the role of citizens is limited to the voting while it is marked by passivity in the period between elections. The elitist view is depicted by Weber (1919: 42) with the words: "In a democracy the people choose a leader in whom they trust. Then the chosen leader says 'Now shut up and obey me.' People and party are no longer free to interfere in his business . . . Later the people can sit in judgment." Schumpeter (1942: 269) says that, in this kind of democracy, making the deciding of issues by the electorate is secondary to the election of the men who are to do the deciding. It is perhaps in this kind of democracy that dirty hands are easier to occur. I would note that, even in this kind of democracy, the opinion of citizens has a role and cannot be ignored by the leaders and their party. *If voting is to be significant*, citizens should give their vote on the ground of the opinion that they have acquired by actively observing and discussing the behavior of the politicians who have been in charge in the preceding period. Therefore, the citizens may "shut up", but they will continue to observe and to think, and the party in charge cannot ignore their opinion because this opinion will determine the result of the next voting. It follows that, even in this kind of democracy, *the opinion of citizens is of value.* Thus, it is also in the interest of the leaders and of the party in charge that citizens express their opinion during the inter-election period, so that politicians can easily know it and take it into consideration. In any case, not even in this kind of democracy dirty hands cases can be admitted. Perhaps, the occurrence of dirty-hands cases might be favored by what might be called a *pseudo-democracy*, i.e., a system in which citizens are kept uninformed and political discussion is allowed only a few days before the election, and is based on biased information and political pressure, so that *voting is not significant.* A situation like this can be summarized by a modified version of Weber's motto mentioned above, inasmuch as the elected leader would not say "Now shut up and obey me," but would order "Now close your eyes until a few days before election, when I will show you my interpretation of the political facts, on the basis of which you will give your vote." In a *pseudo-democracy* like this, dirty-hands cases might be favored and, perhaps, would easily remain unknown.

3.3.2.2.4—Comments on the Corruption in Political Life

In the preceding pages I mentioned the views of those thinkers who believe that dealing with a corrupted boss is common or unavoidable (or even desirable!) in political life. I believe that the problem of whether political leaders should or should not deal with corrupted bosses is worthy of further comment. We can hypothesize the following political situations, assuming that in the political arena there are two competing parties or groups of parties.

(1) 1ˢᵗ Hypothesis: Most Citizens Are Good. In this instance, citizens are divided into two parties, having slightly different political programs and made of good people (corrupted people being just a small minority). In this situation, it may happen that the prevision is that the two parties have a similar number of adherents, so that buying votes by a corrupted ward boss can determine which part will win the election. I think, however, that in this instance, it is not very important to win, considering that also the opposing party is mainly made of good people. If the leaders of one of the two parts attempt to deal with corrupted bosses, they would be absolutely unjustified, and the honest leaders of the other party would have a good chance to win the competition if they denounced to the citizens the attempts made by the leaders of the competing party to deal with corrupted people. I think that, considering that most citizens are good, the advantage obtained with this denouncement would be greater than that obtained by dealing with corrupted bosses.

(2) 2ⁿᵈ Hypothesis: About a Half of Citizens Are Good (and About a Half Are Bad). If about a half of citizens are good and about a half are bad, it may be possible that the pre-voting previsions suggest that dealing with a corrupted boss may allow to get a government mainly composed of good men, with only a very small component made of bad men; this government may be much better than that made mainly of bad men, as it would be the case if the good party had renounced to deal with the corrupted boss. This is the only case in which dealing with corrupted people may be morally justified, provided that the other party is really "bad" and that the role of the corrupted people is kept to the minimum possible. Yet, the hypothesis that about a half of citizens are good and about a half are bad is unrealistic, as in the real world no such clear-cut distinction exists—see below, under point "*4*".

(3) 3ʳᵈ Hypothesis: Most Citizens Are Bad. In this case, the duty of the good political leaders is to provide an active opposition to the bad party in power, in the hope to progressively induce an evolution in the minds of citizens, i.e., in the hope to change them from "bad citizens" into "good citizens". Dealing with corrupted bosses would have no sense.

(4) 4ᵗʰ Hypothesis: Citizens Are Distributed Through a Continuum Going from Very Good to Very Bad People. The above situations (points "*1*",

"*2*", and "*3*") are based on the unrealistic hypothesis that the voting population can be sharply distinguished into "good" and "bad" citizens. Actually,
in most instances, citizens are distributed through a continuum going from
very good to very bad (this, of course, is a simplified description; moreover,
each citizen may behave differently according to the various situations and
circumstances). It follows that the boundary between the "good party" and
the "bad party" is placed in a zone of the continuous distribution where
there are people who range from being "slightly good" to being "slightly
bad". We might assume that the voting population can be divided into 100
rather homogeneous groups of various magnitudes, whose moral goodness
will decrease, through a continuum, from group 1, composed of very good
people, to group 100, composed of very bad people. It follows that group 50
is the last of the good groups (although it is only very slightly good) and
group 51 is the first of the bad groups (although it is only very slightly bad).
An extreme idealist good political leader would like to restrict the extension
of his party to include only the groups from 1 to 10 (formed by extremely
good people, almost similar to "Saint Francis of Assisi"); a very good political leader would like to restrict his party to include the groups from 1 to 20,
or from 1 to 30. A good and realistic political leader will attempt to expand
his party to include the groups from 1 to 50. Yet, if, due to the diverse magnitude of the various groups, this is not enough to get the majority of votes
(>50%), the good but realistic leader may attempt to expand his party by
including people that are only "slightly bad"; in other words, the problem
arises about where to fix the boundary of the good party. In this situation,
the good but realistic leader may attempt to move the boundary of his party
toward the bad part of the continuum, in order to include also the groups
from 50 to 52, or from 50 to 55, perhaps from 50 to 58; considering that
these groups are only slightly bad, their inclusion in the good party might be
allowed in order to avoid that the totally bad party wins. The boundary of
the good party, however, should not be moved too much into the "bad zone"
but should be moved to the minimum possible, as required to make it probable to win the elections. Moving the boundary of the good party a
little beyond the 50th group may be morally justified only when restricting
the good party to the groups from 1 to 50 is estimated as insufficient to get
the majority of votes (due to the diverse magnitude of the various groups).
The moral justification descends from the fact that renouncing to expand the
good party to include groups beyond the 50th one would result in the victory
of the almost totally bad party. Due to the fact that the degree of goodness
of the various groups changes through a continuum, the moral judgment
concerning the choice about where to fix the boundary of the good party is
marked by some degree of *approximation*, as indeed occurs with all judgments (ch. 1.1.3.2.1). Moreover, in the actual world, often the two opposing
parties (or groups of parties), rather than being entirely composed of good

people or of bad people, respectively, are composed of a mixture, even if the good people may prevail in one party and the bad ones in the other. This is another factor that makes moral judgment rather difficult and marked by *approximation*. What is sure is that a "good" political leader can deal with "slightly bad" people of the groups from 51 to 58 (perhaps from 51 to 60) but he cannot deal with corrupted bosses (as admitted by Walzer), who belong to the groups from 90 to 100 (or from 95 to 100); indeed, he cannot even deal with people in the groups beyond 60, otherwise he ceases to be a "good" leader.

3.4—INTERNATIONAL POLITICS

3.4.1 –General Concepts and Ethical Issues

3.4.1.1—General Concepts

As an introduction to international politics, the following concepts will be discussed.

(1) Degree of Universality of the Various Political Organizations. We can distinguish political organizations or governments into four levels, based on their *degree of universality.*

(a) Low degree of universality: Cities. This group includes cities and, where existing, the various administrative districts (or wards or quarters) in which a large city may be divided.

(b) Medium degree of universality: Regions, lands, and non-sovereign States. This group includes "regional" governments, which comprise diverse political entities such as the Italian "regioni", the German "lands", the non-sovereign "States" that form the U.S., etc.

(c) High degree of universality: Quasi-sovereign States. This group includes those political organizations that conventionally are defined as sovereign States. The latter definition, however, is not correct. It can only be used with reference to a hypothetical State, raised during the dawn of human civilization, which may not encounter other States or communities in the area where it exerts its actions and influence. However, in any stage of human civilization, more than one State has existed, and each State entered in some relation (of friendship or hostility) with the other States. Even the Roman Empire at the apex of its extension established some kind of relationship with those ill-defined communities generically named "barbarians". It follows that a State, regardless of the stage of human history to which it belongs, cannot be regarded as fully "sovereign", because the mere existence of other States or communities impedes the performance of some actions, under pain of a war. Even if such hypothesized sovereign State can decide to face a war, it cannot avoid its consequences. [Note that the concept of sovereignty coincides with that of freedom from external control or influence]. Thus, we can say that the full sovereignty of a State is somewhat limited by the mere existence of other States. However, once civilization progressed, States have considered the possibility, the utility, and even the necessity to stipulate treatises with other States; and often they did stipulate such treatises. Since treatises, once stipulated, entail some voluntary limitation of the sovereign of the contractor States, the latter should not be defined as sovereign States but rather as *quasi-sovereign States.*

(d) Full universality: The Universal Republic. Prospectively, this group

should include just one entity: the *fully sovereign Universal Republic*. In the present time, there are some international entities, including various institutions (N.A.T.O., U.N.), which represent intermediate steps in the way that will lead, with time, to the Universal Republic. As underlined by George (1998), modern globalization of problems imposes cooperation of the various nations (already required by the *ius gentium*) to secure international common good.

It has been said that if a centralized Universal State existed, no international politics (international society composed of various States) could exist. Indeed, if a Universal Republic existed, what is today understood as international politics should perhaps change its name into universal politics but the matter and problems with which it is concerned would remain, even if under a somewhat different aspect, as they are problems regarding universal cooperation to assure the universal common good, i.e., the promotion of mind evolution at a universal level (*universal mind evolution*).

Natural law theorists maintain that the relationship between governments with various degrees of universality (mentioned above) should be regulated by the *principle of subsidiarity* (George 1998: 64–66), according to which the authority of a world government should be limited to those problems that cannot be successfully dealt with by national governments, the authority of the latter governments should be limited to those problems that cannot be successfully dealt with by regional government, and so on, down to local governments, neighborhood groups and private associations, and families. I substitute this kind of distinction with an *ontological* one, based on the *principle of increasing degree of universality*, according to which a world government should deal with those problems which *are* fully universal (have a full degree of universality and are regulated by international norms or treatises); likewise, national governments should deal with problems that *are* of nation-wide universality (and are regulated by the national laws), regional government should deal with those problems that *are* of region-wide universality (and that are regulated by regional laws), and so on, down to local governments, neighborhood groups and private associations, and families (dealing with problems regulated by rules, regulations, statute articles, contract terms, and even habits and traditions). This distinction corresponds to that of the various communities with different degrees of universality into which human beings spontaneously organize themselves (Table 3.1).

(2) Non-Democratic and Democratic International Society. I think that we should distinguish two types of international society.

(a) Non-democratic international society. This is a society in which a strong state *imposes*, with the use or the threat of *force* (which in this instance should be more properly named *violence*, as defined in ch. 3.1.2.4), to other weaker States to accept and recognize some agreements or treatises.

In this non-democratic international society (like in the non-democratic national societies) the laws or rules can be defined as "orders backed by threats," an expression used by Hart (1961: 6, 16, 19–25) to interpret the view of Austin (1832). More exactly, they are *projects* directed to satisfy the *desires and interests* of the "strong" ruling State and that are enforced by this State by the use or threat of *violence*. The non-democratic international society (like the non-democratic national societies) is *publicly* immoral or amoral, even if it might be judged as morally good from the point of view of some States, e.g., if it promotes mind evolution of some people or populations; this is because its "laws" do not have a *shared* moral content and, therefore, are not publicly (internationally) justified, and are directed to satisfy the desires and interests of the strong ruling State(s).

(b) Democratic international society. This is a society formed of sovereign States (which are actually quasi-sovereign States—see above), which *freely* stipulate *shared* agreements or treatises to regulate their relationships. The trend to create relationships with other States derives from the structure and functioning of the mind; in particular, it is the way through which human actions expand their universality beyond the limits of the national State toward larger areas, thus approaching the full universality, which can only be reached when, in the future, a Universal State will be established. The following discussion in this chapter will always refer to the "democratic" international society.

As in the domestic field, in the international arena the actions of the various democratic States should be guided by the ground moral norm, which prescribes the promotion of mind evolution until the *evolution-allowing condition* is reached. From this, it follows that each of the richer States has the *duty* to help, to the extent allowed by its wealth, the poor States and populations; this duty, in its turn, entails the *right* of the poor States and populations to be helped, at least to a reasonable extent. Otherwise stated, the *right* of the poor populations to be helped arises from their *duty* to promote their own evolution, which in turn entails the *duty* of the richer countries to help them (because *rights* arise from *duties*, and not vice versa—chs. 2.1.5.2.2; 3.1.2.5.2; 4.1.2.2).

3.4.1.2—Ethical Issues in the International Politics

3.4.1.2.1—Ethics in the International Society

The ground moral norm governs all human actions, including public actions exerted in the international arena. This is because every international action can be directed either to promote or to restrain the mind evolution of the involved populations, thus being morally good in the former instance and morally bad in the latter. Moreover, as a State government has the duty to make any effort to ensure that all citizens concretely enjoy the evolution-allowing, involution-avoiding condition (or the best approach to it), so the *universal or world government*, when it is established, will have the duty to do the utmost to ensure that the various populations of the world will concretely enjoy the above-mentioned condition (or the best approach to it). The moral responsibility of private individuals or groups toward the disadvantaged populations exists, even if it is somewhat limited by the rule of the spheres of decreasing moral responsibility (ch. 2.1.5.2.1). Therefore, the contribution of private individuals or groups in helping the disadvantaged populations is not sufficient. Indeed, the moral duty to help needy *populations* belongs to the sphere of *public morality* and should be fulfilled by the various States. Yet, single individuals are involved as citizens of a State, inasmuch as they should support those political parties whose program includes helping suffering populations.

The big problem is that a universal or world government does not yet exist in this stage of the history of the world. Therefore, in this historical period, international politics is still dominated by projects/decisions and by selfish actions of single States, i.e., by the *arrogance* and *violence* of the various States. In other words, international politics is dominated by the *outward* mind activity (or *mind selfishness*), instead of being guided by the *inward* mind activity (or *mind consciousness*) (Fig. 1.1). Yet, this might be a pessimistic view, since today the premises for a future Universal State already exist and are represented by the network of international relationships, treatises, and cooperation and by the international and supra-national institutions, of which the "United Nations" is the most significant. What is lacking is a universal government capable of projecting and then of enforcing public acts directed to ensure the evolution-allowing condition to all the populations of the world. This, however, does not diminish or annul the moral responsibility of the more developed States toward the disadvantaged ones. Indeed, in the present historical period, each State has the opportunity to choose between two opposite lines of conduct: *(a)* promoting the evolution of the still imperfect international institutions toward the formation of a Universal State, so that "international affairs" will be regulated by shared norms and laws (reflecting shared moral principles and values), or *(b)* acting against the evolution of the existing international institutions and, utilizing the present imperfections of these institutions, continuing to manage the international affairs by the criterion of force and violence. Briefly, each State may act to favor or to restrain the evolution toward a Universal Republic, which makes possible the full universalization of human actions.

I note that the selfish (or egoistic) activity of the various States is not necessarily "morally bad", since, as it is the case for individual or private activity (ch. 2.1.5.2.2) and for the political activity at national level (ch.

3.1.1.2, *1*), the selfish activity of a State may be regarded as *(a) morally-bad egoism*, if it consists of promoting *self-strengthening* (i.e., the State power) by ignoring and violating the rights/duties of other countries to develop the minds of their population (thus breaking the ground moral norm), or *(b) morally-good egoism*, if it consists of promoting what could be called *self-development* (or *self-evolution*), i.e., the development of their power while respecting the rights/duties of other countries to promote their own development (in accord with the ground moral norm). In other words, the outward activity of a State should be integrated with, and regulated by, the inward activity, directed to pursue the common good; if these conditions are met, the outward activity becomes part of the prescription of moral norms.

However, even if a Universal Republic does not yet exist, the ground moral norm is fully valid, because it is based on the moral principles and values engraved on the human consciousness. It follows that, even today, it is the duty of the most developed States to actively contribute to the evolution of the world and to act as promoters of a world government through which human action can reach the full universality. In the meanwhile, the rich States should help the needy populations in order to follow the prescription of the ground moral norm, valid in the human world at any level, from individual behavior to the activity of local, regional, national, and supra-national or universal government. I think that it is morally intolerable and unpardonable that the populations of some countries fall ill for excess of food while other populations starve to death. Helping suffering populations means pursuing an objective moral good whereas ignoring their suffering means to be responsible for an objective moral evil.

3.4.1.2.2—Remarks on War

War is a very complex and debated issue (for a review, see: Brian 2006). Based on my ethical and political conceptions, I underline that war is the worse among the morally-bad events, because it entails many deaths, and each death represents the extreme and irreversible mind *involution*. Moreover, even during a war, the inducement of unnecessary killing, injury or suffering to human beings (including the enemy soldiers) should be avoided, because this would mean to induce mind involution. The rule should be to follow the "less bad conduct" possible, during the morally-bad condition called war. In this regard, one should distinguish *private conduct*, which refers to *individuals* involved in a war, from *public conduct*, which refers to the *institutions* and those individuals who represent them. Another point is that war creates an extremely immoral environment, in which many choices belong to the "hard moral cases", for which no clear-cut moral judgments are possible and for which decisions can only be taken on the basis of *ap-*

proximation and *probability*.

Nagel (1971/72), in discussing the moral problems linked to war, points out that the conduct of warfare should be restricted not only on legal grounds but also on a moral basis, and that the moral restrictions are valid from both the utilitarian and the absolutist view. He thinks that in war we should distinguish between fighting clean and fighting dirty; the latter means to direct the aggression not to its true or proper object (enemy soldiers) but to a peripheral target that may be more vulnerable (civilians, food suppliers, medical personnel); uncertain would be the position of other people, such as the drivers of munitions trucks, civilian munitions workers, etc. The same is true, according to Nagel, in any kind of competition, political or even cultural: in political competitions, one should not use the argument that his opponent's wife is an alcoholic. On these grounds, Nagel (1971/72) condemns the killing of harmless people as well as the indiscriminateness of weapons of mass annihilation. He also underlines that the bad consequences of wars should not be allowed, either by *moral absolutists* or by *moral utilitarians*. War bad effects should not be allowed by *moral absolutists*, including those accepting the law of double effect, formulated by the Catholic doctrine (according to which it would be permissible to bring about as a side effect of one's action something that would be forbidden if made deliberately) because the absolutist is concerned with what one ought to do, regardless of the ends. War bad effects should also not be allowed by *moral utilitarians* because the view that any means can be justified to reach worthy ends should not justify the killing of civilians (including women, children, and old people).

Concerning the *absolutist view*, my comment is that, since war consists of a series of *violent* actions, the absolutist should condemn the war as a whole. I note, however, that the absolutist view is based on the universalizability principle, which I have criticized elsewhere (ch. 2.2.1.1.3, *A1*). Concerning the *utilitarian view*, I think that we should distinguish the use of bad means to reach with *certainty* a worthy end (which may be justified) from the use of bad means based on the *approximate probability* that a worthy end may ensue (which is not justified). Let us consider the case of a utilitarian good soldier, who sees an enemy soldier who is firing a machine-gun toward a large group of civilians; if the good soldier promptly kills the enemy soldier, he actually saves the lives of many civilians, and his conduct is justified. On the other hand, let us consider the case of a lieutenant general (or another authority) who decides to kill a hundred of thousands of civilians with an atomic bomb because he evaluates that: (*a*) the enemy will be impressed by the effects of the atomic bomb, and this increases the probability that the enemy decides to surrender; (*b*) peace can be reached within three months instead of within six months; (*c*) the number of total deaths will be lower. I think that the decision of this lieutenant general is *not* justified, because it is based on estimations which are *probable* but not *certain*; indeed, it is highly possible that the enemy turns more ferocious by the effects of the atomic bomb, that peace is not reached within a shorter period, and that the number of total deaths will be *higher*, and not lower. Perhaps many, if not most, of the decisions taken during a war are based on probable, and not certain, evaluations. Indeed, human previsions are always uncertain, and often decisions are taken (especially by military personnel) based on the *presumptuousness* that one's prevision is (almost) certain.

Finally, one should consider that the war as a whole never produces "useful" results, if one conceive usefulness as the promotion of mind evolution and the prevention of mind involution (in any case: for whom are the results "useful"?) and, therefore, it should never be undertaken on a utilitarian basis; only wars of defense from aggressions should be fought.

3.4.2—Classical Theories on International Politics

3.4.2.1—Legal Positivism

As noted by Finnis (1980; 1996), theorists of *legal positivism* are mainly concerned with the *description* of laws whereas *natural law* thinkers are mainly concerned with the *justification* of laws.

Referring to a *democratic international society*, it has been stated that such a society exists if States conceive themselves as subjected to common rules that govern their relationships (Brierly 1963: 41) or if States recognize a set of common customary rules that govern their relationships and the stipulated treatises (Gihl 1937: 57–64; Nardin 1983: 68, 36–37, 271). Thus conceived, international laws would be laws internally endorsed, according to the view of Hart (1961), and not laws depending on international legal institutions. I note that international laws (like domestic laws) are *shared or universal projects* that, as such, are always internally recognized and endorsed; otherwise, they would be "orders". The content of international laws (like that of domestic laws) is composed of a mixture of *particular selfish beliefs and desires*, expressing the (morally-good) *interests* of some States, and of *universal moral thoughts and feelings* (directed to pursue the universal human good, i.e., the promotion of the evolution of the minds of all human beings). In national States, universal moral projects are stated in constitutional norms (or rules of recognition, according to Hart—1961); in international society, they are embedded in international agreements or treatises or are stated in the statutes of the various international institutions. This premise allows us to interpret the statements of some thinkers. Thus, the concept that the justice of a law endorsed by the involved States should be integrated within the law system itself (Oakeshott 1975: 128; 1983: 129) should be interpreted as meaning that the principles of justice should be shared by the majority of the involved States (and reflect the degree of evolution of their *consciousness*). The statement that laws should not be based on abstract moral principles, which actually could undermine the rule of law (Oakeshott 1975: 128; 1983: 129), should be interpreted as meaning that laws should not be based on moral principles that are not shared and recognized by the majority of the involved States. The concept that the *authority*, validity, and binding force of the international law would depend on a rule of recognition or on accepted customary practices (Hart 1961: 213–37) or are derived from a *basic norm* ("grundnorm"—Kelsen 1934: 193–221; 1945: 110–11, 115–22, 124–26, 131–32, 134–35, 395–96) should be interpreted as meaning that the international law must have some shared moral content, fixed in the rules of recognition or expressed by a "basic norm".

The above statements all indicate the unavoidability of referring, explicitly or implicitly, to a shared *basic moral norm*, endorsed by the majority of the involved States, without which only a system based on force and violence is possible. The search for such a basic norm has been difficult. I think that only a norm pursuing an objective moral good, derived from the structure and functioning of the human mind, and hence grounded on an ontological conception, can serve this scope: the ground norm prescribing the pursuit of mind evolution. Without this solid ontological basis, it is impossible to find any justified moral norm. Kelsen was certainly one of the thinkers most involved in the search for a "grundnorm". Yet, he lacked a supporting ontological conception; this led him to admit, in his last and unfinished work (Kelsen 1979: 256), to no longer support his earlier view about the "grundnorm" and to affirm that a legal norm should be considered as based on a sort of necessary "fiction."

Some thinkers believe that international institutions are necessary to enact, interpret, and apply laws (Oakeshott 1983) and that, being these institutions lacking or defective, international laws can only be regarded as weak laws (Oppenheim 1905: 10) and the international society as an anarchical society (Bull 1977). These statements reveal the lack of distinction between laws and their enforcement. Formal international institutions are not necessary for the existence of international laws, which are recognized rules that may arise just from international treatises and that reflect *shared projects*, which, as such, belong to the sphere of *intellect* (chs. 4.1.1.1;4.1.1.3.2, A; 4.2.6.3). Therefore, in the absence of formal institutions, there is no international anarchy, if the latter term is understood as lawlessness. On the other hand, international institutions are required to interpret and apply the laws (international courts, belonging to the sphere of *intellect*) and to *enforce* the laws through the application of sanctions (international executive apparatus or organ, which belongs to the sphere of *power*) (chs. 4.1.1.3.2, A; 4.2.6.3).

3.4.2.2—Natural Law

Natural laws, as conceived in the new classical theory (George 1992), refer to the *basic* or *intrinsic moral goods* (mainly consisting of life, health, knowledge, work, etc.), which should be regarded as *self-evident* (Grizes et al 1987; George 1988; Boyle 1994). This conception of the basic moral goods and of the laws concerned with them would be reached by mere intuition. As I have pointed out elsewhere (chs. 1.1.1.2.4; 2.1.4.1; 2.2.1.1.1, *1*), the basic human good (recognized by our moral thoughts as the *objective* good) consists of the *evolution of mind* in all its three components. It follows that laws concerned with the human good should be directed to promote mind evolution.

Finnis (1980) underlines that the concept of common good entails the assumption of the existence of a universal common human nature, and that, considering the globalization of human life, the individual good seems to be realizable only in an international context and with the help of supranational institutions. In my opinion, the universal human nature should be understood as the property common to all men (as members of the class of men), i.e., the property of being *evolving* conscious entities made of intellect, sensitiveness, and power. The common good should be regarded as consisting of mind evolution. As regards the utility or necessity of the international context or institutions, I note that the passage from a national to an international context means the *evolution* of human actions (created by the *power*) from a lower to a higher degree of universality; this evolution is similar to the evolution of ideas (created by the *intellect*) from a lower to a higher degree of universality, i.e., the evolution from particular ideas to fully universal scientific laws.

George (1998) underlines that the *principle of subsidiarity* entails that the international institutions and laws must respect and protect cultural diversity (the diverse instantiations of the human good), i.e., languages, customs, traditions, and ways of life; repression can only be justified to prevent fundamental injustices (George 1998). I have already given my interpretation of the principle of subsidiarity (ch. 3.4.1.1, *1d*); here I add that the respect for diversity is not linked to the principle of subsidiarity but is rather linked to the ground moral norm (promoting mind evolution) and to the fact that each individual or group or population can only evolve through particular ways (which are linked to its natural endowment and which define its identity) that lead to the great diversity that gives rise to the richness of the human world. Thus, repressing diversities actually means repressing mind evolution, which is against the ground moral norm.

3.4.2.3—Kantianism

As summarized by Laberge (1998), according to Kant (1797) nations should join into a world league of nations, whose law should forbid the use of force. Such a league should include the *free States*, understood as *sovereign States*, which entails that the non-democratic (non-republican) States should be admitted. The next (penultimate) target should be a pan-democratic (pan-republican) world league of nations. The ultimate target would be a World Republic. Other thinkers (Friedrich 1962: 156; Tesón 1992; 1998) underline that Kant's view of international law (the law of nations) is concerned with a federation of free, democratic States that respect human rights and the international rule of law, preserve peace and whose sovereignty lies on their political legitimacy. Allowing that non-democratic States participate in the society of nations would be a regression from the current international law, and would unjustly confer legitimacy to illegitimate governments (Tesón 1998). Non-democratic States might only be accepted in the society of nations as a forced *modus vivendi*. It has been suggested (Laberge 1998) that the U. N. could be an example of the nation's league as viewed by Laberge, whereas the N.A.T.O. could be an example of a league of nations according to the Friedrich-Tesón view. I will focus my discussion on the issues of *(1)* the formation of the Universal Republic, and *(2)* the Universal Republic as compared to a federation of States.

(1) Toward the Universal Republic. I think that the progression from the local or national States toward the democratic Universal Republic (like the progression of less universal scientific laws toward more universal ones) is a complex and unforeseeable process, whose development cannot be fixed in three (or in any other number of) stages. Rather, it should be considered that such a process consists of the progressive universalization of human projects and actions; therefore, it is the *principle of universalization* that should guide the evolution toward the democratic Universal Republic. This entails that including a non-democratic State into super-national institutions and then attempting to change it into a democratic one or, vice versa, waiting until a State becomes democratic before accepting it, may be a matter of evaluation and choice and may depend on many factors. What is important is that any step should be directed to reach the final end: the universal and democratic republic.

Geismann (1983) thinks that, in the Kantian view, the use of violence and war to enforce democracy in non-democratic States should not be allowed, as the World Republic should not interfere with the social and cultural policies of the various States that compose it. Indeed, preservation of linguistic, cultural, and religious diversity may help to prevent the development of a despotic World State (Kant 1795). I object that these are too generic concepts, which refer to two distinct issues: *(a)* the enforcement of democracy in non-democratic States, and *(b)* the preservation of cultural diversities.

(a) Enforcement of democracy in non-democratic States. Concerning the *enforcement of democracy*, I note that non-democratic States deprive their citizens of liberty and therefore restrain their mind development, thus violating the ground moral norm. If democratic States do nothing to change a non-democratic State and treat it normally, they would become parties of the immoral limitation of freedom present in that State. It follows that democratic States should do something. However, they should not use violent means such as war, because this would cause many deaths, which are the worst of the evils, as they represent the extreme and irreversible form of mind *involution*; rather, they should attempt to democratize non-democratic States by means of cultural and political pressure, to which only moderate economic pressure could be added. The scope should be not to impose a given conduct from outside but to induce an internal evolution of minds. Therefore, I disagree with those thinkers (Tesón 1988; 1998; Rawls 1999) who believe that, from the Kantian-liberal point of view, force can be used in defense of democratic States and of human rights against illegitimate, dictatorial governments, provided that the oppressed people agree on the external coercive intervention and that the latter does not cause too much destruction and harm. My objection is that in a non-democratic State it is impossible to ascertain whether the oppressed people agree or not on the external intervention and that, being the effects of violent intervention or of war unforeseeable, it is not possible to establish that these effects do not cause too much destruction and harm. However, even in the case in which citizens accept a non-democratic government, the democratic States should attempt to change it, because the non-democratic government is *objectively bad* (it restrains mind evolution of citizens) and because the citizens who accept it are responsible for doing nothing to attempt to develop their own minds (see the concept of *moral responsibility toward oneself*, in ch. 2.1.5.2.2).

(b) Preservation of cultural diversities. The preservation of cultural diversities is morally good if it is intended as referring to the particular, individual forms of mind evolution (in the sphere of intellect, sensitiveness, and power) leading to the great variety of individual and population properties, which make the richness of the human world. Yet, preservation of cultural diversities would be morally bad when referred to some cultural habits that are against mind development and therefore against the fundamental moral norm; an example might be the habit of some populations of preventing the education of women. Thus, the bad habits or "bad claims", should not be recognized but rather contrasted, again not through violent intervention but through cultural, political, and even moderate economic pressure.

(2) Universal Republic versus a Federation of States. According to

Tesón (1988; 1998), Kant would not propose a global community of individuals forming a centralized World State, because this super-State, being unopposed, might become tyrannical; rather, he looks at a society of free and democratic nations that allows trans-boundary movement of individuals, because individuals are the ultimate subjects of morality and justice. Other thinkers have discussed whether international institutions should be based on individual vote of all citizens or as the union of State-governments (Grimm 1995; Thompson 1999). It has been said that difference in language can obstruct a deliberative discussion among citizens of different States, which would speak in favor of the union of State-governments (Grimm 1995; Thompson 1999).

I do not think that difference in language is meaningful, since the problems of international institutions can be discussed by the citizens of each participating State in their language. Instead, two distinct concepts should be discussed: *(a)* whether a global community of individuals (i.e., a Universal Republic) is preferable to a society of States, and *(b)* whether a Universal State, being unopposed, is subjected to become tyrannical.

(a) I think that we do not have to choose between a Universal Republic and a society of States, because the fully Universal Republic should be conceived as including the political organizations with a lesser degree of universality (ch. 3.1.1.1.2), i.e., local States, regional governments, and city governments, each exerting his own political and legislative function based on the principle of subsidiarity (according to some thinkers), or based on their ontological nature (according to my theory—ch. 3.4.1.1, *1d*). Rather, what is to be defined is whether the government of the Universal Republic should be directly elected by the citizens or by the governments or parliaments of the various participating States; more generally, whether the government with a higher degree of universalization should be elected by the governments or by the citizens of the States with a lesser degree of universalization. My opinion is that, once a Universal Republic is established, it is the right of the citizens of the world to elect their representatives and their government (as happens today for elections of the parliament of the European Union—all European citizens participate in the election of their representatives). Voting exerted by all citizens has the advantage that the "weight" of each of the participating States is proportional to the number of its citizens and that all citizens count equally. In this regard, it should be kept in mind that any political organization (from the city to region, to State, to Universal Republic) represents the way through which the actions of the *individuals* or *citizens* reach a progressively higher degree of universalization. However, during the (necessarily long) period required for the creation of supra-national or international institutions, it might be temporarily allowed (if required to facilitate the creation and initial functioning of the international government) that the burden of choosing the international gov-

ernment is left to the governments of the various States, provided that the elected leaders of such governments had included in their political electoral program, and discussed with the citizens before their election, the general line of conduct regarding the adhesion to supra-national institutions or the election of supra-national governments.

(b) Concerning the possibility that a Universal State, being unopposed, may become tyrannical, I think that no such possibility exists, because the democratic or tyrannical nature of a State does not depend (or depends very little) on whether such a State has or not the opposition of other democratic States, but rather on the ability and willingness of his citizens to defend their freedom and their other rights. Thus, the future, desirable, constitutional Universal Republic may well be democratic if human beings are able to defend their rights and liberties.

3.4.2.4—Contractarian Thought

As summarized by Brown (1998), according to Charvet (1998) the relevance of contractarianism to international society starts from the premise that society is based on mutual advantage, requiring adherence to moral, overriding norms, which with time are recognized as the product of human invention, i.e., as willed for creating and endorsing rules under ideal conditions of equal treatment. This would produce the classical *civil rights* but not the principles of *distributive justice*, because the initial position involves equal access to assets and resources. Even Rawls (1971; 1999) proposed an international contract that produces the principles supportive of fundamental freedom, human rights, equality of States, self-determination, respect of treaties, non-aggression, self-defense, etc., but not the *difference principle*. Here my critique is directed to the concept of contract, understood as a contingent tool to reach some ends (ch. 3.1.1.1.1). I think that the international society is the necessary result of the trend of human actions toward universality; thus, international "contracts" are the means through which human actions reach a higher degree of universalization (higher than that reached with the establishment of the national States). Moreover, I reject the claim that "contracts" should not produce distributive justice: *first*, because it is not true that the contractor States initially have equal access to assets and resources, since contracts may actually be stipulated between States with diverse access to assets and resources; *second*, because the ground moral norm, by prescribing the promotion of mind evolution, requires that help is given to poor States, which have a more limited access then other States to assets and resources (otherwise stated, which have not yet reached the evolution-allowing condition). This requirement of the ground moral norm serves to reject the claim of Brown (1998), according to whom the contract, as seen by Charvet (1998), has no founding value but only legitimates an existing scheme of cooperation. Brown (1998) claims that such a contract may exclude disadvantaged people, and affirms that this exclusion, unsatisfactory in the domestic context, would be useful in the international context for building a supra-national State. In my opinion, the exclusion of disadvantaged people is against the ground moral norm both when it occurs in the domestic as well as in the international context. Recourse to the ground moral norm gives support to the defenders (Beitz 1979; Pogge 1989; 1994) of the difference principle (which limits inequality) in the international context, and serves to contrast the claim (Beitz 1983; Barry 1989) that the extension of the difference principle to the international society would lead to radical changes and may not be justified, considering that the world cannot be regarded as a cooperative venture for mutual advantage. Actually, the world should be conceived as ruled by the ground moral norm, which prescribes not merely the pursuing of mutual advantage but primarily the pursuing of mind evolution for all humans, which entails special attention toward the disadvantaged people; this includes the pursuit of selfish interest by the States, provided this pursuit of selfish interests is integrated with, and regulated by, the moral norms, so that all populations are enabled to pursue their selfish interests in a harmoniously integrated international system. This is the concept of *morally-good selfishness*, which is valid at individual or private level (ch. 2.1.5.2.2), and at public or political level, both in the national politics (ch. 3.1.1.2, *1*) and in the international context (ch. 3.4.1.2.1).

3.4.2.5—The Cosmopolitan Conception (Cosmopolitanism)

I will expound some *general concepts*, followed by a discussion of various aspects of *cosmopolitan justice*.

(1) General Concepts. The *cosmopolitan conception* is rather opposite to the concept of nationhood and points out the undeserved difference between rich and poor countries; it underlines the need for the conception of a *cosmopolitan distributive justice* or *moral cosmopolitism* (Beitz 1979; 1994; 1999; Carens 1987; Barry 1989: 434–63; Pogge 1994b; Tan 2000) and for the creation of the required international *cosmopolitan institutions* (Shue 1988) in order to make possible projects like the opening of boundaries to all (Carens 1987; Barry and Goodin 1992; Pogge 1994b; 1997; Schwartz 1995; Cole 2000) or to implement global principles of justice. *Cosmopolitan citizenship* is a concept linked to the need for an international conception of justice, security, environment preservation, and economic globalization (Held D. 1995; Shapiro and Hacker-Cordon 1999; Heater 1996; Robbins 1998; Hutchings and Dannreuther 1999; Carter 2001). My brief comment on the cosmopolitan conception is that it represents a way through which

human *actions* achieve a higher degree of universality (or a closer approach to full universality) than can be achieved within the limits of a national or local State. The trend toward cosmopolitanism, therefore, is in agreement with the prescription of the ground moral norm (prescribing the promotion of *mind evolution*), inasmuch as expanding the universality of human actions represents an *evolution* of the *power*. Based on my theory on the structure of the mind (chs. 1.1.1.1; 1.1.2; Fig. 1.1), human selfish actions (outward activity of power or *practical selfishness*) cannot be separated from human *moral acts* (inward activity of power or *practical consciousness*— ch. 2.1.3.3.3). This means that the more universal actions that can be performed in a super-state area make possible both more universal selfish actions and moral acts; this possibility of performing both actions and moral acts of higher degrees of universality is itself morally good. Of course, these moral acts, which possess a higher degree of universality, may be morally-good or morally-bad acts according to whether they are directed to promote or to restrain mind evolution. Cosmopolitanism, therefore, should always be conceived as *moral cosmopolitanism*. As a conception that overcomes the limits of the nationhood, the cosmopolitan conception is an important step toward the final end: the democratic Universal Republic.

(2) Principles of Cosmopolitan Justice. It has been pointed out that *moral cosmopolitanism* requires impartial treatment, according to principles of justice that emerge from a negotiation situation marked by equality and freedom of the negotiators (Barry 1998), i.e., according to those principles of justice that would not be rejected by somebody who is motivated by the desire of finding principles that others similarly motivated could not reasonably reject (Scanlon 1982: 103–28). No particular individuals, groups or country should have special standing, and any matter should be looked at apart from personal attachments, from a larger human perspective (Hill 1987: 132). However, according to Barry (1998), it is possible to acquire some obligations toward some people and not toward others, provided that this special treatment can, in principle, be accepted by those who are excluded. I think that, similarly to what is the case in the private sphere (ch. 2.1.5.3), the principle of equal treatment should be substituted with the principle of ensuring (or, of making any effort to ensure) to all participating States an *evolution-allowing, involution-avoiding condition*, i.e., those concrete conditions that allow all the participating States to attempt to develop the minds of their citizens according to their natural endowment. *Equality* concerns the right to enjoy an evolution-allowing condition, which will lead to the expression of the natural *inequality* or *diversity*, linked to the particular properties (natural endowment) that define the identity of each individual or group or population (chs. 3.2.2.1.1; 3.2.2.1.2).

Barry (1998) thinks that, in the international context, choices should be made by individuals and not by the States, because it is quite possible that govern rules are just within a State but the rules governing relations between States are unjust. I have already expounded my opinion on this issue. I think that it is the right/duty of the citizens to participate (through voting) in all the political choices; thus, each citizen should vote for the local, regional, national and international "governments", since each citizen has the right/duty to contribute to solve all the political problems (from local to international) because all problems affect him. However, in the long-lasting intermediate stages in the way toward a universal, democratic republic, voting about international problems may be temporarily devolved to the representatives (governments) of the various participating States (provided that the international problems were included in the program presented to the voters and were publicly discussed before the voting), if this may facilitate the advancement toward the final end (ch. 3.4.2.3, *2a*).

Barry (1998) proposes to follow four principles of justice. *(a)* The principle of *presumption of equality* (which concerns *persons* and their rights): all inequalities of rights, opportunities, and resources should be justifiable in ways that cannot reasonably be rejected by those who get least, in a hypothetical ideal-choice situation. *(b)* The principle of *personal responsibility* and *compensation* (which concerns *deserts*): compensation is due for differences produced by involuntary causes (nature or misfortune) but not for difference resulting from truly free choices (against the Rawlsian principle that inequality may be justified if the minimum is as high as is feasible). *(c)* The principle of the *priority of vital interests* (which concerns *needs*): primarily the physical health, nutrition, medical care, adequate clothing and shelter, and adequate education. *(d)* The principle of *mutual advantage*, according to which departure from the three above principles is justified if it maximizes the gain of those who gain least from the departure. This principle, which is based on the priority of the worst off, should not be regarded as a return to utilitarianism, because it is subordinated to the other three principles. It endorses Pareto improvements over the baseline set by the operation of the other three principles. Moreover, according to this principle, the worst off is defined in relation to the baseline created by the application of the other principles (Barry 1998).

Other thinkers have proposed a global resource dividend (Pogge 1997), or a universal basic income (Van Parijs 1995: 223–28; 2001).

Once again, I note that all the above proposals, directed to promote the principles of equality and priority of the worst off (by considering the rights, deserts and compensation, vital interests, and mutual advantage) are complex and yet inadequate attempts to implement principles of justice (ch. 3.2.6). The same is true for the proposals of assuring a global resource dividend and a universal basic income (which should be the minimum to be assured?). In contrast, my theory about the evolution-allowing condition, which should be ensured to all, is simple and flexible (the evolution-allowing conditions should take into account both the extremely diverse natural endowments of individuals as well as the concrete conditions and the degree of development of the society—chs. 2.1.5.3; 3.1.2.5.1, *3*) and is derived from the unique ground moral norm: promoting mind evolution.

Miller (1998) underlines that the principles of justice may be distinguished into *comparative* principles, as are the principles of equality ("It is unfair that teachers are paid less than bank clerks"), and *non-comparative* principles, as are the principles of human rights ("It is unjust for people to be executed for theft") (Miller 1998: 169). Referring to Barry's principles of justice, Miller (1998) observes that the first (*presumption of equality*), the second (*personal responsibility and compensation*), and the fourth (*mutual advantage*) are comparative principles, whereas the third one (*the priority of vital interests*) is non-comparative. I observe that the concept of "comparative" principles of justice derives from the false conviction that justice entails equality among individuals and, in addition, is limited to the economic aspect. Actually, justice and, more generally, a morally-good condition is not linked to comparison between individuals (or States) directed to realize equality but consists of assuring to all individuals *equality* in the enjoyment of an *objective* condition allowing the *evolution of mind* in all its components, which leads to the expression of natural *diversities* (linked to the degree and specificity of mind evolution in each individual, group, or population), as they result from natural endowment.

(3) Implementing Cosmopolitan Justice. According to Barry (1998), presently in the world there are undeserved and excessive inequalities, and there is also the need to preserve the natural resources of the planet for the future generations. To this end, the current production level is unsustainable; if the total production is to be reduced, then the poor countries' production can increase only if that of rich countries decreases. However, Barry maintains that the present inequalities should be compensated by high rates of taxation, according to the principle of *personal responsibility and compensation* (see above). In his view, the claim that high taxation, or the transfer of resources from rich countries to poor countries, may limit economic growth and cause everyone to lose is unjustified, as shown by the experience within the European Union (Barry 1998). I note that all the above proposals refer to the distribution of *resources*. Yet, resources belong to the sphere of power, and thus refer to only one of the three mind components whose evolution should be promoted. Thus, the proposal of distributing resources is vague (no criterion is stated about the amount of resources that should be given) and incomplete (it refers only to the sphere of *power*, and ignores the spheres of *intellect* and *sensitiveness*). In contrast, my proposal, that we should ensure the evolution-allowing condition, provides at the same time the end to be reached (ch. 3.1.2.5.1) and the limit of the helper's responsibility (ch. 2.1.5.3); it gives a criterion to establish the minimum

amount of resources that should be given and underlines the further need to help the disadvantaged populations (and individuals) to develop their mind in all its three components.

It has been pointed out that unjust internal distribution because of corruption might even justify an external intervention, because very bad governments do not deserve the respect of their autonomy (Barry 1998). The same would be true in the case of passive acceptance of internal injustice (Barry 1998), as often occurs in "soft States" of underdeveloped countries, such as India (Myrdal 1968). On the other hand, the presence of unjust but "accepted" social conditions (which may result, for instance, from religious beliefs) would not justify external intervention, although it is highly improbable that well-informed people will accept such unjust conditions (Barry 1998). I observe that even "accepted" unjust conditions should be changed (e.g., the existence of castes in India), because, if they are unjust, they restrain mind evolution (i.e., they are objectively bad) and, therefore, are against the ground moral norm. The duty toward oneself prohibits "accepting" a condition that restrains one's own mind evolution (chs. 2.1.5.2.2; 3.1.2.5.2; 4.1.2.2). However, as I have stated elsewhere (ch. 3.2.12, *4*), external intervention should be limited to non-violent means, such as cultural, political, and (moderate) economic pressure, because violent intervention (war) may produce more evil than the bad situation that the intervention is directed to change. Moreover, the degree of injustice that would justify a violent intervention is a matter of difficult and unavoidably arbitrary evaluation, and may apparently justify external interventions actually directed to other covert, and often bad, ends.

(4) Other Aspects of Cosmopolitan Justice. Miller (1998) suggests that we should distinguish a less plausible *strong cosmopolitanism*, equally concerned with the moral claims of all human beings, and a more plausible *weak cosmopolitanism*, which is committed to libertarian morality that imposes to respect the rights of life, liberty, and property of everybody. I observe that it is not enough to respect the *universal human rights* of everybody; it is much more important, especially with regard to the disadvantaged individuals or populations, to fulfill the *universal human duties* (chs. 3.1.2.5.1, *3*; 3.2.2.1.2). The latter have a different sphere of application according to whether they refer to *(a)* private individuals, or *(b)* public institutions and governments.

(a) Each individual has the duty to promote or favor, to the largest possible extent (depending on his personal wealth or power), mind evolution both in his own person and in that of all those who he knows and with whom he can in some way interact, although the moral responsibility of an agent decreases in proportion to the decrease in his closeness toward the people to be helped (see the concept of the *spheres of decreasing moral responsibility*, in ch. 2.1.5.2.1).

(b) Governments have the moral duty (which should be stated in the constitutional norms) to promote mind evolution of *all* citizens in the domestic field and to contribute, together with the governments of other States and in proportion of their power, to promote mind evolution of *all* human beings, primarily those living in underdeveloped countries. The principle of universal human duties, just expounded, helps to confute the claim that the "law of peoples" is based on principles different from those valid for domestic justice, as they would not include the principles of distributive justice (Rawls 1999).

Miller (1995: 53–55; 1998) maintains that *comparative* principles of justice (see above) operate mainly within national boundaries (and also within international associations such as, for instance, cultural societies) whereas *non-comparative* principles also operate across national boundaries. I have questioned above the concept of "comparative" justice and its distinction from the non-comparative justice; here I would like to add, once again, that there is just one principle of justice (ensuring to all human beings an evolution-allowing condition) derived from the unique ground moral norm (prescribing the promotion of mind evolution), and that this principle is valid both within and across national boundaries.

(5) Causes of Underdevelopment. Causes of the underdevelopment of some countries should also be considered; they include *excessive population growth* and inefficient or *unjust economic and political systems* (Miller 1998). Uncontrolled population growth is a serious problem: if the world population is not kept under control, it will be limited by natural forces such as starvation. According to Hardin (1993), this raises the question as to whether there is a moral duty to help individuals from poor countries where there is an uncontrolled increase in the population. On these grounds, it has been suggested that, when non-coercive policies for the control of procreation fail and the needs of the growing population cannot be met by redistributive measures, coercion of procreative decisions would be justified (O'Neill 1986: 158). I argue that coercive measures are ineffective unless they are associated to (or, better, preceded by) adequate education. Once again, I note that my proposal, consisting of promoting the evolution of the mind in all its components, includes the education of citizens and, therefore, will limit and, with time, eliminate the excessive population growth (as it has happened in the developed countries). However, especially during the period before full development is achieved, some kind of intervention may be temporarily justified.

Concerning other factors, such as political stability, appropriate economic and cultural framework, and institutions, it has been suggested that they should be favored by external policies as well as by investment in technology and stable trading links (Miller 1998). I agree on this point, since it is in line with the promotion of the evolution of the mind, in all its components.

As a weak cosmopolitan, Miller (1998) maintains that we should be aiming for a diverse world in which independent political communities can pursue different projects and conceptions of justice, provided that the basic human rights of their members are protected. I object that there is only one conception of true justice, which requires that not only the "basic rights" but also *all* the rights that need to be enjoyed to make possible mind evolution be recognized to all citizens.

CHAPTER 4

Public Ethics and Philosophy of Law

4.1– A New Conception of Laws

4.1.1—Laws as Universal and Collective Projects

4.1.1.1—Defining Laws

In chapter 3, I attempted to show that society and its institutions are the way through which the universalization of human actions and moral acts takes place. The universality of *personal actions* concerns the *agents* of the actions (actions are *universal or shared* if they are performed by all or most of the agents belonging to a class, e.g., all citizens of a State); the universality of *moral acts* concerns both the *agents* and the *recipients* or beneficiaries of the acts (moral acts are *universal and collective* if they are collectively performed by, and if they affect, most members of a class, e.g., most citizens of a State—see ch. 1.1.3.2.5). Both personal actions and moral acts consist of the accomplishment of *projects* (personal projects and moral projects, respectively) (chs. 1.1.1.2.3; 1.1.1.2.4; 2.1.1.3; 2.1.3.3). Thus, universal actions and acts require the previous creation of the respective *universal projects*; in a democratic State, these universal projects are the *laws*.

It is noteworthy that laws are indirectly linked to knowledge, as they are *shared projects* and, as all projects, are created by the *project-making activity of intellect* through the utilization of the previously acquired knowledge; personal projects are linked to ideas, produced by the outward activity of intellect, while moral projects are linked to the moral thoughts, produced by the inward activity of intellect (chs. 1.1.1.2.1; 1.1.1.2.4; 2.1.1.1; Fig. 1.1).

Projects may be *particular* or *universal* (ch. 1.1.3.2.1, 2). Laws are *universal* moral projects with regard to both the agents (they are *projects* of acts *collectively* endorsed by all—or most of—the community members or citizens) and the recipients (they are also *projects of moral acts* directed to affect all—or most of—the community members or citizens). Indeed, as projects of moral acts, laws are not only *universal as to their objects* (they are directed to affect all citizens) but also *universal as to their agents* (i.e., *collective*), because they are collectively and simultaneously endorsed by many or all the members of the community (ch. 1.1.3.2.5). Considering that a moral event is always the product of a single individual (ch. 2.1.2, *A1*), the concept of collectiveness serves to distinguish laws from the universal moral act carried out by a single, private individual (e.g., a gift made by a rich man to *all* the members of a community) (ch. 2.2.2). Thus, laws could be defined as *universal (as to the objects) and collective projects*, which define the kinds of actions and acts that must (or must not) be performed by the members of society. Briefly, laws are "*universal/collective*" *projects*.

Since a law is a project (more exactly: an idea-of-project or a thought-of-project), it actually is an idea of class (generated by the *intellect*) that creates its own members; the members of such a class are the actions defined and prescribed by that law, and the *shared properties* common to all such members consist of the end(s) or purpose(s) or finality(ies) to which the actions prescribed by the law are directed. In other words, each law creates a class of actions; within that class, each individual action will differ from the other actions by its particular properties but will share with them the common properties represented by the finality expressed by the law (for the concept of *class*, see ch. 1.1.3.2.1). Thus, as mentioned elsewhere (Belfiore 2004: 265–68), a law that prescribes to pay a tax is a *project* or, more exactly, an *idea-of-project* that creates a class having as members many individual actions (carried out by the single members of the community) which may differ with respect to many particular properties, as a citizen may pay the money at one bank, another citizen at another bank, another one may pay well in advance, still another may pay the last allowed day, etc.; yet, all these actions share the common property of being all directed to pay some amount of money to the government. Even the laws referring to certain actions that might occur also in the absence of any law, such as the law that forbids and punishes murder, create their own members. In fact, a man may kill another man (e.g., during a fight) both in an organized society regulated by laws or in a hypothetical unorganized population in which there are no laws. From the standpoint of natural science these would be two similar events (a man who kills another man); yet, from the standpoint of the philosophy of law, they are different because, of these two events, only the former represents a member of the class created by the law that forbids and punishes murder. Thus, laws could be defined as *universal/collective projects that create classes of actions*.

There is some similarity between a law or norm issued by a competent authority and a scientific law elaborated by a scientist. In fact, both the issued law, on the one hand, and the discovered scientific law, on the other, defines a class of similar events, i.e., a class of similar human actions in the case of the law issued by a competent authority, and a class of similar natural events in the case of a scientific law. Yet, a scientific law and a norm differ from each other inasmuch as, while scientific laws (being descriptive laws) are ideas-of-classes that are created by the intellect after the observation of several pre-existing events (that are the members of such classes), the authority-issued laws (being normative laws) are ideas-of-classes that create their own members (the actions), and therefore pre-exist to them.

It should be pointed out that the intellect defines in an *approximate or imprecise manner* the shared properties of the classes that it creates, allowing a range of variations (ch. 1.1.3.2.1). This is true for both the classes of natural events (as defined by the biological scientific laws) and the classes of human actions (as defined by the authority-enacted laws). It ensues that the laws define in an approximate manner the shared properties of the actions that they regulate; this is the origin of the *indeterminacy of laws* (chs. 4.2.3; 4.3.1.1, *1a*).

4.1.1.2—Criteria for the Judgment of Laws

4.1.1.2.1—The Value Criterion

As stated elsewhere (ch. 1.1.3.2; Table 1.1), all products of the mind can be evaluated by the general criterion, valid for all of them: the *value criterion*, which allows the distinction between *particular* and *universal*. Projects are no exceptions, and neither are laws. Laws, however, are by definition *universal* projects; therefore, subjecting a law to the value criterion to establish whether it is universal or particular actually means to establish whether it is a law or not. It should be underlined, however, that in the real world a law is never fully "universal" (i.e., endorsed by *all* the citizens); referring to a democratic State, a law is the project that obtains the highest percentage of favorable votes, i.e., the project that, compared to the competing projects, possesses the highest degree of universality and, therefore, represents the *best approach to universality*. [I note that, again, there is a similarity with biological scientific laws, as the latter laws also define only in an approximate manner the properties possessed by *most* members of a given class of objects or events (ch. 1.1.3.2.1)].

In a democratic State, in order to be *universal* (or community-endorsed), a law should be elaborated by the competent authority (the representatives of citizens, say, the parliament), and should be made known to all members of the community, thus becoming a collective, universal project (or population project). Thus, a law, as an ontological entity, exists in the mind (intellect) of all the members of a community: at first, only in the mind of the members of the issuing institution (the elected members of the parliament, in a democratic State) and, after the law is promulgated, in the minds of all members of the community.

4.1.1.2.2—The Specific Judgment Criteria

As any mind product, projects (and, hence, laws) can be evaluated by specific criteria (ch. 1.1.3.1; Table 1.1). Laws (and the executive power that enforces them) have a two-fold nature (see ch. 4.1.1.3.1, below), as they are both *moral* and (good) *selfish* projects.

As good selfish projects, laws should be judged by the *efficaciousness criterion* as *efficacious* or *inefficacious*, depending on whether they are conceived in a way suitable for reaching the scope to which they are directed. Provision of a sanction is one of the elements that increase the efficaciousness of a law. In other words, a collective project (or law) should not only define the shared property(ies) of the class of actions that it creates, but it should also be suitable to be applied and should establish the means to force the society members to observe the law itself and the sanctions to be imposed to those who do not observe it. If, for any reason, the law is unsuitable to be realized or if sanctions are not provided, the law should be judged as *inefficacious*, whereas if the law is suitable to be realized and sanction can be inflicted the law (project) should be judged as *efficacious*.

It should be noted that laws should be distinguished from their enforcement, i.e., from the function of the apparatus that serves to force citizens to observe the law (the enforcement apparatus), which, in contrast to the laws (which, being projects, are created by the *intellect*), is a general action exerted by the State apparatus and, as such, belongs to the sphere of the *power*, and should be judged by the *strength criterion* as *strong* or *weak*.

On the other hand, since laws are also projects directed to affect minds (that is, the citizens), they are actually *universal* and *collective moral* projects and, as such, should be judged also by the *morality criterion* as *good* or *bad* (chs. 1.1.3.1; 2.1.1.1; 2.1.3.1.2; Table 1.1).

4.1.1.3—The Two-Fold Nature and the Binding Force of Laws

4.1.1.3.1—The Two-Fold Nature of Laws

Since the laws of a community are universal moral projects, they are directed to reach, through the corresponding acts, some ends. Thus, the problem of the *finality of the law-regulated acts* arises. To clarify this issue, we should recall that a project is always a *selected project*, i.e., is the project that is selected among the various possible alternative projects. Therefore, the true problem to be solved concerns the choice among various possible projects. Since the laws are projects directed to affect the minds of citizens, this choice unavoidably is (or is also—see below) a *moral choice* (which, of course, may be a *good* or a *bad* moral choice). To understand the finality of laws we should know which are the forces that determine such a choice.

Both in private or individual life and in public life, the choice between alternate *projects* is determined by the balance between *personal or selfish sentiments* (which prompt the agent, or groups of agents, to choose according to his, or their, own prevailing desires, preferences, and interests) and *moral feelings* (which stir-up the choice that favors mind evolution, which in the public sphere is indicated as the common good). Although, of course, the rational component of the mind, i.e., selfish ideas and moral thoughts, also participates in the choices, the emotional component, i.e., selfish sentiments and moral feelings, is prevailing in selecting the project to be realized and, hence, in the creation of laws.

Thus, we can say that public institutions and their laws regulate both public *selfish actions* (here we refer to the *morally-good* selfish actions), which are prompted by the prevailing (good) *desires or sentiments* of individuals, groups, or parties belonging to the law-governed people (directed to reach the objects of their desires or interests) as well as the collective *moral acts* of these people, which are stirred up by *moral feelings* (directed to induce changes, be them evolution or involution, in the minds of citizens).

As mentioned elsewhere (Belfiore 2004: 301), in an ideal world, these two components would be well balanced, as public good *selfish actions* (directed to satisfy legitimate personal or group desires) should be allowed and favored since they, being good, do not interfere or contrast with public *moral acts*, directed to accomplish the common good (promoting mind evolution of all citizens). In this regard, it should be noted that the selfish actions (of individuals or of groups or parties) are morally good if directed to promote the evolution of the agents' mind without interfering with the evolution of other minds (see the concepts of *morally- good egoism* and of *moral duty toward oneself*—chs. 2.1.5.2.2; 3.1.2.5.2; 4.1.2.2). In other words, in an ideal world, *integration* would be achieved between personal (or group) desires and moral feelings and, consequently, between selfish actions and collective moral acts (ch. 3.1.1.2, *1*). In the real world, we can distinguish: *(a)* laws that are based almost exclusively on community-shared moral feelings, and hence should be directed to promote mind evolution of citizens (by ensuring the fundamental rights of the individuals, required to allow an acceptable evolution of their mind); and *(b)* laws that are affected, to some extent, by (good) selfish desires and interests of those individuals or groups belonging to the majority party. As we will see later on, the former laws are mainly represented by the *constitutional norms* while the latter ones are mainly represented by some of the *ordinary laws* and rules. Although ordinary laws must respect the limit posed by the constitutional norms, and despite the obligation of the majority party to consider and respect the activity and opinion of the minority party (in order to reach the best approach to universality—ch. 3.1.2.1, 2), in practice a certain degree of discretion exists, so that it may happen that selfish (personal or group) desires and moral feelings compete with each other in determining the final outcome of legislative activity.

The above reasoning shows that laws are unavoidably linked to moral principles and values. In fact, even if *ordinary laws* are mainly created by the majority party, they should have a moral content in order to adhere to the shared moral principles and values (produced by the consciousness of the community), stated in the *constitutional norms.* This entails that ordinary laws, though they may be affected, to some extent, by the (legitimate) desires and interests of the people belonging to the majority party, should also take into account the fundamental rights of the minorities, i.e., they should pursue the common good. Thus, *the ultimate basis of laws is morality.*

It should be added that ordinary laws, even if affected to some extent by selfish desires and interests, once enacted, must be respected, even by the dissenting citizens (until the latter obtain that the unaccepted laws are changed—ch. 4.1.1.3.2, *B*); this is because laws represent the way through which human actions evolve toward (i.e., reach or approach) universality; universalization of actions is a component of mind evolution (the moral good), together with the evolution toward universality of ideas and of sentiments. In other words, the *evolution* toward universality of the *outward* mind activity is itself a component of the moral good. This concept is close to that of the moral value of selfishness, as a means to develop one's own mind (see ch. 2.1.5.2.2 on the *morally-good egoism* and the *duty toward oneself*), and to that of the moral value of a democratic legal system, as the way through which human acts/actions can evolve toward universality.

As to the *executive apparatus*, which applies and enforces the laws, it belongs to both the *inward* and the *outward activity of power* (*bi-directionality of the mind*), because it, at the same time, performs universal/collective moral acts (directed to pursue moral ends) and favors the morally-good selfish actions of citizens, while itself acting as a selfish and efficacious agent.

4.1.1.3.2—Validity, Efficaciousness, and Binding Force of Laws

The following issues should be considered.

(A) Validity of Laws.

As already mentioned, a law, being a shared *project* created by the *intellect,* can be judged as efficacious (by the *efficaciousness criterion*) if it is made in such a way that (if enforced with sufficient strength) it will reach the end to which it is directed. So conceived, a law is distinct from its *enforcement* by the State and from its *observance* by citizens, which, being actions exerted by the State and by citizens, respectively, belong to the sphere of the *power*, and can be judged as strong or weak by the *strength criterion* (chs. 1.1.3.1; 2.1.3.1.2; Table 1.1). Thus, a law is *ontologically distinct* from its *observance* as well as from its *enforcement*.

The *observance* of a law depends on the magnitude of the majority that has approved it as well as on the *efficaciousness* of the law itself (which includes the provision of a sanction) and on the strength of the *enforcement apparatus*.

Thus, if a law exists (i.e., if it has been enacted by the largest possible majority of democratically elected representatives), it is necessarily valid; for a law, *existence* and *validity* coincide. This means that a law *exists* and is *valid* even if it is inefficacious, is weakly enforced by the enforcing apparatus and, consequently, is unobserved by a variable percentage of citizens.

Yet, the existence and validity of a law has some relationship with its observance. Because, being a law a project shared by the *majority* of citizens (actually, by the majority of citizens' representatives), it should be observed at least by 50.01% of citizens. Therefore, in the case that a weakly enforced or non-enforced law is largely unobserved (it becomes a "dead letter"), we should distinguish whether or not the unobservant citizens are more than 50%, thus being the majority. If the unobservant citizens are not the majority, the law is still existent and valid, and there is the moral and legal obligation to observe it. If the unobservant citizens are *truly* the majority, the law can no longer be valid (a law is a project endorsed by the majority of citizens, even if the endorsement is expressed indirectly, through the representatives of citizens in the enacting assembly). Yet, we should consider that often the unobservant citizen might fail to observe a law not based on a reflective decision (i.e., on a *fully-reasoned, deeply-felt, and enduring decision*) but under the pressure of momentary and superficial beliefs, desires and interests (i.e., based on a *little-reasoned, impulsive, and mutable decision*). If the unobservant citizen is called to carefully evaluate the law that he has just ignored, he may recognize its validity. Therefore, the inobservance of a law should be widespread and persistent to be regarded as the result of a convicted decision of the majority of citizens. Thus, in a well-functioning democracy, parliament (or the equivalent law-enacting assembly) and all the government organs should always be vigilant, in order to notice those laws that are largely unobserved and to re-evaluate, in a reflective manner, their validity, and should attempt to favor the prevalence of *fully-reasoned, deeply-felt, and enduring decisions*. If this vigilance does not occur, uncertainty may arise as to whether a given law is still existent and valid [the existence and validity of a law can only be judged with *approximation*, as happens in most fields of human activity (ch. 1.1.3.2.1)].

(B) Binding Force of Laws.

The unavoidable moral nature of laws entails that laws are morally binding, i.e., that laws should be obeyed because they pursue the common good. Since in a constitutional State (to which we refer) ordinary laws must respect constitutional norms, and since the latter express the shared moral projects and feeling (i.e., shared moral principles and values) of the community, the obligation to obey the law is based on moral grounds, i.e., on the duty deriving from the fact that laws are directed to realize the moral projects and feelings endorsed by the majority of the community members, i.e., to implement the shared moral principles and values. Moreover, the acceptance and observance of the laws in a constitutional State is morally good in itself, since it entails the evolution from an isolated, individual-centered or group-centered way of life into a conception of life integrated in the society, in which human actions and moral acts can achieve the largest possible degree of universalization (ch. 3.1.1.2, 2).

For this reason, there is no obligation to obey the laws issued by a non-democratic government, because in this instance laws represent the project of the governing minority, which should not prevail over the oppressed majority because the latter, being the majority, possesses a higher degree of universalization.

While in an ideal world the common good is the good recognized by all citizens, in the real world the common good is that recognized by the largest possible majority of citizens, i.e., it is actually the *best approach to the universally recognized good.* It follows that a certain percentage of citizens may not endorse some of the norms stated in the constitution and, consequently, some of the ordinary laws. Thus, for this minority of citizens, some norms and laws may not be morally good. Moreover, some citizens may consider unjust or unjustified some of the ordinary laws, even if these respect the accepted constitutional norms (due to the unavoidable indeterminacy of the latter). This raises the problem of whether a *dissenting citizen* can refuse to obey the laws. We should consider separately *(1)* the dissent from ordinary laws and *(2)* the dissent from constitutional norms.

(1) Dissent from Ordinary Laws. The case of citizens who dissent from ordinary laws may concern: *(a)* ordinary laws that are in contrast with constitutional norms, or *(b)* ordinary laws that respect constitutional norms.

(a) Dissent from ordinary laws that are in contrast with constitutional norms. This case is relatively simple because when an ordinary law is in contrast with the constitutional norms (which reflect the moral principles and values as conceived by the large majority of citizens) it must be repealed. Of course, deciding whether an ordinary law is, or is not, in contrast with the constitution is not the task of single individuals, as this decision

must be taken by a specifically designed official organ, such as the constitutional court, which is created in the manner provided for by the constitution itself. As mentioned elsewhere (Belfiore 2004: 302), a citizen who *believes* that a law is unconstitutional is certainly entitled to point out the problem and he may contribute to initiate the official procedure which will be concluded with the decision of the constitutional court. Before a law is declared unconstitutional by the court, it must be obeyed, because at this stage the unconstitutionality of the law is only *hypothesized* or *believed* by one or more individuals, but is not officially proved. If one or more citizens refuse to obey a law because they *believe* that it is unconstitutional, they actually attempt to substitute their individual decision to that of the large majority of citizens (and, therefore, of the State), thus exerting *violence*. Therefore, with regard to ordinary laws, the statement made by St. Augustine in his *City of God* (bk. xix: 21; as quoted by Aquinas in his *Summa Theologica,* I–II, Q;96, Art.4—see Pegis, 1965) that "An unjust law is no law at all" should be changed into "A law that is declared unconstitutional must be repealed."

From the above, it follows that in a constitutional democratic State, since ordinary laws must respect constitutional norms, which express shared moral principles and values (such as the protection of basic human rights), laws cannot be publicly overtly unjust, i.e., overtly unjust by the publicly-shared moral criteria stated by the constitution, because, if a law is recognized as unconstitutional, it will be abrogated. There is, however, room for some degree of "injustice", due to the indeterminacy (or open texture) of the constitutional norms and the unavoidable discretion of constitutional judges.

(b) Dissent from ordinary laws that respect constitutional norms. Apparently, if an ordinary law, enacted in a democratic constitutional State, respects the constitutional norms, it should be accepted by all citizens. This is certainly true in most instances. Yet, due to the indeterminacy of the constitutional norms (and of the laws in general—chs. 4.1.1.1; 4.2.3; 4.3.1.1, *1a*), it is possible that a given ordinary law lies at the boundary of the field delimited by the constitutional norms, i.e., that it is borderline. In this instance, the dissenting citizen is allowed to express his view and to propagandize it in the hope that he succeeds in convincing others with the final scope of obtaining that the law is changed by parliament, or that the law is judged by the constitutional court, whose sentence should be accepted as final (until the existing constitution is in force).

(2) Dissent from Constitutional Norms. It should be kept in mind that moral principles and values expressed in the constitutional norms reflect the moral thoughts and feelings shared by a large majority of citizens (but not by *all* of them) in a given period, i.e., reflects the consciousness of the majority of the community. Moreover, consciousness (inward mind activities), like selfishness (outward mind activities), evolves with time (decades, centuries or millennia), as there is not a moral conception that can be defined as

the highest possible or as absolutely good (likewise, there is not a stage of knowledge that is final, in which all is already known). Therefore, it may be the case that one, a few, or a group of citizens consider(s) one or more constitutional norms as bad or unjust, i.e., they may dissent from the laws pursuing the common good as conceived by the founders of the constitution and expressed in the constitutional norms. This means that there may be a *moral gap* between the "personal" and the "shared" conception of the good. This may happen for two reasons: *(a)* because the consciousness of the dissenting citizen(s) is less evolved than the community consciousness (as reflected by the shared constitutional norms), or *(b)* because the consciousness of the dissenting citizen(s) is more evolved than that of the community. In both instances, the dissenting citizen has the duty to observe the norms shared by the majority of citizens, even if he does not endorse some of them (because the norms shared by the majority of the community members represent the best approach to universality). The dissenting citizens who believe that a given constitutional norm is "bad" have the right to propagandize their view and to contribute to initiate the official procedure (usually provided for by the constitution itself) for re-discussing a given moral norm and, if the support of a large majority is reached, for changing it. This is the way through which the good citizens become *promoters of the evolution of the consciousness of the community* and of the change of the constitution. Indeed, through time (decades and centuries) the moral principles and values of a population evolve and, when they are no longer reflected by the constitution in force, the latter will be changed with a procedure provided for by the constitution in force or defined (either directly or indirectly) by a large majority of the population.

When the dissenting citizen promotes a change that represents an evolution of the community's consciousness, his action (exerted in the sphere of politics and, therefore, of the *power*) will be comparable to that of scientists, who promote science (sphere of *intellect*), or to that of "artists", who promote literary, musical or visual arts (sphere of *sensitiveness*).

It should be stressed that, before a constitutional norm is changed, i.e., when it is only *believed* by an uncertain percentage of citizens that a given constitutional norm is bad, it must be obeyed; otherwise, if a group of citizens, that has not proved to represent the majority, refuses to obey a constitutional norm, it would exercise *violence* (as defined in ch. 3.1.2.4).

4.1.1.4—Re-Definition of Laws

As a conclusion of the preceding discussion, we may attempt to re-define what laws actually are. Conventionally, a law is regarded as a binding rule of conduct or actions formally prescribed by a recognized (and, in democratic systems, publicly justified) community authority. In my view, the *ideal law* should be an *efficacious, long-lasting, morally-good, universal and collective* (or *universal and publicly-shared*) *moral project* (created by the *inward activity of intellect* or *rational consciousness*) endorsed by the largest possible majority of citizens, defining a *class of actions* and directed to implement good moral principles (again created by *rational consciousness*) and moral values (created by the *inward activity of sensitiveness* or *emotional consciousness*), and enforced by a strong executive apparatus (created by the *inward activity of power* or *practical consciousness*) (Fig. 1.1). Thus, laws are produced by consciousness in all its three components (rational, emotional, and practical) and are directed to regulate citizens' behavior by controlling, but not repressing (indeed favoring), citizens' *selfish actions* (produced by the *outward activity of power*) which, when exerted within the limits of the laws, actually are morally good and contribute to mind evolution (see the concepts of *morally-good egoism* and of *duty toward oneself*—chs. 2.1.5.2.2; 3.1.2.5.2; 4.1.2.2).

4.1.2—Laws and Rights in a Democratic Constitutional State

4.1.2.1—More on Laws in a Democratic Constitutional State

I am expounding and discussing the Philosophy of Law by referring to a modern *democratic* and *constitutional* State (as I did in discussing Political Philosophy, in Ch. 3). This means that I will consider: *(a)* the *constitutional norms*, which express the moral principles and values shared by the large majority of citizens and define the structure of the State required to implement those principles and values; and *(b)* the *ordinary laws*, which are directed to implement the constitutional norms by defining and regulating the particular or specific problems and the corresponding public actions.

In a State, the presence of a *democratic constitution*, based on *universal suffrage*, changes the nature of the laws or, more exactly, makes it possible to have true laws; indeed, as it will be mentioned in the following chapters, in the absence of a democratic constitution the claimed "laws" actually are "acts of public arrogance" and their enforcements are "acts of public violence" (ch. 3.1.2.4). Some thinkers could object that this statement is too strong because, considering that most States became democratic and constitutional only during the last century, with the notable exceptions of ancient Greek cities and of Great Britain (even if in the latter country the universal suffrage was introduced only some decades ago), this statement would entail that true laws and legality have been absent from human history until recent times. My reply would be that this is just what I think. In fact, the pre-constitutional, pre-democratic era actually is a historical phase in which there was no legitimate power but violence, not laws but orders backed by threat. This is because, in the absence of free voting with universal suffrage, there are not public justified institutions that can issue laws expressing the projects shared by the largest possible majority of the community members.

I add that this is not the only example of an important field of human activity that has only recently developed. Considering the fundamental parallelism between the activities of the three mind components, I will clarify this statement by comparing the recent development of law and of the executive apparatus of the state (which belong to the sphere of the *intellect* and of the *power*, respectively) with the recent development of an important branch of science, i.e., medicine (which belongs to the sphere of *intellect*). Medicine, until the 19th century, was not a science whose statements were "universal" scientific laws supported by large scale experiments (i.e., laws which were true for most events belonging to a class), but consisted of non-demonstrated affirmations, based on inadequate personal observations; some of these statements were later proved to be true, many others were shown to be false. Likewise, laws issued by non-democratic, non-constitutional governments have not been proven, through voting by universal suffrage, to be universal laws or, more exactly, the best approach to universal laws (i.e., projects shared by the largest possible majority of citizens). Therefore, they are arbitrary orders (issued and enforced by arbitrary authorities, lacking public justification) which, like the claims of the pre-scientific medicine, may often not be universal (community-shared) even if sometimes, by chance, some of them may actually be shared by the community. This means that even a non-democratic government may sometimes issue some laws that are shared by the population. Indeed, voting and democratic elections are like experiments in science: the former serve to prove the universality and collectivity of the enacted laws, the latter the universality of scientific laws.

At this point, an important reflection is in order. The passage from non-democratic to democratic States is the result of a major step in the *continuous evolution of human consciousness* that occurs through time. Therefore, when studying human history, one should always keep in mind that if, on the one hand, history is a main source of knowledge about human nature, on the other hand, it is also true that facts and behaviors that may be judged as justified in past historical periods may no longer be justifiable in the present time, due to the evolution of human consciousness. This means that examples drawn from past historical periods cannot be invoked to justify political acts that are no longer acceptable by human consciousness. Thus, the fact that slavery was accepted during the Roman Empire, or that monarchical absolutism was accepted in past centuries cannot be invoked to justify illiberal and non-democratic political behavior in the present time, both in the domestic and international field. The desire to imitate (or to draw inspiration from) great politicians of the past reveals either (or both) a failure to understand history and/or the attempt to justify a non-democratic or violent political behavior that is actually driven by selfish forces while ignoring the demands of the consciousness.

Before further discussing the philosophy of law, an overview of the various types of "laws" may be useful. In a democratic constitutional State, we should distinguish: *(1)* constitutional (or secondary) laws, and *(2)* ordinary (or primary) laws.

(1) Constitutional (Secondary) Laws. These may be distinguished into *(a)* constitutional moral norms, *(b)* constitutional structural-administrative laws, and *(c)* constitutional functional-administrative laws.

(a) Constitutional moral norms. These are those norms that express the shared moral principles and values (ch. 4.1.2.3). They are initially enacted by a special assembly (constituent assembly) and changed with special procedures, provided by the constitution itself through some of the laws considered here below.

(b) Constitutional structural-administrative laws. These are the laws that define the structures of the administrative system. They are directed to define the nature and function of the organs that, altogether, form the "State".

(c) Constitutional functional-administrative laws. While the "moral" norms (mentioned above, under point "*a*") prescribe those acts that preserve or develop mind evolution and forbid those acts that directly or indirectly induce mind involution of citizens, other constitutional laws regulate the functioning of the administrative system, i.e., of the various organs of the State. They, therefore, concern human actions that are only indirectly linked to mind evolution/involution. However, the respect of the administrative laws is essential for the functioning of the administrative system, which, in turn, makes it possible to put the moral norms into practice; hence the moral obligation to observe the administrative laws.

(2) Ordinary (Primary) Laws. These are laws that regulate "ordinary" citizens' actions capable of affecting mind evolution and have the scope of implementing the fundamental, constitutional norms (thus putting them into practice). So, for instance, an ordinary law that forbids the unlawful restraint of an individual is in actuation of the fundamental constitutional norm that every individual must be free (within the limit defined by the system of laws), because freedom is an essential condition for enabling a citizen to develop his own mind.

Even laws regulating inter-individual relationship, such as the laws that prescribe to keep promises (either written or oral promises), are based on the moral principles and values expressed by the constitutional norms (directed to promote mind evolution), since failure to keep a promise will cause a "damage" (mind involution) to the individual who expected that the promise was kept and who organized his activity on the basis of this expectation (and also because failing to keep a promise breaks the "mini community" formed by the promisee and the promiser—ch. 3.1.2.3.3).

Ordinary laws must respect the more general constitutional norms. The task of deciding whether a law is in accordance with the constitution or not is accomplished by a special organ of the State, whose structure and functioning should be provided by the constitution itself (e.g., a "constitutional court", or an equivalent organ). The process concerning the verification of a claimed discordance of a given law from the constitution must be carried out according to a procedure that, again, should be provided for by the constitution itself.

Finally, it should be noted that a democratic legal system, being the way through which human actions *evolve* toward universality (law-regulated actions represent the best approach to universality), is itself "a *moral good*", and any breaking of a democratic law, undermining the legal system, is morally bad.

4.1.2.2—Duties as the Source of Rights in a Democratic Constitutional State

In the preceding chapter, I mentioned that ordinary laws must respect the constitutional norms, and that the latter express the shared moral principles and values. This means that any norm or law is grounded on a moral basis. We know that the ground moral norm prescribes the promotion of the evolution of the mind, including the mind of the agent himself. If any citizen has the *duty* to promote his own mind, then he has at the same time the *right* to enjoy those concrete conditions that make the promotion of his mind possible (chs. 2.1.5.2.2; 3.1.2.5.2; 3.4.1.1, *2b*). Thus, duties are the source of rights, and not vice versa (Fig. 4.1).

Indeed, any right must be justified, and the only valid justification is that such a right must be recognized for moral reason. The moral reason consists of the duty to promote one's own mind, and this, in turn, derives from the principle (discovered by *moral thought*) that mind evolution is the objective moral good as well as from the fact that mind evolution is felt by *moral feeling* as a moral value.

My conception of the origin of rights from duties shows similarities and differences in respect to that of Hegel, who talked of a coalescence of rights and duties; he wrote:

> [I]n this identity of the universal will with the particular will, right and duty coalesce, and by being in the ethical order a man has rights in so far as he has duties, and duties in so far as he has rights. (Hegel 1821: §155, pp. 109–110)

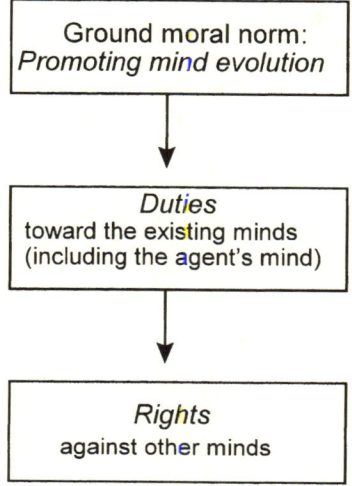

Fig. 4.1. The origin of rights from duties, and of duties from the ground moral norm.

4.1.2.3—Norms, Laws, Rules, and Commands

"Law" is a term that has been used in a generic sense, to indicate any collective or community-shared project (which could also be named as community-shared prescription). However, other terms, such as "norm" or
"rule", are also used with the same or similar meaning. Moreover, the meaning attributed to these terms may be slightly different among the various
countries and languages. For instance, Hart's distinction into "*rules* of obligation" and "*rules* of recognition" would be better defined in Italy as "ordinary *laws*" and "constitutional *norms*". For these reasons, but primarily in
order to better reflect my thought, I think it is useful to define the meaning
that I confer to the terms "norm", "law", "rule", and "command" (Figs. 4.2
and 4.3).

It should be recalled that *moral projects* (or prescriptions), generated by
rational consciousness, are preceded by the generation of *moral thoughts*.
The latter lead the rational consciousness to understand and define the
moral principles, which indicate what is the "good" or the "moral end"
(mind evolution and what it entails). Thus, *moral thoughts* indicate the *ends*
to be pursued; *moral projects* (or prescriptions) define the acts suitable for

pursuing the various "moral goods", i.e., fix the *norms* (and other less comprehensive "rules", see below) to be followed. The norms guide the *moral acts* (directed to pursue the moral end). I have already discussed (chs. 1.1.1.2.4; 2.1.4.1; 2.2.1.1.1, *1*) what is the *moral good* (which should be the end of moral projects and moral acts). The human good can be expressed as *principles* of truth (generated by *moral thoughts*), e.g., by affirming "the principle that mind evolution is the basic moral good," or "the principle that liberty is a moral good." Moreover, the moral good can be expressed as felt *moral values*, (generated by *moral feelings*). This chapter, however, deals with moral projects or prescriptions (which will be realized through moral acts) or, more exactly, with *publicly-shared (or collective) moral projects*, which fix the *moral norms* (and other less comprehensive "laws" and "rules"—see below). Publicly-shared (or collective) moral projects can be distinguished into several classes of various extensions (according to the number of *moral goods* that they are directed to realize and the number of individuals to which they are directed), and can be ordered, in a decreasing order of extension, into norms, laws, rules, and commands, as indicated below (Figs. 4.2 and 4.3). In the following text, I will indicate any norm, law, rule or command with the expressions "publicly-shared or collective" moral project or "public prescription" or "law" (inside double quotation marks).

Let us now define *(A)* norms, *(B)* laws, *(C)* rules, *(D)* commands, and *(E)* the extension and indeterminacy of the various kinds of "laws".

(A) Norms.

The term *norm* should be reserved to the most general publicly-shared or collective moral projects, which are directed to pursue the fundamental moral goods, i.e., to *implement moral principles and values*. Thus, there is the ground norm of pursuing *mind evolution*, i.e., the evolution of the mind in all its components: intellect, sensitiveness, and power (this is the fundamental moral good).

It is noteworthy that even more important than the promotion of mind evolution is the preserving of the existence of the mind and avoiding its partial or total involution, i.e., avoiding physical harm or death, which represent "possibly irreversible" and "total and irreversible" mind involutions, respectively. Indeed, the promotion of mind evolution, prescribed by the ground moral norm, entails the necessary presupposition of avoiding mind involution, which means avoiding primarily physical harm and, especially, death, which, as just said, represents the extreme and irreversible mind involution. It follows that the duty to defend (and the right to have preserved) life and health should always prevail over other duties and rights. Briefly, *the right to life and health should prevail over other rights*.

The ground norm, prescribing the promotion of the evolution of mind in all its three components, defines a class of norms whose members are less comprehensive norms prescribing the pursuit of sub-classes of moral goods (as defined by moral principles and values); these are: *(1)* the norm of pursuing the evolution of the *intellect*, *(2)* the norm of pursuing the evolution of the *sensitiveness*, *(3)* the norm of pursuing the evolution of the *power*, and *(4)* the norm of pursuing the basic conditions required for mind evolution: *liberty* and *equality of rights*. Each of these norms, in turns, defines a sub-sub-class of norms, expressing the duty to pursue a sub-sub-class of moral goods. Thus, referring to Figs. 4.2 and 4.3, *norm-1* (pursuing evolution of *intellect*) includes: *(a)* the norm of pursuing the evolution of intellect in the field of mathematics, *(b)* the norm of pursuing the evolution of intellect in the field of biological sciences, *(c)* the norm of pursuing the evolution of intellect in the field of social sciences, etc. *Norm-2* (pursuing the evolution of *sensitiveness*) includes: *(a)* the norm of pursuing the evolution of sensitiveness in the field of literary arts, *(b)* the norm of pursuing the evolution of sensitiveness in the field of musical arts, *(c)* the norm of pursuing the evolution of sensitiveness in the field of visual arts, etc. *Norm-3* (pursuing the evolution of *power*) includes: *(a)* the norm of pursuing the evolution of power in the field of the health and of economic condition, *(b)* the norm of pursuing the evolution of power in the field of politics, *(c)* the norm of pursuing the evolution of power in the field of the social status, etc. *Norm-4* (pursuing liberty) includes: *(a)* the norm of pursuing *liberty of thought and of believing*, *(b)* the norm of pursuing *liberty of expressing one's own desires and preferences*, *(c)* the norm pursuing *liberty of acting* as a single individual or as an association of several individuals, etc. (Figs. 4.2 and 4.3).

Thus, we could give the following definition: *norms* are general public moral projects directed to pursue the various moral goods as defined by the moral principles and values; briefly, *norms are directed to implement moral principles and values*.

(B) Laws.

Law is the term that should be used to indicate publicly-shared or collective moral projects referring to those *moral acts* required to implement or put into practice a moral norm (and, hence, a moral principle or value). This means that, while norms are general moral projects that indicate *what is the good* to be pursued, laws are less comprehensive (moral) projects that indicate the *(moral) acts required for implementing a norm* (Figs. 4.2 and 4.3).

Indeed, although laws (like rules and even commands) actually are "moral projects" that define "moral acts", we could name them simply "projects" that define "acts" or "procedures", since their "moral" nature is indirect, i.e., depends on the fact that laws (like rules and commands) serve to implement the norms, which directly pursue the moral good.

Laws define "general acts", i.e., acts of general relevance, in contrast to rules and commands, which refer to "specific" and "particular" acts, respectively. Thus, laws can be regarded as sub-classes of the classes defined by the moral norms. In other words, while norms could be defined as first-order universal/collective moral projects (or prescriptions), laws could be regarded as second-order universal/collective projects (or prescriptions). For instance, the norm of pursuing the evolution of the intellect defines a class of laws whose members are: the particular and specific laws ensuring, to all citizens, the availability of school buildings, their maintenance, the functioning of the teaching activity, the accessibility to education, the possibility of choosing the field more appropriate to one's aptitude, etc. Likewise, the norm of "pursuing liberty of thought" defines a class of moral projects (or prescriptions) whose members are: the particular and specific laws to assure freedom of press, the laws to assure freedom of teaching, etc.

(C) Rules.

As each norm defines a class of laws, so each law defines a class of rules. Thus, a rule indicates the publicly-shared (universal/collective) project (or prescription) referring to the "specific" *acts* required to *implement a law*; it can be regarded as a sub-class of the class defined by a law. For instance, a law directed to assure freedom of press defines a class of moral acts whose members are: the rules to assure freedom of newspapers; rules assuring freedom in publishing books; etc. (Figs. 4.2 and 4.3).

From the points discussed above, it follows that there is a parallelism between the system of classes and sub-classes of "laws" (norms, laws, and rules) and the system of classes and sub-classes on the various moral goods that are pursued by the "laws" (Table 2.1).

(D) Commands.

The smallest possible publicly-shared project or prescription is that directed to the performance of a single act; this prescription is the *command* (or *order*). As laws are directed to implement norms, and rules are directed to implement laws, so commands are directed to *implement rules* (Figs. 4.2 and 4.3). Despite the fact that a command refers to a single act, it may be directed to one, a few or many people (e.g., a command or order of the head of a department may be directed to just one person, for instance, a secretary, or may be directed to all the people working in the department).

(E) Extension and Indeterminacy of the Various Kinds of "Laws".

(1) Extension of "Laws". The distinction into norms, laws, rules, and commands is linked to the fact that public moral projects (or prescriptions), i.e., "laws", can be regarded as defining classes of decreasing extension, inasmuch as each class of prescriptions has, as members, sub-classes of prescriptions, each of which, in turn, define a sub-sub-class of prescriptions, and so on, down to the orders or commands, which refer to a single prescription concerning a single act to be performed by a category of individuals or just by one individual. This means that a *norm* is implemented through several laws; a *law* is implemented through several rules; and a *rule* is implemented by several particular *orders* or *commands*. Figs. 4.2 and 4.3

show the hierarchical arrangement of the various kinds of publicly-shared moral projects (or prescriptions): norms, laws, rules, and commands.

It is noteworthy that a class defined by a norm, or by a law, or by a rule is not only based on the extension of the "prescriptions" (i.e., of the prescribed or prohibited actions) that form the members of such class but also on the extension of the class of citizens involved. In other words, while a norm always directly involves all citizens (e.g., all citizens have the duty of not harming or killing others), laws, rules, and commands (in decreasing order) involve the citizens who belong to a defined class or who are in a defined condition (e.g., the laws and rules defining the duties of physicians). Thus, a norm is always universal, i.e., it refers to all the members of the class of men (within a State). A law may refer (i.e., may be directed) to a sub-class of men. A rule may refer to a sub-sub-class of men. It should be added that the rules issued by some executive authorities are directed to relatively small classes of citizens defined by their activity (such as the class of physicians) or by their territorial distribution (such as the inhabitant of a given city); examples are the *regulations* concerning the activity of some categories of citizens (e.g., the rules concerning the duties of physicians), or the *municipal ordinances*, issued by local governments, etc.

Moreover, since any action entails the existence of an agent as well as of a recipient, each norm, or law, or rule defines a class of actions as well as two corresponding classes of citizens: the agents and the recipients. Thus, the law about murdering will create at the same time a class of actions (the class of murders) and two classes of citizens (the class of the murderers and that of the murdered). Sometime there is (apparently) only one class of citizens (the agents), as in the case of the law that forbids pollution or the law that prescribes a class of citizens to pay a given tax at a given time. However, even if indirectly, all laws potentially affect some, many or all citizens, i.e., there is always the class of the "recipient" citizens ("recipient" of the action prescribed or forbidden by the "laws"); referring to the examples just cited, it is clear that pollution damage many and potentially all citizens, and that paying taxes serves to support the entire legal system and therefore indirectly affect all citizens. It should be noted that, concerning laws and rules, there is no close parallelism between the extensions of the prescribed actions and that of the citizens involved.

A final point is that the distinction into norms, laws, rules and commands should be regarded as a simplified scheme. Actually, a continuum between the various kinds of "laws" does exist. Moreover, I have not considered the point in this continuum that separates the "laws" enacted by the parliament from the "rules" or "regulations" issued by the Executive power.

(2) Indeterminacy of "Laws". Another important point is that the degree of *indeterminacy*, or of "open texture", decreases going from norms to laws, rules and commands (see chs. 4.1.1.1; 4.2.3; 4.3.1.1, *1a*).

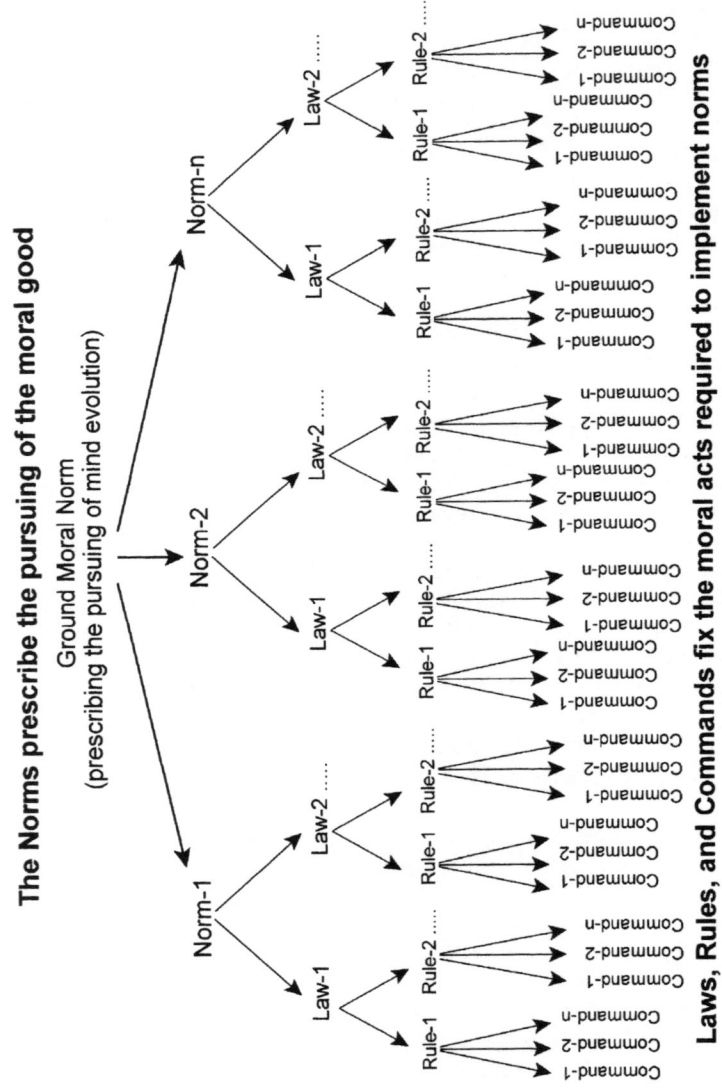

Fig. 4.2. Scheme showing the relationship between norms, laws, rules, and commands. The "ground moral norm" defines the largest class, comprising sub-classes (norm-1, norm-2, etc.), each of which comprises sub-sub-classes (law-1, law-2, etc.), each of which comprises sub-sub-sub-classes (rule-1, rule-2, etc.), each of which comprises several commands (hierarchical arrangement of norms, laws, rules, and commands).

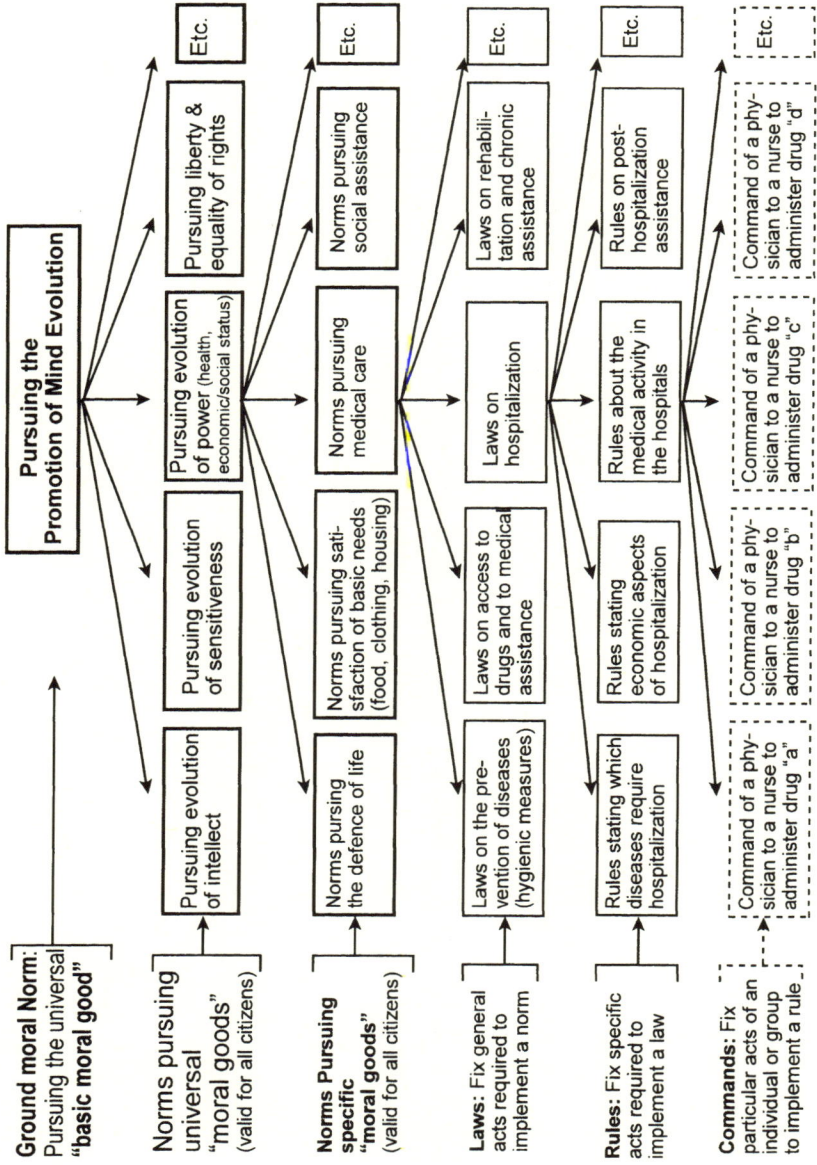

Fig. 4.3. Scheme showing the relationship between norms, laws, rules, and commands (hierarchical arrangement of norms, laws, rules, and commands), together with representative examples.

4.2—LEGAL THEORIES: CRITIQUE AND REINTERPRETATION

Defining the essence and nature of laws has been a difficult task, as it appears from the available literature (Austin 1832; Kelsen 1934; 1945; Hart 1961; Waldron 1990; Murphy and Coleman 1990; Leiter 1998; Bix, ed., 1999; Murphy 2006; Bix 2009; Marmor 2011). In the pages that follow, I will comment on, and reinterpret, some of the main legal theories.

4.2.1—Natural Law Theory

4.2.1.1—Classical Views on Natural Law

Traditionally, *natural law* has been conceived as concerning the laws created by God and, as such, morally just and superior to, and forming the basis of, any other law (Aquinas 1272: 76–157; Blackstone 1765–1769: 38, 41; Lisska 1998: 100–103). As classically stated by St. Augustine and by Aquinas, there is an essential link between law and morality, because moral validity would be required for legal validity. In his *City of God* (bk. xix:21) St. Augustine, as quoted by Aquinas *(Summa Theologica,* I–II, Q;96, Art.4— see: Pegis 1965), said that "An unjust law is no law at all." Aquinas added that a just law is a law that is in accordance with right reason (as it is rooted in eternal and natural law), so that if a law deviates from reason it is an unjust law; in such a case, it is no law at all, but rather an assertion of arrogance. A less radical view maintains that laws are not directly deduced from natural law and yet they are binding even if not fully just (Finnis 1980).

I think that the view that laws should be in accordance with reason raises some problems, since being in accordance with reason is a claim that lacks objectivity, so that different people, by following the "law of reason," may arrive at different conclusions. The affirmation by Aquinas that natural law consists of doing good and avoiding evil does not clarify this point, because there is no objective definition of what is "good" and what is "evil". The validity of the *principle of universalization* and of the maxim prescribing *to treat men as ends* and not as means, both proposed by Kant, have been questioned in previous chapters (chs. 2.2.1.1.3, *AI*; 2.2.1.1.5).

I underline that *the problem of the morality of law primarily concerns constitutional norms,* which express *(a)* publicly-shared *moral principles* (defined by moral thoughts, created by the rational consciousness), and *(b)* publicly-shared *moral values* (felt through moral feelings, created by the emotional consciousness) (Fig. 1.1).

(a) Publicly-shared *moral principles*, generated by moral thoughts, would correspond to the dictates of "reason", invoked by Aquinas. They represent the rational aspect of "natural laws". In my conception, however, moral principles, created by moral thoughts, consist of the awareness that the objective human *good* is the *evolution of mind*, which entails the ground moral norm of *promoting mind evolution*. Because of its *objectivity*, grounded on the essential property of the mind (of being capable of evolution), the ground moral norm that I propose could be regarded as the "true natural moral law". If we consider the "good" as the "evolution of one or more minds", we have an objective criterion to define what the "good" is. This, of course, does not avoid the existence of conflicting views about particular situations. Indeed, the ever increasing complexity of the human world makes it impossible to reduce the innumerable moral problems arising in the individual or social life to a simple one that can be easily resolved by following a well definite moral norm (chs. 2.1.6; 2.1.7; 3.1.2.5.3). This is especially true of the situations that entail *difficult moral choices* (chs. 2.2.1.5; 3.3).

(b) Publicly-shared *moral values*, felt through moral feelings, represent the emotional aspect of "natural laws". They express the profound feelings of the human soul and are available even to uneducated people; moreover, because of the internal coherence of the human mind, they are most often in keeping with moral principles (ch. 2.1.4.1, *b*).

Laws that are felt as "non-natural" (because they do not conform to moral principles and values) are not endorsed by most citizens, who may not *feel* and *recognize* themselves as obligated to obey these laws. These concepts help to distinguish *legal obligation* (being obliged) from *moral obligation* (recognizing and feeling to be obligated). Pure legal obligation (which actually is an alleged obligation) relies only upon the fear of the sanction (the violence exerted by power); moral obligation arises when an agent recognizes (through moral thoughts) and feels (through moral feelings) that a law should be obeyed because it is just (it conforms to the publicly-shared moral principles and values). Of course, legal and moral obligations co-exist in most instances of true *democratic* laws.

It should be remembered that, in the real world, constitutional norms (which express shared moral principles and values) are not endorsed by all, but by the largest possible majority of citizens and thus represent the *best approach to universality*. Moreover, it should be kept in mind that the restless evolution of the mind components, including the evolution of the consciousness, will lead through time to a progressive evolution and a greater degree of universalization of the publicly-shared moral norms. This should be reflected in changes in constitutional norms.

Considering that constitutional norms express the shared moral principles and that ordinary laws must respect constitutional norms, we could change St. Augustine's phrase, quoted at the beginning of this chapter, into the following two statements: "A constitutional norm which is not approved by the (largest possible) majority of citizens is not a constitutional norm at all"; and "A law that is anti-constitutional must be abrogated." In this new form, I think that no one could refuse to accept St. Augustine's motto.

4.2.1.2—Modern Views on Natural Law

4.2.1.2.1—The Ethical Basis of Law

(1) The Moral Content of Laws. The link between law and morality is a much-debated issue. It has been claimed that laws should be distinct from moral principles (Fusser 1996), or that laws may include moral principles although their validity does not depend on them (Raz 1979), or that laws should include both social criteria and the best possible moral justification (Dworkin, 1977; 1982; 1986). However, the close relationship between law and morality is recognized even by legal positivists, as shown by Hart's theory of the *minimum content* of natural law (Hart 1961: 193–200) (ch. 4.2.2.4). Likewise, Fuller (1964) notes that, though a system of laws may include some immoral laws, the majority of the laws should follow moral principles of justice and fairness ("internal morality of law" or "morality that makes law possible"), otherwise it is not a system of laws. These rather vague statements about the moral content of law should be changed into the statement that the moral content of law is the one defined by the constitutional norms; the moral content of the constitutional norms, in turn, reflects the shared (by the majority of citizens) moral principles and values. The latter express the *degree of evolution of the consciousness of the community*, which is the ultimate determinant of public morality; in my opinion, these principles and values are those that recognize mind evolution as "the good" and that can be attained by all men through their inward or moral activity.

(2) Dworkin's Position. Dworkin (1977: 17–45; 1986) contrasts Hart's conception according to which the legal system is based on *rules*, of which some could be safely and simply applied while others would be *open-textured* and would leave uncertainty especially in borderline cases; in these cases, judges would legislate by creative discretion to usefully cover a gap in the legislative system. According to Dworkin (1977: 31–39, 68–71), there is not such a creative legislation by judges, as in difficult or borderline cases, judges actual appeal to the general moral *principles* that are basic for the legal system and society. In addition, Dworkin (1977; 1986) maintains that a "principle" is "a standard that is to be observed, not because it will advance or secure an economic, political, or social situation deemed desirable, but because it is a requirement of justice or fairness or some other dimen-

sion of morality" (Dworkin 1977: 22). Moreover, principles are defined "by appealing to an amalgam of practice and other principles in which the implications of legislative and judicial history figure along with appeals to community practices and understandings" (Dworkin 1977: 36).

According to my theory, the above concepts should be reinterpreted as follows. Instead of distinguishing rules that can be simply applied and others that are open-textured, we should consider that the legal prescriptions (which are publicly-shared moral projects) possess a various degree of indeterminacy that decreases going from *norms* to *laws*, to *rules*, and to *commands* (chs. 4.1.1.1; 4.1.2.3; 4.2.3; 4.3.1.1, *1a*). I think that both Hart's theory of the "minimum content of natural law" and Dworkin's appeal to principles that refer to the "requirement of justice or fairness or some other dimension of morality" actually express the recognition of the necessity to provide *a moral basis for the law*. Concerning the indeterminacy of principles, I note that any legal prescription (be it a norm, a law, a rule, or a command) has always some degree of indeterminacy because a prescription defines a *class* of actions or acts that are similar but not identical to one another, and because any class is always determined by our intellect with *approximation* (ch. 1.1.3.2.1). Thus, the distinction between rules that are simple to apply and rules that are open-textured should be regarded as very uncertain. Moreover, Hart's open-textured rules should be regarded as roughly corresponding to Dworkin's "principles" or general moral values. Since the moral principles (and the norms that express them) are rather indeterminate, a certain degree of judicial discretion cannot be avoided (ch. 4.3). A central point is that the moral principles and values to which judges should refer in difficult cases are not just those that are basic for the legal system and society (as maintained by Dworkin) but should be the moral principles and values expressed by the constitutional norms, because these norms express the principles *publicly-shared* by the community and therefore are the only justified meter to elaborate *public* moral judgments (private or individual moral convictions, which with time may even prove to be the right ones, cannot be used to make *public* judgments—ch. 4.1.1.3.2, *B*). Thus, the moral principles on which judges can rely are only those stated in the constitution. Referring to the publicly-shared moral principles, as expressed in the constitution, overwhelms also the critique by MacIntyre (1981), who notes that in the field of morality there are many disagreements, so that there may not be a shared moral first principle in our society; actually, if it is true that there are not "universally" shared moral principles, it is also true that there are the (constitutional) principles publicly-shared by the "largest possible majority of citizens."

4.2.1.2.2—Political Obligation (Reasons to Obey the Law)

According to Hare (1989b: 8–20), there are several moral reasons to obey the law, based on the logical properties of the moral concepts, primarily on the *universalizability principle*. He distinguishes: *(a) social* moral obligations and duties, which are not derived from politics or laws but are linked to the respect for the interests of others (such as the duty to observe hygiene to prevent diseases to others); and *(b) political* moral obligations, which are linked to the existence of laws (e.g., the obligations related to property and theft). Hare (1989: 19–20) thinks that, in the case that a law is *not enforced*, there is a moral obligation to observe it if the law is still widely respected out of law-abidingness, whereas there is no obligation if the law has become a dead letter and if the law makes no difference to people's behavior.

Concerning *political* obligations, linked to laws, I would observe that (in a democratic State, to which I refer) laws have always a moral basis, inasmuch as the constitutional norms directly express the shared moral principles and values, and the ordinary laws (which must respect the constitutional norms) are directed to implement the constitutional norms in specific fields, thus ensuring that the constitutional principles and values are turned into practice. The laws of the State cover most of the "social" duties (such is the case of the duty of observing hygiene) that, therefore, are actually also political and legal duties; otherwise, they should be regarded as belonging to *private* ethics. Concerning the *non-enforced laws*, we should recall that laws (which are collective *projects* generated by the *intellect*) are ontologically distinguished from their enforcement (which is accomplished by the *executive* apparatus, whose activity belongs to the sphere of *power*) (chs. 4.1.1.3.2, *A*; 4.2.2.3.2, 2). Thus, even if not enforced, a law remains a law (i.e., a publicly-shared, collective project) and, as such, should be observed.

Hare (1989b: 7–20) discusses some instances in which breaking the law might appear, at first, as non-dangerous or even useful. Concerning the law about property, he considers the case in which the victim of theft is rich and the thief is poor; he notes that the claim that, in this condition, the theft would create a net gain in utility cannot be accepted, because this gain in utility would be outweighed by the increase in the cost to cope with an increased number of thefts (Hare 1989b: 16). Indeed, the case of a poor thief and a rich victim is rather complex, inasmuch as one should take into account how much poor is the poor thief, how much rich is the rich victim, and what are the conditions in which the theft occurs. I will just mention that an extremely poor man, who is dying because he does not have enough money to buy some bread, may be justified if he takes from a rich man the minimum he needs to survive, provided that no other possibilities are available. In cases like this, it seems ungenerous to say, as Hare does, that the utility would be outweighed by the increase in the cost to cope with an increased number of thefts. Of course, there are cases of uncertain evaluation (depending on the degree of the need of the poor thief and the richness of the rich victim, as well as other conditions). Yet, I add that each breaking of a law has, besides other effects linked to the specific moral value that any law protects, the general, morally-bad consequence of contributing to undermine the good functioning of the *legal system*, which, being the means through which human actions evolve toward universality, has an intrinsic moral value.

Hare (1989b: 16) also mentions the case of a person who uses electricity for space heating (contrary to government order) in a power shortage, without causing power stations breakdown (i.e., without any disadvantage to others) so that, from a utilitarian point of view, utility would be increased. However, Hare notes that, in this case, there is a disutility consisting of the frustration of a *desire* that nearly all of us have, namely, the desire not to be taken advantage of; in other words, nobody would accept the universal-prescriptive principle that people should be imposed upon, as it occurs in this case (Hare 1989b: 17). I object that the frustration of a *desire* cannot be the basis for a moral obligation. Rather, I note that the person who uses electricity for non-allowed scopes in a power shortage cannot know whether other persons do the same, which may cause power stations breakdown; thus, the illegal user of electricity actually increases the probability of a power stations breakdown, which would interfere with the practical activity of many people, i.e., would induce an *involution* of their *power* (besides contributing to undermining the legal system, which bears an intrinsic value—see above). Hare (1989b: 17) also mentions another kind of case: that of a person who picks primroses in the woods knowing that (most) others will not; Hare thinks that, even in this case, he who breaks the law takes advantage of those who observe it, thus frustrating their desire not to be taken advantage of (Hare 1989b: 17). I observe that picking primroses in the wood is a (very small!) bad moral action because it contributes to diminishing (to a very small extent) the beauty of the wood, which all citizens have the right to enjoy; in other words, picking primroses will diminish the *power* of citizens to enjoy a beauty that they are entitled to enjoy. In addition, there is the contribution to undermine the legal system and its moral value.

4.2.1.2.3—Interpretation of "Prior Law"

Dworkin (1982) argues that the work of judges is similar to that of *chain novelists*, i.e., a group of novelists engaged in writing, one after another, a chapter of a novel by interpreting what has been written by the prior writers in order to make continuing the novel better as a novel (i.e., they aim at reaching the best *aesthetical* standard). He thinks that judges act in a *chain of law*, by making creative decisions that, however, should be "going on as before" rather than start in a new direction; a judge must read what other judges in the past have written, in order to reach an opinion about what they have collectively done and give the best interpretation of past judicial decisions, i.e., the interpretation that shows these decisions in the best *political* light, coming as close as possible to the correct ideals of a just legal system (Dworkin 1982). Here, once again, I note that Dworkin's position lacks reference to a basic ontological conception. Indeed, I object that the comparison between novelists and judges is inappropriate, because novelists express their sentiments (thus acting in the sphere of *sensitiveness*) and, if they fail to express profound sentiments, they will just discredit *themselves* as novelists, whereas judges must apply the publicly-shared norms and laws (thus acting in the sphere of *intellect*) and, if they fail to apply appropriately these shared norms and laws, they will cause damage to *others*, since their decisions are not merely theoretical affirmations, but will be enforced by the executive apparatus (which belongs to the sphere of *power*), thus affecting the involved people. Moreover, I note that, instead of referring to "the best political light" or to "the correct ideals of a just legal system," judges should refer to the publicly-shared moral principles and values, stated in the constitution. In States where a written constitution does not exist (or leaves some areas uncovered), a situation of uncertainty arises. Even in these cases, however, judges should refer to the moral principles and values shared by the majority of the members of the community; they should be clever, careful, and sensitive observers of society to capture the moral principles and values shared by the majority of the community, and then they should apply these principles and values as fully and honestly as possible. The prior law should be considered as a body of authoritative examples of this effort to capture the shared principles and values.

Dworkin (1982) distinguishes two dimensions in the interpretation of prior law. *(a)* One is the *best-fit* dimension (an interpretation should fit the data it interprets), which raises several questions concerning how many prior decisions can an interpretation set aside as mistakes, whether later decisions should have more weight than the older, whether the interpretation should fit the opinions judges write as well as the decisions they take (these are *formal* issues). *(b)* The other dimension of interpretation contains the substantive ideals of political morality on which a judge relies (this is a matter of *substantive* justice):

A thoughtful judge might establish for himself . . . a rough 'threshold' of fit which any interpretation of data must fit . . . if more than one interpretation . . . meets this threshold, the choice . . . should be made . . . by choosing the interpretation which is 'substantively' better, that is, which better promotes the political ideals he thinks correct. (Dworkin 1982: 171)

Again, I note that a judge should refer not to the "political ideals he thinks correct" (because he is not making a personal or private judgment), but to the publicly-shared moral principles stated in the constitution norms (or otherwise captured), because he is exerting a public function.

4.2.2—Legal Positivism

As it is known, *legal positivism* is the doctrine that refers to the "positive law," i.e., to law as it is, or as it has been *posited* by humans (*analytical jurisprudence*), to be distinguished from the law as it ought to be (*normative jurisprudence*). The authority of laws would derive from the *will of a sovereign* that promulgates it and imposes sanctions (Austin 1832), or from defined *procedural rules* (Fuller 1964), or from criteria based on *social conventions* (Raz 1980). In the following pages, I will comment on, and reinterpret, some of the main concepts and theories about legal positivism.

4.2.2.1—Laws as Orders Backed by Threats

I will briefly discuss the view that laws are orders backed by threats, as it was conceived by Austin and by Kelsen.

(1) Austin's View. Austin (1832), the leading English legal positivist, hold that laws are *commands* (command theory of law), which are *general* commands (with regard to people and to acts), issued by the *sovereign*; they would be formed by two components: the *will* or *desire* of the sovereign (that a given action is made or not), and the ability of the commander to inflict a *sanction* to those who do not observe sovereign's will or desire. It is noteworthy that, according to Austin (1832), in a democracy, the electors, and not their elected representatives, form the free sovereign. Moreover, Austin thought that most of the constitutional law is *positive morality*, which he distinguished from the "critical morality". Thus, in the order (or command) backed by threats there would be the key to the science of jurisprudence (Austin 1832: 21); these orders should be *general* (as they refer to a class of person and a general type of conduct), *enduring*, and should be issued by an *authority* (person or body) internally supreme and externally independent, which is generally obeyed (toward which there is a general habit of obedience) (Austin 1832). This view has been considered valid not only for *rules of the criminal law*, which imposes duties, but also for those *rules that confer power* to private individual and to public officials and courts. This is possible if the meaning of the sanction is widened to include the nullity of a legal act when it does not adhere to the rules that govern it.

Thus, as noted by Hart (1958), according to Austin (1832) the conception of law is based on the simple *trilogy* of *(a) command, (b) sanction, (c) sovereign*, to which a fourth component could be added: *(d) the "pedigree"*. In my view, all three of Austin's concepts are questionable, as they are not framed into a conception grounded on an ontological basis.

(a) Austin's "commands". A command is an order given by an individual or a body *"a"* to another individual or body, *"b"*. In an absolute monarchy, the King can issue an order directed to the population (i.e. to all citizens), because the status of the King differs from that of the population. In a democratic State, however, as recognized by Austin himself, the electors (i.e., the citizens), and not their elected representatives, form the free sovereign; indeed, the elected representatives represent the citizens, so that they cannot issue "orders" directed to the citizens, because this would mean that citizens (through their representatives) give "orders" to themselves. Thus, in my opinion, when citizens, through their representatives, enact a law, they actually create a *publicly-shared* (or *collective*) *project*, i.e., a project endorsed by the majority of citizens about some action that should, or should not, be done by all citizens (ch. 4.1.1.1) (laws, being projects, are produced by the *intellect*).

(b) Austin's "sanctions". In an absolute monarchy, the King summarizes in himself the legislative, the executive and the judiciary powers. In a democratic State, however, these three powers should be separated. Actually, in a democratic State, the sanctions are applied by "officials" belonging to the executive apparatus, which represents the *power* component of the mind; in contrast, the legislative organ (parliament), being the organ that enacts the laws, i.e., that created *publicly-shared* (or *collective*) *projects*, expresses the project-making activity of *intellect*. Therefore, sanctions (which belong to the sphere of the *power*) are *ontologically distinct* from laws (which belong to the sphere of *intellect*) (ch. 4.2.6.3).

(c) Austin's "sovereign". In an absolute monarchy, the King represents the sovereign. In a democratic State, however, the citizens form the sovereign. Thus, in an ideal condition, a law should represent a project endorsed by all the citizens. In the real world, no law is approved by *all* the citizens. Therefore, the enacted laws represent the projects endorsed by the *majority* of the citizens; for each law, the issuing organ should attempt to obtain the approval by the *largest possible majority* of citizens, which represents the *best approach to universality*. What is important to note is that, in a democratic State, the "sovereignty" which enacts the laws coincides with those who should obey the law, as both are represented by all citizens (not only by voting citizens, because the latter also represent those who do not vote, such as those under age).

At this point, a mention should be made to the possibility, envisaged by Crenshaw et al. (1995), that even in a democratic State the laws are actually influenced by the culture and interest of the prevailing groups, such as whites, males, etc. (which would represent the true sovereign). I object that no prevailing group can exist if the government is fully democratic (and, therefore, respects the freedom of thought, speech, press, association, etc., of the minority), and if it expresses the projects of the majority with the respect and consideration for the minority (ch. 3.1.2.1, 2).

(d) The "pedigree". Based on the consideration that laws must be emanated by a sovereign, positivists maintain that a law "can be identified and distinguished," to use the words of Dworkin (1977: 17), "by specific criteria, by tests having to do not with their content but with their *pedigree* or the manner in which they were adopted or developed." Thus, a law would be a command with a *pedigree,* i.e., a command whose origin can be traced to the sovereign, i.e., to those individuals (or to that individual) who, *de facto,* define with their activity the legality in a given legal system. This view cannot be accepted for two reasons: *first,* because laws are not commands, as discussed above; *second,* because instead of just a pedigree, laws should have a *publicly justified pedigree,* i.e. they should be enacted by a *publicly justified sovereign* (such as a democratically elected parliament), and not simply from a *de facto* sovereign, and through a procedure defined by *publicly-shared* norms and laws.

(2) Kelsen's View. Kelsen (1934; 1945), in his conception of law, confers weight to the sanction. He considers the "law as a coercive order" (Kelsen 1945: 18), which enacts "coercive measures as sanctions," in contrast to other orders whose "efficacy . . . rests not on coercion but on voluntary obedience" (Kelsen 1945: 19), although the distinction between the two orders is not a clear-cut one. Moreover, Kelsen (1945: 38) says: "General legal norms always have the form of hypothetical statements. The sanction stipulated by the norm is stipulated under certain conditions." Kelsen (1945: 112–13) also distinguishes: a "static system of norms," consisting of norms that can be derived from the basic norm, which should be obeyed because of their content, whose validity and obligatory nature are regarded as self-evident; and a "dynamic system of norms," consisting of norms that cannot be derived by intellectual operations from the basic norm. They "may have any kind of content . . . The validity of a legal norm cannot be questioned on the ground that its contents are incompatible with some moral or political value." (Kelsen 1945: 113). Moreover, according to Kelsen (1945: 122) "law is anything that has come about in the way the constitution prescribes for the creation of law." Yet, through the same constitutional procedure established for the enactment of laws, other acts can be created that have no legal character, such as the recognition of the merits of a statesman; a law is such "if it purports to regulate human behavior, and if it regulates human behavior by providing an act of coercion as sanction" (Kelsen 1945: 123). The efficacy and the validity of a norm would be distinct and yet correlated:

A norm is considered to be valid only on the condition that it belongs to a system of norms, to an order which, on the whole, is efficacious. Thus, efficacy is a condition of validity; a condition, not the reason of validity. A norm is not valid *because* it is efficacious; it is valid *if* the order to which it belongs is, on the whole, efficacious. (Kelsen 1945: 42)

The above considerations suggest that Kelsen regarded the various laws as *conditional orders* to officials to apply the sanctions, i.e., as *hypothetical conditions* the occurrence of which must be followed by the application of sanctions. Kelsen (1934; 1945) maintained that it is enough that the sanction (which may be punitive or *privative* sanctions) is stipulated or predetermined by the law; hence, the claim that "law is the primary norm, which stipulates the sanction" (Kelsen 1945: 61). Thus, the conception of Kelsen is characterized by a very close relationship between the "law" and the "sanction", which, on the contrary, I think are distinct entities, because the former is a *publicly-shared project* produced by the *intellect* whereas the latter is a coercive public action produced by the *power*.

4.2.2.2—The Internal View of Laws

According to Hart (1961: 82–91), laws must be obeyed not because we are afraid of the sanctions (in which instance we could say that we were *obliged* to obey) but because we think (or we feel) to have the *obligation* to obey (so that failure to obey is associated with shame, remorse, and guilt, as well as with blame from the community). Thus, Hart (1961) maintains that we should distinguish between being *obligated* (or having the duty) to obey a command, and to be *obliged* (or forced by violence) to obey. Hart (1961: 88–91) notes that to think or to feel that we have an obligation or duty means that we have an *internal view* of the rules or laws. Some individuals may have an *external view* of laws and obey them only for fear of punishment. It follows that *to have* an obligation should be distinguished from *to feel* obligated, as it is possible that an individual who has an obligation does not feel to have it.

Let us analyze Hart's concept of the *internal view* of laws (entailing that one *thinks* and/or *feels* to have the *obligation* to obey the laws) by discussing the following three aspects.

(1) The "Internal View of Laws" as a Moral Obligation. If having an internal view of laws means to think and/or to feel to have the obligation to obey laws, such that failure to obey is associated with shame, remorse, and guilt, and with blame from the community, this means that the obligation to obey laws is a *moral obligation*. It follows that Hart's conception does not merely allow a minimum content of natural law, but should be regarded as a conception that regards laws as fully *moral laws* and the obligation to obey

laws as a fully *moral obligation*. Moreover, in order for citizens to think and feel to have the obligation to obey laws (i.e., to endorse laws), laws must reflect moral principles and values shared by citizens (or by most of them), i.e., laws must be enacted by a democratic government, which, as such, is recognized by citizens as representing (most of) themselves; otherwise, if the government were non-democratic, there would be no reason why citizens should think and feel to have the obligation to obey laws (in a non-democratic State, citizens might only have an *external view* of laws, and would obey for fear). Only occasionally could the laws of a non-democratic State be endorsed by citizens. It should be pointed out, however, that in a democratic State laws only represent the projects (directed to implement moral principles and values) of the majority of citizens, so that a minority of citizens may not approve some of the laws. This minority, however, is bound to obey the laws because laws, being approved by the majority, represent the best approach to universality and, therefore, fix the standard for *public morality*. In other words, the minority of citizens must obey laws because they recognize the democratic *system*, which, allowing the universalization of human action, has itself a moral value (chs. 3.1.1.2, 2; 4.2.1.2.2). Certainly, citizens belonging to the minority are entitled to follow their own principles and values in their *private life* (i.e., as far as their behavior as individuals is concerned) but in *public life* (i.e., concerning their behavior as citizens) they have the duty to follow the public standard of morality, fixed by the norms and laws in force. In other words, *public morality*, defined by norms and laws, should be distinguished from *private morality*, based on personal rules, which reflect personal principles and values (ch. 4.1.1.3.2, *B*).

(2) The Meaning of Thinking (or Feeling) to Have an Obligation. The statement that citizens should "think" and "feel" to have an obligation to obey the law can be given an ontological explanation. I mentioned above that Hart's conception could be regarded as actually considering laws as *moral laws* and the obligation to obey laws as a *moral obligation*. A moral obligation or duty is a product of *consciousness* and has two components (Fig. 1.1): *(a)* one consists of a *moral thought* (produced by the *rational consciousness*) that leads to "think" or recognize something (in this instance, a law) as morally good; *(b)* the other consists of a *moral feeling* (produced by the *emotional consciousness*) that leads to "feel" that something (in this instance, a law) is morally good and should be pursued.

(3) The External View of Laws as an Immoral Position. Here two conditions should be considered separately: *(a)* In a *democratic State*, if thinking and feeling that laws must be obeyed is a moral duty, obeying laws only for fear of punishment means to be in an immoral position, both concerning *moral thought* and *moral feeling* (apart from the case of the good dissenting citizen—ch. 4.1.1.3.2, *B*). *(b)* In a non-democratic State, where laws are

merely arbitrary orders (not publicly justified), the reverse is true, as moral-ly-good citizens do not think or feel that they are obligated to obey unjust and unjustified laws, and only immoral citizens may endorse these laws.

4.2.2.3—The System of Primary and Secondary Rules

4.2.2.3.1—The Distinction of Primary from Secondary Rules

According to Hart (1961: 79–99), a legal system should consist of *primary rules*, or *rules of obligation*, as well as of *secondary rules* or *rules of recognition, of change, and of adjudication*. This is because a society with only primary rules, Hart notes, would have some defects, which are corrected by secondary rules. Hart's considerations about a society with only primary rules can be summarized in the following three points.

(1) It would be a society with a *static character*, because changes in rules can only occur by the slow process of changes in habits. This defect is corrected by the secondary rules of *recognition*, which provide an authorita-tive way to recognize the existence of a rule as well as its true meaning and scope, thus introducing a criterion for legal validity. Indeed, in modern, complex, legal systems there may be multiple criteria for identifying the law, which are ranked in an order of relative subordination and primacy, so that one of them is *supreme*.

(2) It would be a society marked by *uncertainty*, because doubts may arise about the meaning and precise scope of a given rule. This defect is prevented by the secondary rules of *change*, which define the person or body entitled to introduce new rules as well as the procedures for such changes.

(3) It would be a society marked by *inefficiency* in ascertaining the vio-lations of rules and in administrating the punishment. This defect is correct-ed by the secondary rules of *adjudication*, which confer judicial power and empower individuals to make authoritative determinations about the break-ing of primary rules.

I think that actually a society with only primary rules cannot exist. To clarify this statement, it should be considered that the various kinds of "rules" identified by Hart actually have an *ontological basis* (Table 4.1), and, therefore, they *must* be present in all societies. As also discussed later on (ch. 4.2.2.3.2), this is shown by the following considerations.

First, the secondary rules of recognition represent the constitutional moral norms, which express the shared *moral principles* and *values* pro-duced by the *consciousness* (the *rational consciousness* and the *emotional consciousness*, respectively—Fig. 1.1). There is no society without a con-sciousness and, therefore, without some shared moral principles and values.

Second, the secondary rules of change and of adjudication represent the constitutional *structural norms*, which define the structure and functioning of the legislative and judicial organs required to make it possible to implement moral principles and values.

Third, the primary rules of obligations represent ordinary laws (again, produced by the *rational consciousness*), which regulate human actions and acts by implementing the constitutional norms (Fig. 1.1); since a society consists of a certain number of individuals whose actions are regulated by laws, there is no society that does not have laws (written or unwritten).

Thus, instead of speaking of hypothetical societies with only primary rules, one should speak of societies in which the various kinds of rules are undistinguished and enacted and applied by just one "organ". This perhaps happened in some of the ancient *direct democracies*; examples might be some ancient City-States in which the popular assembly acted as the legislative and judicial organ. This might also hypothetically happen in representative democracies, where an elected assembly would act as the legislative authority (for both primary and secondary rules) and as the judicial organ. In contrast, in the modern *constitutional democracies* there is a distinction between *(a)* ordinary laws and rules (Hart's primary rules) and their issuing organ and/or procedure, and constitutional norms (Hart's secondary rules of recognition, change, and adjudication) and their issuing organ and/or procedure. Moreover, the distinction of rules is related to that of powers (ch. 4.2.6.3), since the rules of changes are related to the activity of the *legislative organ* whereas the rules of adjudication are related to the activity of the *judicial organ* (both belonging to the sphere of the *intellect*). I also note that in the conception of Hart there might be an overlooking of the separateness of the laws (of adjudication—belonging to the sphere of *intellect*) from their enforcement by the executive apparatus (belonging to the sphere of *power*).

Hart (1961: 79–99) also underlines the following points:

(a) The rules of changes have some relationship with the power-conferring rules, i.e., rules that confer to individuals a limited legislative power, i.e., the "power" to make such acts as wills, contracts, transfers of property, etc. (Hart 1961: 96). I note that the so-called power-conferring rules are actually laws that protect some rights of citizens (in the example cited, the right of property).   ˙

(b) The rules of adjudication are also rules of recognition, because determining if a rule has been broken entails also determining what that rule actually is (Hart 1961: 97). This statement seems questionable, since it is quite possible that an organ determines whether a rule (whose validity has been certified by a different organ) has been broken in a particular case. The judicial organ does not ascertain what a law or rule is, because a law or rule is the *definition of a class* of actions (a definition that is always *approximate*—ch. 1.1.3.2.1), whereas the task of a judge is to ascertain whether a

particular action is, or is not, member of a given class of actions. In other words, the determination of what a law or rule is can only be done by focusing on what a *class of actions* is, whereas the determination whether a law or rule has been broken in a particular instance is done by focusing on a *particular action*, to verify if it is a *member of a class* of actions (in doing this, a certain discretion cannot be avoided—ch. 4.3). The statement that the rules of adjudication are also rules of recognition is only valid when referred to the constitutional court.

(c) Hart (1961: 58–66) also underlines that a legal system requires that there is *continuity* between the legislator and his successor as well as *persistence* of laws over generations of both legislators and population. I object that lack of "continuity" and "persistence", as defined above, can only occur in a non-democratic State (say, an absolute monarchy or a dictatorship, and is linked to the "going to power" of a new King or a new dictator) but not in a democratic State because, in the latter, laws are enacted by the body of the representatives of the community (laws are community-shared, or collective, projects) on behalf of all citizens, i.e., of society. This entails that there is no passage from a legislator and his successor, but only a slow, continuous change in practical interests and moral values of society that will be reflected in corresponding changes in the laws enacted by the representatives of society (members of parliament). Therefore, a law remains valid until a new law suppresses or changes or substitutes it. In other words, if a new generation of the population no longer likes a law, it has just one way to express this desire and to implement it: to introduce, through the elected representative, the desired changes into the existing body of laws.

4.2.2.3.2—The Nature of Secondary Rules (Rules of Recognition)

In the lines that follow, some issues concerning the "rules of recognition" will be discussed.

(1) "A Matter of Fact" versus "Best Approach to Universal Moral Norms". According to Hart (1961: 100–110), the rules of recognition are ultimate rules because, whereas they provide criteria for the assessment of the validity of other rules, there would not be rules providing criteria for the assessment of the legal validity of the rules of recognition. Thus, the validity of rules of recognition could be assumed but not demonstrated. Accepting a rule of recognition would not be a matter of legal validity but rather a sort of assignment of value; it would be the recognition that a rule is "accepted as appropriate . . . [and that] its validity is assumed but cannot be demonstrated" (Hart 1961: 109) and that it is applied by the general system. Moreover, whereas a primary rule exists even if it is generally disregarded, a rule of recognition exists only if it is generally endorsed, i.e., generally

recognized, from an internal point of view, and applied. "*Its existence is a matter of fact*" (Hart 1961: 110). I observe that the concept that rules of recognition are "a matter of fact" is the result of the "observation" of what, according to Hart, rules of recognition (i.e., the constitutional norms) actually are: they are norms recognized as appropriate and applied by the general system. This definition, given by Hart (1961), may be satisfactory for jurists or lawyers but not for philosophers. The latter are engaged in understanding *why* constitutional norms are accepted as appropriate, and by *whom* they are accepted. In this regard, the following points are of interest.

(*a*) A *constitutional norm* is produced by the *consciousness* of the community, and is directed to realize universal and collective (or publicly-shared) *projects* directed to implement moral principles and values. The latter are moral thoughts and moral feelings produced by the inward activity of the intellect (*rational consciousness*) and by the inward activity of the sensitiveness (*emotional consciousness*), respectively (Fig. 1.1). As such, constitutional norms are directed to pursue the "common good", as defined elsewhere (chs. 1.1.1.2.4; 2.1.4.1; 2.2.1.1.1, *1*; 3.1.2.5.1, *3*). Thus, constitutional norms express the common consciousness and, as such, have an *ontological basis*. This means that any free community necessarily has moral thoughts and moral feelings shared by the majority of the community members; these moral thoughts and feelings indicate what is the shared common good and are expressed by the constitutional norms.

(*b*) I have already mentioned that constitutional norms should be endorsed by the largest possible majority of citizens, so that they can represent the *best approach to universality*. By using Hart's words, we could say that constitutional norms should be "accepted as appropriate" by the largest possible majority of citizens. This means that there may be a minority of citizens that does not endorse the constitutional norms; yet, even these citizens are bound to obey the constitutional norms because these norms represent the best approach to universality; if the view of this minority of citizens was adopted as a constitutional norm, it would possess a *lower* degree of universality and, therefore, accepting it would be morally bad. From this reasoning, it follows that the statement by Hart (1961: 109), referring to a constitutional norm, that "its validity is assumed but cannot be demonstrated," is not true. If a constitutional norm does not pass the test of possessing the highest possible degree of universality, it is not valid. Thus, if a proposed constitutional norm receives 80% of favorable votes and a different one a much lower percentage of favorable votes, the former has been proved to be valid, in virtue of *the principle of the best approach to universality*. The validity of a constitutional norm can be demonstrated during the work of the constituent assembly (when a constitution is created) or subsequently through procedures that should be provided by the constitution itself, consisting either of an approval by a "qualified" majority of votes by parliament or by a referendum.

Thus, Hart's concept that accepting a rule of recognition means accepting it as appropriate, should be changed into the concept that creating, and therefore accepting, a constitutional norm means to define the moral principles and values shared by the largest possible majority of citizens; such a norm, therefore, should represent *the best approach to universality*. Thus, *the ultimate justification of constitutional norms* (and hence of the publicly-shared moral principles and values) *lies in the fact that they are the best approach to universality*; it is impossible to go beyond this limit. Of course, through time, often through centuries, the community's consciousness (like the other components of the mind) evolves, and this will be reflected in changes in constitutional norms. An example is the right to vote, which was not recognized to women in the past (in Switzerland until recently) but that today, due to the evolution of the *consciousness*, is recognized in all Western democracies.

(2) Validity (Existence) and Efficacy of Laws. As it has been noted (Murphy and Coleman 1990: 32), Hart's rules of recognition, by providing a *norm* to establishing the existence of a given law, make it possible to distinguish the *normative* existence of a law from its *factual* existence: a law is such if originated as defined by the rules of recognition, even if nobody obeys it. Thus, the "validity" of a law should be distinguished from its "efficacy" (the fact that a given law is obeyed more often than not) (Hart 1961: 100–110). I have discussed the relationship between the existence, validity, efficacy (I would say *efficaciousness*), observance, and enforcement of a law in chapter 4.1.1.3.2, *A*. Here I recall that a law (being a universal and collective project) is created by the *intellect*, and therefore is *ontologically distinct* from its enforcement, which belongs to the sphere of the *power*. What Hart calls the "efficacy" of a law, i.e., the degree of its observance, will depend both on factors inherent to the law itself (its "efficaciousness") and external to it (the "strength" of the enforcing apparatus).

(3) The Search for a Basic Norm: Kelsen's "Grundnorm" and the "Ground Norm Prescribing the Promotion of Mind Evolution". In chapter 4.1.2.3, I presented a hierarchical arrangement of "laws", ordered into a system of classes and sub-classes depending on the most general *ground moral norm*, prescribing the promotion of mind evolution. I also distinguished norms (which are actually constitutional norms, and which prescribe the pursuing of moral principles and values) from laws, rules, and commands (which prescribe some practical acts directed to implement norms) (Figs. 4.2 and 4.3). Thus, my *ground moral norm* is the basic and unifying norm of the legal system.

The search for a "basic norm" capable of justifying the entire legal system has been the worry of jurists.

Kelsen (1945: 112–13) distinguishes: *(a)* a "static system of norms" (roughly corresponding to constitutional norms), consisting of norms that can be derived, by means of an intellectual operation (inference from the general to the particular) from the basic norm ("Grundnorm"), which should be obeyed "by virtue of their contents," whose validity and obligatory nature are regarded as "self-evident," like the principle of truthfulness or a still more general norm such as that of living in harmony with the universe (example: "You must not lie"); and *(b)* a "dynamic system of norms" (roughly corresponding to ordinary laws), consisting of norms that cannot be derived by intellectual operations from the basic norm, and that are valid by virtue of the fact that they are created according to a definite rule. He says:

> Law regulates its own creation . . . Since a legal norm is valid because it is created in a way determined by another legal norm, the latter is the reason of validity of the former . . . The legal order . . . is . . . a hierarchy of different levels of norms . . . [T]he creation of one norm—the lower one—is determined by another—the higher—the creation of which is determined by a still higher norm, and . . . this *regressus* is terminated by a highest, the basic norm which, being the supreme reason of validity of the whole legal order, constitutes its unity. (Kelsen 1945: 124)

But, what is this basic norm? It should be a norm whose validity and obligatory nature is "self-evident" (see above); or perhaps is it derived from moral norms or political principles? Kelsen says:

> The expression 'source of law' is finally used also in an entirely non-juristic sense. One thereby denotes also all those ideas which actually influence the law-creating organs, for instance, moral norms, political principles, legal doctrines, the opinions of juristic experts, etc. . . . [T]hese 'sources' do not as such have any binding force [unless they are converted into legal norms]. (Kelsen 1945: 132)

But, which are these hypothesized moral norms and political principles? Actually, Kelsen did not clarify this point and, in his last and unfinished work, he considered the *grundnorm* as a necessary "fiction" for accounting for legal normativity (Kelsen 1979: 256). He wrote:

> [T]he Basic Norm of a positive moral or legal system is not a positive norm, but a merely thought norm (i.e. a fictitious norm), the meaning of a merely fictitious, and not a real, act of will . . . the assumption of a Basic Norm . . . is also self-contradictory, since it represents the empowering of an ultimate moral or legal authority and so emanates from an authority—admittedly, a fictitious authority—even higher than this one . . . [T]he Basic Norm is not a hypothesis . . . but a fiction. A fiction differs from a hypothesis in that it is accompanied—or thought to be accompanied—by the awareness that reality does not agree with it." (Kelsen 1979: 256).

Likewise, Hart, although he attempts to provide a justifying basis for his secondary rules through the theory of the *minimum content* of natural law

(Hart 1961: 193–200), actually recognizes that the existence of secondary rules (constitutional norms) *"is a matter of fact"* (Hart 1961: 110).

These failed attempts to find a "basic" norm as a support of a legal system indicate that, without a reference to an ontological conception, it is impossible to find a justification for both moral principles and values, and the corresponding moral and legal norms. My ontological conception of the structure and functioning of the mind allows me to recognize what is the objective moral good, i.e., to recognize moral principles and values, which converge into the *ground moral norm prescribing the promotion of mind evolution*, and the norms derived from it; the latter norms, in turn, justify laws, rules, and commands issued for implementing them.

(4) The Continuum Linking the Secondary to the Primary Rules. Hart (1961: 79–99) introduced the distinction between primary and secondary rules, which roughly corresponds to the distinction between ordinary "laws" and constitutional "norms". I underline that there is an ontological basis for distinguishing norms from laws, rules and commands. In fact, while both norms and the other forms of "laws" are publicly-shared projects created by the inward, project-making activity of intellect, they differ as far as their objects are concerned. Indeed, norms are general projects that concern the moral principles and values (which are moral thoughts and moral feelings created by the inward activity of *intellect* and of *sensitiveness*, respectively) whereas laws, rules and commands are specific projects that concern the concrete acts and actions (i.e., the procedures), belonging to the sphere of the power, directed to implement the norms. Yet, this distinction should be understood as a flexible (and not a rigid) one, because intermediate steps do exist and, therefore, all kinds of "laws" (understood in a broad sense) can actually be arranged along a *continuum*, going from the ground norm to the more particular commands.

Table 4.1 compares Hart's "rules" with my "publicly-shared projects" (i.e., norms, laws, rules, and commands—see also Fig. 4.3). Table 4.1 shows that the distinction made by Hart is based on the functional scope of the various "rules" whereas mine is made on an ontological basis (it establishes what the various kinds of "laws" *are*). In other words, Hart's view is that a society should *decide* to equip itself with different kinds of "rules" in order to avoid the static character, uncertainty, and inefficiency of a system with only primary rules. In contrast, my position is that the various kinds of "laws" *are* ontologically distinct, as they are concerned with the products of the different mind components: typically, "secondary rules of recognition" (constitutional norms) are concerned with the *moral principles* and *values* (produced by the inward activity of *intellect* and *sensitiveness*, respectively) that should be implemented whereas the "primary rules" (ordinary laws, rules and commands) are concerned with the *moral acts* and the morally-good *actions* (sphere of *power*) required to implement norms.

Table 4.1. Hart's "rules" (and their functional distinction) *versus* my "laws" or "universal/collective projects" or "universal/publicly-shared projects" (and their ontological distinction)

Classification of Hart's "Rules"		Ontological Classification of "Laws" (or "Universal/Collective Moral Projects")	
TYPES OF RULES	FUNCTIONAL SCOPE	TYPES OF SHARED PROJECTS	ONTOLOGICAL BASIS
Secondary rules of recognition[1]	To ascertain the existence and meaning (validity) of rules	Constitutional *moral norms* (pursuing the *common good* as defined by moral principles and values, valid for all men)	They are *universal/publicly-shared moral projects*[2] that pursue the common good, by implementing *moral principles* (produced by the *inward* activity of intellect[3]) and *moral values* (produced by the *inward activity of sensitiveness*[3])
Secondary rules of change	To define the authority that introduces and changes rules	Constitutional *structural norms* (or *shared projects*) on: *(a)* legislative organs that create norms and laws, and *(b)* executive organs	They define: *(a)* the organs that enact *publicly-shared projects*, and *(b)* the organs forming the executive apparatus, belonging to the *inward activity of power* and favoring citizens' good *outward actions*[4]
Secondary rules of adjudication	To confer judicial power	Constitutional *structural norms* (or *publicly-shared projects*) on judicial organs	They define the organs that enact judgments (created by the *outward activity of intellect*) on the *belonging of a particular action to a law-defined class of actions*
Primary rules of obligation	To impose obligations and duties	*Ordinary laws* including rules, regulations, commands, etc. (refer to "classes of men"[5] of variable comprehensiveness[6])	They are *universal/publicly-shared projects* (created by the *inward activity of intellect & sensitiveness*[3]) that define public *moral acts* needed to implement norms (while favoring citizens' morally-good selfish *actions*)

1. No justification of these rules is given; their existence is a matter of fact.

2. They are the ultimate standard of public or *shared morality*. Through time, they may evolve together with the *evolution* of the *community consciousness*.

3. *Inward activity of intellect* and *inward activity of sensitiveness* represent the *rational consciousness* and the *emotional consciousness*, respectively, and, together with the *inward activity of power* (or *practical consciousness*), form the *consciousness* as a whole (Fig. 1.1).

4. The executive apparatus (which applies and enforces the ordinary laws) belongs to both the *inward* and the *outward activity of power*, because its activity consists in exerting universal and publicly-shared *moral acts* (directed to pursue moral ends) and in regulating and favoring the morally-good selfish *actions* of all citizens (while acting itself as a selfish and efficacious agent) (chs. 4.1.1.3.1; 4.2.6.3).

5. Each law or rule defines a class of actions as well as two corresponding classes of citizens: the agents or actors and the recipients. Sometime there is (apparently) only one class of citizens (the agents); yet, even if indirectly, all laws affect some or all citizens (ch. 4.1.2.3, *E1*; Fig. 4.3).

6. Commands may refer to small classes of citizens or even to a single citizen.

4.2.2.4—Laws and Morals

4.2.2.4.1—The "Minimum Content of Natural Law" Theory

According to Hart (1961), naturally good actions can be defined, apart from deep philosophical assumptions, by reference to survival of the involved individuals, considering that a basic human desire is the desire to live and survive. He says:

> The actions which we speak of as those which are naturally good to do, are those which are required for survival; the notions of a human need, of harm, and of the *function* of bodily organs or changes rests on the same simple fact . . . [W]e can . . . discard . . . the notion that this is something antecedently fixed which men necessarily desire because it is their proper goal or end. Instead we may hold it to be a mere contingent fact which could be otherwise, that in general men do desire to live, . . . (Hart 1961: 191, 192).

He thinks that this elementary but diffusely recognized principle may be considered as the minimum content of Natural Law, which is defendable because it is based on the elementary truth that the aim of human beings is survival. The "aim of survival" (Hart 1961: 191) would be the basis for most of the requirements of both law and morals. In particular, Hart (1961: 193–200) points out the following.

(a) Human vulnerability, together with the aim of survival, would be the basis for prohibition, by both law and morals, of injuring human body or of killing (Hart 1961: 194–95). I underline that the aim to survive is just one of the requirements of morals, the basic or minimum one; yet, other largely recognized requirements do exist, such as the requirements of being free, of receiving education and information, of having a minimum of welfare, etc. Who would deny that (in addition to injury and death) extreme ignorance or extreme poverty should be regarded as bad, even if they allow a mere survival? Indeed, in my view, preserving life represents the initial, starting point of *mind evolution*, which is a continuous and endless process that involves not only physical health and the wealth (sphere of the *power*) but also the evolution in the field of knowledge (sphere of the *intellect*) and the sensitivity of the soul (sphere of the *sensitiveness*). Moreover, in addition to the *outward* activity of intellect, sensitiveness, and power (i.e., the selfish mind activity), one should also consider their *inward* mind activity (i.e., the moral mind activity), which represents the activity of the *consciousness*; thus, both the outward and the inward mind activity should be considered. In more philosophical terms, moral requirements are those that make possible the concrete enjoyment of an *evolution-allowing, involution-avoiding condition*, i.e. that allow the evolution of the mind in all its components, which represents the true *moral good* (chs. 1.1.1.2.4; 2.1.4.1; 2.2.1.1.1, *1*). Limiting the requirements of morals to the aim to survive is too limited a

view and reveals the lack of a supporting philosophical conception. A society that pursues and defends, through its laws, the mere survival of its citizens would be a very miserable society! Of course, it is highly possible that in a primitive community the publicly-shared moral principles and values were limited to the defense of survival, and that this was reflected in the issued laws. However, public morality evolves through time (decades, centuries, or millennia), reflecting the *evolution of the consciousness* of the community. Thus, in modern, democratic States (to which I refer), publicly-shared norms and laws are not limited to the defense of survival, but also include the pursuing of most of the "universal human rights"; in other words, they include all those norms and laws required to ensure the equal enjoyment of the *evolution-allowing, involution-avoiding condition* to all citizens.

It is noteworthy that, in order for moral requirements to shape legal rules, they must be moral requirements accepted by the majority of citizens, i.e., they must be moral principles and values whose pursuing is included in the constitutional norms; this is because laws should reflect *public* morality.

(b) The *approximate equality* in strength among men would be the basis for "a system of mutual forbearance and compromise which is the base of both legal and moral obligation" (Hart 1961: 195); conversely, the difference in strength between States would have made international laws to be limited to minor issues and has prevented the organization of sanctions (Hart 1961: 198). The claim that men are approximately equal in strength may be accepted if one refers to physical strength. Yet, it is not the mere physical strength, but the degree of the evolution of the *power* that counts, which depends (apart from physical health) on economic, political and social factors; so understood, "strength" (actually, the "power") varies to a great extent among citizens. Thus, "a system of mutual forbearance and compromise" is not based on the equality of strength but on the moral principle that all humans are equally entitled to enjoy the *evolution-allowing, involution-avoiding condition*.

(c) According to Hart (1961: 196), the *limited resources* available to men make the institution of property necessary, and this entails some form of forbearance. This statement is questionable. Although I recognize and defend the principle of private property (ch. 3.2.3.2), I note that the limitation of resources could make necessary, for the "survival" of all the citizens, the suppression of private property in favor of public property. Moreover, I note that, in any case, private property is not closely linked to the "aim of survival" but rather to the maintenance or to the increase of one's own power (this may be an expression of both *morally-bad* or *morally-good egoism*—ch. 2.1.5.2.2); this confirms that the "aim of survival" is too limited an aim to explain the requirements of morals and of laws.

(d) Hart (1961: 196–97) notes that the above-mentioned rules are *static*.

Other rules are *dynamic*: they are the *obligation-creating rules*, and include rules enabling transferring, exchanging, or selling products, as well as recognizing promises as a source of obligation. I note that the first part of this statement is related to private property (mentioned above), and concerns those activities directed not to assure survival but, most often, to enhance one's own economic power, whereas the last part introduces an entirely new and important factor (promises as a source of obligation), which is complex (I discuss it in ch. 3.1.2.3.3) and, again, shows that values other than mere "survival" are part of the moral as well as legal requirements.

(e) Limited understanding and strength of will would prevent some men from adhering to some prohibitions in view of long-term benefits; hence the necessity of sanctions; in general, however, according to Hart (1961: 197–98) "what reason demands is voluntary co-operation in a *coercive* system." In my opinion, the necessity of sanctions is not only linked to the existence of citizens who do not adhere to the laws because they are "bad" citizens or citizens with a weak will, but also to the fact that, while laws reflect the moral principles and values shared by the majority of citizens (public morality), single individuals may adhere to *personal moral principles and values* different from the publicly-shared ones. These "morally dissenting citizens" have the right to behave as described in ch. 4.1.1.3.2, *B*, i.e., the right to propagandize their ideas in the attempt to change the publicly-shared moral principles (and the corresponding constitutional norms). Before this change occurs, the "morally dissenting citizen" has the duty to observe the laws in his public life and, if needed, he should be *coerced* to observe them (to ensure the functioning of the legal system), while he may follow his own principles in his private life, to the extent that this does not interfere with publicly-shared norms and laws.

4.2.2.4.2—Other Views on the Law-to-Morality Relationship

(1) Laws and Moral Obligations. Based on the possibility that some citizens or groups of citizens may be oppressed by the law, Hart (1961: 202) considers the claim that the adhesion of law to morals should be more extensive and not limited to the *minimum content* of Natural Law. In this regard, the following points are of interest.

(a) It has been asserted that a legal system should be based on a sense of moral obligation (Hart 1961: 202). However, as noted by Hart (1961: 203), never has it been demonstrated that there cannot be legal obligation unless associated with moral obligation; thus, the influence of morality on law should be conceived as a factor merely increasing the stability of the system (Hart 1961: 204). I observe that, by using the terms proposed by Hart himself, without "moral obligation" (i.e., if laws do not reflect public-

ly-shared moral principles and values) citizens can only feel to be "obliged" to observe the law but they cannot feel to have the "obligation" to observe the law; in other words, citizens can only have an "external view" of laws but not an "internal view". Here, again, the important distinction between private and public ethics should be introduced. A given citizen may have personal or private moral principles and values that differ from the publicly-shared ones, as stated in constitutional norms (and, hence, also in ordinary laws). In this case, this citizen has the right to follow his private moral norms in his private live (provided his norms do not have effects in contrast with publicly-shared norms), yet in his public life (i.e., as a member of a society or as a citizen of a State) he has the moral duty of being "obligated" to obey the laws; this is because in a democratic State laws represent the *best approach to universality*. Only in non-democratic States can a citizen claim to be obliged, but not obligated, to obey the laws. Thus, the legal obligation coincides with the *public* moral obligation. The problem linked to the possible gap between private and public morality is discussed elsewhere (ch. 4.1.1.3.2, *B*).

(b) Hart (1961: 204) says that judicial decisions, required because of the open texture of laws, often involve a choice between moral values, and the adjudication should be regarded as just if it is based on the impartial consideration of the possible alternatives. Here I note that judges should not simply choose between vaguely defined moral values but they should choose between publicly-shared moral principles and values, as expressed by constitutional norms. Only in the case when constitutional norms leave some area uncovered, can judges refer to what they, in good faith, think are the most community-shared moral principles and values; I note that no uncovered area can exist if constitutional norms include my ground moral norm (pursuing mind evolution), which comprises *all* kinds of good moral norms and laws (Figs. 4.2 and 4.3), which, in turn, are directed to pursue all kinds of moral goods (Table 2.1).

(c) Hart (1961: 206) notes that "a minimum of justice is necessarily realized whenever human behavior is controlled by general rules publicly announced and judicially applied." This type of control, exerted according to the *principles of legality*, would entail an *inner morality of law* and, hence, a necessary connection between law and morality. Yet, Hart himself adds that this connection "is unfortunately compatible with very great iniquity" (Hart 1961: 207). I object that the "inner morality of law" depends on the fact that a legal system is the only way through which human actions can evolve toward universality, and therefore it is inherently good. This is so provided that laws are not merely "publicly announced" but that they are *publicly justified*, i.e., endorsed by the largest possible majority of citizens (through their representatives) and that, therefore, they represent the *best approach to universality*, as occurs in democratic States.

(d) Several thinkers have suggested that there is an obligation to obey laws as such, irrespective of their moral content, based on *gratitude* toward benefits received from the government, or based on a *duty of fair play* derived from mutual benefits (Rawls 1964), or on *implicit consent* derived from continued residence, or because of the *general utility*. None of these criteria are valid unless laws are enacted by a publicly justified democratic government and therefore express the moral principles and values of the largest possible majority of citizens, i.e., represent the best approach to universality. This is because the utility gained by being a citizen of an organized State depends to a large extent on the democratic nature of the State (the utility is minimal in a tyrannical State), and also because the claimed implicit consent derived from continued residence is actually a forced consent, due to the practical difficulty of changing residence. Thus, the ultimate basis for the obligation to obey laws is their content of shared moral principles and values. This is in keeping with the view that, since morality is one of the major binds of society, a system of laws directed to preserve shared moral principles is justified (Devlin 1959). On a similar basis, according to some thinkers, a legitimate paternalism would be allowed (e.g., to avoid harm recognized as such by all or most rational individuals) (Dworkin G. 1972), as would be the laws directed to avoid not only injury or harm but also offense or psychological discomfort (offense principle) (Feinberg 1985). Yet, according to Hart (1963), this might entail an undue limitation of personal freedom. I recall that this possible limitation is linked to the unavoidable problem of the possible discordance between private and public (publicly-shared) morality, as discussed in chapter 4.1.1.3.2, *B*.

(2) *The Problem of "Unjust Laws"*. Hart (1961) draws the attention on the possibility that some laws, although properly enacted and valid according to the established criteria of a system, may be morally iniquitous. In the face of this problem, legal positivists make assertions like the following ones:

> The existence of law is one thing; its merit or demerit another . . . A law, which actually exists, is a law, though we happen to dislike it, or though it varies from the text, by which we regulate our approbation and disapprobation. (Austin 1832: 157)

or

> The law of a State or other organized body is not an ideal, but something which actually exists. It is not that which is in accordance with religion, or nature, or morality; it is not that which ought to be, but that which is. (Gray 1909: 94)

or "Legal norms may have any kind of content" (Kelsen 1945: 113). According to Hart (1961: 209), two solutions are possible: to consider as valid laws all the rules that are valid by the formal tests, or to refuse to acknowledge as laws those rules that are clearly morally iniquitous. In the latter instances, instead of stating "This is in no sense law," it would be more appropriate to state "This is law, but too iniquitous to obey or apply" (Hart 1961: 210). Thus, according to Hart,

> [Men] should preserve the sense that the certification of something as legally valid is not conclusive of the question of obedience, and that, however great the aura of majesty or authority which the official system may have, its demand must in the end be submitted to a moral scrutiny. (Hart 1961: 210)

Here two distinct situations should be considered. *(a)* In a democratic State, in which laws reflect public morality, a law can be defined as immoral on the basis of personal moral beliefs. This is the case of the "morally dissenting citizen", discussed elsewhere (ch. 4.1.1.3.2, *B*). *(b)* In a non-democratic State, in which all laws are unjustified and expressions of arrogance and violence exerted by the non-democratic government, citizens are entitled to say: "This is not a publicly justified law, but an arbitrary order; moreover, it is too iniquitous to obey or apply." This should be "said" by the citizens; the latter, however, would have to face a morally difficult choice about what "to do", in concrete and particular instances. Indeed, a non-democratic government creates an immoral environment, where moral choices may be very difficult. Hart (1961: 211) thinks that those who did bad actions under bad laws should not be punished, especially when this entails a retroactive punishment. This statement seems to me in contrast with what, according to Hart (1961), citizens should say when faced with bad laws ("This is law, but too iniquitous to obey or apply"). I think that, unless under severe threat, citizens are responsible for serious immoral actions, even if performed to obey unjustified, non-democratic laws.

4.2.2.5—Dworkin's Rules, Principles, and Policies

Dworkin (1977; 1986) distinguishes between *rules*, *principles*, and *policies*, and argues that positivism focuses upon rules and misses the important roles of those standards that are not rules. Dworkin further argues as follows.

(1) Rules, Principles and Policies. Dworkin distinguishes *(a)* rules, and *(b)* principles and policies.

(a) Rules. According to Dworkin (1977), "rules" (contrary to "principles") "are applicable in a 'all-or-nothing' fashion. If the facts a rule stipulates are given, then either the rule is valid, in which case the answer it supplies must be accepted, or it is not, in which case it contributes nothing to the decision" (Dworkin 1977: 24); e.g., if the requirement of three witnesses is a valid legal rule, then it cannot be that a will signed by only two wit-

nesses is valid (Dworkin 1977: 25). Moreover, while principles have "weight", "Rules do not have this dimension . . . [so that] if two rules conflict, one of them cannot be a valid rule" (Dworkin 1977: 27).

(b) Principles and policies. Dworkin (1977: 22) defines a *policy* "that kind of standard that sets out a goal to be reached, generally an improvement in some economic, political, or social feature of the community," while he calls a *principle* "a standard that is to be observed . . . because it is a requirement of justice or fairness or some other dimension of morality." Principles would differ from rules because they do not set out legal consequences that follow automatically when the conditions provided are met (example: no man may profit from his own wrong); they would state reasons that argue in one direction but do not necessitate particular decisions (Dworkin 1977). Moreover, principles would have the dimension of "weight" or importance, and may conflict with one another, in which case the principle that has more weight or importance should prevail. He says:

> I call a 'principle' a standard that is to be observed, not because it will advance or secure an economic, political, or social situation deemed desirable, but because it is a requirement of justice or fairness or some other dimension of morality" (Dworkin 1977: 22) . . . "[P]rinciples . . . do not set out legal consequences that follow automatically when the conditions provided are met" (Dworkin 1977: 25) . . . "A principle . . . does not even purport to set out conditions that make its application necessary. Rather, it states a reason that argues in one direction, but does not necessitate a particular decision . . . There may be other principles or policies arguing in the other direction . . . [It follows that] Principles have a dimension that rules do not—the dimension of weight or importance. When principles intersect . . . one who must resolve the conflict has to take into account the relative weight of each . . . [T]he judgment that a particular principle or policy is more important than another will often be a controversial one. (Dworkin 1977: 26)

Thus, principles may have a different *weight* in different cases and may be in conflict with one another. Moreover, "we make a case for a principle, and for its weight, by appealing to an amalgam of practice and other principles in which the implications of legislative and judicial history figure along with appeals to community practices and understandings" (Dworkin 1977: 36).

On the above grounds, Dworkin (1977: 17–45; 1986) contrasts Hart's conception according to which the legal system is based on *rules*, of which some could be safely and simply applied while others would be *open-textured* and would leave uncertainty, especially in borderline cases; in these cases, judges would legislate by creative discretion to usefully cover a gap in the legislative system. According to Dworkin (1977: 31–39, 68–71), there is not such a creative legislation by judges, as in difficult or borderline cases judges actually appeal to the general moral *principles* that are basic for the legal system and society, so that judges would have little discretion.

I think that Dworkin's distinction between rules and principles is rather vague and reflects the lack of a supporting ontological conception. I think that Dworkin's distinction should be contrasted with the general "classification of laws" (i.e., classification of *publicly-shared projects*) that I discuss in chapter 4.1.2.3 (Figs. 4.2 and 4.3). Actually, Dworkin's "rules" correspond to my *laws*, *rules* and *commands*, whereas Dworkin's "principles" correspond to my *norms*.

From the above, it is apparent that Dworkin fails to distinguish "moral principles", which are *moral thoughts* defining what is good (e.g., the principle that "liberty is a human good"), from "norms", which are *moral projects*, prescribing the pursuing of a given good as defined by the corresponding moral principle (e.g., the norm prescribing the pursuing of liberty). Moreover, Dworkin does not consider the different degrees of extension and indeterminacy of the various kinds of "laws" (as discussed in chs. 4.1.1.1; 4.2.3; 4.3.1.1, *1a*).

(2) Principles and the Rules of Recognition. According to Dworkin (1977; 1986), moral principles on which legal systems are based cannot be validated by the "pedigree test", i.e., on the basis of some rule of recognition; he says:

> Most rules . . . are valid because some competent institution enacted them . . . But this test of pedigree will not work for . . . principles. The origin of these as legal principles lies not in a particular decision of some legislature or court, but in a sense of appropriateness developed in the profession and the public over time. (Dworkin 1977: 40)

Thus there would not be rules of recognition for legal principles. Here I object the following. *(a)* Moral principles valid in public life are *only* those enacted by the "competent institution" (the constituent assembly, or the parliament through special procedures), i.e., those defined by constitutional norms; otherwise, it would be impossible to establish which of the various principles that may be held by different citizens or groups of citizens should be followed. *(b)* The claim that principles originate from the sense of appropriateness developed in the profession and the public over time must be clarified. As I stated above, judges should not choose between vaguely defined moral values but they should choose between publicly-shared moral principles and values, as expressed by constitutional norms. Only in the case when constitutional norms leave some areas uncovered, can judges refer to what they, in good faith, think are the most largely shared moral principles and values: those moral principles and values that have developed over time and that are *firmly established* among citizens, so that they *work as unwritten constitutional norms*. I underline that reference to unwritten norms always entails the risk of arbitrary interpretations; indeed, it may undermine the basis of any legal system. Moreover, I note that no uncovered area can exist if constitutional norms include my ground moral norm (pursuing mind evolution), which comprises *all* kinds of good moral norms and laws (Figs. 4.2 and 4.3), which are directed to pursue all kinds of moral goods (Table 2.1).

4.2.3—The Indeterminacy of Law: Legal Formalism and Legal Realism

Hart (1961: 124–36) underlines that both "laws" and "precedents" have an *open texture*, i.e., they entail uncertainty, and hence require a choice, in their application to particular instances (*indeterminacy of law*). Hart (1961: 136) states that

> In every legal system a large and important field is left open for the exercise of discretion by courts and other officials in rendering initially vague standards determinate, in resolving the uncertainties of statutes, or in developing and qualifying rules only broadly communicated by authoritative precedents.

As it is known, the indeterminacy of law has led to two opposing doctrines: *legal formalism*, on the one hand, and *legal realism*, on the other. To understand these doctrines we should recall that a law is a publicly-shared *project*, which creates a *class* of actions (ch. 4.1.1.1). Thus, a law defines the *common properties* of those particular events (actions) that constitute the *members* of a class. As stated in chapter 1.1.3.2.1, a class, be it a class of physical events (which is created by the intellect after the observation of several similar objects) or a class of actions (which is created by a law of a legal system), is always defined with *approximation*, and their members, although similar, differ from one another as they are *variable events*, with unique and unrepeatable characteristics; hence the *indeterminacy of laws* (chs. 4.1.1.1; 4.3.1.1, *1a*).

It is noteworthy that, besides defining classes of *events* (actions), laws may also define classes of *objects* that are involved in the events. For instance, a law that forbids bringing a wild dog without a muzzle into a public place is a law that defines an action (bringing a dog into a public place) but also two "objects", i.e., the "wild dog" and the "public place". Of course, objects are also defined with *approximation*, since adjectives such as "wild" are indeterminate.

On these grounds, *legal formalism* has developed as the doctrine that recognizes a preeminent role to the *common properties* of the actions that form the members of the class, as defined by a law, whereas *legal realism* has developed as the doctrine that recognizes a preeminent role to the *specific properties* of each of the actions that form the members of the class defined by a law; the specific properties give rise to the *variability* among the actions that are members of a law-defined class (ch. 4.1.1.1).

4.2.3.1—Legal Formalism

4.2.3.1.1—The Thesis of Legal Formalism

Frank (1930: 35) recalls that according to the *conventional view* (or *formalist view*), law is a complete body of existing rules, which can be changed only by legislature; judges are not to make or change the law but to apply law, which pre-exists judicial decisions (otherwise, they would be guilty of usurpation of power). In the 18th century, Blackstone (1765-1769, Book 1: 69) pointed out that judges are not delegated to pronounce new laws but to maintain and expound the old ones, so that when a new decision overrules an old one what has happened is not the making of a new law or the change of a law, but only the vindication of law from misrepresentation. I object that no one would deny that judges are not to make or change the law but to apply the law; the problem arises when one attempts to understand what *applying* a law actually means. This is because a law is always marked by *approximation*, since it attempts to *approximately* define a class of events (actions) that are similar (but not equal) to one another. Thus, a law according to which who kills a person should be punished with sanction "*x*" is a law that makes an *approximate* statement, because a person may be killed with or without premeditation, with or without brutality, with or without provocation, for trifling or serious reasons, etc. Moreover, referring to provocation, one can ask how strong it was; or referring to brutality, one can ask to which extent a given act has been brutal, and so on. Of course, the legislator attempts to restrict the approximation of a law, by making laws with a lesser degree of approximation (i.e., defining sub-classes of actions which include less variable members); yet, some degree of approximation will always remain, because it is linked to the fact that human actions, even those that belong to the same class, differ from one another. What is important, however, is that *the unavoidable approximation of laws, and the consequent discretion of judges, can be restricted to a small, and hence acceptable, extent.*

Honoré (1995) points out that, unlike the interpretation of the utterance of a friend of ours, *legal interpretation* is a formal interpretation because it is in writing, because it has authority, because legal interpretation will make a difference to someone's rights and duties, and because there is an official interpretation of legal texts. Here Honoré seems to overlook the fact that a formal interpretation (although it is in writing, has authority, influences rights and duties, and is official) necessarily entails some degree of *discretion*, because a law is necessarily marked by *approximation*, since it gives *one* general definition referring to innumerable and variable events (actions) and objects.

Honoré (1995) maintains that legal interpretation can be made by two approaches.

(1) The *textual approach* holds that: *(a)* a text must be understood in its ordinary sense; *(b)* when technical or scientific terms are used, their meaning is what they ordinarily mean to the experts; *(c)* only when the textual approach leads to absurd results can a different approach be tried (Honoré 1995). I note that after a text has been understood in an ordinary sense, and its technical terms have been given the meaning indicated by the experts, the resulting interpretation is always and necessarily marked by some degree of approximation; indeed, it is the *decision of the legislator* itself that is approximate. This is because any law refers to (or defines) the innumerable and different events that form a class (reality is made of different and variable events, and nobody can change it). Concerning the claim stated above, under point "*c*", that in the case of absurd results one can try a different approach, it seems too vague a statement to be commented on.

(2) The *purposive approach* gives priority to the purpose of the statute, or contract, or treaty, or will, or regulation, as well as to the general aims of the legal system such as justice, security, and efficiency (Honoré 1995). Both the textual and the purposive approach have been regarded as different ways to get the *intention* of the author of the text (Honoré 1995). Again, I note that it is the *purpose and the intention of the legislator* themselves that are marked by *approximation* and, hence, that require interpretation in their application to particular events, because of the variability of the events (already mentioned) to which the purpose and intention refer.

Honoré (1995) gives two examples concerning the role of interpretation.

(a) Suppose that a statute lays down that a policeman may require someone who *is driving* a vehicle to take a blood test; considering that a man is driving a vehicle only if the vehicle is moving, may a policeman tell a driver to take a blood test after that the vehicle has been stopped? This does not seem to me a good example. One should note that, since a high level of blood alcohol persists for some time, a policeman can tell a driver to take a blood test *soon after* that the vehicle has been stopped (because the result indicates whether the alcohol level was high while the man was driving), but not *much time after* (because the result would be irrelevant to the situation during the driving). Thus, the problem is that reference should be made to the time curve of alcohol disappearance from blood, which, however, can only be known with approximation because the (scientific) law that defines the time course of blood alcohol (like any other law) is an *approximate* statement, which, however, allows us to say with certainty that, if the blood test is made within a few minutes and is positive, it is certainly

valid as proof that the blood alcohol level was high when the driver was driving. Yet, if the test is performed after a certain time, its result may be of uncertain meaning. Thus, as stated elsewhere, the approximation or imprecision that marks human knowledge and previsions prevents us from making precise affirmations and prevision (concerning the precise time when alcohol disappears from blood and when the test gives a reliable result) but allows us to define the condition within which we can make *affirmations* based on *statistics*, i.e., that are true in a high percentage of cases (alcohol persists in the blood for a certain time in most cases), and *previsions* that possess a high degree of *probability* (there is a high degree of probability that the blood test performed soon after that the vehicle has been stopped will yield reliable results).

(b) Suppose that a statute lays down that no one can hunt elephants and hyenas without a license; would this mean that one may hunt either elephants or hyenas without a license? Obviously, in this case there is a mere mistake ("and" has been used instead of "or"); judges have the power of correcting obvious mistakes. This, too, seems to me a not very significant example; nobody would question that judges have the power to correct obvious mistakes. However, I would stress the fact that in some instances what may indeed be a mistake (e.g., a missing comma) may significantly change the meaning of a law. This, however, is not a problem of philosophical relevance; it concerns the possible ignorance of some legislators or the incompetence of those who printed the text of the law.

Hart (1961: 124–54) notes that, by following *legal formalism* (or *conceptualism*), which seeks to minimize the need for choices in the application of a law to particular cases, judicial interpretation of laws or of precedents may be too formal and thus may fail to consider the differences between cases. I would say, in a very schematic way, that formalism might lead to consider all cases of murder alike (or, shifting to a lesser degree of approximation, all cases of "murder after a provocation" alike). Indeed, disregarding the differences between cases entails a profound injustice. The task of a judge is to understand and define the *particular event* (similar to, and yet different from any other) that he has the duty to evaluate.

4.2.3.1.2—Legal Formalism and the Individuality of Judges

Legal formalism seems to ignore another cause of uncertainty in legal interpretation and of the consequent judicial discretion: the individuality of judges. As I will discuss in a next chapter (4.3.1.1, 2), judges are members of the class of judges (which is a sub-class of the class of men). Although they have some common characteristic derived from the common cultural education and experience, they necessary differ from one another because of their "individual properties", which make each judge unique and unrepeatable member of a class of individuals (chs. 1.1.3.2.1, *1*; 3.2.1). Thus, the decision of each judge differs from the decision that another judge would make about the same case. What is important is that the uncertainty that results from the approximation of laws and from the uniqueness of events and of judges is kept to an acceptable minimum.

4.2.3.2—Legal Realism (Rule-Skepticism)

4.2.3.2.1—The Thesis of Legal Realism: Judges as Lawmakers

According to the *legal realism* (or *rule-skepticism*), judges actually make law; Frank (1930: 112–13) said that

> Whatever produces the judge's hunches makes the law . . . What are the stimuli which make a judge feel that he should try to justify one conclusion rather than another? The rules and principles of law are one class of such stimuli. But there are many others . . . usually referred to as 'the political, economic and moral prejudices' of the judge.

As discussed by Purcell (1973: 74–94), this theory is based on the empirical observation of how decisions are actually taken by the courts (i.e., according to the *opinions* and *temperament* of judges), rather than on how decisions should be logically derived from laws; this view emphasizes the role of judicial *discretion* and minimizes that of laws. Let us consider the points that follow.

(1) The Judge Decision Process. It has been argued that the belief that judges do not make or change laws is due to the illusion that laws can be entirely predictable (Frank 1930: 37), and to the awareness that accepting that judges make law actually entails that the rights and obligations of the parties to a given case are decided *retroactively* (Frank 1930: 38). I note that, whereas a certain (tolerable) degree of unpredictability of laws is unavoidable (because it is linked to the approximation with which our intellect defines a class and to the uniqueness of the members of a class), the observation that judge-made laws would be *retroactive* laws is a serious one. Indeed, if judges make laws, these laws would actually be retroactive laws, inasmuch as they are made after the judges know the events to which these laws should be applied. Fortunately, as I will show later, this is not the case.

Frank (1930: 108–9) thinks that the process of judging seldom begins with a premise from which a conclusion is derived, but rather it is worked out backward, starting from conclusions tentatively formulated, and then trying to find premises and arguments which will substantiate them. I think that these statements are misleading. It is true that a judge may start from conclusions tentatively formulated. This is what every man does; we make rapid judgments by unconsciously utilizing the knowledge and principles that we already possess, and then we analyze in a deeper way our judgment to verify whether our first judgment actually conforms to our knowledge and principles. In the case of judges, the knowledge and principles that they possess are the *publicly-shared* norms, laws, and rules that form constitutional norms and ordinary laws and rules (and not personally-created rules that reflect personal convictions); their tentatively formulated conclusions are based on these norms, laws, and rules that they have learned through their cultural education and professional training, and are *not* based on *ad hoc* laws, retroactively made and applied by judges.

Frank (1930: 109) quotes two examples by some jurists.

(a) A considerable portion of a class of young mathematicians, despite the fact that the answer that in the book was reported as right was wrong, succeeded in reaching it, even at the cost of a resort to very un-mathematical processes. I object that this example is not pertinent. Judges do not have an authoritative (stated by a book) and already given solution when they are faced with a case, but only norms, laws, and rules. Their position, therefore, is different from that of the young mathematicians, mentioned in the above example.

(b) A driver who was drunk and who severely injured a man was condemned because of "reckless driving" in one state and because of "assault with intent to kill" in another state, and yet the sanction was similar in both cases; this would be because the penalty provided for "reckless driving" was too light in the latter state, so that in order to give an adequate punishment the two courts followed a different reasoning. Like the former example, this example is not pertinent, because it clearly refers to the case of dishonest judges who, instead of applying the penalty according to the *publicly-shared* norms and laws, deliberately classified the action that they had to judge as a more severe one, in order to be able to apply the punishment that, according to *their own personal* convictions, was adequate.

Frank (1930: 112) quotes the description made by judge Hutcheson of the judicial process:

> The judge really decides *by feeling and not by judgment, by hunching and not by ratiocination*, such ratiocination appearing only in the opinion . . . [The judge] having so decided, enlists his every faculty and belabors his laggard mind, not only to justify that intuition to himself, but to make it pass muster with his critics. (Italics added).

Frank (1930: 160) also quotes the view by H. Yntema that

> [D]ecision is reached after an *emotive experience* in which principles and logic play a secondary part. The function of juristic logic and the principles which it employs seem to be like that of language, to describe the event which has al-

ready transpired.

Once again, I think that the views of both Hutcheson and Yntema about judge decisions are untenable. They are based on the distinction (perhaps, on the contraposition) between the decision stirred up by the feeling of judges and that provided by their ratiocination. To clarify this point, we should refer to the structure of the mind and should recall that, besides the *rational consciousness* (or inward activity of intellect), which produces *moral thoughts* which define *moral principles* (e.g., the principle that "education is good") and *moral projects* (e.g., the project of "pursuing education"), there is the *emotional consciousness* (or inward activity of sensitiveness), which produces *moral feelings* which "found" moral values (chs. 1.1.1.2.4; 2.1.1.2; 2.1.3.2; Fig. 1.1). As I stated elsewhere (ch. 2.1.4.1, *b*), because of the internal coherence of the mind, moral feelings are most often coherent with moral thoughts and, consequently, with moral projects. In the case of judges, since they play a public function, they should refer to *publicly-shared moral principles* (produced by *moral thoughts*) and *moral values* (produced by *moral feelings*), as expressed in the norms, laws, and rules. Thus, not only should judges follow publicly-shared moral *thoughts* (as expressed in norms, laws, and rules), even if they think differently, but they should also consider that the norms, laws, and rules also express publicly-shared moral *feelings*. In other words, judges should behave as if they share both publicly-shared moral principles and the publicly-shared moral feelings (otherwise stated, judges should recognize shared moral principles and should respect shared moral feelings). However, in most instances, judges endorse themselves the publicly-shared moral feelings, so that their feelings are spontaneously in keeping with the principles and values expressed by norms and laws. Only in the case that a judge's moral feelings differ from (or contrast with) the shared moral feeling can his personal sentiments affect his decision. This, however, should only rarely happen for two reasons. *First*, considering that judges are people devoted to the exercise of justice, they should belong to morally-good people and, therefore, should endorse moral thoughts and feelings expressed in norms, laws, and rules. *Second*, if a judge has moral feelings that contrast with the publicly-shared ones, he is *certainly* aware of this contrast, because he experiences it daily during his professional work, and even before, during his training period. Thus, if a judge decides according to his own feelings, he is certainly aware of neglecting publicly-shared moral projects and feelings, and is a guilty judge.

Frank (1930: 113) affirms that rules and principles of law are just one class of the stimuli that prompt a judge to justify one conclusion rather than another, together with judge's political, economic and moral prejudices. Again, this statement overlooks the "public *versus* private distinction", i.e., it reveals confusion between *public* principles of law, which judges should follow, and *private* or personal political, economic and moral prejudices, which judges should *not* take into account, on pain of being guilty.

(2) The Role of Precedents. It has been pointed out that the use of *precedents* is illusory, because, considering the uniqueness of the facts and of the judge's reaction thereto, almost any case is actually an un-provided case (Frank 1930: 162); moreover, it has been maintained that courts can find earlier decisions which can be made to appear to justify almost any conclusion (Frank 1930: 163). Here Frank emphasizes differences between cases; he, however, overlooks the truth that different cases do share common characteristics, which are defined, even if with approximation, by laws. Thus, the differences between individual cases only result in the unavoidable existence of a small and tolerable degree of uncertainty and of discretion.

(3) The Judge as a Wise Arbitrator. Legal realism does not maintain that judges are insincere, but that most of them sincerely believe that they are logically applying rules and principle derived from earlier cases (Frank 1930: 164). However, Frank (1930: 168–69) thinks that a judge, at his best, is a wise arbitrator, who does equity in the sense expressed by Aristotle in his *Rhetoric*: "It is equity to pardon human failings, and to look to the lawgiver and not to the law . . . to prefer arbitration to judgment, for the arbitrator sees what is equitable, but the judge only the law." Aristotle's statements, endorsed by Frank, are questionable. Let us consider separately *(a)* the concept that "It is equity to pardon" and *(b)* the concept of "the judge as a wise arbitrator".

(a) Pardon is unrelated to the pursuing of justice and has a sense only after justice has been done. This is because what can be pardoned is the guilt for faults or offenses; and guilt, in order to be pardoned, must exist. In order to establish whether guilt exists, we need the judgment by a court; of course, here we consider guilt as conceived on the basis of the publicly-shared standard, and not guilt as it might be conceived by someone on the basis of his own personal, arbitrary standard of conduct, often including prejudices.

(b) The acceptance of the concept that a judge should be a *wise arbitrator* depends on what we intend by "wise". An individual may be judged as wise according to an ethical conception, and unwise according to another one. Among racialist minorities, a "wise" person would think that rights should not be equal between individuals of different races. Thus, the concept of the "wise" arbitrator can only be accepted if "wise" is understood as wise according to *publicly-shared* moral principles and values, reflected in norms, laws, and rules. Thus, a wise arbitrator should be a judge who follows the "laws" (norms, laws, and rules), and his wisdom should consist in using his unavoidable, little discretional power to interpret, as best as he can, these "laws"; this means that the wise judge should adapt with wisdom the existing laws to the particular, unique, and unrepeatable case he is judg-

ing. In other words, judges should use wisdom in dealing with their unavoidable, little discretion resulting from the indeterminacy of laws, the variability of the events to be judged and the individuality of judges themselves
(ch. 4.3).

(4) The Law According to Legal Realists. In the attempt to define what
is a law, Frank (1930: 131) reports the statement by J. C. Gray who affirms:

> Thus far we have seen . . . that rules for conduct which the courts do not apply
> are not Law; that the fact that the courts apply rules is what makes them Law;
> that there is no mysterious entity 'The Law' apart from these rules; and that
> the judges are rather the creators than the discoverers of the Law. (Gray 1909:
> 121)

According to Gray, it is only words that the legislature utters when it enacts
a statute: it is for the courts to say what those words mean. There would be
limits to the courts' power of interpretation, but those limits would be vague
and undefined; and that is because statutes, according to Gray, would be not
part of the Law itself, but only a source of law.

Gray's thesis, that seems to be endorsed by Frank (1930), will be clarified if discussed by referring to: *(a)* my concept of law (chs. 4.1.1.1;
4.1.1.3.1), in turn based on the concept of *class* (ch. 1.1.3.2.1); and *(b)* the
distinction between *laws* as *universal and long-lasting projects* and the *particular project* that precedes any particular action.

(a) A law is a *universal and collective* (or *publicly-shared*) *project*, produced by the *activity of intellect*; this project, in turn, is an idea of *class* that
creates its own *members* (the actions prescribed or prohibited). Thus, as an
ontological entity, a law exists in the mind of citizens (first in the minds of
the members of the organ that issues the law, then in the minds of all citizens). Therefore, a law is not a mysterious entity (to use the words of Gray,
cited above), but is a "non-physical" or "mental" object, i.e., an idea-of-
project. The members of the class created by a *law* (i.e., by a publicly-
shared *project*) are some particular, *specific projects* and the corresponding
particular, specific *actions* and *moral acts* of citizens. The adjudication is a
process through which judges verify whether a given action and its preceding specific project is a member of a class or not (e.g., whether an action is a
member of the class of the "murders" or is a member of the class of the "actions of self-defense"). It may be that Gray considered laws (which are ideas
of projects that define a class) only the judicial act through which actions
(which are the members of the classes defined by the laws) are assigned to a
class or to another one. Briefly, Gray would consider only the *members* of
the class defined by a law (i.e., a given action), overlooking that the *members* of a class can only exist if the *class* that defines them already exists.

(b) Laws as *universal and long-lasting projects* should be distinguished
from the *particular project* that precedes any particular action accomplished

by a particular individual. Perhaps, Gray's assertion that "the fact that courts apply rules is what makes them Law" should be interpreted as indicating that Gray focused his attention on the application of rules to the particular actions under judgment and the corresponding particular projects (which are *members* of a class), and overlooked the *class* (i.e., the law, which is a universal and *long-lasting* idea-of-project) that has defined them and that, therefore, must exist.

Transferring these concepts from public to private life, we could say that Gray considers the specific and particular projects that precede any *action* made by a man, but ignores the more *general life projects* that necessarily precede and define the particular projects that precede single actions (Gray could say: the *life projects* of a man actually consist of his *particular projects* and decisions and actions). Referring to my classification of "laws" (as classes whose extension progressively decreases going from norms, to laws, to rules, down to commands), we could say that Gray ignores norms, laws, and even rules, and focuses his attention on particular rules, very close to commands. Yet, commands exist as part of a particular rule, a particular rule exists as part of a more general rule, the latter exists as part of a law, a law exists as part of a norm, and a norm exists as part of the ground norm (promoting mind evolution).

Finally, Frank (1930: 133) recalls that in 1897 Holmes wrote that the prophecies of what the courts will do in fact, and nothing more pretentious, are what he means by "law". Thus, as noted by Frank (1930: 134), whereas according to Gray the law is made up of rules for decision, laid down by the courts, according to Holmes law is made up of the decisions themselves; all such decisions are law. Again, transferring these concepts from public to private life, we could hypothesize that Holmes could say: the *projects* of a man actually consist of his actions. Yet, projects actually are ideas-of-projects and are produced by the *intellect* whereas actions are produced by the *power*; therefore, projects and the corresponding actions are *ontologically distinct* entities (chs. 1.1.1; 1.1.2; 4.1.1.1; 4.2.6.3); moreover, actions could not exist if not preceded by a project (an action consists of turning a project into practice). Returning to the public sphere, we should note that a decision couldn't exist if the law, which is implemented by that decision, does not pre-exist.

4.2.3.2.2—Legal Realism and the Binding Character of "Rules"

Hart (1961: 136) notes that the existence of a court entails the existence of secondary rules; hence, legal realism (or rule-skepticism) does not deny that there are statutes, but regards them as mere *sources* of law, and only denies that statutes are law until applied by courts (Hart 1961: 137). Thus, according to Hart (1961: 138), legal realism (rule-skepticism) might be regarded as a theory of the function of rules in judicial decisions; according to this theory, there would be nothing to circumscribe the area of open texture of laws, so that it would be false or senseless to regard judges themselves subject to rules or *bound* to decide cases as they do. Hart (1961) argues that those who follow this theory are perhaps disappointed by the fact that because men, being not gods, cannot anticipate all possible combinations of facts, the open texture of laws is unavoidable. However, the view that rules must be literally binding or they are not rules is untenable. In this regard, Hart (1961: 139) says:

> It does not follow from the fact that such rules have exceptions incapable of exhaustive statement, that in every situation we are left to our discretion and are never bound to keep a promise. A rule that ends with the word "unless . . ." is still a rule.

Here I refer to my classification of "laws" as classes of various extensions (ch. 4.1.2.3, *E*), and I recall that, going from the ground norm to norms, to laws, to "wide rules", to "narrow rules", down to commands, while the *extension* progressively decreases, the *binding force* progressively increases (binding force here means "binding toward judges"). Therefore, judges are rather closely bound when they apply "narrow rules"; when narrow rules referring to the case under scrutiny are not available, judges should resort to the lesser closely-binding "wide rules" (covering the field to which the missing rule should belong); when no suitable "wide rules" are available, judges should resort to the medium-binding "laws"; when no suitable laws are available, judges should resort to the loosely-binding "norms"; finally, when no suitable norm exists, judges should resort to the very loosely-binding "ground norm" (prescribing the promotion of mind evolution). It follows that, in a well-developed legal system, judges should find the "narrower rule" regulating the case under scrutiny, so that their discretion is kept to the unavoidable (and acceptable) minimum. It is only when the necessary "narrow rules" are lacking that judges resort to "laws" defining larger classes of actions and, therefore, allowing larger discretion. The lack of a specific, narrow rule, however, is possible if the legislative authority has so decided (otherwise the lacking rule would had been enacted). Resorting to a "law" of higher level, however, is a *duty* of judges, because the alternative would be the *arbitrary* resort to their personal principles. Concerning the unavoidable, small, and acceptable discretion allowed even by the "narrow rules", it should be underlined that it should not be regarded as undermining justice, but as the only possible way to do justice, or as the best possible approach to justice. An example may be useful. Suppose that in the world there are only two judges who are both *expert* and *honest* and who, for some reason, are called to judge the same case. Comparison shows that the decisions made by the two judges are similar but not identical, since judge "*A*" takes the decision "*x₁*" whereas judge "*B*" takes the decision "*x₂*". It would be nonsense to ask which of the two decisions is better or more just, since there is not in reality such a mysterious entity called "the just decision", because there is not such a mysterious entity called the "just judge" (of course, I am excluding the case in which judges are inexpert or dishonest). The class of judges is composed of individual judges, who are similar but not identical to one another, each of them being a unique and unrepeatable instance of the *class* of judges (chs. 1.1.3.2.1, *1*; 3.2.1). Thus, both decision "*x₁*" and decision "*x₂*" are equally just; both are the best approach to the "just decision", as their (small) difference is due to the unavoidable difference between individual judges.

As pointed out by Hart (1961: 139), the fact that deviation from the rules will not draw down on the judge a physical sanction is often used to support the thesis of the legal realism. In my opinion, the fact that deviation from the rules will not draw down on the judge a physical sanction may affect the behavior of the dishonest judge but not that of an honest judge; and the honesty of judges is the necessary premise to any reasoning about justice. Judges, however, cannot be divided into honest and dishonest judges, according to a "yes-or-no" criterion, because honesty is distributed among humans through a continuum that goes from the fully honest to the fully dishonest man (the extremes, clearly, being hypothetical instances). Thus, the problem arises concerning the *degree of honesty* of judges; this problem will be discussed in chapter 4.2.4.2, devoted to the "Critical Legal Studies".

4.2.3.2.3—Legal Realism and the Internal View of Laws

As underlined by Hart (1961: 138), the thesis of legal realism is in contrast with the "internal point of view" from which most individuals look at laws. In order to endorse laws, i.e., to look at them from an internal point of view, citizens must believe that laws do exist, and that the courts and other officials will decide and behave in certain regular and hence predictable ways, in accordance with the rules of the system. Interpreted according to my theory, this statement means that the citizens should be confident that judicial decisions are directed to *turn into practice publicly-shared projects* expressed by the laws, i.e., to establish whether a given particular action is, or is not, a *member* of the *class of actions* defined by a law.

4.2.3.2.4—Legal Realism and the "Final" Decisions

Hart (1961: 141) notes that legal realism (or rule-skepticism) is also based on the fact that the decision of a court has the unique characteristics of being authoritative and, in the case of supreme tribunals, final. He points out that, although against a decision regarded as unjust it is possible to appeal to a higher authority, this must end somewhere in a final, authoritative judgment. The latter, being made by human beings, will always carry with it the "risk of honest mistake, abuse, or violation. It is impossible to provide by rule for the correction of the breach of every rule" (Hart 1961: 143). I think that the problem of the "final decisions" is often misunderstood. It is based on the false assumption that a *fully just* decision can be reached and, therefore, must be reached. As mentioned above, the causes that may prevent full justice are honest mistakes, abuse, or violation, to which self-deception should be added. This important issue will be discussed in chapter 4.2.4.2, devoted to "Critical Legal Studies".

4.2.3.2.5—The Ultimate Criteria of Legal Validity

An important question concerns the ultimate criteria of legal validity. Indeed, questions may arise about the legal competence of the supreme legislature itself; the ultimate rules of a legal system may thus be in doubt, and the courts may be called to resolve these doubts. At some time, apparently paradoxical situations may occur, as when the judges of a court, exercising creative powers, settle the ultimate criteria by which the validity of the very laws, which confer upon them jurisdiction as judges, must itself be tested. Hart (1961: 153) notes that:

> The truth may be that, when courts settle previously unenvisaged questions concerning the most fundamental constitutional rules, they *get* their authority to decide them accepted after the questions have arisen and the decision has been given. Here all that succeeds is success.

To understand the role of the courts in these extreme, hard situations, it is necessary to understand the nature of the function of judges. As mentioned elsewhere (chs. 4.3.1.1; 4.3.1.2), judges "study" a concrete, *particular action* to verify to which of the *classes of actions* defined by the various laws it belongs. This study can be profitably accomplished because judges have a *specific competence* and *suitable means*, and because they devote all their working time to it. A judge's competence, of course, is in the legal field; however, when in studying a case the judge encounters problems that require competence in other fields, he may ask the opinion of experts in that field. Thus, the authority of judges in settling difficult problems derives from the fact that they possess *high specific (legal) competence*, have available *means of investigation* suitable to know the problem to be settled, and spend all their working time to this end. For this reason, access to the position of judge should be through examinations open to all citizens possessing a law degree (and having shown good conduct), so that those who pass this examination represent the best possible group of experts in law and judicial problems that the society is capable of providing. Thus, *the authority of judges derives from their specific competence and the availability of means of investigation* (which allows deep knowledge of the facts); otherwise stated, judges' decisions are *informed and competent, and hence authoritative, decisions*. Since judges have to make competent judgments, it would be nonsense to select judges by election, instead than by open examinations.

Of course, true justice requires that honest mistakes, self-deception, and dishonesty (abuse and violation) do not occur among judges. While honest mistakes and self-deception are difficult to prevent and to detect, judge dishonesty can be prevented and detected by rigorous rules internal to the judiciary system and by a control internally exerted by the judiciary system itself. This control should suffice, unless the majority of the judges are corrupted; however, if the majority of judges, who are selected from all adequately trained citizens, were corrupted, this would mean that the majority of citizens are corrupted too. In this rare instance, there would be no remedy and what could be done is to wait that, through time (decades or centuries), the *evolution of the consciousness* of the community will generate more honest citizens and, then, more honest judges. In any case, no control on the judges external to the judiciary system should be allowed; this is because the judiciary system is an institution ontologically distinct from the legislative organ(s) and the executive apparatus (see ch. 4.2.6.3 on the separation of powers), and also because, being judges the controllers, they cannot be controlled by people who are subjected to their control.

To clarify the role of judges, we can contrast it with the role of parliament and that of the executive apparatus. The *executive organ* represents the *power* of the community, and it performs, and forces citizens to perform, the *actions and moral acts* that have been projected by parliament through laws. The *legislative organ* (parliament) freely creates *projects* (laws) that are then realized through actions performed by the executive apparatus and by citizens. As a free creator of projects, the legislative organ represents the *intellect* of the community; not the intellect as creator of ideas (knowledge), but the intellect as free creator of *projects* that are realized by actions, i.e., it represents the intellect as support of the power; more exactly, it represents the *project-making activity of intellect*, whose projects support the actions performed by the power. Considering that a project is always a selected project, i.e., that it entails a decision, the legislative activity actually represents the *free decisions* of citizens, expressed as laws, about which projects should be realized. On the other hand, the judicial organ exerts a *cognitive function* (which belongs to the *cognitive activity of intellect*) concerned with the study of some concrete, particular actions, and expresses *informed, competent and, then, authoritative judgments* about their belonging to one or another of the classes of actions created by the laws. Thus, parliament expresses the *free project-making* activity of intellect; judges express a *cognitive function* of intellect (applied knowledge) through judgments; and the executive apparatus expresses the *power* to perform public actions.

Going back to the uncertainties that may arise when judges face extremely difficult situations, like the one mentioned above (settling the ultimate criteria by which the validity of the very laws, which confer upon courts themselves jurisdiction as judges, must itself be tested), we can say that judges are the most competent people who can decide about difficult cases, and they should perform this hard task by resorting to the most general constitutional norms, which should, even if indirectly, cover all fields of human activity. This is the *ground norm* that I propose in my ethical theory, i.e., the norm of *promoting mind evolution*, which covers all spheres of human activity. Thus, in a well-constructed legal system, there should not be legally "empty spaces" to be filled by the creativity of judges. When judges encounter a particular situation not regulated by a specific law, they can resort to a more general law or norm that covers the same field, even if in a less definite manner. Only in ill-constructed legal systems (i.e., in States with a defective constitution) can true legally "empty spaces" occur, which may be filled by the judge's decisions (always interpreting the moral principles and values most largely shared by the citizens—ch. 4.2.2.5, 2). In general, it should be pointed out that, if legal empty spaces exist, this is the result of a decision by the legislative organ (and, indirectly, by citizens), otherwise the lacking laws would have been issued. Therefore, in these situations, what actually happens is that the legislative organ issues only a general norm and *tacitly delegates* the judges to settle, by using their discretion, the particular cases that belong to the sphere of that general norm.

The above discussion, which clearly distinguishes the function of judges and that of legislative organs, also helps to avoid the suspicion that judges "exert power". This suspicion arises in some citizens mainly in special situations; for instance, when a court, in particular the "constitutional court" (or an equivalent organ), is called to decide whether a law enacted by parliament respects or not constitutional norms. In this situation, it may appear that the court has the "power" of declaring a law under scrutiny as valid or as non-valid and, therefore, has a "power" that overwhelms that of parliament (which has enacted that law). Indeed, judges do not have, and do not exert, any "power"; their task is to decide, by using their *knowledge* (both their general knowledge in the juridical field and specific knowledge gained through the deep study of the object of their decision), whether a

particular case (or a particular ordinary law) belongs or not to a class created by a law (or by a constitutional norm). This is shown by the hypothetical
case in which, after a court has judged a law issued by the legislative organ
as non-valid (i.e., unconstitutional), the legislative organ (through the procedure provided for by the constitution itself) changes the constitutional
norm that was violated by the law under scrutiny, after which the legislative
organs can re-issue the previously unconstitutional law, which, if re-
evaluated by a court, *must* now be declared as valid. Thus, judges exert a
function linked to their specific *knowledge* whereas legislative organs express their *free decisions* (i.e., they create projects, or laws), which will be
realized by *actions* performed by the executive apparatus and by citizens. In
other words, the activity of judges belongs to the sphere of *knowledge* (*intellect*); that of the legislative authority belongs to the creation of "laws",
i.e., of *projects* (*intellect*); and that of the executive apparatus belongs to the
sphere of *actions* (*power*) (ch. 4.2.6.3). It may be pointed out that, since any
action *must* realize a project, the executive apparatus, although representing
the *power*, must follow the projects/decisions (laws) created by legislative
organs about general matter, and the decisions of judges on how to apply
the laws in particular cases. Thus, the executive apparatus must follow the
free and *general* projects/decisions (norms, laws, and rules) created by legislative organs, concerning *classes* of actions, as well as the *particular* and
law-bound decisions taken by judges, concerning particular *members* of the
classes of actions defined by "laws"; in other words, the executive apparatus
must follow the decisions of legislative organs for general matters, and judicial decisions for particular cases (ch. 4.2.6.3).

4.2.4—Other Legal Theories

4.2.4.1—Kantianism

Kantianism aims at the defense of the principles that *ensure rights* of the
individual, even if these rights may cause unhappiness of others or disadvantage to society. These rights are linked to, and derive from, human nature, the nature of human beings who are able to make *free and rational
choices* and possess a *dignity* (Kant 1788; Rawls 1971; Dworkin 1977). I
think that a necessary premise to the discussion of this topic is to remember
that the rights of individuals are not of categorical nature but are directed to
the fundamental moral end, i.e., to the promotion of mind evolution (ch.
2.1.5.2.2).
    Concerning the defense of the rights of the individual, the problem of
the possible contrast that may arise between the rights of one or more individuals and those of others should be considered. In this regard, we should

keep in mind the hierarchical arrangement of moral principles and values (ch. 2.1.4.2; Table 2.1) and of the corresponding norms, laws, and rules (ch. 4.1.2.3; Figs. 4.2 and 4.3). Two situations should be distinguished: *(1)* conflict between rights of the same kind, and *(2)* conflict between different rights.

(1) Conflict Between Rights of the Same Kind. This kind of conflict may occur *(a)* between two groups of individuals numerically equal, or *(b)* between two groups numerically different.

(a) Let us consider the situation in which a physician has only one dose of a medicine that can save the life of one of two patients affected by the same disease. In this instance, there is a true contrast between two groups numerically equal (both include just one patient) concerning rights of the same kind (the right to life). Therefore, the choice is difficult or, perhaps, almost indifferent, since whichever is the choice, one patient will survive and one will die. Here the choosing agent my only resort to minor, questionable, and largely subjective arguments concerning the difference between the severity of the disease in the two patients (patients with the same disease always differ to some extent between one another) or the difference in the characteristics of the two patients themselves (such as the age). In any instance, this would be a difficult choice (chs. 2.2.1.5; 3.3).

(b) Suppose that a physician has 10 doses of a medicine that can save the life of patients affected by the disease "x" if administered within two hours, and that one of such patients is 100 km North from the physician's location while 10 of such patients are 100 km South. In this situation, the right in question is of the same kind (the right to life) but the two groups are numerically different. Hence, the right to life of the group of 10 patients should overwhelm that of the single patient. As noted by Murphy and Coleman (1990: 90–91), when a court defends a fundamental right of an individual against the desire or the interest of a group of individuals (or the entire society) it may appear in some way *antidemocratic* (indeed, in these instances, if the rights involved are equal, both the legal and the moral norms demand that the larger group should prevail). This, however, may be true when the right involved is the right to life, whose violation has effects which are irreversible and which occur in a yes-or-no manner. Things are different when other kinds of rights are involved. Suppose that a father of three sons, who has to choose whether he should utilize the amount of money that he possesses to allow that one of his sons gets a PhD degree whereas the other two sons are forced to stop at high school level, or utilize his money to allow that all three of his sons reach the law graduation level. Well, this father should decide by taking into account the *basic* right to equal treatment, on the one hand, and the merit shown by each of his sons, which raises merit-acquired rights, on the other. In most instances, the choice may be difficult (often moral choices are not an easy matter!) (chs.

2.2.1.5; 3.3).

(2) Conflict Between Different Rights. When the conflict is between rights of a different kind, the hierarchical arrangement of moral principles and values (ch. 2.1.4.2; Table 2.1) and of the corresponding various kinds of "laws" (ch. 4.1.2.3; Figs. 4.2 and 4.3) may be of help. Again, we should distinguish conflicts occurring between groups of individuals that are *(a)* numerically equal, or *(b)* numerically different.

(a) Contrast of different rights between groups of individuals numerically equal may occur when, for instance, a father has to choose between spending the little money he possesses on buying medicine that will save the life of one of his sons who is severely sick, or utilizing the money to send the other of his sons to school. Here the two groups of individuals concerned are numerically equal (both are made of one individual), but the rights involved are different; being the right to life prevalent over that to education (this descends from the ground moral norm, prescribing the pursuing of mind evolution, since death is the most severe and irreversible mind *involution*), the father should spend his money on buying the medicine for his sick son.

(b) Contrast of different rights between groups of individuals numerically different may raise very difficult problems. However, the right to life and that to health should always prevail over other rights, because of the sure irreversibility (concerning life) or possible irreversibility (concerning health) of the effects of their violation (ch. 4.1.2.3, *A*). When other rights are involved, the rights of the larger group and those concerning more general moral principles and values should prevail, even if, in this situation, the choice can only be made with approximation and, again, in special cases, very difficult moral choices (moral dilemmas) may arise.

4.2.4.2—Critical Legal Studies

The critical legal study movement consists of a severe criticism of the *formalism* and *objectivism* of traditional legal and moral theories and of the alleged general (i.e., shared by all or most human beings) principles of justice, fairness, and equality; these principles would be elaborated to justify or rationalize the injustices that necessarily arise from the *power relations* of the various components or groups of society (Unger 1986; Kelman 1987). The components or groups whose power relations determine the moral and legal principles would include: *(a)* The various classes existing in modern Western societies; *(b)* the classes as conceived by Marx (1859), according to whom the alleged moral principles are ideological superstructure elaborated by the dominant class; *(c)* the "masters" and the "slaves" as conceived by Nietzsche (1886: 156), according to whom there would be a *master mo-*

412 *Public Ethics and Philosophy of Law*

rality (for which strength is the major virtue) and the *slave morality* (for which love, humility, and justice are the major virtues); and *(d)* men and women, according to the so-called *feminist jurisprudence*, which underlines that conventional principles reflect dominance of men over women (Baier 1985; West 1988), as it would be shown by the jurisprudence about rape (Estrich 1987).

The above theories are all based on the concept that social moral principles and values, and the corresponding legal rules, are imposed by the dominant group (be it a class or a party or a gender), of which these principles and rules would express desires, interests, and preferences. To evaluate this position, we should distinguish the situation occurring in the non-constitutional non-democratic States (which prevailed in most parts of the world until a few decades ago) and the situation occurring in modern democratic and constitutional States. In the former group of States, arbitrary imposition of desires, interest or preference of the dominant group (be it a large or a small group) may indeed occur, since in these States society is governed by violence, and not through publicly-justified (shared) legal rules based on shared moral principles and values. Things are different in democratic and constitutional States. Here constitutional norms (being moral projects publicly-shared by the largest possible majority of citizens) represent the best approach to the *principle of universality* of laws, i.e., they are publicly-shared by the largest possible majority of citizens and cover moral principles and values largely shared because they express the common good, i.e., what is good for *all* the members (or for most of them) of the class of men (in my conception: mind evolution, in all its aspects), and not for one or more sub-classes into which society may be divided. Of course, there may be minorities that do not adhere to the constitutional norms. These may be "bad minorities", which refuse to recognize the moral values expressed by the constitutional norms. An example of "bad minorities" may be racialist minorities existing in some countries, which would like to discriminate some ethnic groups. On the other hand, these minorities may be "good minorities", which indeed would like to "improve" the constitution, i.e., to change it so that it may reflect what, *in their opinion*, are higher moral principles and values. These minorities (*dissenting citizens*), while having the duty to respect all the democratic laws (included the ones that they do not endorse—because the democratic laws represent the best approach to universality) are entitled to promote, by democratic means (which should be provided for by all constitutions), their opinion in the hope that it will become the opinion of the majority and will be included, through legal ways (again, provided for by the constitution itself), into the legal system (ch. 4.1.1.3.2, *B*). An example of "good minority" may be represented by those citizens who in Switzerland promoted the right of women to vote and, a few decades ago, succeeded in changing the law accordingly. Thus, the only way open to the "good minorities" that feel that they are "oppressed" by the existing laws is to hope for the evolution of the consciousness of the community, which they are entitled to stimulate, so that the undesired laws can be changed.

4.2.4.3—The Rule of Law

According to Raz (1979), in order for the rule of law to be effective and significant, the following principles should be respected.

(a) Principles directed to enable the law to effectively guide actions: all laws (as well as the particular legal orders and commands, such as those enacted by a police constable, or an authority granting a license, or other offices of the executive apparatus, etc.) should be prospective, open, clear, and relatively stable.

(b) Principles directed to avoid (and to remedy for) distortion in the enforcement of law: judiciary must be independent, justice should be exerted accordingly to natural justice (open and fair hearing, absence of bias, etc.), courts should have review powers and should be easily accessible (since high costs, long delays, etc., may turn law into a dead letter), and the discretion of the crime-preventing agencies (police and prosecuting authorities) should not be allowed to pervert the law.

Raz (1979) notes, however, that strict conformity to the rule of law is impossible, as some vagueness is unavoidable, and perhaps desirable, as some controlled administrative discretion is better than none. I fully agree with Raz's above statements; what I would like to comment on is the affirmation (Raz 1979) that the *rule of law* is an inherent virtue of the law but not a moral virtue; this would be so because, although the rule of law prevents arbitrary power, it should not be confused with democracy, justice, equality, human rights or respect of a person, since a legal system may not respect these principles and may still conform to the requirements of the rule of law. Here I ask myself whether the rule of law can exist without democracy, justice and respect of human rights. As correctly stated by Raz, the rule of law requires that judiciary is independent and that courts have review powers. Yet, in a non-democratic, non-constitutional State, there is no warranty for the separation of powers and, hence, for the independence of the judiciary, nor is it possible that the courts exert judicial review. Moreover, how can a non-democratic State assure justice? (Here I refer to *public* justice, not to one or another of the possible *private* conceptions of justice). Actually, the publicly-shared conception of justice is that defined by constitutional norms (i.e., the one supported by the largest possible percentage of citizens and, therefore, representing *the best approach to universality*), so that in a non-constitutional State, no public justice can exist.

Likewise, publicly recognized human rights are those stated by constitutional norms (which, again, represent *the best approach to universality*); hence, in a non-constitutional State there is no way to establish which are the human rights to be recognized. Thus, it seems to me that the democratic, constitutional State is the appropriate environment where the rule of law can be fully realized. Thus, *rule of law actually is synonym of implementation of the principle of the best approach to universality.* What the rule of law can assure in a non-democratic State is that arbitrary power is exerted by means of open and relatively stable laws and legal procedures.

One of the requirements of the rule of law is that laws should not be applied retrospectively. In this regard, Hart (1958) recalls a case related to the horrors of the Nazi regime; in commenting on the decision of the court of appeal, which held guilty a woman who had denounced her husband for insulting remarks about Hitler (thus violating the Nazi statute), he notes that the decision of the court was based on the consideration that the statute "was contrary to the sound conscience and sense of justice of all decent human beings." According to Hart, this decision (while responding to the largely shared desire of punishing an outrageously immoral act) actually meant to apply a law retrospectively, i.e., to sacrifice a very precious principle of morality endorsed by most legal systems. Here my comment is that the claimed "laws" issued by the Nazi regime were actually arbitrary orders backed by violence, because the Nazi Germany was not a democratic State (there was no freedom of thought, discussion, and press nor truly free political voting) so that its "pseudo-laws" did not express moral principles and values publicly-shared by the majority of citizens, but desires and interest of a violent minority (imposed on misinformed citizens). Thus, the denounced husband had not broken any true law, but had only expressed his contempt for a bloodthirsty dictator; the court did not apply a law retroactively, since the Nazi statute had arbitrarily substituted the previous legitimate legal system (which surely did not regard the contempt for bad persons as a crime), which should be considered as still in force. If one hypothesizes that a democratic legal system did not exist before the Nazi regime, then it would be justified to resort to the basic instances of the human soul (as did the court of appeal in the above-cited case). Indeed, referring to the hierarchical arrangement of laws (ch. 4.1.2.3), it should be remembered that the non-retroactivity of laws, like the maxim "Nulla pena sine lege," is valid for rules and laws, but not for the most basic norms expressing the most basic moral principles and values, common to all men (at least to all the men belonging to the same stage of evolution of human consciousness, which prevents us from despising a citizen of ancient Rome for being a slave-owner); this is because moral judgment is unavoidable in the human world and because the human consciousness, with its basic moral principles and values, is the ultimate source of law.

4.2.5—Law and Economics

(A) The Basic Thesis.
According to the *law and economics movement*, the rules of any system of positive law (and perhaps any sphere of human activity) could be best described, explained, and evaluated by the principles of economics (Altman 1995: 170–71). This is because the rationality of an agent's decision and action would be a function of its *costs* and *benefits*; the latter should be conceived as including not only financial gains and losses but also any kind of *preference*, and nevertheless they would be susceptible to being measured by a common unit, money (Altman 1995: 171).

According to my conception, because of the close inter-relationship between the three mind components (intellect, sensitiveness, and power), consisting of the fact that each of these components needs for its activity the support of the other two (chs. 1.1.1.1, 6; 1.1.2, 2nd proposition), any event occurring in one of these mind-components is associated with a supporting event in the other two. Since money is a measure of the power (i.e., of the ability to act), it is apt not only to measure major events produced by the power in its activity (such as economic events directed to increase the power) but also minor actions that support the activity of intellect and of sensitiveness. Yet, the activity specific to the power should be distinguished from the supporting activity that the power provides to the intellect and the sensitiveness. Therefore, money cannot measure events specifically produced by intellect (knowledge) or by sensitiveness (sentiments). If I buy a valuable picture for $100,000 and a music compact disc of Beethoven's 9th symphony for $20, I have made two actions (belonging to the sphere of power) that have very different monetary values but a similar value from the point of view of the sentiment (belonging to the sphere of sensitiveness), as both give me a high aesthetic enjoyment.

According to Posner (1972; 1990: 353–54), all people, either consciously or unconsciously, are rational *maximizers of their satisfactions*, both monetary and non-monetary, in all their choices. I think that this is a general and vague statement, which can be usefully discussed if we refer to my ontological theory about the structure of the mind. "Satisfactions", both monetary and non-monetary, in a broad sense, refers to the satisfaction of *sentiments* (desires or preferences), which are produced by *sensitiveness*. Thus, we should conclude that human life is primarily driven by *sensitiveness*, which would override the other two mind components: *intellect* and *power*. To discuss this view, we should consider *(a)* the various kinds of satisfaction (or of sentiments to be satisfied), and *(b)* the close relationship between sentiments (produced by *sensitiveness*), ideas or knowledge (produced by *intellect*), and actions (produced by *power*).

(a) Satisfaction may refer to different kinds of "sentiments", inasmuch

as we should distinguish *personal* or *egoistic sentiments*, produced by the *outward* activity of sensitiveness (or *emotional selfishness*), and *moral feelings*, produced by the *inward* activity of sensitiveness (or *emotional consciousness*) (Fig. 1.1). We should also consider that both sentiments and moral feelings might vary from light or superficial to deep or universal (according to the distinction based on the *value criterion*), or from "bad" to "good" (according to the distinction based on the *morality criterion*) (Table 1.1). Thus, maximizing one's satisfaction may have very different meanings according to which kind of "sentiments" (light or deep personal sentiments—such as desires or preferences—or moral feelings) are satisfied (this is exemplified in the discussion that follows—section "*B*", point "2").

(b) Human life is not primarily driven by sentiments, as produced by sensitiveness; rather, any human event is the product of all the three mind components, which cannot operate separately, due to the unit of the mind; it is true, however, that any human event (action, or idea, or sentiment) is primarily produced by one of the three mind components, with the support of the other two (chs. 1.1.1.1, 6; 1.1.2, 2nd proposition). Both law and economy belong to the sphere of the *power*, since "law" refers to the *laws*, which, though they are the product of the project-making activity of intellect, regulate citizens' *actions* and allow them to get or approach universality, and *economy* refers to the economic activity, which is one of the ways (together with political activity) through which the power of individuals or groups (i.e., the ability to act) expresses itself. Human actions are produced by the *power* with the support of *sensitiveness* and of *intellect*, since any action is directed to realize an *idea-of-project* (created by *intellect*) and is prompted by a *sentiment* (desire), created by *sensitiveness*, toward that project. [Likewise: any human *sentiment* toward an object needs the support of intellect, in order to know that object, and of power (body structures), in order to be able to know the object. Similarly, any human *idea* about an object needs the support of the power (body structures) in order to be able to know that object, and of sensitiveness, in order to desire to know the object]. Thus, the co-existence of all the three mind components is always present.

The basic thesis of the "law and economics" movement led Altman (1995: 171–98) to develop his views about: *benefit* ("net" and "expected"); *cost-benefit* (evaluated by utilitarian approach, or by the "Pareto optimality" and "Pareto superiority" concepts of efficiency, or by the "Kaldor-Hicks' criterion"); *contracts, torts* and *property*; and *productive efficiency and wealth maximization*. The last concept is worthy of a short comment.

(B) Wealth Maximization.

According to Posner (1990: 356), wealth maximization refers to wealth conceived as the sum of all tangible and intangible goods and services, weighted by offer prices and asking prices; this view leads to the striking conclusion that a desire not backed by the ability to pay "has no standing," because it is neither an offer price nor an asking price. If person "B" is willing to sell his stamp collection for any price above $90, and "A" is willing to pay $100 for B's stamps, then, according to Posner, the following consideration can be made:

> Before the transaction A had $100 in cash and B had a stamp collection worth $90 (a total of $190); after the transaction A has a stamp collection worth $100 and B has $100 in cash (a total of $200). The transaction will not raise measured wealth—gross national product, national income, or whatever—by $10 . . . But the real addition to social wealth consists of the $10 increment in non-pecuniary satisfaction that A derives from the purchase, compared with that of B. This shows that 'wealth' in the economist's sense is not a simple monetary measure . . . (Posner 1990: 356).

Posner's views, mentioned above, are questionable. Let us consider the following points.

(1) The above example is flawed because the statement that "A" was willing to sell his stamp collection for any price above $90 is too vague to be meaningful; indeed, if "A" sold his collection for $100, this means that, at the time of transaction, he asked $100 (it is unrealistic to think that he asked $90 and yet "B" gave him $100!). Thus, there was not the "real addition to social wealth consisting of $10," as claimed by Posner.

(2) Desires (more generally: *sentiments*) are of different "quality", as they may vary, according to the *value criterion* (ch. 1.1.3.2.2; Table 1.1), from light or particular to deep or universal. Suppose that an artistically educated person is willing to sell a valuable picture for $10,000 and that a rich but uneducated person is willing to buy it (just to show his richness) for the same price, and he buys it. In this case, the transaction does not change the measured wealth, yet the satisfaction of a "high" aesthetic sentiment has been substituted with the satisfaction of a "low" sentiment, i.e., a change in *ontologically existing entities* (sentiments) has occurred. If the buyer were an artistically educated person, a different situation would have arisen: the exchange would have produced the substitution of the satisfaction of a high sentiment with that of another high sentiment. This shows that money is a measure of power, and not of sensitiveness or of sentiments. Moreover, it should also be born in mind that desires may change with time (as individual minds continuously change or evolve), which introduces a complicating factor.

(3) Suppose that an educated man must sell a valuable picture because he needs money to cure his sick son; he asks a very low price, say $100, in order to sell the picture quickly. The picture is bought by an uneducated man, who is willing to pay exactly $100. In this case the transaction has not changed the measured wealth, but has caused a great dissatisfaction (in the seller) and a low-level satisfaction (in the buyer). Money is definitely not a suitable measure of desire-satisfaction.

(4) Posner (1990: 357–58) also maintains that transactions need not be Pareto superior (i.e., they should not necessarily entail that at least one person should be better-off and nobody worse-off); he thinks that if an accident, whose probability of occurrence is 0.01, inflicts a cost of $100 and if avoiding it costs $3, the accident can be considered as a wealth-maximizing "transaction"; the contrary is true if the costs were reversed. This, again, is a deduction based only on economic aspects (belonging to the sphere of power) of an accident; yet, an accident (by producing, for instance, psychological stress or physical disability) may exert effects in the sphere of sentiments (belonging to sensitiveness), and even in the sphere of knowledge (belonging to intellect) that cannot be evaluated by economic measures, or can be evaluated by economic measures only in part.

I underline that maximization of wealth, actually, means promoting the evolution of one of the mind components, the *power*. Maximization of one's own power may be expression of *morally-bad egoism* whereas, if pursued in accord to moral norms, it may be an expression of the *morally-good egoism* and is one of the duties toward oneself (ch. 2.1.5.2.2); therefore, maximizing one's own power may be one of the ends prescribed by the ground moral norm, together with the promotion of the evolution of *intellect* and of *sensitiveness*.

(5) There are *political aspects of wealth maximization* that should be considered; as summarized by Altman (1995: 189–90), it has been objected that *(a)* wealth maximization is biased against the poor, because the wealthy are able to spend more money than the poor on what they desire, and *(b)* economic efficiency as a criterion for evaluating the law is biased in favor of the right-wing political party. I note that giving preeminent weight to money and to the economic aspects of life (sphere of power) and to the satisfaction of desires and preferences (which are personal sentiments produced by the *outward* activity of sensitiveness—or *emotional selfishness*), will favor those who have much money and then much power, who will be able to satisfy their desires. The point is that this view neglects other aspects of the human mind, e.g., the role of moral feelings (produced by the *inward* activity of sensitiveness or *emotional consciousness*—Fig. 1.1), which is not directed to maximize wealth but to promote mind evolution (which may include pursuing wealth only as expression of the *morally-good* egoism).

Posner (1972; 1990) observes that economic efficiency may be best promoted by liberal rather than by conservative policies. Thus, social programs to help the poorest (*welfare programs*) may prevent the latter to commit crimes and, therefore, avoid social expenses to contrast and to prosecute crimes; and government intervention is preferable to private charity in order to avoid the "free-rider" problem. I think that welfare programs have not (or, at least, not only) the scope of avoiding expenses for contrasting crimes, but the scope of creating a morally higher environment and of ensuring that all citizens may enjoy the evolution-allowing condition that enables them to develop their mind in all its components, according to their natural endowment (i.e., the scope of implementing the ground moral norm).

Wealth maximization would support individual rights better than utilitarianism (Posner 1972; 1990); thus, what a slave produces goes to the owner, which is an incentive for the slave to work unproductively. Again, I observe that slavery should not be opposed to just because it causes unproductive work but because it severely restrains the evolution of a slave's mind, in all its three components (intellect, sensitiveness, and power); the increase in productivity should only be a (minor) component of the various motives for opposing slavery.

It is noteworthy that, as summarized by Altman (1995: 192–93), liberals give priority to *social justice* over efficiency (which requires redistribution from the free-market outcomes); on the other hand, conservatives maintain that justice is not a priority value, that the outcomes of a free-market are essentially just (perhaps correcting the transaction costs when they limit the efficiency), and that justice and other moral values can be reduced to personal preferences that serve to evaluate what is most efficient (i.e., what maximizes the satisfaction of preferences). I note that pursuing the satisfaction of preferences actually refers to the satisfactions of the people who have power (at the expenses of the weak citizens), and that justice should not be conceived as limited to pursue wealth maximization (i.e., development of the *power*, with no consideration for intellect and sensitiveness) but should consist of the recognition that all citizens possess the right to enjoy the evolution-allowing condition, which enables them to develop their mind, in all its components.

(C) Additional Aspects.

According to Posner (1972; 1990), to understand "*law and economics*", the following assumptions, concerning *legislators* and the *judiciary and the courts*, should also be considered.

(1) Legislators. Legislators would also be rational maximizers of their satisfaction, just like everyone else; they would not be motivated by public interest but by their will to be elected (Posner 1990: 354). To reach this end, they would search the following supports.

(a) Support by organized groups. Posner (1990) points out that, in order to be elected or re-elected, legislators need money, which is more likely to be forthcoming from well-organized groups. He says:

> [T]he rational individual will have little incentive to invest time and effort in deciding whom to vote for. Only an organized group of individuals . . . will be able to overcome the informational and free rider problems that plague collective action. [An interest group will] trade the votes of its members and its financial support to candidates in exchange for an implied promise of favorable

legislation; [this results in] a statute transferring wealth from unorganized taxpayers . . . to the interest group . . . The unorganized are unlikely to mount effective opposition . . . On this view, a statute is a deal. (Posner 1990: 354–55)

Posner's above view is centered on two concepts: *first*, the "organized
groups"; and, *second*, the "unorganized taxpayers".

First concept: The organized groups. To understand what the organized
groups actually are, I will refer, again, to my ontological conception. The
citizens of a State, according to their natural aptitudes (and the environmental opportunities), tend to divide into three large categories: those who primarily develop their *intellect*, those who primarily develop their *sensitiveness*, and those who primarily develop their *power*. In each category, citizens will reach a different degree of evolution, going from a low level to a
high level of evolution. Among the citizens who primarily develop power,
those who reach a high level represent what Posner calls the "organized
groups". The behavior of these "organized groups", like the behavior of any
human being, may be "good" or "bad", according to *the morality criterion
of judgment*, to which no individual or group can escape. The behavior described by Posner would be a "bad" one, since these groups would give
their financial support to candidates in exchange for an implied promise of
favorable legislation, which would result in a statute that is a deal, i.e., that
transfers wealth from unorganized taxpayers to the interest group. Yet, the
"organized groups" could also show a "good" behavior, i.e., they could give
their support to those candidates who promise a legislation favorable to their
interest framed into a general project for the development of all kinds of
economic enterprises and taking into account the interest of all citizens,
which would result in an increased welfare for all, i.e., in the *promotion of
mind evolution* (and not in a transfer of wealth from unorganized taxpayers
to the interest groups). Here I underline that the prescription of the moral
norm to promote mind evolution refers to all minds, i.e., be individuals or
groups. Thus, the pressure exerted by the "organized groups" changes its
meaning according to whether it is directed to increase personal or group
interest at the expense of other citizens or to promote the general interest of
the community (including the interest of the acting agents), in accordance
with the prescription of the ground moral norm. This confirms that, without
reference to the *structure of the mind* and to the *ground moral norm* prescribing *mind evolution*, nothing of the human world can be understood and
evaluated. It is noteworthy that excessively powerful "organized bad
groups" may exert an excessive weight in political life and undue pressure
over the government and other political or social institutions, and may even
undermine the fundaments of democracy. For this reason, a limit in the economic growth of individuals or groups should be established by specific
laws, which should have the rank of constitutional norms (ch. 3.1.2.2.2).

Second concept: The unorganized taxpayers. These are not, as thought by Posner, rational individuals who have little incentive to invest time and effort in deciding whom to vote for. Actually, they represent a composite group, which includes not only those citizens who primarily operate in the sphere of power and who have reached a low or medium degree of evolution, but also those citizens who primarily operate in the sphere of intellect (producing knowledge) or of sensitiveness (producing arts). Of these, some have reached a high degree of evolution and represent well-organized groups in their field. In the sphere of the activity of *intellect*, we have the "scientific group or community", represented by the academic community (scientific faculties), scientists working in research centers, research groups, scientific societies, etc.; in the sphere of the activity of *sensitiveness*, we have the "artistic community", represented by those working in the literary, artistic or musical academies, in theaters, etc. Since the power is supported by the intellect and by the sensitiveness, both these communities may exert their political pressure, which, as in the case of Posner's "organized groups", may be directed to a "good" or to a "bad" end. It will be a "good" pressure if it is directed to spread the knowledge that may help to better understand political problems and to promote the desire to improve social life; it will be a "bad" pressure if it is directed to sustain a political party through a biased propaganda in exchange for the concession of some advantages. Moreover, even citizens who have not reached a high level of evolution can get organized (e.g., trade-unions and similar associations) and can exert political pressure. Finally, it should be noted that most of the "unorganized taxpayers" belong to the worse-off groups and are *very interested* in making the right choice about whom to vote for.

(b) Support by the unorganized people. Posner (1990: 355) points out that legislators are also interested in defending rule-of-law virtues and in providing basic public services (national defense, crime control, dispute setting, etc.) because voters want them. It is after these services have been provided and means of taxation and redistribution have developed, that "the formation of narrow interest groups and the extraction by them of transfers from unorganized groups become feasible" (Posner 1990: 355). Translated into my conception, this means that legislators take into account not only the pressure of the "organized groups" but also the request of all voters, who ask for rule of law and basic public services (which may include taxation and redistribution), i.e., they take into account all citizens. Indeed, legislators would take into account firstly the needs and desires of all the voters, and then would accept the pressure of the "organized groups", which is in contrast with Posner's supposed preeminence of the latter groups in political life. What Posner indicates as rule of law and basic services actually are, or should be, those concrete conditions that make possible for all citizens to attempt to develop their mind (*evolution-allowing, involution-avoiding condition*). When this condition is realized, citizens will develop

their mind according to their natural endowment. Those who are primarily prone to develop their power, if they succeed in reaching a high degree of evolution, will form Posner's "organized groups". If the consciousness of the community is developed enough, politicians who accept bad pressures of the "organized groups" should not be voted.

(2) The Judiciary and the Courts. Posner (1990: 355) points out that legislation needs interpretation and application, which is the role of the courts; the latter are agents of the legislature. Three points should be commented about Posner's view concerning the courts:

(a) He notes that judiciary must be independent to impart credibility and durability to the deals that the legislature strikes with interest groups, as well as to provide a basic public service by resolving disputes in a way that encourages trade, freedom of action, etc. (Posner 1990: 355). I think that judges should impartially apply laws, which should define the rights/duties valid for all citizens, including both the common citizen and the ones belonging to the "organized groups"; it follows that the impartiality of judges cannot serve "to the deals that the legislature strikes with interest groups" (unless "wrong" laws have been enacted by the legislative organs, or the judges in charge are "bad").

(b) There would be an efficient division of labor between the legislative and the judicial branches, as the former concentrates "on catering the interest-group demands for wealth distribution," and the latter "on meeting the broad-based social demand for efficient rules governing safety, property, and transaction" (Posner 1990: 360). I note that the "efficient rules" that judges apply are enacted by the legislative organs (even precedents are framed into principles stated by laws); therefore, it is the legislative power that should respond to both the "broad-based social demand" and the "interest-group demands". If the latter demands are lawful and directed to promote economic enterprises in a frame of general development (i.e., if they ensure that all citizens enjoy the evolution-allowing condition), it is good that they are satisfied because, in this instance, they would be an expression of personal talent and will enhance the wealth of the community (see the concept of *morally-good egoism*—ch. 2.1.5.2.2). On the other hand, if the demands of the "interest groups" are directed to egoistically favor their interest, they should not be satisfied, because they would be an expression of violence against weaker citizens. Thus, again, it all depends on whether the finality is good or bad, i.e., if it is consistent, or not, with the promotion of mind evolution of all citizens.

(c) Finally, Posner (1990: 360) affirms that possible goals of judicial action, besides efficiency and redistribution, such as "fairness" or "justice", are actually labels for wealth maximization or for redistribution in favor of powerful interest groups. I think that fairness and justice are the goal of judges in their application of the existing laws. It is the legal system that can

be directed to wealth maximization, which, however, should be correctly conceived; the legal system, however, reflects the degree of evolution of the consciousness of the community and is under the control of the voters. A legal system should be directed to promote not only wealth (produced by the *power*) but also knowledge (produced by the *intellect*) and literary, musical and artistic experiences and creativity (produced by *sensitiveness*), i.e., it should be directed to promote the evolution of all the three mind components.

4.2.6—*Constitutionalism*

4.2.6.1—Moral Philosophy and Constitutional Law

The constitution (i.e., the body of the constitutional norms) can be regarded as the founding act through which a community organizes itself as a democratic State, by defining moral principles and values that the organized community intends to pursue and the structure and functioning of the State apparatus required to this end. The ideal constitution should be created by a *constituent assembly*, which should represent all citizens, and should be composed of elected members. Yet, at the time when a constituent assembly is elected, there are no publicly-shared rules for such an election, because the State has not yet been founded. Thus, at the origin, a *provisional authority* is required to provide for the first organization steps needed to elect the members of the assembly and to create and maintain a minimum of environmental order that allows the accomplishment of the election. Thus, it could be objected that the initial step for the birth of a democratic State is not itself democratic. But this is not true. Indeed, the origin of a democratic State lies in the will of the large majority of the members of a community to organize themselves into a State. This shared will is the basis for the new State and manifests itself by expressing and accepting a spontaneously formed provisional authority (if a spontaneously formed authority does not meet the shared will of the community, it will not be recognized and obeyed). I underline that this initial shared will of the members of a community to organize themselves into a State is *morally good*, because the organized society is the way through which human actions evolve toward universality, inasmuch as the particular actions of individuals become universal actions of the community (ch. 3.1.1.1.1). The universalization of actions means *evolution* of the *power*, and is therefore in accordance with the prescription of the ground moral norm, of *promoting mind evolution*.

The main scope of the constituent assembly (besides the definition of the structure and functioning of the State) is to freely choose the *moral principles* and *values* that the organized community (or society) intends to pursue, and to state them in the constitutional norms; the latter, therefore, are general (or universal) *projects* directed to pursue the chosen moral ends, as defined by the shared moral principles and values. This is because the constitutional assembly is not concerned with particular problems regarding some groups or classes of the community, but with the general problems regarding all men who belong to the community, i.e., the problems related to the essential properties shared by all men and that define the class of men (even if this class is limited to the men belonging to the community). According to my conception, the essential property of all men (which defines the entire *class of men*), which, as such, is shared by any community of men, consists of the fact that men are minds formed of *intellect, sensitiveness,* and *power*, and capable of *evolution*. Evolution, entailing the change into ever "better states", is the objective human good as defined by moral thoughts (moral principles), felt by moral feelings (moral values), and prescribed by the ground moral norm (ch. 2.1.4.1), from which human rights are derived (ch. 2.1.5.2.2). Here a comparison can be made with the metaphor of the social contract. The members of the constituent assembly are the true contractors; they need not to put themselves behind Rawls' *veil of ignorance* (Rawls 1971: 118–23), but need only the awareness that they are called not to make choices concerning particular groups (not the desires, interest or preferences of the group of the rich, or of the group of poor, or of the group of intelligent people, or of any other group). Rather, the members of the constituent assembly are called to make choices concerning all the people and, therefore, based on the essential properties of the class of men, the ability to undergo *evolution*. The task of the constitutional assembly is to identify the moral principles and values to be pursued and to state the corresponding *norms* (which, consequently, are essentially *moral norms*). The latter will serve as guide for the enactment of the ordinary laws, which can be regarded as members of the class of laws defined by each moral norm (see ch. 4.1.2.3; Figs. 4.2 and 4.3, on the hierarchical arrangement of laws).

The picture that I have just described refers to a hypothetical, ideal condition in which the community, and the members of the constitutional assembly that represent them, share a fully developed moral consciousness, producing moral principles and values like those proposed in this book. However, it should be recalled that the *consciousness of the community* (like its selfishness) *evolves* through time (decades, centuries, and millennia) so that, at a given historical period, the shared moral principles and values express the level of the evolution reached by the consciousness of a community. Like knowledge and desires, which evolve through time as the expression of the evolution of the outward mind activity (selfishness), so the recognized moral principles and values change with time as the expression of the evolution of the inward mind activity (consciousness). Thus, each constitution reflects the degree of evolution reached by the consciousness of a community at a given time. Since evolution (which is the fundamental property of the mind) means changing, a constitution should always be amendable through procedures provided for by the constitution itself, so that constitutional norms can follow the evolution of the community consciousness.

The creation of constitutional norms (and their changes) should be approved by a *large* majority of citizens, because these norms are concerned with the basic rights and duties of *all* men. Referring to the classification described in a previous chapter (ch. 3.1.2.1.2, *1*, *2*), constitutional norms certainly belong to the "1st rank laws". Moreover, constitutional norms should be issued not through voting by all citizens (which is a complex and expensive process that cannot be repeated until a large majority is attained), but through voting by the members of an elected assembly, where voting may be preceded by a *competent* and *interactive* discussion (the representatives have the duty to spend the time required to study and discuss the proposed projects that, if approved, will become constitutional norms) and, when the required majority of approving votes is not reached, the proposed norm can be modified and voting can be repeated until the required majority of the voters will approve the norm (project). Only subsequent changes to the constitution, concerning single issues suitable to be presented to the voters in a clear and simple manner, can be made through voting by all citizens (referendum).

The ability of citizens to understand political events is very important. Waldron (1990: 56–87; 1998: 273–74) underlines that, as it has also been noted by others (Marshall 1984), especially in the U.K. but also in countries where there is a written constitution, such as the U.S., a political event that will prove to fundamentally affect political life may not be understood as such (only a carefully study of political events may allow to discern those that will have normative significance). Therefore, a change that will prove to have constitutional relevance may be democratically approved and yet the constitutional change cannot be defined as democratic. I note that this can be avoided if two conditions are met: *first*, constitutional norms and ordinary laws are enacted by the representatives of citizens (democratically elected assemblies); *second*, the vote of citizens is directed to choose the people to be elected (considering their personal qualities and the party to which they belong), or to take decisions about very basic and simply-presented issues (as occur with referendums). This is because often the decisions concern very complex matters; whereas the representatives of citizens have the duty to spend the required time and to make the necessary effort to study and understand, through interactive discussion, every "object" of political decision, citizens, engaged in their every-day activity, may not have the possibility or the ability to make such a study and to reach a full understanding of the various political issues at stake. For these reasons, the modern, complex society requires indirect, *representative* democracy.

The ideal condition would be that constitutional norms be approved by all the citizens (through their representatives), and that each voter should be fully and objectively informed and free from any influence. In the real world, this never happens; yet constitutional norms should be approved by a large majority (say, 4/5) of the voters; the larger the percentage of the approving votes the better, because the end to be pursued is *the best approach to universality*. Thus, an ideal, fully moral constitution will never be realized in the real world (likewise, a complete knowledge will never be reached); yet, through history, constitutional law should progressively evolve, together with the evolution of the consciousness of the community, toward ever better stages, with regard to both the percentage of the approving voters and the completeness of the moral principles and values pursued (see the similar concept about the degree of democracy of a government, in ch. 3.1.2.2.1, *4*).

The above discussion shows that constitutional norms actually express moral principles and values shared by the large majority of the community; hence the link between constitution and moral philosophy. Thus, any constitution presupposes the adhesion (either conscious or unconscious) to a moral conception. This has long been recognized, as indicated by the statement of Austin (1832: 216) "Constitutional law is positive morality merely" and by Kelsen's postulate about the necessity of a ground norm ("grundnorm"). Yet, since both thinkers lacked a reference to a basic philosophical conception, Austin limited himself to a reference to a "positive morality", and that's that; and Kelsen, late in his life, ended by considering legal norms as based on a necessary "fiction" (1979: 256). Dworkin, too, attempted to find a moral foundation for something comparable to constitutional laws, by appealing to principles that refer to the "requirement of justice or fairness or some other dimension of morality" (1977: 22; 1986). The problem is that there is not a generally accepted moral theory. MacIntyre (1981: 204–25) proposed that the foundation of ethics is based on community-shared sets of values and is thus linked to historical evolution of the culture of a community. I underline, however, that in Austin's above cited statement, the term "positive" should be understood as meaning "publicly-shared by the majority of the community members," and the term "morality" as meaning "the pursuing of mind evolution". The latter norm is not in contrast with MacIntyre's view, since the moral instance of pursuing mind evolution develops historically, together with the evolution of the *consciousness* of the community. This is reflected in an ever-fuller recognition of moral principles and values (and in the enacting of the corresponding legal norms). The point is that, in my conception, the evolution of consciousness leads to progressively understand (or discover) the objective moral good, mind evolution, and this will be reflected in the progressive introduction of constitutional norms directed to pursue it.

Hobbes (1668: 202) claimed that "auctoritas, non veritas, facit legem" ("authority, not truth, makes the law"), which means that laws are based on violence. Weber (1922: 866) holds that constitution law is a positive law that, as such, derives its authority and binding force from its being originated by a legitimate lawgiver. I note that the only legitimate lawgiver is an assembly that represents all citizens, and that the enacted norms are legitimate only if they are approved by the largest possible majority.

Preuss (1996) points out that constitutional law relies on its formal-procedural quality as the result of a more or less arbitrary enactment, unrelated to morality; here I note that there is no "arbitrary enactment" if constitutional laws are enacted by the largest possible majority of an assembly representing all citizens. Preuss (1996) adds that laws, as such, should be general and stable, and should include universally valid truths and reflect the spirit of the whole polity (the law would essentially be reason and not will, *ratio* and not *voluntas*) (Preuss 1996). I observe that laws are indirectly linked to truth and to reason, inasmuch as they are *publicly-shared projects* produced by the activity of *intellect* through the utilization of the previously acquired knowledge about truth (chs. 1.1.1.2.1; 4.1.1.1). The statement that laws should reflect the spirit of the whole polity (see above) should be understood as meaning that laws should reflect the shared *moral principles* (created by *moral thoughts*) and *moral values* ("founded" by *moral feelings*) of the community.

Preuss (1996) maintains that constitution laws are separated from morality and other social relations, since they bind all citizens regardless to their moral, religious, or political beliefs. I think that we should keep moral principles distinct from religious or political beliefs. The publicly-shared moral principles are the basis of constitutional law and, therefore, of the State itself, and should be recognized by most citizens because moral principles are linked to the *universal*, essential properties common to *all* men. In contrast, religious or political beliefs concern *particular*, individual properties that define the individuality of each citizen (or group) and, as such, should be allowed to freely develop toward a rich spectrum of diversities, without any pressure by laws. However, it should be underlined that, besides *public* (i.e., publicly-shared) moral principles, which should be recognized by most citizens, there may be (and, indeed, there are) personal or *private* moral principles, which are those principles endorsed by a minority of citizens or by single individuals. These "private moral principles", of course, are ignored by constitutional norms. Private moral principles may be "better" or "worse" than the publicly-shared ones. The worse of these principles are those endorsed by the "bad" citizens, whereas the better ones are those endorsed by citizens with a greatly developed consciousness and may, with time (when the community consciousness develops further), be publicly recognized and then incorporated into the constitutional law (e.g., in

Switzerland, the right of women to vote was a private moral principle, not publicly recognized until a few decades ago, when it was introduced in the law after a referendum) (see also ch. 4.1.1.3.2, *B*, on the *dissenting citizens*).

4.2.6.2—The Nature and Function of Constitution

4.2.6.2.1—The Constitution and the Hierarchy of "Powers"

Defining the nature and function of the constitutional law has proven to be a very complex issue (Rosenbaum, ed., 1988; Greenberg et al. 1993; Bellamy, ed., 1996; Alexander, ed., 1998). Gaus (1994b) says that the constitution limits the sovereign power of the lawmaking authority by requiring that the government rules both *through* laws and *by* law; this means that the obligation of the ruler to employ the form of the law for his acts is itself an obligation of the law (Preuss 1996). Likewise, Preuss (1996) thinks that there is not the need for a legal hierarchy but rather for a reflexive mechanism by which it is possible the making of rules for rule making (Hart's secondary rules would be the result of a reflexive mechanism), which would occur through the separation of powers (Preuss 1996). In contrast with these views, I think that the conception of the democratic, constitutional State does entail a hierarchy of powers; this is because the authority that enacts constitutional norms (typically, a constituent assembly, or an equivalent) is "higher" than the other lawmaking authorities, which must respect those norms; a constituent assembly, while it limits with its norms the legislative activity of other lawmaking authorities (typically, Parliament and Senate), is not limited by any authority; it makes free choices through which it expresses moral principles and values shared by the community (which it represents). Its activity is of a *moral* nature and serves to found a State and to define its moral norms. After the moral norms and the structure of the State have been created, the ordinary legal activity can take place. Gaus (1994b) thinks that constitution does not function by imposing a super-sovereign power, and notes that the need to limit such a super-sovereign power would lead to infinite regression. I observe that constitution does represent the supreme power, originating from the collective consciousness; the infinite regression mentioned by Gaus has an end, at the level of the consciousness of the community as expressed by the largest possible majority of its members.

We could say that the constituent assembly has a supreme authority because: *(a)* it should enact laws that pass with a *large* majority of votes, i.e., larger than the simple majority (>50%) required for the enactment of laws by parliament (constitutional norms certainly are "1st rank laws"—ch. 3.1.2.1.2); and *(b)* it enacts *universal* laws, i.e., laws that express the *universal* moral principles and values derived from the essential properties of *all* men as evolving conscious entities made of intellect, sensitiveness, and power (ch. 4.1.2.3; Fig. 4.3). In other words, the constituent assembly enacts norms that express the content of the *community consciousness*. Thus, although both the constituent assembly and parliament are elected assemblies that represent all citizens (who are the ultimate source of authority), the former is superior to the latter.

4.2.6.2.2—The Constitution and the Hierarchy of Laws

As already discussed in chapter 4.1.2.3, the various kinds of "laws" are hierarchically arranged in the decreasing order of their "extension", going from the ground norm to universal norms, to laws, rules, etc. The constitutional assembly enacts the "laws" that stay in the top zone of the hierarchy, i.e., it enacts the ground norm and universal norms (Figs. 4.2 and 4.3).

4.2.6.3—The Ontological Basis of the Separation of "Powers"

In the preceding chapter, I mentioned that constitutional norms, besides moral principles and values to be pursued, also define the structure and functioning of the State, i.e., define the "organs" that form the State apparatus and the norms that regulate their functions. I will not discuss in detail this complex issue, but will only mention the problem of the separation of powers, i.e., the separation of the legislative, executive, and judicial powers, each of which should be represented by separate and independent bodies. The separation of powers has been proposed and defended (Montesquieu 1748) because it would better safeguard liberty and security of citizens and would prevent the "abuse of power" through a system in which separate powers will check one another. As stated by Montesquieu (1748: 150), "Constant experience shows us that every man invested with power is apt to abuse it . . . it is necessary from the very nature of things that power should be a check to power." Thus, the separation of powers would be the result of a choice between concentration or separation of powers, made to obtain a scope (greater liberty and security). My approach is different; I am interested in knowing whether legislative, executive and judicial powers *are*, or not, distinct entities, i.e., I am interested in defining the ontological nature of these three powers. It follows that my position about the separation of powers will be the result of a *discovery*, and not the consequence of a choice, made for obtaining a scope.

I will briefly discuss *(1)* the powers of the state and the mind components, and *(2)* the powers of the state and the inward and outward mind activities.

(1) The Powers of the State and the Mind Components. Referring to my ontological conception (chs. 1.1.1; 1.1.2; Fig. 1.1), I underline the following points. *(a)* The *legislative power* is an entity that creates laws, which are universal and collective (publicly-shared) *projects* (each of which creates a *class* of actions) produced by the *intellect* and selected and adopted under the pressure of sentiments and moral feelings produced by *sensitiveness.* *(b)* The *judicial power* is an entity that examines single (or particular) actions in order to get *ideas* or *knowledge* (produced by *intellect*) about them and to establish their belonging to one or another of the classes of actions created by laws. *(c)* The *executive power* is an entity that performs *universal actions* and *moral acts* (concerning all citizens or all the citizens of a class), produced by the *power*, including the enforcement of laws. At the level of peripheral administrative offices, the executive power also exerts *actions* that are *particular*, because they refer to the relationship of the public administration offices with single citizens or small groups of them (Table 4.2).

Shortly: legislative power creates collective, universal *projects*; judicial power creates *ideas* about particular actions; and executive power creates universal *actions* and *moral acts.* Therefore, the three powers (or organs) are ontologically distinct entities; however, while executive power, being a creator of actions, belongs to the mind component that I name *power*, the legislative organ (which creates projects) and the judicial organ (which produces ideas or knowledge about particular cases) belong both to the mind component that I name *intellect.* Yet, despite their belonging to the same mind component, the legislative organ is distinct from the judicial organ because their products (projects and ideas, respectively), despite being produced by the same mind component (intellect), are distinct entities (Fig. 1.1). Moreover, the legislative organ by selecting a given project expresses also the sentiments and moral feelings produced by *sensitiveness.* It is noteworthy that the three organs or "powers", although distinct from one another, are not separate entities; this is because the structure of the mind is such that its components are distinct and yet interrelated, rather than separated (chs. 1.1.1.1, 6; 1.1.2, 2nd proposition). Therefore, instead of the term "separation of powers" we should use the term "distinction of powers" (or, better, "distinction of the organs of the State").

From the above, it follows that only the executive apparatus should be indicated by the term "power" (of the State), whereas the legislative and the judicial apparatus should be both indicated by the term "organ" (of the State). Perhaps, "organ" is the preferable term also for the executive apparatus. Thus, we should distinguish *(a)* the *executive organ*, which performs *universal actions* and *moral acts*, and thus belongs to the sphere of *power*; *(b)* the *legislative organ*, which creates *universal projects* and thus belongs to the spheres of *intellect* (and of *sensitiveness*); and *(c)* the *judiciary organ*, which produces *particular ideas* or knowledge about particular actions and thus belongs to the *intellect*. Therefore, we can conclude that the legislative, the executive and the judicial organs represent components of the State which *"are" ontologically distinct, and yet interrelated, entities*.

(2) Powers of the State and the Inward and Outward Mind Activities. The activity of each organ of the State, including the constituent assembly, may mainly belong either to the outward mind activity (mind selfishness) or to the inward mind activity (mind consciousness), even if, because of the *bi-directionality of the mind*, both activities are actually involved, as indicated below.

(a) The *constituent assembly* exerts an activity that belongs to the *inward* mind activity or *consciousness*, more exactly the activity of rational and emotional consciousness (Fig. 1.1; Table 4.2), since this assembly defines the moral projects shared by the largest possible majority of citizens, i.e., the norms, directed to implement moral principles (created by moral thoughts) and moral values (felt by moral feelings).

(b) The *legislative organ* (or parliament) exerts an activity that belongs to both the inward and the outward activity of intellect and sensitiveness (Table 4.2), because this organ exerts a dual activity: *first*, it defines publicly-shared moral projects (directed to pursue moral ends), created by the inward activity of intellect (or rational consciousness) and selected by fulfilling moral feelings produced by the inward activity of sensitiveness (or emotional consciousness); *second*, it also defines shared projects directed to satisfy the (good) *selfish* interest and desires of groups of citizens, provided that these projects are not in contrast with the moral project (of general interest), i.e., provided that these projects are directed to satisfy the *morally-good egoism* or to accomplish the *duty toward oneself* (ch. 2.1.5.2.2).

(c) The *courts* (including the constitutional court and the trial and appellate courts) exert an activity that belongs to the outward activity of intellect, since this organ produces *particular ideas* or *knowledge* about the belonging of particular actions to one or another of the classes of actions created by the "laws".

(d) The *government* (or administrative or executive apparatus) exerts a dual activity that belongs to both the inward and the outward activity of the power (Table 4.2), since its activity consists of exerting, at the same time, *collective moral acts* (directed to pursue moral ends), produced by the inward activity of power (or practical consciousness—Fig. 1.1) and *universal (general) actions*, produced by the outward activity of power, involving all citizens and therefore representing the evolution of human actions toward universality (ch. 4.1.1.3.1; Table 4.1, note 4). Moreover, the executive apparatus also exerts less universal actions (involving only some classes of citizens) that belong to the sphere of (good) *selfish* activity and correspond to the implementation of laws prompted by the *morally-good egoism*.

Table 4.2. The ontological bases of the distinction of the various organs of the State (or separation of "powers")

INSTITUTIONS	ONTOLOGICAL BASES	CREATED PRODUCTS	"UNIVERSALITY" OF THE PRODUCTS
Constituent Assembly	Inward activity of INTELLECT and SENSITIVENESS (Rational and emotional consciousness)	Universal and collective moral projects (norms)	Universal
Parliament	Inward and good-outward activity of INTELLECT and SENSITIVENESS[1]	Universal and Collective moral or good-selfish projects (laws)	Universal or prompted by morally-good egoism[2]
Constitutional Court	Outward activity of INTELLECT	Legal judgments	Particular[3]
Trial and Appellate Courts	Outward activity of INTELLECT	Legal judgments	Particular[4]
Government (Ministries)	Inward and outward activity of POWER[5]	Moral acts and actions (universal and collective)	Universal or prompted by morally-good egoism[2]
Administrative Offices	Inward and outward activity of POWER[5]	Moral acts and good-selfish actions	Particular[6]

1. The inward activity of the *intellect* and *sensitiveness* can also be named *rational consciousness* and *emotional consciousness*, respectively (Fig. 1.1). It should be underlined that, because of the *bi-directionality of mind* activities, we should distinguish mind activities that are *mainly* of inward/moral nature and mind activities that are *mainly* of outward/selfish nature, as both kinds of activities most often occur together.

2. These are products directed to satisfy the *morally-good egoism* (see the text, chs. 2.1.5.2.2; 4.2.6.3, *2b* and *2d*).

3. Judgments of constitutional courts are *particular* in a special sense: they concern laws that, while defining a class of actions, are themselves members (or particular instances) of a larger class, represented by a constitutional norm. Laws being *particular instances or members of a class*, specialized and technical competence is required to establish their belonging to a given class (i.e., to a given constitutional norm) (ch. 4.3.1.2).

4. Particular judgments refer to particular properties of individual instances. Being *particular*, they require specialized and technical competence.

5. The inward activity of the power can also be named *practical consciousness* (Fig. 1.1).

6. These are particular moral acts or personal actions because they refer to the relationship of the public administration offices with single citizens or small groups of them.

(e) The *administrative offices* exert, at the particular level, an activity corresponding to that exerted by the executive apparatus at general level (see above, under point "*d*"); this activity consists of particular moral acts or personal actions, produced by both the inward activity of power (or practical consciousness) and the outward activity of power (or practical selfishness), respectively; these moral acts and actions are "particular" because they refer to the relationship of the public administration offices with single citizens or small groups of them.

The ontological bases of the various components of a State are depicted in Table 4.2.

4.2.6.4—Different Constitutions

Different constitutions exist in various countries. It is noteworthy that the constitutions created more recently, such as the French (Bell 1992; Preuss 1996) and the Italian (Esposito 1954) constitutions, are more corresponding to the theoretical requirements; the older constitutions, such as that of Great Britain and that of the U.S., show some peculiarities derived from their historical origin (Preuss 1996).

Thus, the *Italian constitution* (Esposito 1954) was created, after the end of the 2nd world war, by an elected assembly, and was approved with a very large majority of votes. It provides the rules for its own changes. The changes should be approved by both the parliament and the senate with an extraordinary majority of votes (2/3) and voting should be repeated a 2nd time after at least three months; in the case that the majority of 2/3 is not reached, the proposed change may be subjected to a referendum if this is asked by at least 500.000 citizens or by 1/5 of the members of parliament.

In the *British Legal System*, there is a horizontal coordination of the different components of the sovereignty, which are sovereign only through common action, and are bound to one another by mutual rights and duties (Preuss 1996). The right of individual freedom is "inherent in the ordinary law of the land. . . [so that] the right is one which can hardly be destroyed without a thorough revolution in the institutions and manners of the nation" (Dicey 1915: 119–20). In this regard, Preuss (1996: 20) says:

> [T]he constitution of Britain is very much the result of its political culture and not the emanation of one single authoritative source (summarized in a written document). Its legal quality is derived from the ordinary course of the law of the land.

This is rather at variance with European constitutionalism according to which the validity and authority of a law derive from the constitution.

In the *U. S. Legal System*, in contrast to the constitutions of most European countries, the bill of rights with judicial review seems to be undemocratically imposed, inasmuch as it is inherited because it was approved by "a bunch of slave-owning revolutionaries living on the edge of an undeveloped continent at the end of the eighteenth century" (Waldron 1998: 271). I object that, although no constitution can be defined as ideal, one should recognize that those "slave-owning revolutionaries" had the wisdom to create a bill that captures some fundamental moral principles and values, related to *mind evolution* (which is the objective moral good—chs. 1.1.1.2.4; 2.1.4.1; 2.2.1.1.1, *1*), first of all, the value of liberty. In the U. S. system, the constitution is a written document and has the status of a supreme law and the founding act of the nation; it is "a thing antecedent to the government, and a government is only the creature of a constitution" (Paine 1791/92: 122). It has priority even over the will of the people itself; for this reason, some thinkers agree that "there exist a deep, almost irreconcilable tension between constitutionalism and democracy. Indeed, they come close to suggesting that 'constitutional democracy' is a marriage of opposites, an oxymoron" (Holmes 1988: 197). In my view, the point is that constitutions should be created by the large majority of citizens (through their representatives) and should be amendable through special procedures provided for by the constitutions themselves, in order to constantly reflect the evolution of the community's consciousness. Changes of the constitution may be directed to better define principles already included in it or to add norms concerning moral principles and values that were ignored in the original text. Preuss (1996) notes that it is a matter of debate whether the written text of the U.S. constitution should be regarded as a rigid text, or whether this text can be interpreted with reference to the contemporary context. Arthur (1996) observes that the framers of the U.S. Constitution used broad concepts like "due process of law," "cruel and unusual punishment," and "free exercise of religion," which suggests that they believed (in agreement with the Enlightenment views) in the power of reason, and intended that later generations should pursue the ideals of freedom, equality, due process, etc., as interpreted in the light of their own experience and understanding. The point is that it should be the task of the representatives of citizens (parliament, through special procedures), and not of judges, to introduce those changes required by the evolution of the community consciousness. However, I underline that a constitution should be conceived as an amendable text, open not only to the minor changes linked to modern interpretations but also to any change that a large majority of citizens would like to introduce, by democratic means, in accordance with the evolution of their consciousness. However, when a constitution uses broad concepts, this means that the constitution-makers have tacitly delegated to experts (judges) the task to interpret vague norms by taking into account the changing conditions of society, as stated by Arthur (1996).

4.3—ADJUDICATION

4.3.1—Defining Adjudication

I will briefly consider two issues: the *adjudication* by trial and appellate courts, and the *judicial review* exerted by constitutional courts.

4.3.1.1—Adjudication by Trial and Appellate Courts

We already know that the creation of a law is focused on defining a *universal* project, which is the idea of a class of actions; in contrast, adjudication is focused on *particular* actions which are members of that class, i.e., is directed to establish the belonging of a given action to that class. In other words, adjudication is directed to establish whether a given action lies within one of the classes of actions allowed, prescribed or forbidden by the existing laws or whether it differs from such actions (and, in what aspect and in which measure). Thus, as I mentioned elsewhere (Belfiore 2004: 269), the work of a judge is somewhat similar to that of the clinician, as both analyze particular cases to determine to which class they belong: the clinician attempts to understand to which class of altered functions (diseases) the particular pattern of symptoms and signs he observes in a given patient belongs; the judge attempts to understand to which class of actions (laws) the particular actions that he examines belong or from which class of actions they diverge.

Adjudication is a very difficult task, which raises the question whether an *absolutely objective adjudication* is possible. Some thinkers (Altman 1986) underline that, being laws most often *indeterminate*, legal facts do not lead to a unique outcome but rather to various and even opposing outcomes, which are influenced by social or personal ideology of judges. Others (Leiter 1998) hold that, due to the indeterminacy of laws, judges often affect or make laws through extensive use of *interpretation* of laws and consequent *discretion* (this issue has been discussed in ch. 4.2.3.2 and its sub-chapters).

To understand the complexity of the adjudication process, we should take into account that two kinds of "classes of entities" are involved: *(1)* the various "classes of actions" as defined by various laws, and *(2)* the "class of judges" as defined by constitutional norms concerning the judiciary.

(1) The "Classes of Actions" as Defined by Laws. We should consider *(a)* the *indeterminacy* of laws that define the various classes of actions, *(b)* the *variability* of the actions that are members of the classes defined by laws, and *(c)* some *special problems in adjudication.*

(a) The indeterminacy of laws. Laws are collective projects, i.e., collec-

tive ideas-of-projects, which define a class of actions. Similarly to scientific laws of the biological world, laws create classes by defining their members (a given kind of action) only in an *approximate* or *imprecise* manner (ch. 1.1.3.2.1). Indeed, the definition of a class (i.e., the definition of the *inclusion criterion* for a given class) is *approximate* both because the inclusion criteria refer only to shared properties (ignoring the particular properties that characterize each individual member of a class) and because shared properties are defined in an approximate way in order to cover the range of variations occurring across the various members. Thus, the indeterminacy of a law is unavoidable (chs. 4.1.1.1; 4.2.3), as it derives from the functioning of the *intellect* and coincides with the *approximation* with which the intellect defines classes. The indeterminacy of laws is (together with the variability of actions—see point "*b*") one of the factors that make unavoidable the *interpretation* of laws.

(b) The variability of actions (or legal facts). The analysis of a particular "object" or "event" and its recognition as a member of a given class is a difficult operation; this is especially true for human actions, which are complex, and whose characteristics (including the circumstances in which they occur) *differ* from one case to another. The *variability of human actions*, which are members of the classes of actions defined by laws, is similar to the variability occurring among "events" which are members of a scientific law, which (excepted the members of the classes of the physical-chemical world) differ from one another by many particular properties (specific of each member) and by the different degree to which the shared (or common) properties are present, as they may occur under a large range of variations (ch. 1.1.3.2.1). This makes the assignment of a particular action to the appropriate class (law) a very complex process, for which the approximate knowledge of the shared properties of the actions belonging to a class does not suffice, and the *interpretation* of the actions (or legal facts) is required.

Thus, when faced with a case of murder, a judge should evaluate how the specific law defines murder, on the one hand, and the particular properties of the particular case of murder he is examining (presence and degree of intentionality, awareness, educational, emotional, and environmental influencing factors, etc.), on the other. Each of these factors (e.g., having lived in a degraded family and neighborhood) is very difficult to evaluate as far as its occurrence, features and extent are concerned, so that some degree of interpretation is necessary.

The necessary interpretation of laws and of legal facts (linked to the indeterminacy of laws and to the variability of human actions), and the consequent discretion of judges, has led to the debate about the claimed law-making power of judges (ch. 4.2.3.2 and its sub-chapters). Dworkin (1977: 84) discusses the claim that, since judges are not elected, it is unjust in a democratic system that they have law-making power, especially considering that their law-making activity is retroactive (*post facto*). On the other hand, Dworkin (1977: 82–90) defends his *right thesis*, according to which judges in their decisions should attempt to protect rights (of the litigants) based on *moral principles*, as opposed to *political principles* (or "policies") such as the general interest of the community. Rights should be protected even if they may be in conflict with the interest of the majority. Dworkin fails to recognize that, while in private life one can recognize some rights to others even if this is not stated by public laws, judges, due to the fact that they exert a *public* activity, must refer not to ill-defined moral principles, but to the *moral principles shared by the majority of the community* and expressed in the constitution, otherwise they would act not according to the *public* morality (as is their duty), but according to their personal morality (which may differ from the morality recognized by citizens).

Hart (1994: 275–76) points out that: *first*, the law-making power of judges is limited to specific problems arising from particular, hard cases; *second*, the delegation of limited law-making power is common in the democratic systems; and *third*, the decision of judges in hard cases cannot be judged as unjust since there are no clearly established laws that could justify a given expectation.

My comment is that, when the hierarchical arrangement of norms, laws and rules is considered (ch. 4.1.2.3; Figs. 4.2 and 4.3), it is clear that there are no "empty spaces" not covered by the legal system because, when a specific "law" is lacking, there is always a "law" of higher order and of larger extension that covers a given issue. Thus, even in the hardest cases and in areas where existing "laws" are more indeterminate, judges will always find a norm or law to serve as a guide for their judgment. This allows that judicial interpretation and discretion are kept to an acceptable (and unavoidable) minimum.

(c) Special problems in adjudication: Publicly indemonstrable facts and borderline behavior. The great variability of human actions and behavior (legal facts), together with their complexity, raises at least two problems, which are briefly considered here.

First, there is the problem of *publicly indemonstrable (or undemonstrated) facts*. These are those facts that, although well known by one, some, or many citizens cannot be publicly demonstrated (because the proofs were destroyed, or the witnesses were killed, etc.) and, therefore, cannot be prosecuted and punished. A typical case is that concerning "Al Capone", the cruel gangster who dominated organized crime in Chicago in the twenties; although most citizens knew what he was, he could not be prosecuted and punished for his murders and massacres, but could only be indicted for tax evasion in 1931. This means that, until 1930, he was officially a "normal" citizen and enjoyed all the rights of U.S. citizens. Thus, for instance, he could have entered a political competition for, say, the position of mayor of

Chicago. Had this happened, the citizens of Chicago would have had the duty to recognize his right to enter the competition, but they would *not* have had the duty to vote in his favor. Instead, the "good citizens" of Chicago would have had the duty not to support him. Indeed, publicly indemonstrable facts raise a big moral problem that can only be solved by distinguishing the demonstrated facts, which *must* be necessarily recognized (in force by the law), from the publicly indemonstrable facts, for which each citizen is *free* to behave according to his own moral principles. Moreover, sometimes the indemonstrable or undemonstrated "bad fact" is strongly suspected but not certain, which increases the difficulty in the citizen's choice. Yet, I think that, while concerning demonstrated facts citizens *must* recognize them (in force by the law), concerning indemonstrable or undemonstrated facts each citizen is *free* to behave in the manner that he thinks is most appropriate, thus revealing the degree of evolution of his consciousness (freedom always entails responsibility). It is true that, when faced with indemonstrable or undemonstrated facts, our consciousness can only rely on *suspicions*, which should more appropriately be named *hypotheses*. Therefore, someone might observe that giving weight to suspicions leads to a "society of suspicion", in which everyone doubts everyone. I object that we should confer weight to the hypotheses, because hypotheses are the way through which our mind approaches and hopefully reaches knowledge in all fields, including the scientific field (e.g., the first step in the reasoning that leads a physician to a diagnosis is the diagnostic "suspicion" or "hypothesis"; if no hypothesis is made, diagnosis cannot be reached). After all, *trust* and *distrust*, which play an important role in human relationships, are based on the uncertain prevision of the future behavior. Those who refuse to give weight to suspicions or hypotheses actually want to ignore or secretly approve bad behaviors. Certainly, evaluating hypotheses require wisdom and prudence; yet, through the manner in which hypotheses are freely evaluated and dealt with, citizens reveal what they actually are: *(a)* morally coarse and often secretly accepting bad behaviors; or *(b)* excessively suspicious; or *(c)* sensible to ethical issues and capable of isolating those responsible for morally-bad acts, and of denying support to those involved in well-grounded suspicions.

Second, there is the problem linked to facts and behaviors that lie at the borderline zone between the legal and the illegal area. The great (and ever growing) complexity of human society makes "borderline" cases ever more frequent. An example may be useful. Suppose that a law obliges the manufacturer of a given product "*x*" to stick a warning label on the packet with a few words explaining the characteristic of the product. Obviously, these words can be written by using fonts of various sizes, from very big and, therefore, easy to read, to extremely small and almost impossible to read, especially by old people. The "cunning" manufacturer might choose a very small font size which, while avoiding that he is prosecuted for having not obeyed the law, enables him to deceive a certain number of people (mainly the elderly) who might not easily read the label. Another example may be that of a member "*A*" of an assembly, who has the legal obligation to make a short but important declaration, like this: "I inform you that the fact '*x*' has happened." During the session, "*A*" makes the declaration, but he speaks in a very low voice while there is a noise of voices, so that nobody hears him, except his friend and accomplice "*B*", who is ready to testify that "*A*" has made the due declaration. These examples show that, due to the complexity of the human world, within the boundaries that limit the area of legal behavior, there is room for all honest men as well as for some (or many) dishonest ones. Again, it is the free and wise choices of the "good citizens" that can restrain the activity of these "dishonest citizens within the law", by isolating them.

(2) The "Class of Judges". We should consider *(a)* the *indeterminacy* of the norm that defines the class of judges, and *(b)* the *diversity* of the various judges who are members of the class of judges.

(a) The indeterminacy of the norm that defines the class of judges. Within a legal system, judges are the members of a class defined by the constitutional norm that establishes the Judiciary. Due to the indeterminacy with which our intellect defines classes (except the classes of the physical-chemical world), the class of judges is only approximately defined. Referring to the Italian legal system, judges are those citizens who have proved, by open examinations, to possess specific knowledge in legal matter, who have accepted to be impartial in applying laws, and whose behavior has been blameless. It is clear that these are generic and approximate parameters that define in an approximate way the class of judges.

(b) The diversity of judges as members of a class. The discretion of judges. Judges are members of the class of judges, which may also be regarded as a sub-class of the class of men. As members of a *heterogeneous class* (as are all classes, except those concerning the physical-chemical world), judges differ from one another with regard to their *individual properties*, which define their personal identity and make each judge a particular (unique and unrepeatable) instantiation of the class of judges; the individual properties can be understood as consisting in the degree of evolution and specificity characteristic of each mind (chs. 1.1.3.2.1, *1*; 3.2.1). This entails that the outcome of an adjudication process will depend to a significant extent upon the ideas, moral thoughts, personal sentiments, and moral feelings of the particular judge that creates the adjudication. This is the origin of one of the factors contributing to the *discretion* of the judges. To avoid discretion, judges should have no personal characteristics; yet, a judge without personal characteristics is a judge who does not exist. Otherwise stated, any judge has his own personal ideas and feelings about the issues with which he is faced, and these ideas and feelings unavoidably affect the outcome of

the adjudication.

Thus, while deliberate deception (and self-deception) by judges (to favor their own "ideology" or "interests") is doubtlessly to be condemned, it should be recognized that judges couldn't be *absolutely* objective. It should be pointed out, however, that the variability among the decisions that different judges would take concerning the same action is restrained within an acceptable range. This approximation or imprecision is somewhat like that occurring in the application of scientific biological laws to particular events (ch. 1.1.3.2.1).

Therefore, discretion, together with interpretation, is required, and the outcome of a process of adjudication is always based on *probability* (which, in legal terms, is indicated as presence or absence of *reasonable* doubt or certainty). We may conclude that *it is impossible to judge by an absolutely objective criterion* (just as it is impossible to achieve an absolutely objective knowledge).

In summary, the adjudication process can be defined as follows: *The adjudication is a decision through which a unique and unrepeatable member of the class of judges evaluates a unique and unrepeatable event to establish whether or not that particular event is a member of a class that is only approximately defined.*

4.3.1.2—Constitutional Constraint and Judicial Review

In the preceding chapter, I mentioned that the decisions of judges always concern a *member* of a class of actions, as defined by a law. This statement would seem to be untenable when one refers to the constitutional court, which exerts judicial review, i.e., which takes decisions concerning the validity of a *law* issued by the legislative organ, and not concerning the evaluation of a *particular case*. To clarify this point, we should take into account the hierarchical arrangement of the various kinds of "laws" (ch. 4.1.2.3; Figs. 4.2 and 4.3); in particular, we should consider that a "law" of a given rank (while defining a class that possesses its own members) is a member of the class defined by the "law" of higher rank. Constitutional norms lie in the top region of the hierarchy of "laws", so that all laws enacted by the normal legislative authority are of lower rank, and therefore are *members* of the class of laws defined by a norm. In other words, an ordinary law is necessarily a member of a class defined by a constitutional norm. When a constitutional court judges the validity of an enacted law, it actually evaluates a *particular member* of the class of "laws" defined by a constitutional norm. Thus, like other courts, the constitutional courts examine the *particular members* of a class, i.e., they examine a "law" as a member of a class defined by a constitutional norm.

4.3.1.2.1—The Constitutional Constraint

Waldron has elaborated a *pre-commitment view* of constitutional constraints: constitutional constraints (and judicial review) may be viewed as
"precautions that responsible rights bearers have taken against their own
imperfections" (Waldron 1998: 274); these "imperfections" might lead
them, especially when driven by panic or anger, to act badly (e.g., against
minorities), i.e., in a way that their moral capacity condemns in advance.
This is in agreement with the view that the respect for individual rights is
not compatible with a purely predatory image of legislative majorities
(Waldron 1993). Likewise, Arthur (1996) talks of *self-incapacitating rules*,
which prevent elected officials from acting against basic rights. Freeman
(1990) defends a similar justification of judicial review. Waldron (1998:
275) mentions the example of Ulysses, who "decided that he should be
bound to the mast in order to resist the charms of the Sirens." Clearly, here
reference should be made to the control of will and to concepts like second-
order desires (Frankfurt 1971; Elster 1984: 36; Taylor 1985a) as well as to
other aspects of the concept of pre-commitment (Elster 1989: 196). I think
that the above statements by Waldron reveal confusion between laws
(which are publicly-shared *projects*, produced by the *intellect*) and their enforcement (which consists of public *actions* and *moral acts*, produced by the
power) (chs. 4.1.1.2.2; 4.2.2.3.2, 2; 4.2.6.3). "Precautions" against wrong
acts that might be done in special circumstances (e.g., when driven by panic
or anger) should be taken by setting up a strong *enforcing apparatus* (e.g.,
the police) capable of forcing people to follow the law. Constitutional
norms have a different function: they define the classes of principles and
values (shared by a *large* majority of citizens) that should be pursued
through ordinary laws that parliament enacts in its normal activity (and not
in a particular state, such as the state of panic or anger), when it is driven by
the balance between the interests and desires of individual, groups or parties, on the one hand, and moral principles and feelings, on the other. The
possible contrast between an ordinary law and a constitutional norm is not
due to transient, exceptional situations (e.g., situations of panic or anger) but
to the complexity of the decisions that parliament has to take (which sometimes require the special evaluation by the constitutional court), or to the
influence or pressure arising from the interests and desires of the majority
party (and its supporting political or economic groups) which, even if possessing only a slight majority, may attempt to ignore the rights of the opposing (minority) party.

Waldron (1998) points out that often the pre-commitment operates
through judgment and decision of other persons (the friend who received the
car key from a heavy drinker at the beginning of a party, with the strict instruction not to return it when it will be requested at midnight). Likewise,

constitutional constrains would work "by vesting a power of decision in some person or body of persons (a court) whose job is to determine *as a matter of judgment* whether conduct that is contemplated (say by legislature) at t_2 violates a constrain written down at t_1" (Waldron 1998: 278). Here, again, I underline that, concerning judicial review, a court is not called to contrast the behavior of the legislative body (this would be a public *action* that could only be exerted by the executive apparatus, belonging to the *power*); nor to create free *projects/decisions* (i.e., laws), because this is the task of the legislative body (including the constituent assembly); rather, it is called to ascertain, by employing its specific juridical competence and by spending the due time to study the case, whether or not a particular law enacted by the legislative body is in contrast with the more basic constitutional norms (publicly-shared by a *large* majority of citizens), i.e., whether or not a particular law is a member of the class defined by one of the basic constitutional norms. If constitutional judges ascertain such a contrast, there are two possible ways to be followed: the law may be abrogated or modified, or the constitution may be changed by the parliament (if the required *large* majority so decides) by following the procedure provided for by the constitution itself. Thus, the final *free decision* about which way to follow is always taken by the required majority of citizens, through their representatives (legislative power), who remain the only ultimate source of free, collective decisions. It is true, however, that constitutional norms may be too vague or abstract; thus, according to Dworkin (1985: 69–71; 1996: 72–116), the U.S. Bill of Rights embodies abstract moral principles that clearly entail the judiciary judgment for their practical application. In these instances, judges may exert their discretion, which should always be directed to interpret, in the most faithful manner, the meaning of constitutional norms. Yet, I repeat that constitutions should be amendable, through special procedures, so that if the judgment of constitutional judges appears to most of the citizens (or their representatives) as unacceptable, they have the authority and the means to change constitutional norms in order to make them clearer and less vague. Indeed, when a constituent assembly defines a norm in a vague manner, it actually delegates its interpretation to judges; therefore, judges would act as delegates of citizens' representatives. The same is true when a parliament enacts a law that is too vaguely defined: in these cases, the parliament (tacitly) delegates to others the task of interpreting the vague law when it must be applied to particular cases. On these grounds, one can reject Waldron's view according to which, in difficult cases, investing the judiciary with an "overriding power of judgment . . . amounts *pro tanto* to a refusal of self-government. It amounts to the people's embrace of what Aristotle would call 'aristocracy', . . . [or it amounts to a] 'mixed constitution'" (Waldron 1998: 280).

Waldron (1998: 280) maintains that judicial review cannot be defended on the grounds that otherwise the majority would act as "to be 'judge in their own case', in determining whether a piece of legislation violates the rights of a minority," because people are presumably *authorities* (not judges) on what they have pre-committed themselves to. This is true, but I note that, in constitutional matters, the majority is an authority (and not a judge) only if it is a *large* majority (i.e., the majority required for constitutional changes), publicly ascertained through voting, and if it acts through legitimate procedures (again provided for by the constitution itself). Constitutional judges do not compete with the authority and power of the majority or of the legislative body but merely ascertain, by their capacity as *authoritative experts*, the existence of contrast between ordinary laws and constitutional norms.

4.3.1.2.2—The Judicial Review and the "Power" of Judges

Here I will discuss arguments against and in favor of the "power" of judges.

(1) Against the "Power" of Judges. Rehnquist (1976), in discussing his notion of "living constitution" (i.e., a constitution that can be changed to follow the evolution of society), notes that a living constitution may allow that non-elected federal judges address themselves to a social problem that other branches of government have failed or refused to settle. He argues that judicial review may have an antidemocratic character and may be "genuinely corrosive of the fundamental values of our democratic society" (Rehnquist 1976: 706). This view is untenable because judicial review is directed to ascertain contrast between ordinary laws and constitutional norms; or to clarify the meaning of a law by referring to a more general norm. Their decision can be annulled by changing the constitutional norms that impose a given constraint (through legal procedures, usually requiring a qualified majority).

Referring to the constitution of the U.S., Arthur (1996) argues that, since that constitution contains provisions referring to substantive rights (such as banning "cruel and unusual punishment" and "unreasonable searches and seizures," or assuring to all citizens a "due process of law" and the "free exercise of religion"), their interpretation and enforcement through the power of unelected judges may seem to contrast democratic values. Moreover, concerning the view that constitutional norms should be regarded as *self-incapacitating rules* (which prevent elected officials from acting against basic rights), according to Arthur (1996), considering that citizens may be unaware of the court's decision or disagree with it, this view cannot easily justify judicial review. Here I observe the following. *(a)* Judges *must* be "unelected judges" (recruited through an open competition, based on their specific competence), because the elected officials would not pass a test of competence and might be influenced by their constituents. *(b)* Judges do not exert "power" but make ascertainments by using their knowledge and by spending time studying the cases under scrutiny, an activity that belongs to the sphere of *intellect*. *(c)* The work of judges entails interpretation but not enforcement, the latter being exerted by the executive apparatus belonging to the sphere of *power*. Thus, judges do not constrain the actions of the legislative power but only state whether or not an enacted law is in contrast with the constitutional norms. *(d)* If the constitutional norms are vague and, therefore, require interpretation (which entails discretion) by judges, this is not due to the will of judges but to the free will of the constitution makers (which are, or should be, representatives of the citizens); moreover, considering that the constitution should be amendable (even if through special procedures), in order to follow the evolution of the community consciousness, constitutional norms can be changed and new ones can be created if a large majority of citizens, through its representatives, freely decides so.

(2) In Favor of the "Power" of Judges. In contrast to Rehnquist, Dworkin (1977: 81–149) attempts to justify the judicial review in cases of controversy about constitutionality of laws. He notes that the U.S. constitution is not based on a majoritarian theory but is designed to protect individual rights against certain decisions that a majority of citizens might want to make. Its clauses should be understood as appealing to moral concepts and, therefore, should be applied by an active court, prepared to frame and answer questions of political morality (Dworkin 1977: 147); a fusion of constitutional law and moral theory would be required (Dworkin 1977: 149). Here I object that, since individual rights (and, more generally, moral principles and values) may be understood in different manners, what the constitution protects are the individual rights publicly recognized by the largest possible majority of citizens. Thus, some rights may not be covered by existing constitutional norms (e.g., the right of women to vote in Switzerland, before the recent introduction of the universal suffrage) and may be introduced when the evolution of the consciousness of the community demands it. Nevertheless, constitutional norms do protect against certain decisions that a majority of citizens might want to make; this is because constitutional norms, although approved by a (hopefully large) majority, are directed to establish the rights of *all* citizens, i.e., those rights linked to the *essential properties* of the class of men (the properties linked to *mind evolution*) and, therefore, possessed by *all* men. Thus, even if a constituent assembly is made of a majority of members who are racialist white and by a minority of members who are black, it should answer questions like these: Should *all* men have the right to life? Should *all* men have the right to freedom? Should *all* men have the right to education? And so on. Reference to *all* men makes it impossible to enact norms that favor a particular sub-class of men (the white, the rich, the intelligent, etc.) that, as such, does not include

all men. Constitution should concern *general, fundamental moral principles and values* and the ensuing rights, which should be equally enjoyed by *all* citizens. In this way, each individual may evolve according to his natural endowment, which leads to the diversity among individuals as far as their degree and specificity of mind evolution are concerned, and gives rise to particular (individual or group) rights (ch. 3.2.2.1.2).

Arthur (1996) underlines the following points. *(a)* The power of unelected judges to enforce constitutional limits on legislative power may enhance, rather than contrast, democratic values such as fairness, by protecting those who criticize officials and their policies. *(b)* Judges are *legally* better situated than members of legislature to make the decision, because the latter may be party of a dispute when citizens challenge legislators. *(c)* Judges would also be *politically* well situated, because they are independent of political pressure. *(d)* Should judges not act according to principles and laws, they would carry a stigma that would not be present in the case of a legislator (Arthur 1996). Apart from the fact that judges do not "enforce" constitutional norms (see point "*a*"), but ascertain whether they contrast with ordinary laws, all four points are linked to the independence of judges from both legislative organs and executive apparatus. This independence, which leads to the favorable effects indicated by Arthur, is grounded on ontological bases, i.e., on the fact that judges belong to an organ which is *ontologically distinct* from the legislative organ and the organ made of government officials (ch. 4.2.6.3).

4.3.2—Sanctions and Punishment

(1) Premise. One should distinguish *crimes*, *torts*, and *contract breaches*, according to the offending entity, the kind of violated law, the enforcement-initiating agent, the enforcing agent, and the scope of the sanction. The distinctive elements of crimes, torts, and contract breaks are shown in Table 4.3.

As summarized by Murphy and Coleman (1990: 112), criminal law prohibits the violation of *inalienability rules* (which refer to rights whose violation is prohibited and cannot be compensated, such as killing or severe body-injury or causing terror) and is initiated and enforced by the State; inalienability rules should be distinguished from *property rules* (which refer to rights that can only be changed through negotiation), as well as from *liability rules* (which refer to rights whose violation requires compensation). Criminal law also refers to some compensable harms (e.g., car theft) because they represent an attack against the State (i.e., against mechanisms of economic exchange).

Table 4.3. Distinction between crimes, torts, and contract breaches

	CRIMES	TORTS	CONTRACT BREACHES
Offended entity	State	Private party	Private party
Violated law	Public law	Public law	Private rules and the public law of contracts
Enforcement-initiating agent	State	Private party	Private party
Enforcing agent	State	State	State
Scope of sanction	Punishment of the criminals	Refund of victim's losses	Rectification of wrongful gains and losses

(2) Punishment. Punishment may be justified in two ways (Murphy and Coleman 1990: 117–24). *(a)* In *utilitarian* terms, because it maximizes right protection and increases security and happiness by *(i)* inducing *special deterrence* (concerning those who have committed a crime) and *general deterrence* (concerning all citizens), *(ii)* keeping criminals (thus impeding the commitment of other crimes), and *(iii)* providing the opportunity to implement rehabilitative programs (this utilitarian view, however, would justify the punishment of an innocent if this leads to social utility!). *(b)* In *retributive* terms (based on justice and respect for rights), because the criminal deserves a just punishment in obedience to a categorical imperative (Kant 1797). This raises the problem of defining the "just" punishment and to explain why the State is interested in it; in this regard, it has been noted that punishment prevents that the criminal takes unfair advantage of loyal citizens who obey laws (Morris 1968; Murphy 1979). I underline that, according to my theory about the illusory nature of the free will and about the existence of moral responsibility without freedom (chs. 2.4.1; 2.4.2), punishment should always be conceived in educational terms, i.e., punishment must be directed to promote, to the possible extent, the mind evolution of the criminal.

(3) Responsibility. Responsibility (or *liability*), which is the basis for punishment, is a very complex issue that has been deeply analyzed (Hart 1968; Murphy 1979; 1985; Wasserstrom 1980). According to Murphy and Coleman (1990: 126), we can distinguish: *(a)* a *strict liability system*, based on a causal relation to an injury or harm, regardless of the agent's intention or choice (this system seems unfair and too demanding, and is therefore implemented only in areas of potentially high danger to public welfare, such

as food processing, banking, etc.); and *(b)* an *excusing system*, which appears as preferable in most areas, based on the agent's mental states (intention, knowledge, recklessness) or character defects (negligence) and which recognizes some *excuses* (such as insanity or compulsory impulses). Again, I underline that, according to my theory about the illusory nature of the free will and about the existence of moral responsibility without freedom (chs. 2.4.1; 2.4.2), the two systems should be combined into just one, which should consider both the severity of the harm caused by an agent and the severity of the potential harm of his negligent behavior.

(4) Criminals as Sick Persons. According to some thinkers (see in: Murphy 1985; Murphy and Hampton 1988), criminals are sick persons who should be cured and, therefore, punishment should be replaced by *therapy*, or other measures such as *forgiveness and mercy*. According to Murphy and Coleman (1990: 129–30), this view is difficult to accept for the following reasons.

(a) This view would entail that all those who violate criminal law are mentally sick. I note that this conclusion is based on the false assumption that men can be sharply divided into "healthy" and "sick". Actually, a continuum exists between these two extremes, so that while, say, a "serial killer" or a "mafia man" who has killed dozens of people are certainly "sick", those who are only responsible for minor violation of law may, at most, be regarded as having a slightly abnormal personality. It follows that the term "therapy" is suitable to indicate the treatment that should be reserved to the sick criminal, whereas for those who are only lightly guilty one should talk of rehabilitative or educational programs, which should promote, to the possible extent, the *evolution of the minds* of those to whom they are directed.

(b) This view would also lead to consider people like Gandhi and Martin Luther King Jr., who were civil disobedient activists, as sick persons! I think that this is not true. Gandhi's struggle was against a publicly *unjustified*, non-democratic political condition, linked to imperialism. He faced no justified laws to obey; rather, he promoted, through pacific means, the implementation of universal human rights and, therefore, he helped mind evolution of his fellow countrymen. Martin Luther King Jr. attempted, again through pacific and democratic means, to actually implement universal human rights (equality, among others) that, in principle, are recognized in the U.S., and his civil disobedience cannot, by any means, be regarded as criminal and, hence, he cannot be regarded as sick. It is the minority of Americans who still show some tendency toward racialism that actually disobey constitutional principles (and may perhaps be sick!).

(c) In addition, whereas criminal law provides due process protection, the view of "criminals as sick persons" might lead to the adoption of "therapies" which might entail deprivation of liberty and which would depend on

the decision of "experts", say psychiatrists, whose judgment may well be fallacious. I note that the opinion of "experts" is already utilized in the current system to ascertain or exclude mental insanity. Indeed, when crimes are regarded as the result of the way in which a person is made, experts are no long required to distinguish the mentally healthy from the mentally insane, but only to prepare graduate educational programs; in other words, prisons should be changed into special educational institutions.

(d) Finally, considering the criminal as a sick and non-responsible person would mean to degrade them from the moral standpoint. This is true only if one assumes that morality necessarily requires free will, but not if one adheres to my theory, which admits the existence of moral responsibility without freedom (ch. 2.4.2).

(5) Contract Breaches. Contract breaches have been variously considered (Kronman 1980; Fried 1981; Kessler and Gilmore 1986). The interest of the State in enforcing private and self-imposed rules of contracts may be justified on a *utilitarian* basis (respect of contracts are necessary for the functioning of markets) or, as Fried (1981) maintains, on a *moral* basis (promises are morally binding). Thus, contract law, besides enforcing promises, would also enforce an external standard of utility or of justice; the latter may refer to *corrective* justice or, as maintained by Kronman (1980), to *distributive* justice. I think that the "utilitarian" and the "moral" bases actually are two faces of the same medal. This is because the moral binding force of a promise (contract) derives from the fact that failing to keep a promise has two morally negative effects: *(a)* it may cause a damage (mind involution—involution of power in the case of a promise concerning economic matters) to the person who expected that the promise was kept, and *(b)* it breaches the mini-society, or mini-community, that arises from the promise (a mini-society made of the contractors and regulated by the "rules" of which a contract essentially consists). Since society is the way through which human actions *evolve* toward universality, any breach of rules that govern a society, including the rules of a contract, is morally bad (ch. 3.1.2.3.3). This is because universalization of actions means *evolution* of the power, which is one of the factors contributing to *mind evolution*.

It is noteworthy that there may be duties even in the absence of contracts, as in the cases considered by the theory of *promissory estoppels* (Kessler and Gilmore 1986), i.e., cases where legitimate expectations are induced without explicit promises made in a contract. This would be one aspect of my theory on *informal mini-societies* (ch. 3.1.2.3.3).

4.3.3—*International and Supra-National Laws*

(1) Premise. Laws are *publicly-shared projects*, i.e., projects shared by all, or most of, the members of a society that has organized itself into a State. It follows that international laws should be conceived as projects shared by all, or most of, the members (States) of the international society that have organized themselves into a *supra-national State*. The ideal political organization of the world should be the *Universal Republic*; yet, in the present stage of the history of the world there are only States that attempt to establish relationships between them. Thus, we are at present in a transition stage, in which the relationships between States are comparable to those between the members of a primitive community, prior to the organization into the form of State. Hence, the present condition of the international society is marked by the uncertainty that characterizes any transition stage. For general reviews, see: Evans (ed., 2006); Carty (2007); and Shaw (2008).

Hart (1961: 224) discusses the problem of how it is possible that, despite the absence of a Universal State (and of sanctions—see below), the sovereign States in which the world is presently organized may be limited by, and bound to, an international law; he considers and criticizes the view that international law should be regarded as "self-imposed [obligations] like the obligation that arises from a promise" and the resulting binding to observance as "auto-limitation" (a sort of social contract between States). He argues that this would presuppose the existence of rules (Hart 1961: 225). I believe that the binding force of international laws can be better understood if we think about the fundamental trend of the mind toward universalization, which, in the political field, means the trend toward a Universal State. This trend manifests itself through the willingness of the various States to undertake relationships between them as a first step toward a further progression in the universalization of human actions. Yet, in the present stage, international laws are often vague and conflicting enough to give rise to uncertainty about the limitations imposed to the States to which they refer.

(2) Primary and Secondary Rules in the International Society. The fact that there is not yet an organized Universal State, entails that the so-called international laws do not form a complete legal system, composed of constitutional norms (Hart's secondary rules of recognition, change, and adjudication) and ordinary laws (Hart's primary rules). Only "rules" like the latter would be present, i.e., international laws would be "a set of separate primary rules of obligation," which includes the rule that gives binding force to treaties (Hart 1961: 233); they would have binding force in that they are accepted and function as such (Hart 1961: 235).

On the other hand, Kelsen referred to his concept of "grundnorm" (1934: 193–221; 1945: 115, 117–18) and claimed that international law must possess a *basic norm* (i.e., a rule of recognition), which unifies the system and provides a criterion for the validity of its rules (Kelsen 1934: 214–17).

I think that a basic *moral* norm is always present, in a conscious or unconscious manner, in any human community (as well as in the life of every individual), as it is needed as a guide for acting; according to my conception, it is the *ground moral norm* prescribing the promotion of mind evolution, which is the source of all other moral norms and political laws, and which represents the tacit premise of any human action.

The moral nature of international laws cannot be questioned by arguing, as by Hart (1961: 229–30), that these laws, like municipal laws, also refer to particular and arbitrary facts apparently unrelated to morality (e.g., the width of territorial waters). These are rules agreed upon to allow the functioning of an organized (national or international) society, which is itself a moral value (because the organized society allows the universalization of human actions, which is in keeping with the prescription of the ground moral norm—chs. 3.1.1.2, 2; 4.2.1.2.2).

It has been observed that, in contrast to municipal law, international law recognizes the validity of agreements imposed by violence. This, however, is due to the fact that the international society is presently in a transitional stage (see above); like national States in the pre-democratic and pre-constitutional era, in which "laws" were imposed through violence by non-democratic governors and were forcefully "recognized" (indeed, simply obeyed), so in the present stage of the history of the world, some agreements imposed by some strong States through violence are "recognized" by other weak States.

(3) The Sanctions in the International Society. Presently, in the international society there is no international court that has the jurisdiction to investigate about what is right and what is wrong and, consequently, there are no centrally issued sanctions. This, however, would question the existence of international laws only if we consider, after Austin, laws as orders backed by threats; yet, laws are publicly-shared projects that, as such, are distinct from the enforcing sanctions (ch. 4.1.1.1).

Hart (1961: 218) maintains that sanctions are possible in the various States because, in a State, society is made of individuals of approximately equal physical strength and vulnerability, so that a malefactor or association of malefactors would not be able to overcome the control by the legal system. On the other hand, due to the great difference in the power of the various States, it is possible that a single very strong state or an association of States may overcome those States defending the international order (Hart 1961: 219). I observe that, concerning municipal laws, what should be considered is not the physical strength of individuals but their political and economic power, which greatly differs among individuals or groups and can resist, and even overcome, the legal system. Concerning international laws, this could happen even more easily. However, one should consider that, like the municipal society, the international society could only exist if its constituent members are willing to build it (by following the ground moral norm that prescribes to pursue a progressive universalization of actions). For this reason, international rules should be regarded as binding, inasmuch as they are voluntarily endorsed by the contracting States and, as stated by Hart (1961: 220), are conceived as entailing obligation to obey, and their breach is thought to justify compensation, reprisals, and countermeasures.

CHAPTER 5

Concluding Remarks

At this point, after having expounded my thought about the philosophy of ethics, politics, and law, as based on my ontological conception of the structure and functioning of the mind, a brief comment on the entire project is possible and even useful.

Starting from the internal observation that the mind is an *evolving, conscious, triadic entity*, made of *intellect, sensitiveness,* and *power*, which exert rational, emotional, and practical activities, respectively (Fig. 1.1), I have attempted to further develop the knowledge of the mind, by means of the observational method (the only suitable to acquire new knowledge), thus becoming aware of the centrality of the *inward activity* of the three mind components, i.e., of *consciousness*. Indeed, of the three fields considered in this book, ethics is clearly linked to the activity of the consciousness as a whole. Politics and law, on the other hand, are mainly concerned with the *inward* activity of the power (or practical consciousness); however, due to the close relationship between the inward and the outward mind activity (bidirectionality of the mind), both politics and law include also the (good) outward activity of the power (morally-good practical selfishness). Moreover, because of the close interrelation between the three mind components, the products of the inward and outward activity of the intellect (moral *thoughts* and *projects* and good-selfish *ideas* and *projects*) and of the sensitiveness (moral *feelings* and good-selfish *sentiments*) required for the practical activity (moral acts and good-selfish actions), have also been considered. The various "objects" discussed in this book (such as human actions and moral acts exerted in private and public life as well as the related moral thoughts, projects, and feelings and the good-selfish ideas, projects, and sentiments) have been conceived as products of the various mind components, i.e., have been interpreted as the expression of the structure and functioning of the mind. On these grounds, it may be justified to hope that the original project of giving ethics, politics, and law an ontological foundation has been realized.

As a philosopher, I have attempted to attain a deeper understanding of the mind and its components through my *rational* activity: first, the *outward activity* of the intellect, by which I gained knowledge about the structure of the mind as the most complex among the observable "objects" and as a continuously changing entity; then, the *inward activity* of the intellect (or rational consciousness), which allowed me to learn about the mind itself as a whole and, especially, about its most inner and unitary aspect, consciousness, and its most notable property: the ability to undergo *evolution*. This rational activity (*moral thoughts* produced by the *inward activity of intellect* or rational consciousness) led me to understand, through a process of *comparative evaluation*, that mind evolution, which entails changing to ever better states, is an intrinsic property of the mind and constitutes the moral good. In this way, the ground *moral principle* has been established, consisting of the proposition "mind evolution is the objective moral good." This principle, although obtained by the activity of the intellect, concerns all three mind components, since mind evolution includes the evolution of the sensitiveness and of the power, besides that of the intellect. Indeed, through rational activity, I understood the roles of *moral feelings* and of *moral acts*, produced by the emotional and the practical consciousness, respectively. Moral feelings make the human soul feel that mind evolution is the moral good, thus "founding" the basic *moral values*; moral acts implement moral principles and values by pursuing mind evolution through *good deeds*. Moreover, politics and law were shown to consist of the interplay between collective moral acts and selfish actions (and the related projects) as exerted in a community or society, and therefore are the expression of both the inward and the (good) outward activity of the power.

Thus, through *rational* activity, I understood the major role played by the *emotional* and *practical* mind activities, primarily the emotional and practical consciousness. The practical consciousness, which gives rise to human moral acts, can only be expressed through the concrete behavior in everyday life. The emotional consciousness, which produces moral feelings, although serving as a guide for moral acts, may also be expressed through language; for this reason, before I end this book, I would like to voice my moral feelings.

Several thinkers (such as Kant, Rawls, and others) have defined the human person as a "rational being", which is too limited a conception, as it only takes into account the rational mind component, minimizing the other components, specifically the emotional component and moral feelings, which, in contrast, I recognize as factors playing a major role. Others have searched the basis of moral values by looking outside the human soul, primarily to God. While I do not comment on the latter issue (as it belongs to the "noumenal" sphere, which is outside the reach of human thinking), I am happy to underline that I found the source of moral values and human dignity in the core of the human soul: the consciousness. By looking deeply in the human consciousness, mine and that of those I know well, I discovered something like a wonderful treasury, a shining light that illuminates and guides human life in its most meaningful steps, a true "first cause" of mankind evolution: moral feelings and their role in moral choices (I attempted to represent this "light" by the image of a star in the center of Fig. 1.1). This "light" is most often in keeping with the indications of reason, due to the internal coherence of the mind; yet, it has a major role in human choices, which are primarily determined by the balance between moral feelings and selfish desires. This enlightening guide, together with reason, indicates the moral ends (those linked to the marvelous characteristic of the human mind: the *endless evolution*) with sufficient certainty to reject some postmodern views supporting a sort of moral relativism. Actually, as mentioned in other chapters of this book, uncertainty may exist only about particular actions and moral acts required to reach an end, but not about the ends to be reached. Thus, human behavior can be said to consist of *uncertain particular acts to reach certain general ends*. Indeed, human moral feelings categorically refuse any claimed uncertainty that justifies wrong or unjust acts directed to reach morally-bad ends; and there is nothing that can repress this powerful voice arising from the core of consciousness. Indeed, I am profoundly impressed by this "divine light" that sheds from human consciousness; it is the cause of the evolution of human moral behavior through the decades, centuries, and millennia. The development from the violence of absolutist power of the past centuries to the modern democracies, from the once justified slavery to the now diffusely accepted recognition of universal human rights, is primarily due to the evolution of moral feelings produced by the human consciousness. The same is true for the further moral improvement of human beings which, hopefully, will take place in the future. Indeed, I would wish that these lines be as a paean to human moral feelings, otherwise named human "conscience", which are the only hope for the future of mankind. Being unable to find the suitable words to express my deep feeling about the "divine light" arising from human consciousness, may I help myself by drawing some verses from Dante; he looked at God to search what I found in the core of human consciousness: the light of the moral values. When, at the end of the Divine Comedy, he attempted to describe his vision of God (which I compare to my looking at the light of consciousness), Dante says:

> My mind in this wise wholly in suspense,
> steadfast, immovable, attentive gazed,
> and evermore with gazing grew enkindled.
> In presence of that light one such becomes,
> that to withdraw therefrom for other prospect
> it is impossible he e'er consent;
> because the good, which object is of will,
> is gathered all in this, and out of it
> that is defective which is perfect there. (Dante, *The Divine Comedy*, Paradiso, Canto 33, lines 97–105)

This clearly describes the deep admiration that I feel for human consciousness and its light. Dante continues:

> Within the deep and luminous subsistence
> of the High Light appeared to me three circles,
> of threefold colour and of one dimension; (Dante, *The Divine Comedy*, Paradiso, Canto 33, lines 115–17).

In these verses there is even the description of a "High Light" which is one and trine ("threefold colour" and "one dimension"), reminiscent of my conception of the mind as a triadic and yet unitary entity.

As to the interdependence that links the three mind components (intellect, sensitiveness, and power), it seems to be expressed by the following Dante's passage (which refers, again, to the "three circles, of threefold colour and of one dimension", quoted above):

> And by the second seemed the first reflected
> as Iris is by Iris, and the third
> seemed fire that equally from both is breathed. (Dante, *The Divine Comedy*, Paradiso, Canto 33, lines 118-20)

Of interest are also the following verses:

> O Light Eterne, sole in thyself that dwellest,
> sole knowest thyself, and, known unto thyself
> and knowing, lovest and smilest on thyself! (Dante, *The Divine Comedy*, Paradiso, Canto 33, lines 124–26)

Here Dante, besides his admiration for the "Light Eterne", seems to talk of something similar to what I name the reflexivity of consciousness, concerning both the moral thoughts ("known unto thyself and knowing") and the moral feelings ("lovest and smilest on thyself").

Finally, concerning the primary role of human moral feelings as promoters of the moral evolution of the world, I would like to refer to the last line of the Divine Comedy, to compare moral feelings to "The Love which moves the sun and the other stars."

References

Ackerman, B. (1980). *Social Justice in the Liberal State*. New Haven, CT: Yale University Press.

Ackerman, B. (1991). *We the People: Foundations*. Cambridge, MA: Harvard University Press,.

Ackerman, B. and A. Alstott (1999). *The Stakeholder Society*. New Haven, CT: Yale University Press.

Addis, A. (1992). "Individualism, Communitarianism and the Rights of Ethnic Minorities." *Notre Dame Law Review* 67: 615–76.

Alexander, L. (ed.) (1998). *Constitutionalism: Philosophical Foundations*. Cambridge: Cambridge University Press.

Allett, J. (1995). "Bernard Shaw and Dirty-Hands Politics: A Comparison of Mrs. Warren's Profession and Major Barbara." *Journal of Social Philosophy* 26: 32–45.

Altman, A. (1986). "Legal Realism, Critical Legal Studies, and Dworkin." *Philosophy and Public Affairs* vol. 15: 205–35.

Altman, A. [1995]. "Law and Economics." In *Arguing About Law*, by A. Altman. Belmont, CA: Wadsworth, 2000, pp. 170–98.

Anderson, B. (1983). *Imagined Communities: Reflections on the Origin and Spread of Nationalism*. London: New Left Books.

Anderson, C. W. (1993). "Pragmatic Liberalism, the Role of Law, and the Pluralist Regime." In *A New Constitutionalism: Designing Political Institutions for a Good Society*, edited by S. L. Elkin and K. E. Soltan. Chicago: The University of Chicago Press, pp. 96–116.

Anscombe, G. E. M. (1958). "Modern Moral Philosophy." *Philosophy* 33: 1–19. [Reprinted in *The Definition of Morality*, edited by G. Wallace and A. D. M. Walker. London: Methuen, 1970].

Anscombe, G. E. M. [1961]. "War and Murder." In *Nuclear Weapons and Christian Conscience*, edited by W. Stein. London: Merlin Press, 1965, pp. 45–62. [Also in *The Many Faces of Evil: Historical Perspectives*, edited by A. Rorty. London: Routledge, 2001, pp. 295–302].

Anscombe, G. E. M. (1981). *Ethics, Religion and Politics*. Minneapolis: University of Minnesota Press.

Applbaum, A. I. (1992). "Democratic Legitimacy and Official Discretion." *Philosophy and Public Affairs* 21: 240–74.

Applbaum, A. I. (1999). *Ethics for Adversaries: The Morality of Roles in Public and Professional Life*. Princeton, NJ: Princeton University Press, pp. 240–74.

Aquinas, T. [1272]. "Summa Theologica." In *Aquinas: Political Writings*, edited by R. W. Dyson. Cambridge: Cambridge University Press, 2002.

Arendt, H. [1951]. *Origins of Totalitarianism*. New York: Harcourt Publishers, 1973.

Arendt, H. [1954]. "Truth and Politics." In *Between Past and Future*, by H. Arendt. New York: Penguin, 1968, pp. 227–64.

Arendt, H. [1955]. *Men in Dark Times*. New York: Harcourt Publishers, 1970.

Arendt, H. (1958). *The Human Condition*. Chicago: University of Chicago Press, 1958 and 1998.

Arendt, H. (1971). "Thinking and Moral Considerations." *Social Research* 38: 417–46.

Arendt, H. (1972). "Lying in Politics." In *Crises of the Republic*, by H. Arendt. New York: Harvest/Harcourt, Brace, Jovanovich Book, pp. 1–47.

Aristotle [~330 B.C.]. "Nicomachean Ethics," "Politics" and "Rhetoric." In *The Complete*

Works of Aristotle, edited by J. Barnes. Princeton, NJ: Princeton University Press, 1984.

Arneson, R. (1981). "What's Wrong with Exploitation?" *Ethics* 91: 202–27.

Arneson, R. (1987). "Meaningful Work and Market Socialism." *Ethics* 97: 517–45.

Arneson, R.(1993). "Market Socialism and Egalitarian Ethics." In *Market Socialism: The Current Debate*, edited by P. Bardhan and J. Roemer. New York: Oxford University Press, pp. 281–97.

Arrow, K. J., A. K. Sen, and K. Suzumura (eds.) (2002). *Handbook of Social Choice and Welfare* (vol. 1). Amsterdam: Elsevier-North-Holland.

Arthur, J. (1996). "Judicial Review, Democracy and the Special Competency of Judges." In *Constitutionalism, Democracy and Sovereign: American and European Perspectives*, edited by R. Bellamy. Aldershot, UK: Ashgate Publishing Co., pp. 61–76.

Audi, R. (1997). "Intuitionism, Pluralism, and the Foundations of Ethics." In *Moral Knowledge and Ethical Character*, by Robert Audi. Oxford: Oxford University Press, pp. 32–65).

Audi, R. (2004). *The Good in the Right: A Theory of Intuition and Intrinsic Value*. Princeton: Princeton University Press.

Austin, J. [1832]. *The Province of Jurisprudence Determined*, edited by W.E. Rumble. Cambridge: Cambridge University Press, 1995.

Ayer, A. J. [1936]. "Critique of Ethics and Theology." In *Language, Truth, and Logic*, by A. J. Ayer. New York: Dover Publications, 1952, pp. 102–20.

Baier, A. (1985). "What Do Women Want in a Moral Theory." *Nous* 19: 53–63.

Baier, A. (1986). "Trust and Antitrust." *Ethics* 96: 231–60.

Baier, A. (1987). "Hume, the Women's Moral Theorist?" In *Women and Moral Theory*, edited by E. F. Kittay and D. Meyers. Savage, MD: Rowman and Littlefield, pp. 37–55.

Bailey, J. (1997). *Utilitarianism, Institutions, and Justice*. Oxford: Oxford University Press.

Baker, J. (1987). *Arguing for Equality*. London: Verso Books.

Banting, K. (2000). "Social Citizenship and the Multicultural Welfare State." In *Citizenship, Diversity and Pluralism*, edited by A. C. Cairns, J. C. Courtney, P. MacKinnon, H. J. Michelmann and D. E. Smith. Montreal: McGill-Queen's University Press, pp. 108–36.

Barber, B. (1999). "The Discourse of Civility." In *Citizen Competence and Democratic Institutions*, edited by S. Elkin and K. Soltan. University Park: Pennsylvania State University Press, pp. 39–48.

Barcalow, E. (2007). *Moral Philosophy: Theories and Issues* (4th edition. Belmont, CA: Wadsworth Publishing.

Barry, B. (1989). *Democracy, Power, and Justice: Essays in Political Theory*. Oxford: Oxford University Press.

Barry, B. (1991). *Liberty and Justice*. Oxford: Clarendon Press.

Barry, B. (1998). "International Society from a Cosmopolitan Perspective." In *International Society: Diverse Ethical Perspectives*, edited by D. R. Mapel and T. Nardin. Princeton: Princeton University Press, pp. 144–63.

Barry, B. (2001). *Culture and Equality: An Egalitarian Critique of Multiculturalism*. Cambridge: Polity.

Barry, B. and R. Goodin (eds.) (1992). *Free Movement: Ethical Issues in the Transnational Migration of People and of Money*. University Park: Pennsylvania State University Press.

Barry, N. (1990). "Markets, Citizenship and the Welfare State." In *Citizenship and Rights in Thatcher's Britain*, edited by R. Plant and N. Barry. London: IEA Health and Welfare Unit, pp. 43–53.

Bauböck, R. (1994). *Transnational Citizenship: Membership and Rights in International Migration*. Aldershot: Edward Elgar.

Beauchamp, T. L. (2001). *Philosophical Ethics: An Introduction to Moral Philosophy* (3rd edition). New York: Mcgraw-Hill College.

Beiner, R. (1983). *Political Judgment.* London: Methuen.

Beiner, R. (ed.) (1995). *Theorizing Citizenship.* Albany: State University of New York Press.

Beitz, C. (1979). *Political Theory and International Relations.* Princeton: Princeton University Press.

Beitz, C. (1983). "Cosmopolitan Ideals and National Sentiment." *Journal of Philosophy* 80: 591–600.

Beitz, C. (1994). "Cosmopolitan Liberalism and the State System." In *Political Restructuring in Europe: Ethical Perspectives,* edited by C. Brown. London: Routledge, pp. 123–36.

Beitz, C. (1999). "International Liberalism and Distributive Justice: A Survey of Recent Thought." *World Politics* 51: 269–96.

Belfiore, F. (2004). *The Structure of the Mind. Outlines of a Philosophical System.* Lanham, MD: University Press of America.

Belfiore, F. (2012). *The Democratic Society and Its Founding Concepts.* Lanham, MD: University Press of America.

Bell, D. A. (1993). *Communitarianism and Its Critics.* Oxford: Oxford University Press.

Bell, D. A. (2000). *East Meets West.* Princeton: Princeton University Press.

Bell, J. (1992). *French Constitutional Law.* Oxford: Clarendon Press.

Bellamy, R. (ed.) (1996). *Constitutionalism, Democracy and Sovereignty: American and European Perspectives.* Aldershot, UK: Avebury Publishing.

Benn, S. I. (1983). "Private and Public Morality: Clean Living and Dirty Hands." In *Public and Private in Social Life,* edited by S. I. Benn and G. F. Gaus. London: Croom Helm, pp. 159–69.

Benn, S. I. (1988). *A Theory of Freedom.* Cambridge: Cambridge University Press.

Benn, S. I. and S. P. Richard (1959). *Social Principles and the Democratic State,* London: Allen and Unwin.

Bentham, J. [1789]. *Introduction to the Principles of Morals and Legislation,* edited by J. H. Burns and H. L. A. Hart. New York: Oxford University Press, 1996.

Bentham, J. [1802]. *The Theory of Legislation,* C.K. Ogden (ed.), London: Kegan Paul, Trench, Trubner & Co, 1931.

Berlin, I. (1969). "Two Concepts of Liberty." In *Four Essays on Liberty,* edited by I. Berlin. Oxford: Oxford University Press, pp. 118–72.

Bertens, H. and J. Natoli (eds.) (2002). *Postmodernism: The Key Figures.* Oxford: Wiley-Blackwell.

Bix, B. (2009). *Jurisprudence: Theory and Context* (5th ed.). Durham, NC: Carolina Academic Press.

Bix, B. (ed.) (1999). *Analyzing Law: New Essays in Legal Theory.* New York: Oxford University Press.

Blackburn, S. [1971]. "How to Be an Ethical Anti-Realist." In *Essays in Quasi-Realism,* by Simon Blackburn. Oxford: Oxford University Press, 1993, pp. 166–81.

Blackburn, S. (1984). *Spreading the Word.* Oxford: Oxford University Press.

Blackburn, S. [1985]. "Supervenience Revisited." In *Essays in Quasi-Realism,* by Simon Blackburn. Oxford: Oxford University Press, 1993, pp. 130–48.

Blackburn, S. (1988). "Attitudes and Contents." *Ethics* 98: 501–17.

Blackburn, S. (1993). *Essays in Quasi-Realism.* Oxford: Oxford University Press.

Blackburn, S. (1998). *Ruling Passions.* Oxford: Oxford University Press.

Blackstone, W. [1765-1769]. *Commentaries on the Law of England,* "Introduction" and "Book 1," 4th edition. Oxford: Clarendon Press, 1770. [Reprint: Chicago: The University of Chicago Press, 1979].

Blackstone, W. T. (ed.) (1969). *The Concept of Equality.* Minneapolis, MN: Burgess Publishing Company.

Blum, L. (1988). "Gilligan and Kohlberg: Implications for Moral Theory." *Ethics* 98:

472–91.

Bohman, J. *(*1996*)*. *Public Deliberation: Pluralism, Complexity and Democracy*. Cambridge, MA: MIT Press.

Bok, S. (1978). *Lying: Moral Choice in Political and Private Life*. New York: Pantheon Books.

Bowden, P. (1996). *Caring: Gender-Sensitive Ethics*. London: Routledge.

Boyd, R. N. (1988). "How To Be a Moral Realist." In *Essays on Moral Realism*, edited by Geoffrey Sayre-McCord. Ithaca, NY: Cornell University Press, pp. 181–228.

Boyd, S. (ed.) (1997). *Challenging the Public/Private Divide: Feminism, Law and Public Policy*. Toronto: University of Toronto Press.

Boyle, J. (1994). "Natural Law and the Ethics of Traditions." In *Natural Law Theory: Contemporary Essays*, edited by R. P. George. Oxford: Oxford University Press, pp. 3–30.

Bradshaw, L. (2000). "Principles and Politics." In *Cruelty and Deception: The Controversy Over Dirty Hands in Politics*, edited by P. Rynard and D. P. Shugarman. Peterborough, ON, Canada: Broadview Press, pp. 87–99.

Brandt, R. (1963). "Toward a Credible Form of Utilitarianism." In *Morality and the Language of Conduct*, edited by H.-N. Castaneda and G. Nakhnikian. Detroit, MI: Waine State University Press, pp. 107–43.

Brandt, R. (1969). "A Utilitarian Theory of Excuses." *The Philosophical Review* 78: 337–61.

Brandt, R. (1971/72). "Utilitarianism and the Rules of War." *Philosophy and Public Affairs* 1: 145–65.

Brandt, R. [1979]. *A Theory of the Good and the Right*, revised edition. Amherst, NY: Prometheus Books, 1998.

Brandt, R. (1992). *Morality, Utilitarianism, and Rights*. Cambridge: Cambridge University Press.

Braybrooke, D. (1974). *Traffic Congestion Goes Through the Issue Machine*. London: Routledge and P. Kegan.

Braybrooke, D. and C. E. Lindblom (1970). *A Strategy of Decision: Policy Evaluation as a Social Process*. New York: Free Press of Glencoe.

Braybrooke, D., B. Brown, P. K. Schotch and L. Byrne (1996). *Logic on the Track of Social Change*. Oxford: Clarendon.

Brian, O. (2006). *The Morality of War*. Peterborough, ON, Canada: Broadview Press.

Brierly, J. L. (1963). *The Law of Nations*. Oxford: Oxford University Press.

Brighouse, H. (1996). "Against Nationalism." *Canadian Journal of Philosophy* 22 (Suppl.): 365–405. [Reprinted In *Rethinking Nationalism*, edited by J. Couture, K. Nielsen and M. Seymour. Calgary: University of Calgary Press, 1998].

Brink, D. O. (1989). *Moral Realism and the Foundations of Ethics*. Cambridge: Cambridge University Press.

Brittan, S. (1988). *A Restatement of Economic Liberalism*. London: Palgrave MacMillan.

Broad, C. D. (1952). "Egoism As a Theory of Human Motives." In *Ethics and the History of Philosophy*, by C. D. Broad. New York: The Humanities Press. [Previously published in *The Hibbert Journal* 48 (1950): 105–14].

Brown, C. (1998). "Contractarian Thought and the Constitution of International Society." In *International Society: Diverse Ethical Perspectives*, edited by D. R. Mapel and T. Nardin. Princeton: Princeton University Press, pp. 132–43.

Brown, H. P. (1988). *Egalitarianism and the Generation of Inequality*. Oxford: Clarendon.

Bubeck, D. (1995). *Care, Gender, and Justice*. Oxford: Oxford University Press.

Buchanan, A. (1975). "Revisability and Rational Choice." *Canadian Journal of Philosophy* 5: 395–408.

Buchanan, A. (1982). *Marx and Justice: The Radical Critique of Liberalism*. London: Methuen.

Buchanan, J. M. (1975). *The Limits of Liberty: Between Anarchy and Leviathan*. Chicago: University of Chicago Press.

Buchanan, J. M. and G. Tullock [1962]. *The Calculus of Consent: Logical Foundations of Constitutional Democracy*. Indianapolis: Liberty Fund Inc., 1999.

Buchanan, J. M. and R. Congleton (1998). *Politics by Principle, Not Interest*. Cambridge: Cambridge University Press.

Bull, H. (1977). *The Anarchical Society: A Study of Order in World Politics*. London: Macmillan.

Butler, J. [1726]. *Fifteen Sermons* (six sermons added in the 1749 edition). Partially reprinted in *British Moralists, 1650–1800*, Vol. 2, edited by D. D. Raphael. Indianapolis: Hackett Publishing Co, 1991.

Butler, J. and J. W. Scott (eds.) (1992). *Feminists Theorize the Political*. London: Routledge.

Cahn, S. M. and P. Markie (eds.) (2002). *Ethics: History, Theory, and Contemporary Issues*. New York: Oxford University Press.

Calhoun, C. (2000). "The Virtue of Civility." *Philosophy and Public Affairs* 29: 251–75.

Callan, E. (1997). *Creating Citizens: Political Education and Liberal Democracy*. Oxford: Oxford University Press.

Campbell, T. (1983). *The Left and Rights: A Conceptual Analysis of the Idea of Socialist Rights*. London: Routledge and Kegan Paul.

Camus, A. (1954). *The Rebel: An Essay on Man in Revolt*. New York: Alfred A. Knopf.

Canovan, M. (1996). *Nationhood and Political Theory*. Cheltenham, UK: Edward Elgar.

Card, C. (ed.) (1999). *On Feminist Ethics and Politics*. Lawrence: University of Kansas.

Carens, J. (1987). "Aliens and Citizens: The Case for Open Borders." *Review of Politics* 49: 251–73.

Carens, J. (1989). "Membership and Morality: Admission to Citizenship in Liberal Democratic States." In *Immigration and the Politics of Citizenship in Europe and North America*, edited by W. R. Brubaker. Lanham, MD: University Press of America, pp. 31–49.

Carey, G. (1984). *Freedom and Virtue: The Conservative/Libertarian Debate*. Lanham, MD: University Press of America,.

Carr, D. (1986). *Time, Narrative and History*. Bloomington: Indiana University Press.

Carritt, E. F. (1973). *Ethical and Political Thinking* [1947]. London: Greenwood Press.

Carter, A. (2001). *The Political Theory of Global Citizenship*. London: Routledge.

Carter, I. (1999). *A Measure of Freedom*. Oxford: Oxford University Press.

Carty, A. (2007). *Philosophy of International Law*. Edinburgh: Edinburgh University Press.

Chambers, S. and W. Kymlicka (eds.) (2001). *Alternative Conceptions of Civil Society*. Princeton: Princeton University Press.

Charvet, J. (1998). "International Society from a Contractarian Perspective." In *International Society: Diverse Ethical Perspectives*, edited by D. R. Mapel and T. Nardin. Princeton: Princeton University Press, pp. 114–31.

Christiano, T. (1996). *The Rule of the Many: Fundamental Issues in Democratic Theory*. Boulder, CO: Westview Press.

Clement, G. (1996). *Care, Autonomy and Justice: Feminism and the Ethic of Care*. Boulder, CO: Westview.

Coady, C. A. J. [1991]. "Politics and the Problem of Dirty Hands." In *A Companion to Ethics*, reprint edition, edited by P. Singer. Oxford: Blackwell, 1993, pp. 373–83.

Coady, C. A. J. (1995). "Dirty Hands." In *A Companion to Contemporary Political Philosophy*, edited by R. E. Goodin and P. Petit. Oxford: Blackwell, pp. 422–30.

Cohen, G. A. [1979/1991] "Capitalism, Freedom and the Proletariat." In *Liberty*, edited by D. Miller. Oxford: Oxford University Press, 1991, pp. 163–82. [Previous version in *The Idea of Freedom*, edited by A. Ryan. Oxford: Oxford University Press, 1979]

Cohen, G. A. (1986). "Self-Ownership, World-Ownership and Equality: Part 2." *Social Philosophy and Politics* 3: 77–96.

Cohen, G. A. (1988). *History, Labour, and Freedom: Themes from Marx.* Oxford: Oxford University Press.

Cohen, G. A. (1989). "On the Currency of Egalitarian Justice." *Ethics* 99: 906–44.

Cohen, G. A. (1990a). "Marxism and Contemporary Political Philosophy, or Why Nozick Exercises Some Marxists More Than He Does Any Egalitarian Liberal." *Canadian Journal of Philosophy* 16: 363–87.

Cohen, G. A. (1990b). "Self-Ownership, Communism, and Equality." *Proceedings of the Aristotelian Society* 64 (Suppl.): 25–44.

Cohen, G. A. (2000). *If You're an Egalitarian, How Come You're So Rich?* Cambridge, MA: Harvard University Press.

Cole, P. (2000). *Philosophies of Exclusion: Liberal Political Theory and Immigration.* Edinburgh: Edinburgh University Press.

Collins, A. (1997). *In the Slip Room.* Toronto: Key Porter Books.

Connolly, W. (1993). *The Terms of Political Discourse.* Princeton: Princeton University Press.

Cragg, A. W. (2000). "Bribery, Business, and the Problem of Dirty Hands." In *Cruelty and Deception: The Controversy Over Dirty Hands in Politics,* edited by P. Rynard and D. P. Shugarman. Peterborough, ON, Canada: Broadview Press, pp. 175–86.

Crenshaw, K., N. Gotanda, G. Peller, and K. Thomas (eds.) (1995). *Critical Race Theory: The Key Writings That Formed the Movement.* New York: The New Press.

Croce, B. [1909]. *Philosophy of the Practical: Economic and Ethic,* translated by D. Ainslie. New York: Biblo and Tannen, 1969.

Crowley, B. (1987). *The Self, the Individual and the Community: Liberalism in the Political Thought of F. A. Hayek and Sidney and Beatrice Webb.* Oxford: Oxford University Press.

Cuneo, T. (2006). "Moral Facts as Configuring Causes." *Pacific Philosophical Quarterly* 87: 141–62.

D'Agostino, F. (1996). *Free Public Reason: Making it Up as We Go Along.* Oxford: Oxford University Press.

D'Agostino, F., and G. F. Gaus (eds.) (1998). *Public Reason.* Aldershot: Ashgate.

Dahl, R. A. (1989). *Democracy and Its Critics.* New Haven, CT: Yale University Press.

Dahrendorf, R. (1962). "On the Origin of Social Inequality." In *Philosophy, Politics, and Society,* 2nd Series, edited by P. Laslett and W. G. Runciman. Oxford: Blackwell, pp. 88–109.

Dancy, J. (1992). "Caring about Justice." *Philosophy* 67: 447–66.

Dancy, J. (1993). *Moral Reasons.* Oxford: Blackwell.

Dancy, J. (1995). "Why There Really Is No Such Thing as the Theory of Motivation." *Proceedings of the Aristotelian Society,* suppl. vol. 95: 1-18.

Dancy, J. (2000). *Practical Reality.* Oxford: Oxford University Press.

Daniels, N. (1979). "Wide Reflective Equilibrium and Theory Acceptance in Ethics." *Journal of Philosophy* 76: 256–82.

Dante, Alighieri [1308–1321]. *The Divine Comedy,* translated by H. W. Longfellow. Boston and New York: Houghton, Mifflin and Co., 1867. [Recently reprinted— Whitefish, MT: Kessinger Publishing, 2010].

Darwall, S. (1998). *Philosophical Ethics.* Boulder, CO: Westview Press.

Darwall, S. (ed.) (2003). *Consequentialism.* Oxford: Blackwell.

Davis, J. B., D. Wade Hands, and Uskali Mäki, (eds.) (1998). *The Handbook of Economic Methodology.* Cheltenham: Edward Elgar.

De George, R. T. (1993). *Competing with Integrity in International Business.* New York: Oxford University Press.

Descartes, R. [1637]. "Discourse on the Method." In *The Philosophical Writings of Descartes* (Vol. I), edited by J. Cottingham, R. Stoothoff, and D. Murdoch. Cambridge: Cambridge University Press, 1999, pp. 111–51.

Descartes, R. [1641]. "Meditation 2." In *The Philosophical Writings of Descartes* (Vol. II), edited by J. Cottingham, R. Stoothoff, and D. Murdoch. Cambridge: Cambridge

University Press, 1999, pp. 16–23.

Deveaux, M. (1995). "New Directions in Feminist Ethics." *European Journal of Moral Philosophy* 3: 86–96.

Deveaux, M. (2001). *Cultural Pluralism and Dilemmas of Justice*. Ithaca, NY: Cornell University Press.

Devlin, P. [1959]. *The Enforcement of Morals*. Oxford: Oxford University Press, 1996.

Dewey, J. (1916). *Democracy and Education*. New York: Macmillan.

Dicey, A. V. [1915]. *Introduction to the Study of the Law of the Constitution*, 8th edition. Indianapolis: Liberty Classics, 1982.

DiQuattro, A. (1983). "Rawls and Left Criticism." *Political Theory* 11: 53–78.

Donagan, A. (1984). "Consistency in Rationalist Moral Systems." *The Journal of Philosophy* 81: 291–309. [Reprinted in *Moral Dilemmas*, edited by C. W. Gowans. New York: Oxford University Press, 1987, pp. 271–90].

Donagan, A. (1997). *The Theory of Morality*. Chicago: The University of Chicago Press.

Doppelt, G. (1981). "Rawls' System of Justice: A Critique from the Left." *Nous* 15: 259–307.

Dorn, E. (1979). *Rules and Racial Equality*. New Haven, CT: Yale University Press.

Dreier, J. (1996). "Expressivist Embeddings and Minimalist Truth." *Philosophical Studies* 83: 29–51.

Drolet, M. (ed.) (2003). *The Postmodernism Reader: Foundational Texts in Philosophy, Politics and Sociology*. London: Routledge.

Dryzek, J. (1990). *Discursive Democracy*. Cambridge: Cambridge University Press.

Dryzek, J. (2000). *Deliberative Democracy and Beyond: Liberals, Critics, Contestations*. Oxford: Oxford University Press.

Dworkin, G. (1972). "Paternalism." *The Monist* 56: 64–84.

Dworkin, G. (1988). *The Theory and Practice of Autonomy*. Cambridge: Cambridge University Press.

Dworkin, R. [1977]. *Taking Rights Seriously*. London: Duckworth, 2005.

Dworkin, R. (1978). "The Rights of Myron Farber." *New York Review of Books*, 26 October.

Dworkin, R. (1981). "What is equality? Part I: Equality of Welfare; Part II: Equality of Resources." *Philosophy and Public Affairs* 10: 185–246 and 283–345.

Dworkin, R. (1982). "Natural Law Revisited." *University of Florida Law Review* 34: 165–88.

Dworkin, R. (1985). *A Matter of Principle*. Cambridge, MA: Harvard University Press.

Dworkin, R. (1986). *Law's Empire*. Cambridge: Harvard University Press.

Dworkin, R. (1989). "Liberal Community." *California Law Review* 77: 479–504.

Dworkin, R. (1993). "Justice in the Distribution of Health Care." *McGill Law Journal* 38: 883–98.

Dworkin, R. (1996). *Freedom's Law*. Cambridge, MA: Harvard University Press.

Dworkin, R. (2002). *Sovereign Virtue: The Theory and Practice of Equality*. Cambridge: Harvard University Press.

Elshtain, J. B. (1981). *Public Man, Private Woman: Women in Social and Political Thought*. Princeton: Princeton University Press.

Elshtain, J. B. [1993]. *Democracy on Trial*. New York: Basic Books, 2003.

Elster, J. (1983). "Exploitation, Freedom, and Justice." In *Marxism: NOMOS 26*, edited by J. R. Pennock and J. W. Chapman. New York: New York University Press, pp. 277–304.

Elster, J. (1984). *Ulysses and the Sirens: Studies in Rationality and Irrationality*. Cambridge: Cambridge University Press.

Elster, J. (1985). *Making Sense of Marx*. Cambridge: Cambridge University Press.

Elster, J. (1989). *Solomonic Judgments: Studies in the Limits of Rationality*. Cambridge: Cambridge University Press.

English, J. (1975). "Abortion and the Concept of a Person." *Canadian Journal of Philosophy* 5: 233–43. [Reprinted in *Feminism and Philosophy*, edited by M. Vetterling-

Braggin, F. Elliston, and J. English. Totowa, NJ: Rowman & Littlefield. 1977].

Epicurus [~341–271 B.C.]. "Letter to Menoeceus and Principal Doctrines." In *Epicurus: The Extant Remains*, translated by C. Baily. Oxford: Oxford University Press, 1926. [Reprinted in *Moral Philosophy: Selected Readings*, edited by G. Sher. Belmont, CA: Wadsworth, 2001, pp. 615–21].

Esposito, C. (1954). *La Costituzione Italiana*. Padova (Italy): Cedam.

Estrich, S. (1987). *Real Rape*. Cambridge: Harvard University Press.

Evans, M. (ed.) (2006). *International Law*. New York: Oxford University Press.

Exdell, J. (1977). "Distributive Justice: Nozick on Property Rights." *Ethics* 87: 142–49.

Feinberg, J. (1973). *Social Philosophy*. Englewood Cliffs, NJ: Prentice-Hall.

Feinberg, J. [1978]. "Psychological Egoism." In *Reason and Responsibility*, by J. Feinberg, 11th edition. Belmont, CA: Wadsworth, 2001, pp. 547–58.

Feinberg, J. (1985). *Offense to Others*. Oxford: Oxford University Press.

Feinberg, J. (1986). "Abortion (and the Conflict of Claims)." In *Matter of Life or Death: New Introductory Assays in Moral Philosophy*, 2nd edition, edited by T. Regan. New York: Random House, pp. 256–93. [Reprinted in *Moral Philosophy: Selected Readings*, edited by G. Sher. Belmont, CA: Wadsworth, 2001, pp. 735–48].

Feyerabend, P. (1975). *Against Method*. London: Verso Books.

Fierlbeck, K. (1991). "Redefining Responsibilities: The Politics of Citizenship in the United Kingdom." *Canadian Journal of Political Science* 24: 575–83.

Finnis, J. (1980). *Natural Law and Natural Rights*. New York: Oxford University Press, pp. 3–22 and 351–68.

Finnis, J. (1996). "The Truth in Legal Positivism." In *The Autonomy of Law: Essays on Legal Positivism*, edited by R. P. George. Oxford: Clarendon Press, pp.195–214.

Firth, R. (1952). "Ethical Absolutism and the Ideal Observer." *Philosophy and Phenomenological Research* 12: 317–45.

Fishkin, J. (1983). *Justice, Equal Opportunity, and the Family*. New Haven, CT: Yale University Press.

Fishkin, J. (1987). "Liberty versus Equal Opportunity." *Social Philosophy and Policy* 5: 32–48.

Foot, P. (1972). "Morality as a System of Hypothetical Imperatives." *Philosophical Review* 81: 305–16. [Reprinted in *Virtues and Vices, and Other Essays in Moral Philosophy*, by P. Foot, new edition. Oxford: Oxford University Press, 2003, pp. 157–73].

Frank, J. [1930]. *Law and the Modern Mind*. Gloucester, MA: Peter Smith, 1970.

Frankfurt, H. (1971). "Freedom of the Will and the Concept of a Person." *Journal of Philosophy* 68: 55–81. [Also in *Free Will*, 2nd edition, edited by G. Watson. Oxford: Oxford University Press, 2003, pp. 322–36].

Frankfurt, H. (1987). "Equality as a Moral Ideal." *Ethics* 98: 21–43. [Reprinted in H. Frankfurt. *The Importance of What We Care About*. Cambridge: Cambridge University Press, 1988, pp. 134–58].

Fraser, N. (1998). "Social Justice in the Age of Identity Politics: Redistribution, Recognition and Participation." In *The Tanner Lectures in Human Values*, vol. 19, edited by G. Peterson. Salt Lake City: University of Utah Press, pp. 1–67.

Freeman, S. (1990). "Constitutional Democracy and the Legitimacy of Judicial Review." *Law and Philosophy* 9: 327–70.

Fried, C. (1981). *Contract as Promise: A Theory of Contractual Obligation*. Cambridge: Harvard University Press,.

Friedman, M. [1962]. *Capitalism and Freedom*, 40th anniv. edition. Chicago: University of Chicago Press, 2002.

Friedman, M. (1987). "Beyond Caring: The Demoralization of Gender." *Canadian Journal of Philosophy* 13 (Suppl.): 87–110.

Friedrich, C. J. (1962). "L'essai sur la paix." In *La Philosophie Politique de Kant*. Paris: Presses Universitaires de France.

Fuller, L. L. [1964]. *The Morality of Law*, revised edition. New Haven, CT: Yale University Press, 1969.

Fusser, K. (1996). "Farewell to Legal Positivism: The Separation Thesis Unravelling." In *The Autonomy of Law: Essays on Legal Positivism*, edited by R. P. George. Oxford: Clarendon Press, pp. 119–62.

Gadamer, H.-G. (1976). *Philosophical Hermeneutics*. Berkeley, CA: University of California Press.

Galston, W. (1980). *Justice and the Human Good*. Chicago: University of Chicago Press, pp. 55–56 and 279–80.

Galston, W. (1986). "Equality of Opportunity and Liberal Theory." In *Justice and Equality: Here and Now*, edited by F. S. Lucash. Ithaca, NY: Cornell University Press, pp. 89–107.

Galston, W. (1991). *Liberal Purposes: Goods, Virtues, and Duties in the Liberal State*. Cambridge: Cambridge University Press.

Gaus, G. F. (1983). *The Modern Liberal Theory of Man*. New York: St. Martin's Press.

Gaus, G. F. (1994a). "Property, Rights and Freedom." *Social Philosophy and Policy* 11: 209–40.

Gaus, G. F. (1994b). "Public Reason and the Rule of Law." In *The Rule of Law*, Nomos XXXVI, edited by I. Shapiro. New York: New York University Press, pp. 328–64.

Gaus, G. F. (1996). *Justificatory Liberalism: An Essay on Epistemology and Political Theory*. New York: Oxford University Press.

Gauthier, D P. (1986). *Morals by Agreement*. New York: Oxford University Press.

Geach, P. (1956). "Good and Evil." *Analysis* 17: 33–42. [Reprinted in *Theories of Ethics*, edited by P. Foot. New York: Oxford University Press, 1967, pp. 64–73].

Geach, P. (1960). Ascriptivism." *Philosophical Review* 69:221–25.

Geach, P. (1965). "Assertion." *Philosophical Review* 74: 449–65.

Geismann, G. (1983). "Kants Rechtslehre von Weltfrieden." *Zeitschrift für philosophische Forschung* 37: 363–88.

Gellner, E. (1983). *Nations and Nationalism*. Oxford: Blackwell.

George, R. P. (1988). "Recent Criticism of Natural Law Theory." *University of Chicago Law Review* 55: 1371–429.

George, R. P. (1998). "Natural Law and International Order." In *International Society: Diverse Ethical Perspectives*, edited by D. R. Mapel and T. Nardin. Princeton: Princeton University Press, pp. 54–69.

George, R. P. (ed.) (1992). *Natural Law Theory: Contemporary Essays*. Oxford: Oxford University Press.

Geras, N. (1989). "The Controversy about Marx and Justice." In *Marxist Theory*, edited by A. Callinicos. Oxford: Oxford University Press, p. 211–67.

Gert, B. (1998). *Morality: Its Nature and Justification*. New York: Oxford University Press.

Gewirth, A. (1973-74). "The 'Is-Ought' Problem Resolved." *Proceedings and Addresses of the American Philosophical Association* 47: 34–61. [Reprinted in *Moral Philosophy: Selected Readings*, edited by G. Sher. Belmont, CA: Wadsworth, 2001, pp. 52–67].

Gewirth, A. (1978). *Reason and Morality*. Chicago: University of Chicago Press.

Gewirth, A. (1982). *Human Rights Essays on Justification and Applications*. Chicago: University of Chicago Press.

Gewirth, A. (1996). *The Community of Rights*. Chicago: University of Chicago Press.

Gibbard, A. (1985). "Moral Judgment and the Acceptance of Norms." *Ethics* 95: 5–21.

Gibbard, A. (1990). "Normative Logic." In *Wise Choices, Apt Feelings*, by Allan Gibbard. Cambridge, MA: Harvard University Press.

Gibbard, A. [1990]. *Wise Choices, Apt Feelings: A Theory of Normative Judgment*. Cambridge, MA: Harvard University Press, 1992.

Gibbard, A. (2003). *Thinking How to Live*. Cambridge, MA: Harvard University Press.

Giddens, A. (1998). *The Third Way*. Cambridge: Polity Press.

Gihl, T. (1937). *International Legislation*. Oxford: Oxford University Press.

Gilligan, C. (1982). *In a Different Voice: Psychological Theory and Women's Development*. Cambridge, MA: Harvard University Press.

Glazer, N. (1988). *The Limits of Social Policy*. Cambridge, MA: Harvard University Press.

Glendon, M.-A. (1991). *Rights Talk: The Impoverishment of Political Discourse*. New York: Free Press.

Glendon, M.-A. and D. Blankenhorn (eds.) (1995). *Seedbeds of Virtue: Sources of Competence, Character and Citizenship in American Society*. Lanham, MD: Madison Books.

Goldberg, D. T. (ed.) (1995). *Multiculturalism: A Critical Reader*. Oxford: Blackwell.

Goldman, A. (1977). "The Principle of Equal Opportunity." *Southern Journal of Philosophy* 15: 473–85.

Goodin, R. (1982). *Political Theory and Public Policy*. Chicago: University of Chicago Press.

Goodin, R. (1988). *Reasons for Welfare*. Princeton: Princeton University Press.

Goodin, R. (1995). *Utilitarianism as a Public Philosophy*. Cambridge: Cambridge University Press.

Gordon, S. (1980). *Welfare, Justice, and Freedom*. New York: Columbia University Press.

Gowans, C. W. (ed.) (1987). *Moral Dilemmas*. New York: Oxford University Press.

Gray J. C. [1909]. *The Nature and Sources of the Law*, 2nd edition (from the author's notes), by R. Gray. Gloucester, MA: Peter Smith, 1972.

Gray, J. (1986/1995). *Liberalism*. Minneapolis: University of Minnesota Press, 1986; 2nd edition 1995.

Green, T.H. [1895]. *Lectures on the Principles of Political Obligation* [1895] *and Other Writings*, edited by P. Harris and J. Morrow. Cambridge: Cambridge University Press, 1986.

Greenberg, D., S. Katz, M. B. Oliviero, and S. C. Wheatley (eds.) (1993). *Constitutionalism and Democracy. Transitions in the Contemporary World*. New York: Oxford University Press.

Greene, I. and D. P. Shugarman (1997). *Honest Politics: Seeking Integrity in Canadian Public Life*. Toronto: James Lorimer.

Greenspan, P. S. (1995). *Practical Guilt: Moral Dilemmas, Emotions, and Social Norms*. New York: Oxford University Press.

Griffin, J. (1986). *Well-Being: Its Meaning, Measurement, and Moral Importance*. Oxford: Oxford University Press.

Grimm, D. (1995). "Does Europe Need a Constitution?" *European Law Journal* 1: 282–302.

Grimshaw, J. (1986). *Philosophy and Feminist Thinking*. Minneapolis: University of Minneapolis Press.

Grisez, G., J. Boyle, and J. Finnis (1987). "Practical Principles, Moral Truth, and Ultimate Ends." *American Journal of Jurisprudence* 32: 99–151.

Grondin, J. [1991]. *Introduction to Philosophical Hermeneutics*, translated by Joel Weinsheimer. New Haven, CT: Yale University Press, 1994.

Guéhenno, J.-M. (1995). *The End of the Nation-State*. Minneapolis: University of Minnesota Press.

Gurr, T. (1993). *Minorities at Risk: A Global View of Ethno-political Conflict*. Washington, DC: Institute of Peace Press.

Gutmann, A. (1980). *Liberal Equality*. Cambridge: Cambridge University Press.

Gutmann, A. (1987). *Democratic Education*. Princeton: Princeton University Press.

Gutmann, A. (ed.) (1992). *Multiculturalism and the "Politics of Recognition."* Princeton: Priceton University Press.

Gutmann, A. and D. Thompson (1996). *Democracy and Disagreement*. Cambridge, MA: Harvard University Press.

Haber, J. G. (ed.) (1994). *Absolutism and Its Consequentialist Critics*. Lanham, MD:

Rowman and Littlefield.

Habermas, J. (1979). *Communication and the Evolution of Society*, translated by T. McCarthy. Boston: Beacon.

Habermas, J. (1985). "Questions and Counter Questions." In *Habermas and Modernity*, edited by R. J. Bernstein. Cambridge, MA: MIT Press, pp. 192–216.

Habermas, J. (1996). *Between Facts and Norms: Contributions to a Discourse Theory of Law and Democracy*. Cambridge, MA: MIT Press.

Hampshire, S. (1989). *Innocence and Experience*. Cambridge, MA: Harvard University Press.

Hampton, J. (1997). *Political Philosophy*. Boulder, CO: Westview Press, pp. 191–209.

Hampton, J. (1998). *The Authority of Reason*. Cambridge: Cambridge University Press, pp. 83–122 and 207–14.

Hardimon, M. (1992). "The Project of Reconciliation: Hegel's Social Philosophy." *Philosophy and Public Affairs* 23: 165–95.

Hardin, G. (1968). "The Tragedy of the Commons." *Science* 162: 1243–48.

Hardin, G. (1993). *Living Within Limits: Ecology, Economics and Population Taboos*. New York: Oxford University Press.

Hardin, R. (1988). *Morality Within the Limits of Reason*. Chicago: University of Chicago Press.

Harding, S. (1982). "Is Gender a Variable in Conceptions of Rationality? A Survey of Issues." *Dialectica* 36: 225–42.

Hare, R. M. [1952]. *The language of Morals*, reprint edition. New York: Oxford University Press, 1991.

Hare, R. M. (1963). *Freedom and Reasoning*. Oxford: Oxford University Press.

Hare, R. M. (1967). "Geach: Good and Evil." In *Theories of Ethics*, edited by P. Foot. New York: Oxford University Press, pp. 74–82.

Hare, R. M. (1971/72). "Rules of War and Moral Reasoning." *Philosophy and Public Affairs* 1: 166–81.

Hare, R. M. (1978). "Justice and Equality." In *Justice and Economic Distribution*, edited by J. Arthur and W. Shaw. Englewood Cliffs, NJ: Prentice-Hall, pp. 118–32.

Hare, R. M. (1981). *Moral Thinking: Its Levels, Methods and Point*. New York: Oxford University Press.

Hare, R. M. (1984). "Rights, Utility, and Universalization." In *Utility and Rights*, edited by R. Frey. Minneapolis: University of Minnesota Press, pp. 106–20.

Hare, R. M. (1989a). *Essays in Ethical Theory*. New York: Oxford University Press.

Hare, R. M. (1989b). *Essays on Political Morality*. Oxford: Clarendon Press.

Harman, G. (1975). "Moral Relativism Defended." *The Philosophical Review* 84: 3–22.

Harman, G. (1977). "Ethics and Observation." In *The Nature of Morality: An Introduction to Ethics*, by G. Harman. New York: Oxford University Press, pp. 3–10.

Harman, G. (1986). "Moral Explanations of Natural Facts—Can moral Claims be Tested against Moral Reality?" *Southern Journal of Philosophy* 24 (Suppl.):57–68.

Harsanyi, J. (1976). *Essays in Ethics, Social Behavior and Scientific Explanation*. Dordrecht: Reidel.

Harsanyi, J. (1985). "Rule Utilitarianism, Equality, and Justice." *Social Philosophy and Policy* 2: 115–27.

Hart, H. L. A. (1958). "Positivism and the Separation of Law and Morals." *Harvard Law Review* 71: 593–629.

Hart, H. L. A. [1961]. *The Concept of Law*. Oxford: Oxford University Press, 1994.

Hart, H. L. A. (1963). *Law, Liberty and Morality*. Oxford: Oxford University Press.

Hart, H. L. A. (1968). *Punishment and Responsibility*. Oxford: Oxford University Press.

Hart, H. L. A. (1994). "Postscript." In *The Concept of Law*, by H. L. A. Hart, 2nd edition. Oxford: Oxford University Press, pp. 238–76.

Hausman, D. M. (ed.) (1994). *The Philosophy of Economics: An Anthology*, 2nd edition. Cambridge: Cambridge University Press.

Hausman, D. M. and M. S. McPherson (2006). *Economic Analysis, Moral Philosophy and Public Policy*, 2nd edition. Cambridge: Cambridge University Press.

Haveman, R. (1988). *Starting Even*. New York: Simon and Schuster.

Hayek, F. A. [1944]. *The Road to Serfdom*, 50th edition. Chicago: University Of Chicago Press, 1994.

Hayek, F. A. (1960). *The Constitution of Liberty*. London: Routledge and Kegan.

Hayek, F. A. (1976). *The Mirage of Social Justice*. Chicago: University of Chicago Press.

Hayek, F. A. (1978). "Liberalism." In *New Studies in Philosophy, Politics, Economics and the History of Ideas*, by F. A. Hayek. London: Routledge and P. Kegan, pp. 119–51.

Heater, D. (1990). *Citizenship: The Civil Ideal in World History, Politics and Education*. London: Longman.

Heater, D. (1996). *World Citizenship and Government: Cosmopolitan Ideas in the History of Western Political Thought*. New York: St Martin's Press.

Heater, D. (1999). *What is Citizenship?* Cambridge: Polity Press.

Hegel, G.W. F. [1821]. *The Philosophy of Right*, new edition, translated by T.M. Knox. New York: Oxford University Press, 1967.

Hekman, S. (1995). *Moral Voices, Moral Selves: Carol Gilligan and Feminist Moral Theory*. Cambridge: Polity Press.

Held, D. (1995). *Democracy and the Global Order: From the Modern State to Cosmopolitan Governance*. London: Polity Press.

Held, V. (1984). *Rights and Goods*. Chicago: University of Chicago Press.

Held, V. (ed.) (1995). *Justice and Care: Essential Readings in Feminist Ethics*. Boulder, CO: Westview.

Herzog, D. (1986). "Some Questions for Republicans." *Political Theory* 14: 473–93.

Heyd, D. (1982). *Supererogation: Its Status in Ethical Theory*. Cambridge: Cambridge University Press.

Hill, T. E. (1987). "The Importance of Autonomy." In *Women and Moral Theory*, edited by E. Kittay and D. Meyers. Totowa, NJ: Rowman and Allanheld, pp. 129–38.

Hinman, L. M. (2005). *Contemporary Moral Issues: Diversity and Consensus* (3rd Edition). Upper Saddle River, NJ: Prentice-Hall.

Hinman, L. M. (2008). *Ethics: A Pluralistic Approach to Moral Theory* (4th edition). Belmont, CA: Wadsworth Publishing.

Hirsch, H. N. (1986). "The Threnody of Liberalism: Constitutional Liberty and the Renewal of Community." *Political Theory* 14: 423–49.

Hobbes, T. [1642]. *De Cive* (English version: 1651), edited by H. Warrender. Oxford: Clarendon Press, 1984.

Hobbes, T. [1651]. *Leviathan* (with selected variants from the Latin edition of 1668), edited by E. Curley. Indianapolis: Hackett Publishing Company, 1994.

Hobbes, T. [1668]. *Leviathan: the Latin Version, Opera Philosophica quae Latine scripsit omnia*, Vol. 3. London: J. Bohn, 1841.

Hollis, M. (1982). "Dirty Hands." *British Journal of Political Science* 12: 385–98.

Holmes, S. [1988]. "Precommitment and the paradox of democracy." In *Constitutionalism and Democracy*, edited by J. Elster and R. Slagstad. New York: Cambridge University Press, 1993, pp. 195–240.

Holmstrom, N. (1977). "Exploitation." *Canadian Journal of Philosophy* 7: 353–69.

Honoré, T. (1995). *About Law* (Chapter 9). Oxford: Clarendon Press, pp. 87–95.

Hooker, B. W. and M. Little (eds.) (2000). *Moral Particularism*, Oxford: Oxford University Press.

Horgan, T. and M. Timmons (1991). "New Wave Moral Realism Meets Moral Twin Earth." *Journal of Philosophical Research* 16: 447–65. [Reprinted in *Rationality, Morality, and Self-Interest*, edited by John Heil. Savage, MD: Rowman & Littlefield, 1993].

Horgan, T. and M. Timmons (1992a). "Troubles on Moral Twin Earth: Moral Queerness Revived." *Synthese* 92: 221–60.

Horgan, T. and M. Timmons (1992b). "Troubles for ew Wave Moral Semantic: The 'Open Question Argument' Revived." *Philosophical Papers* 21: 153–75.

Horgan, T. and M. Timmons (2000a). "Copping Out on Moral Twin Earth." *Synthese* 124: 139–52.

Horgan, T. and M. Timmons (2000b). "Nondescriptivist Cognitivism: Framework for a New Metaethics." *Philosophical Papers* 29: 121–53.

Horgan, T. and M. Timmons (eds.) (2006). *Metaethics after Moore*. Oxford: Oxford University Press.

Hospers, J. (1961). *Human Conduct*. New York: Harcourt, Brace & World.

Howard, K. W. (1977). "Must Public Hands be Dirty?" *The Journal of Value Inquiry* 11: 29–40.

Hume, D. [1739/40]. *A Treatise of Human Nature*, edited by L.A. Selby-Bigge and P.H. Nidditch, 2nd edition. New York: Oxford University Press, 1978.

Hutchings, K. and R. Dannreuther (eds.) (1999). *Cosmopolitan Citizenship*. New York: St Martin's Press.

Ignatieff, M. (1993). *Blood and Belonging: Journeys into the New Nationalism*. New York: Farrar, Straus and Giroux.

Jackson, F. (1998). "The Supervenience of the Ethical on the Descriptive." In *From Metaphysics to Ethics: A Defence of Conceptual Analysis*, by Frank Jackson. Oxford: Oxford University Press, pp. 118–29.

Jaggar, A. and I. M. Young (eds.) (1998). *A Companion to Feminist Philosophy*. Cambridge: Blackwell.

Janzen, W. (1990). *Limits of Liberty: The Experiences of Mennonite, Hutterite and Doukhobour Communities in Canada*. Toronto: University of Toronto Press.

Jefferson, T. [1809]. "To Henrì Grégoir" (letter). In *Jefferson: Political Writings*, edited by J. Appleby and T. Ball. Cambridge: Cambridge University Press, 1999, pp. 491–92.

Joyce, R. (2001). *The Myth of Morality*. Cambridge: Cambridge University Press.

Judt, T. (1998). "Counsels on Foreign Relations." In *New York Review of Books* XLV:13: 54–60.

Kagan, S. (1989). "Constraints." In *The Limits of Morality*, by S. Kagan. Oxford: Oxford University Press, pp. 24–32.

Kant, I. [1785]. *Groundwork of the Metaphysics of Morals*, edited by M. J. Gregor. Cambridge: Cambridge University Press, 1998.

Kant, I. [1788]. *Critique of Practical Reason*, translated by M. J. Gregor. Cambridge: Cambridge University Press, 1997.

Kant, I. [1795]. "Perpetual Peace." In *Perpetual Peace and Other Essays*, translated by T. Humphrey. Indianapolis: Hackett, 1983, pp. 107–43.

Kant, I. [1797]. *The Metaphysics of Morals*, translated by M. J. Gregor. Cambridge: Cambridge University Press, 1996.

Kaus, M. (1992). *The End of Equality*. New York: Basic Books.

Kelman, M. (1987). *A Guide to Critical Legal Studies*. Cambridge, MA: Harvard University Press.

Kelsen, H. [1934]. *Reine Rechtslehre*, 2nd edition, translated by M. Knight as *Pure Theory of Law*. Berkeley: University of California Press, 1967.

Kelsen, H. [1945]. *General Theory of Law and State*, reprint, translated by A. Wedberg. Cambridge, MA: Harvard University Press, 1999.

Kelsen, H. [1979]. *Allgemeine Theorie der Normen*, translated by M. Hartney as *The General Theory of Norms*. Oxford: Clarendon Press, 1991.

Kessler, F., G. Gilmore, and A. T. Kronan (1986). *Contracts: Cases and Materials*, 3rd edition. Boston: Little Brown.

Keynes, J. M. [1936]. *The General Theory of Employment, Interest and Money*. London and Cambridge: Macmillan and Cambridge University Press, 1973.

Kim, J. (2002). *Supervenience*. Aldershot: Ashgate/Dartmouth Publishing.

Kittay, E. F. (1995). *Equality, Rawls and the Inclusion of Women*. New York: Routledge.

Kittay, E. F. (1999). *Love's Labor: Essays on Women, Equality and Dependency*. London: Routledge.

Kittay, E. F. and D. Meyers (eds.) (1987). *Women and Moral Theory*. Savage, MD: Rowman and Littlefield.

Korsgaard, C. M. (1986). "Skepticism about Practical Reason." *Journal of Philosophy* 83: 5–25.

Korsgaard, C. M. (1996). "Reflective endorsement" and "The authority of reflection." In *The Sources of Normativity*, by Christine M. Korsgaard. Cambridge: Cambridge University Press, pp. 49-89 and 90–130.

Kramer, E. M. (1997). *Modern/Postmodern: Off the Beaten Path of Antimodernism*. Westport, CT: Praeger Publishers.

Kronman, A. T. (1980). "Contract Law and Distributive Justice." *The Yale Law Journal* 89: 472–511.

Krouse, R. and M. McPherson (1988). "Capitalism, 'Property-Owning Democracy', and the Welfare State." In *Democracy and the Welfare State*, edited by A. Gutman. Princeton: Princeton University Press, pp. 79–106.

Kukathas, C. (1992). "Are There any Cultural Rights." *Political Theory* 20: 105–39.

Kymlicka, W. (1989a). "Liberal Individualism and Liberal Neutrality." *Ethics* 99: 883–905.

Kymlicka, W. (1989b). *Liberalism, Community, and Culture*. Oxford: Oxford University Press.

Kymlicka, W. (1995b). *Multicultural Citizenship: A Liberal Theory of Minority Rights*. Oxford: Oxford University Press.

Kymlicka, W. (1998). *Finding Our Way: Rethinking Ethno-cultural Relations in Canada*. Toronto: Oxford University Press.

Kymlicka, W. (2001). *Politics in the Vernacular: Nationalism, Multiculturalism and Citizenship*. Oxford: Oxford University Press.

Kymlicka, W. (2002). *Contemporary Political Philosophy. An Introduction*. Oxford: Oxford University Press.

Kymlicka, W. (2004). "Nation-Building and Minority Rights: Comparing Africa and the West." In *Ethnicity & Democracy in Africa*, edited by B. Berman, P. Eyoh and W. Kymlicka. Oxford: James Currey, pp. 54–72.

Kymlicka, W. (ed.) (1995a). *The Rights of Minority Cultures*. Oxford: Oxford University Press.

Kymlicka, W. and M. Opalski (eds.) (2001). *Can Liberal Pluralism be Exported? Western Political Theory and Ethnic Relations in Eastern Europe*. Oxford: Oxford University Press.

Kymlicka, W. and W. Norman (2000). *Citizenship in Diverse Societies*. Oxford: Oxford University Press.

Laberge, P. (1998). "Kant on Justice and the Law of Nations." In *International Society: Diverse Ethical Perspectives*, edited by D. R. Mapel and T. Nardin. Princeton: Princeton University Press, pp. 82–102.

Landes, J. (ed.) (1998). *Feminism, the Public and the Private*. Oxford: Oxford University Press.

Lane, H. and D. Simpson (1984). "Bribery in International Business: Whose Problem Is It?" *Journal of Business Ethics* 3: 35–42.

Lapidoth, R. (1996). *Autonomy: Flexible Solutions to Ethnic Conflicts*. Washington, DC: Institute for Peace.

Larabee, M. J. (ed.) (1993). *An Ethics of Care: Feminist and Interdisciplinary Perspectives*. London: Routledge.

Leiter, B. (1998). "Naturalism and Naturalized Jurisprudence." In *Analyzing Law: New Essays in Legal Theory*, edited by B. Bix. Oxford: Clarendon Press, pp. 79–106.

Lemmon, E. J. (1962). "Moral Dilemmas." *The Philosophical Review* 70: 139–43 and 148–58. [Reprinted in *Moral Dilemmas*, edited by C. W. Gowans. New York: Oxford University Press, 1987, pp. 101–14].

Levinson, M. (1999). *The Demands of Liberal Education*. Oxford: Oxford University Press.

Lisska, A. J. (1998). *Aquinas's Theory of Natural Law: An Analytic Reconstruction*. New York: Oxford University Press.

Little, M. O. (1995). "Seeing and Caring: The Role of Affects in Feminist Moral Epistemology." *Hypatia* 10: 117–37.

Little, M. O. (1997). "Virtue as Knowledge: Objections from the Philosophy of Mind." *Noûs* 31: 59–79.

Locke, J. [1689]. "A Letter Concerning Toleration." In *John Locke on Politics and Education*, edited by H. R. Penniman. New York: Van Norstrand Co., 1947.

Locke, J. [1690]. *Two Treatises of Government*, 3rd std. edition, edited by P. Laslett. Cambridge: Cambridge University Press, 1988.

Lomasky, L. (1987). *Persons, Rights, and the Moral Community*. Oxford: Oxford University Press.

Lomasky, L. (1998). "Libertarianism as if (the Other 99 Percent of) People Mattered." *Social Philosophy and Policy* 15: 350–71.

Lucas, J. R. (1965). "Against Equality." *Philosophy* 40: 296–307. [Reprinted in H. Bedau *Justice and Equality*. Prentice-Hall, 1971, pp. 138–51].

Lucas, J. R. (1966). *The Principles of Politics*. Oxford: Clarendon Press.

Lucas, J. R. (1977). "Against Equality Again." *Philosophy* 52: 255–80.

Lukes, S. (1985). *Marxism and Morality*. Oxford: Oxford University Press.

Lyons, D. (1965). *Forms and Limits of Utilitarianism*. Oxford: Oxford University Press.

Lyons, D. (1981). "The New Indians Claims and Original Rights to Land." In, *Reading Nozick*, edited by J. Paul. Totowa, NL: Rowman and Littlefield, pp. 355–79.

Macedo, S. (1990). *Liberal Virtues: Citizenship, Virtue and Community*. Oxford: Oxford University Press.

Macedo, S. (1999). *Deliberative Politics: Essays on Democracy and Disagreement*. Oxford: Oxford University Press.

Machan, T. (1989). *Individuals and Their Rights*. Chicago: Open Court.

Machiavelli, N. [1513]. "The Prince." In *Selected Political Writings*, edited and translated by D. Wootton. Indianapolis: Hackett Publishing, 1994, pp. 5–80.

Machiavelli, N. [1531]. "Discourses." In *Selected Political Writings*, edited and translated by D. Wootton. Indianapolis: Hackett Publishing, 1994, pp. 81–217.

MacIntyre, A. [1981]. *After Virtue: A Study in Moral Theory*. Notre Dame, IN: University of Notre Dame Press, 2nd edition, 1984, pp. 204–25.

MacIntyre, A. (1998). *A Short History of Ethics: A History of Moral Philosophy from the Homeric Age to the Twentieth Century*. London: Routledge.

Mackie, J. L. [1977]. *Ethics: Inventing Right and Wrong*, reprint. London: Penguin Books, 1990.

Mackie, J. L. (1984). "Rights, Utility, and Universalization." In *Utility and Rights*, edited by R. Frey. Minneapolis: University of Minnesota Press, pp. 86–105.

MacKinnon, C. (1987). *Feminism Unmodified: Discourse on Life and Law*. Cambridge, MA: Harvard University Press.

MacLeod A. (1975). "Equality of Opportunity: Some Ambiguities in the Ideal." In *Equality and Freedom*, edited by G. Dorsey. New York: Oceana Publications.

MacLeod C. (1998). *Liberalism, Justice and Markets: A critique of Liberal Equality*. Oxford: Oxford University Press.

Macpherson, C. B. (1972). *Democratic Theory: Essays in Retrieval*. Oxford: Oxford University Press.

Malpas, S. (2005). *The Postmodern*. London: Routledge.

Mansbridge, J. J. (ed.) (1990). *Beyond Self-Interest*. Chicago: University of Chicago Press.

Marcus, R. B. (1980). "Moral Dilemmas and Consistency," *The Journal of Philosophy* 77: 121–36. [Reprinted in *Moral Dilemmas*, edited by C. W. Gowans. New York: Oxford University Press, 1987, pp. 188–204].

Marmor, A. (2011). *Philosophy of Law*. Princeton, NJ: Princeton University Press.

Marshall, G. (1984). *Constitutional Conventions: The Rules and Forms of Political Ac-*

countability. Oxford: Clarendon Press.

Marshall, T. H. (1965). *Class, Citizenship and Social Development*. New York: Anchor.

Marx, K. [1859]. "A Contribution to the Critique of Political Economy." In *The Marx-Engels Reader*, edited by R. C. Tucker. New York: Norton, 1978, pp. 3–6.

Marx, K. [1861-63]. *Theories of Surplus Value*. In *The Marx-Engels Reader*, edited by R. C. Tucker. New York: Norton, 1978, pp. 443–65.

Marx, K. [1867]. *Capital*, Vol. I. In *The Marx-Engels Reader*, edited by R. C. Tucker. New York: Norton, 1978, pp. 294–438.

Marx, K. [1875]. "Critique to the Gotha Program." In *The Marx-Engels Reader*, edited by R. C. Tucker. New York: Norton, 1978, pp. 525–41.

Marx, K. and F. Engels [1848]. "Manifesto of the Communist Party." In *The Marx-Engels Reader*, edited by R. C. Tucker. New York: Norton, 1978, pp. 469–500.

Mason, A. (1993). "Liberalism and the Value of Community." *Canadian Journal of Philosophy* 23: 215–40.

Mason, H. E. (ed.) (1996). *Moral Dilemmas and Moral Theory*. New York: Oxford University Press.

May, L. and S. Collins-Sharratt (eds.) (1994). *Applied Ethics: A Multicultural Approach*. Englewood Cliffs: Prentice Hall.

McConnell, T. (1978). "Moral Dilemmas and Consistency in Ethics." *Canadian Journal of Philosophy* 8: 269–87. [Reprinted in *Moral Dilemmas*, edited by C. W. Gowans. New York: Oxford University Press, 1987, pp. 154–73].

McConnell, T. (1988). "Interpersonal Moral Conflicts." *American Philosophical Quarterly* 25: 25–35.

McConnell, T. (1996). "Moral Residue and Dilemmas." In *Moral Dilemmas and Moral Theory*, edited by H. E. Mason. New York: Oxford University Press, pp. 36–47.

McDonald, M. (1991). "Should Communities Have Rights? Reflections on Liberal Individualism." *Canadian Journal of Law and Jurisprudence* 4: 217–37.

McDonald, M. (2000). "Hands: Clean and Tied or Dirty and Bloody?" In *Cruelty and Deception: The Controversy Over Dirty Hands in Politics*, edited by P. Rynard and D. P. Shugarman. Peterborough, ON, Canada: Broadview Press, pp. 187–97.

McDowell, J. (1979). "Virtue and Reason." *Monist* 62:331–50.

McDowell, J. (1985). "Values and Secondary Qualities." In *Morality and Objectivity: A Tribute to J. L. Mackie*, edited by Ted Honderich. London: Routledge & Kegan, pp. 110–29.

McKerlie, D. (1989). "Equality and Time." *Ethics* 99: 274–96.

McNaughton, D. (1988). *Moral Vision: An Introduction to Ethics*. Oxford: Blackwell.

Mead, L. (1986). *Beyond Entitlement: The Social Obligations of Citizenship*. New York: Free Press.

Mellema, G. (1991). *Beyond the Call of Duty: Supererogation, Obligation, and Offence*. Albany: State University of New York Press.

Mendus, S. (1989). *Toleration and the Limits of Liberalism*. Atlantic Highlands, NJ: Humanities Press.

Merleau-Ponty, M. [1969]. *Humanism and Terror: An Essay on the Communist Problem*, translated by J. O'Neill. Boston: Beacon Press, 1990.

Mill, J. S. [1843]. *A System of Logic: Ratiocinative and Inductive*. University Press of the Pacific, 2002.

Mill, J. S. [1848]. *Principles of Political Economy*, edited by J. Riley. Oxford: Oxford University Press, 1994.

Mill, J. S. [1859]. "On Liberty." In *On Liberty and Other Essays*, edited by J. Gray. New York: Oxford University Press, 1991.

Mill, J. S. [1861]. *Utilitarianism*, 2nd edition. Indianapolis: Hackett Publishing Company, 2002.

Miller, A. (2003). *An Introduction to Contemporary Metaethics*. Cambridge: Polity Press.

Miller, D. (1994). "Equality and Market Socialism." In *Market Socialism: The Current*

Debate, edited by P. Bardhan and J. Roemer. New York: Oxford University Press, pp. 298–314.

Miller, D. (1995). *On Nationality*. Oxford: Oxford University Press.

Miller, D. (1998). "The Limits of Cosmopolitan Justice." In *International Society: Diverse Ethical Perspectives*, edited by D. R. Mapel and T. Nardin. Princeton: Princeton University Press, pp. 164–81.

Miller, D. (1999). *Principles of Social Justice*. Cambridge, MA: Harvard University Press.

Miller, D. (2000). *Citizenship and National Identity*. Cambridge: Polity Press.

Mills, C. (1997). *The Racial Contract*. Ithaca, NY: Cornell University Press.

Milo, R. (1995). "Contractarian Constructivism." *Journal of Philosophy* 92: 181–204.

Mises, von, L. (1951). *Socialism*, translated by J. Kahane. New Haven: Yale University Press (reprinted 1962).

Montesquieu, C. [1748]. *The Spirit of the Laws*. Amherst, N. Y.: Prometheus Books, 2002.

Moon, D. (1993). *Constructing Community: Moral Pluralism and Tragic Conflicts*. Princeton: Princeton University Press.

Moore, G. E. [1903]. *Principia Ethica*, 2nd edition, (Chapter 1), edited by T. Baldwin. Cambridge: Cambridge University Press, 1993, pp. 53–88.

Morris, H. (1968). "Persons and Punishment." *The Monist* 52: 475–501. [Reprinted in *Punishment and Rehabilitation*, 2nd edition, edited by J. G. Murphy. Belmont: Wadsworth, 1985].

Mouffe, C. (2000). *The Democratic Paradox*. London: Verso Books.

Mouffe, C. (ed.) (1992). *Dimensions of Radical Democracy: Pluralism, Citizenship and Community*. London: Routledge.

Mueller-Vollmer, K. (1988). *The Hermeneutics Reader: Texts of the German Tradition from the Enlightenment to the Present*. New York: Continuum.

Mulgan, G. (1991). "Citizens and Responsibilities." In *Citizenship*, edited by G. Andrews. London: Lawrence and Wishart, pp. 37–49.

Munzer, S. R. (1990). *A Theory of Property*. Cambridge: Cambridge University Press.

Murphy, J. G. (1979). *Retribution, Justice, and Therapy: Essays in the Philosophy of Law*. Dordrecht and Boston: D. Reidel.

Murphy, J. G. (1988). "Constitutionalism, Moral Skepticism, and Religious Belief." In *Constitutionalism: The Philosophical Dimension*, edited by A. S. Rosenbaum. New York: Greenwood Press, pp. 239–49.

Murphy, J. G. (ed.) (1985). *Punishment and Rehabilitation*, 2nd edition. Belmont: Wadsworth.

Murphy, J. G. and J. Hampton (1988). *Forgiveness and Mercy*. Cambridge: Cambridge University Press.

Murphy, J. G. and J. L. Coleman (1990). *Philosophy of Law*. Boulder, CO: Westview Press.

Murphy, M. C. (2006). *Philosophy of Law: The Fundamentals*. Wiley-Blackwell.

Myrdal, G. (1968). "The 'Soft State' in Underdeveloped Countries." *UCLA Law Review*, Vol. 15, No. 4, June. [Reprinted in *Unfashionable Economics: Essays in Honour of Lord Balogh*, edited by P. Streeten. London: Weidenfeld and Nicolson, 1970, pp. 227–43].

Nagel, T. (1971/72). "War and Massacre." *Philosophy and Public Affairs* 1: 123–44.

Nagel, T. (1973). "Rawls on Justice." *Philosophical Review* 82: 220–34.

Nagel, T. [1979]. *Mortal Questions*. New York: Cambridge University Press, 1991, pp. 24–38.

Nagel, T. (1980). "The Limits of Objectivity." In *The Tanner Lectures in Human Values*, Vol. 1, Lecture 2. Salt Lake City: University of Utah Press, pp. 97–139. [In part reprinted as "Value" in *Moral Philosophy: Selected Readings*, edited by G. Sher. Belmont, CA: Wadsworth, 2001, pp. 257–70].

Nagel, T. (1981). "Libertarianism without Foundations." In, *Reading Nozick*, edited by J.

Paul. Totowa, NJ: Rowman and Littlefield, pp. 191–205.

Nagel, T. (1986). *The View from Nowhere*. New York: Oxford University Press.

Nagel, T. (1991). *Equality and Partiality*. New York: Oxford University Press.

Nardin, T. (1983). *Law, Morality, and the Relations of States*. Princeton: Princeton University Press.

Narveson, J. (1988). *The Libertarian Idea*. Philadelphia: Temple University Press.

Natoli, J. and L. Hutcheon (eds.) (1993). *A Postmodern Reader*. Albany, NY: State University of New York Press.

Nelson, W. N. (1991). "The Moral Point of View." In *Morality: What's In It for Me?*, by W. N. Nelson. Boulder, CO: Westview Press, pp. 39–58.

Nickel, J. (1987). *Making Sense of Human Rights*. Berkeley: University of California.

Nielsen, K. (1981). "Violence and terrorism: Its Use and Abuses." In *Values in Conflict*, edited by B. M. Leiser. New York: Macmillan Publishing, pp. 435–49.

Nielsen, K. (1985). *Equality and Liberty: A Defense of Radical Egalitarianism*. Totowa, NJ: Rowman and Allenheld.

Nielsen, K. (1988). "On Not Needing to Justify Equality." *International Studies in Philosophy* 20: 55–71.

Nielsen, K. (1990). *Ethics Without God*. Amherst, NY: Prometheus Books UK.

Nielsen, K. (1992). "Rights and Consequences: It All Depends." *Canadian Journal of Law and Society* 7: 63–92.

Nielsen, K. (1996a). "There is No Dilemma of Dirty Hands." *South African Journal of Philosophy* 15: 1–7.

Nielsen, K. (1996b). *Naturalism Without Foundations*. Amherst, NY: Prometheus Books.

Nietzsche, F. [1878]. *Human All Too Human*, 2nd edition, translated by R. J. Hollingdale. Cambridge: Cambridge University Press, 1996.

Nietzsche, F. [1883-85]. *Thus Spoke Zarathustra*, translated by W. Kaufmann. London: Penguin Books, 1978.

Nietzsche, F. [1886]. *Beyond Good and Evil: Prelude to a Philosophy of the Future*, translated by M. Faber. Oxford: Oxford University Press, 1998.

Nietzsche, F. [1887]. *On the Genealogy of Morals*, translated by W. Kaufmann. In *On the Genealogy of Morals and Ecce Homo*, reissue edition. New York: Vintage, 1989, pp. 24–198.

Noddings, N. (1984). *Caring: A Feminine Approach to Ethics and Moral Education*. Berkeley and Los Angeles: University of California Press.

Noddings, N. (1989). *Women and Evil*. Berkeley: University of California Press.

Nozick, R. [1974]. *Anarchy, State, and Utopia*. Oxford: Blackwell, 2001.

Nussbaum, M. (1988). "Non-Relative Virtues: An Aristotelian Approach." In *Midwest Studies in Philosophy*, Vol. 13: *Ethical Theory, Character and Virtue*, edited by P. A. French, T. E. Uehling, Jr. and H. K. Wettstein. Notre Dame, IN: University of Notre Dame Press, pp. 32–53. [Reprinted in *Moral Philosophy: Selected Readings*, edited by G. Sher. Belmont, CA: Wadsworth, 2001, pp. 492–516].

O'Neill, O. (1986). *Faces of Hunger*. London: Allen and Unwin.

O'Neill, O. (1996). *Towards Justice and Virtue: A Constructive Account of Practical Reasoning*. Cambridge: Cambridge University Press.

Oakeshott, M. (1975). *On Human Conduct*. Oxford: Oxford University Press.

Oakeshott, M. (1983). "The Rule of Law." In *On History and Other Essays*, by M. Oakeshott. Oxford: Basil Blackwell.

Okin, S. (1999. *Is Multiculturalism Bad for Women?* Princeton: Princeton University Press.

Okun, A. M. (1975). *Equality and Efficiency: The Big Tradeoff*. Washington: The Brookings Institution.

Oldfield, A. (1990). *Citizenship and Community: Civic Republicanism and the Modern World*. London: Routledge.

Oppenheim, F. E. (1970). "Egalitarianism as a Descriptive Concept." *American Philo-*

sophical Quarterly 7: 143–52.

Oppenheim, L. (1905). *International Law*, Vol. 1. London: Longmans, Green and Co.

Ormiston, G. L. and A. D. Schrift (eds.) (1990). *The Hermeneutic Tradition: From Ast to Ricoeur*. Albany, NY: State University of New York Press.

Paine, T. [1791/92]. *Rights of Man*. In *Rights of Man, Common Sense and Other Political Writings*, new edition. New York: Oxford Paperbacks, 1998, pp. 83–332.

Parfit, D. [1984]. *Reasons and Persons*, reprint edition. New York: Oxford University Press, 1986.

Parfit, D. (1997). "Equality and Priority." *Ratio* 10: 202–21.

Paris, D. (1991). "Moral Education and the 'Tie that Binds' in Liberal Political Theory." *American Political Science Review* 85: 875–901.

Pateman, C. (1989). *The Sexual Contract*. Palo Alto, CA: Stanford University Press.

Pegis, A. C. (ed.) (1965). *Introduction to St Thomas Aquinas* (with selections from *Summa Theologica* and *Summa contra Gentiles*). New York: McGraw-Hill Education.

Peters, R. S. and S. I. Benn (1959). *Social Principles and the Democratic State*. London: Allen and Unwin.

Pettit, P. (ed.) (1993). *Consequentialism*. Aldershot: Dartmouth.

Pfaff, W. (1993). *The Wrath of Nations: Civilization and the Furies of Nationalism*. New York: Simon and Schuster.

Phillips, A. (ed.) (1998). *Feminism and Politics*. Oxford: Oxford University Press.

Phillips, D. (1993). *Looking Backward: A Critical Appraisal of Communitarian Thought*. Princeton: Princeton University Press.

Plantinga, A. and N. P. Wolterstorff (eds.) (1984). *Faith and Rationality: Reason and Belief in God*. Notre Dame, IN: University of Notre Dame Press.

Plato [~380 B.C.]. *Protagoras*. In *Plato's Thought*, by G. M. A. Grube. Indianapolis: Hackett Publishing Company, 1998.

Plato [~360 B.C.]. *Republic*, Book 2, translated by G. M. A. Grube. Indianapolis: Hackett Publishing Company, 1974.

Pogge, T. (1989). *Realizing Rawls*. Ithaca, NY: Cornell University Press.

Pogge, T. (1994a). "An Egalitarian Law of Peoples." *Philosophy and Public Affairs* 23: 195–224.

Pogge, T. (1994b). "Cosmopolitanism and Sovereignty." In *Political Restructuring in Europe: Ethical Perspectives*, edited by C. Brown. London: Routledge, pp. 89–122.

Pogge, T. (1997). "A Global Resource Dividend." In *Ethics of Consumption: The Good Life, Justice, and Global Stewardship*, edited by D. Crocker and T. Linden. Lanham, MD: Rowman and Littlefield, pp. 501–36.

Pojman, L. (1997). "On Equal Human Worth: A Critique of Contemporary Egalitarianism." In *Equality: Selected Readings*, edited by L. Pojman and R. Westmoreland. New York: Oxford University Press, pp. 282–99.

Popper, K. (1945). *The Open Society and Its Enemies*. London: Routledge.

Porter, J. (1987). *The Measure of Canadian Society*. Ottawa: Carleton University Press.

Posner, R. [1972]. *Economic Analysis of Law*, 4th edition. Boston: Little, Brown, and Company, 1992.

Posner, R. (1990). "The Economic Approach to Law." In *The Problems of Jurisprudence*, by R. Posner. Cambridge, MA: Harvard University Press, pp. 353–92.

Potter, N. T. and Timmons, M. (eds.) (1985). *Morality and Universality*. Dordrecht: Kluwer Academic Publishers.

Preuss, U. K. (1996). "The Political Meaning of Constitutionalism." In *Constitutionalism, Democracy and Sovereignty: American and European Perspectives*, edited by R. Bellamy. Aldershot, UK: Avebury Publishing, pp. 11–30.

Pufendorf, S. [1673]. *On the Duty of Man and Citizen According to Natural Law*, edited by J. Tully. Cambridge: Cambridge University Press, 1991.

Purcell, E. A. Jr. (1973). *The Crisis of Democratic Theory: Scientific Naturalism and the*

Problem of value (Chapter 5). Lexington, KY: University Press of Kentucky.

Putnam, H. (1973). "Meaning and Reference." *Journal of Philosophy* 70, 699–711.

Putnam, H. [1975]. "The meaning of 'meaning'." In *Philosophical Papers*, Vol. 2: *Mind, Language and Reality*. Cambridge: Cambridge University Press, 1979, pp. 215–71.

Rachels, J. [1986]. "The Challenge of Cultural Relativism." In *The Elements of Moral Philosophy*, 4th edition, by J. Rachels. New York: McGraw-Hill, 2002, pp. 16–31.

Rae, D. W. (1981). *Equalities*. Cambridge, MA: Harvard University Press.

Railton, P. (1986). "Moral Realism." *Philosophical Review* 95: 163–207.

Raphael, D. D. (1970). *Problems of Political Philosophy*. London: Pall Mall.

Raphael, D. D. (1981). *Moral Philosophy*. Oxford: Oxford University Press.

Rawls, J. (1964). "Legal Obligation and the Duty of Fair Play." In *Law and Philosophy*, edited by S. Hook. New York: New York University Press, pp. 3–18.

Rawls, J. [1971]. *A Theory of Justice*, revised edition. Oxford: Oxford University Press, 1999.

Rawls, J. (1977). "The Basic Structure as Subject." *American Philosophical Quarterly* 14: 159–65. [Reprinted in *Values and Morals*, edited by A. Goldman and J. Kim. Dordrecht: Reidel, 1978, pp. 47–71].

Rawls, J. (1980). "Kantian Constructivism in Moral Theory: Construction and Objectivity." *Journal of Philosophy* 77: 554–72. (See also "Political Constructivism." In *Political Liberalism*, by J. Rawls. New York: Columbia University Press, 1993, pp. 89–129).

Rawls, J. (1985). "Justice as Fairness: Political, not Metaphysical." *Philosophy and Public Affairs* 14: 223–51.

Rawls, J. (1987). "The Idea of an Overlapping Consensus." *Oxford Journal of Legal Studies* 7: 1–25.

Rawls, J. (1988). "The Priority of Right and Ideas of the Good." *Philosophy and Public Affairs* 17: 251–76.

Rawls, J. (1993). *Political Liberalism*. New York: Columbia University Press.

Rawls, J. (1999). *The Law of Peoples, with "The Idea of Public Reason Revisited."* Cambridge, MA: Harvard University Press.

Rawls, J. (2001). *Justice as Fairness. A Restatement*. Cambridge, MA: Harvard University Press.

Raz, J. [1979]. *The Authority of Law: Essays on Law and Morality*, reprint edition. New York: Oxford University Press, 1983, pp. 210–31.

Raz, J. (1980). *The Concept of a Legal System: An Introduction to the Theory of Legal Systems*. Oxford: Clarendon Press.

Raz, J. (1986). *The Morality of Freedom*. Oxford: Oxford University Press.

Raz, J. (1998). "Multiculturalism." *Ratio Juris* 11: 193–205.

Rehnquist, W. H. (1976). "The Notion of a Living Constitution." *Texas Law Review* 54: 693–706.

Reiman, J. (1987). "Exploitation, Force, and the Moral Assessment of Capitalism: Thoughts on Roemer and Cohen." *Philosophy and Public Affairs* 16: 3–41.

Reiman, J. (1989). "An Alternative to 'Distributive' Marxism: Further Thoughts on Roemer, Cohen, and Exploitation." *Canadian Journal of Philosophy* 15 (Suppl.): 299–331.

Rescher, N. (1966). *Distributive Justice: A Constructive Critique of the Utilitarian Theory of Distribution*. Indianapolis: Bobbs-Merrill.

Rhode, D. (1997). *Speaking of Sex: The Denial of Gender Inequality*. Cambridge, MA: Harvard University Press.

Robbins, B. (ed.) (1998). *Cosmopolitics: Thinking and Feeling Beyond the Nation*. Minneapolis: University of Minnesota Press.

Roberts, M. (1996). *Analytical Marxism: A Critique*. London: Verso Books.

Roemer, J. (1982a). *A General Theory of Exploitation and Class*. Cambridge, MA: Harvard University Press.

Roemer, J. (1982b). "Property Relations vs. Surplus Value in Marxian Exploitation."

Philosophy and Public Affairs 11: 281–313.

Roemer, J. (1982c). "New Directions in the Marxian Theory of Exploitation and Class." *Politics and Society* 11: 253–87.

Roemer, J. (1988). *Free to Lose: An Introduction to Marxist Economic Philosophy.* Cambridge, MA: Harvard University Press.

Roemer, J. (1993). "A Pragmatic Theory of Responsibility for the Egalitarian Planner." *Philosophy and Public Affairs* 22: 146–66.

Roemer, J. (1994). *A Future for Socialism.* London: Verso Books.

Roemer, J. (1996). *Theories of Distributive Justice.* Cambridge, MA: Harvard University Press.

Roemer, J. (1999). "Egalitarian Strategies." *Dissent,* summer issue, pp. 64–74.

Roemer, J. (ed.) (1986). *Analytical Marxism (Studies in Marxism & Social Theory).* Cambridge: Cambridge University Press.

Rosenbaum, A. S. (ed.) (1988). *Constitutionalism: The Philosophical Dimension.* New York: Greenwood Press.

Rosenblum, N. (1998). *Membership and Morals: The Personal Uses of Pluralism in America.* Princeton: Princeton University Press.

Ross, W. D. [1930]. *The Right and the Good,* 2nd edition. New York: Oxford University Press, 2003.

Ross, W. D. (1939). *Foundations of Ethics.* Oxford: Clarendon Press.

Rothbard, M. (1982). *The Ethics of Liberty.* Atlantic Highlands, NJ: Humanities Press.

Rothstein, B. (1992). "Social Justice and State Capacity." *Politics and Society* 20: 101–26.

Rothstein, B. (1998). *Just Institutions Matter: The Moral and Political Logic of the Universal Welfare State.* Cambridge: Cambridge University Press.

Rousseau, J.-J. [1755]. *A Discourse on Inequality,* translated by M. Cranston. London: Penguin, 1995.

Rousseau, J.-J. [1762]. *The Social Contract* [1762] *and Discourses,* translated by G. D. H. Cole. New York: Dutton, 1973.

Rubio-Marin, R. (2000). *Immigration as a Democratic Challenge: Citizenship and Inclusion in Germany and US.* Cambridge: Cambridge University Press.

Ruddick, S. (1984). "Maternal Thinking." In *Mothering: Essays in Feminist Theory,* edited by J. Trebilcot. Totowa, NJ: Rowman and Allanheld, pp. 213–30.

Ruddick, S. (1987). "Remarks on the Sexual Politics of Reason." In *Women and Moral Theory,* edited by E. F. Kittay and D. Meyers. Savage, MD: Rowman and Littlefield, pp. 237–60.

Russell, B. [1945]. *A History of Western Philosophy.* London and New York: Routledge, 2004, reprinted 2006.

Ryan, A. (1984). *Property and Political Theory.* Oxford: Basil Blackwell.

Sandel, M. (1982). *Liberalism and the Limits of Justice.* Cambridge: Cambridge University Press.

Sandel, M. (1984b). "The Procedural Republic and the Unencumbered Self." *Political Theory* 12: 81–96.

Sandel, M. (1996). *Democracy's Discontent: America in Search of a Public Philosophy.* Cambridge, MA: Harvard University Press.

Sandel, M. (ed.) (1984a). *Liberalism and Its Critics.* New York: New York University Press.

Sartorius, R. (1975). *Individual Conduct and Social Norms.* Belmont, CA: Wadsworth.

Sartre, J.-P. [1948]. "Dirty Hands." In *No Exit and Three Other Plays,* reissue edition, translated by S. Gilbert and L. Abel. New York: Vintage, 1989, pp. 125–242.

Savellos, E. E. and U. D. Yalcin (eds.) [1995]. *Supervenience: New Essays.* Cambridge: Cambridge University Press, 2007.

Scanlon, T. (1982). "Contractualism and Utilitarianism." In *Utilitarianism and Beyond,* edited by A. Sen and B. Williams. Cambridge: Cambridge University Press, pp. 103–28.

478 *References*

Scanlon, T. (1998). *What We Owe to Each Other.* Cambridge: Harvard University Press.

Scarre, G. (1996). *Utilitarianism.* London: Routledge.

Schaar, J. (1967). "Equality of Opportunity, and Beyond." In *Nomos IX: Equality*, edited by J. Pennock and J. Chapman. New York: Atherton Press, pp. 228–49.

Scheffler, S. (ed.) (1988). *Consequentialism and Its Critics.* Oxford: Oxford University Press.

Schlesinger, A. (1992). *The Disuniting of America.* New York: Norton.

Schmidt, A. (1997). *The Menace of Multiculturalism: Trojan Horse in America.* Westport, CO: Praeger.

Schumaker, M. (1977). *Supererogation: An Analysis and Bibliography.* Edmonton: St. Stephen's College.

Schumpeter, J. A. [1942]. *Capitalism, Socialism and Democracy.* New York: Harper Perennial, 1962.

Schwartz, A. (1973). "Moral Neutrality and Primary Goods." *Ethics* 83: 294–307.

Schwartz, W. (ed.) (1995). *Justice in Immigration.* Cambridge: Cambridge University Press.

Searle, J. (1964). "How to Derive 'Ought' from 'Is'." *Philosophical Review* 73: 43–58. [Reprinted in *Theories of Ethics*, edited by P. Foot. Oxford: Oxford University Press, 1967, pp. 101–14].

Sen, A. (1970). *Collective Choice and Social Welfare.* San Francisco: Holden-Day.

Sen, A. (1992). *Inequality Reexamined.* Oxford: Clarendon Press.

Sen, A. and B. Williams (eds.) (1982). *Utilitarianism and Beyond.* Cambridge: Cambridge University Press.

Shachar, A. (2001). *Multicultural Jurisdictions: Preserving Cultural Differences and Women's Rights in a Liberal State.* Minneapolis: University of Minnesota Press.

Shafer-Landau, R. (2003). *Moral Realism: A Defence.* Oxford: Oxford University Press.

Shafer-Landau, R. (2006). "Ethics as Philosophy: A defense of Ethical Nonnaturalism." In *Metaethics after Moore*, edited by Terry Horgan and Mark Timmons. Oxford: Oxford University Press, pp. 209–32.

Shafer-Landau, R. (ed.) (2006-2011). *Oxford Studies in Metaethics*, Vol. 1 (2006), Vol. 2 (2007), Vol. 3 (2008), Vol. 4 (2009), Vol. 5 (2010), and Vol. 6 (2011). New York: Oxford University Press.

Shafer-Landau, R. and T. Cuneo (eds.) (2007). *Foundations of Ethics. An Anthology.* Malden, MA: Blackwell Publishing.

Shafir, G. (ed.) (1998). *The Citizenship Debate: A Reader.* Minneapolis: University of Minnesota Press.

Shapiro, I. and C. Hacker-Cordon (1999). *Democracy's Edges.* Cambridge: Cambridge University Press.

Shaw, M. N. (2008). *International Law* (6th ed.). Cambridge: Cambridge University Press.

Sher, G. (1987). "Other Voices, Other Rooms? Women's Psychology and Moral Theory." In *Women and Moral Theory*, edited by E. F. Kittay and D. Meyers. Savage, MD: Rowman and Littlefield, pp. 178–89.

Sher, G. (2001). *Moral Philosophy. Selected Readings* (2nd edition). Belmont, CA: Wadsworth/Thomson Learning.

Shue, H. (1988). "Mediating Duties." *Ethics* 98: 687–704.

Shugarman, D. P. (1990). "Ethics and Politics: The Use and Abuse of Politics." In *Moral Expertise: Studies in Practical and Professional Ethics*, edited by D. MacNiven. London and New York: Routledge, pp. 198–231.

Shugarman, D. P. (2000). "Democratic Dirty Hands." In *Cruelty and Deception: The Controversy Over Dirty Hands in Politics*, edited by P. Rynard and D. P. Shugarman. Peterborough, ON, Canada: Broadview Press, pp. 229–49.

Sidgwick, H. [1874]. *Methods of Ethics*, 7th edition. Indianapolis: Hackett Pub. Co., 1981.

Singer, P. (1971/72). "Famine, Affluence, and Morality." *Philosophy and Public Affairs*

1: 229–43. [Reprinted in *Moral Philosophy: Selected Readings*, edited by G. Sher. Belmont, CA: Wadsworth, 2001, pp. 694–704].

Singer, P. (1974). "Sidgwick and Reflective Equilibrium." *Monist* 57: 490–517.

Singer, P. (1981). *The Expanding Circle*. Oxford: Oxford University Press.

Singer, P. (1993). *Practical Ethics*, 2nd edition. Cambridge: Cambridge University Press.

Sinnott-Armstrong, W. (1988). *Moral Dilemmas*. Oxford: Basil Blackwell.

Sinnott-Armstrong, W. (2000). "Expressivism and Embedding." *Philosophy and Phenomenological Research* 61: 677–93.

Smart, J. J. C. and B. Williams (1973). *Utilitarianism: For and Against*. Cambridge: Cambridge University Press, pp. 75–150.

Smith, A. [1776]. *Wealth of Nations*. Oxford: Oxford University Press, 1998.

Smith, H. M. (1986). "Moral Realism, Moral Conflict, and Compound Acts." *The Journal of Philosophy* 83: 341–45.

Smith, M. (1994). *The Moral Problem*. Oxford: Blackwell.

Sorell, T. (1999). *Moral Theory and Anomaly*. Oxford: Blackwell.

Spinner, J. (1993). *The Boundaries of Citizenship: Race, Ethnicity and Nationality in the Liberal State*. Baltimore: Johns Hopkins University Press.

Spinner-Halev, J. (2000). *Surviving Diversity: Religion and Democratic Citizenship*. Baltimore: Johns Hopkins University Press.

Spinoza, B. [1670]. "A Theologico-political Treatise." In *A Theologico-political Treatise, and A Political Treatise*, translated by R. H. M. Elwes. New York: Dover Publications, 1951, 1–278.

Spinoza, B. [1677a]. "Ethics-" In *On the Improvement of the Understanding; The Ethics; Correspondence*, translated by R. H. M. Elwes. New York: Dover Publications, 1955, 43–271.

Spinoza, B. [1677b]. "A Political Treatise." In *A Theologico-political Treatise, A Political Treatise*, translated by R. H. M. Elwes. New York: Dover Publications, 1951, 279–387.

Steiner, H. (1994). *An Essay on Rights*. Oxford: Blackwell.

Stevenson, C. L. (1963). "The Nature of Ethical Disagreement." In *Facts and Values. Studies in Ethical Analysis*, by Charles L. Stevenson. New Haven and London: Yale University Press, pp. 1–9.

Stewart, P. (1975). "Or of the Press." *Hastings Law Journal* 26: 631–37.

Stocker, M. [1990]. *Plural and Conflicting Values*, reprint edition. New York: Oxford University Press, 1992.

Sturgeon, N. L. (1985). "Moral Explanations." In *Morality, Reason, and Truth: New Essays on the Foundations of Ethics*, edited by David Copp and David Zimmerman. Totowa, NJ: Rowman & Allanheld, pp. 49–78.

Styron, W. [1979]. *Sophie's Choice*. New York: Random House, 1998.

Sullivan, W. (1982). *Reconstructing Public Philosophy*. Berkeley and Los Angeles: University of California Press.

Sutherland, S. L. (2000). "Retrospection and Democracy: Bringing Political Conduct Under the Constitution." In *Cruelty and Deception: The Controversy Over Dirty Hands in Politics*, edited by P. Rynard and D. P. Shugarman. Peterborough, ON, Canada: Broadview Press, pp. 207–27. [New version of "The Problem of Dirty Hands in Politics." *Canadian Journal of Political Science* 28 (1995): 479–508].

Tamir, Y. (1993). *Liberal Nationalism*. Princeton, NJ: Princeton University Press.

Tan, K.-C. (2000). *Toleration, Diversity, and Global Justice*. University Park: Pennsylvania State University Press.

Tawney, R. H. (1964). *Equality*. London: G. Allen & Unwin.

Taylor, C. (1979). *Hegel and Modern Society*. Cambridge: Cambridge University Press.

Taylor, C. (1982). "The Diversity of Goods." In *Utilitarianism and Beyond*, edited by A. Sen and B. Williams. Cambridge: Cambridge University Press, pp. 129–44.

Taylor, C. (1985a). "What Is Human Agency?" In *Human Agency and Language: Philosophical Papers*, by C. Taylor. Cambridge: Cambridge University Press, pp. 15–

44.

Taylor, C. (1985b). *Philosophy and the Human Sciences: Philosophical Papers*, Vol. ii. Cambridge: Cambridge University Press.

Taylor, C. (1986). "Alternative Futures: Legitimacy, Identity, and Alienation in Late Twentieth Century Canada." In *Collected Research Studies: Constitutionalism, Citizenship and Society in Canada*, edited by A. Cairns and C. Williams. Toronto: University of Toronto Press, pp. 183–229.

Taylor, C. [1989]. *Sources of the Self. The Making of the Modern Identity*. Cambridge: Cambridge University Press, 1992.

Taylor, C. (1992). "The Politics of Recognition." In *Multiculturalism and The Politics of Recognition*, edited by A. Gutman. Princeton, NJ: Princeton University Press, pp. 25–73.

Temkin, L. (1986). "Inequality." *Philosophy and Public Affairs* 15: 99–121.

Temkin, L. (1993). *Inequality*. Oxford: Oxford University Press.

Tesón, F. R. (1988). *Humanitarian Intervention*. Dobbs Ferry, NJ: Transnational Publishers.

Tesón, F. R. (1992). "The Kantian Theory of International Law." 92 *Columbia Law Review* 53.

Tesón, F. R. (1998). "Kantian International Liberalism." In *International Society: Diverse Ethical Perspectives*, edited by D. R. Mapel and T. Nardin. Princeton, NJ: Princeton University Press, pp. 103–13.

Thiele, L. P. (1997). *Thinking Politics: Perspectives in Ancient, Modern and Postmodern Political Theory*. New York: Seven Bridges Press.

Thompson, D. F. [1987]. *Political Ethics and Public Office*, reprint edition. Cambridge, MA: Harvard University Press, 1990.

Thompson, D. F. (1993). "Mediated Corruption: The Case of the Keating Five." *American Political Science Review* 87: 369–81.

Thompson, D. F. (1999). "Democratic Theory and Global Society." *Journal of Political Philosophy* 7: 111–25.

Thomson, J. J. (1971/72). "A Defense of Abortion." *Philosophy and Public Affairs* 1: 47–66. [Reprinted in *Moral Philosophy: Selected Readings*, edited by G. Sher. Belmont, CA: Wadsworth, 2001, pp. 720–34].

Thomson, J. J. [1976]. "Self-Defense and Rights." *The Lindley Lecture*. Lawrence, KS: University of Kansas Philosophy Department, 1977. [Reprinted in *Rights, Restitution, and Risk: Essays in Moral Theory*, edited by J. J. Thomson and W. Parent. Cambridge, MA: Harvard University Press, 1986, pp. 33–48].

Timmons, M. (1999). *Morality without Foundations*. Oxford: Oxford University Press.

Tinder, G. (1986). *Political Thinking*. Boston: Little Brown.

Tomasi, J. (2001). *Liberalism beyond Justice: Citizens, Society, and the Boundaries of Political Theory*. Princeton, NJ: Princeton University Press.

Tong, R. (1998). *Feminist Thought: A More Comprehensive Introduction*. Boulder, CO: Westview.

Tronto, J. (1987). "Beyond Gender Difference to a Theory of Care." *Signs* 12: 644–63.

Tronto, J. (1993). *Moral Boundaries: A Political Argument for an Ethic of Care*. New York: Routledge.

Trotskii, L. [1936]. *Their Morals and Ours*. New York: Pathfinder Press, 1973.

Unger, R. M. (1976). *Knowledge and Politics*, reissue edition. New York: Free Press.

Unger, R. M. (1986). *The Critical Legal Studies Movement*. Cambridge, MA: Harvard University Press.

Unwin, N. (1999). "Quasi-Realism, Negation and the Frege-Geach Problem." *Philosophical Quarterly* 49: 337–52.

Unwin, N. (2001). "Norms and Negation: A Problem for Gibbard's Logic." *Philosophical Quarterly* 51:60–75.

Urmson, J. O. (1958). "Saints and Heroes." In *Essays in Moral Philosophy*, edited by A. I. Melden. Seattle and London: Washington University Press, pp. 198–216.

Vallentyne, P. (1989). "Two Types of Moral Dilemmas." *Erkenntnis* 30: 301–18.

Vallentyne, P. (ed.) (1991). *Contractarianism and Rational Choice: Essays on Gauthier.* Cambridge: Cambridge University Press.

Valls, A. (1999). "The Libertarian Case for Affirmative Action." *Social Theory and Practice* 25: 299–323.

Van Dyke, V. (1977). "The Individual, the State, and Ethnic Communities in Political Theory." *World Politics* 29: 343–69.

Van Fraassen, B. (1973). "Values and the Heart's Command." *The Journal of Philosophy* 70: 5–19. [Reprinted in *Moral Dilemmas*, edited by C. W. Gowans. New York: Oxford University Press, 1987, pp. 138–53].

Van Gunsteren, H. (1998). *A Theory of Citizenship: Organizing Plurality in Contemporary Democracies.* Boulder, CO: Westview.

Van Parijs, P. (1992). *Arguing for Basic Income.* London: Verso Books.

Van Parijs, P. (1993). *Marxism Recycled.* Cambridge: Cambridge University Press.

Van Parijs, P. (1995). *Real Freedom for All.* Oxford: Oxford University Press.

Van Parijs, P. (2001). *What's Wrong with a Free Lunch: A New Democracy Forum on Universal Basic Income.* Boston: Beacon Press.

Vlastos, G. (1962). "Justice and Equality." In *Social Justice*, edited by R. B. Brandt. Englewood Cliffs, N.J.: Prentice Hall, pp. 31–72. [Also in *Theories of Rights*, edited by J. Waldron. Oxford: Oxford University Press, 1984].

Waldron, J. (1988). *The Right to Private Property.* Oxford: Clarendon Press.

Waldron, J. (1990). *The Law.* London: Routledge.

Waldron, J. (1993). "A Right-Based Critique of Constitutional Rights." *Oxford Journal of Legal Studies* 13: 18–51.

Waldron, J. (1994). "The Advantages and Difficulties of the Humean Theory of Property." *Social Philosophy and Policy* 11: 85–123.

Waldron, J. [1998]. "Precommitment and Disagreement." In *Constitutionalism: Philosophical Foundations*, edited by L. Alexander. Cambridge: Cambridge University Press, 2001, pp. 271–99. [Also in: J. Waldron *Law and Disagreement.* Oxford: Oxford University Press, 1999.]

Walzer, M. (1973). "The Problem of Dirty Hands." *Philosophy and Public Affairs* 2: 160–80. [Reprinted in *Moral Philosophy: Selected Readings*, edited by G. Sher. Belmont, CA: Wadsworth, 2001, pp. 766–81].

Walzer, M. (1983). *Spheres of Justice. A Defense of Pluralism and Equality.* New York, London: Basic Books.

Walzer, M. (1987). *Interpretation and Social Criticism: The Tanner Lectures on Human Values 1985.* Cambridge, MA, and London: Harvard University Press.

Walzer, M. (1992a). "The Civil Society Argument." In *Dimensions of Radical Democracy: Pluralism, Citizenship and Community*, edited by C. Mouffe. London: Verso Books, pp. 89–107.

Walzer, M. (1992b). *What it Means to be an American.* New York: Marsilio Publishers.

Walzer, M. (1994). *Thick and Thin: Moral Argument at Home and Abroad.* Cambridge, MA: Harvard University Press.

Warnock, G. (1971). *The Object of Morality.* London: Methuen.

Warren, M. A. (1973). "On the Moral and Legal Status of Abortion." *The Monist* 57: 43–61.

Warwick, D. (1981). "The Ethics of Administrative Discretion." In *Public Duties: The Moral Obligation of Government Officials*, edited by J. L. Fleishman, L. Liebman and M. K. Moore. Cambridge, MA: Harvard University Press, pp. 93–127.

Wasserstrom, R. (1980). *Philosophy and Social Issues.* Notre Dame, IN: University of Notre Dame Press.

Weale, A. (1982). *Political Theory and Social Policy.* London: Macmillan.

Weber, M. [1919]. "Politics as a Vocation." In *From Max Weber: Essays in Sociology*, edited by H. H. Gerth and C. Wright Mills. New York: Oxford University Press, 1958, pp. 77–128. [Original publication: *Politik als Beruf.* Munich: Duncker &

Humblodt, 1919].

Weber, M. [1922]. *Economy and Society*, edited by G. Roth and C. Wittich. Berkeley: University of California Press, 1978.

Weinstock, D. (2002). "Citizenship and Pluralism." In *The Blackwell Guide to Social and Political Philosophy*, edited by R. L. Simon. Oxford: Blackwell, pp. 239–70.

West, R. (1988). "Jurisprudence and Gender." *The University of Chicago Law Review* 55: 1–72.

Westen, P. (1985). "The Concept of Equal Opportunity." *Ethics* 95: 837–50.

Westen, P. (1990). *Speaking Equality*. Princeton, NJ: Princeton University Press.

Westermarck, E. [1906-8]. *The Origin and Development of the Moral Ideas*. New York: Johnson Reprint Corporation, 1987.

Westermarck, E. [1932]. *Ethical Relativity*. Paterson, N.J.: Littlefield, 1960.

Wiggins, D. [1987]. "A Sensible Subjectivism?" In *Needs, Values, Truth: Essays in the Philosophy of Value*, 3rd edition. Oxford: Blackwell, 1998, pp. 185–214.

Willet, C. (1998). *Theorizing Multiculturalism: A Guide to the Current Debate*. Oxford: Blackwell.

Williams, B. (1962). "The Idea of Equality." In *Philosophy, Politics, and Society*, 2nd Series, edited by P. Laslett and W. G. Runciman. Oxford: Basil Blackwell, pp. 110–31. [Also in *Utilitarianism: For and Against*, edited by J. J. C. Smart and B. Williams. Cambridge: Cambridge University Press, 1973].

Williams, B. (1965). "Ethical Consistency." *Proceedings of the Aristotelian Society*, 39 (Suppl.): 103–24. [Reprinted in *Moral Dilemmas*, edited by C. W. Gowans. New York: Oxford University Press, 1987, 115–37].

Williams, B. (1973). "A Critique of Utilitarianism." In *Utilitarianism: For and Against*, edited by J. J. C. Smart and B. Williams. Cambridge: Cambridge University Press, pp. 75–150.

Williams, B. (1976). "Persons, Character, and Morality." In *The Identities of Persons*, edited by A. Rorty. Berkeley, CA: University of California Press, pp. 197–216. [Reprinted in *Moral Philosophy: Selected Readings*, edited by G. Sher. Belmont, CA: Wadsworth, 2001, pp. 549–62].

Williams, B. (1979). "Internal and External Reasons." In *Rational Action*, edited by Ross Harrison. Cambridge: Cambridge University Press, pp. 17–28.

Williams, B. [1989]. "Internal Reasons and the Obscurity of Blame." In *Making Sense of Humanity*, by Bernard Williams. Cambridge: Cambridge University Press, 1995, pp. 35–45.

Winston, M. E. (ed.) (1989). *The Philosophy of Human Rights*. Belmont, CA: Wadsworth.

Wolf, S. (1982). "Moral Saints." *The Journal of Philosophy* 79: 419–39. [Reprinted in *Virtue Ethics*, edited by R. Crisp and M. Slote. Oxford: Oxford University Press, 1997, pp. 79–98].

Wolgast, E. (1987). *The Grammar of Justice*. Ithaca, NY: Cornell University Press.

Wright, C. (1992). "Realism and the Best Explanation of Belief." In *Truth and Objectivity*, by Crispin Wright. Cambridge, MA: Harvard University Press, pp. 174–201.

Wright, S. (2000). *Community and Communication*. Clevedon: Multilingual Matters.

Young, I. M. (1990). *Justice and the Politics of Difference*. Princeton, NJ: Princeton University Press.

Young, I. M. (2000). *Inclusion and Democracy*. Oxford: Oxford University Press.

Young, M. D. [1958]. *The Rise of the Meritocracy*. New Brunswick, NJ: Transaction Publishers, 1994.

Young, R. (1986). *Personal Autonomy: Beyond Negative and Positive Liberty*. London: Croom-Helm.

Zangwill, N. (2003). "Externalist Moral Motivation." *American Philosophical Quarterly* 40: 143–54.

Zimmerman, M. J. (1996). *The Concept of Moral Obligation*. New York: Cambridge University Press.

Index